# Spirit
### and
# Nature

# Spirit and Nature

### THE SAINT-MÉDARD MIRACLES
### *in* 18TH-CENTURY JANSENISM

## EPHRAIM RADNER

*A Herder & Herder Book*
The Crossroad Publishing Company
New York

The Crossroad Publishing Company
481 Eighth Avenue, New York, NY 10001

Printed in the United States of America

**Library of Congress Cataloging-in-Publication Data**

Radner, Ephraim, 1956-
 Spirit and nature : the Saint-Médard miracles in 18th-century Jansenism / Ephraim Radner.
  p.   cm.
 Includes bibliographical references and index.
 ISBN 0-8245-1991-4 (alk. paper)
 1. Convulsionaries – History.  2. Jansenists – History – 18th century.
3. Miracles – History of doctrines – 18th century.  4. Grace (Theology) –
History of doctrines – 18th century.  5. Eglise Saint-Médard (Paris, France) –
History – 18th century.  6. Paris, François de, 1690-1727 – Tomb.  I. Title.
BX4732 .R33 2002
273′.8 – dc21

                                                          2002014876

1   2   3   4   5   6   7   8   9   10        06   05   04   03   02   01

# CONTENTS

### SECTION TWO
### MIRACLES AND SANCTITY

### SECTION THREE
### THE FIGURE OF REJECTION

# PREFACE

The present study grows out of a concern on my part for the fate of Christian belief in the West, in particular of ecclesial belief. The question posed by Jesus in Luke 18:8 — "and yet, when the Son of Man comes, will he find faith on earth?" — remains a deliberately troubling goad to such concerns. It is a concern, furthermore, whose conscious or unconscious compulsion seems to have moved many Christians to fractured, and often opposing, attempts at an experientialist reversal of the perceived alienation of God from modern culture. These attempts, from charismatic renewal, to movements for social justice, to the reminting of traditional spiritualities in contemporary currencies of discourse, all betray their deep ecclesial nostalgias and fears, even as they use logics of human sensibility to pry from the Church novel spaces for autonomous believing. Theologically, much of this self-contradictory reaction to the unraveling of ecclesial belief has been explained and justified in terms of the doctrine of the Holy Spirit.

The broader aim of this study, then, is to examine pneumatology in the context of ecclesial uncertainty and faltering belief. My goal in this is as much to test the usefulness of contemporary appeals and recourse to the Holy Spirit's supposed mission in the midst of ecclesial disarray, as to illuminate more specifically the pneumatological contours of that disarray itself, as it is experienced within the concrete details of our communal existence. The issue is clearly not one to be engaged solely within dogmatic categories, but tackled primarily, at least in its investigative apprehension, from a descriptive analysis of the Church's actual life. Such an analysis, of course, is properly achieved only at the end of time. That I have chosen Jansenism, and a limited episode of miraculous experience within Jansenism in particular, as the vehicle for pursuing this broader goal is on one level only an arbitrary response to the larger task's temporal impossibility.

But this basic limitation granted, the chosen episode for this study can nonetheless recommend itself as an appropriate object for investigation *pro tempore*, through its acknowledged participation in the very historical process we can identify as defining the "fate" of ecclesial belief in the West. Not only do the miracles and convulsions of Saint-Médard represent a paradigmatic case of confusion over the nature of the divine supernatural in the eighteenth century, and thus set themselves in the midst of a by-now famous debate over the shape of modern theism, but, more pertinently, they constituted an experiential focal point in the Church's struggle to confront its own cultural and even physical demise within modern Europe. Inscribed in a larger historical movement, known

ix

as "Jansenism," that is now commonly noted as itself reflective of deep
and lasting changes in Christian religious attitude,[1] the episode of Saint-
Médard and its theological context offer a discrete realm of experience in
which to examine what is arguably a developing trajectory of ecclesial existence, in its pneumatically informed shape, that may still be identified
in today's disquieted questioning of the Church's future.

One might be able, of course, to offer methodological justifications
for the present choice of material analogous to those provided by Kolakowski in his monumental study of individual seventeenth-century
mystics, choices that formed a phenomenological basis for much larger
claims about religion in general.[2] But in the end, the reader must judge
the usefulness of this study less because of the nature of its methodological
buttressing than according to the fit it exposes between a set of particular
events, their apprehension, and the perceived character of contemporary
struggles in the Church over Christian believing. And even if such a fit
is missed, I hope that this study's analysis of Jansenist theology on the
question of pneumatic self-disclosure will prove in its own right a stimulat-
ing historical contribution to the reassessment of pneumatology's proper
boundaries. These are boundaries that, it seems to me, have been too often
flouted or ignored at present, to the detriment of the Church's assaulted
common life of faith.

Let me offer a note with regard to citations and quotations from primary sources used in this study. The secretive and collaborative nature of
Jansenist writing in the seventeenth and eighteenth centuries resulted in
their generally anonymous publication. Attributions of most books were
made, however, in works of the day like the *Nouvelles Ecclésiastiques*
and in subsequent bibliographies and dictionaries (e.g., by Barbier and
Picot). While some of these attributions have been challenged by modern
scholars, except in rare cases of obvious uncertainty, I have followed the
traditionally ascribed authorship, as it has been maintained in accessible
reference works like the *Dictionnaire de Théologie* or the *Union Catalogue*. In order to aid the reader unfamiliar with French, I have chosen to
translate even the more substantial quotations from original works, while
noting here and there key vocabulary. In doing so, however, I realize that
I am obscuring what is semantically significant rhetoric, as well as, on occasion, abridging aspects of the original meaning. Jansenist and Appellant

---

1. See the comments on Jansenism at the end of Louis Dupré's *Passage to Modernity*
(New Haven: Yale University Press, 1993). In another work of my own, I have turned to
Jansenism as a paradigmatic example of a certain kind of response to ecclesial "division" in
the West in particular, a reality that I see as one of the defining elements of modern Christian experience. See Ephraim Radner, *The End of the Church: A Pneumatology of Christian
Division in the West* (Grand Rapids: Wm. B. Eerdmans, 1998). The pneumatological interest
of the present essay, however, is much broader than the practical ecclesial focus of the last-
mentioned book, despite the latter's relegation of Jansenism to a purely illustrative role. See
also my article "Jansenism" in Trevor A. Hart, ed., *The Dictionary of Historical Theology*
(Carlisle/Grand Rapids: Paternoster/Wm. B. Eerdmans, 2000), 277–79.

2. Leszek Kolakowski, *Chrétiens sans Église: La conscience religieuse et le lien confessionel au XVIIe siècle* (Paris: Gallimard, 1969), chapter 1.

literature is often complex in its period formalism; but it is also uniquely vigorous and spiritually substantive. It is worth reading, where possible, in its original. In both citations and quotations where French vocabulary is noted, I have maintained the original unstandardized orthography, except in those rare cases where obvious typographical errors obscure the grammatical sense of the phrase. Finally, all quotations from the Bible are from the RSV, except where the original Latin Vulgate has a peculiar sense, in which case the translation is my own, unless otherwise noted.

This study stands as a slight revision of a doctoral dissertation accepted at Yale University in 1994. I have chosen to keep its basic structure and the method of its argument intact, despite its somewhat academic tone, because the overall purpose of the book requires, I believe, the kind of detail and cumulative reflection given in the original endeavor. Since I first worked on the essay, Catherine-Laurent Maire has published a major examination of eighteenth-century Jansenism, whose material coincides with a good bit of my own.[3] This work is a wonderful contemporary study and deserves careful review, especially for its detailed uncovering of primary sources, and their analytic positioning within a framework of historical development. Maire's interests and approach, of a more social-historical character, do not, however, supplant the more strictly theological focus of the present work, and I continue to feel that the religious questions raised by the Jansenist debate over miracles properly open up the sort of broad Christian ecclesial reflection this book intends. A decade of pastoral and teaching ministry since first writing this essay has not lessened my sense of its conclusion's relevance, if not necessarily its final accuracy. The continued misapplication of pneumatological concepts to constructive and practical theology, with blinding results, furthermore, strengthens my suspicion that the life of the Holy Spirit in the Church demands far more reticence in its description than we have been willing to maintain, perhaps because of the modern historical obtuseness this study takes pains to underline.

The book's initial accomplishment was due, in no small measure, to a number of individuals whose intellectual stimulation, encouragement, and assistance supported my work: to Prof. George Lindbeck, the original dissertation's director, whose theological rigor and patience, placed in the service of his passionate love for the Church, has been a gift to me and to the whole Body of the faithful; to Prof. Cyril O'Regan (now of Notre Dame University), who generously and critically read and corrected my manuscript, offering much encouragement along the way, and whose subsequent sense of the essay's usefulness prodded it toward publication; to

---

3. C.-L. Maire, *De la Cause de Dieu à la Cause de la Nation: Le Jansénisme au XVIIIe Siècle* (Paris: Gallimard, 1998). I have chosen not to engage this substantive study in the course of the present work's rewriting, in large measure because Maire's concerns maintain their own proper focus, different from my own, and most of the issues of historical interpretation associated with her perspectives that I do tackle are already covered in the current discussions.

Prof. Louis Dupré, who first introduced me to the Jansenists, alerted me to their positive and ongoing importance for the Church, and has continued to challenge theologians with a basic concern over Christian believing in the modern world; to my colleagues George Sumner, Kathryn Greene-McCreight, and R. R. Reno, for their ongoing intellectual engagement; to the Yale Divinity School Library, whose collection of seventeenth- and eighteenth-century *Jansenistica* is unique in the United States and offered a coherent literary context in which to pursue my research; to the Library's staff, especially Joan Duffy, Susan Burdick, and Martha Smalley, for their unfailingly good-humored and forthcoming assistance; to the Libraries and staff of Harvard and Princeton Universities; to Dr. B. Robert Kreiser, for his encouragement and for the remarkable fruits of his scholarship; to John Jones, of The Crossroad Publishing Company, for seeking this work out and encouraging its publication. Finally, I must offer profound thanks to my wife, the Rev. Annette Brownlee, for her continued and inspiring strength and generosity of spirit, especially during the time of this work's writing and fallow waiting; it is above all an honor to her that it was ever completed. I dedicate it to her, with a deep sense of gratitude for, in this case, the Spirit's absolutely clear use of her for good.

# INTRODUCTION

## The Phenomenological Basis of Pneumatology: Aspects of a Historical Study of the Holy Spirit

The present book could be taken as a kind of commentary on St. Paul's words concerning the "demonstration of the Spirit" embedded in 1 Corinthians 2:1–5:

> When I came to you, brethren, I did not come proclaiming to you the testimony of God in lofty words or wisdom. For I decided to know nothing among you except Jesus Christ and him crucified. And I was with you in weakness and in much fear and trembling; and my speech and my message were not in plausible words of wisdom, but in demonstration of the Spirit and of power, that your faith might not rest in the wisdom of men but in the power of God.

The form of "demonstration" to which Paul alludes here is that of manifestation, or appearing, and this essay seeks to be a limited study of such appearing by the Holy Spirit. As a study of the Spirit's appearing, we will engage, to manipulate Hegel's notion, in a kind of pneumatological "phenomenology," the science in which we know the Spirit as it is in itself through the study of the ways in which it appears to us — St. Paul's *in ostensione Spiritus*. We will pursue such a phenomenology of the Holy Spirit by taking a limited historical episode that by all accounts raises the question of pneumatic appearance — the eighteenth-century miracles and convulsions associated with the Jansenist deacon François de Pâris and his tomb at Saint-Médard in Paris — and by examining its potentially pneumatological features as they are presented to us in time.

It is well to see in advance what we will be dealing with, what are the events from which we shall be culling pneumatic appearance. An admirably clear contemporary account of 1752, from across the Channel, is provided by John Douglas, the bishop of Salisbury. Oddly enough, Douglas tells us of these events in a book which attempts to overthrow the very claims to the Spirit on the basis of which we shall pursue our study. Since we shall be providing no further summaries of these matters, and since their very clarity to someone like Douglas will be a subject of concern to us later on, we will cite his description at length. Who first were the Jansenists?

> The Jansenists are so denominated from Jansenius of *Ipres*, who died 1638. His opinions gaining ground in France were complained of by the Jesuits,

1

to Rome, and condemned by Innocent the Xth in 1653, and by Alexander the VIIth in 1657. In the bulls of these two popes, five propositions, said to be extracted from Jansenius' book, called Augustinus, were condemned, and as they contain the distinguishing tenets ascribed to the Jansenists, by their antagonists, I shall insert them here. *First,* Some of God's commands are impossible to be fulfilled by righteous men even though they endeavour with all their power to obey them, because the grace by which they should be enabled to fulfil them is wanting. *Secondly,* In our present state of corrupt nature, man never resists inward grace. *Thirdly,* In our present, corrupt state, it is not requisite in order to a man's having merit or demerit, that he should have such a freedom of will as excludes necessity; that which excludes compulsion is sufficient. *Fourthly,* The Semi-Pelagians admitted the necessity of inward preventing grace not only to the beginning of faith, but also to every future act of it; but they were heretics because they asserted that this grace might be resisted. *Fifthly,* The Semi-Pelagians are heretics, for saying that Christ died for all men in general.

The condemnation of these five propositions gave rise to vast animosities and controversies in France, till, at last, in 1668, the Pope was prevailed upon to require no more from the Jansenists, than that they should subscribe to the condemnation of the five propositions in general, without mentioning their being contained in the book of Jansenius. This they agreed to; and this transaction is usually called the Peace of Jansenism. But the calm was of short duration. For so early as 1679, we find Mr. Arnaud, the famous Champion of Jansenism, retiring out of France, not thinking himself safe, any longer there. He was followed in his retreat by Pasquier Quesnel, a priest of the Oratory, whose *Moral Reflections on the New Testament,* published in Brussels in 1698, occasioned the revival of the disputes with greater violence than ever. An approbation, prefixed to this book, by the Bishop of Chalons (afterward the Cardinal de Noailles and Archbishop of Paris) occasioned the condemnation of it. For the Jesuits bearing this prelate a grudge, immediately began their intrigues, and after several unsuccessful applications, at length in 1713, got Clement XIth to publish the famous bull or constitution, usually called *Unigenitus,* because it begins with these words, Unigenitus Filius Dei, &c. &c. By this bull *one hundred and one propositions,* said to be extracted from Father Quesnel's book, were condemned [ . . . ] But though the Pope threatened excommunication to those who received not the constitution, Cardinal de Noailles and his party, disregarded the thunder of the conclave, and appealed to a general council: hence they were called *appellants.*[1]

As for the specifically pneumatic events arising within the Jansenist struggle to which we shall refer, the miracles of François de Pâris in particular, Douglas goes on to describe what took place with an irony that will inform any pneumatological conclusion to be ultimately drawn:

It may not be unentertaining to give some account of [de Paris], to whose intercession so many wonders have been ascribed — The *Abbe Paris* was a

---

1. John Douglas, *The Criterion; or Rules by which the True Miracles Recorded in the New Testament Are Distinguished from the Spurious Miracles of Pagans and Papists* (1752), new edition (London: T. Cadell and W. Davies, 1807), 120ff.

gentleman of very good family of the robe, and eldest son of a counsellor of the parliament of Paris. From his earliest youth he discovered a remarkable turn for the extravagancies of devotion. As he grew up, this got so far the better of his reason, that he relinquished all pretensions of succeeding to his father's post, to a younger brother, and dedicated himself to the church, mortifying himself with continual fastings, and scarcely ever stirring from before his crucifix. Not thinking this enough to insure his salvation, he quitted every advantage his birth had given him, and having sold his estate, buried himself in a obscure retreat, known only to the sick and needy whom he administered unto, and relieved. With all this sanctity he was, in his own opinion, the greatest of sinners. This diffidence was the grand principle of his conduct; it made him punish himself with the most severe penances, tear his flesh with the most cruel flagellations, in short, practise all the extravagancies of the wildest fanatic; a name, which, if a weak judgment and a warm fancy be characteristics of fanaticism, belonged to the blessed Deacon, an appellation which our Abbé was honoured with, who thought himself unworthy of the higher order of priesthood.

Having acquired a vast reputation of sanctity among the Jansenists, he died on the first of May 1727 [ ... ] and was buried in the church-yard of St. Medard at Paris, near the South wall of the church, a tomb-stone being put up that covered the extent of his grave, which, from the time of this death, was frequented by his admirers. The number of worshippers increasing daily, an opinion of the efficacy of worshipping there gained ground also. By degrees it was rumoured about, that the sick had by their prayers at the tomb been restored to health; and cures of an astonishing nature had been wrought by the intercession of the blessed Deacon; till, at length, in the year 1731 these reports having put the whole city of Paris in ferment, and St. Medard's Church-yard being crouded from morning to night with sick praying for relief, the civil magistrate, unable by any other means to stem the torrents and close the list of miracles, fell upon the expedient of debarring all approach to the scene of wonders, by walling up the sepulchre. It was on this occasion, that the following frequently repeated distich was made, and put upon the wall.

> De par le Roi — defence à Dieu
> De faire miracles en ce lieu.

Our saint's miracles, after this, become less frequent, though some were attributed still to him [ ... ]; and even to this day, he performs wonderful feats among the *Convulsionaries*, whose extravagancies have done so much discredit to the cause of Jansenism, that the sober part of that sect have not only disclaimed all connexion with them, but have also employed some of their ablest writers to expose their frantic absurdities. These convulsionists well deserve this appellation; for they have amongst them adepts who can, with pleasure, work themselves up to the strangest agitations and convulsions, practising feats which would entertain a Bartholomew-fair audience. [ ... ] In the year 1749 being at Paris, I was invited to go to one of their meetings, where I was told I should be entertained with the exploits of one of their famous heroes, who could not only bring on convulsions when he pleased, but when he was in that state, would lie on the floor and allow his breast to be beat with a stone or hammer. Though my curiosity was not so great as to make me a witness of this myself, the person whom I had my information from, had seen the operation.[2]

These are unusual events, they are largely forgotten today, and, as Douglas indicates, they form a part of a larger theological, devotional, and political agony within the Church. For some, they may even evoke wonder in advance as to how "the demonstration of the Spirit and of power" in their regard could prove anything other than the "extravagant" pursuit of fancy. But in the very oddity of the incident lies, at least in theory, the test for St. Paul's method.

What would it mean to come to know the Spirit through an examination of its appearance in an episode such as this? For the purposes of this study, we can define the contours of the Holy Spirit's "appearance" as shaped by four categorical terms, each of which is expressed by St. Paul in vv. 6–16 of 1 Corinthians 2, as he speaks of the Spirit: the "gifts" of the Spirit (*charisthenta*), their meaning as revealed by God's Spirit (*apokalypsis dia tou pneumatos*), their rejection by those without the Spirit (*hoi anthropoi psychikoi*), and their historical fate in being known or negated, given in the eternal decree of God (*hen proorisen theos pro ton aionon*). The "phenomena" of the Spirit which we shall examine in the case of eighteenth-century Jansenist miracles, then, will include the following: primary "pneumatica," such as the Church, her offices and teachings, as well as secondary pneumatica, such as miracles and prodigies proper; the positive theological and devotional reflection given to these pneumatica; their negative contesting on the part of opponents; and finally the historical outcome to the appearance of these contested pneumatica and their contested apprehension.

None of these categories, of course, are properly applied in a historically sequential fashion, and our study will not attempt to follow such a sequence. Temporally prior reflections on the nature of pneumatica in general, both primary and secondary, often provide the basis for identifying subsequently manifest pneumatica; reflections negatively critical of only some elements of such general understandings can lay the ground for their subsequent positive formulations; while the historical fate of pneumatica and their reflection can, if grasped prospectively (i.e., in overt prophecy or implicit structures of theological expectation) determine in some measure the very shape of pneumatic manifestations and their apprehension in time.

A phenomenology of the Holy Spirit like the present study must therefore be prepared to move freely among these abstracted categories of appearance that form the single event *in ostensione Spiritus*. Fortunately, much of the basic historical work demanded by an examination of our first category with respect to Jansenist miracles, the pneumatica themselves, has been done by other scholars like Dedieu, Kreiser, and Maire, using primary descriptive sources that are among the richest available on record for

_____

2. Ibid., 123ff.

any pneumatic episode within the Christian Church.[3] This study, then, will gratefully assume much of their work, and that of others who have examined historical aspects of the social, political, and biographical elements of the Saint-Médard events and their surrounding context. Such elements ultimately form essential aspects of any full phenomenology of the Holy Spirit, although we shall not be examining them to any extent here, and our own conclusions, therefore, can only be considered partial. The categories of theological and devotional reflection, negation, and historical fate, however, have received less careful scrutiny by scholars, and they will, therefore, form the main object of our examination. And because we are engaging in a study of phenomena, moored in time, much of this examination, analytic as it may be in the main, will fall within historical and descriptive bounds. The essay, on one level, may thus be read as a discourse in historical theology, whose purpose is to lay out a range of thinkers, their thinking, and their implicit theological frameworks, with respect to a specific historical issue — the miracles of Saint-Médard.

But as a phenomenology of the Holy Spirit, our study's ultimate object is to know the Spirit as it is in itself, and not just to describe appearance. To this end, we will be organizing our descriptions and analyses with a view to the culminating and last of our phenomenological categories, the "historical fate" of the pertinent phenomena. This is a category of ostensive display that functions most clearly only as a kind of cumulating gaze over the other phenomena, providing the grasp of self-"demonstration" that the Spirit effects in time. The pneumatic *meaning* of events, theological reflections and debates, and the cognitive outlooks that inform them — our final aim at recovering — is therefore something to be gleaned from the larger mass of historical and analytical descriptions only through a cumulative process of rethinking and rescrutinizing. The process itself, as it encompasses the variously categorized contours of *ostensio Spiritus*, is its own *demonstratio*.

While such a process does entail the extended and involuted format of this essay, the shape of the study itself can at the last be justified in

---

3. Joseph Dedieu, "L'agonie du jansénisme (1715–1790)," *Revue d'Histoire de l'Église de France* 14 (1928): 161–214; B. Robert Kreiser, *Miracles, Convulsions, and Ecclesiastical Politics in Early Eighteenth-Century Paris* (Princeton: Princeton University Press, 1978); Catherine-Laurence Maire, *Les convulsionnaires de Saint-Médard: Miracles, convulsions et prophéties à Paris au XVIIIe siècle* (Paris: Gallimard/Julliard, 1985) and *De la Cause de Dieu à la Cause de la Nation: Le Jansénisme au XVIIIe Siècle* (Paris: Gallimard, 1998). Maire's last book represents the fullest treatment, from a history-of-ideas perspective, of Appellant attitudes we will be examining more theologically. Particular note should also be made of Daniel Vidal's *Miracles et Convulsions Jansénistes au XVIIIe Siècle: Le Mal et sa Connaissance* (Paris: Presses Universitaires de France, 1987). While Vidal's volume is rarely referred to in the present study, it is not only useful, but necessary reading for the Saint-Médard episode. The book remains the only sustained and detailed examination of the convulsionary miracles in print. But its approach to the material, a kind of social semiotics of the experience of evil in individual and group consciousness, so fully leaves aside the confessional and theological frameworks of the participants' self-understanding, that not only its conclusions but even its descriptive concerns render the study difficult to integrate in general with our own investigative focus.

the result of a knowing, the knowing of the Spirit in itself. As I will try to show, such knowing ends in a very restricted "something," according to St. Paul's own account: "I decided to know nothing among you except Jesus Christ and him crucified." This means that our exposition of historical phenomena, ostensibly demonstrating the Holy Spirit, must be seen in their assembled specifics and forms in order to subject themselves to their "decreed" *ostensio* of self-effacement in the face of Jesus Christ, and Him crucified, decreasing in the course of their temporal appearance that He might increase. It is this paradox of final (that is, purposive) and reductive form given only in the specified range of phenomena that will govern the elaborate explication of material in this study.[4]

## Pneumatology and History: Some Alternatives

The approach I have adopted here with respect to pneumatology is, in its presuppositions, hardly novel, except in the depth with which I attempt to investigate certain particular phenomena. This exception, however, is crucial and worth exploring here. Studies of the Holy Spirit have traditionally tended toward being studies of history in at least partial or sometimes even wholesale ways. One of the more popular books on pneumatology in the last forty years was that of Léon Joseph Cardinal Suenens, *A New Pentecost?*[5] Sympathetically prompted by the charismatic movement in the Catholic Church, the volume introduced many readers, in an accessible manner, to a broad exposition of pneumatological themes. Cardinal Suenens did this, however, within the framework of a study in historical discernment: "Everything points to the fact that we are living at a turning point in the history of the Church, in which the Holy Spirit is revealing, to a degree unknown before, a mystery of death and resurrection. [ . . . ] The pages which follow are an attempt to highlight some of the signs of this renewal and to discern the future to which they point."[6] In line with this promise, Suenens moors his subsequent pneumatological reflections in brief, often anecdotal descriptions of events ranging from renewal groups

---

4. To speak of a "phenomenology of the Spirit" obviously creates Hegelian resonances. As will become quite clear, however, what is at issue in this study is not the disclosure of some "ontophany" in the historical process, in the philosophical sense employed by some Hegelian thinkers, but, in the figuralist mode which we shall examine in Jansenist thinking, the revelation of specific scriptural forms in historical experience within the Church especially. For some general discussions that touch on the tensions at work in this distinction, see *Manifestation et Révélation* (Paris: Éditions Beauchesne, 1976), especially the contributions by Stanislas Breton ("Révélation, Médiation, Manifestation") and by Jacques Marello ("Création-Révélation et Manifestation"); see also *Le Mythe et le Symbole de la Connaissance Figurative de Dieu* (Paris: Éditions Beauchesne, 1977), esp. the essays by Ephrem Dominique Yon ("Le Symbole et la Croix"), Stanislas Breton ("Mythe et imaginaire en théologie chrétien"), and Dominique Dubarle ("Pratique du Symbole et Connaissance de Dieu"). For an example of what this study will *not* pursue, that is, the use of figuralist language appropriated to contemporary Hegelian categories, see Peter Hodgson, *God in History: Shapes of Freedom* (Nashville: Abingdon Press, 1989).

5. Joseph Cardinal Suenens, *A New Pentecost?* (New York: Seabury Press, 1974).

6. Ibid., xii; see also 216.

at Duquesne University to Vatican II. Faced with what he perceived to be an extraordinary time in the history of the Church — and world — the cardinal sought to outline the congruence of pneumatic meaning with particular events linked to this prophetically discerned moment in time. Similarly, when John Paul II presented his encyclical *Dominum et vivificantem* on the Holy Spirit in 1986, he did so in the expressed shadow of a historical moment of discerned divine significance, the "end of the second millennium after Christ," an "epoch" "calling" the Church to "announce the Spirit" before the world as it entered the mystery of a historical *novum*.[7] While lacking the specificities of Suenens's book, the encyclical is nonetheless replete with references to the particularities of the present times within the economy of God's revelation to the Church in history:[8] "this prayer ['the Spirit and the Bride say to the Lord Jesus, Come!' — Rev. 22:17] is directed at a precise stage in history marked by the Year 2000, a moment at which is brought into relief 'the fullness of time.'"[9] Implicit references to world events and the longings and needs of peoples shaped by these events crop up throughout these passages. The very act of speaking about the Holy Spirit is bound in widely disseminated expositions like these with the articulation of its phenomenal contours, as apparent in the present and usually as evocative of a particular future.

However traditional the assumption that, in some aspects at least, a phenomenology of the Holy Spirit is both possible and also necessary to a proper pneumatology, nonetheless the tradition of pneumatology as a systematic practice has tended to deform the method by which this assumed *ostensio Spiritus* could become critically manifest. In large measure this has happened through theologians' objectification, not of the historical phenomena themselves, as ought to have been the case, but of the abstracted historical *character* perceived as defining the Holy Spirit's nature. With universal history parsed dispensationally from the time of the early Church, the Holy Spirit was very quickly identified with the special "age" of the Church (something already the case with Irenaeus), even if, against the Montanists, this age was rarely seen as wholly discontinuous in its pneumatic character with the past. And once identified with the "age" of the Church — whether in the so-called "Three Age" Trinitarian scheme, in the "Four Age" scheme of Pre-Law, Law, Grace (i.e., Church), and End, or the "Seven Age" scheme in the which the sixth is given over to the Church — the Holy Spirit came to function as a kind of principle of historical experience for Christianity, and practically speaking, for apprehended history as a whole. The Spirit was given a historical "character" in that the Spirit was made the historical agent of Christ's *innovatio*, through a continuous process of Christian *renovatio* in the Church.[10] Whether or

---

7. Paragraph 2. I have used the text given in a French translation, with an introduction by Yves Congar, as *L'Esprit Saint* (Paris: Éditions du Cerf, 1986).

8. See ibid., paragraphs 25f., 49ff., 65f.

9. Ibid., 66.

10. A Three Age (or Four Age, depending on what you emphasize) scheme is found in

not the full manifestation of the Holy Spirit in its acts awaits an epoch still to come (Joachim) or is already with us (Irenaeus), the Holy Spirit has very often been rendered theologically as a principle of historical "tendency," either pushing the Church in an experienced direction as fully present, or drawing it in an identifiable way as eschatologically anticipated. This last construction is most clearly evident in Jürgen Moltmann's pneumatology, *The Spirit of Life,*[11] a volume that typifies the degree to which pneumatological study has cloaked the particular temporal phenomena of the Spirit's appearing with a fabricated historicizing principle of pneuma. Because typical, the unfortunate results of the kind of thinking Moltmann represents merit at least a passing notice.

In earlier works, as part of an explication of Trinitarian theology in terms of "God's trinitarian history," Moltmann had more or less followed a traditional trinitarian schema in giving over to the Holy Spirit a special period of time in which to "complete" Christ's work in the world, by uniting all things and drawing them together in the Father.[12] In *The*

Gregory of Nazianzus (Theological Oration 5:15f.), but is only later made explicitly Trinitarian (the third age is "Christ's," and this includes the work of the Spirit in the Church). The Four Age scheme is generally traced to Paul, and continues to be espoused by Aquinas. The Seven Age scheme is a mostly Western elaboration (but see Basil's *Hexameron,* whose symbolic form, if not content, lies behind one tradition of this numerological construal of time), based on Augustine's construction, and although the latter did not attach the sixth age of the Church's millennium to the Holy Spirit in any particular way, later medieval writers did, if in an increasingly complex fashion, as they attempted to relate various numerological symbolisms one to another. Thus Honorius of Autun divided three ages each into six periods, with the fourth/seventh age standing beyond history, while Rupert of Deutz used an explicitly Trinitarian three-age scheme that is itself internally (and variably) structured according to seven periods. Many of these schematizing theologians of history were linked to reformist movements within clerical orders (e.g., Anselm of Havelaberg, Eberwin of Steinfeld, Bonaventure), and their discussions of historical development and the Holy Spirit were spurred by the felt need to understand the nature of change in the life of the Church. Joachim of Fiore is the most famous, and perhaps idiosyncratic, in this lineage. For some background to this material, see A. Luneau, *L'Histoire de Salut chez les Pères de l'Église: La Doctrine des Ages du Monde* (Paris, 1964), and Marjorie Reeves, *The Originality and Influence of Joachim of Fiore,* in *Traditio,* 1980.

11. Jürgen Moltmann, *The Spirit of Life* (Minneapolis: Fortress Press, 1992).

12. Moltmann articulated a theology that affirmed the narration of Jesus' history as, in his words, "the history of God, i.e., as the history between the Father, the Son, and the Spirit, from which is constituted who God is; and this, to be sure, not only for men but also already in his existence itself" ("Der gekreuzigte Gott, Neuzeitliche Gottesgrage und trinitarische Gottesgeschichte," in *Concilium* [1974], 412, translated in John J. O'Donnell, S.J., *Trinity and Temporality: The Christian Doctrine of God in the Light of Process Theology and the Theology of Hope* [Oxford: Oxford University Press, 1983], 131). The Incarnation "brings about something 'new' even within the Trinity, for God himself" (*The Future of Creation* [London: SCM Press, 1979], 93), just as does the sending of the Spirit from the wreckage of the crucifixion. The Spirit, in this view, is given to the world in time in a special way at the Cross, for its perfecting work in relation to Christ's mission. It is a work of being given and of giving life and of uniting creation that constitutes its own Trinitarian being (see *The Trinity and the Kingdom of God* [San Francisco: Harper and Row, 1981], 127). It should be noted that Moltmann, in a way that is not wholly consistent with his premises concerning the temporal givenness of the crucifixion from which the Spirit is "sent" in a "new" manner, wants to adapt Joachim's historically sequential (and "modalistic") trinitarian pattern into a more synchronic schema of "continual" transitions between the "kingdoms" of the three Persons (see ibid., 209; also *The Spirit of Life,* 232).

*Spirit of Life*, a full-fledged pneumatology, Moltmann goes further, and extends the Holy Spirit's historical work, by defining it as the basis for inter-subjective consciousness, a mode of being that finally underlies the fact of all created relational existence established primordially in the divine Trinity.[13] Moltmann's point in all of this is to found the personhood of the Holy Spirit, and our epistemological access to this Person, in human "experience," broadly understood. And his pneumatology proper thereafter expands along the lines of described experiential phenomena. No longer are the phenomena themselves given heuristic precedence in understanding the Spirit, however, but because they themselves derive from an embedded metaphysical structure of creation, only certain phenomena are chosen for pneumatic reference as being particularly exemplary of the principle and capable of representing the "life-giving" reality of the Trinity's own relational being. Indeed, because "it is appropriate [ . . . ] to recognize the operation of the Life-giving Spirit of God in the *trend* [emphasis added] to relationship in created things,"[14] and evolution itself reflects the "goal" of "differentiated community which liberates the individual members belonging to it,"[15] the phenomenology of the Spirit which his own method would seem originally to demand is reduced to the illustration of an abstraction.[16]

In a major respect, this marks a departure from, perhaps even a betrayal of, the search for theodicy that fueled Moltmann's earliest writings. For how can we apply a pneumatology like that elaborated in *The Spirit of Life* to events where, on the basis of his own *The Crucified God*, the Cross obviates any *visible* "tendency" to anything other than chaos? More importantly for our purposes, we must ask how a pneumatology like Moltmann's can coherently emerge from such events. Here is where our own study attempts a more critical project, using as its basis particular happenings given in the specific historical incident of the miracles of Saint-Médard. While historical overviews like Hegel's are no longer fashionable because of their seemingly inevitable descriptive procrusteanism, even he provided a more experientially nuanced description of the French Revolution in the service of his larger abstractions, for instance, than does Moltmann's passing (and inaccurate) use of that episode as a type for the "principle" of the Spirit's liberation still unintegrated with conscious religious understanding.[17] The example is critical, given that, in our study, the Revolution forms a historical frame to a set of explicitly pneumatic phenomena, a frame that, as we will see, in itself must contribute *peculiarly* to the previous manifestations of the Spirit in time, and not so

---

13. Moltmann, *The Spirit of Life*, 31ff.

14. Ibid., 225.

15. Ibid., 228.

16. It is odd how Moltmann lapses into the this "evolutionary" vision of the Spirit in history, when the very notion of "evolution" was one he has long repudiated, not only in his earliest works, but in something as recent as *The Way of Jesus Christ* (Minneapolis: Fortress Press, 1993, 292–305), written immediately before *The Spirit of Life*.

17. Moltmann, *The Spirit of Life*, 107. For Hegel, see his *Philosophy of History*, IV:iii:3.

only generally. Moltmann's approach therefore will contrast starkly with the placement of the Revolution within the prophetic discourses of both prospective and retrospective observers among the Jansenists. And while the loss of the (pneumatically) prophetic use of temporal particulars in theologies like Moltmann's certainly contributes to a gain in schematizing clarity, it does so through the subversion of their purportedly phenomenological goal, which must remain necessarily concrete. May it not turn out, in fact, that what we fear in giving pneumatic particulars heuristic priority over functional principles — the possibility of restricted, because phenomenologically incoherent, pneumatologies — actually leads to an increased understanding of the Holy Spirit itself? Our own study will attempt to demonstrate how a rigorous phenomenology of the Holy Spirit in a case like Saint-Médard and its Jansenist circumstances will yield obdurate obscurities about the Comforter, before which pneumatology as a discipline will need to bend and even suffer.[18]

That pneumatology does not do so in so many contemporary theologies, despite their commitments to "history" as the proper field for such inquiry, is simply the mark of a failure of phenomenological nerve. The failure of nerve, it must be added, also has a theologically systematic embodiment, one that has been long warned against in the venerable patristic principle that divine "works" performed in creation ought properly to be

---

18. How then *shall* we "see" the Spirit in such events? An example related to our chosen historical topic, the case of St. Benedict Joseph Labre, provides a parallel to the kinds of phenomenological limits within which an honest pneumatology must take shape. Labre has been generally seen as a "saint" for a strange new time, a pilgrim and a beggar from France in the late eighteenth century, whose mendicant poverty in the slums and churches of a decaying Rome elicited from the populace the spontaneous acclamation of his sainthood at his death in 1783. Occurring at a centennial turn of the ages, awash in the confusions of revolution spawned amid various rationalist faiths, Labre's miracles and life of holy poverty and homelessness strike even secular historians of our era as disclosive of an epochal reaction and transformation, mysterious finally in its significant movement (see Yves-Marie Hilaire, ed., *Benoît Labre: Errance et sainteté, Histoire d'un culte 1783–1983* [Paris: Éditions du Cerf, 1984]). Pneumatic holiness as a concrete phenomenon, if approached merely on this larger historical plane, however, is easily swallowed up in interpretations designed to typify the events. But a more pertinent picture can be gleaned by exploring the phenomenal details of Labre's pneumatic history in the manner we have earlier outlined, carefully sifting their occurrence as part of a textured *ostensio Spiritus* that involves reflection and negation. Such a labor, performed already in part by Bernard Plongeron (see his "Benoît-Joseph Labre au miroir de l'hagiographie Janséniste en France [1783–89], in Hilaire's collection), would demonstrate how Labre's holiness and miracles were part of an intricate fabric of contested claims about the Spirit and about history, in which Jansenists and Jesuits, Gallicans and ultramontanes, revolutionaries and royalists all vied to possess the saint as their own. Yet in the midst of these arguments, Labre's earlier prophetic visions, filled with images of France's, of Rome's, and of the Church's imminent catastrophic destruction, were turning into reality, sweeping away with them the lives and sensibilities of rich and poor alike from all competing parties. Although Labre's authentic sanctity was quickly established by the official Church, the exact nature of his pneumatic existence, the directions of the Spirit's impulses in his life and message, and the substance of its revelations in Labre's person remain shrouded by just the violent circumstances of his historical location and by the contested character of his sanctity's prophetic import. This is exactly the same case with Saint-Médard, although given in a more cutting relief. Such cases as these, however, are not occasional accidents of pneumatological investigation: from a phenomenological perspective, they must provide the strict parameters for pneumatological discourse.

assigned to all three persons of the Trinity, and not just to one (*opera trinitatis ad extra sunt indivisa*). To heed the warning, however, is not to give up describing individual divine works, for fear of constricting their Trinitarian origin, an approach that only falls back on the generalities that lead away from "seeing," e.g., the Spirit in its promised appearances. Rather, the way to avoid the systematic pitfall of identifying a divine work in the world with a single member of the Trinity is through a more rigorous phenomenology of just such works, not a looser one. For although it might seem that pneumatica especially, as personally disclosive acts, ought to prove uncertain vehicles for knowing the Holy Spirit in itself, in that they are supremely works *ad extra* whose Trinitarian origins cannot be properly assigned, a simple phenomenology of the Holy Spirit need not succumb to the functionalizing reductions that pneumatological schemata like Moltmann's ultimately present. For all that is asserted in this method is that the Holy Spirit appears in particular phenomena, not that the phenomena themselves are *singular* indicators of the Spirit; all that is asserted is that a simple phenomenology of the Spirit has no a priori commitment to coherence in the *ostensio Spiritus* and is even willing to submit its gathered particulars to the resulting limits of pneumatological reticence.

This is all it asserts. But, more positively, if this is so, such reticence itself will prove to be an aspect of the Spirit's self-demonstration, a possibility granted seriousness by the fact that it accords with St. Paul's own implicit establishment of the ridiculed Christ as the sole pneumatic object of disclosure. Our investigation will, in fact, take us to this end. The conclusion to our study will attempt to outline positively what *ought* to be the shape of a pneumatology that took seriously its phenomenological limits, ones that defer in their theologically systematic character to the priority of the Christological assertion of Crucified Savior. Following our examination of the Saint-Médard miracles and their Jansenist theological context, then, we will argue that a pneumatology that properly adheres to its phenomenological base will most adequately restrict its enunciatory reach to those scriptural appellations of the Spirit and its work whose coherence lies exclusively in their attachment to the narrative of Christ's self-giving. This kind of "kenotic" pneumatology falls within the traditional lineage of Cappadocian reflections as they were appropriated by someone like Pavel Florensky. But while we can perhaps expect this result, as a confessional presupposition in the wake of St. Paul's words, it remains to be *seen*, of course, and thereby made known concretely as something of the Spirit in itself.

## The Shape of the Present Study

Our study will be structured according to three sections, each of which respectively corresponds broadly to the phenomenal categories of pneumatica, reflection and negation, and historical fate (although not in that order), but which also in itself takes up aspects of these perspectives at once. In their course, we will attempt to let the actual pneumatic center of the miracles of Saint-Médard be seen as refracted phenomena of the Holy Spirit's self-demonstration. This discursive and wide-ranging method of exposition is designed not only to reflect in some small way the historically textured reticence of pneumatic self-disclosure, but engage the reader in that kind of discipline in attentive sifting that alone can move toward an apprehension of the Spirit's display in time. Summaries at the beginning of each chapter will, I hope, provide clarifying indications of the movement taken in the course of such an exercise of viewing.

As Bishop Douglas's "disinterested" summary suggests, the prodigies associated with François de Pâris are properly viewed in the context of disputed Jansenist theologies of grace in particular, and to this theology we will devote our first section. By exploring the matter conceptually, we will be able to observe the way in which such a theology not only structured the specific discourse of miraculous phenomena, but was itself, in its enunciation, a contour to the events in question, stripping away traditional scholastic distinctions between created and uncreated grace, and preparing for the cognitive identification of historical phenomena with the direct manifestation of the Spirit. In our second section, we shall look closely at the traditionally designated "pneumatic" phenomena of miracle and holiness as we try to see how this peculiar theology of grace and the data of the historical experience of particular "graces" or gifts confronted each other and arranged themselves descriptively in an integrated vision of divine appearance within time, understood in terms of scripturally figured form. Finally, in our last section, we shall assume this "figural" mode of viewing that was associated with a specific exegetical practice, explore its character, and see how the vision it orchestrated was itself an element of prophetic experience that eventually subsumed the phenomenal events of the miracles and of their rejection by the Church into a broad posture of pneumatic reticence.

Thus, through a cumulative seeing, which will pass through particulars of theology, pneumatica, and the historical scope of prophetic vision, the present study's examination of our episode, acknowledged by all parties to be pneumatologically challenging, will end by testing and even revealing to some degree the limits placed on pneumatological affirmation by the Spirit's own display. The episode of Saint-Médard is one which centers on a saintly deacon, François de Pâris, known for his penitential self-lacerations and for an obstinate adherence to those Jansenist clergy who refused to subscribe to the 1713 papal bull *Unigenitus* that had condemned many of their teachings; it centers on de Pâris's unremarkable life and death, on the furious theological polemics that formed a conceptual cloak to his and many other similar lives, both those that preceded and those that followed his; it centers on the miracles of healing and the convulsions that erupted at de Pâris's death in 1727, and continued for many years even after the official closing of the Saint-Médard cemetery where his tomb was kept; it centers on discussions of grace and manuals of devotion, on catechisms and biblical exegesis, all of which, however unintentionally, formed the spaces in which the *ostensio Spiritus* could take place, or not, and if it did, be structurally formed by the scaffolding of events far into the future. But to say that this study is given over to an episode so centered is also to say that its *ostensio Spiritus* is given over to a mode of appearing best characterized by the problem of its own obscurity and tendency to forgottenness, already *apparent* in a summary like Bishop Douglas's and in the whole course of Saint-Médard's reassertion in historical memory. A phenomenology of the Spirit in such events so characterized must therefore face the manifest obscuring of its object within the very events deemed crucial to its demonstration.[19] And a derived pneumatology, based on such phenomena, can only adjust itself according to the problematic nature of such pneumatic veiling. Our own concluding suggestion for a "kenotic" pneumatology is a response to just these problematic qualities of the Spirit's ostensive self-display.

Indeed, the problematic nature of the Saint-Médard episode, in its wider reach, is acknowledged even by those with no overt theological interests in the matter. Contemporary scholars have introduced us to the intricately confusing political elements involved;[20] others have fastened the events precariously to understandings of social change in eighteenth century France, amid the larger historical evolutions of cultural *mentalités*;[21] even at the time, observers in France and England like Voltaire and Hume saw the purely intellectual and disconcerting challenges posed by the miracles and convulsions to philosophical perspectives increasingly framed in independence of theistic categories.[22] That one of the clearest, most succinct, and generally accurate summaries of our episode is that

19. From 1712, when the last building of Port-Royal des Champs — the symbolic focus of Jansenist life — was destroyed by royal edict and the bodies of its heroines and saints exhumed and dispersed, these "centers" of the continuing Jansenist movement, some yet to take flesh, were figuratively linked to an increasingly difficult process of wresting spiritual power from the historical drift that instead led to their concealment. Soon after, the abbé d'Étemare and others propelled the drive of Jansenist resistance to *Unigenitus* through a series of "cries" against forgetting, with their *Gémissements d'une âme vivement touchée de la destruction du saint monastère de Port-Royal-des Champs* (3rd edition, n.p., 1734); see also d'Étemare's *Quatrième Gémissement d'une âme vivement touché de la Constitution de N.-S.P. Clément XI* (n.p., 1714); manuals of pilgrimage to Port-Royal and other Jansenist shrines, like that of Gazagnes in 1767, pressed remembrance against an inevitable tide to the other side (*Manuel des Pèlerins de Port-Royal Des Champs*, ["Au Desert," 1767]); Grégoire's nineteenth-century *Les Ruines de P.-R. des Champs*, taking up a rediscovered manual like this, attempted for post-revolutionary France to revivify the meaning of a now-lost Jansenism (corrected edition, Paris: Lavacher, 1809); just as, in 1816, Miss Schimmelpennick's *Narrative of the demolition of the monastery of Port-Royal des Champs* did the same for a bemused English audience, curious over a vanished holiness. And so on, through Sainte-Beuve and others, until today, when the people, places, and writings of these events have settled permanently into the store-bins of scholarly marginalia.

20. See Kreiser, *Miracles, Convulsions, and Ecclesiastical Politics in Early Eighteenth-Century Paris*.

21. See Maire, *Les convulsionnaires de Saint-Médard*.

22. See Voltaire's remarks on the convulsions in the *Philosophical Dictionary*. Hume reflects on Saint-Médard in Section X, "Of Miracles," in his *An Enquiry Concerning Human Understanding*.

provided in 1752 by an English bishop, John Douglas, whom we have already quoted, is itself revealing, for Douglas's descriptive piece is given in the service of *confuting* all post–New Testament miracles, whatever evidences in their favor, in order to save the Bible's historical truths from both papist distortions and Deist attacks. The result, as Leslie Stephens writes, "illustrates most completely the illusions under which the semi-rationalists attempted to banish from the world all supernatural agency but that which they favored in absolute confidence in the impregnability of their cause,"[23] an example thus of the way that even "seeing" these phenomena clearly translated almost immediately into a difficult contest over their obscure significance. As with the case of St. Benedict Joseph Labre, though to a far more extended degree, a phenomenological study of the Holy Spirit in these events of Saint-Médard will expose a *lack* of pneumatological coherence, derived directly from the nature of pneumatic self-definition itself.

Our conclusion regarding kenotic pneumatology, then, much in the wake of St. Paul's words, will aim at revealing the *coincidence* of this pneumatological incoherence with the *scandalon* of the manifest Cross of Christ, mentioned by St. Paul in 1 Corinthians 1:23, and in 2:2 as the being the object of the Spirit's own appearing in power.[24] To speak of "coincidence" here, however, is to distinguish the simply described appearance of the Spirit in "Christ crucified" from a definition of the Spirit's "function" or "role" or "work" as one of "revealing." It is to say, rather, that the theology of the Holy Spirit ends at this point, for this is the place where the *ostensio Spiritus* is consummated for us. By way of contrast, it could be argued, for instance, that Luther, who also linked the Spirit's life with the revelation of the Cross, did so rather in terms of a "characteristic" pneumatic work. As a result, the historical phenomena of such appearance were also abstracted into their "characteristic" qualities: the Spirit, in some of Luther's writing, becomes the agential energy of God's *opus alienum* in its entirety, and the various elements characteristic of this "work" begin to define the Spirit in terms of their principle.[25] As with modern theologies like Moltmann's, *pneuma* in such a construct becomes or may become the basis for an agenda governed by an a priori theological principle. The notion of pneumatological incoherence coincident with the phenomenon of the Cross as I shall formulate it, however, is not meant so much to link Spirit and Cross in a characteristic manner as merely to limit the former by the latter in terms of revealing phenomena. It is not meant to deny identifiable pneumatic events or pneumatic works — far

---

23. Leslie Stephen, *History of English Thought in the Eighteenth Century* (New York: G. P. Putnam's Sons, 1876), 1:404.

24. The most moving, and original aspect of John Paul II's encyclical, Section II, deals with just this theme, taking as its basis John 16:7–8, where the Spirit's disclosure of sin, justice, and judgment to the world is shown to involve primarily the unveiling of the reality of the crucified Savior.

25. See Regin Prenter's *Spiritus Creator* (Philadelphia: Muhlenburg Press, 1953), especially chapter 1.

from it! — but only to say what is the object of their appearance, what it is they display when they are seen. It is not meant to void reference to the Spirit of proper semantic substance, but rather to limit the "usefulness" of such substance theologically for anything beyond the bare enunciations of fact attached to the more extensive discursive breadth of Christological affirmation.

This corresponds, as St. Paul indicates, to a way of describing Christ that carries with it the pneumatic phenomena which, as we have been given them, end by constituting the scriptural record of simple juxta-position between the Spirit's limited appearance and the more fully rendered form of Jesus the Christ. The systematic implications of this kind of conclusion point toward an "emptied" pneumatology, a "kenotic" pneumatology in a peculiar application of the term, and we shall pursue something of its meaning in our final chapter. But as a normative judg-ment about what pneumatology ought to look like, as a conclusion about limits to be drawn and respected in talking about and reflecting on the Holy Spirit, our final reflections remain at base but an attempt to train the eye to see the world and God at once, without flinching.

# CAUSA GRATIAE: CHARACTER, FORM, AND SPIRIT

# Chapter One

# THE QUESTION
# OF GRACE

Jansenism, as Bishop Douglas noted for his English readers, was a movement within French Catholicism defined by a particular theology of grace.
The Jansenist miracles of Saint-Médard, which are the ultimate object
of our phenomenological investigation of the Holy Spirit, were basically
informed by this theology of grace. And as the first section of our study explores this theology, it will do so with an eye to the particular structuring
relationship that Jansenist attitudes toward grace held for the subsequent
experience of miracle, attitudes that construed divine grace peculiarly in
terms of its historical character, its sensible figure, and its pneumatic nature. We will devote a chapter to each of these terms, which together
provide a foundational reflection on the character of pneumatic experience itself, the Jansenist perspective upon which we examine in our second
section.

It will be useful, before embarking on this first section, to offer some
general remarks on how, as a reflection upon pneumatic experience, Jansenist understandings of grace do in fact mark one aspect of the *ostensio
Spiritus* we are attempting to identify. Such remarks are in order first, because the connection between a presupposed theological framework, like
the concept of divine grace, and a description of pneumatic experience,
like bodily healing, is not immediately evident; and they are in order, second, because the very notion of a consistent "Jansenist theology of grace,"
spanning the seventeenth and eighteenth centuries in such a way as to
scaffold the events of Saint-Médard, is not unanimously accepted among
scholars.

To respond to these two issues let us begin with the 1731 miracle
whose account opens Carré de Montgeron's sprawling defense of the Saint-
Médard phenomena, and attempt to see how the conceptuality of grace is
embedded in the narrative. Carré de Montgeron starts things off with a
summary of the event:

> Dom Alphonse de Palacios's right eye had begun to succumb to the same
> problems that had caused him to lose the sight of his left eye in 1725,
> and now he was suffering intense pain because of an inflammation of the
> retina. The fact that it was now beginning to dry out announced the on-
> set of incurable blindness. At this point he was struck by the account of

miracles accomplished through the intercession of Monsieur de Paris. His Spanish origins were not enough to prevent him from seeking the help of this Holy Appellant, whose divine favor God had declared through undeniable miracles. God's mercy began by opening the eyes of the spirit and heart of this young Spanish lord. Despite the fact that his sufferings redoubled and that he experienced a total blindness during the first days of his novena, his confidence could not be shaken. And he soon received the prize: on the morning of the eighth day of the novena, his right eye was suddenly and perfectly healed. Prayer was the sole means.

After long pages of critical argument concerning the authenticity of the miracle, Carré de Montgeron ends with an almost devotional defense of the religious significance of Dom de Palacios's healing. Here, in part, is what he writes:

Finally, *holiness* [*sainteté*] and *truth* [*vérité*] were made manifest in this miracle in the most tangible [*sensible*] and consoling of ways. It is an aspect proper to God that He should strengthen and illuminate the eyes of the soul by providing sight to the body. It is also the case that through this miracle, Dom Alphonse acquired an intrepid courage, that allowed him to trample upon all the most brilliant promises of fortune, to make himself vulnerable to all things for the sake of the love of the Truth, and to suffer with an invincible patience and generosity his captivity and the solicitations of his home. The way he expresses these feelings in his letters reminds us of the constancy and faith of the first Christians of the early centuries.

It was on seeing this prodigy, further, that M. Roulié de Filtieres was happily touched by a powerful grace, one which brought him back to a sense of himself and of eternity; which led him to renounce the pomp and seductive pleasures of this age to which, until then, he had been so open [*auquels il avoit été si sensibles*]; and which, finally, led him to perceive another kind of happiness and another set of goods for which he would willingly sacrifice the goods of this earth.

[...] In all these characteristics we must recognize the works of the Master of hearts, of the God of power, who appears all the more admirable in the operations of his grace even than when, in healing bodies, he renders obedient that clay that supports them.

[...] How thick is the darkness, in the midst of which, instead of offering thanks to the Almighty for such a brilliant healing, a bishop mockingly says that "the real Miracle would have been to open the left eye [...] but the new Saint," as he says a little later, "limited himself to healing the eye that still worked!."

[...]We should rather tremble in the face of these terrible judgments, insofar as God did not choose to heal all at once the two eyes of Dom Alphonse. Take note, with fear, how His justice always accompanies His mercy, and thus how He wished to leave a cloud next to the light in order to blind those who would be blind. The pillar of cloud which illumined the trembling Israelites was, at the same time, destined to blind the proud Egyptians. The Truth is given to righteous hearts, and while she grants them sufficient light for her apprehension, she always allows to those other hearts sufficient darkness for her rejection and misunderstanding.

This, O Savior of men, is how your own poor and obscure life served as the basis upon which the haughty Pharisees denied and blasphemed your works. How useless it would be, O my God, were you still in our day to strike the eyes of our flesh by the spectacle of your marvels, unless you also deigned to soften our hearts by the unction of your grace, and to illuminate our darkness by the light of your spirit. Alas! We have eyes, but we do not see, because we are not worthy to see. But, Lord, say to our souls: See!, and they will see.[1]

In all of this, of course, grace (as the Truth) is presenting a "work" whose very shape acts as a kind of argument, one that Carré de Montgeron claims to relate in the character of the lawyer that he is. The shape is the miracle itself, to be sure, but it is just this identification that provides the notion of "grace" here a wide, but still peculiar, definition.

In the first place, there is a group of characteristics that we might relate to the "tangible" — in Carré de Montgeron's terms, the *sensible*, experience as it grips and moves us. God's holiness and truth are "tangible and consoling"; the body itself, in the miracle, gives way under the pressure of grace, and even more broadly, stands as a kind of sensitive sheath for the human soul; in all, that which is invisible in the spirit touches the eyes figuratively through the shape of the body, and the dramatic changes in character that take place under the influence of the miracle — the touching of the "heart," the pull away from other "tangible attractions" — sparkle to the eyes of onlookers.

Next is a group of descriptions of grace in which the element of historical particularity is prominent: dates, days, the durations of novenas, letters, the creation of a chain of events that moves from a history of suffering and courage, through the miracle, to a series of changed lives in an ever-widening circle of acquaintance. And in all of this, the present lifts up the image of the past, the experience of Israel, the "first centuries" of the Church's life, now revivified, so that the particularities emerge from a profound historical continuity with the original figure of Christ's redeemed life in His Body, typified as well in the dispensation of the Exodus.

Finally, grace is tied to and even identified with a group of descriptions of God that emphasize the two above categories as being embodiments of the divinity itself: God is the "master of hearts," the "creator of being" and the "molder of clay"; God "strikes" the soul through the figure of the body, and adopts a relationship of ordered judgment and mercy toward collectives and individuals as they make their way through time. Light and dark dispensed from God's side, the weight of God's hand thrust into a life, the power of God to reorganize the organs of flesh and spirit, to be manifested in these changes — all of this too is described as the being of grace.

---

1. Carré de Montgeron, *La Verité des Miracles opérés à l'intercession de M. de Pâris et autres Appellans, démontrée contre M. L'Archevêque de Sens* (Utrecht, 1737), vol. 1, 61–2.

Carré de Montgeron's descriptive rendering of grace in terms of the *sensible* of divine history was not unique, and, however reflective of developing eighteenth-century semantic parameters, relied on language already well in place early in the century. The Abbé d'Étemare, for instance, contributed two enormous volumes to a series devoted to the doctrines condemned by *Unigenitus*, written before the miracles occurred and long before Carré de Montgeron's immersion into the further gestural extravagances of the convulsions. At one point, driven by the piling up of his prose to give a definition of grace, d'Étemare produces this: "grace is a feeling [*sentiment*], that softens the heart, that penetrates it, that grips it [*qui l'intéresse*], that pleases it; it is a holy unction, that strengthens the heart at the same time, that causes it to taste the purest joy."[2] The general parallels of this definition, it could be argued, to the description of grace that attends Dom de Palacios's healing are real.

But the parallel is ultimately with dogmatic formulations of the matter. D'Étemare had earlier proposed an image of a trial between God and human creatures over the issue of grace, and we can see there at least a hint of the way in which a strict and narrow set of theological propositions about grace — the "Jansenist" credo — might be linked to the kind of loose, swirling, and sensuously gripping rivulets of the *sensible* we have just dipped into.[3] The divine dispute, says d'Étemare, is after all, derived from the promulgation of the bull *Unigenitus*. D'Étemare is writing his lengthy volumes as a contribution to the defense of Quesnel's *Réflexions Morales*, from which were drawn the propositions the bull condemned. We *are* dealing with doctrine, then, "propositions" to be exegeted, argued over, and supported with reference to Scripture and tradition.

This is a divine dispute, then, but in this context, it is defined in terms of a dispute over doctrine. The doctrine, however, we are told, comes down to this: "God's omnipotence and His domain over men, the right He has to dispose of His own work, and to decide the fate of his own creature." And this, we are further told, is St. Augustine's view of the matter at issue in the Pelagian controversy:

> Is God really God, or isn't He? Further (and this is a horrible thing to think), is Man a God? Here, properly speaking, is the point of the whole question. For there isn't any middle ground: either man is master of his will, of his fate, and of his salvation, or God is. [ . . . ] What is at stake in this dispute, then, are the most intimate rights of God over His creature. And what is remarkable is that Man pretends, not only to strip God naked, but to invest himself with all he has taken away from Him. For what he takes away from God, he grants to his own free will. It is, thus, for his own rights that he

---

2. Jean-Baptiste Le Sesne des Ménilles d'Étemare, *Remarques en forme de dissertations sur les Propositions condânées par la Bule Unigenitus. Ou IV Colone des Hexaples. Dans laquelle on fait la comparaison de la nouvele Doctrine des Jesuites autorisée par la Bule, avec la Doctrine de l'Eglise établie par l'Ecriture, les Sains Péres et les Auteurs Eclesiastiques* (n.p., 1723), vol. 1, 409

3. See ibid., xii ff.

disputes with God. And God is rightly, therefore, in dispute with man, and man is in dispute with God.[4]

D'Étemare now elaborates: not only is God's power in general in dispute, but more particularly is the character of Jesus Christ as Savior. Only if Christ is truly Savior can we claim that God's love and plans are not "useless" and His promises not "empty." Therefore, we are in dispute over "who decides salvation," God or human free will. If through the law of works, then "the promises are made of no effect" (Rom. 4:14) and Christ as died "in vain."

And so the "matters of grace" are "fundamental to the Christian faith." But how so in particular? Look at the case of Paul, that is, the "dispute" in which he played a role: the Jews claimed salvation through the work of the human will, aided by the law. Paul, instead, contended for Jesus Christ, insofar as Jesus Christ *changes souls and heals them interiorly.* "He is the author and distributor of justice," Paul claimed, and in so doing, Paul provided the criterion of the true Messiah, the Messiah in dispute, the *causa Dei* of the first century: the real Messiah changes hearts.[5]

"In all these elements and features, we must recognize that Master of our hearts," as we quoted Carré de Montgeron above, whose grace is even more wonderful in *this* respect than in the healing of our bodies. And the "way of faith," according to the abbé d'Étemare, is this very "doctrine of grace," whose acceptance founds and is founded by the work of a Messiah who changes us from within.[6]

The claim is made, then, that there is one single *causa*, from Paul, through Augustine, through others like Bradwardine, through (as we shall note) the Congregatio *De Auxiliis*, through the Formulaire on the Five Propositions of Jansenius, through *Unigenitus*, through Saint-Médard. Carré de Montgeron will claim this, along with others. The *causa* is grace, a doctrine that provides its own argument, whose utterance offer its own effect, whose effects proliferate. Not only does this claim assert the providential connection between a particular doctrinal construction and experienced historical phenomena like pneumatic healings, but it asserts that the doctrinal construction itself is consistently informative of an ecclesiastical tradition wedded to its defense over time.

Those who dispute the existence of a continuous "Jansenist" outlook through much of the eighteenth century, defined especially by a constant understanding of divine grace, have tended to downplay historical summaries by participants like d'Étemare.[7] In their apt attempts to respond to

---

4. Ibid., xii–xiii.

5. Ibid., xiv–xv.

6. Ibid., xvi.

7. There are at least three major objections to the claim for theological constancy made by contemporary scholars of Jansenism. The first objection argues that any accurate answer to the question "What is a Jansenist?" must render useless any attempt to suggest a theological structure as being "constant" in their thought (Orcibal and Ceyssens). A second objection, of a more limited scope, argues that particularly on the topic of grace, no such constant can

anti-Jansenist caricature, so prevalent in nineteenth- and early twentieth-century scholarship and so willfully blind to nuance, modern scholars have tended to pass over the unavoidably pressing and consistent self-witness of Jansenists themselves. The enormous theological significance of the bull *Unigenitus*, and its power to rally the opposition, lay exactly in its condemnation of a set of doctrinal propositions to which a broad array of clergy and other Christians were committed just *because* of their his-torical sympathies with specific elements of Jansenist thought (whether or not they considered themselves members of the movement). The purpose of the bull, after all, was to reassert, in as broad a way as possible, the heretical nature of the Five Propositions of Jansenius, papally condemned in 1653.[8] And it was precisely because the disputed doctrine that lay be-hind the Propositions was still a matter of conviction that the bull hit home for so many French Catholics.

Thus, we *do* find a vein of concern that unites the earliest defenders of Jansenius to the later Appellants;[9] by the same token, we also find a consistent attempt on the part of these defenders, from very early on, to apply orthodox theological categories, like those of the neo-Thomists to explicate and to justify their defense. A late Appellant like Carré de Montgeron lists the elements of the *causa gratiae Dei* as follows:

be articulated (Orcibal, Cognet, Dedieu, Maire). Finally, while some students of the Jansenist movement are willing to see a common defining quality at work in the whole, they prefer (sometimes because of the above objections) to identify this quality in terms more of "psy-chological" affinity than strict theological principle (Orcibal, Cognet, Knox, and Campbell). See J. Orcibal, "Qu'est-ce que le Jansénisme?" *Cahiers de l'Association Internationale des Études françaises* 3–45 (July 1953); L. Ceyssens, "Le jansénisme: Considerations historiques préliminaires à sa notion," in *Analecta Gregoriana* 71 (1953); P. Hurtubise, "Jansénisme ou jansénismes," in *Modernité et non-conformisme en France à travers les âges,* ed. Myriam Yardeni (Leiden: E. J. Brill, 1983); Louis Cognet, *Le Jansénisme* (Paris: Presses Universi-taires de France, 1961), 123f.; see also Émil Jacques, *Les Années d'Exil d'Antoine Arnauld (1676–1694)* (Louvain: Publications Universitaires de Louvain, 1976), ix; Dedieu, "L'agonie du Jansénisme," *Revue d'Histoire de l'Église de France* 14 (1928): 164–66 (but severely qual-ified on 167), followed by Catherine-Laurence Maire, *Les convulsionnaires de Saint-Médard: Miracles, convulsions et prophéties à Paris au XVIIIe siècle* (Paris: Gallimard/Julliard, 1985), 23; Ronald A. Knox, *Enthusiasm: A Chapter in the History of Religion with Special Refer-ence to the Seventeenth and Eighteenth Centuries* (Oxford: Oxford University Press, 1950), e.g., 227ff.; Ted Campbell, *The Religion of the Heart: A Study of European Religious Life in the Seventeenth and Eighteenth Centuries* (Columbia: University of South Carolina Press, 1991), 29.

8. See the review of *Unigenitus,* drawing on Ceyssens's vast labors, by Gres-Gayer, "The *Unigenitus* of Clement XI: A Fresh Look at the Issues," *Theological Studies* 49 (1988): esp. 264–70 and 276–78.

9. The term "Appellant," as noted by Bishop Douglas in the Introduction, refers to those French Catholics who rejected or at least questioned the authority of *Unigenitus's* 1713 condemnation of Quesnel's "101 Propositions," and who instead "appealed" to a future General Council in order to rule on the orthodoxy of those doctrines concerned. We shall use the term "Appellant" broadly, as inclusive of virtually all French Jansenists in the wake of *Unigenitus,* recognizing as we do so that there were differences among them as to the political tack they sought to take with respect to the bull. Appellant theology itself is varied, having only the doctrine implied in the condemned propositions for a common base. Not all Appellants, furthermore, went along with the miracles of Saint-Médard, let alone with the convulsions. Still, there are some major theological structures that link most of the different factions. It is with these that we will be dealing in our first section.

1. "Free predestination," according to Ephesians 1:4–5.

2. "Efficacious grace" for salvation; a grace that works by faith and works with the human will such that "grace does all in the will and the will does all by grace."

3. The necessity of love for God as the motivating and directing force in all of our actions, especially penitence.

4. In particular, the need in this last sacrament, for the sinner to have a "sincere desire" to give up sin.[10]

Bishop Colbert of Montpellier, an earlier supporter of the Saint-Médard miracles and of the first convulsionaries, gives a summary that, although couched in different language, comes down to similar concerns:

1. "God exercises sovereignty over the hearts of men by the force of grace."

2. In particular, "God is almighty in the human heart with respect to matters of salvation."

3. There is "an obligation to refer all of our actions to God by a principle of love."

To be sure, Colbert also adds a further, peculiarly Saint-Médariste, fundamental:

4. "God's marvelous operations, which are made to appear on the body, are an image and figure of those he makes gleam in the soul."[11]

One of our tasks, of course, will be to see how no. 4 is in fact related to no. 1 through no. 3; but we cannot assume that its presence is essentially deformative of the set as a whole. In any case, this set of doctrinal principles is basically at one with other, non-miraculist Appellant creeds.[12]

It should be remembered that these eighteenth-century Appellant summaries, based as they are on a defense of Quesnel's doctrine as condemned in *Unigenitus*, are thus necessarily bound up with the alleged error of Baius that lay behind the original objection to Jansenius. That is, in particular, there is the general "Jansenist" affirmation, for fallen humanity, of the exclusive and irresistible "necessity" of efficacious grace (as shown below) to fulfill a person's salvific vocation. It is just this affirmation that remains an essential element understood, by all parties, as being set upon by the later bull.

A glance at one of the earliest defenses of Jansenius, written almost a decade before the papal condemnation of the Five Propositions, can do nothing but confirm the consistent prominence of this notion of efficacious grace from the beginning. In his *Seconde Apologie de Jansenius*

---

10. *La Verité des Miracles*, vol. 2, 48.

11. Colbert, *Instruction Pastorale du 1er Février, 1733*, in *Oeuvres*, vol. 2, 27.

12. See the *Instructions sur les vérités qui concernent la grace de N.S. Jesus-Christ* (Paris: 1747), vol. 1, 312. Here, the propositions are elaborated with respect to the "incarnational" theology that Orcibal wants to see as somehow peculiar to Quesnellism, and thus at a distance from at least much of seventeenth-century Jansenism. But does this theological scaffolding in any way alter the defining centrality of the propositions themselves?

(1645) Arnauld returns continually to the question of "efficacious grace" in his attempt to refute the charges of Habert against the bishop of Ypres. The centrality of the issue and the argument Arnauld uses remains consistent throughout his life: (1) efficacious grace is necessary for any good (salvific) act; (2) is, by definition, irresistible in fact, although not in theory since there always remains in the human will the capacity for opposites; (3) and is not contrary to the freedom of the will, since the will freely, if inevitably, cooperates with the divine love that inspires it. Arnauld draws his justifications not only from Jansenius's own words, but, in his usual method, from Scripture, Augustine, Thomas, and the Dominicans of the Congregatio *De Auxiliis*.[13] In 1686, when Arnauld attacks the entire notion of a "Jansenistic" sect as a "spectre," he is still struggling to defend the same doctrine and still appealing to the same sources.[14] A perusal of Quesnel's arguments several decades later would reveal how little the fundamental issues have changed, despite the now more extensive formulations of them that must be confronted, given the 101 condemned propositions of *Unigenitus*.[15]

Some general notion of grace, then, is at the identifying center of Jansenism, and it remains so through the eighteenth century. This is not to say either that articulations of this notion are not varied, and even to such an extent as to provide it peculiar orientations, nor that commitments to this notion as a whole or to aspects of it are not common to theologians who are not considered "Jansenist." But Arnauld can call "Jansenism" a spectre not because he does not self-consciously hold theological commitments in common with other members of an identifiable movement, but because he believes those commitments themselves are in continuity with the Church's traditions as a whole, with which, of course, many other individuals comply. To the degree that perceived enemies of this tradition concerning grace are "anti-Jansenistic," Jansenism stands as an integral theological perspective of positive rebuttal.

And it is just such positive theology that must, if we are to take it seriously as an integral facet of any religious movement that propounds it, somehow be essentially linked to whatever psycho-cultural and culturo-affective orientations one might also perceive as being at work. As Campbell and Knox to some degree affirm, there *is* a continuity of the "heart" from Saint-Cyran to the Appellants, even the Saint-Médardistes, and an attempt to grasp the theological webs of support for such a *sensibilité* is surely called for.

While Arnauld was not, to be sure, well-known for his spiritual writings, even in this consummate controversialist we can gain glimpses of

---

13. The *Seconde Apologie* is found in the reprint of Arnauld's *Oeuvres*, vol. 17. See esp. 180–220.

14. Antoine Arnauld, *Le Fantôme du Jansenisme*, in *Oeuvres*, vol. 25; on the recurrent neo-Thomist argument, see 41.

15. Pasquier Quesnel, *Plainte et Protestation* [after the author's second edition] (1717). See esp. 92ff.

such a web, and one that ought to belie any notions of some great cleav-
age between the classically theological postures of the seventeenth-century
Port-Royal and the later Appellant enthusiasms. Two examples will suffice
to demonstrate this confidence.

In one short work of direction, he answers a question that surely only
a theologically Jansenist Catholic could ask: "Ought I to thank God for
my predestination?"[16] Here Arnauld carefully outlines the way in which
an individual ought to think of her or his relation to God's will. Faith
banishes fear, he writes, while hope exists *with* fear. It is the latter attitude
that God grants with respect to predestination — that is, we may hope that
we are among the elect, but only fearfully, lest, as Thomas says, we become
somehow negligent of our Christian calling for reasons of presumption.

How then is fear properly "hopeful"? First, Arnauld explains, though
our salvation is uncertain, our hope for it is grounded in the historical
fact of Christ's own death for us and the promises He made to us — God's
goodness, His wish to save us, His own sacrifice, all of this testifies to
the *kind* of God we have. But second — and this proves Arnauld's main
argument throughout his life on this subject — we have the "testimony"
of God's love at work in our hearts. Using Paul's language from Romans
(e.g., 8:16), Arnauld emphasizes how the Holy Spirit "gives witness" to our
spirit of the love without which salvation has no meaning or existence.
(This verse, of course, plays an equally important, though less nuanced
role in Wesley's teaching.) Since we "feel" this love at work, and feel it
grow within our lives, our confidence is all the more strengthened as we
look to the Christ who is the source of love.

This "testimony of love" becomes the constant theme of Arnauld's limited writings of spiritual direction. We are to look for it not only in our
lives, but in the lives of others, in the life of the Church itself.[17] Just as
important, however, as these signs of love may be for indicating God's
presence in the hope of predestination, there are also the small signs of
wrath and justice that abut our lives: our sense of sin, the flutter of re-
morse, the vast gulfs that tell us of God's hiddenness and absence.[18] If
we can *recognize* and *feel* the personal weight of God's choices for our
life — and here Arnauld is simply speaking of the conscious identification
of efficacious grace at work, both in its saving and in its efficaciously limited and unsaving modes — choices that inspire fear and trembling and
even bitter disappointment, we can be brought into that place where all is
acknowledged as grace, is experienced to be so, and is thereby made the
carapace of our salvation.

It is precisely because this kind of *sensibilité*, for someone like Arnauld,
was so thoroughly grounded theologically that de Lubac (following Blondel
on this score) could afford to turn his attention wholly to the side of the

---

16. Arnauld, *Oeuvres* 26:95.
17. See ibid., 9–11.
18. See ibid., vol. 1, Letters 58 and 80.

experienced shape of grace as the Jansenists explained it, and concentrate most especially on a conceptual critique of their interpretation of the Augustinian doctrine itself.[19] But this approach, even if it disregards through prejudice half of the story, at least demonstrates the case that I am making: from the earliest moment of Jansenism until its most lurid devolution among the convulsionaries, there is reason to believe in the motivating existence of theological structures that inform the specific attitudes Jansenists themselves would take with respect to their own theological vocation.

In the three chapters that follow, a case will be made for the existence of a set of three broad Jansenist theological structures, which singly and together inform the movement's understanding of grace. These broad structures, I will argue, underpin the more developed and peculiar Appellant view of matter in dispute, the *causa Dei* that is grace. In chapter 2 we will argue for the influence of a peculiarly Jansenistic emphasis on the historical dimension of grace. In chapter 3 we will look at how Jansenism, especially as it appropriated concerns of the French Oratory, saw this

---

19. See de Lubac, *Augustinianism and Modern Theology* (London: Geoffrey Chapman, 1969), 43, on the implications of Jansenius's understanding of Adam's Fall as a kind of "determinism" from below — concupiscence — mimicking the subsequent determinism of redeeming efficacious grace (quoting Blondel): "When man falls, he falls in his entirety, and all of a piece. And he cannot be rescued from the mire save by an experienced attraction, by the domination of an opposite and entirely holy concupiscence. Grace remains extrinsic; it does not fall into the promiscuity of a wholly corrupt nature; it is for this reason that for the saving action to be effected an attraction must be felt and experienced. *And this opens the door to illusions and deceptive exaltations of the individual consciousness*" (emphasis added). The notion that "extrinsicism" in the construal of grace leads to the uncontrolled enthusiasms of, e.g., miracles is a common one, at least as used to describe Jansenists. Bremond's disdain of the Jansenists feeds on this evaluation, and it has been followed by other scholars who see the anti-mystical and anti-contemplative strain of Jansenism as a repressive force whose fracture accounts for later Appellant extravagances. See F. Ellen Weaver's conclusions to her *Evolution of the Reform of Port-Royal* (Paris: Beauchesne, 1978), 154ff. (See also her "Saint-Cyran's 'Prière du Pauvre' vs. Nicole's 'Oraison Mentale': A Conflict over Styles of Prayer at Port-Royal," in *Citeaux: Commentarii cisterciensesi* 24 [1978], where later Jansenism is oddly aligned with the development of systematized mental prayer.) But it is also possible to see the *bête-noire* of Jansenism, that is, "Molinist" construals of grace, as directly contradictory of such blatantly experientialist attitudes as those found among the Saint-Médardistes. This, at least, is the argument of Francis Clark's "Grace-Experience in the Roman Catholic Tradition" (in *Journal of Theological Studies,* New series 25, 1974), which offers a fascinating reading of Molina's scheme as standing quite close to Nominalist-Protestant predestinarian rejections of "sensible grace." The Jansenist example, however, ought to alert us to the difficulty of typifying such construals, for they managed to maintain a strict Augustinian predestinarian outlook, sometimes even joined with a nominalist metaphysic, that, although informed by a distrust in mystical sensibility, was nonetheless strongly affirmative of necessary and particularized actions of grace within time that were capable of apprehension. With respect to this last element, Jansenists stood squarely against the Molinists. But even more crucially, as we shall see, what was at issue was not the reality of "grace-experience" itself, in Clark's formulation, but the character of its contestability within a world of competing experiences. While certainly an Augustinian concern, this is not one de Lubac himself addresses clearly. It must be said, further, that Appellant "experiences" of grace, while rarely located at the level of mystical consciousness of either an individual or corporately contemplative kind, nonetheless bare a resemblance to the "figural" shapes of inner experience detailed by certain spiritual writers like Surin and Grignon de Montfort.

historical dimension of grace as being constrained by a particular set of forms, the forms of Jesus' Mysteries. Finally, in chapter 4 we will see how Jansenism's linkage of both this history and its forms to the Holy Spirit provided Appellant theology with a vision of grace that construed God's immediate presence in terms of the Church's history as it is configurated to the shape of Jesus' scripturally defined life. Taken together, these broad elements of outlook on the topic of grace laid the groundwork for Appellant Jansenism's view of grace as the divine Figure of Christ enacted in history, in part, through the pneumatic reality of miracles and their rejection.

From a historically genetic point of view, we could say that, in large measure, the Appellancy given voice in the Saint-Médard miracle represents the flowering of certain fundamental Jansenist concerns about grace as they are specifically colored by the influence of some broad devotional patterns bequeathed by the "French School" of Bérulle and his followers. We will see, then, especially in chapters 3 and 4 of this section, how Jansenist Oratorians like Quesnel and Duguet prove decisive innovators in this development. However, the crucial role played by the importation of Oratorian concerns must not be seen as minimizing the even more critical force of originally Jansenistic commitments in establishing the shape of Appellant theological experience. This will be our final observation before turning, in the next section, to the question of miracle itself: Jansenism posed a set of affirmations about grace that, in their reception, logically led to certain expectations about their self-promotion and self-defense. If grace is as we have learned it to be, the Appellants reasoned, then given the times in which we live, God through His grace will act in a certain way. In this first section on grace, then, we will outline the boundaries of those expectations, the fulfillment of which carried with it the obscure *ostensio Spiritus* we are tracking.

# Chapter Two

# THE HISTORICAL CHARACTER OF GRACE

## Outline of the Chapter

In this chapter, I will argue that there is a consistent Jansenist view of grace that sees it as that reality which provides a specifically *historical* continuum for the accomplishment of God's loving purposes for the human creature. It is this historical dimension of grace that makes possible, and logically necessary, the later Appellant identification of grace with sensible qualities, a prominent conviction among the supporters of the Saint-Médard miracles and the bridge by which the theology of grace and pneumatic experience are seen as coterminous.

Because of the breadth of the topic, I shall adopt a single focus for the discussion: the developing conceptions among Jansenists of the distinction between Adam's grace in Innocence, and the grace given to fallen human beings. Beginning with de Lubac's negative evaluation of this distinction in Jansenism, I will try to show in response how Jansenism was in fact wedded to a notion of grace's continuity between Innocence and Fall, in such a way as to develop a peculiar insistence on history as the embodiment, in some sense, of grace itself.

In trying to demonstrate the consistency of this point of view among Jansenists, and its axiomatic weight in the rise of Appellant thought, I will examine a number of thinkers, beginning with Jansenius himself, next treating both anti-Thomist and neo-Thomist conceptions held by subsequent Jansenists, and culminating in the work of the Appellant d'Étemare. Finally, in order to provide a more theologically systematic summary to the various attitudes just surveyed, I will ground the "historical dimension" of Jansenist grace in the way in which scholastic categories for grace were fundamentally reinterpreted by a Jansenist like Arnauld.

## The "Historical Continuum" of Grace as an Alternative to de Lubac's Critique of Jansenism

If we are to disengage something of the character of Jansenist understandings of grace, we can do no better than to turn to de Lubac's own critique of that understanding.[1] De Lubac's remains the only serious contemporary wrestling with the theological implications of Jansenist thinking on grace. And, as we noted just above, de Lubac takes seriously enough a theological center of gravity among the Jansenists to affirm its logical generation of the vagaries of *sensibilité*. And the place he implicitly — but unappreciatively — locates that center is in their fierce following of the scent of divine "effects," the scattering and linking of pressing moments of divine exigence upon persons over time.[2]

De Lubac is insistent that the Jansenists' major disorientation derived from their concentration on the fundamental contrast between innocent Adam and fallen humanity. Jansenius set the stage for this, according to de Lubac, by seizing on the "minor" opposition Augustine makes between the divine assistance *sine quo non* — "without which" — Adam could not have willed rightly (but which he was free not to use) and the *adjutorium quo*, the divine assistance directly "by which" sinful people are efficaciously aided toward their salvation. Not only is the emphasizing of this distinction a twisting of Augustine's total thought, says de Lubac — being found only in passing in the late *De correptione et gratia* — but by being made central to their theology of grace, it skews the entire Jansenist understanding of the relation between grace and nature altogether.[3]

It is important to be clear that de Lubac is less interested in the Jansenists for their own sake than he is in rescuing Augustine from their hands so as to adapt him as a model for de Lubac's own view of the relation of grace and nature. And this is a view in which divine love *continuously* initiates, makes effective, and completes all human effort in a relationship of

---

1. De Lubac's seminal 1931 articles on Baius and Jansenius were later incorporated as chapters in *Augustinianism and Modern Theology*, to which we shall refer.

2. The notion that grace ought to be seen as a temporal effect was a traditional scholastic axiom. See Aquinas's definition: "Since God's love means something eternal, it can never be called other than prevenient. Grace, however, signifies an effect in time, which can precede one effect and follow another" (*Summa Theologiae* [henceforth S.T.] 1a2ae 111:3, ad 1). The distinction Thomas makes here between love and grace is one that the Jansenists will usually avoid. The conviction, however, that grace itself is "an effect in time" is one that Jansenists found unavoidable, and that Thomas only comes to stress in the later questions of the *Summa Theologiae* on the Incarnation. The fact that Thomas may here be speaking of "created grace" — this is not clear — while the Jansenists almost universally eschew the distinction "created/uncreated" grace, is itself the final clue that brings into relief the parameters of their general discussion of the *causa gratiae Dei* in relation to other theological construals of grace: the effects of God, in time, argue for a God who is essentially "efficacious."

3. It is interesting to see how a modern scholar of Augustine, largely unaffected by the pervasive mistrust of Jansenism that still dogs a French theologian of an earlier generation like de Lubac, views this question of the "place" of *De correptione* in Augustine's overall theology. J. Patout Burns, for instance, has made a persuasive case that, while the late Augustine's views of grace are indeed distinct from his earliest writings on the topic, the *De correptione* forms a logical outworking of the mature stance on grace Augustine adopted by 418. Thus, the discussion of Adam's grace in Innocence, far from being a potentially misleading obtrusion into an otherwise consistently articulated theory of continual participation in grace by Adam, is really, according to Burns, a coherent element in Augustine's later theology of operative grace. See Burns's *The Development of Augustine's Doctrine of Operative Grace* (Paris: Études Augustiniennes, 1980), Introduction, 129ff., 164ff.

union between the human being and God on the model (and through the guarantee) of the Incarnate Word. The point for de Lubac in all this is that this relationship of gracious love is established *from the beginning* of humanity's creation and is continuous from the state of Innocence through the Fall and Redemption; the relationship of nature to grace is constant and consistently intimate through the history of the human race.[4]

Where de Lubac would argue for continuity, he sees the Jansenists raising up a wall of distinction in the manner of Baius: an almost Pelagian freedom in Innocence, and a graceless natural (or gracious supernatural) servitude after the Fall.[5] But is this contrast really fair to the Jansenists? To be sure, the decisive change in the relation of the creature to divine grace that is marked by the Fall is emphasized by the Jansenists in a way that calls for decisively different judgments, respectively, about the experience of the human creature in the two conditions of innocence and fall. But is there no continuity in the elements that constitute these different experiences? Let us examine this question briefly.

The crux of the problem, for de Lubac, is not that the reality of grace is denied for innocent Adam by the Jansenists, but that they seem, like Baius, to describe it in terms of a necessary "debt" given over by God to Adam for his free use, that is, as an extrinsic "object." Jansenius, says de Lubac, "comes close to asserting" that Adam's original grace was "postulated by essential claims when,

> after saying that God owes it to himself to grant his help to the being whom he has just created, he assigns as reason for it not so much the sublimeness of the end to which God destines him, as the weakness of the creature which, brought out of nothingness, always retains an inclination for nothingness.[ . . . ] In the same spirit Quesnel exclaimed: "Gratia Adami est sequela creationis, et erat debita naturae sanae et integrae [Proposition 35 condemned by *Unigenitus*]."[6]

There is nothing particularly inaccurate about this description of Jansenist thinking in general on the question. De Lubac goes to great lengths to argue that it is a deformation of Augustine's own thought, but for all that, he must continually admit that the saint's explicit remarks in his later writings seem to point in this direction, unless they are placed in the wider context of his theology. The real issue is to decide in what the character of this kind of grace as interpreted by the Jansenists consists, and in what way it logically implies something about the redemptive grace of Christ after the Fall.

As de Lubac notes, Arnauld's *Seconde Apologie* touches directly on this issue. When discussing Article IV of Habert's attack on Jansenius, "On the Grace of Angels," Arnauld takes up the question of the nature of origi-

---

4. Henri de Lubac, *Augustinianism and Modern Theology* (London: Geoffrey Chapman, 1969), 54ff.

5. See ibid., 40ff. and 71ff.

6. Ibid., 41.

nal grace and simply restates, as Jansenius did, Augustine's arguments in the *De correptione* chapter 12. What kind of grace was this? Truly supernatural and essential to life with God in every way: "However healthy and strong a rational creature might be, it is hardly any more possible that he take one single step on God's way without the aid of grace, than it is for the healthiest eye in the world to see without the help of light."[7] But it is not enough to see this "light," to which grace is compared, as an object functionally extrinsic to the being of the creature. For, as Augustine goes on to say (and this becomes Jansenius's motto of sorts), however much the divine light cannot be understood as an intrinsic capacity, it is the very means by which the creature fulfills its created nature and purpose:

> the Free Will suffices for evil; and it is sufficient for doing good only if it is aided by the sovereign and almighty good; just as the eye is sufficient in itself to see nothing and to dwell among the shadows; but whatever clarity it possesses is not sufficient for sight unless it receives from without a greater help and clearer light.[8]

De Lubac cannot see how the stress on the grace "from without" can be anything other than an extrinsic object whose being is here circumscribed by the use to which the creature puts it. But this is clearly not what either Jansenius or Arnauld understand by Augustine's imagery. That this "light" of grace was given over to the angels for the free use of the creature is simply a catholic axiom, clearly stated by Augustine.[9] It constitutes the *adjutorium sine quo non* of life with God, but it does not itself effect the right choices for which it is given to the creature; this choice resides in the unencumbered will of the innocent creature. Still, and this is the point, this grace is no less *intimate* in its presence and effects, to which it is directed by the creature, because it is thus given over to the creature's will. Rather, its very "use" by the creature is constituted by the most intimate bond imaginable: that of the indwelling divine love that gives itself over to its own creature's being. It is a grace such that only by its continual self-giving could it allow "a creature, pulled from nothingness to unite itself, though love, to its Creator."[10]

Thus, Jansenius speaks of the original grace as truly "sufficient," in the sense that its gift was truly adequate to its use because in fact the use was made.[11] Arnauld, even more pointedly, emphasizes the fact that the

---

7. Arnauld, *Seconde Apologie*, 167–68, citing Jansenius.

8. Ibid., 168, citing *De correptione et gratia*, chapter 11.

9. Arnauld appends to his treatise a version of Clement VIII's summary of Augustinian teaching, as the pope presented it to the Congregatio *De Auxiliis* in 1602; Clement's confirmation of the "two helps," although without interpretation, is clearly pertinent to the Jansenist explication. See ibid., 643–44.

10. Ibid., 168

11. See de Lubac, *Augustinianism and Modern Theology*, 41; this contrasts with the "sufficient" grace of scholastic terminology attacked by Jansenius, which, given after the Fall, is determined in its use by the fallen free will of human beings and cannot therefore be anything but "inefficient," given the constraint of sin that operates on the will.

indwelling gift of the Holy Spirit, sanctifying the will, was made to the
angels in innocence.[12] These points make no sense unless they are seen
as attempts to found the possibility of the free use of grace, as given to the
innocent angels and to Adam, on a relationship of divine intimacy that
precedes and accompanies it. In speaking, therefore, of the "debt" to the
creature that is original grace, Arnauld clearly defines this in terms of the
character of a divine presence that has made the gracious decision to live
as the "principle and end" of the creature's loving enjoyment.[13]

What disturbs de Lubac the most, and therefore pushes him to understand this Jansenist conception of original grace in as "ungracious" a way
as possible, is the manner in which the Fall seems to operate, in relation
to this conception, in such a disorienting and distinguishing fashion. If
the wholly efficacious nature of medicinal and salvific grace after the Fall
stands in such contrast to original grace, as it seems to for the Jansenists,
it must mean that original grace is somehow weak, "Pelagian," unimportant, indelectable. But what if we understand the Jansenist contrast not as
an attempt to distinguish the nature of grace itself in terms of its creative
end, of that which it constitutes? What if, instead, we see their distinction
between original grace and the grace of redemption as one that describes
the purely historical character of its human destination? Then we will not
be forced to choose between "continuity" and "disjunction" — as if we
are dealing with a different God and different creations, as de Lubac fears
with the Jansenist model of Innocence and Fall. Rather, we will search for
continuity in the *purely historical* description of how God's grace takes
shape across a landscape of events, in which, to be sure, the Fall stands as
a major chasm, though by no means one that determines the purposive
character of divine grace itself.

If only with respect to the single question of Adam's grace, I think the
search for this kind of continuity is evident throughout the history of Jansenist thought, even as this thought has embraced a number of different
theological styles. We can observe this in both the more "neo-Platonic" attitudes toward the question adopted by the direct followers of Jansenius, as
well as in the positions taken by the more self-consciously "neo-Thomist"
Jansenists of the movement's later period.

## The "Historical Continuum" of Grace
## according to Neo-Platonic Jansenism:
## Jansenius, Gerberon, and the Proximities of God

That Jansenius's theology of grace was shaped by a "platonizing" attitude
deliberately adduced from his study of Augustine, and in direct contrast to
the "philosophy" of the schools, has been one of the important demonstrations given us by Orcibal's labors. De Lubac, as we have seen, does not

---

12. Arnauld, ibid., 174, citing both Jansenius and Augustine, *De Civitate Dei*, 12:9.
13. Ibid., 147–48.

seem willing to grant the importance of this fact because the Jansenist emphasis on the efficacity of redemptive grace seems to point backward, by contrast, to a "merely sufficient" grace in the innocent Adam, which is discontinuous with the grace of Christ. But Orcibal has cogently argued that Jansenius's exemplarist emphasis on the created *imago Dei* of the human being can be joined to an emphasis on efficacious grace precisely because the *imago* is itself based on a gift of supernatural grace given even to the innocent Adam, and without which Adam would not have been wholly "formed" as a creature envisioned for divine love.[14] All nature, according to Jansenius, tends toward nothingness (*deorsum*) apart from grace, which acts as a kind of glorious "rein" on the creature's slide into non-being; further, the gift of the *imago* determined that the rational creature could be satisfied only by God. Therefore, Jansenius made the case that divine grace was an essential and continuous aspect of creation, without which the creature would not only be *informis* but also, in the case of the rational creature, thereby contradicted as to its divine end.[15]

In addition, finally, to such ontological support that underlies the structural role of grace, Jansenius speaks of the "actual" mode of grace, for Adam, which responds to the inherent contingency of the creature in the fact of knowing the good, by revealing that good to Adam, so as to act for its realization or apprehension. In a double sense, then, supernatural grace constitutes the rational creature as formed by God: first, by defining that formation itself and its continuance through time, and second, by adhering the creature to the historical ends of its Creator, in order to reach the term of its purpose.[16] This grace, known as "charity," is the "bond" or "glue" that thus marks the historical contiguity of rational creature and Creator both in innocence and redemption; what the Fall alters is not this relationship, but rather the historical experiences that will determine the contours of its configuration. As a result of the Fall, the attractions of creation now set themselves up as separating objects between God and the human person, and what was merely a tendency *deorsum* in the very reality of creation is now incarnated as a succession of actual alternative ends for love.

Gabriel Gerberon clarifies the relation at work between these elements of continuity and historical particularity in a work that Orcibal has characterized as one of the few attempts at elaborating a devotional system

---

14. Orcibal, "Thèmes platoniciens dans l'Augustinus' de Jansenius," in *Augustinus Magister* (Paris: Congrès International Augustinien 1954), vol. 2, esp. 79ff.; see also his "Néo-platonisme et jansénisme: Du De libertate du P. Gibieuf à l'Augustinus," in *Nuove ricerche storiche sul giansenismo, Analecta gregoriana* 71 (Rome, 1954).

15. For references in the *Augustinus,* see Orcibal, "Thèmes platoniciens," and P. J. G. Healey, *Jansenius' Critique of Pure Nature* (Rome: Gregorian University, 1964), 50–68.

16. See Orcibal, "Thèmes platoniciens," 78, and Healey, *Jansenius' Critique of Pure Nature*, 67.

derived directly from Jansenius.[17] In the opening of his *Miroir de la Piété* (1676), Gerberon outlines the major elements of Jansenius's attitude toward original grace, ones that apply subsequently to *all* historical conditions of the human person: creation *ex nihilo* means that there is a tendency in all creatures *au néant*, toward nothingness; the supernatural and *only* end of the rational creature is the vision of God who is God Himself (and anything done or lived for less than this is, by definition, sin); the freedom of the creature is defined by any movement toward this end, which is equivalent to the movement of love; finally, this movement (which is grace) is given in creation itself, so that whatever its circumstances, the creature is determined by grace. Gerberon, an early editor of Baius's works, does not shy away from the Baianist language of grace as a "debt" to the creature, or of God's "justice" as demanding the conferral of such grace.[18]

But it should be stressed that the direction of such comments leads to an understanding of the relation of nature and grace that is quite opposed to de Lubac's interpretation of their implication. Rather than establishing some kind of independence of nature from grace in the condition of innocence, Gerberon marshals this scheme — in which "debt" and "justice" refer to both the ontological and historical creative purpose of God — for the description of a creation that is shot through with the divine presence of grace itself. Baianism, in this context, serves the purpose of elucidating an almost trembling encounter with the fragility of creation, which discloses creation as a translucent being-in-grace. "True piety," which Gerberon here seeks to explicate, consists in a response to this vision that comprises the attitudes of adoration, thanksgiving, praise, humility, and vigilance. And this kind of piety, in Gerberon's view, was a human vocation even in the state of innocence.

What distinguishes the state of innocence from that of fallenness, then, is not a different vocation in grace, but simply the set of circumstances in which to pursue this vocation. To the degree that God responds to these different circumstances, then, divine grace assumes distinctive shapes, while nonetheless retaining its active relationship with respect to the creative purpose of God over time. The continuity of grace lies both in its end and in its circumstantial constitution. Gerberon, therefore, can describe the state of Innocence as itself being "grace," in that the circumstances of innocence were themselves so ordered by God directly as to be "elevating." No evils or weaknesses or miseries beset Adam — as indeed God had so constructed creation from the beginning — so that there was a perfect and unimpeded congruence between the ontological support of Adam's being and the path by which humanity would move over time toward consummated beatitude.[19]

---

17. See Orcibal's comments in his article on Gerberon in *Dictionnaire de la Spiritualité*, vol. 6 (1967), col. 289–93.

18. Gerberon, *Miroir*, 1–30.

19. Ibid., 42–46.

This lack of circumstantial impediment provided the defining structure to human love: it moved toward God of its own, because it was initially established with this focus. "Of its own," of course, means according to the "free use of the human will," and, like all Jansenists, Gerberon here speaks of the way in which innocent Adam was given grace to use according to his own choices, in such a way as to move to his end through "merit." But this is not simply Pelagianism thrown back into Paradise. The premise for this kind of assertion is not the supposed integrity of Adam's independence from grace, but rather the originally established and unimpeded intimacy of God *with* and even within Adam. Gerberon uses an extreme and striking expression for this reality: in Innocence, God "abandons" his grace, God "abandons" predestination and merit, into the free will of humanity; by contrast, in redemption, we "abandon" ourselves, or rather, are so abandoned through divine love, to God's victorious grace.[20] No more seamless form of proximity, short of identity, could evoke the continuity of this intrinsically creative relationship of grace than the character of abandonment to the other; yet only the formal distinctions in the respective manners of handling such abandonment — in Innocence and Fall — could capture the defining peculiarities that historical locale provides the notion of grace, or that grace itself takes on.

To be sure, Gerberon uses terms like the "natural grace of innocence" as opposed to the "efficacious" grace of redemption, and he stresses several times the way in which original grace "helped" — that is to say, was efficacious in its own right — only within the realm of ontological maintenance.[21] But again, we must beware of thereby assuming the existence of some "space" of human experience in which grace was not operative, and in which instead the human will had some kind of extensive sway. Rather, it was just the *lack* of such a space, it was just the pressing closeness of creature and creator in innocent Adam that defined human free will as salvific love itself. Only sin, according to Gerberon, can institute such space, by deliberately interjecting a creature between the human heart and God (who is, after all, not an object whose extension can be measured in any case). Indeed, sin provides in history not only the invention of distance, but distance, in what concerns the relation between God and humanity, is never to be measured except in terms of infinity: "the abyss of sin attracts only the abyss of grace."[22] Just as there is not now, so there has never been a middle term between cleaving to God and whole alienation. Insofar as sin introduces a space between the rational creature and God, it is an unbounded emptiness, in which flow each of the proliferating works of God as imperfect ends for love.

---

20. Ibid., 58 and 101ff.
21. See ibid., 100.
22. Ibid., 108.

## The "Historical Continuum" of Grace according to "Neo-Thomist" Jansenists: Quesnel, Boursier, d'Étemare, and the Realm of the Divinely Sensible

We have here, then, a positional reading of the relation of creature to God, within which grace is defined according to the ontological concerns of a neo-Platonism tempered by Christian creationism. The schema, however, turns out to be no different when described in the neo-Thomist terms of efficient causality. As noted earlier, it is not immediately clear that the basic Jansenist commitments on grace are fundamentally altered because of the adoption of certain alternative metaphysical orientations by members of the movement.

As a first example, we can cite Quesnel, who is frequently described as having made a distinctive turn away from the ontological "pessimism" of Jansenius toward a more traditional Thomistic attitude.[23] Tans lists several of these Thomistic turns that would have been unacceptable to Jansenius: e.g., Quesnel's description of human liberty in terms of a *potestas ad utrumlibet*, that is, as a kind of indifference toward alternative contraries;[24] his explication of Christ's universal salvific will in terms of the distinction between antecedent and consequent divine willing and between the sufficient and efficient character of the blood of Christ; and finally, his description of original grace in terms of a kind of actual "union" with God, rather than as an ontological support within a realm of intimacy.[25] But what Tans says about Quesnel's attachment to Jansenius — that it is based less on an attitude of theological discipleship than on a sense that he must defend a co-defender of Augustine — is equally true of Quesnel's theological resort to Thomistic arguments. This is evident in, for instance, Quesnel's short history of the *De Auxiliis* dispute. His explication and defense of the Dominican position, as well as his examination of the Council of Trent's Decree on Justification, are all obvious and uncomplicated attempts at emphasizing the basic Augustinian character of their respective teachings on grace, a character that is sustained from the basic Jansenist perspective: "All the doctrine [on grace] of St. Augustine and St. Thomas boils down to [*se réduit à*] the doctrine of free predestination and the true efficacity of the grace of Jesus Christ necessary to every action of Piety."[26]

23. See the chapter by J. A. G. Tans, "Quesnel et Jansenius" in *L'Image de C. Jansénius jusqu'à la fin du XVIIIe siècle*, ed. E. J. M. van Eijl (Louvain: Leuven University Press, 1987).

24. See Gerberon's clear discussion of this issue from Jansenius's perspective, in his *Miroir*, 4, 96ff., and 182–202. From this perspective, human liberty is defined simply as "the sway [*empire*] of the will over its actions," to accomplish them when it will and not when it does not will them (187). In this sense, freedom of the will is simply the will as it wills what it wants as an action, without any bow to the character of "indifference to contraries." The fact that fallen humanity *always* "wants" sin, therefore, does not compromise the will's liberty, since in inevitably willing sinful actions, the will nevertheless is doing just what it wants.

25. Tans, "Quesnel et Jansenius," 143, 147, and 138ff.

26. Quesnel, *Abregé de l'Histoire de la Congregation De Auxiliis, C'est-à-dire, Des secours*

With respect to our present topic, the grace of Adam, Tans's attempt to mark some distance between the basic commitments of Jansenius and Quesnel seems to miss the more fundamental unity. Drawing from a late apologetic work in response to the condemnations of *Unigenitus*, we can briefly outline Quesnel's attitude on the question.[27] It is true that Quesnel stresses, in his attempt to defend his orthodoxy, the "separability" of Adam's original grace from his created "nature — such grace being thus wholly "supernatural."[28] There is no concern here, as with Jansenius, to avoid the whole concept of "pure nature" on the ontological grounds of nature's tendency *deorsum*. Instead, Quesnel sets up a contrast between the grace of Adam and the grace of Christ that is framed in terms of its being "singular" and "communally mediated." With respect to Adam, he writes that he is talking about

> a grace that [Adam] received in his own person, and which everyone who would be born from him and from his posterity would also receive in their own person. [ . . . ] Adam received sanctifying grace for himself alone, independently of every other creature that came from God. In contrast, the Christian is sanctified in Jesus Christ. For God has placed in this Head, worthy of adoration, the totality of graces that He destined for his members, and none of [his members] receive of these graces except as they derive from Christ's plenitude and in a manner dependent upon him.[29]

The question of grace's mediation, then, is what is at issue. And in lifting up this contrast, by implication Quesnel is characterizing the sanctifying grace that is "separable from nature" as being, *in both* states of Innocence and Fall, essential to the loving purposes lying behind God's creation of

---

*de la Grace de Dieu* (1687), 96. At this point in the debate, we continue to see the obsessive attacks on the Jesuits as a major framework for posing the theological problem of grace: the reason why the Jesuits have failed to accept the consistent magisterial defense of Augustine's doctrine of efficacious grace is their desire to "please people" with "soft" theology. The unambiguous Jansenist platform is evident, for instance, in the following description of this "soft theology" of the Jesuits: it is "a theology that is gentle, human, insinuating, accommodated to the reason and ordinary ideas of men; that sheds grace abroad in all directions, from an abundant supply; that renders the free will master of its own operation and of the very operation of grace itself; that places the salvation of people in their own hands; that widens the road to heaven; that doesn't in any way alarm sinners with the worry of God's judgments and His penal withdrawal of grace; that finds nothing difficult in the conversion of the greatest of sinners, because they are always assured of having all the graces necessary for converting themselves, without having to make use of tears, prayers, and groans to obtain them; and since they always have a good opinion of the disposition of all Christians, they will send off and prod these folk, no matter what condition the people are in, to the Holy Table. And all this is done *in order to expand their own power*" (78–79). By contrast here, almost every element of Jansenist concern is glaringly brought into relief.

27. Quesnel, *Plainte et Protestation du Pere Quesnel contre La condamnation des Cent-une Propositions*, 2d ed., n.p., 1717.

28. Ibid., 175.

29. Ibid., 174f. The issue here is not whether the grace of Adam is somehow "other" than the grace of Christ — this is denied. Rather, Quesnel is trying to make the obvious point that there is a difference between the two graces with respect to their *historical mediation*: the fact of the Incarnation and its particular forms defines the remedial grace of Jesus Christ in the Church in a unique material fashion.

the human person. Thus, despite his defense of the separability of original grace from nature, Quesnel avoids any construal of "pure nature" by insisting on the "simultaneous infusion" of a sanctifying grace (i.e., the *adjutorium sine quo,* which is distinguished from the "grace of creation itself"[30]) at the moment of creation, in order that Adam could advance, individually, along the path of "friendship" with God for which he was created. Without this simultaneous infusion of grace, Adam would have "fallen" into sin *immediately,* that is, in a sense, "faultlessly."[31] Indeed, it is the historical dimension that determines the moral quality.

This is a somewhat curious turn in Quesnel's reasoning, but it marks his attempt to explicate the troubling Baianistic phrase (removed from later editions of the *Réflexions Morales*) concerning Adam's grace as a *sequela creationis et debita naturae sanae et integrae,* a consequence of creation and a debt to healthy nature. These words had been condemned in *Unigenitus,* and someone like de Lubac considers them to be an epitome of the Jansenist error.[32] Quesnel, while admitting the ambiguity of the now eliminated phrase, nevertheless insists on the bad faith of those who grasped at its supposed Baianism:

> When I said in the first editions [of my work] — which have been reformed by His Eminence — that *this grace was due to nature, in its health and wholeness [la nature saine et entiére],* how could one imagine that I intended to speak of a true debt in the ordinary sense of the word? For there could never be any promise on God's part [in this regard], nor any merit on man's part. It was rather a figure of speech, such as human beings often use, and it meant, with respect to God, that it was something "fitting" to His wisdom, "worthy" of His goodness, and something one might expect of His Providence.[33]

By "providence," Quesnel here means the evident "purposes" of God, evident according to the retrospective understanding we have of the created goal for humanity, as it is subsequently revealed to us in Christ. And it is thus a purpose that informs the condition of innocent Adam from the moment of his creation. It is characterized by a relationship of immediate intimacy between God and the creature, but one that is structurally provided by God, and not somehow intrinsically bound up with the being of the creature itself. Thus, Quesnel stresses both the individual and particular receipt of grace, in this innocent condition, as well as the separability of the grace from created nature itself: it is given *particularistically and temporally* to Adam, and it is its extrinsic quality that guards these two elements. Quesnel variously calls this grace "supernatural," "sanctifying," "conserving," and "independent," and each of these descriptions serves to constitute the world of particulars in which Adam is created to "rejoice" in

---

30. Ibid., 176.
31. Ibid., 180.
32. De Lubac, *Augustinianism and Modern Theology,* 41.
33. Quesnel, *Plainte et Protestation,* 177.

"a profound peace with God."[34] The grace of redemption, by contrast, does not in any way reconstitute this world of historical particulars in which the human being is created for friendship with God; instead, it simply provides a different figure according to which the grace of friendship is mediated, that is, the form of the Body of Christ. In both cases, however, grace is understood as the motor for the providentially desired historical existence of creation.

We shall explore in the next chapter some of the implications to this contrast of "forms" for the mediation of grace. But apart from this, it should come as no surprise that the peculiarly temporal and particularistic dimension of this vision of grace should find the language of efficient causality congenial. In making use of such language, however, Jansenists did not, it seems to me, stray very far from the "positional" framework that we saw as informing Gerberon's contrast of Innocence and Fall: given the historical continuity of God's plan for the human creature, what distinguishes original from redeeming grace is determined by the configuration of particulars of creation in relation to God's immediacy. The neo-Thomist appeal to "physical predetermination" in explaining the relation of grace and free will had already been noted approvingly by Jansenius and the early Arnauld (see the latter's *Seconde Apologie*, 183f.), but this was never taken up systematically at the time. By the eighteenth century and in Quesnel's wake, however, such appeals were put to deliberate use by Jansenist apologists. Among the most consistent of these attempts to apply the category of efficient causality to a discussion of grace was a work by Laurent-François Boursier. Boursier became one of the guiding theological figures behind the Appellant defense of the Saint-Médard miracles and early convulsions, but he gained a significant reputation early in his career with the publication of a massive investigation of grace described almost obsessively under the rubric of neo-Thomist "physical premotion."[35]

While space does not allow us a full description of this fascinating work, its place as a type in subsequent discussion demands that we at least mention its main argument. Boursier draws on the purported Thomist premise that God acts on the human free will through actual (not merely habitual) "physical" aids, aids that have "efficacious force by their own nature," but whose working does not detract from the will's capacity to act within the "liberty of indifference." This divine premotion in grace, however, mirrors the mechanism of created life in general, which takes its

---

34. Ibid., 179.

35. Boursier, *De L'Action de Dieu sur les creatures: Traité dans lequel on Prouve La Premotion Physique par le Raisonnement. Et où l'on examine plusieurs questions, qui ont rapport à la nature des esprit et à la Grace* (n.p., 1713). On Boursier and his relations to Cartesian philosophy, see Bouillier, *Histoire de la Philosophie Cartésienne*, vol. 2, 311–26. In many respects Boursier was closer to Malebranche than to Thomas, especially in his occasionalist explications of human knowledge and action. Near the end of his life at this point, Malebranche was persuaded to write a negative response to Boursier, in which, in particular, he argued for independence from grace of the actual act of the will's consent to an action. It was his last work, *Réflexions sur la Prémotion Physique* (1715).

form from the welter of forces — material, intellectual, and spiritual — acting upon creatures. Boursier elaborately describes human beings in terms of a psychosomatic unity wherein the shape of human life is ultimately determined by this divinely configured orchestration of forces that end in particular nerve impulses. In created Innocence, this orchestration was unimpeded in its effects, and Adam lived in a free and utter intimacy with God, in which the divinely given forces at work upon his life were received with a delectable immediacy analogous to an immersion within a garden of blossoms. At the Fall, however, the advent of concupiscence marked the disruption of this intimacy by a radically opposing set of forces, acting now as impediments to the human creature's receptivity of God's configurated premotions. Within this scheme, Boursier could speak — familiarly, in Jansenist terms — of redemptive grace not as a novel power or relationship, but as God's premotive force moving now "over a greater distance" than before, in overcoming the obstacles of sin. Indeed, Boursier dares to make explicit the full erasure of the Augustinian distinction between the *adjutorium sine quo* and the *adjutorium quo:* all grace, even in Paradise, is an *adjutorium quo.*[36]

However much a self-styled "neo-Thomist" like Boursier relies on the language of efficient causality, then, he presents a perspective on grace that differs little from Gerberon's in describing its unified creative power: grace constitutes the world of historical particularities according to which God is present to His creature(s). In fact, in that they function as equivalent terms, one could go so far as to identify this grace, so peculiarly conceived in the Jansenist outlook, with that constituting and constituted history itself.

I shall want to take a last look, in some greater detail, at the way in which Jansenism could fundamentally redefine grace in such historically constitutive terms. But before doing so, it is worth noting how Boursier's neo-Thomist categories themselves were immediately relativized by other Jansenists in an effort to distinguish the underlying commitments Boursier was upholding with respect to the positional nature of grace's continuity in its movement through Innocence and Fall. D'Étemare's *Remarques,* for instance, deal at some length with Boursier's work, and he is taken to represent, with others, the "Thomist" understanding of grace that contrasts, to some degree, with the two other major "systems of grace," the "Molinist" and the "Augustinian." While most of the time d'Étemare tries to establish the full compatibility of the Thomist and the Augustinian systems, over and against the innovations of Molinism, he cannot deny the differences between them on many counts, and there is no question but that the "Augustinian" system accords most fully with the doctrine of Quesnel's *Réflexions,* which he is defending from the attack of *Unigenitus.* Still, in trying to ferret out the basic commonalities that remain despite these differences, he brings into relief some of the key Jansenist at-

---

36. See Boursier, *De L'Action de Dieu sur les creatures,* vol. 1, 316, 319, and 342ff.

titudes that persist beneath the different "systems," a commonality that he recognizes as bringing thinkers like Boursier into the Jansenist (and thus "orthodox") camp.

Many of the features that distinguish the different systems of grace, according to d'Étemare, revolve around the relationship between Innocence and Fall. The Thomists, he claims, insist on a complete continuity in the metaphysical relationship of creature to Creator through all conditions, whether of innocence, fallenness, or redemption. "Because humanity has come from nothing and is infinitely weak, it stands in need of an extremely powerful help; and because it is God who brought humanity out [of nothing], He exercises over it a sovereign domain."[37] In this sense, "efficacious grace" represents the means by which human beings exist, act, and move to their respective destinies in every respect. "Physical premotion" as grace, in the sense that Boursier uses the term, can therefore provide the explanatory framework in which the whole of human history, whether naturally or religiously understood, plays itself out.[38] As in Boursier's scheme, there is really no difference whatsoever in the structure of grace in Paradise or in redemption. Predestination is "free" of determination by merit even in innocence, since every act of perseverance even then derives from the free and efficacious gift of consent. What needs to be explained, rather, is the way in which sin itself freely arises in a non-deterministic fashion.

The Molinist system, by contrast, explains the human creature naturalistically, as a being created into a realm of freedom from determination, *except* in those things pertaining to life with God, that is, to his supernatural end.[39] Thus, Adam in Paradise existed in full possession of capacities for free willing within a limited sphere of the "natural" — this sphere of capacity and its objects is called "pure nature" — but, by a gratuitous "supernatural grace," Adam was at the same time elevated to a wider life in communion with God. In losing this added supernatural grace at the Fall, human beings are now universally left to that state of "pure nature," where they can freely choose and act toward the limited "natural goods" that pertain to this sphere. To the degree that God provides a means for the attainment of a human being's supernatural end, God does so by supplying supernatural graces to an individual that can, in the same naturalistic fashion, be used or rejected freely. This kind of redeeming grace was dubbed by neo-Thomist and Jansenist critics of the system as "versatile grace," that is, as divine grace whose use was given over to the free determination of the creature. Predestination in this condition after the Fall is not "free" here, because it refers only to the divine foreknowledge of how individuals will in fact make use of such gifts, and in no way embodies the sovereign divine decision to provide efficacious means to

---

37. D'Étemare, *Remarques*, vol. 1, 133.
38. Ibid.
39. See ibid., 134–35.

salvation to this or that individual irrespective of his or her capacities to use them.

With these two contrasting outlines in place, d'Étemare can simply construct the Augustinian system out of its rearranged elements.[40] Simply put, the Augustinians are "Molinists" with respect to the state of Innocence, and Thomists with respect to the state of sin and redemption. In Paradise, supernatural grace is "versatile" in the sense of being given over to the free use of Adam — this is the "baianistic" principle — but after the Fall, all grace works efficaciously and freely. This is so for two reasons: first, the scope and power of the fallen free will is hindered by the universal introduction of concupiscence; and second, the guilt deriving from original sin breaks the bond of the divine commitment to that offering of grace which had held initially at creation (the *debitum* of grace in Innocence). Predestination is, as in Gerberon's term, "given over" into the hands of Adam in Innocence, as personal right decisions acquire or make use of the graces of perseverance; in Fall and Redemption, however, predestination is wholly "free," since human beings now "deserve" no more than condemnation.

There is nothing very surprising in all this, at least from the Appellant point of view, except perhaps the brazen clarity of its explication. Few Jansenist writers would be willing to adopt the Jesuit notion of "versatile" grace in no matter what form. More interesting is the way d'Étemare tries to locate the Thomist and the Augustinian views in a broader way to the side of Molinism regardless of the particular historical order in which each group might decide to arrange the elements of gratuity and self-determination. To do this, d'Étemare goes after the idea of "pure nature" which he has identified as being somehow central to Molinism.[41]

The crucial issue defining the two sides, d'Étemare argues, lies less in the explanation given to the mechanism of grace in the state of innocence — whether it be efficacious or not — than it does in the assessment one makes about what counts as a properly human life, in *any* condition. And on this question, Boursier's unimpeded divine premotion and Quesnel's *debitum* of grace are agreed: the life to which the human being was created is one in which a fundamental intimacy with God is assumed as determined, purposed, or "providential." D'Étemare goes into elaborate — and exegetically sophisticated — detail in analyzing Augustine's own developing views as to the kind and extent of divine aid offered to innocent Adam.[42] He concludes, simply, that there is an ambiguity as to whether Augustine posited an "efficacious" grace moving the "first desire" of Adam, which would then determine the use of the *auxilium sine quo* (Boursier) or whether, in fact, that first desire was part of the constituted "good will" of Adam's creation that thereby founded the versatile use of the *auxilium*

---

40. Ibid., 135–37.

41. For what follows, see ibid., 137–47; and vol. 2, 4–7.

42. Ibid., vol. 2, 19–30.

(Quesnel). But however one comes down on this interpretive question, there can be no quibbling with the fact that the very existence of Adam, as purposively created, was to dwell in unity with God.

Of course, the Molinists insisted that Adam was granted a supernatural elevation from the moment of his creation that made possible this life in unity. How does this differ from the Jansenist commitment? It is not, obviously, the end of such an elevation to which d'Étemare objects. Rather it is the implication derivative of the notion of "elevation" itself that is pernicious, an implication that leads to the presupposition of an originally created "non-elevated" nature that can somehow be subsistent in its integrity apart from a life with God altogether. The pernicious implication of the claim for supernatural elevation in innocence, then, is the idea of a "pure nature," a fundamental condition to which human beings after the Fall and the loss of that supernatural elevation revert. This natural condition after the Fall, according to the tag, differs from original creation (apart from supernatural elevation) *tamquam spoliatus a nudo*, only as someone robbed of his clothing differs from someone who is naked. Although without any essentially ongoing connection to God, through grace, this natural condition is good insofar as it represents one term in God's creative purpose. The condition is shaped by its own, more limited, character, capacities, and ends, whose use and attainment is good in itself. Put simply, the Fall makes effective upon humanity the limits of its created nature, no more, and the fallen life is a limited life in which, for the most part, God lies outside the boundaries.

It is the absolute *horror* of such a conception of livable if limited independence that so shocks d'Étemare. Could any life on earth without God ever be called "natural"? Further, could such a life without God ever be experienced as anything other than profoundly grotesque?

> Does Scripture really reduce the change wrought on human nature by sin to this? The image Scripture paints in so many places, of the misery, the weakness, and the corruption into which man has fallen since Adam's sin — is all this to be reduced to teaching us simply that man has returned to his natural condition, a condition that is good in itself, even if less elevated than that to which Adam had been called?[43]

> For is there anything that could have greater repercussions than to strip man of the relationship he stands in, either toward God or toward true righteousness, that provides him his worth? or than to give him different duties to accomplish [i.e., natural, not divine duties], different virtues to acquire, different rewards to expect, and different punishments to fear?[44]

Life without God is pure misery. That is the simple point d'Étemare wishes to make. To pretend otherwise is wholly to misunderstand both the nature of God and of God's purposes, as well as the vocation of human beings. If nature is God's creation, then pure misery cannot be pure nature. This

---

43. Ibid., vol. 1, 141.
44. Ibid., 140.

is all that is meant by Quesnel's *debitum;* and this is all that is meant by the proliferating flowers of Boursier's garden. If God created human beings, such creation embodies at the least a set of circumstances that can only be described in terms of utter glory — the glory of proximity and conversation, of vision and encounter. And since d'Étemare pushes his discussion of grace back to this point, with this kind of logically necessary embodiment, brushing aside the distinctions between efficacity and versatility in Paradise, it appears that the concept of grace is designed to serve this set of circumstances, and in a wide variety of ways: "grace" stands for its simple description; it stands for its enjoyment; it stands for the elements of relationship that characterize it, including its initiating players (i.e., God); it stands for its motive genesis and conservation. And, as we have already seen in every other Jansenist figure we have examined, "grace," as a term, represents the circumstantial embodiment of all these aspects as it persists or is reconstituted through time, across the chasm of the Fall, and through its continued redemptive movement.

What we found earlier in d'Étemare's definition of grace, that is, the qualities of a certain *sensibilité,* whatever their peculiar characters, flow directly from this fundamental Jansenist perspective. If grace is a "feeling," that "softens," "penetrates," "grips," and "pleases" the heart,[45] it is not so simply because it is power that works on the emotions or at best the affective character of the will. Rather, grace "works," in the sense of forming the relational *gestalt,* the very situation in which the history of a "ravishing" relationship takes its shape. It is formatively subsuming, in this respect, of every particular element that can be identified as constituting that relationship, of every divine "effect" in the world. The quality of *sensibilité* that informs its description is precisely that: the descriptive process itself as it locates the facets of the subsumed whole, that points each one out, that distinguishes each peculiarity as it presents itself in time. It is not so much the affective, as opposed to the intellectual character of this descriptive apprehension that is being stressed in calling grace a *sentiment,* as it is the purely "sensible," that is really discrete, quality of each facet. Only sensible experience — as opposed to the atemporal abstractions of intellectual cognition or even formless passions — correlates to the historical particularities that mark the providential continuity of God's purpose, that is, to grace. Although Jansenists relate this to the Augustinian category of "love," it should be clear how deliberately they have stressed the potentially temporal aspects surrounding love's realization.

## Jansenistic Grace as a Historical Category: Arnauld's Systematic Definition

When Jansenists think of grace as an "effect in time," as Thomas put it, they will not be led to consider the "created" nature of such effects,

---

45. Ibid., vol. 1, 409.

as these effects might normally be understood, but rather the historically subsuming quality of any reality at all that shapes the relational effects of God's providential purpose. We have noted how Jansenists avoided the distinction between created and uncreated grace altogether preferring to attribute this traditional scholastic division to a matter of perspective, uncreated grace being seen from the initiating side of God, and created grace being understood from the finite reception of that relationship by a creature. But taken strictly, "grace" refers to the single orchestrating reality of the relationship as a whole: it is of "one nature," being the single "movement" that brings the human soul into a place of rejoicing in God and creature for God's sake, *however this is to be understood particularly.* [46]

From the narrowly systematic point of view, then, we ought to see Jansenists simplifying the categorizations of grace given by the Schools and relying on a single conceptuality that will emphasize the continuously historically creative and directive character of God's presence to the human creature. *Sensibilité*, in the sense that we have begun to elucidate the term, will depend on such a simplification and focus. And this is just what proves to be the case.

It is with this systematic observation that we can give some final support to my explication of the Jansenists' historicization of grace. And one of the clearest expressions of this more comprehensive systematic move is also one of the earliest, Arnauld's 1656 treatment of Thomas on grace. [47] Written at a time when Arnauld was seeking to defend himself against censure from the Sorbonne, the work marks the first careful attempt to reread Thomas's treatise on grace in the *Summa Theologiae* from a Jansenist perspective. While the issue here is that of "efficacious grace," the topic is not approached through Thomas's metaphysic of causality as was usually the case with neo-Thomist discussions of grace since the Congregatio *De Auxiliis*. Rather, Arnauld is far more concerned with an examination of what it means for God to "will" something for His creatures, to lay out the particular elements making up the fulness of the divine plan. [48]

From the first, Arnauld wishes to emphasize the fundamental distinction in Thomas between habitual grace and the grace, more generally understood, by which God acts to fulfill the divine will. Thus, although he admits that Thomas is usually referring to habitual grace when he uses the term "grace," Arnauld is himself more interested in the *auxilium Dei*

46. See [Hugot], *Instructions*, vol. 1, 451 and 176ff.

47. Arnauld, *Vera S. Thomae De Gratia Sufficiente et Efficaci Doctrina Dilucide Explanata* in *Oeuvres*, vol. 20; a longer version, covering the same material in more detail, quickly followed, the *Vindiciae Sancti Thomae circa Gratiam Sufficientem*.

48. However one judges the adequacy of treating grace from this alternative slant, a proper appreciation of Jansenist thinking is not helped by ignorning the reality of the alternative altogether, and reading Jansenism merely as a deformed theory about divine *causality*. This kind of reading stands as a significant drawback in Abercrombie's discussion of the relationship of Jansenism to Thomism in his *The Origins of Jansenism* (1935), which to this day remains the only major theological treatment of Jansenism in English.

*moventis,* that grace by which, according to Thomas, all other specific graces are made possible or are given ground for action.[49]

Governing Arnauld's reading of texts from the *Summa* is one basic definition Thomas gives in *De Veritate* 24:14: the free will is unable to reach the good beyond human nature (salvation) without grace, and while we use the word "grace" here, we must distinguish it from our more common use of the term as "habitual grace"; for this grace by which the creature moves to its divine end is rather the very mercy of God, through which He works an interior motion in the spirit and ordains exterior events for the salvation of an individual.

Drawing on texts from 1a2ae 106 and 109 of the *Summa Theologiae,* Arnauld describes habitual grace in Thomas's terms as that which "heals" human nature, "elevates it," and gives it the capacity (*posse*) to fulfill the commandments and avoid sin. But his emphasis in describing this habitual grace is on the fact that a habit, even of grace, need not be used at all: it is, as Thomas himself makes essential to the definition, something subject to the free will. "A habit by definition is something we use when we will," as Arnauld quotes it.[50] And, as he goes on, he contrasts this kind of habit with what Thomas describes as the direct work of God the Holy Spirit moving in love within the soul.[51]

It should be pointed out, however, that love normally considered, for Thomas, *is* a habit, and is not the direct movement of the Spirit in the human spirit, precisely because such love must be free.[52] We can observe already, then, that by pressing the metaphysical imperfections of habitual grace seen in terms of its effect, Arnauld is moving his sights away from the reality of the Christian life as understood subjectively — created grace — toward the realm of God's own purposes in shaping that life as a whole.

This can be noted further as Arnauld explains in more detail the historical limitations constraining the scope of habitual grace. A habit need not be used, he says, which means simply that a person can still sin who lives under the habit of grace alone.[53] It is only God's *direct* help that is ever infallible, infallibility being a characteristic that cannot pertain to the contingent instruments of human existence. While habitual grace confers a capacity, it cannot confer the actual willing of the good itself; that is, habitual grace confers the capacity "sufficient not to sin," but is not in itself a confirmation in righteousness.[54]

Arnauld turns to Thomas's Question 109 as his key text for introducing the notion of a "special" grace that is both prior and subsequent to

---

49. In what follows, I will simply outline Arnauld's explication, in order, of Thomas's ideas, noting in particular those texts to which Arnauld refers.

50. Thomas Aquinas, *S.T.,* 1a2ae 78:2 resp.

51. See ibid., 2a2ae 24:11.

52. See ibid., 2a2ae 23:2.

53. Arnauld, *Vera S. Thomae De Gratia,* Article 4.

54. Thomas Aquinas, S.T., 1a2ae 106:2 ad 2.

habitual grace, the grace of the *auxilium Dei moventis*. Thomas is himself somewhat unclear at this point on the relation between these two *temporal* aspects of the *auxilium*, a fact that allows Arnauld to subsume all grace that is not explicitly habitual, according to Thomas, into the one form of efficacious divine willing.

In the first place, Thomas presents God as the cause of every "motion," whether physical or spiritual, and this in two senses: both as prime mover, and as the "primary actuality" of every formal perfection.[55] "However perfect a physical or spiritual nature is taken to be, it cannot proceed to actualize itself unless it is moved by God." This kernel for the later neo-Thomist ideas of physical premotion, however, is qualified by Thomas in terms of its historical outworking: "this actual motion is in accordance with the order of His providence, not according to natural necessity." To Arnauld's mind, it is a qualification that moves in the direction of predestination and away from purely metaphysical mechanisms of causality.

In 109:2, Thomas then draws the distinction between Innocent Adam and the condition of fallen humanity. "Intact human nature" (*natura integra*) required the grace of divine assistance, as prime mover, "to do or to will any good at all." While "in respect of the sufficiency of his capacity to perform actions, man could by his natural endowments will and perform the good which was proportionate to his own nature" (i.e., acquired virtue), nonetheless intact nature was unable to will or to perform the "transcendent good" (i.e., infused virtue) without special divine assistance.[56]

Fallen nature needs grace in an additional sense: in order to "heal" its natural capacities so as to perform the natural goods which were accessible to the powers of the *natura integra*. At this point, the contrast seems small, since in both states human nature needs grace to will supernatural goods (these derive from the infused virtues as directly wrought by God — the *auxilium?*), as well as the *auxilium* of the prime mover to will anything at all. In any case, it is this "healing" grace that Arnauld latches onto as "habitual grace" strictly speaking.

Arnauld finds his ammunition by which to dispense of this healing grace, as being anything other than ancillary, in 109:9, which he quotes almost *in toto*. Thomas points out that, even when once healed *in mentem*, fallen nature "continues to be spoiled and infected as regards the flesh," as well as mired in "a kind of darkness of ignorance in the understanding." This fact reveals our need for the continuous grace of God moving and protecting us as we proceed as *viatores* through life. On this basis, we are

---

55. Ibid., 109:1.

56. What is the actual relationship, as Thomas conceives it, between this last "special assistance" and the first "assistance" of God as prime mover? None is spelled out; and one can see how, on the basis of texts like this, neo-Thomists, Molinists, and Jansenists, as they ordered themselves into parties, were able to launch themselves off from a common authority.

both helped in knowing for what to pray, and we are helped in persisting in that prayer, in order that we might be defended from temptation and so act according to God's will. For "God knows all things and can do all things."

This continual aid of grace, Thomas makes clear, is *subsequent* to the gift of habitual grace. And Thomas goes so far as to say that, in a sense, habitual grace is "imperfect," in that "it does not totally heal" a person. The grace given subsequent to healing, that is, subsequent to habitual grace, represents the work of the entire Trinity as it "moves and protects us" in the course of our lives as they wind their ways through a world itself beset by imperfection. And as both Thomas and Arnauld emphasize,[57] the *auxilium* as it is understood at this stage is indistinguishable from the grace of perseverance. This being so, Arnauld can attach to the *auxilium* as a whole the attribute of infallibility or efficaciousness. While Thomas himself does not emphasize this fact, Arnauld can now subordinate the purposes — and thus "efficacity" — of habitual graces that can, by definition, be lost through sin (and this includes infused forms and powers), to the gift by means of which these graces are made to persist in the course of a life.

Since, as we saw, Thomas places the work of the *auxilium* within the order of providence, Arnauld now is able to have the entire working of grace — in the perfections and "imperfections" of its applications that are nothing else but the form of God's historical will and purpose — subsumed under the category of predestination. From one perspective, Thomas himself does this, but the emphasis has clearly shifted with Arnauld. Turning more explicitly to Augustine now, Arnauld discusses the visible and experienced effects of the *auxilium* within the large drama of God's historical will for an individual or for a people.[58] There is, he writes, not only the "universal movement" of God's grace at work in all creatures, but also the "special grace" that determines the limits and contours of the creature's movement toward salvation as it is instantiated historically.[59]

It is worth asking to what degree Arnauld has distorted Thomas's own thought here. Thomas, as we have seen, uses the notion of God's "motion" both in a more naturalistic sense — as prime mover and formal cause of actuality — and in more particular senses of special graces for particular motions of willing and acting within the schema of holiness and salvation. Arnauld ends by collapsing these two senses into the one efficacious will of God's providence and predestination. Efficacity is now applied *in a primary sense* to the whole of God's historical will (what Thomas usually calls God's "consequent" will), which includes in a subordinate way the metaphysical aspects of the divine motion within it. Thereby the whole issue of the "permission" of sin and the occasional withdrawal, in indi-

57. See 109:10.
58. Arnauld, *Vera S. Thomae De Gratia*, Articles 9–17.
59. Ibid., Article 19, drawing on Thomas Aquinas, S.T., 1a2ae 9:6 ad 3.

vidual instances, of the specifically efficacious grace for salvation becomes merely the historical embodiment of the larger efficacious grace of God's providential governance of all things, in predestination and in reprobation. Habitual graces, where even a matter of concern, are relegated to mere instrumentalities in this subsuming history of relationship.

In some ways, this collapsing of senses, this simplification of the concept of grace itself, follows the development of terms as Thomas uses them in his treatise on grace as a whole. For there is a clear shift at work from the early part of the treatise, where the *auxilium Dei moventis* is used rather strictly to refer either to the metaphysical aspects of the divine motion or to the initial converting movement of the will in preparation for the sanctifying grace of justification.[60] What Thomas calls "justifying grace," however, is identified, not with the *auxilium* but with "healing grace," that is, with habitual grace.[61]

Soon after this, we find Thomas describing "justification" as a whole in terms of a joint working of habitual grace and the *auxilium*, although each aspect is carefully distinguished.[62] By Question 113, however, Thomas seems to be emphasizing the underlying priority of the *auxilium* throughout the reality of justification, characterizing the whole as a gradual "movement," in itself, of the soul to justice, under the influence of the *Deus movens*.[63] Almost every stage or aspect of this process is now tied to the *auxilium Dei moventis*, including the infusion of virtue.[64] Grace *is* the *Deus movens*, God moving as the Holy Spirit indwelling the human soul.[65]

Simply collapsing the various distinctions among types of grace, then, is something Thomas himself is willing to do. But even this kind of simplification need not necessarily lead in the direction Arnauld takes. The final moment in Thomas's discussion, where grace becomes consonant with the indwelling Holy Spirit, could easily be interpreted according to the kind of neo-Platonic categories of participation and possession that many have wanted to see as predominant in the later Thomas.[66] What is crucial is how one is going to assess the character of the Spirit in his description. And this is the critical thing to be gleaned from our examination of a Jansenist appropriation of Thomas: once Arnauld, as he does, takes the image of "movement" versus "indwelling" as the primary shape of divine grace, then the landscape in which this grace is effective will be determined by aspects of proximity and event, that is, by historical relations. And we can see how the adoption of such a framework for the understand-

---

60. Thomas Aquinas, S.T., 1a2ae, 109:6.
61. Ibid., 109:7–8.
62. Ibid., 109:9; 111:2.
63. Ibid., 113:1.
64. Ibid., 113:6.
65. Ibid., 113:6; 114:3; 114:6.
66. See, among others, Rondet's interpretation, along these lines, of Thomas on grace in his *The Grace of Christ* (Westminster, Md.: Newman Press, 1967).

ing of grace establishes a fundamental systematic basis for conceiving the Pauline *ostensio Spiritus* in terms of phenomenal events *in general*, as well as in the particulars of historical pneumatica.

That the Jansenists aimed at explicating the continuity of grace from Innocence through Fall and Redemption seems to me irrefutable. It is not, however, a continuity governed by participation, as de Lubac suggests it ought to be, participation through a nature engraced by the expansive and overarching reality of the Word to be incarnate. Rather, the continuity lies simply in the ordering of history according to a purposive set of proximities between God and creature. Proximities of delight and wonder and intimacy, to be sure; but distinct encounters, nonetheless, that somehow leave the shapes of creation clearly defined and intrinsically independent of any nature not their own, except insofar as such natures "come close," one to another. This historical ordering of distinct creatures is, of course, the "predestination" to which the Jansenists held firmly. The very "freedom" of its ordering, its amenability to a variety of possible configurations in the hands of God's purpose, testifies to the discrete natures involved, each limited enough to be turned to some purpose and some order larger than itself.

But just this freedom, this set of distinctions, this ordering within the context of a temporal dimension that demands specific relations between bodies — just this array of elements that make up what we call history — witness to the distinctive power of order over time and creature that holds together the limits of creation and its consummation. And in Jansenist thinking, if the continuity of God's grace is to be understood primarily in historical terms, then we are free to take seriously — that is to say, religiously — what in fact *does* snare our attention in the world: the experience of pain, of incapacity, of dreadful, even willful, impotence. To call the constituted history of such experience grace itself is to claim that God's love arises *here* first, instead of demanding an explanation for experience only as an afterthought to love. The *ostensio Spiritus* in this schema is essentially tied to its own "apparently" phenomenal contradictions.

There is more to this than "pessimism," the easy and profoundly misdirected complaint so frequently launched against the Jansenists, as if, when all is said and done, their real fault was to have been too gloomy, beset by the great "temptation of despair."[67] To take the historical shapes of the world more seriously even than the atheists, more seriously even than the hedonists and epicureans, to uphold this set of distinctions and particularities as the environment and stuff of love in a primary sense, and not merely its props, was at the least a claim to take back history, to take back its jolts and its bruises for God, in God's near shadow. Such a claim, finally, stands as the human articulation of a rigorous phenomenology of the Spirit such as we are pursuing.

---

67. See Knox, *Enthusiasm*, 208.

*Chapter Three*

# THE FORM OF GRACE

## Outline of Chapter

Having argued in the previous chapter that Jansenists saw grace as having essentially a historical dimension, we will now go on to show how the Appellant understanding of grace assumes, in addition, that it have a particular historical form. It is this historical form, or set of forms, encompassed by the Incarnate Christ that further buttresses theologically the particularly sensible aspects of the later miracles as a significant aspect of the *ostensio Spiritus.*

We will use as a focusing theme for this chapter the eighteenth-century idea of *sensibilité* developed theologically in terms of a set of constraining forms. Having sketched something of *sensibilité*'s importance in this regard, we will indicate the idea's pertinence to Jansenist discussions of grace through a brief examination of some works by the Appellant doyen Jacques-Joseph Duguet, who forms an important link (along with Quesnel) between the earlier and later periods of Jansenist thinking.

With these remarks in place, we can go back, historically, and trace the way in which this later Jansenist view of grace's sensible form derives from a marriage, largely the result of Quesnel's influence, of Berullian themes pervasive in the French Oratory, and the Jansenist insistence on the historical dimension of grace. While the resultant combination is unique, we will end by suggesting that it remains consistent with theological structures fundamental to the earliest period of Jansenism.

## The General Concept of *Sensibilité* and Its Theological Significance

In the last chapter, we defined a broad and general character in the context of which to approach the link between the Jansenist understanding of grace and the quality of *sensibilité* that later Appellants in particular seemed to attach to this grace. This peculiarly characterized conception of grace, I argued, is defined by its specifically historical dimension. What marks off the Jansenists, of course, is not simply that they claim a historical dimension to grace, but that they see this dimension as being something so subsuming of its governing reality as to make the phenomenon of grace, at times, a term almost synonymous with the constituted shape of history itself. The "constituted" aspect of history, in this case, was a logical ground for Jansenist claims for the "efficacity" of grace. More specifically, I argued that our examination of the relationship, as the Jansenists saw it, between the grace of innocent Adam and the redeeming grace offered to fallen Adam pointed to an understanding of this divinely constituted history/grace as that ordering by God of His temporal proximity to His creatures. Such an ordered sequence of divine proximities is what gives the spatial and objective circumference to the "world" of creaturely encounters and experiences. *Sensibilité*, in this wholly general theological context, is merely the expression of the relation of creature to this world that is founded on the history of God's loving proximities.

We opened our section on grace, however, with a formal pneumatic event, a miracle described by Carré de Montgeron, and it was the issue of *sensibilité* as it expressed the *causa gratiae Dei* through the circumstances of the miracle that first attracted our attention. We can return to this feature of his writing by now applying our limited characterization of grace to his reflections on Dom de Palacios. Thus, that the context of historical relations between God and human beings should characterize the very nature of grace, as we have seen, dovetails readily with the conviction that God's purposive relation to the world itself should take grace as both its object and its very agent, grace marked through its array of historical effects. And therefore, that there should be a *milieu sensible* expressing this argument is a logical motivation to Carré de Montgeron's description of miraculous events.

But we must go further than such generalizations and try to distinguish how the specifically theological quality of *sensibilité* that is peculiar to the Appellant insistence on the miraculous expression of the divine purpose separates itself from the connotations of the term as it was used only "generally" during the period. This is necessary, given the fact that the very concept of *sensibilité* was part of an eighteenth-century cultural code, whose presence in the vocabulary of the Saint-Médardistes is, in itself, unremarkable. Only in making this distinction can the quality of divine grace as itself *sensible* be located for the Jansenists in a realm apart from the purely affective religiosity to which the label of "enthusiasm" has recently consigned their attitudes. That is, a theological notion of *sensibilité* will itself provide for a perspective on miracle, on the uttered *causa*, that transcends the phenomenological category of enthusiastic religion as it is applied to specific supernatural outbreaks and derived from deformed doctrine.

Baasner has characterized some of the ways seventeenth-century theologians and religious moralists gave to the term *sensibilité* a set of connotations that were to open up new avenues of meaning for later eighteenth-century secular writers.[1] In general, following Mesnard's the-

---

1. Frank Baasner, "The Changing Meaning of 'sensibilité': 1654–1704," *Studies in Eighteenth-Century Culture* 15 (1986): 77–96; This article represents a more extensive treat-

sis,[2] Baasner attributes to an Augustinian reaction against neo-Stoicism a reassessment of the role of the affections and passions that allowed for their (limited) positive reevaluation. Besides the more neutral definition of *sensibilité* in terms of physiological sensitiveness,[3] theologians like the Oratorian Senault as well as the Jansenist Nicole sought to ascribe to human emotive capacities the fundamental element necessary for ethical love and even for religious compassion. As opposed to the kind of passional "indifference" (leading to a pernicious *insensibiité*) that antique Stoic writers recommended, and that was being promoted by contemporary Stoic revivalists, Senault, for instance, insisted that a human being required *sensibilité* in order to respond to the demands of the human needs of others, as well as respond to God. In this sense, *sensibilité* functioned as a passive capacity of vital responsiveness, touching not only the physical senses, but the "heart," the seat of ethical and spiritual love.[4] "Tenderness" quickly became the secular equivalent to this religiously founded *sensibilité*, and both types, through the seventeenth century, functioned most frequently in the context of discussions concerning various kinds of love.

It should be noted that by tying *sensibilité* to the "heart," seventeenth-century theologians like Senault were not forging into territory foreign to traditional Catholic formulations of Christian existence. Pascal's juxtaposition of "reason" and the "heart" in this respect is hardly novel. Mesnard stresses the Augustinian background to much of these attempts to rehabilitate the passions as a vehicle for the religious life, and certainly the *caritas* focus of so many theologians, and not only of the Jansenists, was decisive. One might also cite just as obviously the broad devotional traditions of the late Middle Ages, wherein both mystical and popular commendations concerning the priority of loving union over purely intellectual contemplation provided a general outlook that was still influential through much seventeenth-century spiritual counsel.

The turn to the eighteenth century, according to Baasner, finds *sensibilité* undergoing a broadening of reach, and a leap beyond the religious confines of mere receptivity for love. While seventeenth-century preachers, for instance, still felt the need to point out how an untrained *sensibilité* could lead to "sensuality," eighteenth-century writers outside the Church now saw the entire fabric of social relations as depending upon this universal capacity. Not only love, but sociability, responsibility, duty, and virtue were all conceived as being contained in this single power, given by na-

---

ment and overview of some of the issues presented in the early chapters of his large work, *Der Begriff 'sensibilité im 18. Jahrhundert: Aufstief und Niedergang eines Ideals* (Heidelberg: C. Winter, 1988).

2. Jean Mesnard, "Le classicisme Français et l'Expression de la Sensibilité," in *Expression, Communication and Experience in Literature and Language*, ed. Ronald G. Popperwell (London: Modern Humanities Research Association, 1973), 28–37.

3. E.g., "the disposition of the senses to receive the impressions of objects," according to Antoine Furetière's *Dictionnaire Universel de la langue française* (1690).

4. See Baasner, "Changing Meaning," 83–84.

ture for the very efflorescence of civic life. Certainly, the optimistic turn to nature stands in sharp contrast to thinkers like Senault, whose classic *L'homme criminel* could entertain the value of *sensibilité* only in the light of redemptive grace.

Nonetheless, one aspect of the eighteenth century's positive expansion of *sensibilité* that proved convenient or at least coincident to certain interests of some Jansenist thinkers was the subsuming physiological reading given to *sensibilité* by thinkers whose concerns ultimately gave rise to sensationalist systems like Condillac's.[5] Much of the impetus, philosophically, to this development derived from attempts to deal with tensions inherent in the Cartesian opposition between reason and feeling, with *sentiment* ultimately predominating by the eighteenth-century as the primary constitutive motive to social meaning.[6] In line with this, then, we recall how easily the theory of physical premotion as a defense of efficacious grace resulted, in the hands of Boursier, in a picture of the human person as a system of nerve impulses and traces orchestrated, ultimately, by God. Yet it was precisely this seeming physiological reductionism that allowed Boursier to describe a created world in historical continuity between Innocence and Fall, a world defined in terms of the changing relationships of proximity between God and the particularities of creation and creature. This very coincidence, however, must make us wonder to what degree the Appellant rehearsal of miracle stands in closer contact with the Jansenist quest for the historical continuity of grace than with the cultural drift toward affective materialism. The purely theological use of *sensibilité*, then, remains to be extricated from these kinds of coincidences.

## The Jansenist Linkage of Sensible Historical Form to Grace: The Case of Duguet

By the third decade of the eighteenth century, popular Jansenist handbooks began to circulate widely. Many of these volumes, some of great length, were modeled on the welter of devotional material aimed at parish clergy and educated laypeople that had proved so successful in France since the mid-1600s — manuals of prayer, confessionals, meditations, and spiritual counsel. What distinguished the Jansenist contribution to this genre was its formal theological focus. Appellant devotionals were generally written with an explicit pedagogical, and even dogmatic, aim, harnessing the rhetorical structures of spiritual instruction for the purposes of inculcating right belief on the many topics associated with the embattled movement. Adopting the language of *sensibilité* to this purpose

---

5. On the psychological and phsyiological trajectories of the concept, see Baasner, *Der Begriff.*, 237–57; see also Ernst Cassirer, *The Philosophy of the Enlightenment* (Princeton: Princeton University Press, 1979), 93–120.

6. For a discussion of this motivating tension in the realm of aesthetics, see Francis X. J. Coleman, *The Aesthetic Thought of the French Enlightenment* (Pittsburgh: University of Pittsburgh, 1971), 3–46.

proved one obvious aspect of this adaptation of devotional discourse, but one that was particularly congenial to the Appellant marriage of dogmatics and spirituality. Works like the *Instructions sur les vérités qui concernent la grace de N.S. Jesus-Christ,*[7] for instance, attempt to explicate the errors of *Unigenitus*'s condemnations, but do so through standard meditative applications of the "forms of Jesus' Mysteries," which are used to ground the moral and ascetic lives of readers. The presentation of scriptural shapes of Jesus' and the Church's life as objects of devotional conformance is used as an explicit method by which to render *doctrine* subjectively "gripping" (*intéressantes*), as its truths, in the forms of Christ's life, take hold of the heart and its *sentiments,* evoking *tendresse* and sympathy.[8]

The forms derivative of a traditional *imitatio Christi* are thus coupled with perspectives elicited by the language of sensibility. And in fact, the necessary connection between form and *sensibilité* was a constant theme in much eighteenth-century writing. Receptivity, responsiveness, and finally the active pursuit of the lines of social duty were frequently discussed in terms of some set of constraining forms. What is universally the case, however, is that when such formal aspects to *sensibilité* are brought forward, they are understood to be the forms imbedded in or derived from or produced by Nature. Eighteenth-century aesthetic and moral theories of imitation (or approximation or appropriation) abound, but they are always dealing with imitations of Nature and the forms of Nature, however beautified or standardized.[9] If there is a peculiarly religious attitude adopted toward the forms of imitation, it will not unexpectedly adopt postures that are distinguishable from Nature; and if this attitude is peculiarly Jansenist, it will perhaps involve a redefinition of formly *sensibilité* along the lines of particular historically constituted shapes.

A simple example of how this structure does in fact lie implanted in Jansenist thinking can be observed in a few passages from Duguet. By examining how this senior member of the Appellant movement progresses from a purely theological argument for the Jansenist conception of grace toward the devotionally infused commendation of this conception, akin to the later *Instructions,* we can see more precisely how the *constraints* of a peculiar form lie at the essence of grace's characterization.

Duguet's *Lettre sur la grâce générale* (1701) was one of many pieces that came out (although this one was not released to the general public until 1737) to refute Pierre Nicole's theory of General Grace. Nicole, who along with Arnauld was deemed one of the pillars of seventeenth-century Jansenism, had posited some kind of universally distributed divine capacity — a "physical power" as he termed it — to accomplish the good

---

7. Attributed to N. Hugot and published in two volumes in 1747 (n.p.).

8. See ibid.,vol. 1, viii and 47ff.

9. See Coleman, *The Aesthetic Thought of the French Enlightenment,* chapter 3; see also Bernard Tocanne, *L'Idée de Nature en France dans la Seconde Moitié du XVIIe Siècle: Contribution à l'histoire de la pensée classique* (Paris: Klincksbieck, 1978), 304–24, on later seventeenth-century attitudes with respect to the "imitation" of Nature.

as commanded in the natural law. Such a "grace," as he was willing to define it, removed from all people that "natural impotence" which otherwise would provide people an excuse for sinning. But Nicole, Jansenist as he remained, distinguished this general grace from the efficacious grace of Christ, by which alone the "voluntary impotence" of the will could be overcome so as to do the good for salvific ends. Such virtue, according to Nicole, is not natural in any case, and thereby he reaffirmed the Jansenist commitment to efficacious grace as it is linked to "free" predestination.[10] Many Jansenists considered all of this either the opening to a muddling of self-contradictions on the matter, or an undermining of their principles altogether. Duguet counted himself among these critics.

We need not enter into the details of Duguet's arguments. Most of them sound predictable Jansenist themes and invoke the categories of Augustine's debate with the Pelagians. Jansenius's own attacks on "sufficient" graces, graces that are in fact sufficient only for sin, are rehearsed once again. Nicole's system, we are told, cannot deliver what it promises, that is, a means to satisfy those sinners who complain that Augustine's doctrine is "too hard," precisely because in it Nicole offers a grace that, while universal, is still inefficacious for salvation. What then is the *fundamental* problem? Nicole's general grace "cannot change hearts," but can only provide a capacity for willing whose universal and voluntary misuse leads to pervasive sin.[11] We are in familiar territory.

But Duguet is less interested in the notion of efficacity in itself than in clarifying the context in which the "changing" of hearts can be discerned. To do this, he must bring into relief the opposition of nature and grace with respect to the realm of the heart. And while such an opposition between the natural and the supernatural is traditional enough, where Duguet's emphasis lies in its elucidation is on the aspect of grace's discrimination *within* nature, *among* natural objects. Following various texts from Thomas's *Summa Theologiae*, Duguet enumerates the features of the "natural": when human beings live by reason and in society, they are living "naturally." Such living proceeds from natural realities like the "basic [logical] laws of reasoning," ethical laws of "social life" (e.g., rewarding the good, the priority of the general good, etc.), conscience and its troubling or tranquility, and finally instincts like family bonding.

Now, while the grace of Christ can be considered as a perfecting work upon and among these realities, Duguet insists that such grace can never be equated with nature as such. And while created nature is a good, for which we thank God — and this nature includes the *Imago Dei* in which we are formed — none of this can be called "grace" without confusing the character of our religious existences. Nature does not equal grace,

---

10. On Nicole's theory, and the debate it provoked, see E. D. James, *Pierre Nicole, Jansenist and Humanist: A Study of His Thought* (The Hague: Martinus Nijhoff, 1972), 7–31. On Duguet's discussion of the overall theory, see the *Lettre*, 4ff. and 94ff.

11. Duguet, *Lettre*, 11–12.

nor is there *any* middle ground between nature and the grace of Jesus-Christ. The latter stands on faith, and faith is something "not all have" (2 Thess. 3:2).[12] Here are the key terms for Duguet's point: there is an absolute *distinction* between grace and nature — "il n'y a point de milieu" (no middle ground) and "rien d'equivoque" (nothing equivocal) in this differentiation — and this distinction is represented by the concrete lives of individuals within the world. That grace is distinguished from nature is embodied in the distinction between human creatures, one from another. Thus, Duguet's working definition of grace comes down to this: "a gift that distinguishes one man from another and is far from common to all; that establishes a difference between the good and the bad and is far from being equally present in the one and the other."[13]

It is this distinction within the world that allows Duguet to relate the abstract nature of grace to the particularity of divine grace as it is made real in Jesus Christ. Grace of course, as for Augustine, is emphatically defined only in terms of the Incarnation and death of Jesus, the particular man and particular savior.[14] Just this particularity stands as the problem that Nicole is trying to overcome, with his proposal for a universal endowment that will "justly" take away the complaints of sinners *distinguished* from the elect. Yet, as Duguet never tires of repeating, it is only by grasping the distinctive and discriminating aspect of the person of Jesus — *His* life and *His* work as it touches *this* or *that* person — that we can begin to perceive just what grace is. And so, when Duguet passes toward the end of the *Lettre* to a discussion of the "necessity" of sinning, he fastens on to the distinction between claiming the freedom for particular acts apart from sin, and the inevitability of sin attaching itself to the "sum" of a person's actions, that is, to the very distinctive shape of a life as a whole.[15] That grace distinguishes, that lives themselves take distinctive shapes, all derive from the fact that there is *a* distinctive life and shape that determines individually the form of a person's life for salvation. Salvation is the gracious congruence of these two distinctive forms.

This kind of argument stands as only the abstract logic presupposed in Duguet's main writing vocation, or what became of it in later life, that is, his cumulative "explication" of the "Mystery of Jesus." Made up of a series of theological and devotional commentaries (in the peculiar hybrid that emerged from what is called the "French School" of spirituality) on texts of Scripture relating to Christ, Duguet was never able, or perhaps had no desire, to complete anything beyond the Passion, Crucifixion, and Burial.[16] Yet just these commentaries on the life of Jesus represent the practical religious instantiation of his insistence on distinguishing and

---

12. Ibid., 20–25.
13. Ibid., 26. Duguet stresses the Thomistic character of this formulation.
14. Ibid., 31.
15. Ibid., 125–31.
16. See André Guny's article "Duguet" in *Dictionnaire de la Spiritualité*, vol. 3 (1957), col. 1766.

particularly formative grace. They do so founded upon the principle of *sensibilité* constrained by form:

> Human beings, who were submerged in the senses, needed a divine teacher.
> [...] To lead them out of error, however, they needed something more than
> simple instruction. They needed a teacher who was different than their own.
> They needed God Himself to become visible, to live among them; to speak
> to them in a language they could understand; to attract their wonder with
> miracles, and their love with goodness; to confirm His doctrine, once having
> taught them, by His own examples; and finally, to gather up into a final
> example all the circumstances capable of persuading them that there is a
> life different than this one, that virtue is something super-real, that virtue's
> hopes for an eternal happiness are well-founded, that God deserves to be
> obeyed without limit [...] All this was divinely accomplished by JESUS-
> CHRIST.[17]

Within the realm of the "senses," then, God takes form. To be sure, it is not an arbitrary form, not one that was to be merely instrumental to salvific purposes, but whose shape might be indifferent to specific contours; rather, the Incarnation's form represents the very "truth" of God's life with respect to humanity and stands as that truth's "tangible" and "popular" instantiation.[18] All the elements of Jesus' life, alluded to in popular devotionals as objects for meditation, are in fact the "impressions of grace" — the sensible form communicated to the sensible creature — in such a way that a new form is created in "resemblance."[19] The language of "model" and "image" is here used liberally. But the theological issue is clearly not one of "imitation" in the narrow sense. "We are called to follow Him. Our glory consists in resembling him, and it is by grace that His resemblance is given" as "an image" to the "children" of a model (and in contrast to the model and image of Adam).[20] There is here a merging of participatory concepts and sensible features. And this is exactly the theological point about grace that Duguet wants to exploit: what "impresses" about grace — indeed the fact that grace can be spoken of as an impressing power upon the faculties and the senses is founded on this reality — is that it imparts the particular form of the lived existence of Jesus.

In this light, the larger "Mystery" of Jesus, the great form that His lived existence embodies and communicates, can be viewed in part as the sum of the variety of particular historical forms whose sequential experience constitutes the one category "life of Christ." Duguet, following the tradition, calls these smaller forms "the mysteries," in the plural, and links their discrete shapes to the sensuous turns that grace follows in molding our "sensible" existence in and fastened to their image. Commenting on Galatians 2:10 — "I have been crucified with Christ" — Duguet explores

---

17. Duguet, *Explication du mystere de la passion de N.-S. J.-C., Suivant la Concorde. Jesus Crucifié* (Paris: Jacques Estienne, 1728), 3.

18. See ibid., 11.

19. Ibid., 69, 20.

20. Ibid., 20–21.

the way in which our baptisms have "joined" us to the New Adam so that "we are, from now on, linked to all His mysteries, to all His conditions [ . . . ] During this life, we carry about with us a happy mix of all that has happened to our Head."[21] We should note how, in this phrase, Duguet describes the experiential "mix" of "happenings" as something "carried." Subjective response is only a partial perspective on the workings of this grace, and instead of concerning himself with this, he points to objectified events and discrete elements whose shape is brought together and subsists from without, independent of the creature. The forms — and they are descriptively specific — are Christ's and are identifiably particular in their historical qualification of Christ's experience. We must, in this instance then, begin to see how the "personalization" or "sentimentalization" of salvation evident in the *Instructions*, when defined by the imposition of the forms of Jesus' mysteries, implies less an affective appropriation of religious meaning than the objective receipt (however understood) of a historical form.

We shall have occasion to return to the "states" of Jesus, as Duguet refers to them above. But before we do, we need to be clear that the forms of Jesus' mysteries, making up together His great Mystery, do not merely stand as the representations of particular events in the life of a Savior. They are not simply *granted* importance because of their subject so that they thereby define grace only as accidents. Grace is *sensible* because of the constraint of form; but the form is constraining because of the nature of what it means for God to love a sinful human being in a saving fashion. *Sensibilité*, in this scheme, is somehow essentially linked with salvation from sin.

In the vocabulary of Duguet and his tradition, this link is described by the French translation for *kenosis*, the term Paul uses in Philippians 2:7 for Christ's "self-emptying." *Anéantissement* — "annihilation" — is seen by Duguet as forming, with humiliation, the double model for our Christian existence. In itself, it is the form of the Mystery.[22] Applied to the divine life, however, it gives rise to the sensible logically, though with "no real change in nature":

> Whenever the Divine shows itself, brilliance and glory ought to accompany its manifestation. But should [the Divine] let go of itself, to the point of allowing itself to be mistaken and to be confused with the form of a slave — with which form it truly wished to be clothed — then it has hidden its majesty and has annihilated the exterior and sensible distinction that ought to obtain between itself and the form of the servant that acts as its cloud and clothing.

While sacrificing its glory to its "mercy and its love," divinity instantiates the "humility of the Word." For,

21. Ibid., vol. 2 (part 2, 1728), 14.
22. Ibid., vol. 1, 34–35.

it is in accepting a condition in which the Word will be hidden, in which
its love will not be grasped, in which the form of a slave will appear alone
and will be apprehended as the only existing object — it is in this that the
annihilation of the Word consists [...] Here is our model: *Hoc sentite in
vobis quod et in Christo Jesus* [*have this mind among yourselves which is
yours in Christ Jesus*]. JESUS CHRIST is God: he has annihilated himself.[23]

With respect to the relation of God standing over and against the creature, "glory" itself defines the distinction. Duguet will call it a "sensible"
distinction, but he seems to imply some transcendent form of sensibility. In the case of God's "sacrifice" of glory for the sake of "mercy," this
transcendent distinctiveness too disappears, and all that is left between
God and creature are the distinctions by which human beings themselves
discriminate among objects and subjects, "mere" *sensibilité*, as an almost
purely physiological dimension of particularization. The Divine Word as
saving love becomes "mere form" — this is the meaning of "the form of a
slave" — and only this form "will appear and be taken for the only existing
object." That grace has a historical form, then, is the definitive aspect of
divine love for human sinners. And the Incarnation is not only an instrumentality of love, but the crystallization of the "mere form" itself, glory
squeezed of its juices, of its supra-formalities, the accidents alone, which
can only be God loving.

It should be obvious here that Duguet is moving within a tradition
that is not primarily Jansenist in inspiration. Indeed, he is working within
that tradition of incarnational mysticism that proceeded from a joining of
Pseudo-Dionysian and Augustinian strands of devotion. Within this context, *sensibilité* cannot simply be read as a turn in the eighteenth-century
road of ideas, but as a fundamental *Christian* category for both explaining
the reality and the experience of God's saving love. The inescapable religious logic involved in adopting this category is obvious even today, as is
evidenced by someone like von Balthasar, who states the almost axiomatic
and certainly unoriginal nature of this Christian concept, when he writes:

Perception, as a fully human act of encounter, necessarily had not only to
include the senses, but to emphasise them, for it is only through the senses
and in them that man perceives and acquires a sensibility for the reality of
the world and of Being. And, what is more, in Christianity God appears to
man right in the midst of worldly reality. The centre of this act of encounter
must, therefore, lie where the profane human senses, making possible the
act of faith, become "spiritual," and where faith becomes "sensory" in order
to be human.[24]

Von Balthasar, who is here tracing the general connection between the
carnal senses with the "senses of faith," will press on from this basic implication of anthropology and Incarnation, much in the direction of Duguet,

23. Ibid., 36–39.
24. Hans Urs von Balthasar, *The Glory of the Lord* (San Francisco: Ignatius Press, 1982),
1:365.

by emphasizing the paradoxical nature of divine "self-emptying" as itself the loving establishment of mere form (or "being and its sensibility" in this case) as grace:

> But this, the Word's, flesh encounters man as God's *exinanitio* or "self-emptying." This Servant is comprehensible only as the Lord who came down for our sake. Everything about his sensibility and carnality breathes the Spirit, breathes too the Spirit's humiliation. It is senses that perceive God's humility sensually. [...] Thus all the senses perceive the non-sensual sensually. This is why they are so ready to go through the death of the senses which essentially awaits everything sensual.[...] But in the very midst of this self-renunciation they possess, in the phenomenon of the Incarnate God, the warrant of their own inconceivable resurrection. [...] Hence, at a deeper level, the poverty of Being and of its sensibility reveals the sole treasure Being contains, which is nothing other than — love.[25]

Still, while von Balthasar's expression here of the link between Incarnation and sensible form hardly touches on the reach of his own theology, as stated here it only grasps at the minimal implications of Christian affirmation. For Duguet and other Jansenist devotionals are, as we saw, concerned to disengage these minimal implications as presuppositions for the peculiar historical attachments between individual and Christian forms that truly *is* a Jansenist, or more precisely, Appellant conception. To get a sense, then, of how a traditional incarnational mysticism is adapted by the Jansenists, we need, for a moment, to go back behind the eighteenth-century devotion to the Mysteries of Jesus to its French source in Bérulle and the Oratory of Jesus, which he founded.

## At the Origins of the Appellant *Grâce sensible:* Bérulle and the Mysteries of Jesus

The complexity, as well as the fluidity, of Bérulle's theology demands that we simply outline certain features that were to be taken up thematically, though not necessarily systematically, by his followers.[26] What I wish to suggest in this is that, to the degree that those with Jansenist sympathies took up some of these themes, they clearly did so by resolving some of the tensions in Bérulle's thought in a particularly historicizing direction. This had the result of preparing the way for the application of "form" to the experience of the Church in a way that would prove more radical than Bérulle's own commitments might have allowed or at least urged.

Bérulle is known today for the vigor with which he commended a Christocentric and Incarnational theology and devotion.[27] And while

---

25. Ibid., 406–7.
26. I have found Louis Cognet's chapter on Bérulle the clearest overview of the material; see his *La Spiritualité Moderne* 1 (Paris: Aubier, 1966), 310–59.
27. For standard, and not inaccurate, expositions of this popular assessment, see, for example, John Saward, "Bérulle and the "French School," in *The Study of Spirituality*, ed. C. Jones, G. Wainwright, and E. Yarnold (London: SPCK, 1986), and Michael J. Buckley's

these renewed and, even in their focus, perhaps novel emphases may well stand in some implied connection with more contemporary incarnational concerns,[28] it is important for us at least to place them in their more traditional theological lineages. In this case, we must stress the Dionysian and exemplarist background to the Trinitarian base that undergirds Bérulle's scheme.

In one succinct text, Bérulle orders the immanent relations of the Trinity under the rubric of "communication" of persons.[29] This gives rise to several dialectical Trinitarian oppositions: unity/plurality, origin/emanation, unity/fecundity, unity/society. The major point being made here, of course, is that these inner characters of "communication" form the "cause and exemplar" of God's external communication, which is embodied in the Mystery of the Incarnation. "Economy," then, is an exemplarist phenomenon, and when the Incarnation itself, the historical life of Jesus, is reflected upon, it is usually explicated by Bérulle in terms of the historical image of a particular Trinitarian relation.

Thus, the hypostatic union, which is at the center of Bérulle's theological system, is an external communication founded on the intra-Trinitarian relations of Son to Father, embodying the "perfections" of these relations and bringing them into visibility. Bérulle can go so far as to speak of the hypostatic union in terms of a "second Trinity," although in this case the embodied relations consist "essentially" of "soul, body, and divinity" in the person Jesus, with each element reflecting the divine Persons of God.[30]

Given this exemplarism, Bérulle understands the incarnated reality of Jesus, which includes His historical experience as it is embodied in various events of His life, as reflecting especially the relation of Son to Father in their eternal relations. In an important passage from the *Grandeurs*, the Incarnate life that is to be our model is drawn into a reflective link with four qualities of "filiation" with respect to the Father: procession (=dependence), contemplation ("looking-toward"), referral (of all one's self), and attachment or indwelling.[31] The specific lived elements of the Incarnation — the elements of humiliation, poverty, weakness, passion, obedience, and so on — therefore are seen as instantiations of eternal relationships, whose visible lowliness lies in an embodied contrast to the essential glory of the Son, but whose shape is nonetheless really expressive of that glory, in hiddenness. There are a number of more theoretic aspects to Bérulle's Christology, including what proved to be his trou-

treatment of Bérulle in "Seventeenth-Century French Spirituality: Three Figures," in *Christian Spirituality: Post-Reformation and Modern*, ed. Louis Dupré and Don E. Saliers (New York: Crossroad, 1989), 42–53.

28. See Guillén Preckler's brief remarks on Liberation Christology's affinities to Berullianism, in his *Bérulle aujourd'hui, 1575–1975: Pour une spiritualité de l'humanité du Christ* (Paris: Beauchesne, 1978), 111–14.

29. Bérulle, *Discours de l'estat & des Grandeurs de Iesus*, VII:ii (*Oeuvres complètes*, Montsoult, 1960, reproduction of the 1644 editio princeps [henceforth *Oeuvres*]), 261–63.

30. See *Grandeurs*, III:viii, 207; also Louis Cognet, *La Spiritualité Moderne*, 335.

31. *Grandeurs*, V:ix, 238–39.

bling — troubling, at least, to some of his contemporaries — insistence upon the exclusive divine "subsistence" in the hypostatic union, which penetrated a passive and unsubsistent human nature with divinity. But all of these really stand in subordination to his exemplarist Trinitarianism, in which the character of Sonship demands a relationship of infinite dependence.[32]

A tension appears just here between the historical particularities of the Incarnate life and the more summary image or eternal exemplar of which they are temporal facets. There can be no question but that Bérulle took seriously these particular facets of life: they constitute the "mysteries" that become the foundation to one aspect of his devotional program, whose influence, as we saw, reaches out through the eighteenth century. But they tend, nonetheless, to subordinate their details to the larger form of the Trinitarian archetype. Thus, in the text to which we just referred, Bérulle will distinguish the specific "works and sufferings" of Jesus' "pilgrim life," from the "new State" the Incarnation makes "permanent and eternal in Heaven," that is, the "state" of embodied or visible filiation. While we are to honor these particular acts of Jesus, we are called more intensely toward a comprehensive change of "state," in which the "new man" as a full entity given over in "servitude" to God will stand as a single formal image of the Son.

In this respect, the "state" of Jesus, which may well include the various "states" of the individual mysteries, carries a subsuming ontological meaning, which while "formly" insofar as it denotes a relational configuration, is not so strictly shaped by the historical form of Christ's life in the way we understood the term in Duguet's work.[33]

The tension between limited form and eternal archetype is real, however, in that Bérulle has his definite "historicist" side. While he wavered between descriptions of the Incarnation in terms of a Scotist predetermined perfection of the human creature, apart from the Fall, he would also insist on the particular shapes of the Incarnation's temporal evolution as determined by sinful humanity's need for redemption.[34] Within the context of the Fall, the individual mysteries of the Incarnation become specifically salvific elements. The following text, cited at length, gives a good indication of how the exemplarist Trinitarianism of the hypostatic union can move into the more historically specific aspects of the mysteries themselves, seen as salvific "operations":

> Oh, that I might join myself to your Grandeurs and to your Humiliations, to your Cross and to your Glory, to your Life and to your Death.
>
> This is my desire and my hope. But this is beyond my power, and I further expect it [only] from the new grace of the new man. For [this grace]

---

32. See Cognet, *La Spiritualité Moderne*, 339.

33. On the ontological use of "state," see Guillén Preckler, *"Etat" chez le Cardinal de Berulle: Théologie et spiritualité des "états" bérulliens* (Rome: Gregorian University, 1974), 45–61; 83ff.

34. See Cognet's description of this in *La Spiritualité Moderne*, 342ff.

joins me to Him, and places me in the condition wherein I might not only work, but even more, receive and carry with me His own holy and divine works. Indeed, this grace moves toward an even closer and more intimate communication. For since this new grace emanates from the Incarnation, and therefore resembles its principle and its prototype, it moves me to be in JESUS and JESUS to be in me, just as He is in His Father, and His Father is in Him. Oh JESUS, therefore, be in me, live in me, work in me, form and figure in me your Conditions and your Mysteries, your Actions and your Sufferings.

[ . . . ] You are the image of God. Let me be the living image of you. Let me be made like you, as you conform me to your Mysteries, just as you, in your desire to become like me, conformed yourself to my miseries. Let me carry with me the effects and the characteristics of your Grace and of your Glory, of your Power and of your Life on this Earth.

May your birth cause my rebirth; may your Infancy return me to innocence; may your flight to Egypt have me flee the World and Sin; may your servitude make me your slave; may your bonds unbind me and deliver me from my sins, from my passions, and from myself; may your hidden and unknown Life hide me from the World and Vanity; may your solitude uphold me, your temptations strengthen me, your labors soothe me, your sorrows heal me, your agonies comfort me, your weaknesses console me; and may your death make me live and be reborn to eternity.[35]

In this case, the larger shape of "resemblance" to the prototype is explained in terms of the particular acts that save from sin, and Bérulle returns to the language of "operation" or of causality. In so doing, he is merely restating, and deliberately so, the kind of explanation offered by Thomas Aquinas with respect to the effects of the Incarnation and its mysteries. On several occasions, Bérulle will remind his readers of the way in which Thomas had understood, e.g., the Passion, to be more than simply a "meritorious cause," but also an "efficient" cause of new life.[36] Thomas's remarks on this matter, while consistent, are hardly extended. Not only does he speak of the "efficient causality for salvation" of various aspects of Christ's life, he will at times apply to the mysteries the character of "sacrament," implying their continued efficacity in the assumed flesh of Christ, now taken up in divinity for eternity.[37] Bérulle is willing to assume the model of efficient causality, and go further in the direction of Thomas's sacramental implications, by eternalizing these specific acts of salvific power, and so providing the shapes of these acts with some kind of enduring formative quality.

This is the import of the famous text from the *Oeuvres de Pieté* 76, "On the Perpetuity of the Mysteries of Jesus Christ."[38] Bérulle tells us

35. *Elevation a Iesus sur ses principaux estats and Mysteres* 1 (*Oeuvres*, vol. 1, 530).

36. See his *Oeuvres de Pieté* 29 (*Oeuvres*, vol. 2, 795).

37. For Thomas on the Mysteries, see Joseph Lécuyer, "La causalité efficiente des mystères du Christ selon Saint Thomas," in *Doctor Communis* 6 (1953), esp. 104–20. Key texts include *S.T.* 3a 48:6; 49:1 ad 3; *Compendium Theol.*. 227, 228, 239.

38. In the *Oeuvres*, vol. 2, 886f.

here that the "infinity" of the person (Christ) also "communicates an infinity" in accomplishing the mysteries in his human nature. Although in many respects the mysteries are "past," that is, are discrete historical events whose experience as events is lost to us, yet in other respects they have achieved an eternal "perpetuity." These last aspects of the enduring mysteries include "power" (or "virtue"), "love," "the Spirit," "merit," the "interior state" of the mystery, "efficacity," and "virtuous disposition." In all of this, Bérulle is clearly pointing to what we might call the "spiritual" meaning or force of the events, their "inner" realities as both saving acts and expressions of Jesus' own filial reality. As a result we see that the "forms" the mysteries comprehend are only metaphorically shapely.

Yet while the mysteries in this sense still exist, though in a heavenly way, just as do the bodily scars of the crucifixion, the effect of their heavenly perpetuation extends beyond their (conceptual) representation of spiritual realities and touches also the concrete historical dimension of individual Christians. Bérulle tells us that the mysteries persist and communicate their persistence through the operation in us of an "actual taste," a "vitality" and "living presence" of the disposition in which Jesus historically accomplished them. And so we are led into a realm in which the Christian not only shares "inner" dispositions — "disposition" itself being the term by which to distinguish the historical shape of the mystery from its embodied religious attitude — but also the very "affections" of the living Christ within the mystery.[39] In this context, then, *sensibilité* as the distinctively formal human response to a particular shape embodied in the life of Christ has some place in Bérulle's thinking.

And this becomes more evident too as we note in what way Bérulle's Christocentrism really does reconfigurate the given shapes of historical existence. One of his favorite descriptive terms by which to indicate the subsuming life of Christ achieved in the Incarnation is "world": Jesus is "a world," and indeed represents "the world" itself in its comprehending grasp of life in the presence of God. The New World that is Jesus *is* of greater breadth, beauty, and "durability" than the one world created in six days. It contains within *Jesus*, through the hypostatic union, the "visible, intellectual, and archetypical" worlds that reach beyond even the collection of creatures contained in the world as we understand it.[40] Seen this way, the Christian, by incarnational grace, is brought into an environing realm in which the forms of Christ, including those of the mysteries, set up a context of shapely reconfiguration that contrasts efficaciously to the "sensible" world of the "old" creation: new forms, new pressures, new demands, new impressions, new affections, new proximities, and so on.

This move toward a new universe in Christ, populated by new forms,

---

39. See his remarks on affective sharing in the Mass, in the *Oeuvres de Pieté* 85 (*Oeuvres*, vol. 2, 903)

40. See *Grandeurs*, IX:iv (*Oeuvres*, vol. 1, 316–17); see also Cognet, *La Spiritualité Moderne*, 351, on the Platonic categories of micro- and macrocosm that lie behind some of Bérulle's discussions here.

wherein grace seems to act as the effective repositioner of the individual in almost spatial terms, is as far as Bérulle will go, however, in his assimilation of grace to particular historical forms themselves. Because, for all his devotion to the particular mysteries, he still insists, as we saw, that they are either instrumentalities for some deeper purpose, or bearers of some inner meaning or disposition, whose real significance lies in a metaphysically distant archetype of Trinitarian filiation, whose embodiment in time is real enough, and glorious enough, but only because of its logically prior and independent reality apart from time and creation.

The "historicism" of Bérulle, then, which Cognet rightly identifies with his commitment to theological discussion in light of the Fall, is limited by his exemplarism from taking the "economy" of salvation as definitive of the form of grace. History itself is a vehicle for archetypical form, but cannot claim more than this, is not itself "mysterious," in the way that Jansenist devotionals, following Duguet, imply by linking the "truths of grace" to the experience of its formal appropriation.

In fact, Bérulle will sometimes speak of the "world" that is Jesus as a kind of exclamatory synonym for less concrete epithets, like "life" or "principle." The contrast between the old and the new creation, between the old and the new worlds, between nature and grace, becomes one between created "nothingness" — our "proper" nature as a "nothing" good only for "sin" — and "humble elevation."[41] In effect, we are given "two" natures, one from the Father (nothingness) and one from the Son, our "Father" in grace; we carry each with us, and the relationship between the two is one of reflection: humble elevation being only the visible "perfection" of the annihilated creature in good works.

This comes as something of a surprise, since the concrete nature of the "new life" in Christ was something at least hinted at in the theology of the applied states of the mysteries. But in fact, Bérulle was just as content to describe the history of salvation, the economy, in terms of an alternation of "nothingness" with respect to the human creature. First, God creates the human creature as a "nothing" for the purpose of adoration; Adam's sin reduces this creature to "next to nothing," and the grace of Christ restores the original relationship in a more stable fashion.[42] The history of salvation, in this light, forms not so much an unfolding of particular and distinctive configurations of proximity between creature and God, as it does the mirrored reflection in time of an ontological relationship that asserts and reasserts itself according to the image of the Trinitarian existence. History represents the *néant* of the creature as it rightly "adheres"

---

41. "On the vocation of Christians to holiness," *Oeuvres de Pieté* 110 (*Oeuvres*, vol. 2, 960–65).

42. *Oeuvres de Pieté* 135 (*Oeuvres*, vol. 2., 103f.). For a discussion of Bérulle's views of creation and fall, see Jean Dagens, *Bérulle et les origines de la restauration catholique (1575–1611)* (Paris: Desclée de Brouwer, 1952), 270–90. Bérulle has many things to say about the purpose of human creation and its relation to God that are more positive than simply what I have indicated here; but the adherence of a "nothing" to its creator sets the limits to his thoughts and defines even such dynamic concepts as "love."

to its creator, and it is this form that both defines the Incarnation and is rendered real by the filial image embodied in the Incarnation.[43]

To return to the question of *sensibilité* from this perspective, we can see to what degree the *sensible* has been emptied of any intrinsic significance and how it looms as a concern only insofar as it is relativized by its more perfect ideal forms, in the Platonic sense. Mesnard has drawn our attention to a text from the *Oeuvres de Piété*, "De l'usage qu'on doit faire des sentimens humains [On the use one should make of human sentiments],"[44] in which Bérulle provides a concise set of instructions on the place of human *sensibilité* within the Christian vocation. This brief work was written in response to a woman in a particular situation of suffering, and it is to these "feelings" of pain and "repugnance" that Bérulle addresses his remarks. In general, he divides the world of *sensibilité* into two categories. First, there is the sensitive life of the Christian. This, according to Bérulle, is to be traversed in a state of disinterest, as a "soul that goes simply to God, situated among these things [feelings] but without attachment to them." One acknowledges the realities of suffering experience, indeed, one thinks oneself "deserving" of them, and so is unresistant to their presence. Nonetheless, as personally experienced "affections" and "feelings," they are to be left behind as insignificant elements in a life whose "only object is God, and only feeling is for God." This relativizing of human *sensibilité*, finally, is founded on a humble and lived recognition of God's *grandeur*, and one's own creaturely *néant*. And to this degree, the Christian's *experience*, that is, religiously significant *sensibilité* touching the "soul" or heart of the creature, is an experience of nothingness.

But Bérulle also notes a second category of sensible experience. This includes the affections of the Incarnate Jesus:

> Honor greatly the pains and virtues of our Lord JESUS CHRIST, and most especially [honor] His humility, that was willing to take and carry human experience [*sentimens humains*]. For the History of His life shows us this, as he wept, sorrowed, trembled, was frightened, and troubled at the sight of others. This is so, even if these things may seem better suited to our own infirmity than to the greatness and supreme perfection of his Humanity, deified and personally united to the Divine.

The curious import of this final exhortation to this reader is not only to uphold the only "true" affections as being those of the Incarnate Lord. For given the context of his advice, Bérulle wishes to explain how even the value of these Christic *sentiments* are but the signs of the abnegation of "proper" affection altogether. We may attach ourselves as "nothings" to God, indifferent to our own particular grating experience, precisely *because* Jesus' incarnate life embodied a self-denial of divine experience (however one might characterize such a paradoxical conception). Even the experience of the incarnate mysteries, then, already more "real" than

---

43. On Bérulle's concept of "adherence," see Cognet, *La Spiritualité Moderne*, 349ff.
44. In the *Oeuvres Complètes*, vol. 2, 1059–60.

human *sensibilité*, stands as a pointer to a yet more fundamental "disposition" of *anéantissement* that lies at the relational heart of the divine filiation.

Thus far I have wished only to show that there is embedded in Bérulle's initiation of the mysteries devotional theology a tension between the Trinitarian exemplarist and historicist elements. And I believe that tension presses, in his own thinking, more toward the former than in the direction of the latter. Within Bérulle's thinking, in any case, there could be no appreciation, as with Duguet, of "mere form" as the shape of grace, simply because in large measure the Incarnation is buttressed by what is without form, by the transcendent God who is defined in terms of interior relations imaged ontologically through creaturely dependence. *Anéantissement*, which looms large in Bérulle's thought, though perhaps not so much as in his immediate followers', is defined in terms of creaturely dispositions in the image of these divine relations, for which the Incarnation is a forceful expression. For Duguet, however, we have seen that the *kenosis* of the Word represents the divine reduced to historical act, to love, to particularity aimed at particular people. Divine glory reduced to mere form is in fact what takes place in particular loving. There is no Trinitarian reflection involved if for no other reason than that the distinctiveness of grace does not describe a "disposition" or an "attitude" in Bérulle's sense, but a specific encounter of proximity and vision. Bérulle can call grace "relational" in the "image of the Trinity," that is, the intra-Trinitarian life, of which all reality is a reflection, but this leads him to the astonishing conclusion that, as creatures, we are but the "accidents" of the "substance" that is Jesus Christ Incarnate, the passing shimmerings of that larger current which is God's eternal self-relationship.[45]

This contrast between Bérulle and Duguet can only affirm the fact that, despite the Platonic leanings of even someone like Jansenius, the positing of the Fall as a historical and not an ontological distinction in the definition of human creaturehood determined that the Jansenists erect a set of constraints to the understanding of grace that essentially tied it — and therefore God — to particular historical formalities: events, visible shapes, and experiences. The personalization of Christ's salvific being is thereby strictly externalized according to specific shapes of life experience, to some degree, and at least *primarily* this personalization does not rely on the apprehension of a meaning behind these shapes.

We might state the contrast again in another way. In concert with Bérulle, these "shapes," according to Jansenist discussions of the mysteries as in Duguet, are not external models whose link to the Christian depends on "conformance." This would be a simple restatement of the unvarnished devotions of *imitatio*, wherein the shapes of Christ are "followed" as a "path," a learning. The Appellants follow Bérulle here: the shapes are divine ("perpetual" and "enduring") and divinely present to the

---

45. See *Oeuvres de Pieté* 118 (*Oeuvres*, vol. 2, 976).

Christian. In contrast to Bérulle, however, the Jansenists might stress that the meaning of these shapes lies not in their undergirding dispositions, imaging an archetype of divine relation, but rather that they lie in the very external shape itself, as it is figured in the Christian; they are some-how instrinsically significant. Indeed, the mysteries as they take form in the Christian life are *figures* more than anything else, particular realities molded by God into particular shapes. If they point to anything beyond themselves, it is to their *direct* historical referent, the life of Christ lov-ing. As figures, they are the human and historical equivalent to the "mere form" achieved in the Incarnational self-emptying of the word, no longer "form" in the substantial sense of ontological wholeness and glory, but in the minimal sense of "sign of similitude."

## Toward Appellancy: Quesnel's Transformation of Grace's "Form" to "Figure"

In moving from the terminology of "form" to "figure" here, I am introduc-ing a key concept in Appellant theology, over which we shall be expending some lengthy investigation in later chapters. I will not linger over the dis-tinction here, except to limit its ultimate usefulness from the start. "Form" and "figure," for the Appellants, are in fact used interchangeably, but our discrimination between the two can be helpful if it keeps us aware of the constraining, rather than fulfilling, function that form will play for their theology. This, at least, we can see immediately in the divergence that takes place in the French Oratory between the school of Bérulle's succes-sor as superior, de Condren, and the interests of a younger member of the congregation like Quesnel, whom Duguet followed. The distinction is sharp and easily grasped.

It should be stated from the start that the connection of the Oratory and later Jansenist, especially Appellant, theology is intimate. Not only were strongly influential leaders of the later period, like Quesnel and Duguet (initially anyway), actual members of the Oratory, but many of the prominent figures of the Appellant movement, like Boursier (not to mention François de Pâris, the "saint" of Saint-Médard), were educated at theological institutions directed by the Oratorians, like the seminary of Saint-Magloire.[46] By the time that popular Jansenist handbooks were be-

---

46. The suspicions hovering over the Oratory by the latter half of the seventeenth cen-tury, that it was a haven for Jansenist thinking, were never dispelled. The early friendship of Saint-Cyran and Bérulle initiated the connection in people's minds, and the undeniable Jansenist and Appellant sympathies of many Oratorians by the eighteenth century sealed the charge. Throughout the nineteenth century, and to this day even, writers from or on the Oratory seem bound to defend the group from such perceived aspersions, but pointlessly, it seems. That the Oratory was never as an institution committed to Jansenist positions is obvious, and that many of its prominent members and associates, from de Condren on, were bitter adversaries of Jansenism is also evident. But as the whole debate over the "spectre" that constituted "Jansenism" has shown, the theological lines were never quite so conscious as some would have liked them to be. In any case, that the Oratory and many of its mem-

ing distributed in the first half of the eighteenth century, the devotion to and theology of the Mysteries of Jesus, deriving ultimately from Bérulle, had permeated Jansenist spirituality so thoroughly that its marriage to specifically Augustinian categories of grace and predestination was almost natural, and certainly inevitable. And individuals like Quesnel played an important role in orchestrating this espousal.

But, as Cognet has observed, it was not Bérulle directly who exerted a decisive influence on the subsequent outlook and interests of the Oratory and its friends — his writings were rarely read after the middle of the seventeenth century — but friends and followers of the Oratory's founder.[47] Initially it was François Bourgoing — the third superior general of the Oratory — who provoked the dissemination and popularization of Bérulle's ideas with his own immensely successful *Les vérités et excellences de Jésus-Christ Notre-Seigneur.* The French edition of 1636 is said to have seen over twenty re-editions. In addition, Guillaume Gibieuf contributed to the propagation of some of these conceptions with his 1630 *De libertate Dei et creaturae,* which we know to have been studied by many Oratorians like Quesnel.[48] For our purposes, finally, we must note the enormous role played by Charles de Condren's leadership, as Bérulle's direct successor at the Oratory. Although he wrote and published little, his lectures, direction, and example profoundly colored the devotional interests of the Oratory and its own influence for years to come.

And what this influence amounted to, in large measure, was a strengthening of and emphasis on the Platonic features of Bérulle's thought, reformulated in a decidedly "annihilationist" mode. Cognet characterizes de Condren's thought in this way:

> A double nonentity [*double néant*], due to its created nature and to the sin that marks that nature, humanity nonetheless exists only for God, and owes everything to God. As de Condren sees it, the creature's essential homage due to the Creator involves not adoration, in the first instance, but rather sacrifice, "the essential duty of religion."[49]

The chief source for the articulations of de Condren's particular concerns is a reconstituted version of a talk he gave dealing with the Letter to the Hebrews, which was published after his death in 1677, *L'Idée du Sacerdoce et du sacrifice de Jesus-Christ donnée Par le R. P. De Condren....*[50] The editing of this lecture was done by Quesnel himself, who contributed

---

bers proved an essential element in the development of eighteenth-century Jansenism is now without question. On the history of the Oratory through the early eighteenth century, touching on many of these matters, see Batterel's still-authoritative *Mémoires domestiques pour servir à l'histoire de l'Oratoire* (modern edition by A. M. P. Ingold and E. Bonnardet, Paris, 1902–5, 4 vols.).

47. Cognet, *La Spiritualité Moderne,* 360–61 and following.

48. See Cognet, ibid.; J. A. G. Tans's article, "Quesnel," in *Dictionnaire de la Spiritualité,* vol. 12 (1986), col. 2739.

49. Cognet, *La Spiritualité Moderne,* 387; see also the introduction to the *Lettres du P. Charles de Condren,* ed. P. Auvray and A. Jouffrey (Paris, 1943), xxxvii ff.

50. The rest of the title reads ... *Second Superieur General de l'Oratoire de JESUS.*

a preface and two further sections on the notion of sacrifice. (A first section to the book is provided by an anonymous writer.) Here, then, we have a place to observe the encounter of one authentically Berullian strain of thinking with the first suggestions of a Jansenist appropriation of that strain. And one place of contrast that comes to the fore lies in the category of form and "figure."

De Condren, as Cognet pointed out, bases his reflections on the premise that "sacrifice" is the "essential" religious duty. And this, he says, is because the "obligation is engraved upon the very ground of the creature's being," that is, as a creature created from nothing, whose own paradoxical existence depends upon its losing itself wholly in the Creator, through "annihilation."[51] When de Condren lists the "reasons" for rendering sacrifice today, only the last of essentially five motivations speaks of sin. The rest depend on the inherent nature of created being.[52]

Much of the lecture is given over to an explanation of the form of sacrifice according to the shapes presented in the Letter to the Hebrews. While the use of Hebrews in this context may seem self-explanatory, it is significant that this scriptural example of typological exegesis par excellence should be tethered to a presentation of ontological principles. In the first place, the adoption of the scriptural paradigm for theological explanation, rather than meditation, is a new departure. It marks a development in scriptural application that goes beyond Bérulle's contemplative and "epideictic" attitude to the Bible.[53] But, nonetheless, in the second place, the peculiar historicist basis of scriptural typology, arguably even in Hebrews, is still made to serve an essentially exemplarist theology.

Thus, de Condren will break down the reality of sacrifice into a number of forms, five to be exact: consecration of victim, oblation, immolation, "inflammation" or "consumption," and finally communion.[54] These are described in terms of the mysteries of Jesus' Incarnation, with each form mirroring some aspect of the mysteries. And, to be sure, these forms are also located, typologically, within the realm of salvation history, although in a very attenuated fashion.[55] However, as with Bérulle, the fundamental determinant of these shapes is the inclusive form of Jesus' "heavenly" life with the Father, a continual sacrifice of glory that somehow gives a form of perpetuity to the aspects of relation embodied in the particular mysteries.[56] There is little question that, as an inclusive whole, even when characterized by glory, the single form of Christ's sacrifice remains that of *anéantissement*, and the Christ who rules in majesty remains the "slain"

---

*Avec quelques Eclaircissemens & une Explication des Prieres de la Messe Par un Prêtre de l'Oratoire* (Paris: Jean Baptiste Coignard, 1677).

51. Ibid., 53–54.

52. Ibid., 54–59.

53. The term is Michael Buckley's, in his chapter on Bérulle, "Seventeenth-Century French Spirituality: Three Figures," 49f.

54. *L'Idée*, 62ff., and 81–99.

55. Ibid., 103ff.

56. Ibid., see 105ff.

Christ, upon the throne. This essential form precedes and "encloses" any other specific, such as the sacrifice for sin, which by this point in the discourse has been forgotten.[57]

Quesnel's third section to the book, "Wherein the truths of the preceding discourse are clarified," in no way contradicts any of these concerns, although the Berullian focus on *adoration* is reasserted very clearly, and in contrast to de Condren's own emphasis on *anéantissement.* The sacrifice of the Incarnation is presented as the divinely paradoxical means by which God, "who could not adore himself, and who nonetheless cannot be worthily adored except by himself," contrives to fulfill an eternal vocation called out by the divine glory.[58] And, following de Condren, Quesnel also describes the elements or forms of sacrifice in general in terms that revolve around a more inclusive and single shape of the Incarnate word, whose particular shapes tend toward the historical shedding of specific form in favor of the spiritual reality of awaiting beatitude.[59]

But even in this last case, Quesnel stresses the particularity of the historical figures for sacrifice in the unfolding dispensations of sacred history with a detail and a determinancy that does not interest de Condren. The "exterior shell" that "envelops" the "pure" and "spiritual" truths of the mysteries, which will be possessed "naked and without veils, without signs and figures" in glory, nonetheless are qualified historically by a specificity that must be remarked. And it must be so remarked because, unlike Bérulle and de Condren, Quesnel locates the object of the mysteries as being quite explicitly the Church, as the Body of Christ, and not simply the Christian as a "creature" touched by the Church's baptism.

This ecclesial concern of Quesnel represents a significant point of departure. Despite claims for the French School's innovating (or renovating) thinking with regard to the *Corpus Mysticum* as a central ecclesiological model,[60] the fact remains that this thinking rarely transcended a Eucharistic analogy, and it was the Jansenists in particular who developed the doctrine in a vital and compelling fashion.[61] In the context of the *L'Idée,* Quesnel's turn to the Church as the object of the sacrificial form that is the Incarnate Jesus means that he will take much more seriously the experiential reality of the sacrificial figures embedded in its history, transient though they may be.

It is in his "Preface" [unpaginated] to the book as a whole that Quesnel reveals this shift and its import with respect to de Condren's ontologism. Here he opens his entire discussion by immediately subordinating the cen-

---

57. See ibid., 66–73; 110.

58. See ibid., 160f.

59. Ibid., 159f., and 152ff.

60. See Emile Mersch's *The Whole Christ: The Historical Development of the Doctrine of the Mystical Body in Scripture and Tradition* (Milwaukee: Bruce Publishing Co., 1938), 531–55.

61. We shall be returning to this question in the next chapter. For the moment, we may cite Cognet's two-part article "Note sur le P. Quesnel et sur l'ecclésiologie de Port-Royal," in *Irenikon* 21 (1948).

tral notion of sacrifice to the single purpose of "satisfaction for sin," and in doing so, relativizes the Incarnation itself according to this historical demand: the purpose of the Incarnation is the Priestly Sacrifice of Jesus; but the purpose of this sacrifice is the satisfaction for sin. By stating his premise this way, he turns on its head the Berullian phrase that "Jesus Christ is the Masterpiece of God," through the addition of the historical purpose of such a divine work: " . . . and the masterpiece of Jesus Christ is the Church," the particular "body" that is his own, yet is shaped by the individual and corporate existence of a temporal collective. From the start, then, the exemplarism of filiation is noticeably ignored.

Quesnel provides an unremarkable Anselmian paradigm of satisfaction, to which, however, he adds a remarkable observation. Quoting from the Vulgate (Eph. 2:4), he writes that any satisfaction offered by Christ is one of "excessive love" (*nimiam charitatem*). This means, he explains, that the simplest humiliation of God would have sufficed to pardon the creaturely offense given to God by Adam. In terms of the logic of propitiatory mechanics, there was no "need" for the Passion and Death of Jesus. How then do we explain the *actual* forms of the Incarnate life?

> The zeal inherent in God's glory, and His love for human beings, led Him to make a sacrifice. Despite being rooted in and founded upon love, even the saints cannot comprehend the breadth, the length, the height, or the depth of this sacrifice. Sacrifice: after four thousand years of being promised and figured, it was finally accomplished in the times ordained by God, through His humiliations, by His sufferings, and by His death upon the Cross, by His resurrection, and by His Ascension into Heaven.[62]

In this way, Quesnel *detaches* the mysteries from any ahistorical ontological basis and infuses each with an intrinsic and independent value that springs uniquely from the love of God, rooted in the particular context of experienced sin. It is the Jansenist insistence on the historical pressures working through the Fall from Innocence that transforms de Condren's eternal sacrifice back into a discrete element of historical relation between God and creature.

Further, as he goes on to explain, each mystery itself is displayed figuratively in the "economy" of God's sacred history as it is described in Scripture. And therefore, far from assuming that the typological figuration of sacrifice in the Old Testament has lost its compelling interest, as "shadows" that have given way to the truth, we are encouraged by the very nature of the economy to approach the truth *by way of* the figures. Each stands, historically, as a concrete guarantee of God's love, given fully in the incarnational sacrifice, and that sacrifice itself is apprehended as truth only by means of traversing that concrete experience. Only by moving along the relation from "exterior to interior" is the perfect revealed as perfect.

---

62. *L'Idée du Sacerdoce*, preface (unpaginated).

The "form" of sacrifice, in de Condren's archetypical sense, gives way as an object of experience to the "figures" of sacrifice, as Quesnel delineates them. And "figure" here denotes not simply the "prefiguration" of the type, but also an experienced relation of these specific historical shapes as tied *directly* to the equally specific and independent shapes that mark the incarnate life of Jesus. However important and ultimate may be the "interior disposition," the spiritual and discarnate meaning of the mysteries, Quesnel wishes to stress the perpetually *inescapable* nature of the figure as a place for apprehending and appropriating that meaning. In this respect, the "body" as a figure, including the body that is the Church attached to Christ as its head, becomes figuratively significant as an entity of historical experience.

The contrast with de Condren is here clear enough, I think. And it will suffice at this point in our discussion merely to point to some practical components implied in this turn to the figure by Quesnel. They constitute, it seems to me, the link necessary for grasping the movement from Bérulle to the Appellant attitudes toward the mysteries apparent in Duguet and his followers. In a work of devotional direction for Lent that Quesnel published ten years after the *L'Idée*,[63] we see that the "states" which Bérulle had defined as ontological dispositions to be appropriated spiritually by the individual Christian have now become historical experiences suffered by the *Church* and its members, as identified through particular events and people. These now project into an extended sacred history of the actual "body" of the Incarnate Lord, and this projection of specific form becomes the primary meaning of "figure."

Jesus is first described as the "universal Penitent," who "carried in his Body and in His heart all the effects of [God's] justice and all the dispositions of a true Penitent." This is the attenuated exemplarist model at work. But then Quesnel goes on to explain that the historical "carrying" of these dispositions constitute a peculiar efficacy of the *sensible:* the Body and Heart of Jesus, as they take specific forms, are able to give expression to their shape in a manner that is "alive, pathetic, and touching."[64] Whereas in Bérulle the affections of Christ are noted as self-enclosed signs of the archetype of filial annihilation, to be pressed into a realm distant from the quieted *sentiments* of the Christian, here Quesnel is actually reversing the relationship: the affections of Christ are given their specificity for the exact purpose of *creating* human *sensibilité*.

And just as in the later Jansenist devotionals, this peculiar brand of *sensibilité* is rendered as a constraining force of form, the creation in human history of the figure of Christ's own life, without reference to any further reality.

---

63. *Jésus-Christ Penitent: ou Exercice de Pieté pour le tems de Carême, pour une Retraite de dix jours. Avec des Reflexions sur les sept Psaumes de la Penitence et la Journée Chrétienne. Par un Prêtre de l'Oratoire de Jesus* (Paris: Lambert Roulland, 1688).

64. Ibid., preface (unpaginated).

> For we are His members, in order to continue His life, to carry in us His various conditions, and to have Him fulfill in His Mystical Body the Mysteries that He has already fulfilled in his own natural Body, just as St. Paul himself says: *I rejoice in my sufferings for your sake, and in my flesh I complete what is lacking in Christ's afflictions, for the sake of His body, which is the church* [Col. 1:24].[65]

This is the creation of form, of course, in and as the life of the Church. And thus, a peculiar and fluid relationship is set up in the "figure" existing between what Quesnel had earlier called "the exterior" and "the interior": the "body" as the mystical Body of the Church, stands as a figure for the very "natural flesh" of Jesus, and whatever meaning the figure holds in relation to its original is a strenuously "fleshly" meaning.

Quesnel will continually stress the Berullian connection between the "life mystery" and the "interior disposition" it embodies, but now the flavor of the emphasis is on the "inseparability" of the disposition from the bodily reality, and not vice versa. The embodied figure is inescapable and necessary.

> Finally, since Jesus Christ united members to Himself in order that they might carry His likeness, and in order to make them imitate Him by retracing in them His Mysteries, His qualities, and His dispositions, and by enlivening them with the spirit of His Penitence — therefore, we gaze upon, honor, and imitate Jesus Christ when we gaze upon, honor, and imitate His saints,

that is, the members of Christ's body whose lived existences *in the body* most clearly stand as distinctive figures of the mysteries.[66]

Devotionally, the retreat Quesnel outlines in this manual is organized according to a highly methodical sequence of ten individual daily practices: meditation on one of the "mysteries" of Jesus' life, for our "adoration," and His formation within us; meditation on a quality of Jesus' penitence, including its "use" for us; meditation on specific words of Jesus from Scripture, pertaining to penitence, for study and following; meditation on an interior disposition of penitence, to "work over" in terms of one's own life, and to pray over; taking up an "exterior action" of penitence, to love and to practice; an act of vocal prayer and praise concerning penitence, in order that particular words may be on our lips and in our hearts; mediation on a "terrible truth" of judgment, in order to fear and avoid it; meditation on a "consoling truth" for particular encouragement; meditation on a particular saint, for consideration and imitation; and finally, the recitation of one of the penitential psalms. All of this may well mark the evolving degeneration of devotion, within the French School, into serialized and formalized fashions of spiritualized routine. Still, it is important for our purposes to recognize in this particular example the way in which the organization of the retreat follows a kind of proliferation of concrete

---

65. Ibid.
66. Ibid.

figurating exercises, the sum of which is seen as embodying the working of grace.

Finally, it is already evident, I think, that at least the theological components for Carré de Montgeron's description of Dom de Palacios's healing are available even at this point in the practically limited boundaries of Quesnel's devotional writing: tangible attractions, historical particularities, figured and thus inseparable connections between them that grant to the shape of the flesh an intrinsically significant form as coincident with Jesus' forms, including the flesh of the Body, the Church, ordered relationships over time, and so on. To the extent that, in Appellant theology, there will be discerned a manifested *ostensio Spiritus,* visible as grace working, and that it will impose itself upon the attention of the world, then this *ostensio* will be apprehended in the same proliferation of particular figures, only now somehow pressing and demanding.

Of course, to the degree that Quesnel and Duguet provide the dynamic inspiration to Appellant *figurisme,* the specific form of scriptural exegesis that lies behind many aspects of the defense, and indeed very experience, of the Saint-Médard miracles, we must ask to what degree it is fair to characterize the "form" of Jansenist grace in figurist terms. Certainly, the Oratorian influence provides the essential impetus toward the specifically incarnational figurism that comes to define grace in Appellant minds. But we have also seen that only the engagement with the peculiar historicizing quality of Jansenist grace — the elements of distinguishing and discriminating encounter and proximity between God and creature, the historical ordering of these particular relations — only this coupling with Jansenist structures for viewing grace could have given rise to the *historically* constraining shapes which that grace was seen to render in its own act. For the "form" of grace to be truly *sensible,* that is, for grace to be active as figure — and this, we shall see, *is* the form of the pneumatic event of miracle — Jansenism had to appropriate and redirect, according to its own image, Berullian themes.

It is perhaps odd that the Appellant theology of the Saint-Medardists *is* so rarely tied to the Oratory, except in the person of Duguet, whose ideas have been seen, in any case, to be peculiar. Dedieu can assert, though without explanation, that later "figurism," of the Convulsionaries even, overleaps the Oratory altogether and ultimately derives from Arnauld and even Jansenius and not from the Jansenist transformation of originally Berullian categories.[67] But there is perhaps some truth in identifying the fundamental motor to this development as the Jansenist insistence on the distinctive and subsuming historical line drawn by the figure of the redeeming Jesus. This, after all, was Duguet's own theological starting point, despite his obvious and continued debt to Oratorian devotional forms.

It is, of course, Pascal's as well; and we shall be examining something of

67. Dedieu, "L'agonie du Jansénisme," 167.

his own figural concerns in the second section of this book. But even before Pascal, as if bound by an inner thread, we *do* see Arnauld also hinting at the same reality, and toward the same figural direction, despite his almost full lack of interest in the devotional practices of the Oratory. We see this, for instance, when, in his defense of Jansenius's characterization of the grace of the Old Testament as "impeding," he decides to locate the historical reality of Israel within a realm that is *entirely* figural.[68] Jansenius had called the Old Testament a "grand comedy," something his critics regarded as tantamount to blasphemy. Arnauld retorts that the bishop of Ypres meant this in the best sense: the Old Testament was a "dramatic" "figure," that is, an "animated and vivid representation" of Jesus Christ, in which the "figures" were actual living people and events, each of which, and as a whole, pointed to the single and unique grace of Christ. Hence, there was no grace operative in Israel that was not the grace of Jesus; but at the same time, we can claim no operative grace in Israel that does not actually "figure" specifically and in an identifiably shapely fashion the Christ from Nazareth. If unrecognized and invisible, then there is only "seeming" grace, which is inefficacious and to that degree, "impeding."

As with Duguet, then, so with Arnauld: the grace of Christ distinguishes, constrains, marks out in particularity. As a result, it has a form, a specificity, and, in a historical context such as the Jansenists universally demand in the shadow of the Fall's still-ordered place in God's purpose, grace exists as a set of shapes embodying the contours of a living person. If there is a redeeming love, then there is form, and the world of love is settled into a set of experienced figures whose sensible deployment marks the shape of history. With this conclusion comes also a hint of the pneumatological implications given in this way of conceiving grace: if the Holy Spirit is truly to be *seen*, then it can appear only in the identifiable forms impressed upon historical events by the figure of Christ's life and death, paradoxically — and most clearly — perceptible in the shape of rejection, the Cross's ignominy.

---

68. Arnauld, *Seconde Apologie*, II:4–10, 99ff.

# Chapter Four

# THE SPIRIT OF GRACE

## Outline of the Chapter

This chapter will focus on bringing into relief some of the implied pneu-matological elements central to the Jansenist conception of grace within the limited boundaries in which we have been examining it until now. These elements will constitute a necessary, if only partial, framework for our understanding of the Saint-Médard miracles as evident pneumatic events within the *ostensio Spiritus*, such as we shall be investigating them in the next two sections.

In this task, Saint-Cyran's pneumatology provides us with two basic categories, whose significance we shall trace in later Jansenism: the link between charity and grace, and the historical/ecclesial focus of this char-ity, tied to the Holy Spirit. We will examine how Jansenist catechetical literature develops these two themes, providing elements that will be joined, by someone like Quesnel, with particular Oratorian concerns. Thereby, we will see how Quesnel finally and implicitly reorients, in a sense that is "Jansenistic" with respect to our previous discussions of grace and consistent with later Appellancy, pneumatological concerns that prove important to later Appellant apprehensions of pneumatic self-demonstration.

## Saint-Cyran (1): Charity and Command, and Later Jansenism

A properly adumbrated pneumatology can be formulated only in the wake of the full phenomenal reach of the *ostensio Spiritus*'s apprehension. Such a process, as we have indicated its Pauline structure, must move beyond the categories of observed theological reflection and struggle, through to the grasped *concreta* of pneumatic experience and its negation, and fi-nally to the sense of their collective historical fate. But even within the parameters of abstracted theological reflection of the kind we have been examining in Jansenist conceptions of grace, we can and ought to identify elements of pneumatological discourse whose strictly notional character nonetheless forms an aspect of this larger mechanism of the Spirit's appre-hension, even prior to our encounters with essential *pneumatica*. Indeed, the close conceptual connection between Jansenist theologies of grace and

80

their formal pneumatology is such as to indicate the centrality of both these reflective modes to the experienced shape of the *ostensio Spiritus.*

However abstracted appear the discussions of grace at which we have looked thus far, the conjunction of their theoretical frameworks of "historical form" with the actual ecclesiastical and political contests in which Jansenists were engaged mapped out a realm of religious perception in which larger issues like the nature of the Holy Spirit were bound to be construed. The evolving shape of the struggle over *Unigenitus,* however, a struggle which gradually and sometimes cruelly marked the demise of the Jansenist movement as a whole, meant that whatever forms were discussed as constituting this history would prove to be figures of visible defeat. If grace was itself given in the form of such appearance, as Jansenists were committed to saying in the shadow of the Christic Mystery, even before its experienced embodiment in their ecclesial existences, then other theologically systematic implications to the concept of grace were inevitably characterized in a similar way, pneumatology included.

As an opening observation, we can say that, in general, Jansenism reflected its era in giving little explicit attention to the doctrine of the Holy Spirit. But Pentecost was usually considered as the culminating "mystery" of Jesus' Incarnation, and handbooks like the *Instructions sur les vérités qui concernent la grace,* to which we have already referred, used the figure of the Spirit's gift to the Church as a jumping-off point for discussions of a number of matters, most especially the topic of grace itself.[1] In such discussions we see a merging of usually discrete theological language and referents, as the participatory goal of the mystery devotions is understood to have its temporal fulfillment in the granting of divine efficacity to human creatures: grace, love (or "charity"), and the Holy Spirit itself all become interchangeable terms for the enabling of human conformity to Christ. Topics often dogmatically associated with the Holy Spirit, like the New Covenant, the New Command of love, or the Church's life of sanctification, are always elaborated within this diffuse mingling of terms. The resulting semantic process discloses that underlying and deliberate Jansenist conflation of earlier scholastic distinctions, in the manner we observed with Arnauld's discussion of Thomistic categories of grace.[2] As with Arnauld, however, the outcome to this merging of terms is to give a

---

1. *Instructions sur les vérités qui concernent la grace de N.S. Jesus-Christ.* For discussions of the Holy Spirit in connection with issues like grace and the fulfilling of commands, see vol. 1, 44f., 60, 174ff., 206ff., 268, 285–95, 330ff., 356ff., 371ff., 383ff.; vol. 2, 103.

2. See ibid., vol. 1, 290–93, where we are told that "the grace of Jesus Christ" *is* charity itself; it is not the "cause of charity," nor is it a "capacity" for charity created in the human person. There is no distinguishing term between the two, for grace and charity are identical. This means, of course, that the grace of Jesus Christ is itself the act of *human* loving, and grace is identified with a specific historical engagement, whether understood as an interior disposition or as an exterior deed. Thereby, finally, the scholastic distinction between habitual (created) grace and actual grace — a movement given the soul by God directly — is rendered impertinent. Like Arnauld's reformulation of Thomas, all of grace here is subsumed into the reality of the *auxilium Dei moventis.* The author of the *Instructions* makes this explicit when he rejects Thomas's distinction in favor of Augustine's definition of grace

special prominence to forms of historical experience that act as the distinct definers of these abstract conceptions, the Holy Spirit among them.
Perusing such popular material, we see that pneumatology — speech about
the Holy Spirit — thus devolves into the discernment of particular historical processes that configurate the forms of Jesus' incarnate existence in the
temporal experience of the Church. Not surprisingly, then, a devotional
like the *Instructions* provides as a basic rubric for understanding the relationship of God to His people the connection of the "gift of grace" — that
is, charity in the form of the Holy Spirit's coming at Pentecost — with the
ultimate Return of Christ to the world, a historical moment of conformity
when love is all but "extinguished."[3]

Having made this general observation, we must now examine how, behind this remarkable, if unconscious, constriction of pneumatology, there
lie not only Jansenist theological structures of grace but also the coming together of a number of quite distinct and smaller conceptual moves
made by Jansenist theologians with respect to the doctrine of the Holy
Spirit especially. In particular, what Cognet calls the "pneumatism" of
Saint-Cyran proved an initial and major influence on later pneumatology
within the movement, and even though the substance of Saint-Cyran's
attitudes in this regard was common to other thinkers of the early and
mid-seventeenth century, its example in a hero of emergent Jansenism
warrants attention.[4] Indeed, the role that Saint-Cyran's work played as a
model for later Jansenist catechisms, where almost alone the Holy Spirit
is treated systematically, means that his comments on the matter must
prove fundamental for pneumatological discussions even into the eighteenth century. And, in fact, Saint-Cyran approaches reflection on the
Holy Spirit in two areas that will set the parameters, in a sharply limiting
way, for much of this later commentary. These two areas can be identified
as the link between grace and charity and the historical and ecclesial focus
of this link, in terms of the Holy Spirit. Let us look at each area in turn
and see how Jansenism carries through, in certain respects, with these
concerns, in the direction of a developing Appellant pneumatology.

In the first place, it is Saint-Cyran who intimately links the Holy
Spirit to the discussion of grace as it touches on the keeping of the com-
mandments through love. What is grace? "Grace is nothing else than the
infusion of love and charity itself within the soul, accomplished by the
Holy Spirit which gives itself to the soul with this love and this charity.
For God takes hold of the heart and makes it do and love and hate that
which He pleases."[5] The link between the three — Holy Spirit, Grace, and
Charity — is a constant in Saint-Cyran's writing. From one perspective

as "*every* movement of the soul which carries it to rejoice in God for His sake and in the
creature's for God's sake," this movement itself being "charity" (176ff.).

3. Ibid., 12.
4. Cognet, *La Spiritualité Moderne*, 479ff.
5. Saint-Cyran, Ms. de Rennes, f.180, in Jean Orcibal, *La Spiritualité de Saint-Cyran
avec ses écrits de piété inédits* (Paris: J. Vrin, 1962), 246.

it is a reprise of themes familiar from medieval mystics and not absent from some of the early Schoolmen, whose comments on the identity of uncreated grace with the Holy Spirit, as Trinitarian love indwelling in the soul, are repeated by the abbé without much self-consciousness.[6]

But just as importantly, his remarks about this linkage are often tied to the context of the "law," as in his small piece on "Le coeur nouveau [the New Heart]," where the discussion of grace and the Holy Spirit serves to elucidate the idea of a New Covenant by which the law is self-fulfilling in the Christian.[7] Using as his text Ezekiel 36:26, on the giving of a "new heart of flesh" in the place of the old "heart of stone," Saint-Cyran elaborates a short devotional meditation on the "converted heart" and its dependence upon God's grace, "the grace of Jesus Christ." On this grace depend the actual good dispositions and deeds that are made possible by conversion and to which we are all called. The "new heart" itself, he describes as being nothing else than "His [Christ's] Spirit and His Grace, by which our soul detaches itself from the objects of sense, and lifts itself to God through all kinds of good thoughts and holy affections." And this Spirit and Grace, in turn, are properly called by the name "Charité" and "Amour [Love]."[8] What is interesting to note is how, in the rest of the treatise, the Holy Spirit disappears from view, while Grace as Charity takes center stage, to clarify the nature of a life lived according to the shape of God's will.

Similarly, in the influential *Theologie familiere* — a kind of simple catechism that will lie at the base of many later Jansenist documents — discussion of the Holy Spirit (in the context of the Church, Lesson 6) precedes several long sections on Charity and on Grace (Lessons 9–12) that are oriented, without qualification, and without reference to the Holy Spirit at all, toward the keeping of the commandments of God. Charity is defined as "a power [vertu] that makes us love God above all things, for the sake of loving Him for Himself, and that makes us love our neighbor as ourselves."[9] There follows a long set of questions and answers on the defining qualities of "good" and "bad" loves, of the kinds of acts that embody these qualities, of the circumstances that determine "who" a "neighbor" is and so on. And in all of this, the discussion of charity breaks down into an increasingly categorized set of activities and relationships that in themselves set the boundaries for the will of God, and thus for the demands of the divine law.

Lesson 10 on the Ten Commandments, thereby, logically follows. It opens with the question "What is the true mark of Charity?" and provides this reply: "It is the observance of the Commandments of God: for

---

6. See his *Lettres Chrétiennes et spirituelles* (Lyon, 1674), vol. 1, 450; see Cognet's comments, *La Spiritualité Moderne* 1 (Paris: Aubier, 1966), 477f.

7. Saint-Cyran, *Le coeur nouveau*, in *Theologie familiere, Avec divers autres petits traitez de devotion*, edition nouvelle (Paris, 1647), 127–60.

8. Ibid., 137–38.

9. *Theologie familiere*, 50.

whoever says that they love God, and does not do as He commands, is a hypocrite and mocker of God."[10] After a lesson on the Commandments of the Church (the observance of feast-days, the Mass, Confession, and so on), Lesson 12 gives instruction "on Grace," a catechetical category given independent prominence by the Jansenists in particular. But the point of grace, in this context, is to offer the means of fulfilling the commands of charity:

> Is it enough to know God's commandments in order to keep them? No: for one needs, beyond [such knowledge], to have God's grace, without which we cannot keep the least of the Commandments, neither do anything good, no matter what knowledge we have.[11]

As noted, the Holy Spirit itself is not mentioned through the course of these discussions, though perhaps it implicitly (and only implicitly) undergirds the teachings on charity and grace through its prior explication under the rubric of the Church. Rather, charity and grace are brought into an explicit identification, under the rubric of the "commands of God," and it is the latter reality that predominates.

Immediate followers of Saint-Cyran maintain this predominating focus, although with some variation on the degree to which the Holy Spirit manifests itself in the explication of this interest. Matthieu Fey-deau's *Catechisme de la Grace* (164?), written for the bishop of Amiens, for example, stays clearly within the limits set by the *Theologie fami-liere*. To the opening question "What is Grace?" the answer given is a remarkably concise summary of the nature of the Old Law with respect to the New, and the experiential aspect of the new Law, in the manner of Saint-Cyran's "new heart": "[Grace] is the inspiration of divine love, poured into our hearts by the Holy Spirit, in order that we might accomplish with sweet delight [*suavité*] the things which the Law teaches us."[12] While linked both to love and to the Holy Spirit, this definition and the subsequent discussion of grace are almost wholly concerned with the purpose for which grace is an instrument, that is, the accomplishment of God's willed commandments. The notion of *suavité*, of course, shifts some of this concern toward a quality of obedience's experience, but the experience itself — the unimpeded movement of the will for the good — is understood as an aspect of God's commanding will.

Arnauld's posthumously published *Instruction sur la grace, Selon l'Ecriture et les Peres* (1700) is a far more nuanced (and longer) popular treatment of the question. And in this case the weight of the discussion, although still centered on fulfilling God's will, is far less interested in that will as "commandment" than in its demand for a quality of conformity from the human creature. In other words, doing the good for Arnauld

---

10. Ibid., 60.
11. Ibid., 73–74.
12. 1650 edition, printed in Arnauld's *Oeuvres*, vol. 17, 840.

is treated more in terms of *willing* as God wills than in achieving specific tasks. Thus, his discussion of grace elevates the quality of *suavité* to the very character of charity, and grace becomes a "movement" of the will, a temporally experienced trace of interior conformity with God's own movement. In this context, the Holy Spirit looms much larger, and the concentration on the text of Romans 5:5, as Augustine uses it so extensively — the charity and love of God shed abroad in our hearts by the Holy Spirit which is given to us — transforms grace into an indwelling presence of God rather than an instrumental "aid."[13] A large portion of the *Instruction*, then, is devoted to issues relating to interior dispositions of love and the relation of these dispositions not so much to their practical deeds as to their divine origins.

In some ways, however, the interest of Arnauld's treatment remains unique. And in any case, his reliance in all of this on Augustine's *De Spiritu et littera*, common to many Jansenists, ultimately reveals the limits to which any reflection on the relation of Holy Spirit to Grace will carry. For Augustine, after all, premises his own treatise on the question of "obedience," of fulfilling the commands of righteousness. Arnauld seizes on the dispositional quality of obedience as Augustine discusses it — "love" or "pleasure" as inspired by the Holy Spirit — but the premise itself must finally set the bounds for what kind of interest in the Holy Spirit, as linked to grace, one can pursue. These are bounds that, under certain circumstances, can eventually exclude the Spirit altogether from the discussion of grace, something that Saint-Cyran has already evidenced in some writing even while demonstrating elsewhere an insistence on the vital pneumatological foundation of grace.

It could be argued, further, that the catechetical format itself, through which Saint-Cyran exerted enormous influence on subsequent Jansenist articulations of grace, proved as limiting as Augustine's influence to the exploration of these pneumatological foundations. This, at least, is the case until other and later Jansenist concerns free the format so as to allow it to encourage more creative reflection on the matter. For in large measure, Saint-Cyran inherited a *shape* for catechetical instruction that had already fixed the connection between charity and command and had thereby limited any implied pneumatic essence to charity as grace to one of instrumental accomplishment. Peter Canisius's sixteenth-century catechisms, in particular, lay out the structure for all catechizing for the next two centuries.

Canisius's *Summa Doctrinae Christianae* as well as his shorter catechisms share a common order that remains authoritative in its constraining theological implications: the three Theological Virtues, the sacraments, and "Christian justice." The first section begins with Faith, under the rubric of which the Apostle's Creed is discussed; under the virtue of Hope comes "prayer," especially the Lord's Prayer; finally, under

---

13. See the *Instruction* in ibid., vol. 10, 416ff.

Charity, the teaching of the Ten Commandments and the commandments of the Church is explicated. This proves a neat division by which
to inculcate the memorization and meaning of the several basic Christian
formulae, and it becomes standard. For Canisius, however, reference to
the Holy Spirit is limited to a few remarks on its article in the Creed: it is
a coequal member of the Trinity, and "illuminates, purifies, sanctifies, and
confirms" believers, as well as aiding their "infirmity."[14] Other than this,
and scattered passing references — the Spirit is not mentioned in the section on Charity — one must wait until the final section of the Catechism,
on "Christian Justice," to receive further instruction, here on the "Gifts
and Fruits" of the Holy Spirit. Amid the lists of the Works of Mercy, the
Beatitudes, the Cardinal Virtues and so on, these remarks on the Spirit
have in their sights the elements of an obedient life measured by works
standing in positive contrast to "the flesh."[15] In this, they have in no way,
even implicitly, offered any avenue beyond the obediential concerns that
even a more marked identification of Spirit and Charity would provide, as
in Saint-Cyran, who must still labor under the rigid application of charity
to command.

In large measure, the catechetical division of the three Theological
Virtues touches later Jansenists in the same way, and perhaps through
Saint-Cyran, whose *Theologie familiere* was taken, in some cases verbatim, as the basis for the pioneering Jansenist Catechism "of the Three
Henry's."[16] And when highly influential writers like de Barcos and Nicole
were to turn their attention to popular instructions of the faith, they followed the same format, with the same resultant limitations. "Love" is a
way of keeping the law, and in any case, the Holy Spirit does not figure
directly in this concern.[17]

Nicole, in particular, represents almost the furthest point one might
carry this connection. In his case, all three Theological Virtues have been
subsumed into the process of keeping the Law, and all three now fall under
the rubric of the Decalogue. On the other hand, the actual obediential
framework of the discussion has been itself ordered by a peculiar reading
of Augustinian anthropology: "love" is defined exclusively in terms of an

---

14. *Summa Doctrinae*, edition of 1569, I:xvii (Vienna, 1833; 4 vols.; vol. 1, 78). In later
editions of the smaller versions of this catechism, the Spirit here is said to be conferred
by baptism. See a popular seventeenth-century French edition, *Catechisme, ou Instruction
Familière sur les principales veritez de la Religion Catholique, Par Demandes et Réponses.
Trés-utile aux Nouveaux Convertis* (Paris, 1686), 11.

15. *Summa Doctrinae.*, V, "Ad justitiae partem alteram" sec. 3 (vol. 4, esp. 456).

16. This "Jansenistic" catechism first appeared in 1676 and received its nickname from
the fact that it was composed for the use of the bishops of La Rochelle, Angers, and Luçon,
that is, for Henry de Laval, Henry Arnauld, and Henry de Barillon. The work's full title
is, *Catéchisme, ou Doctrine Chrétienne, imprimé par ordre des Monseigneurs les Evesques
d'Angers, de la Rochelle, et de Luçon.*

17. See [Martin de Barcos], *De la Foy de l'Esperance et de la Charité ou explication du
Symbole, de l'Oraison Dominicale, et du Decalogue* (Anvers, 1688) vol. 2, 1ff.; Pierre Nicole,
*Instructions theologiques et morales, sur le premier Commandement du Decalogue; ou il
est traité De la Foi, de l'esperance, et de la Charité* (Paris, 1710), 84ff.

"inclination" (*pente*) and "weight of the soul," that comprehends all the passions and affections of a person. Charity, as a good love for God above all things, becomes an attachment and an orientation that embraces all particular objects and actions. "Commands" in themselves are secondary manifestations of the contours of such attachments. But as a "weight," however much "assisted" by grace, love remains even in this case intrinsic to the human soul itself, and thereby cannot naturally include the Spirit's presence as anything but an extrinsic movement that initiates direction, rather than recreation. The metaphor is that of "dominion" and not of formation.[18] And in Nicole's case, the oriented nature of obedience ultimately leads to a position at odds with the Appellant valorization of *sensibilité:* "sense," "passion," and "affection" are all *dis*-orienting elements in the soul's demanded attachment to God, whose purity must in the end eliminate formliness altogether, in favor of an unmediated proximity.[19] This kind of view stands in sharp contrast with what we eventually see in Appellant devotionals like the later *Instructions sur les verités*, where our duties of "charity," seen as the effects of grace, are understood wholly in terms of pneumatically constituted "form," i.e., in the forms of Christ, the Scripture, and the Church.

## Saint-Cyran (2):
## The Spirit, the Church, and History

If the implicit connection between the Holy Spirit and grace, abortively rendered through the conception of charity, was to find a place for its expression in Jansenism, then it would clearly have to lie in a category outside that of "love," as it was catechetically located. This in fact proves the case, as pneumatological interest resurfaces within the limited discussion of the Creed. What is interesting to note here, however, is that it is not the Creed understood under the Canisian rubric of the Theological Virtue of "Faith" that provides the new pneumatological context, but rather a reformulation of the Creed's catechetical location in terms of a historical "summary," independently prefixed to the actual discussion of Faith as creedal. Saint-Cyran is a critical influence here, and this leads now to look at the way that Jansenism, in his wake, found an alternative focus for the Holy Spirit as grace and charity in the reality of the Church.

In the *Theologie familiere*, Saint-Cyran opens with a discussion of God, who He is, and how we can know Him (Lesson 1). On this basis, he then presents five additional lessons summarizing the history of salvation, beginning with Creation, and moving through the Fall, Redemption promised in the Old Testament, Redemption given in the life, ministry,

---

18. See ibid., 103.
19. See ibid., 112–29, where even the incarnated mysteries of Jesus are subordinated to a disembodied adherence of the "spirit" to God and are useful only as devotional aids to the immature.

death, and resurrection of Jesus, and finally Redemption embodied in the life of the Church. Only *after* these first six lessons, does he take up the standard catechetical division according to the Theological Virtues. What is odd is that Lesson 8, on the Creed (under the rubric of Faith), merely recapitulates, in abbreviated form, elements from the discussion of the first six lessons, and, *qua* Creed, is of only passing interest. Instead, its content, now seen purely in terms of "story," has been transferred to a foundational and independent position at the head of the catechism.

In this more "historical" context, then, Saint-Cyran does reflect on the Holy Spirit. In themselves, his comments are brief, but they point both to some of the elements that later Jansenists, and the Appellants in particular, will magnify in their own pneumatological explorations. First of all, Saint-Cyran initiates his remarks on the Holy Spirit in the context of Pentecost, that is, in the context of a particular historical event that somehow brings about a distinction in the experience of humanity, and that helps structure the unfolding of the redemptive purpose of God. In fact, he does this in a somewhat negative way, by asking the question as to the cause lying behind the *fruitlessness* of Jesus' incarnate ministry: why was the preaching of Jesus inefficacious during His lifetime? because the Holy Spirit had not yet been given.[20] Once given at Pentecost, however, His new and resurrected life was effectively communicated to human creatures for the first time.[21]

The discussion of Pentecost ends the fifth lesson, "On the Incarnation," and leads into the next section, devoted explicitly to "the Church." The Church, indeed, just as it depends on the Spirit in the creedal structure, is here as well designated as the work and the vivifying residence of the Holy Spirit. "Why was the Holy Spirit sent upon the earth? In order to make perfect the Disciples of Jesus Christ, and to form the body of the Church." And "perfection," in this case, is immediately defined as "the perfection of charity" and "the love of Jesus Christ."[22] Thus, we see how the relation of the Spirit to Charity reasserts itself here as love is embodied in the formation of the Church. Even more than this, Saint-Cyran wants us to press the connection between Spirit and Church (that is, Spirit and loving Christians joined together) to a point close to formative identification:

> How did the Holy Spirit form the body of the Church? By uniting the hearts of the Disciples of Jesus Christ with God, and among themselves by charity, with which they were filled. For the bond and soul of the Church is the Holy Spirit and the fire of its love.[23]

This description of the Church is repeated in Lesson 8, on the Creed, when Saint-Cyran calls the Holy Spirit that which "forms and animates" the Church as Christ's Body.

---

20. Saint-Cyran, *Theologie familiere.*, 25f.
21. Ibid., 29f.
22. Ibid., 30f.
23. Ibid., 31.

The Holy Spirit here is never identified with grace itself. But insofar as Saint-Cyran understands the efficacy of Christ's life to be embodied in the formative presence of the Holy Spirit, that identification is closely implied. Further, this presence literally does "form" the Church as Christ's Body by temporally establishing the embodied "bonds" that are identified with charity itself. One could claim that an additional implication of these formulations, then, is that the Holy Spirit somehow constitutes the historical features of that Body, whose forms are the forms of love. Such an implication, at any rate, is in line with explicit comments of later Appellant writings like the *Instructions*.

Saint-Cyran's nephew de Barcos comes closest, among his followers, to reiterating these themes most clearly. But it is interesting to see how he has begun to extend some of his uncle's remarks in a historically broader dimension. We have noted how for de Barcos, in his *De la Foy de L'Esperance et de la Charité*, the actual discussion of charity excludes, through its emphasis on command, any explicit concern with the Spirit. But the context of the Creed, understood in a fashion as a historical recital — the rubric of "Faith," under which it falls seems ultimately irrelevant — does provide de Barcos with a necessary opportunity for discussing the Holy Spirit in a manner that embraces more pointedly historical form, now pushed back to include foundationally the form of the Incarnation itself.

De Barcos devotes a lengthy section at the beginning of his discussion of the Son, in the Creed, to the affirmation "who was conceived by the Holy Spirit."[24] The "unction" of the Spirit in the Incarnation, indeed, establishes the divinely redemptive character of the man Jesus, as the very person of God, and it does this through the historical imparting of the reality of "infinity" to limited flesh. Thus, the result of Jesus' pneumatic conception is a sequence of characteristics that embody perfection within the temporal sphere: conception without concupiscence means the "formation" of a body by God in a purely unimpeded way; the Incarnation is the most perfect of God's works, just as the Spirit is the plenitude of the Trinity; the Incarnation represents the perfection of loving power, as the Spirit works the embodiment of its own miracle; the Incarnation is the perfection of historical holiness, just as the Spirit is the procession of divine holiness; the Spirit's conception indicates that Jesus was wholly formed as a full human being in the womb, unlike other human beings; etc.

In each instance, de Barcos stresses the way in which the perfection of historical form is given instance in Jesus because of the formative presence of the Holy Spirit. And when he goes on to discuss elements of the life and passion of Jesus, as indicated in the Creed, he does so with a careful attention to the historical particularities to which the Creedal formulations allude: the names of Mary and Pilate, the insistence on death and burial, a limited yet noted number of days in the tomb, the temporal distinction marked by the Ascension, versus the earlier appearances

24. De Barcos, *De la Foy de l'Esperance*, 51ff.

of the Resurrected Jesus, and so on. In all of these details, de Barcos explains how the Creed's affirmations are determined by a resolute commitment to the tangible historicity of the Incarnation's narrated shape. Falling as they do under the banner of the Spirit's unction, all of these historical particularities which mark the arrangement of the Incarnation are thereby, although in this case only implicitly, linked to the perfecting, that is infinitely formative, work of the Holy Spirit.

When dealing with Creed's article on the Holy Spirit itself,[25] de Barcos traces a kind of unequal parallel between this perfecting work in the Incarnation and the temporally completing work of the Spirit in the Just, that is, the Church. He begins with a description of the Spirit in its Trinitarian life as the term of the "love of truth" between the Father and the Son. This is simply the *vinculum* theory of Augustine restated, according to which the Spirit is understood as the "bond of love" between the other two persons of the Trinity. Here, however, de Barcos emphasizes the dynamically teleological nature of this connection, that is, the immanent fashion in which the Spirit "perfects" the life of God's love, seen in terms of attachment and adherence.

When encountered in the realm of the created order, this dynamically perfecting character of the Spirit takes on a historical aspect. We have already seen something of what this means in the case of the Incarnation, where perfection is instanced in discrete events in the life of Jesus, each one perfect in itself. But in the case of human creatures, justified members of the Church, the perfecting work of the Spirit is embodied rather in the *collection* of events of a life, whose particularities tend in a given direction whose term — that is, whose perfected form — is reached only at death. Thus, de Barcos identifies the Holy Spirit's presence in the form of charity "residing" in a "temple" with persevering grace itself.[26]

Finally, this typically Jansenistic historicizing of grace is further worked out in the way de Barcos takes up Saint-Cyran's descriptions of the Church, whose "soul" is the Holy Spirit. In addition to linking the creedal affirmation of the "marks" of the Church to the Holy spirit — One, Holy, etc., as well as the Communion of Saints — de Barcos interpolates the Augustinian notion of the "Two Cities" into his commentary. Just as the individual is perfected by the Spirit through the constitution of an overall form of a life tending to God, so the "Heavenly Church" (i.e., the "City of God") is brought to its perfection by grace through the welter of historical particularities. In this way, de Barcos implicitly draws a connecting line between the Spirit and Predestination — an elaboration of the identification of the Holy Spirit with persevering grace, much in the way Arnauld had done earlier with respect to the *Deus movens*.

De Barcos can press the historically formative aspect of the Spirit back into the Incarnation not only because of the Creedal affirmation con-

---

25. Ibid., 122–32.
26. See ibid., 128–29.

cerning Jesus' conception, but because the logic of an ecclesiology of the Mystical Body demands that kind of parallel. For de Barcos, however, the Incarnational form to which the Spirit gives rise in history is only a secondary theme, which I have had to bring into relief. And by the same token, Saint-Cyran's pneumatic ecclesiology, while clearly stated, is not given a great deal of flesh. What is evident, however, is that in this version of classical Jansenism, the logical possibilities for a connection between Spirit, Incarnation, and Church exist, and indeed conform to the deeper structures of grace as we have examined them in earlier chapters.

## The Holy Spirit and Historical Form: The Oratory, Claude Fleury, and Later Jansenist Catechisms

These logical possibilities are in fact given distinctive actuality in later Jansenist catechetical literature — the literature whose popular and programmatic simplicity will provide the sensible bite that Appellant discourse demonstrates. Two general influences seem to lie behind this actualization: Berullian themes from the Oratory, and the radical development of Saint-Cyran's historical prefix to the catechism by Claude Fleury. Each of these influences bears noting.

Bérulle himself did not formulate a peculiar pneumatology, but some of his Trinitarian comments proved important. In the *Grandeurs de Iesus,* in particular, he advances his original conception of the Spirit as that person of the Trinity who "has this essential characteristic, that he is sterile and fertile [*fécond*] at the same time; sterile in himself, and fertile with respect to what is outside of him."[27] In immanent terms, the Spirit does not give rise to either of the other Persons, as each of them gives rise to the Spirit. Rather, the Spirit stands as the "term" of Trinitarian "fecundity" (much in the manner that de Barcos speaks of it as the "term of plenitude"), whose energy is determined by "unity" (the bond or *vinculum*) and not by creative production. But because, in some sense, the Trinity as a whole, and therefore each Person properly, is "fertility" itself, the Spirit's sterility within the Trinity is offset by its productive creativity outside itself, within the economy of creation.

This particular and proper "fecundity" of Spirit is, according to Bérulle, embodied in the production of the Incarnation, in the creation of the Mysteries of Jesus.

> Since [the Spirit] is sterile in his Divinity because of the condition proper to the Mystery of the Trinity, it is only by a new Mystery that [the Spirit] should be fertile in another and ineffable manner: that is, by providing a new being for the work of the preexistent God (oh strange marvel!) that should from now on exist in a new nature.[28]

27. *Grandeurs*, IV:ii (*Oevures*, vol. 1, 212).
28. Ibid., 213.

The Holy Spirit "creates" Jesus, and thereby is the fullness of Trinitarian love poured out into God's creatures, according to the richness of the Incarnated mysteries, each appearing in time, yet holding that love in the unity of the Trinitarian being.[29]

While de Barcos seemed rather to "push back" the formative character of the Spirit from the historical reality of the Church to the Incarnation, Bérulle works from the other direction. The Trinitarian nature of the Spirit, paradoxically limited in some sense, finds its fullness in creation, and most perfectly in the creation of the Incarnate Son. To the degree, then, that the Mysteries are historically rooted for Bérulle, that rootedness is essentially pneumatic. Further, the outpouring of God's love, whose term in creation is also the "unity" (or adherence) that takes form in the Holy Spirit, means that in some sense "grace," even understood as the "grace of Christ," is creatively established pneumatically.

We will see in a moment how a consideration of the Mysteries of Jesus assumes a central place in later Jansenist catechizing, with some obvious implications for a theology of the Holy Spirit. But we have already expressed some reservations as to the ultimate historical thrust of Bérulle's theology as a whole, and it seems as if these later catechisms would not have taken the shape they did without an additional and perhaps more decisive prod from Fleury's example, or at least from the motivations behind his work. Claude Fleury was an eminent and pioneering historian of the Church, whose even-handed temperament allowed his own Jansenistic theology to work cooly in the shadows of his less partisan and more prominent labors. His 1683 *Catechisme historique, Contenant en Abregé l'Histoire Sainte et la doctrine Chrétienne* proved an enormously popular essay in catechetical method and content, which perhaps single-handedly wrested basic Christian instruction from the format left by Canisius. The work went through at least 468 editions and translations, following its approval for the Archdiocese of Paris.[30]

We have already seen how Saint-Cyran offered a preliminary section to his catechism that was structured according to the sequence of salvation history, but that was not directly linked to the Creed. Fleury in effect elevates and magnifies this kind of historical section to the whole of the catechetical purpose, and, just as important, gives a lengthy and focused rationale for so doing. This long introductory material is what most interests us.

In general, Fleury claims that his goal is purely practical, spurred by a concern for effective pedagogy. In fact, however, his arguments move in a decidedly theological direction, and probably derive in the first place from such a ground. He begins with a question: Why do so many Christians either learn nothing in catechism, or grow up with a distaste for Christian

---

29. Ibid., 214.
30. See remarks by Elisabeth Germain in *Jésus Christ dans les catéchismes: étude historique* (Paris: Desclée, 1986), 61ff.

truth? The answer is simple: most catechetical instruction has been governed by the logical and theological principles of scholastic method, that is, by deductive arguments working from abstractions.[31] Such a method is inherently unsuited to the common Christian for whom such instruction is geared. Its only result is a discourse of "dryness." What then is to be done?

Fleury's answer is, as he claims, one that derives from practical and universal experience: do what people have always done in teaching Religion, that is, use the method of storytelling.

> I find that there has been, more or less, a single method used for teaching Religion. And that is to make principle use of narration and the simple deduction made from facts [*faits*], upon which method is founded dogma and moral precepts.[32]

Basing this judgment on the nature of "oral tradition," which not only defines contemporary teaching, but specifically lies behind the historical creation of the scriptural texts, Fleury notes how from Adam through Moses the teaching of God was passed down from parent to child through the recounting of events, of the *faits* [facts or events] of God's action. Indeed, he points out, the centrally religious reality of the Exodus for Israel was specifically established by the command to "retell" the story from one generation to another, as at the Passover feast. Even the advent of written Scripture did not undercut this vital duty, since Scripture itself existed in part to express the consistent narrative obligation God had given His people.

And far from altering this narrative structure to divine truth and its impartation, the New Covenant brought it into even bolder relief, as that truth itself takes form in the life, miracles, marvels, teachings, and events of the person Jesus.[33] The teaching of the Acts, for instance, is founded on "testimony," the testimony of "eyewitnesses," whose commendation of Christ is effective among their listeners according to the method, as Fleury has put it, of *la déduction des faits* [the deduction made from facts]. The oral recounting of historical facts alone provides the logic for understanding the Christian truth.

Fleury is adamant that even the more "abstract" elements of the Christian faith — the doctrine of the Trinity, of the Incarnation, of Predestination — cannot be properly grasped unless their articulation flows naturally from this method of factual deduction. Here he speaks of "proofs" (*preuves*) that any person can grasp, but what he has in mind is not something that proceeds by a logic of demonstration so much as something that itself can "grasp" that conviction of the person. Doctrines

---

31. *Catechisme historique* (augmented edition of E. H. Fricx, Brussels, 1727), vol. 1, 2–14.
32. Ibid., 14.
33. Ibid., 16f.

are grounded in facts, and these facts "prove" the doctrines somehow, insofar as they are

> evident, illustrious, tangible [*sensibles*] facts: for instance, the creation of the world, the sin of the first man, the flood, the call of Abraham, the exodus from Egypt [ ... ] and other extraordinary facts, such as miracles like those of Moses, of the Prophets, and finally of Jesus Christ and His disciples.[34]

And if this recital of events provides a method of "reasoning" (*raison-nement*) for listeners, it is through a kind of imaginative attraction that touches them. Fleury uses words like "inspire" and "please" in the sense of being *agréable* through the "impressions" of gesture and natural *sentiment*, of conviction and love.[35]

Thus, what is crucial to the proper teaching of the Christian faith are two elements: first, "religious attachment" to the *language* of Scripture, that is, the constant use of the stories of Scripture in their own expression;[36] second, a teacher who enters into these stories, as they are retold, with a visible sense of "penetration" by their sensible force. Fleury's summary method, then, is this: if the catechism is organized, both structurally and in its enactment over time, according to this sensibly communicated narrative that covers the stories of Scripture as they take an overarching shape from Creation to the formation and ministry of the Christian Church, the elements and forms of basic Christian doctrine, which are otherwise promoted in standard catechisms, will reveal themselves in a compelling and clearly apprehended fashion. Speak of the Prophets and their prophecies, speak of the Messiah, speak of the creating and saving God, of the Holy Spirit and those anointed to speak by it — tell these stories clearly and from a heart of tangible belief, and the wealth of divine truth that they contain will flower in the minds of listening children and adults.[37]

The catechism that Fleury composed turns out in actuality to be three separate sets of lessons, the last of which stands in some contrast to the method he had so clearly and painstakingly explained in his long preface. In the first place, Fleury gives what he calls a "small catechism" for the youngest children. This consists of a series of lessons, each devoted to a simple retelling of some portion of the biblical story, with some short questions and answers concerning content appended. Second, there is a longer "family catechism," which simply repeats in more extended detail the stories of the first, and drops the concluding questions and answers. In both cases, though a few doctrinal comments intrude, Fleury is rather strict in touching upon only narrative elements from the Scriptures. But the last series of lessons comprises a discussion of "dogmas of religion" and constitutes about half the entire work (about 150 pages). Here Fleury

---

34. Ibid., 21f.
35. See ibid., 51ff.
36. See ibid., 37, 41.
37. See ibid., 42ff.

follows, more or less, the standard catechetical breakdown of topics, governed by the Theological Virtues. Curiously enough, his presentation of these doctrines, admirably concise though they may be, contain hardly any reference to the narrative history upon which, as he had earlier argued, their compelling articulation is supposed to rest.

From the perspective of our own discussion, it is enough to say that, in his explicit doctrinal sections, Fleury adds nothing new in his discussions of grace and the Spirit. In a manner that stands in the tradition of Saint-Cyran, the Holy Spirit is identified with Charity itself, and this in turn is understood as the grace necessary for keeping the obligations of the divine law. The Spirit is tied to the Church in terms of its "assembling" function, but no real emphasis is placed upon any ongoing character to this activity.[38]

But in the first two narrative catechisms, without doctrinal focus, Fleury's method of discussion inevitably gives a particular effect to his description of the Spirit. Divorced almost wholly from dogmatic categories in this context, the *functional* equivalence of Spirit/Grace/Charity dissolves into a more sharply drawn image of the Spirit as a person who can enter a scene and then orchestrate agentially the action of an unfolding drama. As in Saint-Cyran's historical preface in the *Theologie familiere,* the historical event of Pentecost assumes a central place in apprehending the Spirit. Fleury goes farther, however, through his desire to found his discussion only on narrative elements. For thereby he is able to stress, implicitly, the continuity of purpose and historical detail in such a way that Jesus' life — in the context of the whole of history — and the life of the Spirit and the life of the Church all take their significance from the particular shapes of their temporally founded intersignification. He is able to speak of the Spirit, of the Apostles, and of the Church in terms of "promise" fulfilled, in terms of specific acts — preaching, miracles, courage, conversions, suffering — that derive their meaning from the unfolding narrative character of Jesus' ministry and teaching as it points to a future implied in the shape of the story. Christian existence, caught up in and moved by this Spirit given in time and for specific activities and events, is part of the story only because of this Pentecostal formative presence.[39]

No pneumatology, strictly speaking, is given here of course. But because God, Christ Jesus, and the Holy Spirit are the only historical shapers of the story that undergirds Christian existence, God's life, in this kind of uncommented discourse, takes meaning almost exclusively in terms of particular events to which the narrative's shape provides an evolving set of figurative interconnections. Baldly, and in a completely unelaborated way, Fleury demonstrates practically the Jansenist structures of Christian

---

38. Ibid., vol. 2, 122ff.; 136ff.; 203ff.
39. See ibid., vol. 1, 101ff. ("Petit Catechisme," Lesson 23 on the Descent of the Spirit, and Lesson 24 on the Vocation of the Gentiles).

grace as historical and formly, and now given origin in the shape of God's person, in this case the Holy Spirit as the being of Christian history.

Despite the enormous popularity of his catechism, Fleury's exclusively historical approach (which even he saw fit to expand dogmatically) was not followed by subsequent catechisms. What Fleury's example did encourage, however, was a significant expansion of the historical portions of the standard format. In the case of Jansenists, this meant that, following in Saint-Cyran's footsteps, the historical prefix to the catechism became a major element founding almost all catechetical structures, sometimes distinguished as a "Summary of the History of Religion," or simply characterizing the explication of the Creed in a historically elaborated manner.

In addition, this expanded historical portion of the catechism provided a hospitable context in which to discuss Berullian themes of the Mysteries that had become so devotionally pervasive. And it is this combination of focus on Incarnational form and particular historical event that marks the peculiar direction taken by Appellant thought, a direction that, pneumatologically, will have unusual implications. In large measure, these later Jansenist (and specifically Appellant) catechisms do not offer new articulations to doctrine, in comparison with their progenitors. But their structural weight does give a novel character to their interests.

We may take as a foundational example the early eighteenth-century *Catéchisme du Diocèse de Nantes,* written for the diocese's bishop, Gilles de Beauvau, by a well-known Jansenist theologian, Noë-Mesnard.[40] As had become common, the catechism is really a collection of three different sets of instructions, graded for small children, more advanced children, and, in a more doctrinal format, for leaders of adult missions. The two children's catechisms, which touch on our concerns, follow what is now a common pattern: a long set of lessons dealing with the "history of religion" from creation to the "four last ends," and then a slightly longer portion that deals with more practical doctrinal basics (e.g., the Sacraments, Decalogue, Virtues, Prayer, etc.).

Within the historical section, the lessons dealing with the life of Jesus no longer keep themselves strictly to the details of the scriptural narration, as in Fleury. Instead, the "history" of Jesus is explained in terms of His "mysteries," the historical details of which are retold with explicit encouragements to devotional and existential participation. Further, the mysteries themselves are presented as particular forms that comprehend different historical periods and dispensations. This is the case, however, not in the Berullian sense of archetype, but in a decidedly figural sense, whereby the shapes of Jesus' life are understood as themselves shaping the experienced particularities of salvation history. Thus, attention is given, as it is not either in Bérulle or in Fleury, to the history of the world and to the history of Israel in particular in terms of "figures" for Christ and

---

40. I will be citing the second edition of 1705 (Paris, Louis Roulland).

the Church. Further, the form of the specific historical mysteries of Jesus' life are joined to an explication of the Church's calendar of Feasts, so that the shape of the contemporary Church's devotional life is revealed as a reformation, in subsequent time, of these Christic figures.[41]

The recital of the mysteries, historically rooted, yet figuratively expansive through history, is designed catechetically to lead students to a set of lively experiences: to conform to Christ's example, to love with His love, and to be joined in union with Him. These, we are told, represent the purpose of this portion of the catechism, indeed, of Jesus' own historical existence as apprehended.[42] Only in this context, now, does the historical entry of the Holy Spirit, at Pentecost, reveal its religious significance. For while in Fleury, Pentecost and the Spirit then given assume a meaning based primarily on the structure of the preceding narrative, in the case of the *Catéchisme de Nantes*, Pentecost, the Spirit, and the subsequent life of the Church are structurally tied to a set of transhistorical (although not ahistorical) forms, whose historical persistence is explicitly established in the course of the preceding lessons. And while particular "functions" are still adumbrated for the Spirit — sanctifying, governing, and so on — what is stressed through the catechism's arrangement here is the way the Spirit forms the link between Jesus as Mystery and the Church as the Mystery's continued history. The Spirit constitutes the historical conformance aimed at by the catechism, not functionally, but (as in Fleury's historical outlook) merely and purely personally. This is not quite the same thing as Bérulle's notion of the Incarnation and its shapes as the fruit of the Spirit's "fecundity." But it comes close to such a vision, stripped of its Trinitarian immanentism and left to be viewed on the bare pages of the economy. Bare, and thereby palpably unadorned.

In effect, I am claiming an implicit theological significance to the mere fact of juxtaposition between Mysteries and Spirit, in the context of a historical recital. The juxtaposition itself becomes common in these later Jansenist catechisms, even as each becomes increasingly embedded in the events of Appellancy.[43] The Nantes catechism, in any case, is already mov-

---

41. This integration of the Church's liturgical year into the actual historical instruction of the catechism is notable. Heretofore, feast-days were explained cursorily, if at all. With the flowering of the mysteries devotion, reflection on the calendar gained new prominence, insofar as the liturgical calendar generally follows the sequence of Christ's life and symbolizes the most significant of the Gospel events, that is, the mysteries themselves. Bossuet, for instance, composed for his diocese an entire catechism dealing with the Church's year, the *Catéchisme des fêtes et autres solennités et observances de l'Église* (in his *Oeuvres*, edition of Paris: Vives, 1867, vol. V). But not before these early eighteenth-century catechisms do we see the feast-days integrated with the historical narration of the mysteries themselves, in such a way as to connect figurally the Church's life with the history of Christ's forms.

42. This is comprised in lessons 9–13 of the catechism.

43. See the highly regarded (as well as attacked) so-called "Catéchisme de Montpellier," or more properly the *Instructions Générales en forme de Catechisme où l'on explique en abregé par l'Ecriture Sainte et par la Tradition, l'Histoire et les Dogmes de la Religion, la Morale Chrétienne, les Sacremens, les Prieres, les Cérémonies et les Usages de l'Eglise*, nouvelle edition (Paris: Simart, 1739), 3 vols., esp. the first volume on the "history of religion." See also the later, much shorter, and equally popular (among Jansenists) *Catéchisme du Diocèse*

ing in the orbit of the kind of formly *sensibilité* we have already examined, and, although it does not state the theological structure outright, its pedagogical method is explicitly tied to the pneumatic quality of "story" as formative unit, in the manner suggested by the juxtaposition. In a preface to the catechism on how to teach,[44] the author tells us that "learning" comes through the sensible touch of "story" (*histoire*), which itself takes effective form through the "grace and unction of the Holy Spirit." This fact should both encourage the catechists to rely on scriptural story as well as to add those from their own experience. In this way, divine "truth" takes root in the penetrated hearts of the students. Pedagogy, as Fleury had insisted, thus represents the very shape of salvific history itself: a set of events, orally repeatable through their form, grasps the lives of specific individuals in order to reshape them through and in the Spirit within the history of the Church. This, at any rate, seems to be the term given to the historical orientation Saint-Cyran had first indicated in his *Theologie familiere* by explicitly emphasizing the link between the Spirit and the Church's formation and initial life.

## Quesnel's Figural Pneumatology and the Basis for Appellant Pneumatology

It should be said, however, that what is generally understood by Saint-Cyran's "pneumatism" is a view of prayer, rather than of history or the Church. "Abandonment to the Holy Spirit," in Cognet's analysis, represents a common strand in seventeenth-century French spirituality, given a certain prominence in the Oratory, and emphasized in particular by this friend of Jansenius, so much so that he could be accused of "illuminism."[45] In general, such abandonment refers to the prayerful disposition — the prayer of "poverty" in Saint-Cyran's terms[46] — that does not ask, but awaits in patience only for what objects, encouragements, direction, and transformations the Holy Spirit chooses to give, as the one who truly "prays within us," according to Romans 8. In all of this, however, the governing context of individual prayer means that reflection on the Holy Spirit will generally move in directions somewhat at odds with the historically expansive and ecclesially embodied pneumatology of the catechetical literature. To note how Jansenist predilections reoriented this devotional pneumatism is to gain a final clue as to the fundamental mooring of later Appellant pneumatological understandings of grace.

This pneumatic abandonment proved a central theme in the teaching and example of the Oratory's second leader, de Condren, and of his disciples, Olier in particular. Following Bérulle, the forms of the Mysteries —

---

*de Lyon* (1767) of Malvin de Montazet, which uses the historical explication of the Creed in a similar way.

44. Unpaginated.

45. Cognet, *La Spiritualité Moderne*, 479ff.

46. See *Le Coeur nouueau*, 151ff.

including the *états* of Jesus — were seen as most especially and properly applied to the life of the individual Christian through the free working of the Spirit. The emphasis on the "individual Christian," however, is crucial. Olier is perhaps the most relentlessly "pneumatic" of the school, and his experience of prayer, despite the commitment to the Church's larger mission that ultimately brought him fame as founder of the Sulpician order, was still profoundly private. We are told that, on occasion, he could do nothing for days and was confined to his quarters, until he felt moved by the Spirit to some particular action.

It is important to note, however, that even such practically inclusive waiting still depended on the particular and public notions of the Mysteries. The goal of the Christian life is "conformity to Jesus Christ" and "this conformity consists in resembling Him: first, in His mysteries...."[47] The Holy Spirit is that which effects such conformance, and Olier will even call it "the spirit of the holy mysteries," such is its central role and being with respect to our lives. Yet however well-known the shape of these mysteries — the Passion, the Burial, and so on — they ultimately reduce themselves, in a way that is not unfaithful to Bérulle, to interior dispositions of the soul, to "secret" qualities of relation to God, founded mainly on the kind of theology of annihilation Olier had inherited from his master de Condren. While the mysteries are public, their effect, as Spirit, is hidden within the soul of the individual; not, of course, that this effect would remain without fruit, but nonetheless it must exist in ineffable adherence to the self-emptying Son, as a paradoxical embodiment of personal emptiness.

This is an understanding of the relation between Mystery and Spirit that Jansenism will reformulate. We saw in the last chapter how Quesnel rehistoricizes the Mysteries and their *états* as conceived by de Condren, in large part by understanding them as historical figures, in a typological sense. At the same time, we noted how one figure in particular, that of the Church, became the focal point for the integration of the Mysteries' form into history, at least in the present. In like manner, Quesnel rehistoricizes the pneumatism of the Oratory by insisting on its link to the Mystical Body, which is the Church. Thus, in the *L'Idée du Sacerdoce et du Sacrifice de Jesus-Christ*, we already examined in part, Quesnel includes a long discussion of the Holy Spirit that seems deliberately to move away from the private and secret sense of sacrifice whose character de Condren and Olier had intimated.

Quesnel remains faithful to Bérulle in underscoring the metaphysical motive for unity that lies behind the nature of God's life: "God, who is sovereign and original unity itself — *Principalis unitas* — does all His works in unity, and reduces them, finally, to that very unity that is His."[48] Sacri-

---

47. Olier, *Introduction à la vie chrétienne*, in his *Oeuvres Complètes* (ed. J.-P. Migne, Paris: Ateliers catholiques, 1856), co. 54; see especially the first three chapters of this work.
48. *L'Idée du Sacerdoce*, 158.

fice, in particular, is an activity by which all things are brought into unity, especially the human race brought into unity with God. Thus, Quesnel founds the shape of sacrifice in the immanent being of God, wherein unity finds its source and end. The particular sacrifice of Jesus is then explained in terms of this immanent character: God is thereby eternally adored, through the sacrifice that takes place *dans son sein* [in His bosom], in which the Father is the Temple, the Son is the Altar, and the Spirit is the fire that consumes the victim. All of this moves from the exemplarist Trinitarianism of the Oratory's founder and remains very much at one with Bérulle's orientation. The subsequent discussion of the Temple and the Altar reflects this exemplarism clearly, as the historical sacrifice of Jesus is described in terms of a set of relationships that are eternally established.

But when Quesnel comes to speak at length of the "fire" of Jesus' sacrifice, that is, of the Holy Spirit, he alters the perspective of his comments. To be sure, the "fire of the Spirit" that "comes down from heaven" at Pentecost mirrors the eternal procession of the Spirit within the Trinity. But most of all, Quesnel is now interested in the way this Fire enters history "au milieu des temps [in the midst of time]" in order to reshape the lives of believers who now move into a heavenly future.[49] The goal of human life is to be joined with Jesus in heaven, for all time adoring God in a manner "consumed" by charity, that is, by the Spirit itself. Yet, in presenting this goal, Quesnel wishes to introduce now a history of *vocation* and progress, by which the lives of the faithful *become* "des victimes agreables à Dieu [victims acceptable to God]."[50] Only in this context does Quesnel raise the issue of the relation of charity to command — the Two Great Commandments — a relation reduced to the historically realized vision of unified adoration: we live today by charity a life whose shape is being moved through time toward the communion of praise. Thus is the traditional catechetical subordination of love to the law, so constrictive even in Jansenism, abandoned in favor of a historically tending pneumatism of the Body.

Instead of thinking of this vocation in terms of an increased "conformance" to Jesus, wrought by the Spirit in self-abandonment, in the manner of de Condren and Olier, Quesnel understands the historical movement toward perfect heavenly sacrifice as itself a movement in union, a movement in charity, a movement of Spirit, somehow complete and with its own integrity as *already joined to Christ*. This he can do by turning to the central mystery of the Church as Christ's Body, the historical realization of the unity of love.[51] Writing imaginatively from the mouth of Jesus addressed to His Father, he speaks of the Lord's indwelling in His followers as an act accomplished,

---

49. Ibid., 210ff.
50. Ibid., 211; 215ff.
51. See ibid., 220ff.

in order that the Holy Spirit—who is this eternal love with which you have loved me to the point of uniting my humanity to the Word in unity of Person, and who is the principle and bond that makes of the Son of God and the Son of Man one single Christ — that this Spirit and this love may be given to them for this purpose: to be eternally united in me as members of one body, united to me as members to their Head, united by me to you, as one spirit. *Qui adhaeret Deo unus spiritus est* [whoever is joined to God becomes one spirit with Him]. Finally, [the Spirit is given them] in order that, consuming them with me in unity, this love may make of them a single victim and holocaust, that burns and sacrifices itself to you for all eternity.[52]

The Church as a whole, then, lives Jesus' sacrifice. This is what it means to live "in the Spirit." And this, of course, means that the history of the Church is the history of Jesus' sacrifice, that its history is the shape of consuming love, is the form of the Spirit in fact, as it lives in the adoring reconfiguration of humanity before God.

These early insights of Quesnel, still explicitly tied to the annihilation-ist context of de Condren's outlook even as they transform that outlook on a broader ecclesial canvas, continue to inform his more mature and much more influential popular writing of the *Réflexions Morales*. As the founding, if unwitting, document of Appellancy — as the source of the *Unigenitus* condemnations — the *Réflexions* inevitably color all subsequent public articulations and defenses of Jansenist commitments. And on the central topic of grace, they provide the parameters of the Appellant vision precisely in the terms of historical and ecclesial pneumatism, as linked to the form of the Mysteries, that we have been tracing.

It is in Quesnel's original preface to the work, rather than in the work's body, his extensive commentary and notes on the whole of the New Testament, that we see these parameters most succinctly laid out: moving from Berullian premises, through their historicization and localization in the Church, he draws a picture of grace that is ultimately reducible to the pneumatic participation of the Body of Christ in the historical figures presented by Scripture. So clear is the presentation, that we need only cite each step of the argument:

1. All of Scripture constitutes the palpable voice of the Holy Spirit witnessing to the life and precepts of Jesus.[53]

2. The reason for the Incarnation is that God might have a "sovereign adorer" capable of the infinite adoration due God (Bérulle).[54]

3. The adoration provided by the Incarnation consists in every aspect of Christ's body, soul, and life: every gesture, look, sigh, humiliation, step, and word, as lived and as figured in sacred history.[55]

---

52. Ibid., 221–22.
53. *Le Nouveau Testament en français, avec des réflexions morales sur chaque verset,* (edition of 1727), vol. 1, xxi–xxiv.
54. Ibid., xxvi ff.
55. Ibid., xxxii–xxxiii.

4. These forms of the Incarnation — the Mysteries — including their figures, act as the historical vehicles of grace and the Holy Spirit, insofar as their "virtues" (*vertues*) are accomplished in the person of every faithful member of the Church.[56]

5. It is, however, as Church, and not as individual, that the Mysteries are embodied. Jesus lives in us, in his *états* and *Misteres*, as we are part of the His Mystical Body; He continues to suffer in the Church, and His Passion and Resurrection are "refigured" in the life of the Church, not only through its sacramental life, but through its very history.[57]

6. The forms of this Christic life, the shape of the Mysteries and their refiguration in the Church, are given in Scripture. Scripture itself is a "sacrament," by which the Holy Spirit "retraces" its historical figures in the lives of its readers. Scriptural figuration and its appropriation in the formal life of the Church, then, is the very embodiment of the Grace of Jesus Christ, that is, of the Spirit of God shaping the world. Thus, the figures of Scripture mirror the shape of sacred history, including its events and experiences. And both represent the grace that is the Spirit.[58]

It is within this context that we are to understand Quesnel's more traditionally Jansenistic discussion of the Spirit in the *Réflexions* proper. In one of the most extended passages devoted to this topic, for instance, on the whole eighth chapter of Romans,[59] Quesnel identifies what he counts as twenty-five "effects of the Spirit." Based on the various verses of the chapter itself, he frequently collapses the Spirit into an equation with "grace" and with "the grace of Christ" and with "charity," much in the direction Paul himself points in the course of the text. Most of Quesnel's comments stress typical Jansenistic themes: the force of love over cupidity, fear and hope, love as desire or "taste" (*goût*), and so on. But three elements come to the fore amid these twenty-five effects: the notion of the Spirit's indwelling — the "soul of the soul"[60] — the notion of this indwelling being tied foundationally to the Mystical Body of Christ, His Church,[61] and the notion that, as His Body, the Church and its members will be formed historically by the Spirit into His historical image.[62]

In all of this, then, the Spirit is lifted up as the shaper of Christ's forms for His people. And the reach of these forms stretches both backward into the past, through the types of the Old Testament, and into the future, through the awaiting conformances of the Church to the outplaying Mysteries of Jesus' living image. The scope and effect of this reach is what Quesnel means by the equation of grace and Spirit: God's self carries and imparts the forms of historical existence that Christians hope in, receive,

---

56. Ibid., xxiv–xxxv.
57. Ibid., xxvii–xxx; xxxv–xxxix.
58. Ibid., xli–lv; lx–lxii; lxx ff.
59. Ibid., vol. 6, 86–104.
60. See ibid., 89f.
61. Ibid., 90ff.
62. See ibid., 100ff.

and live through as members of a formally circumscribed Jesus. Grace as charity, or Spirit as charity, describes something similar: not so much the fulfilling of specific commands, love is the formative movement of a set of acts that define the comprehensive shape of a person, most especially of the Church itself. Thrown in the larger historical context that is the unfolding of God's great acts, embodied in the figures of Scripture, charity and its movement of the will, whether by *suavité* or force or *feu* (fire), represent configurating tendencies, rather than punctiliar functions: the Spirit that is love conforms the Church to the shape of Jesus in time.

We are not very far here, finally, from the pneumatological elements that are later so evident in Jansenist devotionals. The "forms of the Spirit," which are occasionally identified in handbooks like the *Instructions* — the Scripture, Jesus, and the Church — are all implied by Quesnel in their central role as the intersignificating and effecting powers of historical grace. Further, what counted in such books' brief description of the Pentecost mystery as the adorative response to divine form-giving is already at root in Quesnel a worshipful astonishment at the shapes of history that are perceived as immediate to God. The Spirit-given form of Christ pervades and confines the forms of the Church's history, and thus, even and because of its abasement in the course of ecclesial experience, that experience on its own becomes worthy of adoration.

It should come as no surprise to find elsewhere in Appellant writing a more visible flowering of this adorative pneumatology located in historical form. In a way that stands at a great distance from the early Saint-Cyran, yet is still connected to his first intimations regarding the link between Spirit and Church in history, someone like Nicholas Cabrisseau can, in 1740, take the format of "instructions on the Creed" and elevate the discussion of the Spirit to a pitch of doxological sonority that is possible only *because* of his presuppositions of grace's pneumatological historicity.[63] Unlike virtually all of his predecessors, Cabrisseau founds his remarks about the Spirit on the vocation that we have to offer the Spirit *worship*.[64] Not only is this argued, as in Basil the Great's early example of this method, according to the Spirit's names in Scripture, the example of the Church's liturgy, and the traditionally articulated effects of the Spirit. Cabrisseau, in the manner of the Jansenists' ecclesial and historical orientation, also and more forcefully stresses how the experience of the Church in its formation and growth to the present — the articles in the Creed that depend on the affirmation of the Spirit — itself embodies realities that call for our praise: miracles, saints, martyrs, holiness, courage, preaching, suffering, healing, etc. It is not so much that these "effects" of the Spirit's work demand our thanksgiving, as it is that their configuration in a continuous history displays the shape of the Spirit as being at one with the

---

63. [N. Cabrisseau], *Instructions courtes et familieres sur le Symbole, pour servir de suite aux instructions courtes et familieres de Messire Joseph Lambert* (Paris: Ph. N. Lottin, 1740), 2 vols., especially vol. 1, 252–75 and vol. 2, 137–94.

64. See ibid., vol. 2, 149ff., 162, 175ff.

shape of Jesus, our "model."[65] The "Mystery of the Incarnation" is, as with the Church, one of the Spirit's "unction," and in the case of both, this "grace of love" is actually something of "glory," that is, a form or set of forms whose shape intrinsically "attracts" our praise.[66]

This is ultimately the question posed by the Appellant pneumatology of grace: is history itself adorable as it conforms to the shape of Jesus Christ? Is it so, as the *Instructions sur les vérités qui concernent la grace* affirms, in such a way that charity "crushed" must take the form of the Church pressed down, as the Spirit's historical shape follows the path of Jesus' own self-emptying? And if this is so, then both the tremors and the lightning, the sighs and the groanings, the sense of ending and the astonished overturning of experienced finality that each mold temporal substance for Jesus' body, as they form the sensible movement of the Church's actions and compose its distinctly uttered syllables of praise, will constitute the unexpected contours of the *ostensio Spiritus*. Such will prove the environing experience of chastened hope in which the miracles of Saint-Médard will offer the presence of God before the unbelieving eyes of a fallen century, according to Appellant reflection. Our next section will mark our transition to a study of the character of such specific pneumatic events as they took shape within a Jansenist sensibility fashioned theologically to discern the edges of this kind of experience.

---

65. Ibid., 153ff., 170ff.
66. See ibid., 181ff.

# SECTION TWO

# MIRACLES AND SANCTITY

*Chapter Five*

# THE QUESTION
# OF MIRACLES

## Outline of the Chapter

Whereas the first section of this book tried to identify some general theological features that may have undergirded pneumatic experience, such as that of miracle, among Jansenists, this section will focus more narrowly, although still somewhat broadly, on the particular reflective vision of the miraculous itself — including prodigious events and human sanctity — that may inform the experience. We focus here, in other words, on a particular Jansenist "theology of miracle."

This first chapter of the section will provide an introductory context in which to explore this theology. After loosely identifying, inductively, certain characteristic features of an Appellant miracle account, we will contrast them with a number of other paradigmatic construals of miracle from among some of Jansenism's immediate forebears and contemporaries, both Protestant and Catholic. In general, I will suggest that the Jansenist experience of miracle, despite its eminently controversial context, actually tended to eschew the traditional functionalist account of the phenomenon common to the era's polemics in favor of a figural explanation. In addition, this non-functionalist perspective was joined to a circumstantialist view of the miraculous event as both non-uniform as well as non-punctiliar, that was peculiar to Jansenism, and that nonetheless upheld in a novel way a traditional Catholic understanding of miracle as divinely epiphanic (the primary basis for accepting an explicitly ostensive version of the Holy Spirit's apprehension). These three features — the circumstantial, the figurative, and the epiphanic — will form the parameters for a subsequent, more detailed discussion of the Jansenist theology of miracle in the two chapters that conclude the section.

## Features of Appellant Miracle

The first section of this book opened with Carré de Montgeron's description of a miracle at Saint-Médard, the healing of Dom Alphonse de Palacios. After reviewing parts of his account, I identified, in a loose fashion, three general categories of qualification that seemed to inform the miracle's description: *sensibilité*, historical particularity, and continuity, and the identification of these last with the character of divine grace itself. In effect, our subsequent investigation of the theological structures of grace that underlie Appellant Jansenism could be seen as a delving into just these categories.

Not that our broad distinctions there mirrored exactly the categories of the miracle account, but they did seem to confirm them in large: what we called "the historical character of grace" comprehended aspects of the *theologically* narrative quality of Carré de Montgeron's description, just as our notion of the "formal constraints" of grace in the person of Christ's figure might well include aspects of the miracle account's interest in the sensible contours of a figurative experience (that is, one that conforms to the phenomenal shape of a scriptural episode or individual). Less obvious, perhaps, but arguably pertinent to Carré de Montgeron's identification of God's presence with the unfolding of the miracle's shape, was our final suggestion of an implied (and developing) Jansenist pneumatology, collapsing Spirit with just these experienced historically and figuratively sensible qualities.

I believe that these are more than fortuitous or broadly trivial convergences. And if they are more than that, we are perhaps encouraged to take these theological structures and the historical particulars that embody their force and ponder their appropriateness for informing our conceptions for the Holy Spirit's self-expression generally. That is the ultimate challenge our investigation will pose. It is a challenge, however, that, were it real, would be merely a reflection of the immediate imposition pressed upon us by an actual instance of an *ostensio Spiritus Dei*. What shall we do with Dom de Palacios and his cohorts? Or better, what will be done with us in their face?

But as we go further into our phenomenological study of the *Holy Spirit*, our goal is certainly not to force the details of particular experiences of such pneumatic appearance into artificial structures of commonality. Rather, we should seek to allow these particular experiences to speak for themselves in a way that might reveal the givenness of their linkage within a divine purpose of expression. The Jansenist "theological structures of grace" that we sketched in the first section, then, indicate possible parameters within which these experiences might begin to be understood, but they certainly do not demand a detailed applicability. We are, with diverse viewings of its shape, circling a problem rather than defining its constituent parts from within.

To this end, I propose we now pursue a second experiment of viewing, more constricted this time, as we reflect on the general shape of miracle itself within the developing Jansenist experience leading up to Appellancy. Within the broad parameters of a theology of grace, sketched in our first section, can we locate the fact and shape of miracle in a way that is peculiar to Jansenist experience? Does such an experience actually fall within these parameters, as I have just asserted, and in what way? How, finally, will the fact of miracles, so elucidated, help define *in advance* as it were, the Appellant version of the *ostensio Spiritus* that incorporates their proliferation at Saint-Médard? In the rest of this introduction, I wish only to identify some concepts that may help ground the answering of these questions in the subsequent chapters of this section.

Let us then return, for a moment, to Dom de Palacios. If we assume that Carré de Montgeron's account of the miracle is somehow typical of the Appellant experience of miracle at Saint-Médard, can we distinguish in it peculiar features that inform the experience in a way that also typifies? Let me propose three features of the account that touch upon the character of the miracle itself.

First, we should note that, although this is the first miracle Carré de Montgeron describes in his expansive dossier of documentation and reflection, it is clearly and deliberately spoken of as but one miracle taken from an ongoing series. Dom de Palacios is not the first person to be healed at François de Pâris's tomb, and we are told that he seeks the saint's intercession by a gift of grace that allows him to respond to accounts of miracles *already* worked. With this opening miracle, then, Carré de Montgeron, places us in the midst of an already unfolding story of cures.

All that happens to the suffering Spaniard takes place as a piece in a larger drama, the details of his experience gaining meaning by their association with and relation to a greater set of circumstances. Not only is he healed, but his healing then converts M. Roulie des Filtières, and we are given a glimpse of the opening up of connected avenues of grace. By contrast, the healing is also placed within the context of rejection, where bishops and others act particularly in blindness, and more generally as part of a divine scheme of illumination and darkness, spread across the expanding scene of the *causa gratiae Dei* of Appellancy.

I will call this first feature of the miracle, as narrated, its *non-punctiliar* aspect. It is a given miracle, with all of its peculiar and individual details, experienced by a given person the shape of whose life is critical to the miracle's reality. Yet the miracle is firmly set within a frame of other miracles, a set of circumstances whose historical cast makes the miracle itself a part of some larger temporal reach, something greater springing from the historical purposes of God.

A second and related feature of the miracle as told by Carré de Montgeron, can be gleaned from the way the account subtly hides by degrees the actual character of the miracle as *healing* behind the screen of miracle as *figure*. Both Dom de Palacios's and M. Roulie des Filtières's experiences are assumed into the work of "that Master of our hearts," for whom the healing of bodies, and its sensible components, are but signs. Signs of what? The historical frame within which the miracles are set as building blocks is itself something that acts as a larger figure, not of a specific divine action, but of God's encompassing "justice and mercy," in Carré de Montgeron's words.

Within this large figure, of light and dark, of vision and blindness, specific historical shapes take form, moving from the scripturally trans-historical figure of the Exodus to the yet more particular experiences of miracle and its rejection. The account of Dom de Palacios's healing, like all of Carré de Montgeron's dossiers, ends with a prayer in which the particular event, and its experienced details gives way to a heated celebration of figurative praise and petition: bodies signify spirits, events dissolve into the shape of Jesus' life and relationships, and the universe as a whole is gathered up into a single posture within the sovereign hands of God.

This figural transposition of the individual event is surely the most dis-tinctive aspect of the Appellant miracle accounts. It is perhaps so obvious as to have been too narrowly assumed, without reflection: an attacked minority in the Church claims miracles on its behalf as a "sign" of God's favor. On this reading, the miracle as figure is no more than a divine mark of approval. But the figurative construal of the miracle here is pre-cisely what pushes the event beyond *any* "functionalist" understanding of what is happening. Not only is the immediate purpose of the miracle — the healing from physical pain and sickness — transcended by the figura-tive interpretation; so too is the immediate set of circumstances wherein the miracle takes place, that is, the Appellant struggle.

For now, this historical framework, with its particular needs and con-flicts, is subsumed into the figural elaborations of divine history itself, the shape of Israel and of Egypt, of Jesus and the Jews, of God's own transcendent history of light and darkness. Pushed to this extreme, indi-vidual bodies and individual speech, with their purposeful specifications, are hidden behind (or, better, within) a far more glorious and unitary figure of God's creative display in history as a whole. This single fig-ure comprehends even the peculiar aspects of the eighteenth-century *causa gratiae Dei*. To speak of the "purpose" of the miracle is already to subordinate the figure as divine shape to some secondary scheme of accomplishment. Fundamentally, the miracle as figure is supremely *non-functional* in its freedom from an immediate role in furthering specific ecclesiastical ends.

To describe the miracle of Dom Palacios's healing as non-punctiliar and non-functional — that is, as circumstantial and figurative — is simply to propose a third and more inclusive feature of the miracle given shape in this context: the purely revelatory, the broadly theophanic character of the miracle, in which divine hereness is posited. Of course, the qualities of this hereness are fluid, and to this extent somewhat deceptive. In Carré de Montgeron's accounts, the character of the *causa gratiae Dei* predominates within the miracle: the Truth speaking, illumination and blinding, and so on. But this is only to underline that the work of God on His own behalf is itself epiphanic, is a display of grace (and hence of the Spirit of love), and that the figure of its history stands as the shape of God apprehended. Carré de Montgeron appropriately speaks of "holiness" as "manifested" in the miracle, a formulation properly descriptive of the divine glory.

## Protestant Contrasts

One way to test the distinctiveness of these three features of Appellant miracle — circumstantial, figurative, and epiphanic (or "glorious") — is to compare them with other, non-Jansenist descriptions of such events. While this can be done here only in the most general of ways, it will usefully begin to bring into relief the way in which the Appellant vision of God's self-disclosure as grace, informing, for example, Carré de Montgeron's account, is determined by an underlying frame of divine experience within which miracles appear only and necessarily in a certain light.

The most immediate contrast to be noted here is with the whole tradition of dominant Protestantism on the topic of miracles, as it was expressed by Luther and Calvin and known at the time by Catholics in France. In brief, the Reformers largely rejected the occurrence of contemporary miracles altogether. How and why they did so reveals a vastly different conception of what a miracle is within the framework of God's ordering of sensible life.

Luther's discussion of miracles was early linked to the question of whether they might occur in order to confirm particular doctrines. In his dispute with Erasmus over free will, Luther was forced to answer Erasmus's claim that the Church's traditional teaching affirming the existence of free will in men and women was supported by saints working miracles in the Spirit of God.[1] Luther is hardly systematic in his retort, but he provides the following shotgun reply. First, can Erasmus actually *prove* that the people he calls saints really were such, and that the miracles he claims they performed really happened? This is the historical-critical question of evidence. Second, Luther wonders, even if one could certify the saints and miracles as genuine, whether it is possible to prove that the miracles were worked *for the express purpose of confirming* the doctrine of free choice. This seems unlikely, and therefore, third, if a miracle *cannot* be explicitly linked to a particular doctrine, Luther feels that such a doctrine is not to be believed. Fourth, it is clear that a doctrine like human free will *needs* such confirmation, because many heathen who support it (and a good number of other doctrines) *appear* to be wise, talented, and authoritative, and so, on Erasmus's grounds anyway, confirming of the teaching. But, finally, if God wanted to confirm a given doctrine that is now in dispute, why are there no miracles today to back it up?

What Luther says about miracles applies to saints as well, but with a slightly different slant: real holiness lies in humility and weakness dependent upon God (the opposite of the affirmation of free choice), and thus a central feature of sanctity is its "hiddenness." Historically, the "holy" Church of the Creed is preserved from error by Christ, but only in a fashion that masks true saints beneath the veneer of the comprehended

---

1. See Luther's *De Servo Arbitrio*, trans. and ed. Philip S. Watson, in *Luther and Erasmus: Free-Will and Salvation*, ed. E. Gordon Rupp and Philip S. Watson (Philadelphia: Westminster Press, 1969), 144ff.

Body, the wheat mixed in with the chaff. We recognize other Christians as "saints" through the "rule of love," not through "faith" (i.e., not through the demands imposed by papal canonization). Historical "facts" — like sanctity — within this world, are properly a secret when they touch upon salvation.

Thus, while Luther does not deny the reality of miracles and saints, and indeed (at least for the sake of argument) grants their confirming powers with respect to doctrine in theory, he argues for the practical impossibility of ever discerning a miracle or a saint in history, especially as they might be explicitly linked to the confirmation of a doctrine. And Luther's point in all of this is obvious: "What then, are we to do? The Church is hidden; the saints are unknown?"; all that remains is *Scripture* to guide our thinking.[2] It is Scripture as exclusive authority that Luther wishes to establish in the face of Erasmus's appeals to miraculously confirmed tradition.

Without seeing Luther's remarks here as systematically indicative, they do nonetheless display some features that remain consistent in his thought. First, miracles are *historically arbitrary.* That is, to the degree that they happen, their authenticity and meaning is opaque and ungraspable. To the degree that they happen, they cannot be connected with other events, other disputes, other contests or challenges. Miracles as elements of a divine purpose — like the Appellant *causa gratiae Dei* — are rejected from the start. Second, any notion of historical "display," of "glory" manifested, is rejected in favor of a vision of God's power as inherently hidden.

It is no surprise, then, to see Luther, in other works, confining his positive discussion of miracles to *interior* works of God, and consigning, by definition, all exterior works of power — prodigies and wonders — to Satan. (In his 1522 preface to the New Testament, Luther ranks John and Paul above the Synoptics precisely because they emphasize faith over miracles and works.) In his Lectures on the Gospel of John (chapter 14, verses 10–12), he now includes enthusiasts along with papists as among those "seduced" by the devil into following the authority of "majesty," mighty works, prophecies, saints, and holiness. The revelation of God's glory is always Christ, but Christ "masked" by the Word. Any other purported manifestation of God outside the Word is satanic.

This said, Luther resorts to a dispensationalist reading of history to account for the early miracles of both Christ and the Apostles. However genuine their original works — and anything else of the Devil is only counterfeit — "the day of miracles is past" (verse 12). Christians today do not accomplish such works. But not, Luther is quick to add, because they are weaker. Did not Christ promise that His Church would do "greater works" than He? Physical miracles are in fact the *least* important of the works of Christ. More glorious are the works of the Church accomplished in the individual: the sacraments, conversion, instruction,

---

2. Ibid., 158.

comfort and strength, prayer. All these are "greater," not only in their dependence upon interior faith, but in the extent of their field of action,
touching the lives of countless thousands, unlike the constricted scope of
the individual healing.

Luther's stress on the miracles of interiority on the one hand (the
hiddenness of faith) and on the miracles of the institution on the other
(the power of God masked in the institutionally proffered Word) lays an
inescapable fence around the positive outbreak of holy miracles in his own
day. This fact is not even contradicted, substantially, in those cases where
Luther appears to be affirming the miraculous character of the present, as
in his occasional reflections on the eschatological nature of the present
age. In his postil for Advent 2 (Luke 21:25–26), Luther preaches fervently
on the "signs" of the times, which presage the imminent return of Christ.[3]
In his gloss on the various elements Jesus points to as indicators of the
End, Luther initially takes each with utmost literalism: the world has
reached such a climactic pitch of commercial and technical accomplish-
ments, that the end must surely be at hand; we see an increase in solar
and lunar eclipses and a rash of falling stars about us, comets and omens
of all kinds, including the discovery of monsters and the onslaught of new
diseases like syphilis. All these constitute properly miraculous portents of
the concluding rush of history.[4]

What is interesting here is both the way Luther explains the nature
of these signs and where he locates their significance. First, he tells us
that all of these signs represent "natural phenomena." They are empirical
realities that can be observed and measured by astronomers and other
scientists. The notion of miracle as a breach in the "laws of nature" is
explicitly rejected. Rather, Luther advances the view, ultimately deriving
from Augustine (and taken up, in a transformed manner by Malebranche
as we shall see), that, as natural phenomena that are also divine signs,
they were preordained by God from the beginning of creation *within* the
ordering of natural processes: "nevertheless, God, in carrying on his work
in silence, gives us security and moves forward in his plans . . . the course
of the heavens [being] so arranged from eternity that before the last day
these signs must appear."[5] Within the unbroken order of nature, then,
these events are "tokens," whose shape is in no wise distinguished from
any other aspect of history, and whose divine significance is supremely
founded on the faith of the believer who grasps their place in the divine
scheme. As real events, then, the apprehension of their origins is founded

---

3. In *Luther's Church Postil,* trans. John Nicholas Lenker (Minneapolis: Luther In All
Lands Co., 1905), 1:59–86.

4. On Luther's views of the "End," see the summary articles by the Adventist Winifried
Vogel, "The Eschatological Theology of Martin Luther. Part I: Luther's Basic Concepts" and
"Part II: Luther's Exposition of Daniel and Revelation," in *Andrews University Seminary
Studies* 24, no. 3 (Autumn 1986), 249–64, and 25, no. 2 (Summer 1987): 183–99.

5. *Luther's Church Postil,* 65–66.

on the interiority of a kind of fideistic gnosis, rather than derived from the nature of the events themselves.

Further, Luther subordinates the experienced reality of these events, as depicted in Scripture, to what he calls their "spiritual" meaning. In effect, though history will provide real examples of these signs, being ordered natural phenomena, Jesus reveals them in advance to his disciples as a form of allegory: the sun stands for Christ, the moon for the Church, the stars equal Christians, the powers are to be identified with the prelates, and the whole relation of their various veilings and fallings from the heavens are to be interpreted in terms of the apostasy and heresy of the Church of Rome.

To the degree, then, that Luther does have room for a circumstantial reading of miracles, even here it is a reading determined by hiddenness and obscurity and attached, in any case, to the working of satanic powers — the papacy, the Turks, the enthusiasts, and so on. Luther's parsing of history, in which contemporary events often do find a significant place, is always demonized around the negative pole of manifestation. Because of this, where contemporary "miracle" is acknowledged at all, Luther interprets it in an *anti*-epiphanic fashion, and for this reason, miracle stands as a perverted form of functionalism: "wonders" and "prodigies" (and even historical experience as a whole) can only, in their overtness, witness to the Devil.

We should not ignore the profound effect Luther's *theologia crucis* had in shaping this ultimate result: hiddenness, obscurity, and weakness are all elements that must characterize any shape of divine glory because of the form of the Cross, which alone represents saving power. What is interesting to note in passing (and in anticipation), however, is that this determinative focus on cruciformity, which is not unrelated to the formly character of grace as Jansenists came to understand it in terms of the Christic "mysteries," seems to lead in Luther's mind to the obscuring of the divine presence in history's shape: the Christian and the Christian Church alone stand as the places of clear blessing, in the face of satanic manifestation. Here, cruciformity separates the Church from the world. But in Jansenist eyes, at least as Appellancy arises, the cruciform shape of true miracle leads to an opposite conclusion, in which the Church and the world's history share the same figure. Given our discussion in the previous section, might this not be due precisely to the pneumatological appropriation of the form of Christ to the form of history, including the Church's?

In any case, Protestantism quickly seized upon the dispensationalist logic that was perhaps only a secondary implication of Luther's concern with the hiddenness of divine power: that is, that visible and physical miracles, however authentic in the time and at the hands of Christ and his apostles, have ceased in the life of the subsequent Church. "The time of miracles is past." This was Calvin's clear teaching, and it is enunciated with a more sharply drawn functionalist concern with doctrine than even

Luther had evidenced. Further, from the perspective of French Catholics, it is Calvin and his reformed followers who represent the most challenging opponents of miracle.

The controversial context of the fight with Catholicism in which miracle is discussed seems wholly definitive of the problem in Calvin's mind. In the *Institutes'* preface to Francis I, Calvin responds to the by-now common charge of Catholics that the Reformers had no miracles to confirm their doctrinal novelties. He presents what becomes the traditional Protestant case. First, he admits that the miracles of Apostolic times were genuine. However, these were necessary only to confirm the initial preaching of the Word. Once confirmed, and organized into the canonical Scriptures (of the New Testament), no further confirmations were necessary. Miracles have ceased because they have fulfilled their function and are no longer necessary. (Even Augustine, in some of his earlier remarks, had felt this to be the case.) Two results now follow: controversies over doctrine are to be settled by appeal to Scripture, not to miracle; and any miracles that are claimed (i.e., by Catholics) are clearly satanic delusions.

This analysis, which Calvin reasserts throughout his work,[6] provides a clear framework for describing the nature of genuine miracle. The main element in the description hangs on the dispensationalist premise: the miracles of the New Testament were given for a specific *function* that now no longer needs to be filled. The function, in precise terms, is to aid and uphold the initial teaching of the Word of Christ. In the *Institutes* (III, 2:5), for instance, he presents a definition of "implicit faith," against the scholastics, as a "predisposing attitude" to accept the explicit teaching of the Christian religion. "Implicit faith," in other words, is something we might call "teachableness." The example Calvin gives of this, however, is that of people who became "attentive" to Christ's words because of his miracles. Miracles thus perform the function of grabbing our interest, in order that we listen to the truth of Christ's word.

But this predisposing function was necessary only at the beginning of the Gospel's preaching. While theoretically still a function miracles could fulfill, today the Word of Scripture itself in the Church commands sufficient attention and is made efficacious through the work of the Holy Spirit. As with Luther, the original function of physical miracle — which Calvin can still describe in the epiphanic terms of "the power and visible image of the presence of God"[7] — has been transferred to the obscured interior experience of conversion and the formalized exterior works of the ecclesiastical institution. Joined to, then, and implied by the functionalist account of miracle, is a purely punctiliar notion of its occurrence and of divine history as a whole: individual conversions (a general class of experience) take place, each in a uniform but discrete manner, through unrelated

---

6. See *Institutes* IV 19:6, 8; *Harmony of the Gospels* on Mark 16:17. In the *Commentary* on John 14:10–12, Calvin follows Luther's interpretation of the "greater works" done by the Church in terms of converting the world both institutionally and internally.

7. *Commentary* on John 14:11.

immediate (interior) or ahistorically immutable (the exterior dynamics of Scripture and Church) structures; dispensationally, physical miracles are functionally dependent on these realities. It should be obvious that this finally traditional Protestant construal of miracle contradicts, on every count, the related experience of healing given in Carré de Montgeron.

## Catholic Functionalism

That Protestant dispensationalism did not constitute an attack on the functionalist version of miracle, but rather sought to limit the historical scope of miracle's functional value, ought to be clear. But Protestantism shared this basic functionalist view of miracle with its opponents. For one of Catholicism's chief controversial weapons in the wake of the Reformation — as Luther already saw in his debate with Erasmus — was the claim that a consistent theology should apply the confirming aspect of New Testament miracle to the history of the Church as a whole. The Roman Church had miracles, and the Protestants didn't; *ergo* Roman doctrine and tradition were confirmed in the face of the Reformers' attacks. Indeed, post-Tridentine discussions of miracle represent the triumph of pure functionalism, in a way that at least Luther's *theologia crucis* hints at obviating.

Bellarmine is a good example of the stock Catholic view of miracle. In two discourses on the topic he conveniently lays out what becomes the traditional Catholic response to Protestant dispensationalism.[8] In Bellarmine's view, miracles, along with prophecy, represent the functional *discrimen* between the Heavenly Jerusalem that is the Church and the earthly city of which the heretics (i.e., Protestants) are a part. The "glory" of miracles to which Bellarmine refers does indeed have some connection to the epiphanic nature of miracles we discussed earlier, but it is here firmly subordinated to the sole function of discrimination. Miracles and prophecy "shine out" like the sun and the moon, or like the two eyes of the microcosmic human being; but their light, as light, serves a definite purpose. *Exornatio* [beauty] is subsumed by *utilitas*.[9]

With respect to the Protestant attack on contemporary miracles, Bellarmine points out that it is inconsistent to deny the testimony for miracles given by Patristic saints while accepting their doctrinal teaching on other matters, including the interpretation of Scripture. (On this score, the early Church Fathers make better witnesses than do the Protestants.) To claim that purported post-apostolic miracles were probably demonic (Calvin) is to rip the incident of miracle from its circumstantial context, i.e., the context of holiness and conversion described by trustworthy witnesses from the past.[10]

8. "Concio de Gloria Miraculorum" and "Concio de Miraculis Haereticorum," in *Opera Omnia*, ed. Justinus Fèvre (Paris: 1873; repr. Frankfurt: Minerva GmbH, 1965), vol. 9.

9. Ibid., 543.

10. Ibid., 549f.

Should one not recognize that the *results* of subsequent miracles are consistent with their function in the Scriptures, that is, "persuasion" and establishment of faith in Christ? This accepted, it ought to be clear, according to Bellarmine, that miracles today act to distinguish true doctrine from false, the true Church from the false. It is an evasion on the part of Protestants to reject the possibility of authentic post-apostolic miracle. Instead, they ought to join battle with the Catholics *through* miracle, and let miracle decide, just as did Moses and the magicians of Pharaoh, and Elijah and the prophets of Baal. Whose are stronger? The answer is obvious: the Protestants reject miracles because they cannot perform them. While true saints even today die yet are found to have incorruptible bodies, Luther's corpse is putrefying. The only prodigy Protestants can genuinely present in this contest is the fact that Satan has been able to mislead so many from the true Catholic Church.[11]

Bellarmine's vision of a consistent ecclesiastical history, in which miracles continue unabated in an evidential role established scripturally even before Christ is not wholly different in its presuppositions from the Protestants', except in its rejection of dispensational distinctions. What the uniformity of history does provide in contrast is a context in which miracles, by their very sameness, might be perceived as "display" or divine manifestation. That is to say, there is a sense in which the uniformity of miraculous occurrence might undercut a purely functionalist view of miracle. Further, the controversial demand that miracles be judged by their circumstantial effects, however uniformly functional (and thus in some sense still necessarily punctiliar), also represents an *opening* at least to something more bound up with historical possibilities (and hence with larger and distinct historical figures).

But in fact the whole tenor of this kind of post-Tridentine controversial discourse clearly lays the foundation for later Christian apologists of all confessions. Miracles, if and when they occur, "confirm" doctrine; from a Catholic point of view in particular, they "persuade" and lead to faith. As Christian inter-confessional debate gives way to the defense of Christian claims in general against Deists and atheists in the later seventeenth and early eighteenth centuries, miracle's role as "evidence" brings to a vigorous fulfillment its perceived functional nature. This link between the forms of religious controversy stemming from the Reformation and the rise of particularly modern forms of apologetics is by now a commonplace. But to note it in particular with respect to the question of miracle is to further emphasize in what ways Jansenist viewings of religious experience stand to the side of developing Catholicism.

Thus, by the early eighteenth century, Catholic theologians in France had well appropriated Bellarmine's categories of the "discriminating miracle" and firmly applied them to the defense of Christianity in general. Abbé C. Houtteville offers a particularly striking example of what this

---

11. Ibid., 551–55.

might mean in his enormously popular *La Religion chrétienne prouvée par les faits*, first published in 1722.[12] Writing against Deists and self-styled *incrédules* [unbelievers], Houtteville's task is to demonstrate the credibility of specific Christian claims, including claims for the truth of basic "mysteries of the faith." How do this?

Houtteville asserts at the beginning of his long work the following basic principle that governs all human acceptance of any claim whatsoever:

> Only the authority of evidence subjugates Reason. That which is not clearly perceived leaves at least some freedom for doubt. To believe, one must judge; and to judge, one must, above all else, know the object. For to judge what one cannot see is to judge nothing; and to judge nothing is not to judge at all.[13]

The empiricist presuppositions governing this statement are clear enough, and need not concern us. The problem Houtteville faces with respect to the unbeliever is that Christianity claims many things that are not directly subject to visible truth, that are not, in fact, "objects" to be grasped, e.g., the mysteries of the Incarnation, the Trinity, and so on. How can "the authority of evidence" capture the reason with respect to these elements of the faith?

> Our religion is both clear and obscure and the same time; but this clarity and obscurity do not touch the same objects. [...] Now the Christian's "mysteries" are a stumbling block to his reason, but also the matter of his faith. Nonetheless, the certitude of these very Mysteries is tied to truths that are evidently known, and it is inseparable from them. Here is the element that is clear, and as a result, here is where contradictions are dissolved. In a word, we follow the footprints of faith; but faith itself follows the footprints of the Light. [...] Do you wonder, then, what is this kind of proof that is able to conquer the mind's revolts? It is the proof of facts.[14]

There is nothing unusual in Houtteville's claim here: the mysteries of the faith — doctrine — are confirmed by accompanying "facts" that are verifiable according to standard rules governing the credibility of evidence. And the confirming facts in question, he tells us, are miracles, the miracles of Jesus especially. Once one has "proved" such a fact, once one has demonstrated the historical veracity of such an event, then the dispute with the Deist or the unbeliever is resolved on the side of faith without further ado.[15]

---

12. I will be referring to Houtteville's own revised edition of 1740 (Paris, Gregoire Dupuis), 3 vols. On Houtteville in his immediate context, see R. R. Palmer, *Catholics and Unbelievers in Eighteenth Century France* (Princeton: Princeton University Press, 1939), 80ff. For earlier late seventeenth-century versions of Houtteville's evidentialist argument based on "historical facts," by, e.g., Pierre Sylvain Régis and François Lamy, see Tocanne, *L'Idée de Nature en France*, 127ff.

13. Houtteville, *La Religion chrétienne prouvée par les faits*, vol. 1, 3.

14. Ibid., 4–5.

15. Ibid.

Houtteville develops his notion of proof by the facts of miracle in a way that is certainly peculiar to his era (especially as regards the nature of *sensibilité*), and we shall have occasion to return to some of these remarks.[16] In general, however, and despite the empiricist equipment he sports, he has moved no further beyond the traditional functionalist understanding of miracle as the confirmation of doctrine. The application of a Thomistic discussion of the *mechanism* of miracle — that is, that as a witnessed fact judged to be "beyond" the natural order of the universe's created powers, it is clearly miraculous — allows him to treat miracles as demonstrable evidence for the divine origin of the teaching they accompany.[17] But Houtteville's carefully defined notions of evidence and their historical credibility[18] do little to alter the basically functionalist notion of miracle that was already well-founded in the Church.

Only when he must confront the objection that the miraculous gifts of the Holy Spirit seem to have become less universal after the first centuries of the Church (a section he added to this later edition, and hence after the Saint-Médard episode had run much of its course), does he reveal in what way the experience of the recent Church's life might require some attenuation of the model of uniform evidential purpose. While he acknowledges (like Calvin) that miracles are no longer necessary for the conversion of the world, as they were early on, he denies as a consequence that they have stopped. Miracles are not taken away; rather they have become more *hidden* (*secrètes*) — and more "marvelous" for that fact — in order that, by veiling His own gifts, God might both encourage faith and discourage pride. One day we will see clearly the Wisdom of God's providence in this mysterious ordering of manifestation.[19] This is an ultimately Augustinian argument, but its use here reflects a new appreciation of the fact that miracles, for all their sameness in function, actually do "appear" according to providential designs, whose character is as much informed by obscurity as by evidential clarity. It is not, however, an insight that does anything more than peep out from among the hundreds of pages in Houtteville's multivolume work.

It should not surprise us, however, if the controversial and apologetic

---

16. Houtteville defines a number of different forms of demonstration — "metaphysical" (i.e., logical), "through *sentiments*," "moral" (i.e., through the coincidence of a variety of circumstances and aspects), and finally demonstration through "fact." It is the last, synonymous with confirmation by miracle, that Houtteville claims is the most "persuasive," *frappante* [striking], and *pénétrante* for all people. Why? Precisely because "facts," as elements that are *palpable* and *sensible* are, of all things, universally accessible to public confirmation or disconfirmation. They are subject to universally apprehended rules of evidence, deriving from the experience of vision and self-consciousness. (He claims that even Descartes had to base his system of truth on the apprehension of the "fact" of self-consciousness, open to the tribunal of public scrutiny. See ibid., 6–18).

17. Ibid., 21ff.

18. See ibid., 29ff., where he gives "seven characteristics" that establish a fact, rules by which he will, in the course of the rest of the first volume, "prove" the veracity of the Gospel miracles as historical evidence.

19. Ibid., vol. 2, 473ff.

edge present in all the remarks on miracles we have just examined did not inevitably demand the kind of abstract functionalist views we have found on the subject by a kind of academic logic. To work as part of an argument, on whatever side, miracles must be rendered in the appropriate shades of utility. To this depiction, supporting nuances of historical uniformity or dispensationalism can play a role, though only the most subordinate one. And from the beginning, the experiential impetus of epiphanic display has been banished precisely because of its intractable discreteness. Now where miracle will play a role in the *ostensio Spiritus*, or *causa gratiae Dei* in particular, as with the later Appellants, we should expect as well that the functionalist account of miracle will predominate. Will this prove the case, and to what extent?

## The Catholic Experience of Miracle

As I have earlier noted, this expectation of Appellant functionalism has guided the scholarly assessment of the debate over miracles around the Saint-Médard episode. Nor is it, in fact, an unimportant element in Jansenist thinking about miracles in general: what do they *do*, what purpose do they serve, how can we distinguish true from false, so that they may fulfill their own proper discriminating function? These are questions people like Pascal will ask, and ask as sharply as anyone. Still, I have claimed that the functionalist account of miracles, as it is linked with views of the uniformity of history and the less than obvious manifestation of God within history's shape, simply does not square with classic descriptions of miracle like Carré de Montgeron's. In large part, our discussion thus far, because of its confinement to the concerns of theological controversy, has failed to touch on the most important element in miracle's evaluation: its experiential immediacy, that it has happened to a person, with particular effects whose meaning is significant only because of its personal (though perhaps wholly public) character. Descriptions of miracles like that of Dom Alphonse de Palacios are from the beginning specific events whose descriptive experience in effect precedes theological definition and ultimately must determine such definition on its own terms.

To gain a still more accurate perspective on the distinctive features I have suggested for the Appellant miracles, we ought now to consider other descriptions of particular miracles rather than look only at the controversy over definition and use. To be sure, the ways in which such controversy eventually overshadows the theology deriving from description are not without significance. Pascal himself struggles mightily to escape the bonds of pure definitional logic and scholars today still remain tied to an abstract definitional notion of miracle that demands the subordination of all descriptive power to the consequent task of adumbrating a functionalist model.[20]

---

20. When Orcibal came to analyze the notion of miracle as it was expressed at Port-

To the extent that the controversial theologians did not carry off a full-scale victory over religion itself, miracles remained discrete phenomena that resisted abstract typifications. And to this extent, traditional understandings of miracle, supported by Thomas, though not distinctive to him, remained viable and experienced realities.[21] I want to underline the fact that Thomas's treatment of miracles comprehends a number of traditional attitudes, since, as someone like Orcibal shows, it has been possible to see the "Thomistic" perspective on miracles as an exclusive vision that somehow denies "Augustinian" epiphanic concerns any theological reflection.

It was van Hove who first made so much of the difference between a so-called Augustinian view of miracles based on the *experience* of "subjective" wonder, predominating in the tradition through the Middle Ages, and Thomas's novel formulation of miracle according to a strict model of efficient and divine causality.[22] There is no reason to dispute the advent of a new precision with Thomas, but we should still realize that his comprehensive — and broadly scattered — discussions of miracle are not aimed at proposing innovating schemes for understanding the phenomenon. All of Augustine's subjective interests remain present too, and Thomas himself is forced to acknowledge them in large measure because he continues to take seriously the experiential integrity and context of miracle. Miracles are still firmly associated with saints and holiness, with thaumaturgic power, with theophanic wonder, and with the whole range

Royal, he did so by applying a set of opposing Augustinian and Thomistic *definitions* ("La signification du miracle et sa place dans l'ecclésiologie pascalienne," in *Chroniques de Port Royal*, nos. 21–22 [1972], 83–95]. Trying to see how Pascal fit into these purportedly exclusive models proved a difficult problem. One wonders if Orcibal misjudged what was at issue. Did not the use that Houtteville made of Thomistic categories of causality to support his evidentialist arguments derive from an emerging concern with definitional models in the seventeenth century that had already begun to shut out the descriptive priority in evaluating miracles?

21. The material on traditional conceptions of miracle up to and including Thomas is extensive. In large measure it approaches the question definitionally, which has meant in practice that functionalist understandings of miracle have been emphasized. See John Hardon's helpful overview, "The Concept of Miracle from St. Augustine to Modern Apologetics," in *Theological Studies* 15 (1954): 229–57. On Augustine, there are the seminal articles by Paul de Vooght, "La notion philosophique de miracle chez saint Augustin," *Recherches de Théologie Ancienne et Mediévale* 10 (1938): 317–43; "Les miracles dans la vie de saint Augustin," in ibid., vol. 11 (1939): 5–16; and "La théologie du miracle selon saint Augustin," in ibid., 197–222. See also John Mourant, "Augustine on Miracles," in *Augustinian Studies* (1973): 103–27, and the introduction by A. Trapè, R. Russell, and S. Cotta to Augustine's *La Città di Dio* (Rome: Città Nuova Editrice, 1978), xlii–liii. On Thomas, see the still definitive work of Aloïs van Hove, *La doctrine du miracle chez saint Thomas et son accord avec les principes de la recherche scientifique* (Paris: J. Gabalda, 1927).

22. Van Hove, *La doctrine du miracle chez saint Thomas*, passim, esp. 1–26. The Augustinian definition, based on a short passage from the *De Utilitate Credendi* (16:34), had emphasized the aspect of subjective astonishment and wonder: "I call a miracle anything which appears arduous or unusual, beyond the expectation or ability of the one who marvels at it." Thomas's basic definition, on the other hand (see the *Summa Theologiae* 1a 105:7), although cognizant of Augustine's stress on the marvelous, takes off from the notion of the "beyond," but locates such transcendence in the divine causality: a miracle is that caused directly by God, exclusive of all other *possible* or naturally impossible causes.

of circumstances that elicit and are defined by the action of *admirare*. This aspect, which forms the psychological basis for later exploration of causal origin, also provides the experiential foundation for the *persuasio* whose confirming power with respect to doctrine later apologists and controversialists stressed so exclusively.[23] Admittedly, these Augustinian elements form only limited elements in Thomas's discussion of miracle as a whole.[24]

Even Augustine's own treatment of miracle is itself sufficiently fluid as to comprehend most of the distinct points upon which Thomas will later elaborate precisely, without thereby confining the phenomenon to a definitional, and thereby potentially a purely functionalist role. His interest in causality, which has sparked much debate over his notion of the *seminales rationes*,[25] tends to break down and dissolve as he confronts specific instances of experienced grace.[26] His seemingly strict apologetic concerns with respect to miracle — the confirmation of doctrine — also dissipate in the face of the proliferation of lived prodigies.

The famous text at the end of the *City of God* (22:1–9), for instance, founds its remarks on the problem of miracle as a means of conversion. But this question, in turn, has been raised by Augustine in order to illustrate the possibility of the resurrection of the flesh: the power of Apostolic miracles demonstrates the power of God that raised Jesus from the dead. Augustine darts back and forth between questions of credibility and evidence and persuasive force and causal origin. What he finally ends up presenting to the reader, however, is an extended and intriguingly detailed account of a whole series of *contemporary* miracles associated with the relics of St. Stephen, recently removed to North Africa. These are miracles of healing and transformation that Augustine knows first-hand: we hear of fistulas, blindness, conversions, gout, possessions, dangling eye-balls, the power of prayer, baptism, relics, and holy soil. There is neither order nor systematic sifting of these miracles according to type and form. Each story holds its own, and finally each is given a role to play, not so much in some grand apologetic scheme, as in a more subtle, yet divinely ordered display of divine power, of new Life itself. As if exhausted simply by the narrative effusion, by the details laid one upon the other, by what he himself calls the "sensible" "eloquence" of these divine words in the flesh, Augustine falls back merely to *view* and to be touched, with the reader, by this humanly uncontrolled though humanly specific, manifestation of God.

This experience of autonomous life (and thought) giving way to divine control, which creates of its own new and particular stories, the

---

23. See, among many instances in the *Summa*, 1a2ae 41:4; 111:4; 2a2ae 5:2; 171:1; 178:1; 180:3; 3a 15:8; 43:1.

24. The treatment in *De Potentia* Bk. III, q. 6, represents Thomas's most sustained discussion of miracle from the perspective of causality (although even here not without touching on other traditional aspects).

25. See the key texts in Augustine, *De Genesi ad litteram* 8:26; 9:16–18; *De Trinitate* III:8.

26. See the convincing discussion in Mourant, "Augustine on Miracles."

details of which conform to a marvelous power imprinting upon human life its own determined figures, is precisely the movement into a realm in which miracle defies functionalist reduction. It is also the realm of miracle as it asserts itself in the lives of the Church's living faithful. One thing that Benedicta Ward's account of medieval miracle shows is the way in which the theoretical concerns, subdued in any case at least until the thirteenth century, were always practically subordinate to the highly diverse expressions of lived miracle that the Church persistently retold because persistently presented to her common life: Eucharistic wonders, healings, shrines, relics, pilgrimages, the presence of living saints.[27] She rightly draws our attention, in closing, to Gregory the Great's depiction of St. Benedict, which can stand as a kind of summary for the experiential articulation of miracle as it could be stated for the Church as a whole: standing in a new relation to God, through the Spirit given in the incarnated and resurrected flesh of Jesus, the saint (and through him the Church) found his own sensible life — body and speech — transformed into a conduit of divine light and glory.[28] The epitome of this kind of lived relation between redeemed Church and controlling Spirit is a vision given to Benedict at the end of his life, in which the whole world is gathered up as in "a single ray of light" — an event Gregory interprets in terms of the gift of "seeing with the eyes of God."[29]

Miracle, then, is the sensible outworking of a kind of divine viewing: it takes in details and circumstances whose interwoven fabric constitutes the stories of saints and other people in given times, and whose existence stands outside any function other than the epiphanic display of God's creative and providential power. To this degree, the popular experience of miracle, and its religious articulation, stand in much closer relation to the features of Carré de Montgeron's account. The recent work of cultural historians of the seventeenth and eighteenth centuries has demonstrated the steady continuity of experience that exists through these periods, underneath the spume of theological debate over definition.[30]

To take a well-known example, we might consider the work of Henri Platelle, who in 1968 published a collection of documentary accounts of thirty-two authenticated miracles taken from churches in seventeenth-century Lille.[31] These stand as only a fraction of a much more significant number of alleged miracles in the city that were never given official approval for publication for various reasons, but whose experience was at

---

27. Benedicta Ward, *Miracles and the Medieval Mind: Theory, Record, and Event 1000–1215* (Philadelphia: University of Pennsylvania Press, 1987).

28. Ibid., 216ff.

29. See Gregory the Great, *Dialogues*, trans. Odo John Zimmerman, O.S.B. (New York: Fathers of the Church, Inc., 1959), 58, 73, 82, 96, 98, 105ff. (Dialogue II).

30. See the bibliography given in Louis Chatellier's "Le miracle baroque," in *Histoire des miracles* (Angers: Presses de l'Université d'Angers, 1983), 92f.

31. Henri Platelle, *Les chrétiens face au miracle: Lille au XVIIe siècle* (Paris: Les Éditions du Cerf, 1968).

least as pressing as officially corroborated prodigies. The character of these miracles — healings and exorcisms mostly — follows several clear features.

First, the importance of specific circumstances to the formal meaning of the various miracles is critical. These circumstances ranged from the larger conflict with Protestantism (and later Jansenism!), the opening of new shrines and the promoting of new devotions (e.g., to St. Ignatius of Loyola), to the carefully detailed stories of the sick and their search for relief, tales of despair and extended failure, the orchestration of prayer and the temporal embodiment of faith on the part of friends and colleagues within the Church.

Second, we see in all of these accounts ways in which the miracle forms part — often a motivating part — of a larger community configuration of sensible shape. Groups of people are brought together not only around new devotions, but into sets of relationships that render actual physical forms: new spaces and buildings, choreographed prayers, and the decoration of spaces through *ex-voto* images and official art. Most such artwork provide sensual displays of healing and divine power whose multiplication redefines the context of communal prayer into a physical figure in which the human body and its weakness mirrors the intimate inclusion of God. Chapels are crowdedly filled with hanging replicas of legs and children, with small paintings detailing the stories of relief brought and the images of saints and heaven through whom graces have been received. The stories and circumstances themselves become literal figures of the encroaching presence of God.[32]

Finally, and most obviously, all these miracles give rise, in the midst of these individual lives, to testifying expressions of "joy," "astonishment" and "wonder," to effusions of prayer and delight, to the fast-spreading fervent tales of divine visitation throughout the city: God has acted, God is here in this or that place, God has made His touch and His visibility one and the same. The miracles are, supremely, acts of divine manifestation, whose appearance stands on its own and elicits reactions dependent on nothing but the hereness of God.

In all of this, we should acknowledge how the elements of the official *inquiries* into the miracles represent concerns divergent from these popular features, but also how they remain strangely ancillary to the effect of the dossiers as a whole. The testimony of witnesses, of medical doctors, and of Church leaders all seem to be governed by just the kinds of evidentialist concerns that, on a more abstract scale, will characterize the theoretical concern with miracles taken by theological controversialists. But their roles are small, and clearly serve a limited purpose, one that ultimately is designed to unveil yet more fully a marvel that was always initially clear, yet until this point confined to the experience of a few.

---

32. On the sensual construction and recreation of a miraculous world through the proliferation of *ex-voto* images, see Bernard Cousin, *Le miracle et le quotidien: Les ex-voto provençaux images d'une société* (Aix-en-Provence: Sociétés, Mentalités, Cultures, 1983).

The inquiries serve as a form of publicity, just as much as they fulfill the function of discerning and exposing imposture.[33]

These primary characteristics of the popular experience of miracle, however, cannot simply be identified with those features we proposed for the Appellants. The epiphanic aspect predominates, as do the circumstantial elements. Still, they do so in a very constricted fashion: these are small stories, and the grace of God revealed through them seems cut to scale. To some degree, the figurative quality of the miracles and their arrangement within communities represent both a meaning so broad as to be almost indistinct — the body as locus of divine communication — and so personal as to be grasped only in isolation. Unlike the case of Dom Palacios, a blinded eye in this world does not display the Exodus of Israel and the Church.

In short, however non-functionally the miracle may be experienced, it is nonetheless revealed and grasped in a purely punctiliar fashion. The miracles are not tools; yet nor are they comprehended in the larger figures that constitute the history of God's dealings with the world and the Church. They simply happen in the midst of distinctive (though not uncommon) struggles with pain. Their context, for all its varied particulars, remains static, much like the (differently construed) worlds of historical uniformity in which the Reformers and their opponents did battle.

## Factors Involved in the Development of the Appellant Experience of Miracle

In the light of this comparative overview, it is now possible to trace, by way of contrast, the effects of four factors involved in the Jansenist development toward a general view of miracle like that of Carré de Montgeron. What appears to be a combination of wider historical attitudes, purely Catholic sensibilities, and peculiarly Jansenist theological concerns and experiences seems to provide, in the end, the framework out of which the Appellant experience of miracle can take shape.

---

33. To acknowledge this relationship between inquiry and experience here in the seventeenth century is to raise from the start a note of caution concerning the alleged "positivistic" attitude toward miracles that Carré de Montgeron will evidence, in contrast with, e.g., Pascal. See J. R. Armogathe, "A propos des miracles de Saint-Médard: Les preuves de Carré de Montgeron et le positivisme des Lumières," *Revue de l'Histoire des Religions* 87 (1971): 135–60 (esp. 140–48). That the eighteenth century adopts certain forms of expression, and that Appellants emphasize certain elements of the traditional examination of miracles does not, on the face of it, constitute a "new" understanding of how to relate to the phenomenon of miracle itself. Indeed, it is difficult to see how the "positivistic" detailing of evidence that is present in Carré de Montgeron's dossiers is anything but a more extensive version of the ancillary method of public "unveiling" that was already in place in most post-Tridentine dioceses like that in which Lille was located. Were it the case that the investigation overwhelms the story — as it does in the minds of many who attack the Jansenist miracles — then we could speak of a new relation. In the case of such opponents to Jansenism, however, we are asked to wonder if the relation is determined so much by a cultural mindset as by simple unbelief.

A first and general factor we can identify in this development is the concern for credible evidence deriving from the apologetic construal of miracle as functionally confirming of doctrine. Early Jansenist theologians were no more immune to this prevailing attitude than other churchpeople. Spurred by controversialist energies against Protestants and atheists as well as by desires to establish the historical basis for the authority they claimed supported their primitivist vision of the Church, Jansenist scholars adopted what were to become new standards of modern "critical" investigation into historical documents. Led by hagiographers like Robert Arnauld d'Andilly and others, the great Jansenist historians Le Nain de Tillemont and Claude Fleury were among the models of classical critical demeanor in the face of the Church's past legends and claims, judiciously sifting through the evidence for, among other things, alleged miracles and wonders performed by saints in the past.

In part, this kind of critical reappraisal of the tradition about the miraculous came as a direct response, on its own territory, to the critique of the miraculous in general by sceptics like La Mothe le Vayer and Gabriel Naudé, whose dismissal of so much of the Church's tradition relied less on metaphysical prejudices than on the "incredible" nature of the supporting evidence. Jansenists, like other Catholic apologists, were keen to defend that tradition, but only by acceding to the critical demands of these *libertins érudits*. By the early eighteenth century, the famous Jansenist hagiographer Adrien Baillet could publish his multivolume Lives of the Saints in a form that called into question almost all the more famous miracles attributed to them.[34]

Still, in the spirit of post-Tridentine apology as a whole, this kind of serious reappraisal of the historical tradition was adopted with the sole purpose of burnishing the credibility of the Catholic Church's testimony, not undermining it. If miracles were to function as persuasive evidence for Catholic claims (and later, for peculiarly Jansenist claims as to the authority of certain Fathers of the early Church), such miracles must be specifically identified and critically authenticated. We could call this critical effort, then, not a debunking of miracle, but a clearing up of the historical clutter left by too many spurious prodigies.

From the Jansenists' point of view, therefore — along with other apologists' — the critical task with respect to miracles would be to provide a new context of clarity. This is the second factor we need to distinguish in the development of the particularly Appellant view of miracle. With the deck cleared of legend, true miracles would reveal themselves in all their proper relationships: they could be properly "effective" in their retelling.

---

34. On the "critical" element of Jansenist historiography with respect to miracles, see Tetsuya Shiokawa, *Pascal et les miracles* (Paris: Librairie A.-G. Nizet, 1977), 16–30 (on the *libertins érudits*); Bernard Tocanne, *L'Idée de Nature en France*, 115–27; *Histoire des saints et de la sainteté chrétienne*, ed. Bernard Plongeron and Claude Savart (Paris: Hachette, 1987), 9:22ff.

The critical program was to serve as a prelude to the rendering of divine *sensibilité* in all of its distinctions, in order that faith might become firm.

Arnauld, for instance, in the *Logique, ou l'art de penser* caps the entire work with a discussion of the place miracles (and other historical events) might hold in the process of "reasoning." In a way that presages Houtteville's treatment of the "mysteries" of the faith, Arnauld distinguishes two grounds for appropriate belief in the truth of something: the senses and reason, on the one hand, and authority on the other, whether divine or human. We believe in Christ, for instance, according to divine authority; yet however obscure this may be, it is never blind faith. For we believe

> when we know the cause [of a thing], and because it is a reasonable action when, once He has given us sufficient proofs, we subject ourselves to the authority of God. Such proofs include, for instance, miracles and other prodigies, which oblige us to believe that God Himself has disclosed to us the truths we ought to believe.[35]

Miracles, then, form the "sensible" (and thus "reasonable") basis for religious belief.

What follows next is a set of rules for determining the credibility of a historical event, of which miracles are a sub-species. Arnauld uses a number of examples drawn from contemporary critical research into ecclesiastical and textual history and shows on what basis one might judge one account of an event more credible or at least probable over another. He ends, however, with a long and detailed summary of Augustine's relation of the miracles of St. Stephen's relics drawn from the *City of God*. What is his purpose in repeating these miracle stories? He does not analyze them; he does not subject each to any critical test. It seems instead that Arnauld wishes to provide an example of the *experience* that a *preuve sensible* can offer to one who is contemplating questions of the faith. In this context, the critical establishment of miracle, by way of evidence and for the purpose of evidence, gives way, as we saw earlier, to a lived sense of being "captivated," in Arnauld's term, by the power of God. If this is "evidence," it is a kind of properly "psychological" evidence whose power demonstrates its origin, yet just for that reason eludes a final definition. Hence, Arnauld is willing to speak of "moral certitudes" deriving from the evidence of historical events that, although on one level less compelling than "metaphysical certitudes" of logic, are nonetheless more crucial in the realm of religious belief.[36]

Just this placement of miracle's evidential experience within the realm of the "moral" life — the meta-empirical world of divine communication and sensibility — gives rise to the problematic that informs the third factor in our brief analysis of the developing Appellant experience of miracle. That is, to the degree that we live in a world deformed by pervasive sin,

---

35. Antoine Arnauld, *Logique* (1683), IV:12, in his *Oeuvres*, 41–42: 396.
36. Ibid., chapter 15, 405.

it is exactly within the realm of life where "moral certitude" might function that evidence becomes ambiguous, that experience is warped and
thus misleading. On this issue, the peculiarly pessimistic elements of
the Jansenist theological outlook provide a perspective on miracle that
is unique.

We have already seen how Luther made much of the contestability
and thus inherent ambiguity of miracle as evidence. He speaks instead
of "hidden" miracle and "obscured" holiness, incorporating these religious
phenomena into a more expansive and determining theology of the Cross:
sensible evidence, indeed divine sensibility whether evidential or not —
is not possible *by definition* because of the nature of divine humiliation
in the self-giving of Christ. Jansenists, by contrast, began to see in the
contestability of miracles not so much a reason to reject them altogether
by definition, but yet another manifested embodiment of the reality of
faithlessness in the world, another example of sin. And, in the context of
their Augustinian predestinarianism, they concluded that the visibility of
miracle, its evidential possibilities, its epiphanic being and critical linkage within historically divine configurations depended on the providential
ordering of grace and reprobation, of light and darkness, of illumination
and blindness. That true miracle, anchored in the realm of the psychology
of sensible wonder and astonishment, was also chained in this still-fallen
world to the reality of *aveuglement* [blindness] was the great and motivating Jansenist insight provided through the reflections of Pascal, among
others.

We have already seen in the last section how the Jansenist notion of *sensibilité* eventually settled around the form of Christ in his mysteries — an
understanding of the sensible that collapses the spiritual (the Spirit itself)
into particular and exclusive historical forms of experience. We should
now note the implications of this collapse from the side of the historically
sensible in particular: such sensible experience becomes a compelling element only as it is transfigured through its assumption into the form of
Christ's Spirit. Thus, the distinguishing qualities of a miraculous event,
*frappant, sensible, palpable*, can be grasped as such only as they are spiritually inhabited, only as they have been divinely adopted and distributed
in the *ostensio Spiritus*. Unbelievers are blind to the miraculous in all of
its topography, but not because of some quality inherent in the character
of such events *qua* events. Rather, the configuration of belief and unbelief,
of sight and blindness, of sense and numbness, follows the ordered shape
of the providentially — pneumatically — embodied Christ. Miracles, thus,
mark the boundaries and the lines that shape the map of a *single* divine
history, but because of this fact are not defined by some set of *universally*
sensible arrangements.

This particular Jansenist response to what we might call the "functionalist impasse" of miracle was able to follow its peculiar path, in contrast
with forms of Protestantism, in large measure because of the constraints
imposed upon its articulation by the Catholic tradition and experience

of miracle itself. This constitutes the final factor that must provide the basis for the Appellant experience of miracle. Luther, in particular, used the ambiguity of miracle not only to justify its rejection altogether, but that rejection itself allowed him to differentiate the true Church from the realm of Satan. The strict loyalties for the Catholic Church held by the Jansenists, instead, demanded that any ambiguity, any role or experience of miracle and its rejection that might contribute to a cartography of faith must be exercised firmly *within* the boundaries of the Church itself.

Thus, to some extent, a further ambiguity was inserted by Jansenists into the experience of miracle, whereby its power to trace the lines of configurated destiny in belief and unbelief was to be subsumed in the more comprehensive, yet positive, figure of the Church itself. The fate of miracles and their experience — including their contestability and rejection — in this case, does not mark off parts of history, as with the Protestants; rather, it testifies to the very shape of the Body of Christ in a pneumatically integrated temporal sphere.

This is precisely what Carré de Montgeron is expressing when he speaks of bishops scoffing at Dom de Palacios's healing: the scoffing itself is joined organically to the sensible restoration of sight. As a pair they are held together figuratively by God, as orbs in the sky, as the pillar of cloud and fire, as the Exodus, as the ministry of Jesus among Pharisees, as the unitary work of God's fashioning of history according to the form of Christ's mystery, "in mercy and judgment." But it is *one* form, not the division of history into competing forms.

The three features of Carré de Montgeron's description of miracle — non-punctiliar and circumstantial, non-functional and figurative, and epiphanic — each gain their structural moorings from these factors, just as these factors themselves fit within an abstracted theology of grace that reflectively informs the experience of *pneumatica* for Jansenists. Insofar as they mutually influence and depend upon each other, it is not possible to draw strict lines of genesis between them (especially given the broadly schematic nature of their articulation here). But that has not been the point of this exercise. Beginning with a hypothesis of distinctiveness, I believe we can now offer at least a tentative affirmation of the peculiar character of Jansenist miracle as it is finally experienced in the course of the Appellant engagement in the *ostensio Spiritus*. It is a peculiarity that would seem at first glance to tie in closely with the more purely theological structures of grace we examined earlier, but here bound up with particular events and experiences that, in themselves, are divine givens independent of theological predisposition. In a major sense, it is this last bond between theology and event that must be established if the prior structures are to have any validity. Tracing some of the connections and the divergences of these experiences with other aspects of the surrounding Christian tradition has allowed us to situate Appellant miracle in a general context from whose midst we can now apply a more detailed investigation.

*Chapter Six*

# MIRACLE AND
# CLASSICAL JANSENISM

## Outline of the Chapter

Taking up some of the general features of Jansenist miracle as we have just
outlined them — circumstantial, figurative, and epiphanic — this chapter
will examine in detail how these features were explicated theologically by
early apologists for Port-Royal, by Pascal, and by Arnauld.

The first part of the chapter looks at the 1656 miraculous healing of
Pascal's niece through the presence of a relic at the Paris convent of Port-
Royal. We begin with a small treatise written anonymously by friends
of the nuns in defense of the miracle, not only as being genuine, but as
being a positive sign of divine blessing on the convent. The way these
writers present the miracle, in relation to traditional ways of construing
such events, points to a Jansenist vision that is already moving in the directions earlier indicated as characteristic. Pascal's subsequent reflections
on miracle, spurred also in large measure by the healing of his niece,
carries this movement further and construes miracle in an explicitly figurative manner, as a sensible sign of God's justice and mercy embodied in
the Cross.

In the last part of the chapter, we will look at how Antoine Arnauld
proposed a more general theory about the sensibly figurative character of
miracle, understood as an element of historical providence. Arnauld's reflections on the Port-Royal miracle of the Holy Thorn are less instructive
here than are his more mature philosophical considerations of the relation of God's will to historical experience. These are developed during the
course of his debate with Malebranche over perceptual epistemology and
divine *volontés* (decisions of the will).

The chapter concludes with a question about the controversial implications of this vision of figurative sensibility, particularly as it touches on
the notion of the Appellant ecclesiastical struggle. If divine sensibility, in
its miraculous and epiphanic character, is given primary historical embodiment in the experience of belief and unbelief, how are we to assess the
place of human agency in the course of a critical theological conflict like
that of Appellancy (or any other historically developmental episode that
involves pneumatic direction)? Figuration implies a certain answer to this
question.

# The Miracle of the Holy Thorn

The eighteenth-century editors of Arnauld's complete works were not the first to draw the connection between the Appellant miracles of Saint-Médard and the 1656 healing at Port-Royal in Paris of Pascal's niece, Marguerite Perrier. Bishop Colbert of Montpellier had done so in 1727, publishing for the first time several of Pascal's *pensées* on miracles as an appendix to his third letter to the bishop of Soissons concerning the recent outbreak of Appellant prodigies.[1] Marguerite Perrier herself, then an old woman, saw the new wonders at Saint-Médard as but the manifestation of a grace that had worked in divine continuity with the healing she had received as a girl when lodging among the persecuted nuns of the Jansenist headquarters.[2] But Arnauld's editors, writing in the 1770s, explicitly draw attention to the *theological* continuity and commonality that, in their minds, informed the reflections on miracles from these two different eras. Referring to Arnauld's unfinished *De l'autorité des miracles* of 1657, the editors write with respect to Pascal and Colbert:

> One can see how M. Pascal and M. the Bishop of Montpellier have applied these principles to the miracle of the Holy Thorn, just as the same Bishop has done to the miracle performed in Paris on Madame la Fosse in 1725 by the Holy Sacrament, and to other miracles performed after this in favor of the defenders of true doctrine. We can see how [Colbert's] principles and reasonings are the same as those of M. Arnauld, and we can consider the *pensées* of M. Pascal and the writings of the Bishop as properly filling in the gaps left in Doctor [Arnauld's] Treatise on Miracles, which was never finished.[3]

Neither Pascal nor Arnauld, obviously, lived to see the development of Jansenist Appellancy, let alone the proliferation of miracles associated with the movement that began in the 1720s. And the later eighteenth-century claim for continuity with the "golden age" of Port-Royal was perhaps the rationalization of wishful thinking and self-justification in the shadow of a disintegrated movement covered with opprobrium. Still, identification of some common *interpretive* relation to miracles across these two periods is worth noting, since it is exactly the hypothesis with which we are working. And we can ask now, with respect to Marguerite Perrier, the young girl healed in 1656, and Marguerite Perrier, the eighty-year-old woman watching the unfolding of a new act in the divine drama of which she had

---

1. Charles-Joachim Colbert, *Oeuvres*, vol. 2, 249–68.

2. Kreiser, *Miracles, Convulsions, and Ecclesiastical Politics in Early Eighteenth-Century Paris*, 70–72.

3. Arnauld, *Oeuvres*, vol. 23, "Preface historique et critique," xi. On the editors of this monumental and historically significant series of Arnauld's complete works — Claude-Pierre Goujet, Gabriel du Pac de Bellegarde, and Jean Hautefage — any one of whom may have penned the introduction to this particular volume, see Émile Jacques, "Un anniversaire: l'édition des Oeuvres complètes d'Antoine Arnauld (1775–1783)" in *Revue d'Histoire Ecclésiastique* 70, nos. 3–4 (1975): 705–30.

formed an opening scene, What unifying character is constructed by this chaining of events?

Marguerite's healing forms the symbolic motor to the Jansenist articulation of lived miracle. It stands as the basis for both Pascal's and Arnauld's initial reflections on the topic in general. Although other miracles followed, it was this one in particular, officially authenticated by the Church, that embodied in the minds of many Jansenists an object of divine display that would comprehend the figure of any other miracle that might and would succeed it.

Marguerite was related to Pascal through her mother, Gilberte, who was the writer's sister.[4] The girl's ailment first surfaced when she was six years old, in late 1652. What began as a seeming irritation of her left eye, manifested in a continual teariness, soon developed into an obvious infection of some sort, diagnosed as a "lachrymal fistula." Cauterization was the recommended procedure, but Marguerite's parents hesitated in the face of such a painful operation. Instead they sent her to Paris, to lodge at the convent of the Port-Royal nuns in the city, an order of which her older sister Jacqueline was a member. While there, a doctor had promised to cure her within six months through use of a water treatment.

But the effects of the illness did not ease, and Marguerite's health deteriorated under the regime. There now appeared to be a kind of small tumor beneath the surface of the skin and pus began to drain from the eye, the nose, and into the back of the throat, the smell of which became increasingly hard for others to tolerate. The little girl herself lost the sense of smell, and she was separated from the other girls. While some of the consulting doctors now felt the disease to be incurable, an attempt at the operation "by fire" was finally deemed necessary. Marguerite's uncle, Blaise Pascal, had been looking after the girl's interests while in Paris and informing her parents in Clermont of the doctors' recommendations. At the beginning of March 1656, he pressed the father to come immediately, in order to be with his daughter for the operation. But only days before his arrival, the girl was suddenly cured.

The remarkable healing took place on March 24, on a Friday in the third week of Lent. For the first time, it seems, the convent had put on display in a small side altar in the chapel a reliquary recently donated by a local priest containing a thorn purportedly from the Holy Crown worn by Jesus at his crucifixion. It had been decided to use the relic as a focus of prayer on the Passion of the Lord. The mistress of the girls who lodged at the convent brought in her charges, and they prayed before the thorn. Marguerite herself approached the relic and kissed it. Mistress Flavie, noting how horrible the girl's eye appeared, then took the additional

---

4. For the narrative that follows, I am relying on Shiokawa's discussion in *Pascal et les miracles,* chapter 3 (76–118). Readers will find there ample archival references as well as discussions of other modern investigations of the material.

step of bringing the reliquary down and placing it in contact with the eye itself.

The girls then returned to their rooms. But Marguerite, feeling that a miracle would take place, began to say a novena to the Holy Crown. Within fifteen minutes, she felt the pain disappear. Within two hours, she informed her elder sister and the girls' mistress, Sr. Flavie Passart. They beheld in astonishment a girl whose left eye now seemed completely normal. The swellings had disappeared. They pressed the edges, and no fluids or pus came out. Over the next few days Marguerite was examined by two doctors associated with Port-Royal, who confirmed the cure. Pascal himself saw her on March 29 and called for the official surgeon of the convent, who, upon examination, called the healing "complete and miraculous."

After a few weeks, a dossier of medical attestations was put together, and, in response to this and to the growing public discussion and rumor of the miracle, the archbishop of Paris's vicar general began an official process of verification. The results were positive, and on October 22, 1656, Marguerite's healing was proclaimed by the Church an authentic miracle "beyond nature," worked by the grace of God.

Even before the official authentication was publicized, the miracle of the Holy Thorn had become a subject of lively debate. People began to flock to the Port-Royal chapel to see the thorn, and other miracles of healing were reported. And while the relic was moved outside the convent for devotional reasons, it seemed to bring cures only at Port-Royal itself. Members of the nobility soon began visiting, including the exiled queen of England. The nuns had, at the time, been under intense pressure and persecution over the issue of the Five Propositions supposedly from Jansenius condemned by Pope Innocent X in 1653: Arnauld had already been expelled from the Sorbonne, the Petites Écoles of the Port-Royal de Champs convent outside of Paris dispersed, and the Paris house cited for closure. But now the situation eased somewhat within the flow of these new and exciting events, the queen herself taking an interest in their development. Although originally it was just a momentary and isolated healing, a whole set of circumstances now sprang from Marguerite's little eye that figured, for the nuns at least and their supporters, as a larger miracle of historical intervention on behalf of Port-Royal's cause.

Very quickly, then, the miracle seemed to have become the lynchpin of some larger divine event. Or, at least, the miracle seemed to control larger events according to the mechanics of some divine reason. What was the character of this evolution? It is odd, in perusing the documentary material assembled for a discussion of this question by someone like Shiokawa, to note how the implications of the miracle never surpass the defined shape of the miracle itself. That is, whatever meaning is to be gleaned from the healing seems to be revealed in the minds of the participants only as an image emerging from the accumulation of evidences, of facts, of dates and witnesses, and finally and most importantly, of the details of the healing itself, told, retold, researched, examined, and lifted up. The larger figure of the narrative, if it is to be grasped, can be so apprehended only from the touch of the innumerable points of contact that are to be had from coming close to the passage of a young girl's body from illness to health. What did she feel? What were her symptoms? Who saw them and can describe them in the most exact and vital manner?

Consider this lengthy initial description from the first public polemical defense of the miracle put out by associates of Port-Royal:

> M. de la Poterie was, by title and piety, a churchman. For some time now he had among the relics of his chapel a holy Thorn, from Our Lord's Crown. Having sent it to the Carmelite nuns, who had a holy curiosity to see it, he also sent it to Port-Royal on Friday, March 24th of last year. These nuns received [the relic] with enormous devotion: they placed it in their choir on a table laid out as an altar, and after singing the Antiphon of the Holy Crown, they would kiss it. There was a young lodger at the convent, named Marguerite Perrier. For three and a half years she had suffered from a "lachrymal fistula," and now she took her turn to go up and kiss [the relic]. The nun in charge, who had been more deeply concerned than ever about the swelling and resulting deformity of [the girl's] eye, felt moved to bring the relic in contact with her ailment, for she believed that God was sufficiently good and sufficiently powerful to heal it.
>
> The nun did not think more about it. But the little girl went back to her room, and after fifteen minutes noticed that the ailment had been cured. When she told her companions, they found that indeed, it had disappeared. There was no longer any tumor present: the eye, swollen almost shut and teary all the time over three years, was now as dry, as healthy, as lively as the other eye. The drainage that ran from one moment to the next from the eye, from her nose and mouth, and was in fact running down her cheek just before the miracle — as she attested to in her declaration — had now dried up completely. The bone [of her nose] which had decayed and rotted, was now returned to its original condition, and the foul odor that it had emitted, so awful that the doctors and surgeons ordered that she be separated from the others, had now changed into a breath whose sweetness was like a child's. At the same time, she recovered her sense of smell, which she had lost because of the ill effects of the pus that came from her nose, and all the other problems that resulted from this also disappeared, even to the point that her pallor, so pale and gray, became once again lively and light, just as before.[5]

The *Reponse* from which this is drawn was a hastily written reply to an anonymous attack on Port-Royal's justificatory claim to the miracle, both works appearing during the summer before the offical authenticating pronouncement. Although the editors of Arnauld's works argue for Arnauld's authorship, there is reason to believe that the tract represents a collaborative effort on the part of many theological supporters of Port-

---

5. *Reponse a un ecrit publié sur le sujet du miracle qu'il a plu a Dieu de faire a Port-Royal depuis quelque temps, Par une Sainte Epine de la Couronne de Notre Seigneur* (1656), in Antoine Arnauld, *Oeuvres*, vol. 23, 10.

Royal, including perhaps Arnauld and Pascal together among them.[6] The point, however, is that while the work represents an explicitly *theological* analysis of the importance of the miracle, such analysis is fundamentally circumscribed by the descriptive detail of the healing itself. The careful summary of the illness, paraphrasing, it appears, from the depositions provided by the girl and others — to be used in the official inquiry no less — offers the only basis upon which explicit theological understanding will be gained. In particular, the quantity, origin, and stink of the pus, among other things, limits and informs any further evaluation to be made of the event. Yet, the shape of this suppuration, tied to the minutes of the day, the dates of the year, and the cold surface of a reliquary, provide the justification for the following claim, made immediately after the descriptive summary we have just read:

> In the face of this miracle, which should bring about eruptions and transports of spiritual joy, what person of piety could not join in them in the way that St. Augustine did, when he recounts, in *The City of God*, the healing of a young man who had been cursed by his mother and suffered from an ongoing trembling throughout the limbs of his body? "The Church," he wrote, "is filled and ringing with these cries of joy: Glory to God! Praise be to God!"[7]

While the authors go on to note, in contrast, the discretion of the nuns in the face of Marguerite's healing, their judgment on the event is firmly enunciated through its linkage with Augustine's famous catena of prodigies: each detail of the girl's suffering eye and participation in the transformation of bodily experience marks the inescapable glorification of God.

It is important to stress the character of this axiomatic judgment from the beginning. If the *Reponse* is the first systematic articulation of a Jansenist perspective on miracle — just as Marguerite Perrier's healing stands as the axiomatic moment of Jansenistic miracle itself — then this way of construing its shape will provide a set of limits to the discussion that will play a decisive role for future reflection. The limits themselves can be summarized in the phrase "epiphanic sensibility": whether it be the shadow of the day, or the odor of the breath, or the tincture of the visage, each sensibly felt pressure of the miracle's shape reveals some self-confirming image of the Deity.

The *Reponse* outlines this vision of miracle as epiphanic sensibility in a number of ways. The attack to which it was replying[8] had made much of the fact that miracles, in the history of the Church, were often admonitory events whose power acted as a negative guide for the unbelieving. In other

6. See the "Preface historique et critique" to vol. 23 of Arnauld's *Oeuvres*; see also, Orcibal, "La signification du miracle et sa place dans l'ecclésiologie pascalienne," in *Chroniques de Port Royal,* 88, and Shiokawa, *Pascal et les miracles,* 106f.

7. *Reponse,* ibid.

8. *Rabat-joie des jansénistes ou Observations nécessaires sur ce qu'on dit être arrivé au Port-Royal au sujet de la sainte Epine, par un Docteur de l'Eglise catholique* (1656?).

words, the central purpose of miracles was for the conversion or at least the public overthrow of heretics and infidels. This interpretation was based on a rather tendentious reading of 1 Corinthians 14:22ff. ("tongues are a sign not for believers but for unbelievers"), the point of which was to claim that, while the healing of Marguerite may have been genuine, its occurrence could not be taken as a positive blessing from God on Port-Royal, but must rather be taken as the opposite: a divine warning to the Jansenist nuns that they return to the teaching of the Catholic Church. The *Reponse*'s brief is to establish a normative reading of miracle that understands its primary character in terms of a *positive* and sensible divine self-demonstration. On these terms, the healing's occurrence within the convent of Port-Royal can be grasped only under the rubric of blessing and not of terror.

In specifying their meaning, the authors of the *Reponse* remain faithful to an Augustinian premise, that miracles stand, in some fashion, as the unveiling of the invisible God. Quoting from Augustine directly, they describe divine prodigies as "miraculous works that render visible, as it were, the presence of the invisible God" (Tract. in Joan. 8).[9] The affirmation of *présence*, however, is critical. From the first, and despite subsequent and understandable qualifications, the miracle is here taken as more than a cipher, as more than a sign, whose being serves to lead participants away from itself toward some distanced and otherwise protected truth. In and of itself, the miracle is God's presence, God's own being, rendered "visible."

The authors, again working from Augustinian citations, make much of the sensible distinctions and implications to be drawn from the notion of "visibility" and "presence." In general, they come down to the distinction between "eye" and "ear," a distinction that, on the level of sensibility is not so clear until it is realized that the two organs stand as images of the contrast between bodily sense and intellectual reasoning. Affirming later the "sign" function of the miracle in Thomistic terms — the miracles are "signs [ . . . ] that always signify and mark out some truth to human beings" — the definition is immediately located in presentative terms: "this language is even more divine that words," for God is "the truth itself."[10] Miracles are indeed a language, and hence gain their meaning within a system of signs. But, in Augustine's terms, these are almost "natural" signs, whose own existence presents and encompasses the thing signified itself — a possibility in this case only because the *significatum* (that which is signified) and the *virtus significandi* (the power of signifying) is God Himself: God's language is in fact the presence of God to human flesh.

Thus, the contrast between "body" and "speech" points to a contrast between two realms of being, in which, surprisingly, human reasoning is seen as less divine than the orchestrated and experienced sequence of physical phenomena. "Human beings explain themselves in words, but

---

9. *Reponse.*, 7.
10. Ibid., 15.

God speaks by actions";[11] and, "his [God's] miracles are, as it were, his eloquence, which is understood, not by the ear, but is grasped by the eye and
the spirit [*esprit*]."[12] This kind of overt appeal to physical phenomena and
to the physical senses as a supreme means of divine self-communication
is indeed surprising, given the background neo-Platonist suspicion of the
senses that informs virtually all elements of religious epistemology in the
period. Even the developing, and peculiar, notions of *sensibilité* among
Oratorian and Jansenist writers, such as we have earlier examined, do not
quite prepare the reader for such bald (if, as the literal citations suggest,
still traditionally rooted) assertions. *Esprit* is tied to visibility, to the capacity to see, and presumably to touch; it is therefore an element of the
human constitution that is the most divinely "touchable," or impression-
able — that aspect that moors a person most firmly within the created
environment that is most closely tied to God's immediate direction. *Les
oreilles* [the ears], by contrast, imply a distanced ratiocination according to
conceptual schemes, whose capacity to provide sure knowledge is severely
limited.

It would be a mistake, then, simply to see the primary appeal to the
senses here simply as a reflection of some general and burgeoning empiricism. The primacy of the ocular derives from and is relevant to a
specific set of circumstances in which God takes immediate shape within
the created order. Indeed, such special circumstances are by definition
miraculous. But this peculiar set of limits to the revelatory function of
"sight" itself relies on a particular characteristic of God: "God speaks by
actions," not by words. It is this broader reality that implies a loosening of
the constraints that define the miraculous and opens up the presentative
possibilities of God's self to a larger swath of the generally "historical."

If we remember Arnauld's discussion at the end of the *Logique,* we can
see a more systematically presented parallel to this way of understanding
the appeal to the miraculous as to a special character of revelatory sensibility. Arnauld had distinguished two ways in which we believe something
to be true: according to reason, and according to authority. In both cases,
however, the role of sensibility is central. In the first — knowledge by
reason — he tells us that reason works only by making use of the material furnished to it by the senses. Indeed, while we can speak of such a
thing as "direct" knowledge by the senses, as well as pure "reasoning," in
both forms we actually experience an inextricably joined activity of sense-
reasoning, where it is more a matter of one aspect predominating over,
than of one side excluding the other.

With respect to our belief in some truth on the basis of authority, Arnauld had insisted that only divine authority could adequately found such
knowledge. But if so founded, he stressed, the knowledge was infallible.
Yet, we recall, Arnauld defines divine "authority" as "reasonable" in that

---

11. Ibid., 18, quoting from Augustine's 49th Epistle.
12. Ibid., quoting Augustine, *De Civitate Dei* 22:8.

its human acceptance is based on sense-reasoning. This in turn derives from the encounter with "sufficient proofs, such as miracles and other prodigies, which oblige us to believe that it is He [God] himself who reveals to people the truths that we should believe."[13]

The foundation for Arnauld's claim here is twofold, and is exactly that put forward in the earlier *Reponse*. That is, that, within a given context of events as a whole, the visibility of God is evident in particular events and is to be trusted because "God is no deceiver." Sensibility as divinely presentative — that is, as the properly miraculous — functions only within a *divinely guaranteed set of circumstances*. The *Reponse* turns to this principle of God's reliability in discussing the Thomistic concept of the miracle's causal origin: a miracle is that which is "visibly" beyond the forces of nature and is therefore attributable only to an infinite power, i.e., to God.[14]

Little is made of this causal definition, however, since the polemic here defends not the authenticity of the miracle, but its significance with respect to Port-Royal. In an effort to counter the *Rabat-joie*'s contention that a miracle is primarily directed toward unbelievers (and hence, the nuns of Port-Royal must be considered heretics), the authors now turn to the principle of divine "reliability": an obvious miracle cannot be such as to confuse people about the truth that may be at stake. Would God perform a miracle at Port-Royal, setting off a whole set of events that drew people to the convent in praise and admiration, that seemed to provide consolation and strength, joy and praise to the nuns, if in fact God's purpose had been to confound the Jansenist doctrines supposedly held by the sisters? The principle appealed to here is that used by Jesus himself when the people tried to stone him in Jerusalem: evident miracles *confirm* the person who performs them as divinely approved: "If I am not doing the works of my Father, then do not believe me; but if I do them, even though you do not believe me, believe the works, that you may know and understand that the Father is in me and I am in the Father" (John 10:37–38).[15]

It is interesting to note here that a scriptural principle that, on the face of it, appears to use miracles as punctiliar marks of confirmation for a person who is seen as separate from his circumstances ("... if you do not believe me ... ") is in fact applied by the writers of the *Reponse* to the circumstances themselves, which only subsequently (logically speaking) confirm the miracle in its work as "divine mark." For the premise of God's "reliability" is defined, not in terms of the "work" itself, but in terms of its context: God never lets miracles be done in circumstances that could lead to error.[16] Miracle and context are inextricably bound together in their disclosive power. Thus, the writers affirm the probity of the nuns of Port-Royal in terms of the effects of Marguerite's healing on the

---

13. Antoine Arnauld, *Logique* (1683), IV:12, in his *Oeuvres*, 41–42: 395–96.
14. *Reponse*, 15.
15. Ibid.
16. Ibid.

public: increased devotion to prayer, to the praise of God, to the Passion, to the Eucharist, in short, to the means of salvation offered in the Catholic Church.[17]

Indeed, beginning with a view of miracle as a peculiar phenomenon causally considered, the writers of the *Reponse* have redefined this causality in terms of a configuration of events, whose convicting totality is upheld by the axiom of God's orchestrating direction of contextual circumstance as a whole. And what — to pursue the parallel between the two works — in Arnauld's *Logique* appears at first to be the simple enunciation of a critical standard applied to all historical investigation, is, in this case at least, shown to be dependent on a vigorous belief in the divine configuration of history. "In order to judge the truth of an event and determine whether I should believe it or not, I cannot consider it only in itself, as I might a proposition of Geometry. Rather, I must pay attention to all the circumstances that surround it, whether interior or exterior."[18] This is a principle for *all* historical knowledge; but it is grounded on the more basic foundation that governs the authority of knowledge by "faith" in particular: God does not deceive, and the whole tapestry of events in which revelation is embedded testifies to and indeed embodies this reliability.[19]

The *Reponse*'s unconstrained notion of the miracle as "sign" is thus established not only in its emphasis on the direct presentative character of the event, but in the way this punctiliar epiphanic aspect itself dissolves into a broader web of synthetic circumstance. It is the *whole* of this web that, by the end of the work, begins to be described in miraculous terms. The writers, for instance, agree with their critics that miracles are useful as apologetic elements for the conversion of unbelievers. But they also insist that (primarily?) miracles serve to "justify" believers. In any case, there is every reason to believe that miracles do both at once, and that the only way to determine these different functions is to examine the *circumstances* of the miracles themselves. By what feature do they say that this context is characterized? By *les marques sensibles,* that is, by the very impressive quality that defines the miracle as an epiphanic sign.[20] Context and miracle have become one.

Just through this dissolving of sense into circumstance — of the divine eloquence of the eye into the divine peroration of witnessed history — do the writers of the *Reponse* bring into coincidence their seeming empiricism with the notion of constraining form that we argued as definitive of Jansenist *sensibilité*. For the divine epiphanic character of the miracle of the Holy Thorn has been affirmed by the *Reponse* precisely as it can be construed *figuratively*, that is, not only as part of a larger set of events, but

---

17. Ibid., 16; see 8, where the writers sharply note how Catholic critics of Port-Royal, in the face of the miracle of the Holy Thorn, seem to be perversely adopting Calivinistic reasoning in order to explain the healing away.

18. Arnauld, *La Logique,* 399.

19. See ibid., 395–97; 401–5.

20. *Reponse,* 26–28.

as itself indicative of the peculiarly divine shape of that set as a whole. It is *because* the miracle is part of a context whose specific features have been orchestrated by God — literally in terms of time and place and relic and individuals involved[21] — and *because* this context itself carries a presentative power, that the miracle can be apprehended in a figurative sense, a sense that derives from the form of God's own historical being.

Thus, the miracle is "interpreted" at various points in the tract as a "sign [*presage*] that He [God] wishes to heal our souls, and to sanctify them by the thorns of persecution that now threaten us,"[22] as a *"consolation sensible"* that mirrors the mercy of Jesus,[23] and as an image (in the shape of the healed "eye") of the rectification of sound spiritual "doctrine."[24] The body/soul figure of the healing is perhaps both the most obvious and the most fundamental to subsequent Appellant interpretations of miracle (as we have already noted with respect to Carré de Montgeron). But its compelling appropriateness derives, not from any definition of miracle in general, but from the fact that this particular miracle of the Holy Thorn is buttressed by and subsumed within a series of events that testify to the regeneration of spiritual life among participants. Moreover, the body/soul figure is itself qualified and given substance through the specific elements of the relic, which takes on even more detailed meaning in its figuration of the "thorns of persecution" then threatening the nuns. *Their* history bears the same contours as the figure of the relic and its power.

Finally, the figurative meaning of the miracle goes beyond a creatively metaphorical (and thereby conventional, in the literary sense) application of image to event, but construes the actual shape of the experienced event as supernaturally wrought according to a divine form. In fact, this is the remarkable conclusion to the essay as a whole: the miracle of Marguerite's healing is identified with the *very flesh of Jesus,* the touch of which heals. Both physical object — the relic — and the episode of healing with its consequences are seen as a historical reconfiguration of the incarnate being of the Son, within the world.[25] The ultimate epiphanic nature of the miracle resides *not* in some punctiliar unveiling of deity — in the sense that Benedicta Ward speaks of the miracles of Benedict, according to Gregory, as "chinks in the barriers between heaven and earth."[26] Rather, what is un-

---

21. See ibid., 30–31, where the writers insist that there can be nothing indiscriminately located by God within the context of the miracle, not even the meanest detail, if both miracle and context are to bear their presentative aspect.

22. Ibid., 11; see also 17.

23. Ibid., 8.

24. Ibid., 17.

25. Ibid., 31.

26. Benedicta Ward, *Miracles and the Medieval Mind: Theory, Record, and Event 1000–1215* (Philadelphia: University of Pennsylvania Press, 1987), 216. The writers do cite another work of Gregory, Homily 5 (1) on Ezekiel, which speaks of miracles in this more discretely "blaze-like" image of sharply differentiated rays of light (*Reponse,* 18); but even here, the emphasis on the miracles is in their capacity to play a role in the unfolding battle between God's righteousness and their persecutors. They are never allowed to stand on their own, apart from the larger figure.

veiled is a complete figure, which enbraces an abundantly shaped array of moments and people and happenings, the whole of which alone testifies to the historical form of God's life in Christ.

*In nuce,* then, these first defenders of Port-Royal's miracle of the Holy Thorn laid out the boundaries within which Appellant miracle, as I claimed in the last chapter, would be experienced and described: circumstantial and non-punctiliar, figurative (and by implication only here, non-functionalist), and epiphanic of God's hereness. But the boundaries are not simply generalized. The final conclusion, that these three features of the miracle are best understood in terms of their historical reconfiguration of Jesus' own incarnate flesh, reorients the Jansenist perspective on miracle in a decidedly specific direction. For the shape of Jesus' flesh is in large measure known already, through Scripture, and its historical reconfiguration in the unfolding of a miraculous drama must, more than anything else, constrain the scope and plot of the drama itself. There can be no "new" epiphanies, within a figurated history. And there can, therefore, be no "surprising" miracles in the sense, not of quenching *admiratio,* but of excluding experiences of unexpected conformities to Christ. The writers of the *Reponse* asserted that the Holy Spirit both animates the Church and works the miracles within it.[27] They asserted, at the same time, that the flesh of Christ itself "works" the miracles in their reconfigurating character. We are therefore led, implicitly, to view the Church's historical (that is, Spirit-directed) drama in a way that will starkly contrast with, say, Bellarmine's evidentialist vision of the Church's self-glorifying and miraculous progress through the world. If the flesh of Christ is glorified in history, it is only through a set of darkened circumstances, in which the Holy Spirit displays itself in the figure of the Lord's despised flesh.

## Pascal and Sensible Figure

Pascal most clearly drew out this implication. If miracles — among other things — form an essential element in the reconfiguration of history according to the shape of Christ, then our expectations concerning the functionalist character of miracles — as evidence, as proof, as divinely aimed *virtus* — must be overthrown and replaced. And if the *Reponse* of 1656 already pointed in this direction, leaving Pascal not so much with a problem to be solved as with a set of insights to be unraveled, this is not to deny that, in fact, aspects of the controversy over the Port-Royal miracle themselves forced him, with considerable discomfort no less, to rethink the traditional givens concerning miracles with which all theologians of the time labored. The point in stressing the peculiar elements at work in the *Reponse* is less to discount Pascal's subsequent originality than it is to locate that originality in pursuing leads to conclusions.

---

27. Ibid., 14.

Shiokawa, in any case, has given a persuasive genetic reading of Pascal's views on miracles, which, though it gives short shrift to the existing material of the *Reponse* already available to (and perhaps partly composed by) Pascal, does present a structure within which to view the logical development, at least, of Pascal's interpretation.[28] Shiokawa argues that Pascal began, before the healing of his niece, with a rather uncomplicated notion of miracle as an epiphanic unveiling of God's glory. He had early expressed a respect for saints and relics, and the power of the Holy Spirit to operate through their physical remains as through their living bodies. Shiokawa argues that this conviction was supported in Pascal's mind by his more properly philosophical beliefs concerning the "openness" of the realm of "nature," which ought not to be defined too strictly in terms of a "closed system of physical laws." His research on vacuums had already testified, in his mind, to the severe limitations of human scientific expectation and prediction in the face of unknown natural possibilities.[29]

In the immediate aftermath of Marguerite's healing and as the controversy began to unfold, Pascal started collecting ideas for a work specifically devoted to the question of miracles in general. This, at least, is the reigning scholarly assumption. Such a work would have attempted to provide a more extended and systematic response to critics of Port-Royal in the manner of the quickly prepared *Reponse*. Fragments for this unfinished work now comprise — it is believed — Series XXXII and XXXIII of the unclassified bundles found at Pascal's death.[30] If this is so, the so-called "fragments on miracles" that are today found in most editions of the *Pensées* — some of which Colbert, the bishop of Montpellier, published for the first time in 1727 — do not form part of the larger apologetic work to which they are presently attached in the minds of many modern readers.

Shiokawa argues that the fragments on miracles, coincident with the immediate polemic surrounding the Holy Thorn, point to a developing unease on Pascal's part with the traditional apologetic appeal to miracle. At first insisting that miracles "discern" doctrine, if not establish it outright — the circumstantial context of miracles in this case becomes an essential feature in their apologetic utility — Pascal soon realized that the problem of discerning the miracles themselves, in whatever context, is not as easy as he had assumed. Fr. 830 represents the responses he had received to a set of questions he had put to de Barcos, presumably in an attempt to get clearer as to the arguments opponents of Port-Royal had made concerning the possibility of demonic prodigies. Is there a way to tell divine miracles apart from such evil impostures? The strict Thomistic definition by causality — there are certain events that are beyond the ca-

---

28. The summary that follows of Shiokawa's genetic thesis is drawn mainly from chapter 4 of his work *Pascal et les miracles*, "Pascal devant les miracles."

29. Ibid., 120f.

30. This group of fragments contains #830–912 of the Lafuma numbering of the *Pensées*, to which we shall hereafter refer, according to the "Intégrale" edition of the *Oeuvres Complètes* (Paris: Éditions du Seuil, 1963).

pacity of any created nature, including a demon's or an angel's — seemed inadequate given Pascal's adherence to a view of nature as an "open system": there is no real way to tell in advance what is "beyond" nature's capacities.

The troubling problem of discerning miracles, then, seems to have pushed Pascal toward a more intense reflection on the circumstantial nature of miracle: only a thorough investigation of the times, the persons, the consequences, and the location of these elements within the apprehended unity of God's purpose as demonstrated in the whole of Scripture could contribute to a correct identification of an event as miraculous.[31]

The logical difficulty that Pascal encountered in so circumscribing the evidential power of a miracle was compounded by the growing perception, even in the wake of the miracle's authentication, that Port-Royal was not to be spared persecution just because it was home to divine healings. The whole project of the *Provincial Letters,* in addition it seemed, had failed to deflect the attacks of the convent's aggressors. *Recognizing* a miracle for what it is, therefore, had a good deal more to do with a certain posture of the heart — that is, of faith — than with a carefully measured investigation of either cause or circumstance. In the face of this realization of "resistance" to miracles Pascal, according to Shiokawa, was forced to abandon altogether the apologetic character of miracle in favor of a view that saw miracles in terms of the mysterious outworking of a "hidden God," making use of ambiguous signs by which to demarcate, historically, the elect from the reprobate.[32] Within this world of divinely orchestrated ambiguity, it is possible now to turn the criticism of *Rabat-joie* against its authors: the point of miracles is not to convert unbelievers, but to condemn them in their unbelief (fr. 728).

By this point, however, Pascal seems well into his project for the unfinished *Apology,* and it is interesting to note, as Shiokawa does, that miracles seem to have only a small role to play in the classified bundles that make up the bulk of this work. Their place has instead been filled by prophecy, a reality that acts as the orchestrating mark in history par excellence. But prophecy's mark is now wholly subject to the shadowed ambiguity of a faith defined only in terms of its grasp of history's shape or figure — a grasp that presupposes grace's empowerment but does not itself result in any new appreciation of God's reality.[33]

Given the speculative nature of the reconstructed chronology of the fragments as a whole, and particularly of the relation between the fragments on miracles and those of the evolving *Apology,* I think it unwise to interpret Pascal's reflections in terms of a development that progressively *abandons* one perspective on miracles in favor of another. In fact, from a logical point of view, I would argue that only through his

31. Shiokawa, *Pascal et les miracles,* 136–65.
32. Ibid., 166–76.
33. Ibid., chapter 5, esp. 181ff.

attempt to hold on, by means of a figurating reinterpretation, to the traditional Catholic evidentialist understanding of miracle was Pascal able
to avoid the full-scale rejection of contemporary miracle that someone
like Luther propounded when faced with the functionalist impasse of
contestability. I propose, then, that we take Shiokawa's "stages" and see
them more as theological elements that Pascal will finally place, positively, within a single coherent structure, although one that, because of
its comprehensiveness, will present a now novel and distinctive vision.

In the first place, we should recognize that Pascal's interest in the positive reality of epiphanic sensibility did not desert him even as he began to
organize his *Apology* along lines that muted the evidentialist significance
of miracles. The primacy of the *sensible* in adjudicating true beliefs remained a constant axiom for him, which is precisely why the ambiguity
of the *sensible* became a determinative factor in the shape of his apologetics. In the 18th Provincial Letter (1657), Pascal outlines the way in which
disputes about "facts" (*faits*) are to be resolved. What is envisioned here
is whether or not something is the case within the temporal order, and
this, obviously, includes historical events. (The topic, then, is parallel to
the last section in Arnauld's *Logique*.) At issue is the notorious question
of whether or not the Five Propositions condemned by Pope Innocent X
in 1653 as being heretical *and* taught by Jansenius are really to be found
in the latter's *Augustinus*. While most Jansenists were willing to accept
the right of the pope to condemn the doctrines articulated in the bull —
that is, they accepted the *droit* [right] of the condemnation in its purely
theological terms — they denied that, *in fact* (*en fait*), these doctrines were
taught by Jansenius and could be located in his writings. Was the pope's
decision as to matters of *fait* to be accepted on authority?

Pascal's treatment of the question here is hardly original. But the principle to which he appeals has some significant implications. "From what,
then, do we learn the truth of facts? It will come from our eyes, my Father, which are the legitimate judges of these things."[34] The "eyes," then,
are the means by which the truth of historical facts is determined — the
"eye," here, in the sense of the *Reponse,* as the category inclusive of all
sensible experience. This is in contrast to other types of knowing: the
"reason" determines the truth of "natural things," and "faith" determines
the truth of "supernatural things." Even if the pope says that something
happened or did not, should we determine, through sensible means, that
the opposite is the case and that therefore the pope's instruction is contradicted, we will have reasoned properly. An example Pascal gives provides
a rather banal instance of his point: in the eleventh century, Leo IX — a
canonized saint — had decreed that the remains of Saint Denis had in fact
been removed from France and were now to be found at a monastery in
Ratisbonne; was he correct?

---

34. Pascal, *Oeuvres complètes,* 466.

The French, however, knew this fact to be false according to [the testimony of] their own eyes; for when they opened the reliquary and therein found all the relics intact (as the historians of the day testify), they continued to believe, as they had always believed, the exact opposite of what this holy pope had ordered them to believe, knowing full well that even saints and prophets are liable to be surprised.[35]

Whether or not a given set of relics is in one place or another, however, is a less than ultimate concern for the faith. But, as it turns out, Pascal is willing to subject the interpretation of Scripture to the test of the *sensible* as well, and in a way that seems to move far into the realm of those "supernatural things" that he had earlier confined to the adjudication of faith. Citing Thomas as his authority, he writes:

When Scripture itself presents us with some passage or other, whose initial literal sense turns out to oppose what the senses or reason recognize with certainty, we should not attempt to deny their [our senses' and reason's] force in this encounter [with the text], aiming at subjecting them to the authority of this apparent sense of the Scripture. Rather, we should interpret the Scripture, and try to discover there another sense that agrees with the truth of the senses [*vérité sensible*]. For the Word of God is infallible even in matters of fact [*faits*], just as the relationship between the senses and reason is certain within their proper realm: and these two truths, therefore, must agree with each other.[36]

While Pascal, quoting from Thomas, uses as an example one of scientific fact — whether or not the moon is a "greater light" than the stars, as a superficial reading of Genesis might imply — it is clear that the simple Augustinian principle he enunciates here will elevate the role of the *sensible* in determining matters of *faith* in particular — e.g., the life, works, and destiny of the incarnate Christ — to a level that goes beyond mere questions of observable natural phenomena. Scripture, after all, is "infallible" in matters of fact — that is, historical matters — and therefore the truth of Scripture must coincide with the witness, that is, the evidence, of the senses.

The fragments for the *Apology* continue to make use of this principle. Fr. 189, for instance, represents a lucid summary of Pascal's conviction, now taken to its logical conclusion: the conformity of historical fact as presented in Scripture with the witness of our sensible investigations is the only means of founding the truth of God's existence and being. Only through Jesus Christ is God "known." And why is this? Because the incarnate — i.e., historical — person of Jesus Christ offers the only sensible referent of "fact" by which God's reality can be tested. For Pascal, at this point, the revelatory aspect of this historical test is to be found in the fulfillment of prophecies connected with Christ, which fulfillment

---

35. Ibid., 467.
36. Ibid., 466–67.

he obviously believes to be verifiable according to standards of critical investigation. The point is that since (in Pascal's mind) the fulfillment of prophecies can be established, in the manner that any historical event can be established or refuted, then the scriptural claims for Jesus Christ can be upheld, and as a result so too his teaching regarding God. "But to prove Jesus Christ, we have the prophecies, which are solid and palpable proofs. And since these prophecies are accomplished and proved true by the event, they indicate these truths to be certain, and thus provide the proof of Jesus Christ's divinity. In Him and by Him, therefore, we know God."

What is crucial here is the way Pascal has made the "event" — however it is apprehended — the standard by which divine truth is grasped. With this in mind, it does not make too much sense to impose on his developed thought a major distinction between the evidential power of prophecy and that of miracle. If either is to be "useful," then it is only as each is experienced as a sensible happening. In fr. 903, for instance, from the possibly early reflections on miracles, Pascal speaks of the sufficiency of miracle to "prove" the truth of Jesus, quite apart from prophecy's fulfillment. His purpose here, however, is not to elevate miracle over prophecy, but simply to assert that the foundation of our knowledge of God in Christ is the *immediate* perception by an individual of the sensible power of God. The experience of the man born blind, from John 9, to which Pascal refers here, was to be a favorite among Jansenist apologists for miracles: questioned by the Pharisees with respect to his healing at the hands of Jesus, he answers "whether he [Jesus] is a sinner, I do not know; one thing I know, that though I was blind, now I see" (John 9:24).

Pascal is here referring to the self-authenticating nature of personal experience — but experience whose quality as *palpable* is significant only to the degree that it reveals a supernatural truth. It is important to bear the final aim of this intimately personal experience in mind, since otherwise Pascal would simply be positing a form of evidentialism that assumes some public standard for judging divine causality, in the manner of a caricatured Thomistic definition of miracle. Instead, the notion of "proof" with which he is working elides imperceptibly with the reality of divinely sensible epiphany: "Miracles prove the power that God holds over hearts, through the power He exerts over bodies." This statement of the fundamental figurative significance of healing miracles, central to later Jansenist and Appellant thinking, makes no sense — for there is no a priori connection between the healing of a physical member and the constitution of the heart — unless one assumes the inherent revelatory character of the experience as divinely imposing upon the sensibility of the individual. The "evidence" of the senses, then, at least in its power to convict, is closely entwined with an epiphanic reality that escapes the control of those very senses, and that orders their significance from without.

The very epiphanic nature of sensibility in historical experience is therefore at the root of Pascal's vexed concern with the problem of discerning miracles. For events to be revelatory — and this is what is meant by "proof" for the most part — they must be divinely ordered, even with respect to the shape of the stimuli they provide. In the same fragment as above, 903, Pascal writes: "There are two supernatural foundations to our religion, which itself is wholly supernatural. One is visible, the other is invisible: miracles with grace, and miracles without grace." Here, clearly, Pascal is referring to the fact that, however public a miracle may be, however much it may conform to a describable order of experience, its "visible" — that is to say, epiphanic — character is dependent upon grace. Miracles without grace, while genuinely supernatural, remain hidden somehow, hidden within a set of experiences that do not attain to genuine self-understanding. The paradox here, of course, is that in both cases, the visibility of the event *qua* event is equal. Elsewhere, in fact, Pascal calls "grace" the "interior" foundation of religion, in contrast to miracles' exteriority. Yet only this interior reality can illumine the visible contours of the exterior event.

To discern the miracle, then, is in some sense to discern the presence of an epiphanic purpose. This might seem a begging of the question, assuming what has been proposed for demonstration. But Pascal is not so much trying to use miracles as a means of convincing unbelievers here as he is trying to defend an epiphanic claim for particular events — in this case that of his niece's healing among others. As with the *Reponse,* Pascal must therefore have recourse to the larger context of revelatory circumstance in which to locate the particular event of the miracle. And again, it is *because* of the conformity or coincidence of revelation with historical event that Pascal can insist on the application of the principle of God's reliability in the face of a broad array of experience. To claim, as he does time and again, that "God owes it to human beings that He not lead them into error" (fr. 840) is simply to assert as a fundamental truth the potentially epiphanic purpose of all historically ordered experience. Thereby the task of discerning miracles is included in the act of casting a wider historical net set for the catching of some greater image of divine presence.

The turn to context and circumstance derives from this: discernment becomes a process of entering the world that surrounds a purported miracle and feeling the weight of its details and qualities. This is as true for those in Jesus' time (see fr. 875) as it is in our own. The whole debate over whether miracle confirms doctrine or vice versa — the sterile opposition that the polemic with the enemies of Jansenism had engendered — collapses into this exploration of and suffusion within the shape of an inclusive history. The interplay of mutual confirmation between miracles and doctrine, miracles and individuals, miracles and the history of the true Church — see fr. 841, 846, 855, 856, 901, 903 — boils down less to a set of "rules" of evidence (although Pascal does use this language) than to the transferal of the epiphanic experience onto a larger stage. Explicitly in fr. 854, he provides a model for the discernment of the miracle at Port-Royal, and it is no more than a description of the elements at work in the event as a whole, the form of which carries its own authentication through the imposition of the divine presence on our historical sensibilities:

> Here [*voici*] is a sacred relic, here is a thorn from the crown of the world's savior, over whom the prince of this world has no power at all, and it [the relic] accomplishes miracles by the very power of this blood shed for us. Here is God Himself, choosing this house as a place to radiate His power. These are not human beings who perform these miracles, through some unknown power whose uncertain character obliges us engage in a difficult discernment. It is God Himself, it is the instrument of His only Son's passion, who, although He is in many places, now chooses this place in particular and draws people from every direction to come to it and receive these miracles of relief from their weakness.

"Voici!" Look! Pascal does no more than present us with the objects of the event and ask us to behold. This is enough, for the objects themselves, related as they are to each other in the course of the episode, bespeak the direct involvement of God: "Voici . . . c'est Dieu même [Here [ . . . ] it is God Himself]."

"Discernment" is in fact nothing else than the human side to the coin of "visible" miracle, that is, it is no more than the activity of someone whose location within the historical episode is upheld by the interior aspect of supernatural grace. Pascal will speak of "reason" as a sufficient means by which to discern a miracle (fr. 837), but by this he does not mean so much an intellectual process of movement from premises to conclusions, as the kind of experiential weighing of possibilities, likelihoods, specific events and their qualifications, and finally the receipt of their cumulative shape as divine reality. On one level, this kind of *raison* is equivalent to the "moral certitude" of which Arnauld speaks in the *Logique* with respect to historical knowledge in general. Only in this case, Pascal is clear that we are dealing with supernatural realities whose significance and substance define the very means by which they are grasped: sensereason, as we called it in Arnauld's case, is here the human capacity that best parallels the specific kind of self-communication that God provides within the world.

This moves us to the last element with which Pascal works: the positive quality of miracle's rejection. However much the prolonged controversy over the Holy Thorn healing may have actually discouraged Pascal in his sanguine view of miracle's apologetic efficacy, the very principles he held concerning the divinely controlled sensibility of historical event meant that he would logically have to reinterpret the significance of the historical rejection of miracles. Insofar as the sensible features of a miracle remained supernaturally founded even in cases wherein the interior grace granting the event an epiphanic power might be missing, one must be able to give account, in some fashion, of that residual supernatural quality within the contours of the happening. We have seen that the "reason" that discerns a miracle in its context is no more than a divinely touched capacity to use one's "eyes." Whatever ambiguity surrounds this kind of "evidence" lies less in the contestable nature of the "facts" than in the diverse relations that the epiphanic power of the facts imposes on the human participant. If "certitude" is not possible in the case of miracles, this is because their visible character is "given," according to a divine choice, and not simply extracted by human effort from the quarry of experience. The facts themselves, at least in theory, are indisputable; what distinguishes between those who discern in them the presence of God and those who do not is simply the recognition provided by the gift of faith.

This appeal to God's providential grace — if not God's actual predestinating decree — acts as the organizing form to Pascal's vision of history's shape as a whole. In fr. 835, he summarizes this view in a discussion that includes all facets of the character of *fait*, and in a way that is worth quoting in its entirety:

> Prophecies, miracles themselves, and the proofs of our religion are not of such a nature that we can say that they are absolutely convincing; but at the same time, they are not such that we can say it is unreasonable [*sans raison*] to believe in them. Thus, there is evidence and obscurity to enlighten some and to darken others. But the evidence is of such a kind as to surpass or at least equal any evidence to the contrary, so that it cannot be the reason that determines whether we follow the evidence or not; it can only be the concupiscence and malice of the heart. And in this way, there is enough evidence to condemn, but not enough to convince, so that it is clear that grace, rather than reason, is what makes some people accept [the evidence], and those that run from it do so because of concupiscence and not because of reason.

"Reason" here almost seems a mask for grace, while its rejected availability for those who cannot discern God's sensible presence displays a heart still mired in sin. The "obscurity" to which Pascal refers, then, does not lie in the nature of the "evidence" except insofar as that evidence, the divinely sensible, depends for its efficacy on the mysterious will of God's own choice. Indeed, the whole notion of the "sensible" here, of "facts" and "events," including miracles and their circumstances, is now subsumed in something both far grander and far less tractable than self-conscious experience: the shape of history as God handles it to compose the form of salvation and reprobation. "*Excaecavit*, etc.," Pascal exclaims in fr. 834, referring to the text in John 12:40, where Jesus quotes the prophet Isaiah on the unbelief of the people: "*He has blinded* their eyes and hardened their heart, lest they should see with their eyes and perceive with their heart, and turn to me to heal them."

This history of light and shadow settles into a *single* form that, as Pascal goes on to say in the same fragment, quoting from 1 Corinthians 1:22–23: "*Judaei signa petunt et graeci sapientiam quaerunt. Nos autem Jesus Crucifixum* [The Jews demand signs and the Greeks seek wisdom; but we *preach* Jesus crucified]." To this extent one is reminded of Luther's *theologia crucis*, by which all overt manifestations of glory are rejected in favor of the obscurity of Christ's self-giving. But Pascal then goes on to add his own Latin gloss to Paul's text: "*Sed plenum signis, sed plenum sapientia. Vos autem Christum, non crucifixum, et religionem sine miraculis et sine sapientia* [But full of signs; but full of wisdom. You *preach* Christ, but not him crucified; and *you preach* a religion without miracles and without wisdom]." Far from turning to the Cross as the principle by which all contemporary miracles should be rejected categorically, Pascal sees the Cross as that one place where the single character of divine sensibility manifests itself most fully in its inclusive reach: the nature of the crucified Christ lies in the form it provides to comprehend both epiphanic reasoning and its rejection. Indeed, the one form constitutes the historical center of divine self-disclosure, just as in John's Gospel, the "glorification" of the son in the form of the Cross (e.g., 12:23, 28, etc.) stands not so much as a statement on the paradoxical nature of glory as it bespeaks the shape in which actual divine power is exercised.

If, in fact, Pascal seems less interested in miracles in the fragments destined for the *Apology*, it is perhaps because by this point he has seized upon this subsuming formal nature that lies behind the particular details of a given history, which may or may not include specific miracles:

> This religion is so great in miracles and saints who are pure, irreproachable, scholars and great witnesses, martyrs, established kings (like David), Isaiah who was a prince by blood; [this religion] is so great in knowledge, having laid out all its miracles and all its wisdom. Yet it rejects all this, and says that it has neither wisdom nor signs, but only the cross and folly [ . . . ] and that nothing of all these [other] things can change us and make us capable of knowing and loving God, except [through] the power [*vertu*] of the Cross's folly, without wisdom or sign, and that signs can do nothing without this power. (fr. 291)

But what Pascal has in mind here is not the insignificance of miracle, but the way such significance can only depend upon its placement within the larger figure of Christ's being, which alone provides such signs with the *vertu* or the power of life. In fr. 180, for instance, he stresses again the critical role that miracles played and continued to play in the life of the Gospel. But now he explicitly makes their power depend on the place they hold in historical relation to the unfolding of prophecy's fulfillment. He does this, however, not in an effort to provide a functional buttress to prophecy's apologetic role, but in order to emphasize how the whole of the Church's history must be seen in terms of its figurative imaging of Christ's own being, a form whose linkage to the Cross's humiliation sensibly displays the historical destinies of human souls.

The concern with "figuration" derives directly from this insight into the coincidence of Christ's form with the sensible nature of historical experience. And while "figuration" is the great Pascalian apologetic obsession, it remains, on the whole, so foreign to modern readers of the *Pensées* that the large portions of the work devoted to this theme are usually skipped over entirely. Yet the topic constitutes the core of Pascal's understanding of God's relation with the world and the Church, in a way that logically proceeds from the reflections we have examined on the epiphanic character of historical fact. The form of Christ crucified comprehends the power of divine sensibility orchestrating the receipt of God's self-disclosure in a world determined by grace and sin. In a reciprocal motion, it is necessary to turn back to the actual contours of historical event and see in them the image of that same form, whose surfaces define the range of light and shadow that divine sensibility itself imposes. This particular shape of history is the "figure" about which Pascal speaks at such length in the drafts for the *Apology*.

Pascal opens his section on "foundations" with this reminder to himself: "I must put in the chapter on 'foundations' everything that is in the chapter on 'figuration' [*figuratifs*] as it relates to the reason for figures [*figures*]. Why is Jesus Christ prophesied in his first Coming? Why is he prophesied in a way that is so obscure?" (fr. 223). Figuration is connected with prophecy; yet prophecy is connected with "obscurity," that is, with the fact of diverse epiphanic reckonings. The rest of the series deals with the role of prophecy in history as well as in apologetics. But the principle remains the same as that which determined the final evidential value of miracles in Pascal's mind. "*Blinding. Englightening.* Saint. Aug. Montag. Sebonde. There is enough clarity to enlighten the elect, and enough obscurity to humble them. There is enough obscurity to blind the reprobate and enough clarity to condemn them and make them inexcusable" (fr. 236); and, "We understand nothing of God's works unless we accept the principle that He wished to blind the one group and enlighten the other" (fr. 232). Not surprisingly, to this series belong the famous reflections on the "hidden God" (see fr. 242)

To the degree that prophecy is recognized as such and is recognized in its fulfillment, it plays a role like that of miracle, appealing to the divinely enlightened "reason" of those examining its claims and its fruit. Conversely, to the degree that prophecy is unclear, is vague and ambiguous, ensnares the curiosity and conviction of only a few while repudiating the interests of the many, prophecy and its historical fulfillment rightly form the "blinding" force of God's self-communication. And finally, to the degree that prophecy works in both fashions in a comprehensive way, bringing together into a single shape the various strands of unfolding historical experience that together make up its revelatory character, prophecy demarcates the "figural" nature of history itself. To this ultimate degree, all history — "les ouvrages de Dieu [the works of God]" — conforms to the figure of the crucified Jesus: "Figures. The letter kills — everything happens in figures — it was necessary that Christ suffer — a God who is humbled — here is the symbol [*chiffre*] that St. Paul provides us" (fr. 268; see also 253). The belief that "everything happens in figure" summarizes an attitude toward history that ties the outworking of all events to the scriptural shapes granted ontological substance by the real life and experience of the incarnate Christ. From a very different starting point, Pascal has come to articulate a vision of the relation of grace to Scripture's historical form that is parallel to (and obviously anticipates chronologically) the presuppositions expounded in something like Quesnel's *Réflexions*.

The specific (and prolific) aspects of Pascal's discussion of figure need not detain us here, since we will touch on their implications in a later chapter. Our purpose has been to delineate the way in which a reflection on miracle as circumstantially ruled, even epiphanically, provides a basis on which to interpret its functional role in terms of historical reconfiguration. And this notion of reconfiguration, by the end of his life, assumes for Pascal a dominating primacy over particular elements of historical experience. Miracles take their place alongside a variety of sensible experiences, which only as a whole and together provide for the epiphanic impetus traditionally applied to holy prodigies. From one point of view, Pascal consistently struggled with the functionalist possibilities of miracle: its role in confirming persons, doctrines, communities, and so on. The polemic over the Holy Thorn healings made this inevitable. Even in the fragments destined for the *Apology,* this potential role was never denied. Pascal deliberately enlarges the historical field in which miracle is to be located and discerned, and finally interprets that field in strictly figural terms, terms which derive their meaning from the form of the God "humiliated" in Christ. But in doing this, the confirming and discerning functions of miracle take on the character of lines or gestures that detail the more sweeping colors of an encompassing canvas. It is this larger figure, standing only for itself, complete in its own formliness and without further purpose, that in fact determines the functional efficacy of the miracles themselves — if they will convert, what they will reveal, how they will be grasped and touched.

From this perspective from above, as it were, the functional aspects of miracle, limited as they are, shed their purposiveness in favor of a more independently exhibitive garb, whose shades and timbres — sight and blindness — on their own mark the face of God's self-portrait. This kind of view coherently resolves the seeming tensions at work in Pascal's basic understanding of miracles' epiphanic nature. "I would not be a Christian without miracles, St. Augustine says" (fr. 169); "*Ubi est deus tuus* [Where is your God?]. Miracles show Him and are a flash of lightning" (fr. 878); "Thus, it was not right [*juste*] that He [God] should appear in a way that was manifestly divine and therefore absolutely capable of convincing everyone; but at the same time, it was not right that He should come in a way so hidden that those who genuinely sought Him could not recognize Him" (fr. 149). God's justice and mercy hang from the figure of the Cross — "the gentle Coming [*l'avènement de douceur*]" (fr. 149) — and along its lines is colored the whole extent of divine sensibility.

Does Pascal's central use of the term "figure" cohere with other Jansenist understandings of the term? Although we will be exploring the notion of "figure" more extensively in a later chapter, we are already in a position here to make more precise the general theological significance of the category as it applies to both Pascal and later Jansenists. For in an earlier chapter, we distinguished Jansenist "figure" from a more Berullian understanding of "form," the latter of which was an ontologically divine and ahistorical exemplar to which human life conformed historically only in a metaphysically derivative and incomplete manner. The notion of "figure" that we called "Jansenist," on the other hand — tied to Duguet's "mere form" — we indicated as being simply the historically constricted shape of the Incarnation itself. While later Jansenists used the terms "form" and "figure" interchangeably (as we have done and will continue to do), I think it is now possible to note how Pascal himself limits "form" in the direction we proposed for Jansenism in general.

"Figures," for Pascal, are primarily scriptural, as is natural given the exegetical origin of his vocabulary on this point. But these figures do not represent literary similitudes within the text so much as they do the historically sensible shapes themselves that are depicted in Scripture. In Fleury's sense, they are the historical *faits*, whose descriptions in and of themselves trace shapes that carry a consistent formative power over time. The Incarnation, obviously, is the primary figure at work here; that is, the Incarnation understood as the described shape of Christ's life, ministry, death, and Resurrection.

Now while this figure, and the figures of other scriptural episodes, do not point to further and purer ontological structures of divinity beyond themselves, they do stand as the *same* shapes by which historically sensible human experience *as a whole* is structured. This seems to place them in an odd metaphysical position. For, as with Duguet later, Pascal's figures point only to themselves; yet they also "configurate" the rest of history, and so claim a certain transhistorical significance. And to this extent *only* do they stand as epiphanic vehicles for God. Not, to be sure, for some inner character of God, but for God as God is in history.

But "God as God is in history" is of course none other than the Christ himself, the Incarnate One. The epiphanic character of the figure, therefore, still reveals nothing beyond its primary self (or, in its traditional role, if the figure is explicitly the description of events other than Jesus' life, nothing beyond its Christological antitype), a self that, while truly theophanic, is always constrained in this particularistically historical fashion. With respect, then, to the process of configuration by which the world's temporal shapes cluster about the forms of Christ's life, it could be said that our own historical experience is thereby relativized by the figure according to which it is structured, even while the sensible details of this experience are elevated to the level of Christic patterning. The pattern itself, finally, determines that both shape and detail stand naked before the world in a clarity of self-sufficiency, the apprehension or mistaking of which derives from the figure itself: blindness clings to light at the foot of the Cross.

The idea that God shows Himself in His hiddenness certainly sounds peculiarly Pascalian. To modern ears it may perhaps also ring with a certain existentialist note of preciosity. But the implication of this Jansenist claim, according to our study, is not one of autopathetic anguish; rather, it is that the *ostensio Spiritus* is figural, that is, rooted in the sensibility of the historically divine figure. In any case, it is precisely the figural aspect of epiphanic obscurity that Pascal held in common with other Jansenist theologians reflecting on pneumatic miracle in particular. The rejection of the Holy Thorn's significance as a healing relic and the rejection of the miraculous episodes surrounding its display seemed to have less to do with demanding the articulation of the figural conviction than with providing an intense occasion for that conviction's already apprehended relevance to be given clarity. Thus, Marguerite Perrier's healing maintained a symbolic value for later Jansenists; but it never served as the novel explicator of a previously hidden reality.

I emphasize this point because it is possible to see a Jansenistic reformulation of the same figural principles with respect to miracle that takes its cue, not from the Holy Thorn events at all, but from much more abstract philosophical and theological concerns. This is the case with Arnauld, whose "parallel" interests with the authority of miracle as explained in the *Logique* we have already noted, and to whose more general epistemology we now briefly turn.

## Arnauld, Miracle, and the Providential Figure

Although we cannot be sure that Arnauld assisted in the redaction of the *Reponse,* another work of his written just after it demonstrates how he was fundamentally wedded to a seemingly traditional notion of miracle as evidence.[37] Although ostensibly trying to refute what he saw as the Calvinist implications of attempts at attenuating the evidential power of miracles — i.e., the conclusion that post-apostolic miracles are impossible — what is interesting is the way Arnauld here brings to bear arguments that rely on his belief in the self-authenticating nature of sensible experience.[38] The Calvinist attempt to distinguish Jesus' miracles from subsequent imposture is pointless, according to Arnauld, just because of the universal human capacity to apprehend a true miracle through sense experience

---

37. Arnauld, *De l'autorité des miracles* (c. 1657), in his *Oeuvres,* vol. 23, 33–86. This work was written during the flurry of controversy stirred up by the Holy Thorn events.

38. See ibid., 35–42. Arnauld, following Thomas Aquinas's notion of miracle as *persuasio* that found its end in the reductive efforts of someone like Houtteville in the eighteenth century, understood sense experience to be, by its very nature, the strongest persuasive argument for certain important truths, demonstrable by the facts of history. In this case, he presents two paradigms from the New Testament, to explain the evidential power of miracles: Nicodemus's response in John 3:2, that Jesus' deeds are such as to demonstrate God's power at work — this is miracles judged "on their own terms [*par eux-mêmes*] and by their evidence, and not by doctrine"; the second paradigm, drawn from the response of the man born blind and healed, in John 9:25 ("one thing I know — *unum scio* — that though I was blind, now I see"), points to the subjective ratification of miracle on the basis of personal sense-experience.

that was the basis upon which Jesus' works were properly identified *in the same manner* as other genuine miracles.[39]

Arnauld's discussion of miracle as evidence is thus placed within the context of a general epistemology, and his later philosophical interests in the topic of perception bear directly on the question. Recent studies of his long controversies with Malebranche, derived in part from a renewed interest in the development of Cartesianism, have made it clear that Arnauld consistently pressed for a more "realistic" version of object-perception congruent with a high valuation of the divinely guaranteed knowledge granted by *sensibilité*.[40] Although both Arnauld and Malebranche were occasionalists in their understanding of how the mind apprehends objects, Malebranche's epistemological scheme struck the former as needlessly complex and ultimately prone to skeptical implications. Rather than defining perception of objects through an occasionalistically divine interposition of a representative idea in the human mind, as Malebranche argued — a theory according to which "direct" perception is to be had only of divine ideas grasped in union with God — Arnauld insisted that the human mind perceives objects *directly*, the word "idea" referring not to a representative entity placed by God in the mind, but simply to the mind's *act* of perception. "Sense" qualities like color and so on, while admitted by Arnauld to be modifications of the mind and not inherent elements in an object, are nonetheless understood by him to be immediate mental reactions to the object so sensationally "colored."[41] Since God is the wholly trustworthy — He is "no deceiver" — orchestrator of knowledge, occasionalistically ordering the communication of bodily movements to the mind ("sensible perception" of objective entities), Arnauld could affirm a sufficient basis for our genuine knowledge of an external world. This affirmation stood squarely against Malebranche's contention that external reality's existence must be taken on faith, since we cannot demonstrate that God has actually created bodies even if we can be certain that He exists and is reliable.[42] But, as Arnauld argues, in-

---

39. Ibid., 50.

40. Thomas Lennon has been a major scholar in this field: see his "Jansenism and the *Crise Pyrrhonienne*, ", *Journal of the History of Ideas* 38 (1977): 297–306; "Occasionalism, Jansenism, and Scepticism: Divine Providence and the Order of Grace," *Irish Theological Quarterly* 45, no. 3 (1978): 185–90; see also his translation, with Paul J. Olscamp, with accompanying *Philosophical Commentary*, of Malebranche's *The Search after Truth* (*Recherche de la vérité*) (Columbus: Ohio State University Press, 1980). Two recent translations have appeared, with helpful introductions, of Arnauld's attack on Malebranche's epistemology as presented in the former's *Des vraies et des fausses idées* (1683): *On True and False Ideas*, trans. Elmar J. Kremer (Lewiston, N.Y.: Edwin Mellen Press, 1990) and *On True and False Ideas*, trans. Stephen Goukroger (Manchester: Manchester University Press, 1990). In addition, there is an important recent study of Arnauld's epistemology: Steven M. Nadler, *Arnauld and the Cartesian Philosophy of Idea* (Manchester: Manchester University Press, 1989).

41. See Nadler, *Arnauld and the Cartesian Philosophy of Idea*, 76ff., 108ff., 120ff.; also Kremer's introduction to *On True and False Ideas*, xxii ff.

42. Arnauld, *On True and False Ideas*, tran. Stephen Goukroger, chapters 27 and 28. See also Nadler, *Arnauld and the Cartesian Philosophy of Idea*, 57, with references.

sofar as human experience of the external world is joined to this certainty of God's existence and reliability, its inherent intelligibility depends on an intimate relationship of objective coherence between God's being and human sensibility. Experience in time can only take place within a circumstantial realm that, ordered by God, affirms its own objective existence in the very act of disclosing its divine derivation.[43]

On this basis, Arnauld finally says that we can see how miracles (and other supernatural testimonies like prophecy, sanctity, and Scripture itself) can and do indeed play a "confirming" role with respect to divine truths, since their sensible reality, within a given context of experience, evidences in an immediate fashion their divine origin.[44] Miracles can bring about faith, because faith can indeed follow the divine sufficiency of sensible experience; whereas, for Malebranche, belief in the potential of miracles to confirm faith necessarily presupposes the faith it seeks to confirm, since sensible experience, of which miracles are a sub-species, itself depends on a prior faith in a God who has created bodies.

Miracles can act as sensible proof of divine truths, indeed of God's very presence, as Arnauld had earlier asserted in the wake of the Holy Thorn controversy. This is because sensation itself is divinely established as at all meaningful only within a context of circumstance that is fundamentally epiphanic as a whole, at least when analyzed epistemologically. The implications of this fact are explicitly noted by Arnauld: sensible experience gains its significance insofar as it is understood to be part of an orchestrated historical figure constructed by God; sensible experience is the human aspect of divine providence. Thus, sensible miracle, which depends on the miracle of sensation, can be identified only as such because of its place within the miracle of divinely formed history. God is the cause of all our ideas, Arnauld remarks, as much because He gives us the "faculty of producing them" — an almost trivial observation — "as because, in a thousand ways which are hidden from us, according to His plan for us for all eternity, He arranges in the secret order of His providence all the events of our life."[45] And while the myriad of "ways" may be "hidden" from us, the whole, as it experienced, is a single manifestation and self-authenticating testimony to the subsuming power of God to create the world of our sensible existence at each moment into a coherent whole.

Having raised the topic of divine providence, we are in a position to touch on that aspect of Arnauld's theology that most closely links up with the kind of figural analysis of miracle that the early writers of the *Reponse* dipped into, and that Pascal articulated with such urgency and elaboration. Nadler asks the appropriate (and rarely examined) question of why Arnauld was so set against Malebranche's *epistemology* in particular, a posture that was so antipathetic as to fuel a bitter and prolific contro-

43. Arnauld, *On True and False Ideas*, esp. 213ff.
44. Ibid., 217.
45. Ibid., 209.

versy over many years. Nadler speculatively proposes what he considers to be deeper theological reasons for the animus Arnauld bore toward the Oratorian philosopher's theory of representative ideas. In brief, he suggests that Arnauld found Malebranche's notion of "seeing all things in God," via the distinct representative ideas, as moving in the direction of "divinizing" everyday objects. But Arnauld's morally rigoristic Jansenism, with its ascetic tendencies, reacted, according to Nadler, against such epistemologically divine intimacies in favor of the more "hidden God" made famous by Pascal.[46]

The problem with this interpretation is that the direct realism of Arnauld's own theory of perception is both premised upon and serves to uphold a vision of God's *historically impinging* character. Far from arguing for a more "distant" God — leaving aside the question of "hiddenness" — Arnauld is defending a historically *sensible* God, whose intimacy, however, is defined by the configuration of created sensibility within a comprehensive context of circumstance.

This, in short, is the weight that any elevated doctrine of providence must offer. Returning to a contrast we used in trying to describe Jansenist construals of grace in the face of critiques by de Lubac, we could define Arnauld's epistemological occasionalism as boiling down to one of a *"historical"* nature, as opposed to Malebranche's more "ontological" occasionalist emphasis. In Arnauld's view, God temporally configures sensory "causes" according to an eternal form known and willed "from eternity" for each and every individual. In this way, "knowledge" of the world is taken to be a kind of peculiarly historical experience, rather than the apprehension of a set of ahistorical realities. If one is to speak at all of any kind of ontology governing our process of knowing, Arnauld would confine such reflection to the nature of the configurating causes — the divine shapes into which providential ordering settles in a historical fashion — and eliminate its applicability to the elements of human experiencing itself. The "hiddenness" of this divine ordering in its instrinsic nature, however, is precisely what protects the *intimacy* with which divine presence can be experienced, sensibly or otherwise.

This point is brought home in a later stage of the controversy between Arnauld and Malebranche, dealing in particular with the topic of miracles. Malebranche had published, in 1680, his *Traité de la nature et de la grace*, in which he presented his vision of an occasionalistically ordered universe whose shape imaged the perfections of God's glory. It is a vision of almost breathtaking order and serenity, whose major flaw, seized upon immediately by Arnauld, was its rejection of all historically particular — and thereby sensible — activity by God. What would become of the world whose history Scripture seemed to describe, a world filled with the confusions, hard edges, chances and changes of life lived in encounter with the presence of God through time?

46. Nadler, *Arnauld and the Cartesian Philosophy of Idea*, 136ff.

Malebranche had taken up the metaphor (too avidly, in Arnauld's mind) of God as architect, whose creative purpose was to build for Himself a Temple — Christ — designed to glorify his character. To the construction of this temple, the created universe was a necessary foundation. Such a work would "honor" God in its form and ordering, not only by being constructed in beauty and excellence, but by conforming to God's image through its "uniformity" and "simplicity." This last quality was central to Malebranche's conception of God's characteristic "order": simple ways are more "worthy" of God than proliferated ways.

Thus, God's actions by means of "general laws of nature" are more worthy of Him than particular divine intrusions into and amid the created order. At the creation of the universe itself, God made everything according to "particular decisions" (*volontés particulières*) — creating, for instance, each element of the world, as described in Genesis, by specific fiat. But God did this in such a way that these particular creations contained in themselves the "germs" of all subsequent order, to be unfolded in history according to natural laws. (Malebranche has here taken off from remarks of Augustine regarding the *rationes seminales*, created in the first six days, from which all subsequent and seeming historical interventions, like miracles, have their origin.) Particular decisions are in fact not worthy of God, according to Malebranche, because they are less simple, and in the created order are indicative of the kind of limited intelligence that can do only one thing at a time. Once created by God, then, the world follows the most simple — and thus divine — mode of natural movement. God "rests" after a fashion, while the whole universe forms itself according to natural laws into the glorifying construct it was intended to be, each "particular" happening constituting the "occasion" by which the general law instituted by God instantiates itself.

It is pertinent to our concerns to note that Arnauld initially responded to the *Traité* by defending the "particular decisions" by which miracles were accomplished. In his *Dissertation sur la maniere dont Dieu a fait les fréquents Miracles de l'Ancienne Loi par le ministere des anges*,[47] Arnauld takes issue with Malebranche's claim that the miracles of the Old Testament were, as Augustine had explained in his *De Trinitate* (Bk. III), performed by angels who themselves were but the occasional causes for the fulfillment of general laws of nature established at the creation of the world. The main logical argument Arnauld brings to bear is that it is contradictory to claim at the same time that God does everything and that God also communicates His powers to creatures, like angels, only by making them occasional causes which then determine God's general

---

47. The full title is *Dissertation de M. Arnauld, Docteur de Sorbonne, Sur la maniere dont Dieu a fait les fréquents Miracles de l'Ancienne Loi par le ministere des anges. pour servir de reponse Aux nouvelles Pensées de l'Auteur du Traité de la Nature et de la Grace, dans un Eclaircissement; qui a pour titre: Les fréquents Miracles de l'Ancienne loi, ne marquent nullement que Dieu agisse souvent par des volontés particulieres* (1685), in *Oeuvres*, vol. 38.

will to produce certain effects.[48] If God is truly to be imaged in utter simplicity and power, the contradiction cannot be avoided, for either God has given over the power to determine events to the occasional causes themselves — the angels — in which case the divine causality has been limited and dispersed, or God has in fact determined particular occasional causes — willing that the angels do this and not that — in which case, God has not been spared the complicating superficiality of particular decisions.

Quite apart from this logical problem, Arnauld does not see how Malebranche's God, "who loves His wisdom more than His creatures," squares with the simple witness of Scripture, where individual people are clearly described as being "inspired" in particular ways according to God's will.[49] This problem is really more critical for Arnauld than the other. For it would appear that the whole of salvation history, as it is traditionally understood anyway, crumbles if particular events are not seen as "miraculous," that is, as being the result of particular decisions of God, but are seen instead as creaturely desires that independently determine the particular shapes to be taken by the divine General Will. Did Jesus, who, after all according to Scripture, had the power to give life and to take it up, die and rise according to the *Father's* particular will or not? Did the apostles, who had the power to preach or not, decide to preach in some places and not in others (see Paul, with respect to Macedonia) according to their own desires, thereby determining God's General Will, or did they do so because particularly inspired according to the particular will of God? The mission of angels like Gabriel to Mary, or the angel sent to Peter in prison, were these too not products of particular decisions of God, at least as described in Scripture?[50] The very transition from the covenant of the Law of Moses, "given by angels," to that of Grace cannot represent some decision made by God's ministers apart from a specific divine will. And such a will could act, not according to some principle of simplicity — since this would demand immutability, not change — but only according to its own particular and sovereign decisions whose integrity is founded on no principle beyond its own intention.[51]

Ultimately, it is this scriptural test that is decisive for Arnauld's argument, not simply because it asserts an otherwise inescapable authority, but more practically, because the scriptural witness to the particular actions of God both describes and thereby confirms the experience of the Church through its history. We pray to God, for instance, and not to angels (as common sense would direct us, if Malebranche were right),[52] and this kind of experience, founded on the scriptural historical narrative, has been ratified through, among other things, the very miracles and interventions that have been sought through specific petition. The miraculous experi-

---

48. Ibid., 686ff.
49. See ibid., 696ff.
50. Ibid., 700ff.
51. Ibid., 727ff.
52. Ibid., 732.

ence of the Church, epitomizing the specific and personal nature of divine decisions, conforms to the Scripture's self-description, a description made in terms of a history of particular intentions and their fulfillment by God. Only on this basis can both creation and history together witness to God's existence and glory in the face of the charges of atheists.[53]

Arnauld develops the implications of such an interpretation of scriptural history much more fully in a lengthy work that soon followed the *Dissertation,* his *Reflexions philosophiques et théologiques sur le Nouveau Systeme de la Nature et de la Grace.*[54] Here, especially in the lucid first book of the treatise, Arnauld ponders the significance of applying the quality of "simplicity" to God as a necessary perfection that touches upon His historical creativity — that is, as a perfection that deals with the category of divine "decision" in general. Malebranche seems to believe that it is obvious that the meaning of the phrase "les voies les plus simples [the simplest ways]," applied to God, can be established a priori in such a way as to rule out miracles of any frequency. Malebranche, in fact, admitted that God *did* perform miracles — that is, interventions by particular decisions — but only rarely, and only to "correct" the progress of his General Decisions, in the way, we might say, that preprogrammed satellite flight paths are occasionally corrected by ground control in order to take into account the conjunction of larger forces. On the whole, however, Malebranche rejected the notion that the specifics of historical experience could be attributed to particular decisions by God and argued instead that visible "defects" in creation, for instance — e.g., stillbirths, blindness, earthquakes — were better explained as the necessary (and thereby morally neutral) results of a divine will that operates according to the simplest paths, come what may particularistically.

Arnauld asks in response how we could possibly know in advance what "ways" of God are "simplest" with respect to particular decisions and their corresponding creative events, since we do not know, in advance, anything of God and God's designs.[55] Indeed, the logical foundation for language about "simplicity" is a grasp of some larger context in which elements can be compared according to a comprehensive standard. By definition, it is just such a context, of a historical character in this case, that eludes human creatures governed essentially by temporal and intellectual finitude. We do not know God's plan for our lives, let alone for the world, and are therefore in no position to define the nature of the perfections of divine simplicity and orderliness with respect to history. As for understanding God's willing for the world, we are like feral children, Arnauld writes in a striking simile, who wander into a great town, encountering tremendous pomp and splendor in the churches while in the streets there is nothing but dirt and filth; who see beasts slaughtered in abundance at

---

53. Ibid., 334ff.
54. In his *Oeuvres,* vol. 39.
55. Ibid., 180ff.

festivals, while at other times the populace starves; who cannot grasp the meaning behind consumption and celebration, the scale of social values that determine plenty and scarcity, and the orchestration of a civic existence that is ordered on some design other than momentary physical survival.[56] On the basis of naked historical experience, taken on its own terms, we are without synthetic context, and so approach the level of mere beasts.

But ultimately we *are* more than beats. For, of course, the image of the scriptural design *is* available to us, and its figures alone indicate the *kind* of circumstantial context in which the particular decisions of God can be grasped as appropriately simple and orderly (although, in our personal experience, this rarely happens in an obvious way). The providential action which we know in faith to be determinative of the particularities of our lives is evidently established in general through the witness of those scriptural designs according to which history is shaped—the images of God's concern for, e.g., David, Solomon, and so on. Each of these figures — extended by Jesus even to the birds and the hairs on our head — disclose, if not the individual features of God's providential ordering of our lives, at least the fact that such ordering takes place, and in a way that can be described in terms common to the scriptural history.

In this way, Arnauld is able to link the particularity of God's action — in Malebranche's terms, its purely miraculous nature — to the reality of divine providence, which in turn founds the individual conviction we hold that God's love extends to the detailed specifics of our lives. Ultimately, Arnauld insists that our definition of what is "simple" in God's willing be subordinated to our knowledge of God's *love* for His creation — a principle that is meant to overturn Malebranche's startling adage upholding the priority of simplicity, that "God loves his Wisdom more than His works."[57] But love is particular, something we know not so much by definition, as through our temporal learning of its nature in the experiential conformance of our shaped existences to the particularly construed figures drawn in the history of scriptural events.

In fact, throughout this long discussion, Arnauld allows the question of particular miracle to become subsumed into the larger providential discourse, with prodigies acting as that language's uniform set of phonemes. It is significant to observe the way in which Arnauld attenuates the specifically causal definition of miracle in this fashion. For though he admits the existence of "general laws" of nature, and initially explains miracles in contrast to these as "particular operations" of God, not included in these general laws, that "tend directly to certain effects," he then limits the former in favor of a vastly expansive notion of the latter. "General laws," for instance, include only "certain measures of movement imposed on all matter, and rules of the communication of movement in bodies." But

---

56. Ibid., 191.
57. See ibid., 215; 245–47.

they do not include "new determinations imposed on matter by spiritual agents"; these last belong to God's particular decisions, by which God directly acts upon such agents — angels, demons, and human beings — in ways that carry them to determine matter in specific directions. This form of direct action, Arnauld says, is what is meant by God's "inspiration" of intelligent being.[58] What Arnauld has in mind, however, is not the occasional inspiration of a creature, but the ongoing and utterly inclusive direction of creaturely spirit by the Holy Spirit, according to which the turns and construction of history are built.

The mechanism of providence, then, is divine inspiration, which itself is the instantiation of historical configuration through the infinite application of particular divine decisions. Arnauld next draws three definitional conclusions from this construal of history. First, all of human history is properly understood as "miraculous," in the sense that the circumstances deriving from human decision, impinged upon also by the decisions of angels and demons, spring directly from the particular operations of God's will that are not included in the scope of the general laws of nature.[59] But how shall we describe the character that governs the apprehension of these miracles? This is the second conclusion Arnauld draws: history, as a whole, represents the configuration of what is "hidden" in God's willing. Miracles can be divided into "public" and into "secret" prodigies. The former constitute what is normally understood as miracle: the spectacular healing, or vision, or physical displacement. But "secret" miracles actually make up the bulk of our experience, since in fact God's determination of matter through spiritual creatures — inspiration — grasps the inclusive whole of our histories.[60]

Finally, the quality of "hiddenness" which characterizes the miraculous nature of all human history is founded on the particular figure of God's predestinating and reprobating design. Here Arnauld converges completely

---

58. Ibid., 256ff.

59. Ibid., 259–60.

60. If I am not mistaken, Arnauld here has borrowed his whole discussion of public and secret miracles, understood within the context of divine providence, from Pierre Nicole. Nicole wrote Arnauld two letters, subsequently published, while he was reading a manuscript copy of Book I of the *Reflexions* that Arnauld had circulated among friends for comment before publication. It would appear that the content of these letters, sometimes word for word, was incorporated by Arnauld as chapter 10 of the published book. These two letters of Nicole appear as number xxviii and xxix in the *Lettres de seu M. Nicole pour Servir de Continuation aux deux Volumes de ses Lettres*, forming vol. 8:2 of the *Essais de Morale* (Paris: Guillaume Desprez [1743?]). Nicole himself, however, was not particularly interested in the question of miracles, and tended toward a distanced and critical attitude in the face of actual claims for the miraculous. In general, he viewed such contemporary claims, even on behalf of the Jansenist cause, with the suspicion of one troubled by the possibility of "tempting God" through appeals to sensible demonstration. See vol. 3 of the *Essais*, 71–72 ("Des quatre derniers fins"); vol. 4, 203–9 ("Des diverses manieres dont on tente Dieu"); vol. 8, 194 (Lettre lxxx). See also the discussion of Nicole's view of miracles in E. D. James's *Pierre Nicole, Jansenist and Humanist: A Study of His Thought* (The Hague: Martinus Nijhoff, 1972), 68–73 and 165ff. And unlike Arnauld, Nicole did not pursue the idea of the secret miracles of providence into the figural context of scriptural history's model, according to which sensible experience itself was to hold an epiphanic character.

with Pascal. The particular decisions of God — that is, miracles properly speaking — are experienced as *human* history, and thus are hidden, for one purpose only: in order that God's designs of mercy and justice might fulfill themselves, by which the reprobate are left unknowingly blind and the elect act only by a "faith without evidence."[61] As with Pascal, however, the point here is not to reject the epiphanic character of human history, in all of its sensible aspects, but to transfer that character to the larger (scriptural) figures of historical design, which then subsequently act as forms according to which sense experience can indeed be grasped as miraculous. Arnauld will in fact *exclude* most sense experience from the realm of general laws of nature, at least in its self-conscious significance, since in reality even the physical phenomena which construct the "events" of people's lives — illness, encounters, health, work, suffering, etc. — are products of God's particular decisions, insofar as they are "proportioned" to the divine plan that structures the merits and punishments of human individuals.[62] These raw experiences do not become any less sensible for being subsequently understood according to the providential figures whose forms are elucidated primarily in Scripture. Indeed, the figures themselves gain a sensible center.

Arnauld, to be sure, does not particularize this kind of figural sensibility, founded on hiddenness, in the form of the humiliated God, in the way that Pascal does. Scriptural figures of history, rather, seem to stand in valid multiplicity side by side. But Arnauld does, on occasion, explicitly tie the miraculous character of these figures — their dependence on God's inclusively particular decisions — to the central claims made by the reality of the Incarnation.[63] For only a Christ properly described in terms of the hypostatic union[64] rightly discloses the intimate connection between divine omnipotence and the particularities of specific decisions — however they are causally construed — embodied in human history. In Jesus we find a full coincidence of such sovereign design and the human experience of specific intentions ordering the shape of circumstance and event. Only the reality of such an incarnational conjunction can account for the particularities of distinction so evidently asserted by Scripture, tradition, and experience, between the elect and the reprobate, those saved and those left to their rejection of God. Apart from a God-man, in whom the design of the world is particularly ordered, this salvific distinction would be subject to the same logical contradictions that Arnauld had elsewhere noted were implied in Malebranche's version of historical occasionalism: divine sovereignty seemed to vie with divine vulnerability to determination from without.

61. Arnauld, *Reflexions*, 260.
62. Ibid.
63. E.g., ibid., chapters 16 and 17; and Book III, chapters 6–8 (700ff.).
64. Malebranche is accused of crypto-Nestorianism with respect to his claim that the human will of Christ represents the occasionlist determination — that is, the historical limitation — of God's general will to save all people.

Recasting the argument in terms of providential causality, then, Arnauld does parallel, to some degree, Pascal's vision of the Crucified Savior as the figure whose sensible form in itself determines the shape of light and darkness into which history is constructed as human experience. And to this degree, as with Pascal, Arnauld affirms that the hiddenness of miracle in itself founds miracle's role as epiphany, as the cause of *admiratio:* for the scriptural figures that define the shapes of our historical experience point to the particularities and intimacies by which God forms our lives, to such a level of incessancy and sensible depth as to disappear from normal vision.[65] Such is the necessary hiddenness of this intimacy, curled tautly into the forms of divine experience that are themselves so tightly folded into the objects of daily encounter as to be covered by surfaces of unexcited human expectancy. Yet from such tight corners these divine shapes relentlessly determine every aspect of their circumstantial contexts. Thereby they reappear in the manifestation of a grace whose character renders the conformance of figure and experience palpable along the lines of praise, even as it traces at the same time the design of muted sightlessness. And while the pneumatological aspect of this vision is never explicitly articulated by Arnauld, it is easy to see how his theology of sensible history here, determined in large measure by emerging facts of pneumatic experience like miracle, must be grounded in a comprehensive, if similarly characterized, version of the *ostensio Spiritus.*

## Miracle and the Figure of Contestability

A phenomenological study of the Holy Spirit that takes as its objective referent the experience of early modern Europe must contend with a contemporary assessment of the period's religious evolution that inevitably calls into question the authenticity of *pneumatica* framed by what is supposed to be a transitional cultural *mentalité.* It is still possible, despite a recent scholarly appreciation for the integrity of popular religious experience, to view an era like the seventeenth and eighteenth centuries in terms of a progressive struggle between the forces of sober experimental knowledge and the sluggish appeal of superstitious credulities. (Indeed, such appreciation as cultural anthropology has demonstrated for the pervasiveness of the irrational has only served, from one perspective, to confirm the intractable nature of the battle waged between the modern "scientific" vision of experience and an atavistic and distanced entrenchment in an enchanted universe.) Henri Busson's classic *La pensée religieuse française de Charron à Pascal* offers a still widely accepted statement of this supposed relationship, in which the rise of an "experimental" spirit, seeking to strip phenomena of alleged miraculous elements in favor of physical explanations — even to the point of assuming "occult" natural forces at work behind the evidence of *sensibilité* — gradually moved to overcome

---

65. See ibid., 302ff.

the religious prejudices of the credulous masses. Somewhere in between this opposition, Busson tells us, stood figures like Pascal, torn between a commitment to the experimental basis of demonstration and religious credulity that could not dispense with miracles. To these divided minds is due the eventual division of knowledge and method into distinct realms of science and religion.[66]

In response to a judgment like Busson's, with its distinguishing oppositions, our own examination of miracle among the Jansenists would seem to indicate that the appeal to *sensibilité's* persuasive force was a uniform attitude that joined both the "credulous" and the "incredulous" in a shared response to the world's assertions. Indeed, far from sundering a connection between the demonstrative basis of the physical and the religious sciences, Jansenists like Pascal and Arnauld demanded their coincidence, seeing miracle as precisely that phenomenon that illustrated such commonality. If this were not the case, the traditional Catholic evidentialist potential of miracle could not be upheld, as Jansenists, in their own way, insisted that it should be.

If the terrain of sensibility, then, was shared by both debunkers and defenders of miracles, atheists and believers, it seems that something else was in dispute between the two groups. And if not the centrality of sensibility to knowing, then the nature and origin of such sensitive knowledge itself formed the core of the debate. In this respect, Arnauld's historically particularizing occasionalist view of the miraculous nature of sensory experience and the certainties deriving from it represents perhaps the most extreme version of a commitment to the inclusively divine basis of sensible experience as a whole. But only by recognizing what is common to the dispute can we appreciate how the fact of disputation itself demanded, for Jansenists like Pascal and Arnauld, a reformulation of how sensibility can maintain its primary role as vehicle of truth. If sense experience properly witnesses to the truth of God, and such experience is guaranteed by the particular will of God, then, according to the Jansenist vision, *debates* about the significance of sense experience, *pneumatica* included, must themselves form a part of the experiential witness to God's historical design.

The reality of miracle's contestability, as we have already observed, stood as a problem for a strict evidentialist view of miracle's phenomenal definition. Bellarmine, in the sixteenth century, could urge Catholicism's enemies to join conflict with her by using the swords of competing miracle as their weapons. But with the interpretation of sense experience itself increasingly in dispute, this kind of heroic battle became incoherent. Still, the priority of sense experience, in the minds of all, for establishing the truth meant that, even among seventeenth-century Jansenists, the expe

---

66. Henri Busson, *La pensée religieuse française de Charron à Pascal* (Paris: Librairie Philosophique J. Vrin, 1933). See esp. 304ff., and the discussion of Gassendi, Pomponazzi, Campanella, Varini, and Pascal.

riential demonstration of divine reality, being, or demand could not be simply ignored. What they elaborated in place of the earlier appeal to the punctiliar evidences of miracle, however, is an understanding of the historically interpretive context of miracle as that which defines the significance of sense perception as a whole. And this interpretive context is potent and necessary just because of the sovereign and miraculous nature of God's domain over and presence in the sensible.

Thus, the eighteenth-century editors of Arnauld's works, in their introduction to the *Reponse* and Arnauld's *De l'autorité des miracles*, astutely summarize the attitude of Port-Royal toward the confirming role of miracle in the following way: it is not the case that miracles are ever final authorities in matters of dispute; rather God never allows the truth to be ultimately obscured in a situation of historical contestability, and therefore always provides some clear testimony, whether in teaching or in prodigious event. "For there is always a greater light on the side of the truth than on the side of error."[67] The reference to some "greater light" is significant, in that demonstration, including sensible demonstration, is now described in terms of a religious image of efficacious design. Light, of course, stands in contrast to "darkness," and to the blindness of those who cannot or will not see. Miracle, in this regard, is thereby unburdened of its intrinsic persuasiveness in favor of its position within some scheme of experienced divine choice, a scheme that organizes the shadows and the illuminations of God's truth.

The editors, then, are implicitly upholding the kind of contextual version of miracle that we have examined at length in this chapter. A single sensible phenomenon like a miracle, whose physical contours are the same for believers as for unbelievers, discloses its epiphanic significance only as it is grasped within the divinely choreographed circumstantial whole, the realm of providence, the figured shape of divine willing, that coincides with the form of God's own historical being. *All* sensibility testifies to the incarnate body of Christ. In its very contestability, it conforms itself to His humiliated suffering, one that joins together mercy and judgment, light and darkness, glory and hiddenness in a single figure.

Whether we choose to join ourselves to the religious convictions lying behind this vision of miracle, it should nevertheless be clear that the vision itself embodies a particular and peculiar reading of the nature of the seventeenth century (and eighteenth century, for that matter) religious debate between rationalistic/scientific and spiritual outlooks, as it has been popularly construed. For the Jansenists quite simply insisted that the struggle of and within Christianity in this era lay between belief and unbelief themselves as fundamental categories of human description. They refused, ultimately, to redefine these categories in terms of differing worldviews, or diverse philosophical presuppositions or opposing deductions from common principles. Belief and unbelief, rather, as they struggled to-

---

67. Arnauld, *Oeuvres*, vol. 23, xi.

gether in and around the Church, did so according to their respsective configurated places within a common design, whose shape composed a pattern of light and dark. Because of this, the commitments of the opponents within the debate could never be reduced to the outworkings of some more basic intellectual or cultural components whose meaning was ever independent of their common imaging of the details of Christ's own figure.

Thus, conceptually genetic readings of the theological history of the period — readings like those of de Lubac or more recently of Michael Buckley[68] — must ever stand in a marked contrast to this kind of figurist understanding of theological debate and seem to reverse the relationship of theology to belief in general. For, beginning with a conviction of common sensibility, the figuralist view of the Jansenists would claim that differing theological constructions (or their complete rejection) must historically derive from a divinely figurated orchestration of that unitary sensibility's interpretation; nothing more, and nothing less. Intellectual histories may reveal existing structures for conceptualizing belief and unbelief, but they will never unearth relationships of cause and effect.

This observation must of course alert us to an important fact: even the grand *causa gratiae Dei*, to which the Appellants gave themselves, must, on these their own terms, be subordinated to that providential figure. In it, both polemic and persuasion, not without necessity, are relativized by the further submission to a figurated experiential logic. The Jansenist battle against Molinism, in this light, is explained less in terms of some attempt to explicate and argumentatively overcome a faulty theological theory, whose distorting power perverts the minds of the faithful, than as the experienced participation within the agony of God's self-disclosure within Christ's flesh. The details of the concepts and arguments do not thereby become less intelligible and appropriately discussed; but the expectations and the strategies of those involved must become subordinated to a pattern that will inevitably defy logics of human causality however construed. The meaning of human "agency" shifts into another realm of signification, wherein actors display in particular ways rather than effect to particular ends the character of their purpose.

This was perhaps only a gradually appropriated understanding of the disputational struggle on the part of Jansenists. But it eventually asserted itself nonetheless. To grasp the causality within history as figurally motivated was to move toward a different view of human location within that history, one that stood to the side of causal instrumentality, and firmly within the ambit of the epiphanic event itself. With respect to the happening of miracle, we have seen what this might mean, to some extent, in terms of moving beyond functionalism. But we must now expand our view

---

68. See his *At the Origins of Modern Atheism* (New Haven: Yale University Press, 1987), which argues that the sixteenth- and seventeenth-century French religious apologetic contributed to the dissemination of a priori atheistical presuppositions by their adoption of their opponents' naturalistic categories of argument.

to include those human actors to whom the miracles were attached: not only, for instance, the nuns of Port-Royal, for whom the miracle figured the "thorns of persecution," but even those *from whom* the miracles derived, ostensibly, those "saints" whose experience within the figure implies, not instrumentalism, but holiness, the epiphanic or ostensive moment of the Holy Spirit.

# Chapter Seven

# THE FIGURAL MIRACLE
# OF SANCTITY

## Outline of the Chapter

This chapter explores some of the ways in which the Jansenists' apprehension of the *ostensio Spiritus* was characteristically shaped by their understanding of the "figural" nature of holiness. We begin by noting that, while the phenomenon of human sanctity forms the traditional ground for theological reflection on the Holy Spirit, in fact the orientation of such study in our own era is determined less by systematic concerns than by how one accounts for the shapes that mark a historically particular form of saintliness, that is, by how one explains historically causal origins for the definition of holiness at a given point in time. Because Jansenists applied to sanctity's sensible form the same figuralist framework of genealogy that they adopted for miracles, the pneumatological implications of their hagiology led in a peculiar direction. This direction is instantiated, as we examine the matter, in the accounts of the "saint" of Saint-Médard, François de Pâris, narratives in which his specifically "penitential" sanctity is described not in the usual terms of self-denial's virtue accomplished, but as the figural embodiment of particular scriptural forms within the history of the Church. It is this figural understanding of holiness as penitence that we then trace back to the center of an earlier Jansenist classic, Arnauld's *De la fréquente communion,* a book whose vision of the historical decline of the Church's practical life, given in the shape of Christ's physical suffering, is made the circumstantial framework for the appearance of holy penitence in the lives of saints. Holiness as figurally construed in a prominent stream of the Jansenist movement thus posits the ground of phenomenal *pneumatica* as figural history, a premise that must finally apply to the very shape of the *ostensio Spiritus* as a whole.

## Miracle, Sanctity, and the Holy Spirit

As miracles took on a decidedly functional role in the controversialist designs of Catholic propagandists, so did the saints with which miracles were often linked. For quite apart from the specific issue of veneration, Reformers had initially questioned the formal cult of saints on the same strategic grounds as they had dismissed the authenticity of post-apostolic miracles, that is, with respect to the purported probative value of saintliness for the establishment of doctrine. We remember how Luther exclaimed in the course of his argument with Erasmus over free will, "What, then, are we to do? The Church is hidden, and the saints are unknown!" The teaching of the Church cannot be made to rely on sanctity, Luther argued, for saintliness is contestable, and, in the dispensation of the Cross, the glory of individual holy people is probably hidden from the eyes of the world anyway. But Catholics like Bellarmine refused to grant the undermining power of contestability and urged the Protestants to come forward with the kinds of holy witnesses to their doctrines that, in his mind, alone could justify the sweeping claims and criticisms of the tradition the Reformers had made. Together with miracles, then, saints had a crucial function to fulfill (or be denied) in the battle over divine truths within the divided Church.

Early Jansenists likewise continued, as they did in their experience of miracles, to view the reality of human sanctity in terms of its probative function. We have seen how the miracle of the Holy Thorn at Port-Royal could be interpreted polemically as a sign of divine favor in part because its occurrence was linked to the sanctified life of the nuns among whom its power was displayed. Emphasizing this sanctity had formed one aspect of the apology made against the *Rabat-joie*'s distorted claim that miracles are a sign for "unbelievers," which, in the Holy Thorn's case, therefore demanded the conversion of the nuns from a divinely disclosed heresy. If instead, as Port-Royal's defenders argued, the nuns' conduct was in fact holy, then the miracle in their midst confirmed their life and the doctrinal perspective that undergirded it.

Did the experience of sanctity, however, like that of miracle, gradually assume a non-functionalist character for Jansenists? The question is important, particularly as it bears on the pneumatological underpinnings for the kinds of attitudes we have been exploring up until now with respect to "prodigies" and "wonders." The question, however, is also arguably posed in the first place. On the one hand, the sanctified life has been the traditional — one could say narrowly exclusive — locus for the Church's theological reflection on the Holy Spirit: the spiritual gifts, fruit, and so on. Miracles themselves, as a general category of phenomena, while occasionally overlapping with subdivisions of pneumatic *charismata*, have nonetheless included so many other kinds of occurrences of such theologically enigmatic character that their intrinsic link to the work of the Spirit in particular has never been systematically grounded. Except in the case of miracles actually performed by saints — and this need not even include miracles obtained by the intercession of saints — there is no *prima facie* reason to associate historical phenomena with particular pneumatic realities. To examine a Jansenist understanding of sanctity as yoked to their understanding of miracle on the basis of some common pneumatological ground might therefore mark a fundamentally confused endeavor. On the other hand, even to suggest that sanctity could be defined in the primarily functionalist terms of doctrinally probative value might appear to be an initial reductionism that distorts the enterprise from the beginning by riveting a realm of general Christian experience, for Jansenists as much as for anyone, to a constricted controversial context.

Despite these possible objections, an examination of the linkage between the joint pneumatological fate of sanctity and miracle in Jansenist reflection needs to be pressed. In one sense, a study such as this labors under the weight of expectation demanded by just the kinds of modern construals of historical genesis we touched upon at the end of the last chapter. "Sanctity" is today understood in terms of those very categories of intellectual and social genealogy that are applied to the evolution of *mentalités* from miraculous to scientific worldviews, from the enchanted to the disenchanted. We must wonder, therefore, whether the figural construal of belief and unbelief by which Jansenists gave an alternative explanation to the destiny of miracle's reception might not also apply to understandings of holiness, and in a way that must challenge standard scholarly approaches to the subject. If the clarity of a miraculous event depends primarily on a providential orchestration of human experience according to the figure of Mercy and Judgment (in Pascal's terms), might it not also be the case that human sanctity in the form of perspicuous examples of holiness be understood according to the larger historical shape of a divine figure? If so, then holiness itself cannot be defined in terms of abstract patterns of behavior, subject to culturally genetic descriptions, so much as in terms of providential outcomes to a life. Pneumatologically, sanctity in this case would indeed be a historical figure (determined scripturally), and the Holy Spirit's "mission" would be understood in terms of its circumstantial figural design, and not primarily its affective manifestation in individual experience, whose interpretation would follow evolving schools of theological explanation.

What seems a purely methodological concern, then, will actually determine how we identify the phenomenon of sanctity itself. Two important and recent discussions of Jansenist views of holiness demonstrate the distinction at issue here. René Tavenaux's "Les voies de la sanctification chez les premiers jansénistes" (Paths of sanctification among the first Jansenists) approaches the subject in terms of the social and theological filiation of Jansenist "spirituality."[1] He examines the sociological location of "Christian heroism" among the *solitaires* of Port-Royal who came from the soldiering nobility; he traces relationships of influence in Saint-Cyran's penitential orientation from Tridentine concerns of the seventeenth century, represented in both Francis of Sales and Bérulle, and so on. J.-R. Armogathe's "La Sainteté Janséniste" carefully locates Appellant views of sanctity not only within the unfolding drama of persecution, but also in the lineage of Port-Royalist and local Parisian traditions of

---

1. In *Histoire et Sainteté* (Angers: Presses de l'Université d'Angers, 1982), 95–107.

eremeticism.[2] (Armogathe's piece is itself placed in a broader setting by Bernard Plongeron, who argues for a general kind of eighteenth-century "saint" who stands in a "protest" relationship to developing aspects of European Enlightenment culture.)[3] Both essays properly draw formal historical connections, the cogency of which I would not wish to deny. But both also presuppose that the concept of Christian holiness embodies a set of definable behavioral attitudes that can be abstracted and set within a stream of intellectual evolution: genealogies of spiritual theology, ascetical methods, and sociological determinants form the boundaries within which the meaning of holiness can be grasped. Perhaps inadvertently — for although they are historians, at least some of these scholars are believing Christians — the "life of the Spirit" thereby becomes coterminous with a cultural construction.

In this case, however, the problem is not simply that the historian may wish to describe in terms of secondary causalities what the believer may wish to attribute in terms of primary causality to other (divine) factors. Rather, by applying categories of cultural filiation, the actual object of investigation — the holiness wrought by the Holy Spirit — receives a particular phenomenological shape that may well distort its historical reality, a prospect that a theologian studying this episode must carefully guard against. If, that is, the Jansenist's own figural approach to miracle is applied to human sanctity, then not only how we interpret holiness and its divine ground, but also the historical experience of holiness, will prove peculiarly shaped and will require a peculiar description.

## Sanctity as Penitence: François de Pâris

Just how peculiar can be gauged by considering the "life" of the man whose alleged saintliness became the focus of the Saint-Médard miracles themselves, François de Pâris. In many respects, Pâris's written life follows the format of any number of pious examples of Christian virtue, whose selflessness is held up in popular form in order to spur the laity toward greater devotion. Kreiser's modern retelling of his life stresses these formally recognizable features.[4] In large measure, too, the popular biographies of him written in his day claim nothing more. By presenting a "picture of his virtues [*tableau de ses vertus*]" for meditation, writes the author of one such *Vie*, Christian families are helped in relinquishing their "attachment" to the things of this life.[5] The details of the life are themselves unremark-

---

2. In *Histoire des Saints et de la Sainteté Chrétienne*, ed. Bernard Plongeron and Claude Savart (Paris: Hachette, 1987), vol. 9, part 1, 101–10.

3. See ibid., 27ff.

4. Kreiser, *Miracles, Convulsions, and Ecclesiastical Politics in Early Eighteenth-Century Paris*, 81–90.

5. *Vie de Monsieur de Paris Diacre du diocèse de Paris. Nouvelle Edition Augmentée de plusieurs faits qui ne se trouvent dans aucune des précedentes. En France. 1733*, iv, vi. This version of an original published in 1731 is attributed to Barthelémy Doyen, a sometime companion of Pâris. I shall refer to it simply as "Doyen." Another biography, attributed

able examples of such virtues of devotion. Born in 1690 to a family of the judicial *robe*, François was destined for a legal career, fought with his father over his own preference for a religious life, and finally pursued his desires against his family's objections. Ordained deacon in 1720 and insistent on remaining in this order, he spent the rest of his life until his death in 1727 in ascetic prayer, study, and acts of charity, living in poor neighborhoods of Paris, working at weaving, and distributing as alms what income he continued to receive from his patrimony. Worn out by his labors, he died peacefully in the parish of Saint-Médard, beloved by the surrounding populace. Apart from the fact that Pâris was an ardent Appellant (living, according to Kreiser, in a strongly Appellant area of the city), nothing in these broad details stands out from accounts of other holy recluses.

But the broad details do not tell the whole story, if indeed "story" is the proper word with which to describe the effect of a biography like Doyen's. Apart from the first twenty or so pages, which recount François's conflict with his family (in a manner explicitly reminiscent of Francis of Assisi), the remaining two hundred plus pages of the *Vie* are surprisingly devoid of narrative interest, in part because, it seems, so little happened in François's life itself. Even devotional color is lacking in what instead comprises an almost interminably repetitious account of Pâris's search for an increasingly severe penitential discipline. For the last ten years of his life, the young man apparently does nothing except seek sharper ways to subject himself to ever more rigorous forms of physical mortification. Over and over again we are treated to descriptions of his *pénitences, austeritez, mortifications,* and *macéractions.* We hear of his fasts, the gruel he ate, the sleepless nights, the constant moving from one room or house to another, each with progressively less furniture, less comfort, less hygiene. Hair-shirts, spiked-belts, unwashed clothes abound, but with little variation or dramatic retelling. His friends are, on the whole, nameless props to these earnest rounds. There is a numbing sameness to the recital, as if François himself was intent on flattening out the contours of his existence into one undifferentiated shape of self-inflicted suffering.

Kreiser's modern account plays up the elements of almsgiving and life among the working poor that François pursued, giving us details about the social make-up of the slums he frequented and the economic iconography of the habits he cultivated, associated as they were with Port-Royalist spiritual traditions. But Doyen's contemporary account, by contrast, merges Pâris's voluntary poverty and manual labor with his mortification. It is "charité," of course; but charity as nothing but a subspecies of penitence, of self-conscious unworthiness, of a life unsparingly rubbed into nothing by being dragged along the ground before God's face. It is all of one deliberately woven gray piece. One of his greatest acts of "generosity"

---

to Pierre Boyer appeared at the same time. A précis of one or the other followed shortly thereafter, attributed to Barbeau de la Bruyère, bound together with a number of devotions related to the saint's cult.

to the poor, we are told, is not a gift of money, but the distribution he made among the indigent of countless small volumes of *Instructions de la Penitence!*[6] While he gives the catechism to poor parishioners, he does so reluctantly, and eventually abandons even this service out of a sense of his incapacity and unworthiness. The long explication of his final illness and death are really no more than arbitrary temporal boundaries imposed on an otherwise unitary existence of relentlessly deadening self-obliteration.

This is not really a life for emulation at all, as indeed Doyen indicates at many points in his narrative. "Does this seem like too much?" he wonders aloud with his readers.[7] Is this kind of devotion continuous with the Christian vocation as we normally understand it? God, Doyen, notes, frequently asks of His saints things that necessarily escape our grasp of what is right. If François de Pâris presents a *tableau de vertus*, they are virtues that defy the spiritual categories of usual Christian teaching or appropriation. Doyen quotes the remarks of one of Pâris's confessors: "His great design had always been to give himself over to God so completely that he might seek absolutely nothing else. From this perspective, he always lamented the fact that he was obliged to share his time, even if it was to the benefit of his neighbor. Here was his burden!" This kind of inner torture over objects of love, even of neighbor, is not likely to be, nor is it designed to be imitable within the society of the Church. And while it certainly bears some resemblance to general Jansenist concerns over the duty to love God more than anything else, it also goes well beyond what Jansenist moral theology would ever instruct by setting up an implicit tension between love of God and love of neighbor.

Doyen himself, along with Pâris's other biographers, is writing in the wake of the miracles that proliferated following François's burial in the Saint-Médard parish cemetery. He even mentions these miracles at the beginning and end of his *Vie* and notes how the biography is to be read in conjunction with other accounts of these subsequent healings. But there is something deliberately curious about the utter absence in the *Vie* itself of the enthusiastic *éclat* [brilliance] attendant upon the miracles, whose purpose was, at least on one ostensive level, to bring popular encouragement to the faithful of the Church. The shape of the saint's life rather repudiates, in a basic fashion, the sensible graces offered to the suffering through his intercession after his death. Instead of healing, he embraced physical misery; instead of wholeness, he sought brokenness; instead of the open display of God's power before the Parisian public, he buried himself in dreary anonymity. The way that the saint's life forms an image of oppositeness with respect to his miracles demonstrates the intimate connection and purpose between life and miracle, with each reflection deciphering the other through contrast, and joining together in a single figure of *chiaroscuro*.

---

6. Ibid., 43.
7. E.g., ibid., 83, 111, passim.

In general, then, it is appropriate to speak of a unitary "penitential miracle" in François de Pâris's life. *S'anéantir* [self-annihilation] was a prevalent concern in the spiritual vocabulary of the French School, as we have already indicated. But in this case, self-humiliation before God's glory is described not as a vocation fulfilled, but as a brute fact whose complete realization in the person of François is starkly unnerving. "His sacrifice was complete [*entier*]," Doyen remarks, while reflecting on its perverseness, "and could perhaps be viewed as a true burnt offering," as if other merely spiritual disciplines in that direction could only bear the mark of a replica.[8] No matter how much Doyen will insist, e.g., in his preface, that the *austeritez* of the saint prove the possibility of ascetic virtue for anyone even today, he cannot escape the judgment that this is not an example of the possible, but of "a godly man whom it pleases God to raise up from time to time."[9] This is an instance of historical grace, pure and simple, of the "violence" by which heaven is made habitable by God's "hand" in the face of the otherwise impossible recalcitrance of everyday human existence.[10]

In particular, François's *penitence* itself forms the center of the narrative's miraculous element, a fact that defines the figural nature of the miracle itself. Doyen points to this in two lines of description. The first is the explicit participatory imagery that Pâris himself uses, according to Doyen, to explain the nature of his penitence, imagery which stands somewhat at odds with Doyen's own more moralistic explanations of Pâris's actions in terms of creaturely abasement. While Doyen speaks of a general "unworthiness," he tells us that Pâris spoke instead of his desire "to imitate the condition of childhood in which Jesus Christ desired to be born [ . . . ]. I hope that by this disposition He will also be born in me."[11] Again, the indignity of his living quarters, he confided to a friend, is designed to reenact the "stable in Bethlehem," in which the Lord was born.[12] These sorts of deliberate conformities to the Christic mysteries of the Incarnation, especially those of the Childhood of Jesus, are hardly novel in the devotional context of his time (Pâris was himself educated at the Oratorian seminary of Saint-Magloire, a Jansenist stronghold). But the point is that they demonstrate how the motivating character of Pâris's self-humiliation lies elsewhere than in the mere cultivation of a set of moral dispositions. "What! Shall I not drink the Cup that my Father has given me!"[13] he exclaims on his death bed, as if to seal his experience in unity with the incarnational figure, "the life, the death, the resurrection, and the glory of Jesus Christ, so clearly drawn" in his life.[14]

---

8. Ibid., 111.
9. Ibid., iii.
10. Ibid., v.
11. Ibid., 108f.
12. Ibid., 192.
13. Ibid., 218.
14. Ibid., iv.

We *are* talking about a figure here, in the Jansenist sense, and not about the imitative quality of moral exemplarism. This becomes clear as we see how Doyen, if not Pâris himself, locates the participatory character of penitence in a historical scheme of incarnational re-enactment. Within an era of sinful disintegration, Pâris's austerities were a divine sign of both judgment and hope, by which penance was made for the woeful failures of the Church, even while the possibility of grace was thereby embodied in time, in the middle of Paris, in the midst of the capital of all France.[15] There, in the flesh of a generation sliding away from God, François de Pâris stood as a martyr at one with those who confessed the Truth of Christ, as in the age of Julian the Apostate, as one who was raised up "to lament over the ills of the Church." This life of groaning, says Doyen drawing on figurative texts from the prophet Isaiah, bears upon its body "the noble mark of the Cross of Jesus Christ."[16] Becoming one with Christ, for Pâris, involved the gracious reconfiguration of his experience according to the form of the One condemned for the sin of a fallen world, or a fallen France, or a fallen Church:

> We live in a time when a flood of iniquity overwhelms us from all sides: when a countless number of Christians approach the Sacraments [immersed] in the habits of mortal sin; when they think that communion requires nothing more than having made one's confession, without even assuring oneself of one's conversion by some appropriate trial; when even Ministers climb up to the Altar, despite the fact that their lives place them on the level of penitents. Why should we be shocked to see what God might place within the heart of one of His servants . . . ?[17]

Circumstantially, however, the historical experience of Christians in the present does render the figure in a "shocking" light: the experience of God's chosen servant astonishes precisely in the way that it establishes the figure of the Cross in the midst of its particular degenerate age. To this extent, not only are the figures of the Incarnation directly applicable to the miracle of Pâris's penitence, but so are those of the history of the Church as a whole, which is shaped in a secondary way according to the incarnational forms as it moves through time. Not only do the martyrs of the Church or the Desert Fathers resume their existence in the holy deacon, but more pungently does the apostolic Church, "Primitive Church," the figure in opposition to which the "ills of the Church" of today are given relief.[18] Past and present stand in a recurring relationship of figural reciprocity, the providential cipher of which, in his own day, the saint himself represents.

Just this circumstantial location of the phenomenon of saintliness, as we saw in the Jansenist view of miracle, establishes its figural import.

---

15. Ibid., 117ff.; vii.
16. Ibid., 119f.
17. Ibid., 117.
18. See ibid. xii, 37, 65, passim.

But tied here more explicitly to the shape of the Church's history, that is, to the sequence of events that together constitute the corporate shaping of the "new man" in Christ, this figural reality passes from the Christological realm into that of the Spirit. Conversely, the pneumatic existence of the Church is shown to be immovably fixed to the historical figures of Christ's own existence. The link between the two realms, theologically distinguished though they may be, cannot lie in some instrumental facility that the latter provides the former. "Spirituality," in its modern intrinsically functionalist cast, is simply an incoherent concept in this light. Rather, the relationship between Christological and pneumatological realms can be parsed only in terms of the figures themselves as they can be particularistically articulated, in this case, in the interpreted life of the saint. This is a possibility that cannot be grounded ultimately in anything other than the historical retrieval of scriptural shapes in the lives of God's people. If there is an *éclat* to the elements that make up "sacred" history, it lies in the various instantiations of this retrieval, and to this degree miracle and sanctity — just as with prayer and works — coincide supremely. "I ask only for the grace of God," François de Pâris mutters near his end, "for it is all I need."[19] But this is a judgment on the shape of history that can be figurally established, and in the context of belief, has been so established. It is not a program of piety, however divinely suggested. It is a simple given.

## Figures of the Penitential History of the Church: Arnauld's *De la fréquente communion*

If, therefore, François de Pâris is to be seen as an example of the late Jansenist pursuit of "penitential" spirituality, as he is normally described, he cannot be so in the sense of being an adept of particular ascetic principles. He is a divine event, by which those principles themselves are to be interpreted. This is a crucial reversal of normal explanatory direction.

It is possible, for instance, when encountering remarks like those of Doyen quoted above concerning the evils of the age, to identify stock elements of the Jansenist penitential program: the need to combat the moral laxity of the contemporary Church and the evil habits of taking communion or of presiding at the Eucharist in the state of sin, the necessity of taking the sacrament of confession seriously, and of receiving absolution only after performing appropriate penance beforehand, and so on. Everyone familiar with the seventeenth- and eighteenth-century French Church, as with aspects of ecclesial life in France through much of the twentieth century, will discern in Doyen's observation the shadow of Saint-Cyran and in particular the echo of Arnauld's battle cry against Jesuit confessional practice in his 1643 *De la fréquente communion*. And

---

19. Ibid., 208.

in François de Pâris they will simply see an obsessive product of this program of inculcation of religious "guilt." So Tavenaux and, more pointedly,
a scholar like Delumeau have indicated.[20] But as Delumeau himself and
other scholars point out, the actual encouragement of penitential rigorism
in France was hardly confined to the Jansenists, though they may have
played an important role in the process of its popularization.[21] A major
question that students of Jansenism must ask is how the Jansenist concern with penitential discipline was distinctively framed by its proponents
in an era when Borromean piety was generally accepted by all theological
parties, including in many cases Jesuits. Further, an answer to such a question must take into account the providential embodiments of its practice
that the sanctity of a François de Pâris was seen as instancing. That is to
say, Jansenist penitentialism must be seen in its link to the holy seams of
the figural history that saintliness, in their own view, identifies.

Arnauld's *De la fréquente communion* is both the natural place first
to pose the question, as well as the provider of exactly the sort of answer
the Jansenist tradition, in my mind, ought to suggest.[22] The enormous
popularity of the book for almost a century (over fourteen editions through
the early eighteenth century) makes its presentation of "penitentialism"
paradigmatic for the movement, but also, given its slant, forces one to
reconsider the actual import of Jansenist "penitentialism" as a "spiritual
movement."

The occasion for Arnauld's book is well known. Saint-Cyran was wont,
as a spiritual director, to delay the giving of absolution after confession for
the purpose of giving time for the appropriate penance for sins. This procedure, of course, necessitated periods of abstention from the Eucharist,
and it was this result of the method in particular that eventually came
under attack. The friend of one of the gentlewomen whom the priest directed had told her own more lenient confessor of this rigorist practice,
so provoking a written denunciation of Saint-Cyran and of his penitential standards. With Saint-Cyran in prison at the time, the young Arnauld

---

20. Tavenaux places *le saint diacre Paris* at the end of the line of Jansenist "saints"
whose sanctity is defined in part by this program of *épreuve pénitentielle* (penitential trial);
see "Les voies de la sanctification," 95 and 103. Delumeau's major scholarly goal has been
to detail the ways in which the Church contributed to the process of "dechristianization"
through its construction of a "culture of guilt." In this, the Jansenists played a leading role.
See especially his *Sin and Fear: The Emergence of a Western Guilt Culture, Thirteenth–
Eighteenth Centuries* (New York: St. Martin's Press, 1990), 250 and 320, on Arnauld's *De
la fréquente communion*.

21. See especially Marcel Bernos's essay "Saint Charles Borromée et ses 'Instructions aux
confesseurs.' Une lecture rigoriste par le clergé français (XVIe–XIXe siècle)," in *Pratiques de
la confession: Des Pères du désert à Vatican II. Quinze études d'histoire* (Paris: Les Éditions
du Cerf, 1983), 185–200. Bernos, while acknowledging for instance the critical effect of Arnauld's book in providing fuel to the debate over Penance, nonetheless sees the 1657 decision
by the Assemblée du clergé to promulgate St. Charles Borromeo's *Instructions* throughout
the Church as the real origin of French Catholic penitential rigorism, with lasting results for
the life of the faithful quite independent of the involvement and fate of Jansenism.

22. Originally published in 1643; I will be referring to the edition printed in his *Oeuvres*,
vol. 28.

was enlisted as his point-man in response. The result was *De la fréquente communion*, a work whose almost one thousand pages of paragraph by paragraph refutation of the original attack, buttressed by countless Patristic and scholastic citations, could hardly have been expected to be the best-seller that it became. Written in close collaboration with Saint-Cyran, a fact that has aroused some debate as to the actual extent of Arnauld's originality in composing the work, the book remained one of the most influential documents of the Jansenist moral perspective, in large part because it coincided with existing confessional tendencies among many toward rigorism.

Arnauld gives a summary of the book's argument in a sequel that he published two years later. Despite the profusion of elaboration he had offered, he admits that the points he defended come down to three simple affirmations: first, that it is useful for Christian souls to do penitence *prior* to taking communion, hence the usefulness of delaying absolution after confession until such penitence is performed; second, that while there is no "necessity" to delay absolution until the fulfillment of penitence, except in the case of mortal sins, there might be a "circumstantial" necessity to do so in certain cases, even of venial sins, in order to emphasize for the penitent the horror of sin; finally, that the Christian life is properly considered to be one lived in imitation and "conformity" to the Lord, and hence penitential discipline serves a more fundamental formative function, by training the penitent to follow the dispositions and path of Jesus' own life of humiliation.[23]

On this basis, the book seems indeed to be doing nothing more than promoting a certain set of attitudes with respect to sacramental practice. It may appear odd that someone like Doyen will later construe the destiny of France and of the Church in terms of this practice, but, then, such pietistic reductionism may be something we expect of a religiously blinkered era. Nonetheless, as we examine the kinds of arguments that Arnauld puts forward to justify the practice itself, we realize that something else is going on besides an examination of the propriety of sacramental discipline. These arguments, at their most abstractly theological, revolve around the notion of participation and can be described in terms of the following series of affirmations.

First, the Eucharist is itself something palpably holy and awesome, something which "the Angels behold only with trembling."[24] Here, the very presence of God is shared with human beings, and the danger as well as the graciousness of the gift is inescapable. Those who participate in Communion do so at considerable risk to their own unholy persons. This kind of vision, framed in terms of figures from the Old Testament Temple

---

23. *La Tradition de l'Eglise sur le sujet de la Pénitence et de la Communion*, in *Oeuvres*, vol. 28, 112–13. This work, apart from the long preface, is nothing but a compilation of further texts from the tradition, designed to support the thesis of the *De la fréquente communion*.

24. *De la fréquente communion*, 287.

cult, is familiar enough. The real basis of the assertion of the danger of holiness, however, lies not in the sacrificial parallels of the Old Covenant, but in the straightforward appropriation of a text like 1 Corinthians 11: what is Eucharistic meat for some is deadly poison and condemnation for others, on the basis of their mode of reception in charity.[25]

This marks the second explicit argument for the inculcation of purity before Communion: the holiness of the Eucharist is finally predicated on the fact that it is an actual participation in the flesh of Jesus, the Christ. "Moral purity," in this light, is explained in specifically formal terms, not of preparatory worthiness, but of figural congruence between the individual Christian and the life of Christ. An extended quotation here gives some flavor of this repeated argument:

> Since dwelling in Jesus Christ is, at one and the same time, the preparation and the effect of the Eucharist (as we have already said), the most certain rule by which we might recognize those who deserve to take communion often is to observe what they do, rather than what they say, and to see how they walk in the steps of the world's Savior [ . . . ]
>
> It is for this reason that the Savior of the world wished to live a life in common with others, to live among people, in a way wholly unlike Saint John [the Baptist], who lived in the desert, or as a Penitent when outside the desert. For in doing this, His life resembled more the life of other people, and thus more appropriately served as a model for all Christians, whatever their condition and profession.
>
> Yet for all this, we see today that the greater number of Christians who are committed to the Religion and Rule of Jesus Christ have convinced themselves that it is enough to bear only the outer marks of this. They make no effort to walk in His steps, to imitate His life, and to observe His Rule, which is all bound up with love, with disdain and hatred of the world, and with a life that separates itself from all things that could lead one to offend God.[26]

As Arnauld notes, conformance (as "indwelling") is both preparation *and* effect of Communion. In a sense, then, penitential abstention from Communion is also Communion's fruit, or more properly, an extension of the Eucharistic participation itself. This seeming paradox derives from the fact that a life attuned to the demands of Christ's charity indwelling the soul will recognize the frequent need to reform itself penitentially, and so separate itself from the very source of its life.

This is stressed, primarily, on the basis of a third argument, viz., that communion with Christ's Eucharistic Body is enclosed within one's membership in the Body of Christ which is His Church.[27] Conformity to Jesus' life is not only an affair of individual discipleship, but of immersion in that which is "common" in the life of Christ, that which is governed by the

---

25. Ibid., preface, 81; see also 200ff.
26. Ibid., 589–90.
27. See ibid., 191ff. and 591f., the latter text of which begins a figural comparison of the Church as Christ's Body in relation to the Body of "the Dragon."

boundaries, texture, and relations of the "apostolic fellowship," the image of which is given in the early chapters of the Acts of the Apostles: the "breaking of bread" can only follow the "teaching of the Apostles" and their common life which, as a whole, figure Christ's body.

And this, finally, clarifies the participatory link between the penitential discipline surrounding the Eucharist and the realistic association of membership in Christ with Baptism. In almost every context of the argument, Arnauld ultimately explains how the delay of absolution, conditional on penitence, is founded on the need to restore the communion given in Baptism and "violated" by post-baptismal sin, that is, by any sin whatsoever that a Christian might commit, even granted the important distinction between mortal and venial offenses. All the saints of the Church and her tradition through the Council of Trent agree, Arnauld insists, that "the basis for this rigorous penitence is the violation of Baptism."[28] Made new in Christ within the Church at Baptism, any Christian who sins again, especially in acts considered "mortal" but even in venial ways that become habitual, ruins the New Covenant in the same way that Adam ruined the Covenant of Innocence by his original disobedience. And just as Adam's sin required the penitence of Christ, so the sin against that grace requires penitence, although in this case a penitence through renewed participation in the life of the one Savior, granted through the sacramental discipline of the Church's common existence. Just as Baptism provides the gift of the Spirit that forms one's membership in Christ's Body, so penitence for sin that results (among other things) in one's separation from the Eucharist is the product of a new work of the Spirit, impelling one to the rigors of this "second Baptism by tears."[29]

While none of these four arguments in themselves surprise, taken together, their participatory focus, as it is propelled toward the pneumatological center of the institutional Church, serves to raise a significant logical problem. If unity with Christ is coincident with the unity given in ecclesial participation, and this equation together stands in a holy opposition to the fallenness of human life in general, what is one to do if the Church herself falls short in holiness? The reality of sanctity in its historical constriction looms large as a major threat to the possibility of saving conformance. This is a threat that Arnauld must meet head on. It is, after all, suggested by the very fact that penitential "rigor" stands in historical contrast to the temporal rounds of lassitude in which the Christians of the Church have swirled for centuries. To "defend" a practice that seems at odds with contemporary lenience is to tackle explicitly not so much the charge of innovation — Arnauld can do this easily enough through simple appeal to the tradition — but the significance of the need for reform in

---

28. Ibid., 350. See also 200ff., 291, 357ff., and passim.
29. Ibid., 81f., 191ff., 602ff.; see also *La Tradition de l'Eglise sur le sujet de la Pénitence et de la Communion*, 153ff.

a Body that is guaranteed through the Spirit's presence and guidance as being Christ's own.

In this regard, the preface to *De la fréquente communion* is the most remarkable thing about the book as a whole. In it, Arnauld sets out an entire theology of the history of the Church that appeared shocking to some (judging from subsequent explanations he had to provide in its defense) and that, at any rate, proved strikingly prescient of the theological turn that aspects of later Jansenism were to take.[30] A small treatise in itself, of almost one hundred pages in length, the preface attempts the task of explaining the seeming change in the Church's practice from frequent communion in Apostolic times to the need for penitential abstention in subsequent eras.

Arnauld does not shy away from the obvious explanation here: frequent communion, while a good to be aimed at even today, was possible in the early Church's practice only because the early Church herself was more "pure" than the Church of later times. The Holy Spirit, in a real sense, was more active in the lives of Christians in the Apostolic age, and "carried the faithful at a time when the Church was purer in habits [*moeurs*] and discipline." Christians today, by contrast, are more "weak" (*faibles*) than their forebears and lack the early Church's "force," "vigor," and "virtue."[31] It is not the case that the Sacraments have somehow become *more* holy in our own day and therefore require increased preparatory precautions; rather God and His gifts are ever the same. The Church has instead become herself less worthy of Him. In this explanation, then, Arnauld asserts that a

---

30. The actual authorship of the preface is still uncertain. Following a comment in Clémencet's eighteenth-century manuscript *Histoire littéraire de Port-Royal*, Lucien Goldmann attributes the entire preface to Saint-Cyran's nephew, Martin de Barcos (see Goldmann's *Correspondance de Martin de Barcos, Abbé de Saint-Cyran Avec les Abbesses de Port-Royal et les Principaux Personnages du Groupe Janséniste* [Paris: Presses Universitaires de France, 1956], 608). Norman Kurland likewise cites de Barcos as the author (see his "Antoine Arnauld's First Controversy, *De la Fréquente Communion*," in *The Dawn of Modern Civilization: Studies in Renaissance, Reformation, and Other Topics Presented to Honor Albert Hyma*, ed. Kenneth Strand, 2d ed. [Ann Arbor: Ann Arbor Publications, 1964], 246). Part of the problem here is that de Barcos was called to Rome along with Arnauld to answer questions regarding the book, although it was never made clear at the time as to why he was included in the investigation. Sainte-Beuve tells us that de Barcos merely added several controversial phrases to the preface, which was otherwise the work of Arnauld (*Port Royal* [Paris: Gallimard, 1953], vol. 1 [II:xii], 650). Godefroi Hermant's seventeenth-century *Mémoires*, however, explicitly express mystification as to de Barcos's involvement in Rome's concern, since, as far as Hermant knows, de Barcos had nothing whatsoever to do with the book (*Mémoires*, ed. A. Gazier [Paris: Plon, 1905] vol. 1 [III:xi], 246–47). Finally, we may note that the eighteenth-century editors to Arnauld's *Oeuvres* see no difficulty in attributing the preface in its entirety to Arnauld himself (*Oeuvres*, vol. 26, xxxvii). For what it is worth, Arnauld likewise claims the preface as "his," in the later preface to *La Tradition de l'Eglise*, 91. The coherence of this last work, whose preface no one disputes is Arnauld's, with the preface of *De la fréquente communion* argues for their single authorship in my mind. However, the collaborative nature of many of these early controversial works, along with the acknowledged consultative role of Saint-Cyran and de Barcos at this time, perhaps renders the whole debate somewhat moot.

31. *De la fréquente communion*, preface, 89ff.

principle of consistent historical corruption lies at the root of the whole penitential controversy.

Two aspects of this principle need to be emphasized by Arnauld: the first is the early Church's own innocence and purity, and the second is the subsequent and increasing degeneration of the Church's life. The two aspects, however, are part of a temporal continuum, and it is important to keep this in mind as we assess this particular version of what was to become a standard seventeenth-century assertion of the unchanging authority of Patristic doctrine. Arnauld can affirm, like other proponents of the Apostolic Deposit of his age, the unambiguous role of the "Primitive Church" in authorizing any subsequent doctrinal formulations or disciplinary practices.[32] But the authoritatively paradigmatic character of the early Church is a historically relative phenomenon; it depends on the identifiable and to a degree expected corruption of the Church as it moves through time. "The primitive Church is the Church proper, in her purity and in the exact observing of [her] discipline, such as it was before it was altered by the slackening of the faithful."[33] This "slackening [*relâchement*] of the faithful" alone defines, through contrast, the purity of an earlier age, and it does so, not through some intrinsic principle by which its own character is apparent, but by the simple fact of its historical location in the experience of the Church: the earliest Christians were persecuted for the Truth of Christ, while, after the fourth and fifth centuries, this was no longer the case. Indeed, the writings of an Augustine or an Ambrose prove authoritative for Arnauld primarily insofar as they are the Church's only real witness, through one remove, to the "silent" period of the persecutions, from which few writings survive. "Purity," then, which can be observed among the earliest Christians and which seals their authority for the life of the Church to come, has as much to do with lived conformity to the image of Jesus' Cross, as it does with theological integrity.

Arnauld makes explicit use of figural imagery in explaining this historical fact about the early Church. As the physical body of Jesus was formed in an instant by the Holy Spirit in Mary's womb, grew to maturity within her flesh over nine months, then gave itself over to a life within the world that led inexorably to death, to be witnessed to immediately by the Apostles who model Jesus' own practice, so the Body of Jesus which is the Church follows the same figure: formed in an instant by the Holy Spirit at Pentecost, it grew to maturity, according to God's plan, within the first few centuries of its life, then to assume its ministry in the world leading to Jerusalem, and witnessed to immediately by the Fathers, who are examples of the Apostles' practice. We should note in this figural match between the historical experience of Jesus and of the Church how the most extended temporal portion of the image is carried

---

32. See the classic account of this general seventeenth-century view, with respect especially to Bossuet, by Owen Chadwick, in his *From Bossuet to Newman*, 2d ed. (Cambridge: Cambridge University Press, 1987), chapter 1.

33. Arnauld, *De la fréquente communion*, 125.

by the period of Jesus' life once born, a series of years marked in general by obscurity and directed inevitably to an ignominious death. The Church's experience, apart from its spiritual "gestation" in the "womb" of the first centuries' persecution is thus linked to this long time of hiddenness and slide into demise. Arnauld therefore can stress the historical unity of the Church only by likening it to the process of aging.[34]

The authority of the past for the present is based in this way, not on an ahistorical vision of the Church's immutable character, but on a relentlessly temporalized evaluation of the Church's practice of faith. Arnauld attacks those who defend a more lenient penitential discipline on the basis of the Church "of the present," which they claim is distinct from the past's rigorism. But he can reject this kind of appeal to substantive mutability only because he can insist on the historical continuity of the Body of Christ that takes seriously the temporal reality of "decline." The Church is a single river, he asserts following Augustine, flowing from heaven over the centuries and returning to its celestial origins. But the course of this current is decidedly downhill, until the final gathering up of its waters. More accurately, the Church follows a "revolution of times" more in step with the movement of the sun: a rising that leads inevitably to a twilight and disappearance. Applying Augustine's image of the *mundus senescens* (aging world) to the Church itself, and citing Gregory VII and Bonaventure as his authorities for so doing, he demonstrates how only the discipline of the past could be authoritative for a Church "in the time of her change and of her old age," "of her faltering and her twilight [*couchant*]," wherein a rotted present is intrinsically delegitimized.[35] Such decline is itself contained in the authoritative predictions offered by the Apostolic Church: a time of anti-Christ, of contemporary delusion and deception, when our sole recourse is to Scripture handed down from the first witnesses of Christ's life.[36]

Arnauld's historical framework for upholding the authority of the "primitive Church" is, as presented thus far, significantly different from the purely "static" perspective of authority Chadwick ascribes to someone like Bossuet. But it *remains* a defense of the unchanging authority of that past. Where Arnauld diverges even from the dominant principle of the Apostolic Deposit, however historically located, is in the way he makes his framework ultimately demand a reformulation of that in which authority actually consists. While ostensibly designed simply to defend the reappropriation of ancient penitential discipline in the seventeenth-century French Church, Arnauld's historical argument actually transforms the meaning of penitence altogether, precisely because of the way it defines the Church's temporal "decline" in terms of "practice" according to a figure.

Obviously, Arnauld cannot afford the appearance of claiming that the

---

34. Ibid., 126ff.
35. Ibid., 128.
36. Ibid., 130.

Church of today has somehow wandered from the path of its divinely guaranteed infallibility. In affirming her decline, he must also be able to affirm the Church's authoritative continuity with her past. We have seen that he does this generally by speaking of the Church as shaped according to the figure of Christ's physical body, subject to the vicissitudes of decay to be sure, yet still joined to its Head. But more particularly, Arnauld needs to justify the continuing identity of this figural relationship in ways specific to the penitential controversy. This he does by making the practice of penitence itself an integral part of the figure, and indeed, of the reality of figural continuity through history.

The opening into which Arnauld elevates penitence into this role is found in the distinction he makes between the "truths of faith" and the "truths of practice" within the Church. Only the former are "immutable." A failure to grasp this fact is among the primary motivations to heretical schism on the part of those who cannot accept the possibility of a Church whose life, but not whose doctrine, is corrupted. Is it blasphemy to insist on the fact of ecclesial disorder? Those who think it is,

> have failed to consider that those who defend the Church against heretics are equally obliged to uphold these two truths: first, that the Church is incorruptible in her faith; and second, that she is corruptible in her habits of life [*moeurs*] among the majority of her members, and that she will continually degenerate bit by bit from her original purity, to the degree that she approaches the end of the world [ ... ]
>
> These two principles are so necessary and essential to our Religion that we could say that heretics normally become heretics only because they refuse to recognize them, and that Catholics cannot defend the Church unless they uphold [these principles] against [the heretics]. After all, in recent times what exactly are the reasons heretics have alleged in abandoning the Church? Have they not claimed that the Church has ceased to be the true Church, and that she has become a diseased body? But do they not say this because they have confused the corruption of [the Church's] habits of life with the corruption of the faith [ ... ]?[37]

The decline of the Church, then, is restricted to *moeurs*, to the way Christians actually live out their faith and demonstrate their faithfulness in conformity to Christ. This, after all, is also the basis for privileging the early centuries of the Church, whose experience was demonstrably pure by reason of its consciously embraced persecution. But penitence itself is exactly an issue of *practice*, of "discipline," not of "the faith" or of doctrine. The fate of the early Church's penitential discipline, therefore, coincides with, and indeed traces the figure of increasing corruption in the Church's historical existence.

Penitence thus becomes the preeminent indicator of figural continuity in the Church: positively, by affirming the Church's link to the early centuries' purity wherever such discipline is properly practiced, and nega-

---

37. Ibid., 131.

tively, by qualifying the figure of decline wherever such proper discipline is abandoned or attacked. Further, in its own instantiation in individual lives, penitential discipline, as we have remarked earlier, marks out the dispositions and boundaries of a vocation of conformity to Christ, wherein charity is demonstrated through suffering on behalf of a bleeding Body. Whenever such discipline is engaged, therefore, the historical form of the Church is given its necessary flesh as the figural body of Christ.

The understanding of sanctity in particular to which this historical vision gives rise is unique and can be seen under three aspects. First, the "holiness" of the Church (in the sense of the Creed's affirmation) — which is coincident with her continuity in immutably divine character — is in practice nothing but the repeated historical insistence of "penitence" over and against the temporal forces of corruption. Arnauld speaks of the Church's continual "reform" as being essential to her character, and describes the Councils of the Church in just these terms. But "reform" here is nothing but the attempt to seize anew the purity of the Church's early life of disciplined practice in following Christ.[38] The Church's holiness is defined by the *éclat* of these repeated agonal attempts.

But they are only attempts, after all. And thus, second, the Church's holiness, through the negative role of penitence's figural construction, is marked only within contexts of corrupted opposition to reform, that is, only within the context of persecution, the paradigm of the early Church's purity in any case. With each attempt to bring the Church's life back to the form of integral discipleship, with each attempt made to do so in the face of historically rooted resistances among Christians themselves, with each attempt beaten back and finally struck down, the penitential shape of figural illumination shines ever more brightly.

This, finally, is the reason why Arnauld lays such great stress, throughout the preface, as well as throughout the book as a whole, on the role of individual saints not only in authorizing the penitential discipline Saint-Cyran has followed, but of actually rendering its providential meaning and ultimate destiny transparent. Charles Borromeo is Arnauld's most cited example here, but by no means the only one.[39] In the end, Arnauld upholds less the legitimating character of their teaching on penitence than their role within the reforming circumstance of the Church's continued degeneration. At each stage of this *révolution*, saintliness consists in an overwhelmed struggle to retrace the apostolic figure in the life of the Church, a struggle which in its own repressed result gives reality to the shape it pursues. Individual lives of sanctity, then, derive their own *éclat* only from the place they hold in an expansive *tableau* of Christic *discipline*, traced by the Holy Spirit on the canvas of a devolving temporal fabric.[40]

---

38. See ibid., 137ff.
39. See ibid., 131ff. See also chapters 33–44 in the main body of the work and chapter 42 especially.
40. See ibid., 111.

One of the most fascinating elements of the preface is the way it ends on an intensely apocalyptic note, sounding themes and naming personages that are today associated in Jansenism exclusively with later eighteenth-century Appellant thinking. But given the context of his argument as a whole, the logic of Arnauld's appeal finally to the Book of Revelation is obvious: here Scripture itself summarizes in an explicitly figural way the shape of the Church's penitential holiness. Arnauld suggests how the destiny of Christian *moeurs* will move toward ever greater abandonment to dissipation, until the Church's faithful will be confined to those penitential solitaries driven into the wilderness, "persons both holy and religious, who will not only try to offer God an abundant satisfaction for their own sins, but who will press themselves, through the rigor of their penitence and the continual ardor of their piety, to draw God's mercy upon others by seeking from Him day and night a true conversion of sinners." The consummation of the Church's temporal life then nears its close, as, in the midst of these reduced circumstances, Elijah and Enoch return. They come, not only to preach penitence, but, in their figural conformity to its shape, to embody pleadingly its rejection as the form given by Christ to all history:

> Through a wonderful relationship and harmony of action which, we might say, God has always held within the great designs of His providence and grace, the Church thereby begun in Penitence will end in Penitence. Saint John [the Baptist] came to preach [penitence] before the first coming of the Son of God; Elijah will come to preach it before the second. St. John is said to have come in the spirit of Elijah; we could say the same about Elijah, that he will come in the spirit of St. John. But Elijah will not only be the image of St. John. Even more so will he be the image of Jesus Christ. That is why he will preach penitence like Him; he will be hated for his preaching like Him; he will be killed like Him; he will be resurrected like Him; he will convert people while rising into heaven, just like Him.[41]

No clearer appropriation of individual lives to a divine historical figure could be imagined than this formal symmetrizing of biblical persons within a single consummated picture. And insofar as the picture is described by Arnauld to include the penitential servants of the Church's entire history, set up in a relationship of charitable contrariety to their ecclesial and worldly circumstances, the reality of these instances of sanctity becomes subsumed into those scriptural figures who both frame and characterize the overall image of Christ's Body. Since this overall image conforms to the incarnate Lord's subjection in the flesh to death under the burden of sin, sanctity becomes one discerned side to the double aspect of salvation, much as Pascal described it, to be viewed as penitence because it is tied in the flesh of Christ to salvation's other aspect, the blindness of reprobated sin. Interestingly, Arnauld articulates this larger image in pneumatological terms, as a single "impetuous wind of the Holy Spirit

---

41. Ibid., 149–50.

that breaks the hearts of stone" under the sign of a universal "baptism" of "tears" that is simply appropriated through differing subjective lenses.[42] Figurally speaking "the life of the Christian in general, whether he be innocent or sinful, MUST BE A CONTINUAL ACT OF PENITENCE."[43]

## The Penitential Figure versus the Virtue of Penitence

To apprehend the character of such sanctity, of course, is an act of figural discernment rather than the application of hagiological standards to particular cases. For it is important to note how this turn to the figuralizing aspect of the Spirit serves to place the "innocent" and "the sinner" on the same historical rung. Without thereby rendering indifferent the distinction between the status of each group, penitence itself is essentially a-moralized in favor of a circumstantial reinterpretation of its significance. This amoralization of a practice of sanctity represents the equivalent, in personal terms, of the Jansenist tendency, in the reflection on miracle, to defunctionalize the prodigious event.

It stands, furthermore, as only a peculiar tendency in Jansenism, which was by no means universally followed by members of the movement. By and large, in fact, penitentialism was moralized in keeping with the general outlook of the era, even in the eyes of many whose sympathies were defined by a self-conscious adherence to the principles of Saint-Cyran. Read apart from an understanding of its preface, *De la fréquente communion* could be appreciated purely in terms of the imperative of its rigorist program.[44] In this vein, it must be admitted, a whole strand of Jansenist "spirituality" can be conflated with the generalized penitential piety of the late seventeenth and early eighteenth centuries, irrespective even of the reality of Appellancy.[45] But it is a vein that must be carefully distinguished

---

42. See ibid., 158f., 213ff.

43. Arnauld, *La Tradition de l'Eglise sur le sujet de la Pénitence et de la Communion*, 215; see also 153, 158f., 213ff. This conclusion is also consistent with what we know of Saint-Cyran's own indubitable writings on the subject of penitence. In particular, the relationship of baptism and post-baptismal sin and penitence with the figure of Christ's crucifixion, understood in a historically participatory, even reiterative fashion across time and within the Church, is elaborated in a strongly realistic fashion in, e.g., *La Spiritualité de Saint-Cyran avec ses écrits de piété inédits* (Paris: J. Vrin, 1962), 384; see also 297, 314, 326, 358, 382ff.

44. This fact explains the popularity of a Jansenist like Nicole's work among theological parties of all stripes, writings which reappropriate penitentialism into a scheme of general moral formation quite independent of any figural framework and structured rather as a set of abstracted "virtues" appropriate to the good Christian life. See Nicole's *Instructions Theologiques et Morales sur les Sacremens*, nouvelle edition (Paris: Charles Osmont, 1719), vol. 1, 128ff.; also 295ff.

45. One sees the turn toward moralism already at work in writings of a more purely "Jansenist" cast, in the sense of adhering to the construal of sin in the bishop of Ypres's more strictly neo-Platonic ontological terms. E.g., *Le Catechisme de la Penitence, Qui conduit les Pecheurs à une veritable Conversion* (Paris: Helie Josset, 1676), which may be by Gerberon or Le Tourneux, while it maintains the amoral equivalence of "l'innocent" and "le pecheur," nonetheless does this in terms of a general anthropology of creaturely sin and grace that can ignore the historical figures of the Fall, of the various Covenants, of Christ, and of the

from the original concerns of Arnauldian figuralism, whose perspective alone lies behind the peculiar outcome of miraculous penitence embodied in François de Pâris. Just on the basis of the themes found in the preface to *De la fréquente communion*, it is possible to trace the continuing influence of Arnauld's vision in particular examples of Jansenist penitentialism, a line of concern that even where it does not in fact lead directly to the events at Saint-Médard, does still seem to comment on them from afar.[46] Even here, however, a certain tension exists between the expecta-

---

Church. Its "Exercices" and "Sentiments interieurs de l'ame Penitente" are meditative spurs to feelings of abject creaturely abasement that make virtually no reference to the scriptural images and persons so prevalent in something like Quesnel's almost contemporary Oratorian *Jésus-Christ Penitent*, to which we have referred in an earlier chapter on participation in the Mysteries. Even a prominent later Appellant like Jerôme Besoigne, who not surprisingly stood with those who distanced themselves from the events of Saint-Médard, exemplifies the moralizing tradition of Nicole in its methodical implications in his popular multivolumed *Principes de la Pénitence et de la Conversion, ou Vie des Pénitens*, 3d ed. (Paris: Desaint & Saillant et Simon, 1766), which now defines "penitence" as a set of dispositions and practices preparatory to an ascending movement of Christian "perfection" (see the "Avertissement," v–viii), whose term of "justice" would in theory leave penitence behind altogether. Nothing could be further from the ideas of Saint-Cyran, whose anti-method was designed to leave every Christian enmeshed in the single power of a subsuming historical figure, no matter their moral condition. The common "functionalist" presupposition of this moralizing attitude is made explicit in other, less theologically sophisticated non-Jansenist writings on penitence: in general, we discover, the purpose of rigorous penitential discipline is to regulate the social life of the parish according to a more orderly design of virtuous group-control. See the guide put out by the bishop of Bayeux for the use of his priests, *Conduite des Confesseurs dans le tribunal de la Pénitence, selon les instructions de S. Charles Borromée, et la doctrine de S. François de Sales*, 4th ed. (Paris: Gabriel Charles Berton, 1760), vii ff. By this point, the hardest possible line on delay of absolution and abstention from communion is justified solely in terms of its morally edifying influence with respect to virtue and vice, wholly independent of theological or scriptural imperative.

46. In contrast, for instance, to *Le Catechisme de la Penitence*, mentioned in the previous footnote, a contemporary set of practical instructions from the Diocese of Arras, demonstrates a close link to an Arnauldian perspective, on the basis of the historical and general figural framework of its remarks. The Jansenist, and later Appellant bishop of Arras, Guy de Seve de Rochechouart, provided his diocesan priests with instructions on the sacrament of penance that commend the rigorist position of absolution's delay in terms of the Church's place in a long history of assault at the hands of the Demon, whose purpose it is to attack "the Cross" of Christ precisely in the area of its fullest figural embodiment, penitential discipline (*Premiere Lettre Pastorale de Monseigneur L'illustrissime et Reverendissime Evéque d'Arras, Aux Curez, Vicaires, et Confesseurs de son Diocése Touchant l'Administration du Sacrement de Penitence* [n.d., n.p.], see 9–20, 9–10 esp.). One can find later Jansenists continuing to work with this framework, locating the practice of penitence within an explicitly persecutory history of the Church's dicipline and sanctity. Bit by bit, however, the clear edges of Arnauld's own scheme become attenuated, and the vision reverts from the striking assertion of the Church's figural "aging" into one in which a primitive *age d'or* (Golden Age) is simply contrasted to an undifferentiated and subsequent history of merely fluctuating faithlessness; see the Bishop of Vence Antoine Godeau's *La Vie de S. Charles Borromée, Cardinal du Titre de Sainte Praxede, et Archevêque de Milan* (Paris: Andre Pralard, 1684), preface (unpaginated), and 387ff.; see also the later *Instruction Pastorale de Monseigneur l'Archevèque de Tours, sur la Justice Chrétienne, Par rapport aux Sacremens DE PENITENCE ET D'EUCHARISTIE* (Paris: Guillaume Desprez et Pierre-Guillaume Cavelier, 1749), attributed to the Appellant theologian Gourlin. The *Instruction* follows exactly many of Arnauld's explicit citations upholding the Church's history of "corruption," although, once again, the *age d'or* of the primitive Church is not grounded in anything except the bare assertion of purity. In this case, however, an elaborate theology of union with Christ through the Mystical Body of the Church and the Eucharist, which is ultimately of a figural

tions for programmatic method, available for popular formation, and the conviction that penitence is a wholly miraculous affair in terms of its historically figural constitution. To grasp this tension is to see more clearly how only an undistracted focus on the circumstantial aspects of sanctity, an unabashed and total embrace of figuralism, could lead certain Jansenists beyond this unresolved mix of miracle and moralism to the peculiar phenomena associated with the "self-immolation" of the Deacon Pâris in the midst of a *siècle dégénéré* (degenerate age).[47]

Indeed, the direction in which Arnauld's particular historical framework for understanding holy penitence will find its fullest flowering is one that moves steadfastly away from generalizing attitudes about proper Christian virtue toward the location of individuals in specific circumstances of figural clarity. For the figural approach to sanctity, despite its reliance on the universal efficacy of particular "forms" for construing historical experience, nevertheless insists on their particularity in both scriptural and individual coincidence. Only the examination of specific experiences of oppositional penitence can provide the disclosure of the figural *éclat*. This is a fact that, in the realm of sanctity, parallels the paradoxical role of contested *sensibilité* in the realm of the physically miraculous.

*De la fréquente communion*, with its peculiar preface, traced a history of sanctity that was designed, ultimately, to frame the disclosure of a specific seam of luminosity in the folds of the Church's life: the man in prison, whose confessional practice the book aimed to defend. This is why

---

character, is provided that displays the fullness of later Jansenist reflections on the participatory basis of penitence (see 229ff., 322ff.). This is conflated with a parallel pneumatological explanation, that sets up an Augustinian opposition of Spirit (and Charity) to the World, within which penitential submission takes its form (see 188ff.).

47. Adrien Baillet's monumental *Les Vies des Saints*, most often cited today as an example of rationalism's debunking of the supernatural, is a good example of the tension between moralistic and figuralist versions of sanctity in play even among polemically Jansenist hagiographers. It should be said, first of all, that, along with other Jansenist historians like Tillemont and Fleury, Baillet's critical efforts to sift out the purely legendary from traditional accounts of the saints' lives, derived primarily from a desire to establish the *religious* claims of the Church on unimpeachable *faits*. Still, it is undeniable that when Baillet elaborates a general theory of sanctity, as in the lengthy preface to the series *Discours sur l'Histoire de la Vie des Saints*, he defines holiness in terms of its functional usefulness to the Church in the form of moral exemplarism. Imitability of virtue, Baillet insists, is paramount in discerning authentic saints, and miracles on the whole are secondary, if not utterly distracting elements to be considered. At the same time, however, Baillet has adopted Arnauld's vision of the Church's besieged suffering and decrepitude, and in the course of pursuing this vision, he ends by redefining the moral shape of holy conduct in terms of persecuted martyrdom, the penitential submission to which is seen as almost demanding the extinguishing of pneumatic *éclat*, not only of miracles, but of abstracted imitable virtues as well. The *Discours* as a whole totters uneasily in this unresolved mingling of typical post-Tridentine moralism and Jansenist perspectives. The *Discours* is found in Baillet's *Les Vies des Saints, Composées sur ce qui nous est resté de plus authentique et de plus assuré dans leur histoire, disposées selon l'ordre des Calendriers et des Martyrologes. Avec l'Histoire de leur Culte selon qui'il est établie dans l'Eglise Catholique. Et l'Histoire des Autres Festes de l'année*, 2d ed. (Paris: Louis Roulland, 1704), vol. 1, 7–70. See also the volume's unpaginated dedicatory "Epistre" to Cardinal de Noailles.

the work cannot be read so much programmatically as in terms of its testimony to the election of a set of circumstances for figurative coherence. The "principles" of the Church's historical corruptibility, of penitential contrariety, of humiliated conformity, and so on serve only as heuristic devices to identify, in the order of grace, the establishment through specific histories of God's scriptural realities. The concrete figure of the imprisoned Abbé de Saint-Cyran, assaulted for his fidelity to a discipleship time would scorch, hovers throughout the text as its illuminative key.

In the same way, although now made explicit, the *Vie* of François de Pâris takes the otherwise undifferentiated details of his penitential self-offering and ties them to a set of events and individuals that alone provide the grid through which to glimpse the pneumatic meaning of his sacrifice. I have not mentioned this fact until this point, for its relation to the general figuralist concerns of Appellancy will form the focus for the chapter that follows. But unlike hagiographers of Baillet's sort, whose unshakable concern for universalizable virtue devoid of the marvelous led him to list "simplicity" that was almost *ennuyeux* [dull] as a note of documentary authenticity in a saint's life,[48] Doyen's account of François provides the same dry catena of *obscurités, mortifications, silences,* and *humiliations,* but repeatedly ties them to a specific set of contested examples: the "saints" of Port-Royal. Penitential sanctity is given figural form only insofar as its Christological participation is grounded in an *identifiable* history of opposition. The point here moves far beyond special pleading for the Appellant cause, and a movement's attempt at constructing hagiographic propaganda.

> He [François] would very much have liked to have found a solitude similar to that which had been seen and admired only a few years before at Port-Royal des Champs. He had many times watered the ruins of that place with his tears. But since he was now forced only to mourn its destruction and had no hope of finding a similar place, he struggled to construct one for himself alone.[49]

To enter the history of the saint's own circumstances alone provides access to the figure in which he dwells: that is, to know, for instance, where he walked on pilgrimage, and on what ground his tears were shed, for whom, and on behalf of what exhausted forms of life. Similarly, the scriptural figure is open only to those willing to identify with the narrow lines of historical experience upon whose edges that figure is folded — in this case, the demolished cloister outside of Paris, with its desecrated cemetery stripped of its holy bones.

The full significance of sanctity's peculiar pneumatic meaning, for these Jansenists, is to be found in this coincidence of particular event and scriptural figure, rendered in oppositional terms of light and darkness

---

48. Ibid., 136ff.
49. Doyen, *Vie de Monsieur de Paris,* 37f.; see other references to Port-Royal as François's explicitly penitential model, e.g., 40ff., 65f.

that are gathered in the saving form of the Cross's assumption of sin. Given the dearth of explicit Jansenist reflection on pneumatology, we are left at this stage of our study to summarize on our own the systematic implications of this understanding of pneumatic disclosure as the shape of penitential contestability. To be sure, we are not yet at a point in our investigation when the Jansenists' own view of their experienced apprehension of the Holy Spirit's self-manifestation can be properly summarized; nor for that matter can we ourselves offer a comprehensive assessment of the *ostensio Spiritus* involved in that experience. Nonetheless, we have been led at least to the provisional conclusion that, in a Jansenist perspective, all "appearance" is figurally ordered by God in general, and that pneumatic appearance in particular is epiphanic of such figures. It is not only the case, therefore, that Jansenist perceptions of the world presupposed the possibility that the Holy Spirit could be apprehended phenomenologically in terms of specifically characterized events and objects identifiable as "pneumatic." To this degree, a study of Jansenist theological attitudes only confirms their congruence with the traditional pneumatological assumptions that undergird the present investigation. But in addition, the figural basis, as writers like Arnauld saw it, of human experience in general, typified by the Christian Church as Christ's Body in its dependence on the Lord's incarnate form, demands that *any ostensio Spiritus* will prove epiphanic only insofar as it conforms to the divinely shaped character of such general experience, whose breadth of sensible shape qualified by the distortions of sin is encompassed only on the Cross. The Spirit's appearance according to this understanding, in short, is subject to the *same* (and not only "similar") constraints and contradictions as the Incarnational epiphany of Golgotha. This conclusion is provisional, however, in that the substance of this pneumatological affirmation will emerge only in our final section, as we examine how Appellant reflections on pneumatic figuration in general, drawn within scriptural limits, and their experience of it in particular in the fate of the negated Saint-Médard miracles gave rise to a comprehensive grasp of the Spirit's unveiling in time.

# THE FIGURE OF REJECTION

*Chapter Eight*

# FIGURALISM AND THE BIBLE
## *Figurisme* and the Continuity
## of Its Jansenist Practice

### Introduction and Outline:
### *Figurisme* and Historical Reference

Our study thus far has uncovered a convergence of Jansenist understandings of grace and of pneumatic event in what can be called a figuralist vision of divine history. Because this vision so generally informs the various reflective and experiential aspects of an *ostensio Spiritus* in Jansenist terms, we need to examine the conceptual integrity of its character. Indeed, the figuralist vision of Jansenism does not simply supply accidental elements to the reflective experience of miracle and sanctity, but, in its own theologically systematic breadth, it actually provides the very phenomenological boundaries in which the apprehension of the Holy Spirit becomes possible. From the start, as it were, the notion of historical experience as figurally construed in scriptural terms establishes the descriptive limits within which the historical fate of pneumatic events and its reflection and negation take shape. If pneumatology properly derives from a phenomenology of the Spirit, from the theological encounter with the *ostensio Spiritus*, then in the case of Jansenist Appellancy, pneumatology is also systematically coterminous with figuralism itself.

The purpose of the next two chapters, as earlier promised, then, is to trace something of the theological relationship existing between the Jansenist experience of miracle and sanctity, as embodied historical events, and the Jansenist reading of Scripture in figural terms, a reading which lies at the root of the larger pneumatological orientation of Jansenism. The two chapters together form an integrated attempt at exploring this issue. Initially, however, the reader will discover that our immediate examination of pneumatic figure and Scripture discloses, not the Holy Spirit itself as a central theological issue, but the historical reference per se of the scriptural text. This historical referentiality of the biblical text was always *presupposed* in the connections we drew earlier between a pneumatology of historical forms according to Scripture and the figure of Christ (see our chapter 4 on "The Spirit of Grace"), and throughout the seventeenth century at least, this presupposition needed little defense in order to buttress its effective role as contributor to a vital, if implied, pneumatology of grace. Yet, in the context of a discussion of the Saint-Médard episodes, it is important now to note how an assumption of the Scripture's historical referentiality was integrally coherent with an assumption of the pneumatic character of miracles and sanctity. Not only do we observe how both assumptions were challenged at once in the early eighteenth century — though without the consciousness of their connection — but both were conjointly attacked indirectly through a developing challenge to the figural understanding of Scripture in particular. The next two chapters, then, will see their focus shift in course from holy miracle as figure to figural readings of Scripture and their historical reference in time. Overall, our aim will be to explore the ways in which the figural reading of Scripture adopted by Jansenists and Appellants in particular derived from and also demanded the affirmation of the essential historical referentiality of these figural texts themselves.

The discussion that follows has learned much from and shares with Hans Frei many common historical concerns touching on the fate of biblical interpretation in the eighteenth century.[1] At the outset of my own discussion here, however, I must emphasize in what way my approach to Jansenist figural interpretation of Scripture differs from Frei's positive evaluation of pre-critical exegesis in contrast to its subsequent "eclipse."[2]

Frei's study traces the gradual subjugation in exegesis of the biblical narrative to extra-biblical frameworks of meaning (e.g., to schemes of salvation-history, the pilgrimage of the Christian soul, evolutionary rationalism, Newtonian science, historical philosophy, etc.). Once the text's narrative coherence, traditionally held together by figural/typological interpretation, was lost, there followed its fragmentation in signifying capacity. Especially pronounced was a consequent separation, interpretively, of the text's narrative integrity from its religious meaning and truth, the latter of which was increasingly supplied from some other non-biblical source. The obsession in modern scholarship with the biblical text's historical referentiality is a symptom, according to Frei, of this breakdown of a previously assured identity existing between narrative and meaning. Now, the eighteenth-century controversy in French Catholicism over Jansenist figural readings of Scripture — a controversy Frei himself does not mention — might therefore seem to fit neatly within Frei's historical scheme, with the Jansenists playing either a rear-guard role in defense of the pre-critical tradition of exegesis, or perhaps (less instructively) taking up the historicist intellectual categories of their opponents and donning the garb of today's aggrieved, though thoroughly modern, fundamentalists.

Frei himself, however, as he examines the more theological issues at stake in this development, pays only slight attention to the essentially

---

1. See Hans Frei, *Eclipse of Biblical Narrative: A Study in Eighteenth and Nineteenth Century Hermeneutics* (New Haven: Yale University Press, 1974), esp. chapters 1–7.
2. See ibid., 17–46, 152–54.

formative role played by the text's historical referentiality in sustaining the Scripture's instrinsic susceptibility and perhaps demand for the integrative figural interpretation he so evidently admires. Jansenist exegetes, especially among the eighteenth-century Appellants, were notable for insisting on the mutually dependent character of figure and historical event. But it is an insistence that stands outside the usual limits to the debate over narrative and reference, since it was directed at an affirmation of phenomenal history's inclusive Christoformic nature and derived not simply from a faith in the historical accuracy of the biblical text. Far from either ignoring the historical-critical challenge to Scripture's reference, or from succumbing to its presuppositions and attempting to refute them on its own critical ground, Jansenists not only observed in experience, but articulated in scriptural terms, the enabling power behind the Christian Church's subjection of itself to the affronting logic of this phenomenal Christoformity. Theologically, their hermeneutic program, if we can use such a phrase, is carefully built on a particular understanding of the Holy Spirit, just as we have been intimating throughout this study.

But in the context of the present chapter, the question will turn on the Jansenist appreciation of the necessary conformity of history and text, as figurally verified in the experience of the Church. Sanctity and miracle, therefore, must remain integral to the hermeneutic question, in a way that Frei does not acknowledge, perhaps because the historically objectivist implications of such an asserted connection defy the strict standards of his own post-critical sensibility, a sensibility that locates forms of relative truth within distinct areas of either text, or world (community), or consciousness (subject), but which cannot trust in the possibility of the crisp coincidence of all three in figuring a single reality, divinely rendered as providentially significant, that is, as the Truth itself. From the Jansenist perspective, sanctity and miracle demand a (scripturally) figured phenomenal history, and thus the figural interpretation of Scripture as a whole. This is because the meaning of any divine *éclat*, by definition subversive of historical expectations, lies in and reverts to the elusively providential character of its occasion, which is another way of describing the nature of divine figuration itself. But conversely, a figural interpretation of Scripture (and of scriptural history) must, according to this perspective, also demand the occasion of sanctity and miracle, insofar as any figurated reality must be able to reflect the divine control that is embodied in the historical *éclat* of temporally subversive holiness. Scriptural figure and historical miracle are here, then, but two descriptions of the same phenomenon, and the insistence that figural exegesis of Scripture take as its object historical referents derives from the properly adorative posture adopted in the face of this phenomenon.

In comparison with Frei's focus, therefore, we could say that our current examination will concern itself with how the figural exegesis of Jansenists is informed, not by their understanding of the compositional character of the biblical narrative itself, but by the authorial power of a peculiar divine shape, which they see as making possible and characterizing the coincidental figure of narrative and history together. That this divine author's figurating power is made accessible normatively in Scripture, rather than in historical experience, and hence that the figures of Scripture are formatively and cognitively prior in heuristic terms, does nothing to weaken for Jansenists the historical center created by and embodied in God for both Scripture and its history — the living figure of the incarnate Christ — in its role as the proper and ultimate focus for religious reflection.

In following this course, our investigation will first take us through a more detailed view of the hagiographical publicity given to François de Pâris and of its figuralist presuppositions. It will thereupon involve us in a critical examination of the origins and meaning of explicit Jansenist scriptural exegesis, a discussion that will necessitate a revision of the scholarly assessment of Appellant *figurisme,* as the method was known. From this base, in chapter 9 of the section, we can offer an alternative evaluation of Jansenist construals of scriptural history, which lie at the heart of their experience of the *ostensio Spiritus.*

## Figuralist Practice and Appellant Hagiography

To see something of the landscape discovered in pursuing the direction given to the consideration of sanctity we have attributed to the early Appellants in our last chapter, and to uncover more directly some of its figuralist exegetical presuppositions, let us examine more closely the documentary context in which de Pâris's life was publicized. We have noted how Doyen's original biography traced an almost numbing adumbration of unevolving penitential details, virtually devoid of any of the sensible brilliance normally associated with the outburst of the miraculous that Doyen chose to leave unremarked, although still clearly hovering over the account of the saint. We pointed, in particular, to the effect this had of elevating the quotidian details themselves to the rank of prodigy, yet only within the subdued embrace of the Christic figures to which they were referred and described as instantiating. What penumatic *éclat* might have been claimed for de Pâris's life as whole, then, could be defined only in terms of this deflation into scripturally constrained forms of experience. Further, the repeated tie that Doyen invoked as binding de Pâris to the now diminished past of Port-Royal only served to clothe these same scriptural forms in shades of meaning whose hues did not necessarily brighten the immediacy of the Appellant ordeal in 1731 and after. The *vie écrasée* (crushed life) embodied in the common figure, despite the unspoken effect of the miracles, staked out its historical importance only by burrowing into the experience of unremarkable *petitesse* [smallness] that penitence imposes. For these reasons, the characterization of such a *Vie* as a religious movement's "hagiographic propaganda" — an otherwise pertinent description — seemed to us inapt.

It might seem otherwise, however, with subsequent writings about the saint. Within the year that Doyen's *Vie* appeared, abridged versions of the life were published. Instead of standing on their own and meeting the public as pure offerings of the shape of holiness — however interpreted by someone like Doyen — these short biographies were frequently devotionally tailored and then rebound into small anthologies, whose range of accompanying texts provides what seems a full descriptive vision of the Appellant cause at its factionally most incisive. In this context, sanctity takes on the role of *imprimatur* to the more specific forms of theological and legal arguments that the opponents of the *Unigenitus* bull continued to mount. One such anthology, for instance, which we shall now examine, displays this almost ideological relocation of de Pâris's life most clearly. It opens with a shortened version of the biography[3] — attributed to J. L. Barbeau de la Bruyère — which itself acts as prelude to a longer devotional section containing an extended "meditation" and set of "instructions" and *pratiques* (practices) related to the saint and the Church. This, then, is bound with a small set of prayers concerning grace and the traits of de Pâris's holy life; two long summaries of miracles associated with de Pâris,[4] taken from Archbishop de Noailles's official inquiry; a detailed "chronology" of events connected with the bull through 1732 and the closing of the Saint-Médard cemetery, by Nicolas LeGros;[5] a full copy of the bull's text; and finally, an *explication* in dialogue form, of various theological points in dispute (e.g., the religious powers of temporal rulers, efficacious grace, the reading of Scripture, the nature of penitence, the duty of the laity to involve themselves in such matters. etc.), ending with the most extended question, that of the Saint-Médard miracles themselves.[6] This last work is attributed to Boursier.

The collection as a whole obviously served to propagate the Appellant case in a time — the early 1730s — when increasingly harsh official measures were being taken against the movement. In addition, as the devotional opening demonstrates, the texts are also geared toward supporters whose stamina and informed commitment may have begun to wane. To this degree, we can speak of "propaganda." However, it is critical to observe that, in this instance, the propagandistic element of the anthologizing factor, far from reformulating the character of de Pâris's sanctity as figural coincidence, is rather itself redefined by its own willful subservience to this view of the saint's life and related prodigious effects. Not only do LeGros's chronology and Boursier's dialogue aim their outlines toward concluding pieces dealing with de Pâris and the miracles.

---

3. *La Vie de M. François de Paris, Diacre* (1731).

4. *Recueil des miracles operés au tombeau de M. de Paris Diacre* (1732); *Second recueil des miracles operés par l'intercession de M. de Paris* (1732).

5. *Abrégé chronologique des principaux evenemens Qui ont précédé la Constitution Unigenitus, qui y ont donné lieu, ou qui en sont les suites. AVEC Les CI. Propositions du P. Quesnel mises en parallelle avec l'Ecriture et la Tradition* (nouvelle edition, 1732).

6. *Explication abregée des principales questions qui ont rapport aux affaires présentes* (1731).

This fact alone is significant. But the manner in which this appears to depend on the anthology's extensive opening of hagiographical, devotional, and descriptive texts informs the content of their otherwise more purely historical and theological popular instruction. The events themselves as they are described and defended shape the nature of their publicity, much as Jansenist sanctity, according to our examination, renders peculiar the sensible *éclat* of the miraculous.

Barbeau de la Bruyère's version of the *Vie*, which opens the anthology, adds nothing to Doyen's in the way of factual content. Indeed, in its abbreviation it tends to magnify the enumerated penitential practices of de Pâris into iconic demonstrations of sanctity in a way that inevitably transforms the circumstantially adorative focus of Doyen into something more immediately pedagogic. But even Doyen's catalogue aimed at the tracing of coincidental figures, something the epitomization of detail in the abridgement only makes more explicit. For the pedagogical intent of the work appears less in its application to the Appellant cause than in its formal placement of that cause within the figural construal of sanctity's historical shape. Contemporary events stand in the fore of the presentation, but only implicitly — unlike LeGros's subsequent chronology — as the presupposed object of explication to be grasped by the cipher de Pâris's life represents.

Thus, the *Unigenitus* bull is mentioned only twice, and in passing, in the course of the biography,[7] and de Pâris's status as an opponent to the bull constitutes only one shade of his portrait, informative more of his character than of his activities and at one with other gently outlined contours, like his adherence to the "spirit" of Port-Royal.[8] And as with Doyen's version, even though the miracles after his death are noted, the account remains resolutely concerned more with the substance of the life itself and with the penitential sacrifice it embodied. The healings, popular veneration, and spontaneous search after the saint's relics are related, not for themselves, but to mark the clarity of his faithfulness in the eyes of the populace. Instead, the narrative culmination of the story is given in a translation of the long epitaph placed on de Pâris's tomb by his brother. Here, we are given notice only of his mortifications, with some brief commentary:

> ... he could properly, then, be called a "man of desire"; his delight was in penitence. ... It was through this means that he was victorious over the Demon, that seducer of men ... being rather consumed by the fire of his charity than by that of his fever. We could rightly call him an innocent victim of penitence.[9]

And so it goes. Appellancy is implicitly memorialized here not as a theological program, but as a historical typification of the struggle of divine

---

7. *La Vie de M. François de Paris, Diacre,* 12 and 29.
8. Ibid., 11.
9. Ibid., 34f.

charity within a *monde flatteur* (flattering world) riddled by demonic aggressions. This represents the figure of Christ's Cross[10] and to this degree purposely outstrips the lines that mark the particularities of ecclesiastical dispute.

But ecclesiastical dispute is not thereby relegated to transitory circumstance. Instead, it is subsumed into the elevating motion of sanctity's figural type. It is this dynamic that imbues not only Barbeau de la Bruyère's attempt at venerative pedagogy but the anthology's overall ideological exterior with an unresolved tension between the will to publicize and the divine choreography that has already placed figural limits on motions of even its faithful servants. The preface to the *Vie* and its attached devotions reveal this tension clearly, and with it the elements that give what came to be known as Appellant "figurisme" its peculiar vision within the range of adaptive hermeneutical styles normally associated with besieged minorities.

What we can observe in the combination of accompanying preface and devotional instructions is what happens when the "eschatological figure" which we traced back to Arnauld is explicitly perceived as determinative of the various penitential figures associated with Jansenist Christoform sanctity, or more properly, when the two figures are seen as joined. The opening paragraph of the preface lays out the normative shape of the Church's sensible experience of holiness: although "destined" to raise up saints, through the very "permission" of God "the greatest number of her saints are those whom the world neither knows during their life nor after their death," of whom many are even "driven from her bosom by those granted her authority."[11] Sanctity is thus primarily marked by its hiddenness, by the temporal failure "to see the glory of [the Church's] most faithful servants manifested to the eyes of men." Within the consistent weave of this general fabric that clothes the *éclat* of glory, however, God brings openings through which the brilliance of His power is given light in the public manifestation of a "life altogether astonishing," by which sinners are wakened and the just are consoled. Such unveilings of holiness are rare, and coincide only with those historical moments in the Church's life when evil is most rampant and corruption most embedded. The Arnauldian perspective on sanctity's historical location proves here to be a deeply moving current.

To an era of *ecclesia* and *mundus senescens* (aging Church and world), we are told, the divine gift that is François de Pâris is proffered. In the midst of an age of "indifference," "scandal," the truth "anathematized," the Gospel "annihilated," of "vice," "abomination," and "rejected saints," "God, who watches over His Church, reveals before our eyes a perfect model of penitence, of humility, of total detachment, of patience, and of sincere attachment to the truth." The purpose of the biography that

---

10. Ibid., 29 and 33.
11. The three-and-a-half-page preface is unpaginated.

follows, then, is to present readers with a holy example to be "imitated" in its complete ordering as "a fabric of mortifications, punishments, and austerities." With this brief introduction complete, there follows the actual life of the saint. But a reflective audience cannot help but be puzzled by this paradoxical exhortation to attentiveness. For the very claim to that divine illumination of a particular life for imitation is premised on the fact of a historical landscape that must inevitably cast its brilliance in the drowning shadows. The miracles of healing are not even mentioned here, and the "astonishing life" that is described as planted before the human eye so clearly in this age is that of the penitential self-reduction that necessarily trades visibility for virtues that deliberately remain "unknown." Far from prying open an epoch to divine light, François de Pâris slips into a time when "the examples of the Saints were rejected as useless" and the will of faithfulness fulfills itself only by its submission to this shuttered disdain. Of course, the biography that is traced is an attempt to publicize the nature of this hidden battle with the world's tempter and such a struggle's proper human posture, but the very possibility of its propagandistic success is contradicted by the manner in which God's charity must burn: the special times of glorious "consolation" when God raises up a public saint can only drape themselves more heavily in the folds of history's usual veiling of the holy. The *contrast* first drawn by the preface between the normal course of the Church's shadowed destiny and those rare hours of divine translucence is shown instead to end in unforeseen *coincidence*.

This is not, however, to imply identity. That is, the hope that François de Pâris might be among the shining stars within a firmament otherwise kept outside the eye's reach is not one that is dashed or simply contradicted by the fate of his restricted influence within the Church. Instead, as the devotions which follow the biography reveal, the recognition of, or even just the naming of the coincidence between norm and circumstance — the culling of the figure from its history — itself identifies the light that burns its own distinctive shape through the sequential cloak of temporal events.

The long "Prayer in the form of a meditation" that follows the epitaph's translation extends the canvas of the preface and the figural paradox that it depicts into something more explicitly expressive of the historical moorings given to sanctity's ambiguous reflection. It begins with two scriptural quotations designed to place the subsequent meditation in the realm of such adorative praise as flows from the radiance of divine action in the world: "I will praise you, O my God, because your greatness bursts forth in a wonderful way; your works are wonderful. . . . Who is like you, whose holiness bursts forth so fully, terrible and worthy of all praise, who works wonders?" (see Ps. 139:14, Ex. 15:11).[12] Indeed, as the borrowed voice of Moses here insists, the emphasis is upon the brilliance of miracles in particular, of the saving interventions of God before the face of a disdain-

---

12. Ibid., 35.

ing and defiant human enemy. But, as in the preface, the character of this "brilliance" as it is associated with François de Pâris is immediately unfastened from the sensible astonishment of, say, the condemned Egyptians drowned in the sea and is instead redescribed in terms of the "eyes of faith" that alone can "pierce" the besieging ramparts of "encircling mortality" to behold the "magnificence" of that gratuitous choice that alone could form within the world a life of such complete penitence.[13]

At this point, however, the prayer inserts the miraculous antinomy of glory in its sensible hiddenness within an eschatological figure that has now gained new detail in comparison with the preceding biography's more temporally uniform account of the world's consistent opposition to the grace of sanctity. The saint is recognized not only in his showing forth of Christ, but in his essential relation, as such a sign, to his surrounding era, "these times of decadence for the nations called to enter your Church."[14] What is referred to here, without explanation, is the specific expiration of that vocation of the Gentiles which is to mark the consummation of the ages. This is predicted both by Paul and Revelation, as our author will remark in a later text. Here, it is enough to observe that de Pâris's holiness is spoken of now in terms of "prophecy" within this historic context; his is a form that is identified as Christ's, but also as the pneumatic center of prophetic "zeal" destined for an "immolation" as a victim of the "age." The penitence that figures Christ is thus embodied in another form, that of the precursor to final judgment in the midst of an unfaithful people: "in these last days, when it seemed as if all that remained was for you to strike the earth with [your] curse, you chose for us your Servant [i.e., de Pâris] as a forerunner of the Prophet intended to soften your wrath."[15]

The relationship of miracles to this prophetic form of history's close is described in terms that resonate with Pascalian overtones, as we have identified them in his reflections on divine epiphany. The orchestrating figure of the Incarnate Crucified directs its own manifestation through the sensible display of grace's configurating touch, and this historical "piece" is given experiential body through its command of dark and light, "blindness" and "sight," judgment and mercy. Thus, François de Pâris's penitential submission is properly (and commonly) called a "burning and gleaming light" in part because of its train of miracles worked at the saint's tomb. The prodigies are not simply swallowed up in the well of retiring humility, remaining "unknown" through divine poverty's demand, but emanate "glory" as they penetrate the public's sensibility.[16] Yet the force of such inescapable demonstrations remains conformed to the figure drawn by God's free grace among the hearts of men and women. As with Pascal, the "evidential" power of the Saint-Médard events depends upon, and in large measure itself represents in its historical fullness, the efficacious

---

13. Ibid., 36.
14. Ibid.
15. Ibid., 37, 42f.
16. E.g., ibid., 43.

workings of that providential hold on human lives that is identified as "faith," and whose weak and passing grasp is charged to humankind as lack thereof. It is not surprising, of course, to find praise offered to God for de Pâris's extraordinary instantiation of God's "sovereign grace."[17] Such more narrowly theological elements in an Appellant portrait are to be expected. But informing, as they must, the very sensible character of the miracles as they are perceived in the world, they act as defining props for a more specifically historical stage, one that gains even more particularist figural depth than in Pascal's vision:

> Multiply, therefore, your exterior graces, but without adding to them that anointing that alone softens the heart; and those proud spirits that are full of their own self-sufficiency, even as they harden themselves further, will they not become, just in this, the living proof of that truth of yours they are opposing? You rain down, as it were, miracles; yet have these very miracles not become for many a hail of stones sent to kill and crush them? Has the time arrived for punishing those nations become apostate in their turn? And do these miracles, however much they may console your Church, proclaim to those who have humiliated her with so many insults a kind of Egyptian plague or the punishment of a Babylon?[18]

The miracles themselves give evidence of the shape of God's configurating grace in "softening" the brittle pride directing human vision even as its work brings into relief the sharp edges of that sin which refuses to acknowledge these divine gifts. Not only does this increased "hardening" in the face of epiphanic demonstration point to the healings' simultaneous role in "killing" and "crushing" their detractors, but the episode of Saint-Médard as a whole now becomes a "living proof" of God's own truth, understood theologically in terms of the subsuming reality of efficacious grace, but given factual substance in terms of the scriptural figures of Egypt and Babylon, two nations fallen beneath the weight of God's justice.

As in the case of Pascal, we might well wonder how a "proof" that is rooted in the very rejection of its demonstrative ingredients can act as evidence of anything, and to whom. But the nature of a persuasive religious apology (Pascal) or of divine vindication (de Pâris's miracles) is bound up less with the abstractly quantifiable groups of the convinced than with the manner in which identifiable individuals, whether convinced or not, together compose a larger figure definitive of God's historical display. "Evidence" here boils down to the figural conformity of events, which itself embraces the spectrum of its human recognizability.

---

17. See ibid., 38: "Your Servant found all his joy on this earth in discovering the glory of this grace. By it, he understood and intimately grasped how, without such grace, there is in a person only sin and its outcome, there is only a prideful poverty and a slothful indigence, there is only a general incapacity to do any good or even to ask You for it. He never exalted his free will, for he knew well (as You Yourself had taught him) that it had no power of its own to do anything but destroy itself, and that You do not save a man except insofar as You *save his free will*" (St. Bernard).

18. Ibid., 46f.

But this very fact gives epiphanic form a certain open-endedness, or at least historical fluidity in its configurating power. The images, in the quote above, of an "Egypt" or a "Babylon" are readily gleaned from the circumstances in which the "rain" of miracles at Saint-Médard descends, and these in turn inform as types the specific era of the "nations' punishment" at the end of time. Yet the petitionary genre of these descriptions is designed to lead the reader away from the posture of final assertion such bold interpretations of events might demand, into one, instead, of inquiring submission to the continued molding of the world's arrangement. The question of the eschatological figure raised through the types of Israel's past is resolved in a return to the saint's contemporary intercession, in bowing lovingly to an oppression that, in its very figural integrity, cannot therefore be ruled unredeemable:

> O God, mighty God, terrible God, inscrutable in your counsels, I adore you! But more than anything, my task is to seek your grace and to beseech You for your mercy! Through your only Son, you command us to pray for those who malign us and persecute us; Lord, it is for them that we now pray, with respect to this Holy Brother, whom we know with such power to be your intercessor whom you have given us. And so, Lord, may he pray for those who hate us, and may he ask of you that you do not impute to them the sin of warring against you that they commit in doing so against us.[19]

The figure of sanctity thus moves back from the immovable proclamation of temporal consummation and links this limiting reality to less predictive and more historically typical figures of the past. This is seen in the way the saint is associated with such a broad catalogue of scriptural individuals as to blur the lines of distinction between the various epochs of the Church's history that his life has purportedly illuminated. Praying for one's enemies in the face of devastating punishment and to the point of death, François de Pâris, precursor to the Prophet "in these last days," reveals at the same time the impression of John the Baptist,[20] the martyred deacon Stephen,[21] and finally the divine Servant whose penitence joins sin and its own dreadful wages into one exhausted body.[22] Far from dictating the course of events to follow, the historical enactments of these various figures as they are grasped in their eschatological posture end by harmonizing the conflicting elements of the Saint-Médard experience into a Christic, though temporally non-sequential narrative. We are given a cluster of scriptural figures within which events are ordered, the whole of which is singularly Christ's even while the parts of which appropriately stand as alternating frameworks for particular experience.

Only within this context do the miracles themselves have a properly empowered role. We have already examined something of the Jansen-

---

19. Ibid., 47.
20. Ibid., 43.
21. Ibid., 44.
22. Ibid., 42.

ist insistence on the circumstantial nature of such pneumatic displays. But ironically, although Appellancy seems a crystalization of the limited disputational narrative according to which Port-Royal's writers parsed the miraculous, the shifting play of figural light in which François de Pâris's life was seen, revealed dispute itself to be an ancillary (though indispensable) circumstance to the broader swaths of divine history that Scripture elucidates in temporal repetition. The glory of God composes a durationally embodied lectionary.

Thus, the biography's appended "Prayer in the form of a meditation" is followed by nine "instructions and exercises [*pratiques*] on the Holiness and Miracles of M. de Paris," the whole of which constitutes a description of this demonstrative coincidence between the events of holiness and their figural proliferation in the face of Church and world. The instructions, in effect, encourage readers toward nothing more complicated — although in itself the participating vision of sanctity's display ringed by its opposition — than the single act (*pratique*) of recognizing in its depth this coherence between circumstance and scriptural form. Referring, for instance, to the prophetic figures de Pâris himself explained as informing his ministry, the devotional guide insists that,

> committing oneself to the reading of Scripture along the general lines of his [de Pâris'] outlook and searching there for the consolation that God announces must come after the ills that Scripture predicts, is therefore itself a way to share M. de Paris' own vision, and perhaps even to enter one of the principal purposes of his miracles. For [to do this] is truly to unite oneself with the spirit of M. de Paris and to enter into a holy communion with him (which is the general way in which one brings dignified and useful honor to the Saints).[23]

The instructions, then, provide a wide selection of pertinent figures according to which the participants in these devotions — participants, we are led to believe, in the events of Saint-Médard as well — can join themselves to the "spirit" of holiness whose movement is reflected in the strange vision of a divinely vindicated faith emblematically rejected.

While each of these nine instructions purportedly aims at a distinct devotion, their explications merge into a far more general collection of figural claims whose only development lies in the loose eschatological crescendo of their arrangement. "Understand the gift of God [given] in M. de Paris," which begins the guide, elucidates the figural concert joining, among others, the saint with the birth of Cain through grace (Gen. 4:1) — the first steps of the human race and God's ordering of its course — and with the consolation given to the old age of our history by God's love (e.g., Gen. 37:3, Ruth 4:15, Ps. 92:14).[24] All this is deliberately colored by its placement within the prophetic frame of the Church's own struggle in a disintegrating world (e.g., Ps. 11). The next two devotions,

---

23. Ibid., 73.
24. Ibid., 49ff.

"Recognizing the particular protection God provides to the putative party maligned under the name 'Jansenist'" and "New zeal for the cause of God, which was entrusted to M. de Paris and decided at his tomb,"[25] promise a more pointed and polemically self-interested justification for Appellancy. Instead, references to *Unigenitus,* its condemned propositions, and the theological battles preceding the document, although they are given clear relief, are appropriated into a tableau bounded by the stories of Esther, Daniel and Susanne, and St. Stephen. The entire history of Port-Royal and its followers, configurated in this manner, is then exploded into the prophetically verbal reach of Psalm 2 and Isaiah 59:14ff., even as these figural announcements are contracted into "this little cemetery of S. Medard," where we are exhorted to worship: "let us adore God [here]."[26]

The venerative center to this history exerts a crucial pull on the significance of the prophetic tenor of the explications. "Worship" here is supplied its figural weight in the next five instructions through the repeated linkages of de Pâris's modeling of scriptural form with the evolving shape of the Church's reaction to the miraculous — both in her limited embrace of the healings and in her more extensive repudiation of their truth. We are called to praise God with a "mixture of joy and terror," to remark the "double judgment" of vindication and punishment exercised at the saint's tomb, to prepare for new and fiercer trials despite the victory that sensible holiness represents in the midst of persecution, to join ourselves to the saint's own self-immolating hopes, and finally, eagerly to desire the "double coming" of Jesus Christ yet to be enacted in time, the first to convert Israel of the flesh and the second, after the Jews' own mission to the world on His behalf, to bring to consummation the Kingdom of His saints. In themselves, these vaguely ordered topics point to a predictive claim about expected happenings that might somehow further the justifying role played by the miracles for the Appellant cause. The figural characterizations of these claims, however, impose upon them a temporal freedom whose logic comes less from the certainties of historical sequence than from the glorifying stance adopted in their enunciation of scriptural narrative and profile as they elucidate a conflicted present tethered in their midst. Figures drawn from Exodus, the Psalms, Isaiah, Wisdom, Daniel, the Gospels, Acts, the Epistles, and the Apocalypse all serve to render the features of these devotions; in themselves their deployment combines the historical past and future into a single, but circulating set of contemporary events. The strong outlines of each scriptural reference appear as sensible images individually, to be sure, in such a manner that a list of applications can be grasped by any reader. But only in their *catalogued* sum do they give up an offertory aura, thereby granting to the order of their description an interchangeability that reorients the purpose of their distinctive rehearsal

---

25. Ibid., 52–61.
26. Ibid., 61.

from temporal succession as something oracular to divine expression in
its coherence as something figurally teeming.

The last instruction, then, if taken alone, could seem but a blunt apocalyptic warning based on the previous texts employed concerning, e.g., John
the Baptist, Elijah, and Peter's epistles, and marshaled so as to describe
predictively the divine fashioning of human history around the painful
triumph of Jansenist doctrine:

> God raised up [M. de Paris] like a banner of penitence pointing to the near-
> ness of God's Kingdom and to His great wrath [coming] upon peoples who,
> though within the external bosom of the Church, are far more criminally
> guilty than even the Jewish people were when God was so close to bringing
> upon them ruin. M. de Paris *saw the wrath of God kindled by the Constitu-*
> *tion Unigenitus*; these were his own words, and he took upon himself the
> task of assuaging that anger like another Elijah, of giving himself completely
> over to a devouring zeal and bitterness of heart which penetrated his being.[27]

But this final instruction, the author makes clear, is designed to "summarize" all the devotions and their explications that have gone before in a
single figure which, *in itself*, includes the chronologically adventist props
of the work's concluding statement just quoted. "Do penitence [*faire pen-*
*itence*]" — this is the last devotion's title, explained in these terms: "a
kind of summary of what all the instructions mean that God gives us
in the life and miracles of M. de Paris."[28] But this is only to return to a
present, already set forth in all of its bounded particularity, whose figural
practice in its various forms of saintly coincidence discloses the future
course of events only as it buries itself in the contemporary fractures of
contested sensibility. Within a purely sequentialist understanding of scriptural prophecy, penance may well be a peculiar and responsive vocation
for those who live shadowed by the threatening ax of Doom's unique day.
But as a "summary" (*abregé*) of such prophecy itself, not only a reaction to
it; as a description of the present's frame in instancing predictive acts, not
only the result of such foreseeing; as the sensible kaleidoscope of Scripture's historical forms, not only the external environment making possible
their meditation; as the figured stuff of God's embodied death in sin en-
folding love's engendering life; as all of this at least, penitence, precisely
in the crags that guard its passage beyond a purely human experience, is
a divine showing.

If scriptural figures that span history are themselves thus catalogued
within the fashioning framework of a Christically penitential form defined by the limits of present circumstance, then the act of anthologizing
the arguments of ecclesiastical dispute within the borders of such specific hagiography subjects whole notions like a movement's "propaganda,"
"justification," and self-"vindication" to a reformulating treatment. By

---

27. Ibid., 79f.
28. Idem. Faire penitence.

pointing to the details of the party's experience and theological rationale, the collections of affidavits to the healings, LeGros's chronology, and Boursier's tract all underline the shape of their own historical *dismissal* even as they withdraw into the power of the figures their details alone can, as it were, proclaim before the public.

LeGros, for instance, ends with a notice of the closure of the cemetery in January 1732 and of the disturbed confusion caused by the first convulsions among the healed. His last remark describes a member of the royal court, the Chevalier Folard, "Brigadier in the King's Armies, whose stunning conversion drew the attention of the Court and of foreign countries," who is banished from the realm, presumably just because of this unsettling "brilliance" [*éclat*] in his Christian experience. The order is, however, soon revoked, we are told, not for religious reasons, but in view of Folard's loyal service to the nation.[29] So does political reward, LeGros realizes, drown out the clap of God's offensive thunder. On this hook, according to the author, then dangles the "history" of a movement.

Boursier, last of all, whose theological treatment of the miraculous relies as much on the recently published "notes sur les miracles" of Pascal as it does on Thomas Aquinas, completes his dryly reasoned contribution to the anthology on the same plane of reconceived evidentialism as did his Port-Royal mentor before him: the "extraordinary blasts" of Saint-Médard serve to make faith more "certain" in its claims. Yet "certitude," he tells us, in the wake of de Pâris's figure, is nothing else than "lamenting our sins with a contrite and humble heart."[30] Nothing else. This stands as the enacted summary of the "cause of God" to which he has referred throughout his dialogue, with seemingly typical Appellant self-righteousness. With this conclusion to his work, however, Boursier allows the grand *causa gratiae Dei* to reach its "end" in the reduction of asserted luminosity back into the already adumbrated form of a despised deacon. What *éclat* persists in such a setting? Only that which strains through strings of figures culled from Scripture and left behind to form the mesh, as it were, of that one great net "cast into the sea" that gathered of every kind (Mt. 13:47).

To say with such an image, "so shall it be at the end of the world" — as it seems to me Appellant hagiography does in its repeated relating of prophetic figures to the historically effective immobility of penitence — is to make "endings" and temporal presents cohabitants of sacred history. It is to replace a notion of singular chronological succession in the working out of divine providence with one according to which distinctive scriptural events like the "coming forth of angels" to "sever the wicked from among the just" and the final "wailing and gnashing of teeth" press their sensible forms into the shape of contemporaneity, itself "like unto the Kingdom of heaven," which holds and orders within its grasp the sheath of measured spans men and women call their lives.

29. LeGros, *Abrégé chronologique des principaux evenemens,* 74.
30. *Explication abregée des principales questions* [Boursier], 82.

## *Figurisme* as an Appellant Innovation?

The entire devotional structure given to François de Pâris's public expo-
sure is clearly based on the intricate web connecting scriptural figure and
the Christian life. Already before his death this web had been pulled apart
and the purely exegetical aspects of its reality displayed and debated. That
there is something peculiar about specifically Appellant exegesis, such as
that applied unself-consciously in the de Pâris material, is evident from
the simple fact that it was quickly singled out for attack by Appellancy's
contemporary opponents. Of course, the degree to which the rejection of
Appellancy as an ecclesiastical party encouraged the opposition artificially
to fabricate supposedly Jansenist attitudes and practices that would provide convenient targets for accusation, among which was only a putative
hermeneutical heresy, is difficult to gauge. From an Appellant view, in any
case, such "false" accusations themselves were disclosive of a theological
rift within the Church that sprang from the demonic war raging in her
midst. From the perspective of the Church's defense of truth, then, an
examination of the exegetical battle is called for as a matter of faith. Still,
it is worth noting from the beginning of our discussion that specifically
Appellant hermeneutics as denominated by the term *figurisme* was an
invention of the *anti*-Jansenists, and not a self-designation.

The "method" of Appellant hermeneutics known as *figurisme* was
first publicly attacked — and thereby given a nominal existence — in
two anonymous works of 1727 directed against the exegetical writings
in particular of Duguet.[31] Now generally attributed to an otherwise unknown priest, the abbé Martin-Augustin Léonard, these two volumes of
considerable length are significant for their disclosure of what appear to
be common attitudes toward Scripture among the French clergy, attitudes that are beginning to diverge openly from Jansenist reading of the
Bible that had, until then, been considered unexceptional. Duguet and his
younger colleague Jacques Vincent Bidal d'Asfeld had published a two-part
work in 1716, the *Règles pour l'intelligence des Saintes Ecritures* ("Rules
for understanding the Holy Scriptures"), which had gained considerable
popularity, and, indeed, continued to be used as a hermeneutical guide
well into the nineteenth century.[32] The first section, the "rules" proper,
attempted to summarize within what bounds and according to what gen-

---

31. *Réfutation du livre des regles pour l'intelligence des Stes Ecritures* (Paris: Jacques
Vincent, 1727), and *Traité du sens litteral et du sens Mystique des Saintes Ecritures, Selon
la Doctrine des Peres* (Paris: Jacques Vincent, 1727). An earlier attack on the *Règles* appeared
in 1723, the *Mouââcah, ceinture de douleur, ou réfutation d'un livre intitulé "Règles pour
l'intelligence des saintes Écritures,* under the authorship of the rabbi "Ismaël Ben Abraham,
juif converti," a recognized pseudonym for the linguist and orientalist Étienne Fourmont
(1683–1745). It garnered little interest and no response, and the *Réfutation* and *Traité* are
generally considered the first publicly acknowledged opposition to *figurisme*. On Fourmont,
see the article by J. Richaridt in *Dictionnaire de Biographie Française*, vol. 14, cols. 786f.

32. The text, for instance, was reprinted in J.-P. Migne's *Scripturae Sacrae Cursus Completus* (Paris: Garnier Frères, 1877), vol. 27, and we shall generally be referring to this more
easily consulted edition.

eral principles one might read the Old Testament in particular, in its parts
and in its whole, as figurally referring to Christ. The second section, entitled "Application of the preceding rules to the Return of the Jews," stands
as a self-styled example of such Christocentric reading, using as its limited topic the figural relationship between Paul's teaching in Romans 11
and various Old Testament texts.[33]

While Léonard tells us that *figurisme* as a "system" was first utilized
by Jean-Baptiste Le Sesne des Ménilles, the abbé d'Étemare, in a work
written in 1712 (though not published until 1723),[34] it is Duguet's *Règles*
that he views as the source of menace, laying out a hermeneutic that
has "by now" attracted "many" adherents, especially among the younger
priests.[35] But in what lies the "systematic" character of Duguet's exegesis?
In many respects, Léonard criticizes figurism for its tendency toward the
*un*disciplined imagination, for a *lack* of limiting rules, and for a failure to
structure its exegesis around clear principles of reasoning. In particular,
the elevation of the "mystical sense" as the main sense of Scripture insofar
as it embodies the figural significance of the literal sense, leads to a "mania
for allegories," an "unbridled liberty to seek and find anything one wants
in the Scripture," and that is the "illuminist" opposite of a "methodical"
interpretive venture.[36] As a form of interpretation that claims to be the

33. It has been argued, e.g., by Hervé Savon, that this last portion comes from the hand of
d'Asfeld, and actually represents something of an ill-fitting and not wholly faithful enactment
of Duguet's "Rules." (See Savon's "Le figurisme et la 'Tradition des Pères,'" in *Le Grand
Siècle et la Bible,* ed. Jean-Robert Armogathe [Paris: Editions Beauchesne, 1989], 757–85.
See also our discussion later in this chapter.) For the moment, we can simply note how
the coherence of the work was assumed from its initial publication, by both supporters and
opponents of its perspective. Indeed, the continued authority that the *Règles* maintained
even within non-Jansenist circles, an authority that always included as its base the secondary
"application" regarding the Return of the Jews, should alert us to the theological difficulties
faced by anyone trying to pry Jansenist exegesis loose from orthodox tradition, especially on
the basis of its "prophetical" outlook.

34. D'Étemare is still often cited as the "inventor" of *figurisme* (see the article
"Figurisme" by Mangenot in the *Dictionnaire de la Théologie Catholique*), although, as in
Savon's case, this assertion seems based on a desire to disassociate the mild-mannered and
consistently revered Duguet from the later vagaries of the convulsions with which figurism
became connected, and which d'Étemare for his part in general supported. On the other
hand, opponents of Appellancy at the time, like Léonard (and confirmed by d'Étemare's own
claims), saw the latter as a disciple of Duguet, and one whose views were substantially formed
by the public lectures on Scripture Duguet offered (through others) and by personal conversations with him in Paris in the first decades of the eighteenth century. Much is complicated
in our efforts to sort out origins and influences here by the fact that many works, both by
Duguet and d'Étemare as well as others involved, were written in manuscript and circulated
in a limited way, many years before being published in book form. Goujet, Duguet's first biographer, tells us that the "lectures" standing behind many of Duguet's published works on
Scripture are really "notes" he had written for others to explicate before the public, notably
Rollin at the College de Beauvais and d'Asfeld at the parish of Saint-Roch. See [Claude-Pierre
Goujet] *Vie de M. Du Guet, Prêtre de la Congrégation de l'Oratoire, Avec le Catalogue de
ses Ouvrages,* (n.p., 1741), 19. In any case, the *Règles is* the first published book openly
identified as "figurist," and for this reason, as well as its influence, it continues to deserve
the reputation it soon gained as the "figurist handbook." We shall be returning briefly to the
subject of d'Étemare's relationship with Duguet's thought at the end of this chapter.

35. *Réfutation,* vff.

36. See ibid., 1–11, 109ff., 431, 459.

only means by which to save the Old Testament for the Church's use, figurism ends by embodying an "idiosyncratic fanaticism."[37] Rather than describing a strict system at all, then, even Léonard (for all his gallic enumerative logic) sees figurism, as we do in this chapter, as an identifiable way of approaching Scripture, but one that is not so much constructed on hermeneutical principles as one that emerges to view practically out of or in concert with a set of general theological convictions, many of which we have already examined in Section I, and which inform the devotional world of sanctity and miracle we are now exploring.

Let me then outline three attitudes and interpretive practices exposed in the *Règles* that come under attack by Léonard. Their presence under his fire sets the stage for the concerns my present chapter will thereafter seek to address.

1. Léonard's most specifically theological objection is the assertion he claims to identify in Duguet's work that the Holy Spirit exercises total control over the form and meaning of Scripture. In the first place, Léonard recognizes that Scripture's significant language is often unclear, and hence that the appeal to a "mystical sense" (i.e., a "figural" reading) is both reasonable and acceptable when limited by the strict standards of the Church's tradition and their "judicious" application.[38] But even with this admission, he insists that mystical readings were always understood to be second-best attempts to tackle a scriptural text in eras still reliant on historical tools insufficient to the task of properly comprehending the more primary literal sense.[39] If the Fathers did in fact have frequent recourse to figural interpretation — contrary to their own cautionary principles — it was only because they still lacked the scholarly equipment necessary to "penetrate" many texts on a literal plane, equipment now conveniently available to "modern interpreters." In any case, the mystical sense must be seen as a tenuous and temporary standby for more authoritative literal readings of Scripture.

This is why Léonard cannot stomach the insistence that figural readings of Scripture might derive from the inspiration of the Holy Spirit, that is, from the Spirit's own embedded direction of the text's formation and meaning in history.[40] Even figural readings found to be expounded by Scripture itself — e.g., by Paul — ought only, according to Léonard, to be seen as interpretations governed by the precise historical situations in which the apostle lived and by the limited explanatory objectives he held for his audience. As such, they cannot pretend to any inclusive interpretive embrace of Scripture and scriptural history as a whole.[41] The Holy Spirit's

---

37. Ibid., xii, xv.
38. This fact, and the obviously extensive use made by the Fathers of figural exegesis, lies behind the entire argument of the *Traité du sens litteral*. See also the *Refutation*, chapter 1; also, 100ff.
39. See the *Traité*, 349ff.
40. See the *Refutation*, vii.
41. See the *Traité*, 521ff.

legitimating role in such accepted figures is therefore limited to Paul's own time and does not carry through into our own in any obvious or useful manner. Indeed, the claim to a pneumatic authority behind the *whole* of Scripture as it has come down to us in all of its details, an opinion accurately attributed to Duguet, strikes Léonard as dangerous, precisely because it grants to the obscurities of scriptural language and its referents an infallibility that must lead to imposing and demanding spiritual pressures placed upon present history in its continuity with the past.[42] Léonard accepts the inspiration of Scripture and its pneumatological base, to be sure, but only on the level of its literal meanings' edifying goal. To save the "literal" meaning by limiting the Spirit's subsuming authorial control of the text, is therefore, comfortably to truncate the present age from the chronological past of Scripture, leaving only the bridge of moral instruction to span significantly the years' passage.

2. Léonard's second argument with figurism, then, lies in the disturbing historical logic of the latter's pneumatological premise: if the Holy Spirit infallibly authored Scripture in its whole and detail — in Duguet's view, as referring to the temporally figured Christ — then its whole and detailed referents would, on a purely literal plane, require a historical interpretation — a conclusion rendered clearly preposterous in Léonard's mind, precisely by the mutually disclosed obscurities and incongruities of Scripture's narratives and discourses (e.g., contradictory prophecies, multiple fulfillments, temporally mixed and dislocated historical referents). Figurists resolve the incongruities by adopting mystical readings of the texts that include the very shape of history within their grasp: history, they say, follows the shape of the figures, and not vice versa. Literalists, as Léonard argues, properly resolve the incongruities on the level of literary and historical-critical exegesis, parsing a given text according to its self-enclosed historical situation and compositional genre, so as to segregate biblical imagery into non-intrusive chronological sectors, each of which do not impinge upon the others.

Thus, Léonard astutely explains, the figurists are in fact "too literal," in that they demand a historical referent for every detail of Scripture, turning the text into a vast display of prophetic utterances whose reach must touch the very moments of our own day.[43] Literalists, on the other hand, realizing that the literal meaning rightly reflects what a text's authors and community context "felt" and "understood" in their *own* time, appreciate the central and flexible literary role in Scripture played by genre and compositional "metaphor," whose varied imagery cannot and must not be applied to infallibly identified historical referents in all or even most cases. Paradoxically, therefore, the "literal sense," while it affirms the historicity of the compositional context of Scripture, is careful to limit the historical referentiality of its literal discourse to immediate context, while

---

42. See the *Refutation,* 120ff.
43. See ibid., 100ff.

figurism's displacement of primary authorial causality away from human writers onto the Spirit of God, demands that such literal reference in time be affirmed always, and thus in a way that can be accommodated coherently only by extending the figural grasp of Scripture's particular texts to all of history.

3. These supposed failures of method, finally, lead to Léonard's most intense unease with Duguet's figurism: its willingness, born of logical necessity, to contemporize (or futurize) the referents of biblical figures, in the form of exposing their prophetic congruence with continuing events, especially within the Christian Church's own history and experience. The literalists, however, dissect history into a sequential chronology of discrete events, each occasion of which encloses its own discrete meanings in the form given to its textual composition by historical context. This can only rule out the possibility of a temporally subsuming figure drawn from some particular portion of Scripture that might fashion the shape of the present or future. The present and the past are instead related hermeneutically by the "analogy" of "experience,"[44] and certainly not by the divine coincidence of figural conformance. An affirmation of the latter leads only to the kind of apocalyptic prophetism associated with self-deluding millenarians and unrestrained heretics. Léonard evidently relishes the parallels he is able to draw between the works of apocalyptic Protestants like Pierre Jurieu and Cocceius and the recently published works of d'Étemare.[45] He is particularly pointed in his citations from Arnauld and Nicole, unimpeachable Jansenists both, as even they attacked seventeenth-century "illuminists" for their reliance on figural images of Scripture to "predict" the future. The future, Arnauld admitted, was unknown, and therefore any prophecy of the Bible already accomplished within biblical history or the early Church could not be used to establish post-apostolic events.[46]

Léonard, therefore, uses as a base for his criticism of the figurists a particular judgment about the relation between historical experience and God. In his mind, the Church lives in an era when any scriptural "figure" it might identify within the sacred text is exhaustively and rightly explained in terms of the circumstances of its literary genesis. The Holy Spirit's relation to these figures can be distinguished and limited to the levels of the text's own periodized composition, the text's preservation within the Church over an evolving temporal sequence, and the text's continuing pedagogic adequacy within that history. The pneumatic — that is, divine — significance of a text is therefore not to be located in its historical referent, but in the subjective assimilation by the Church of that text into particular circumstances. Léonard describes the religious contrast this establishes between his "literal" and Duguet's "figurist" exegetical approaches: the

---

44. See ibid., 124–25, where Léonard argues, on this basis, against the use of the Psalms in a figural fashion.

45. Ibid., 429ff., 459.

46. Ibid., 460ff.

first is ruled by "reason" which defines historical referentiality in terms of immediate compositional context whether it be phenomenal or literary; the second, in treating the texts' references as infallibly signifying historical phenomena and thereby demanding figural construals of history itself, is ruled by a need to "multiply miracles at every moment."[47] So it is that the exorcism, by Léonard et al., of figural exegesis is plotted with the banishment of miracle. And both have run afoul of an eschatological unease. That most seventeenth-century Jansenists, like Arnauld, read the Bible in an unremittedly figuralist fashion, following the footsteps of their Patristic mentors, caused, in their own time, few eyebrows to rise.[48] Not until the dust of a destroyed Port-Royal had scattered and *Unigenitus* had unsettled the nation, did the fact of these wielded figures, in all their forms, knocking at the door of the Church's present day impress upon a typical Christian like Léonard the troubling implications of a shape to Scripture's past that might hold power to twist today into its very image.

The moment that figural exegesis of the Bible became associated, as by Léonard, with an "apocalyptic," "illuminist," and "prophetic" hermeneutic, *figurisme* was born in order to be cast away. And following this pattern of association, figurism's phenomenal siblings in the shape of miracle and sanctity were similarly discarded by opponents of Jansenism in the Church, joining the category of objects whose marginal religious integrity, so it seemed, could merit only exclusively historical-critical or psycho-cultural scrutiny. It is a pattern that has survived the particular Jansenist and Appellant struggles and has asserted itself broadly since in

---

47. Ibid., 379.

48. One of the most lastingly popular works of seventeenth-century Jansenism was the so-called "Bible de Royaumont," frequently reprinted, and attributed today to the Port-Royalist Nicolas Fontaine (actual title: *L'Histoire de Vieux et du Nouveau Testament, Avec des Explications édifiantes, tirées des Saints Peres pour regler les moeurs dans toutes sortes de conditions* [Paris: Pierre le Petit, 1680]). This work is nothing other than a summary of the entire Bible (complete with attached chronology) explained according to its traditional "figures": "the sacred histories [ . . . ] that have as their Author the Holy Spirit itself [ . . . ] are painted in figures as very important instructions," according to the explanations of the Fathers (see the opening "Lettre" of dedication to the Dauphin, and the initial "Avertissement"). While a kind of moral exemplarism governs most of the over eighty figural expositions (e.g., the Burning of Sodom, Jacob in Egypt, David and Uriah, Job, etc.), this is not exclusively the case, and some explanations are given more traditionally typological and prophetic casts (e.g., the Fall, Jericho, the Parable of the Wedding Feast, et al.). Furthermore, the overall progress of these moralistic interpretations serves the larger figural purpose, familiar in Jansenist devotion, of guiding the reader to a deeper participation in the "shape" of Jesus Himself. Still, it is the case that texts like this, as well as other popular works of biblical exposition like le Maistre de Saci's appended commentaries to his translations of the Bible into French along with their extended "prefaces" (e.g., on Proverbs and on Genesis), and the prefaces to other Port-Royal translations of, e.g., the New Testament (known as "de Mons," and first published in 1667), for all their overt appeal to Patristic figural exegesis, tended not to press the prophetic aspects of their interpretations in ways that stood out. Such aspects, however, were not ignored nor certainly repudiated by their Jansenist authors, and they are frequently in evidence in the exegesis supporting the more explicitly devotional writings of the group by individuals like the *solitaire* Jean Hamon. "Figures" as the central character of scriptural signification remained an innocuous possibility to the reading public until it assumed the explicated shape of eschatological turmoil.

modern historical studies of pneumatic events written along culturally genetic lines. Our own approach to both Appellant figurism and pneumatic
experience, however, must stand in some tension with such continued
patterns of judgment as they are sweepingly applied even to practical
Christian concerns like humility, penitence, poverty, and the experience
of factional commitment. For we must remember that a major purpose
of this study has been the testing of a specifically pneumatological claim;
that is, that the boundaries of our theological definition of the Spirit are
given textual relief by the vagaries of ostensibly pneumatic experience in
their immediacy and historical fate. To this end, we are granting pre-
sumptive cogency to the particularities of the participants' self-expression
as we experiment in the construction of an, almost *ad hoc*, configurating
framework that can render these expressions theologically coherent precisely as *Christian* history. In a sense, we are asking the pneumatological
"why?" of certain events, a question that cannot but mold the shape of
this study into a form that differs markedly from more standard historical
or theological approaches.

   This point has already been made in our introduction. However, it is
worth making again at this stage, because the pneumatological question
here posed resembles in a peculiar way the very shape of devotional and
exegetical practice given order by Appellant reflection on the apparent fact
of sanctity and miracle. We drew attention at the end of the last chapter
to the Jansenist search for "coincidence" of particular event and scriptural figure, a coincidence that was seen as rendering the significance of
sanctity in its relation to the Holy Spirit. The recognition of just such conformities by Appellant writers represents not only a particular construal
of experienced history, but also the unveiling of such a history's pneumatological character. If the *éclat* of holiness or miracle in this context
is by definition unhinged from some functionalist or moralizing logic,
it nonetheless appears in a form that is describable according to a narratively based scriptural figure. The "why" of the Spirit is thus located
in the historical assertion of biblical form, forms constructed from the
material of contemporary events. This is an understanding that we will
now examine more closely, not only in an attempt to unravel its general meaning, but because, moored in the particular episodes of Jansenist
Appellancy and of the Saint-Médard miracles, the understanding acts
as a kind of prophetic judgment on its own experiential context in the
Church, a judgment which can be weighed in light of the purposes of
this study. This judgment, furthermore, touches the presuppositions of
the study itself and of any other that takes these episodes as their concern; if for no other reason, it fuels the insistence that might otherwise be
absent from the press of penitence and its alleged holy fruit in someone
like François de Pâris. As we examine the "figurist" vision of Appellancy,
especially in its practical consistency within Jansenist thinking, we are
therefore implicitly orienting our study more particularly toward the category of Saint-Médard's historic fate (according to our introductory Pauline

scheme), articulated prophetically by its participants. A specific exegetical practice, in this sense, is shown to be intrinsic to the phenomenal shape of *ostensio Spiritus,* as it is given in the form of contested miracle and penitential sanctity.

I have therefore placed great weight on a particular description of the Appellant view of sanctity, one that is seen in terms of temporally kalei-doscopic scriptural figures which form the shapes of historical experience Christically in a way that does not escape the boundaries of particular events. And my emphasis here has two purposes. The first and less important is the purely scholarly one of attempting to explain as accurately as possible the actual religious concerns embedded in the devotions surrounding François de Pâris, and the theological trajectories launched by these concerns. Second, I am interested in observing how the episodes of these devotions — including the miracles themselves — clothed in the garment of their explicit or implied theological self-understandings, can reflect upon their own historical location within the life of the Church. This last purpose presses into the pneumatological question we have all along been raising indirectly, because it begins to play with the dangerous fire of discernment, not only bearing the burden of asking "why?" as one explores particular forms of Christian experience, but of submitting oneself to a possible answer in one's confrontation with the demands of contested sanctity. The second purpose, however, is clearly dependent upon the accomplishment of the first, and it is here that a brief defensive comparison of my interpretation of the figural devotions of Appellancy must be mounted in the face of recent assessments of Jansenist "figurisme" as we have begun to explore it. For the fact is that the Jansenist theological vision embodied in something like their theology of grace provided a consistent framework in which Scripture's meaning was adduced historically, a framework that already informed the perspectives of seventeenth-century exponents of "classical" Jansenism like Arnauld and other well-known *solitaires* of Port-Royal, who are celebrated today chiefly for their defense of a traditional Patristic exegesis, mistakenly seen to be in opposition to later Appellant hermeneutics.

*Figurisme* was and remains a technical term, as we noted in our examination of Léonard's critique, referring to a style of biblical exegesis practiced by various Jansenist Appellants. But we should recognize that, like the term "Jansenist," it was coined and applied to individuals by their opponents on the whole as a denigratory designation. This is not to say, again as with the term "Jansenist," that it does not refer to a distinct and discernable attitude, but only that *figurisme's* accurate definition of such an attitude is probably to be grasped in going beyond the hostile boundaries normally associated with the word's application. I prefer at the outset, therefore, to call figurism a "style" of exegesis. But opponents of Appellancy, as we saw, and even some Appellants themselves, tended to explain figurism as a "system," promoting the notion that there existed a comprehensive and comprehensively delimiting method for reading the

Scriptures among Appellants that determined their beliefs in a commonly perverse direction.

Whatever its scholastic mustiness, the *Dictionnaire de Théologie Catholique*, for instance, remains one of the few accessible places where a student today can find a discussion of figurism.[49] This is how the article states the matter:

> Figurism is a system interpreting Holy Scripture, based on the multiplicity of meanings [*senses*] presented by the letter of the Bible. In addition to the first meaning given in the "words" themselves, there are others, and not only one (as with the Catholic exegetical notion of a spiritual or figurative sense, provided for as a deeper meaning within the letter); rather, there could be as many as four or five meanings, or more, superimposed upon the first. As a result, all the persons of the Old Testament, their actions and the events of Jewish history, figure different persons, actions, and events of the New Covenant, that is, of the entire Church since its foundation to the end of the ages.

In and of itself, this description seems so general as to apply to the interpretive practices of any number of orthodox commentators over the ages, and one wonders at how the writer here, E. Mangenot, can properly imply that "Catholic" exegesis allows for only a single "figurative" or "spiritual" reading of any given text. But Mangenot's concern is made more explicit later, after having provided a list of representative readings (e.g., taking images of faithful and unfaithful wives in the Bible as figures for the vocation of the Gentiles and the Jews and ordering their use according to the assumption of some mutual interreference):

> Figurism, then, consisted in discovering the Church's future beneath the figurative events and persons of Scripture, or beneath the figures of words and symbols used in Scripture. It abused both the figurated sense and the figurative sense of the Bible, by exaggerating them, and stretching them so as to apply to figures or texts that did not have nor ever could have had the prophetic meaning attributed to them.

Even here, the problem seems to be one of exaggeration and lack of restraint in applying figurative readings. But one is reminded that proliferated figuration, as gleaned by someone like Gregory the Great, was never exiled from the catholic tradition's vision of Scripture. There is, in any case, hardly anything deformatively "systematic" in this approach. Is it the fact that the "future" of the Church was made a referent for these figures that ought to excite our opprobrium? While not in itself a heretical act, Mangenot finally admits that it is in the results of such prophetic interpretations, not the procedure itself, that figurism's defective practice lies:

---

49. E. Mangenot, "Figurisme," in *Dictionnaire de la Théologie Catholique*, ed. A. Vacant, E. Mangenot, and É. Amman, 15 vols. (1903–50), vol. 5:2, cols. 2299–2304.

The abuse was yet more visible in the application of these exegetical principles than in the principles themselves. For, in effect, this system of Scriptural
interpretation aimed not only at recapturing the past history of the church,
figured or symbolized in the two Testaments; it aimed most of all at its own
application to the present and future situation of the Church. This is how it
was able, for instance, to compare certain texts from the prophets of Israel
with symbols from the Apocalypse, and in so doing manage to discover the
final apostasy made in accepting the Bull *Unigenitus,* or to find the teachers
of error in the Last Days among the priests and pope who fought against
efficacious grace, or revivified pelagianism, or who promoted ethical laxity
[ ... ] As a result of all this, the conversion of the Jews was [thought to be]
near, and its prelude, the coming of the prophet Elijah, was imminent. They
saw these two great events proclaimed everywhere in Scripture. And so the
grand mystery of iniquity was about to be consummated, an event to be
followed by the triumph of Jesus Christ and by the Savior's reign on earth
for a thousand years.

Here, then, is what disturbs about figurism: an alleged millenarianism,
some details of which stand in judgment on the institutional Church. It
is true that, since at least the Council of Ephesus in 431, the assertion of
an "earthly" or "carnal" rule of the saints with Christ during the thousand
years mentioned in Revelation 20:6 was officially rejected by the Church.
But, as subsequent arguments over this and other apocalyptic texts demonstrate, much depended on how one defined and envisaged an "earthly"
reign. Even Augustine, frequently cited as an enemy of "chiliasm," is willing to accept a "literal" reading of the millennium in terms of a measurable
duration of human time shaping the created world; where he calls for a figural construal of the term is in its experiential connotations, which must,
in his mind, be viewed in reference to "spiritual" (though by no means
ahistorical) victories by the Church on earth.[50] Jansenists from Arnauld
to the Appellants moved easily within such Augustinian confines, arguing
for the figural realities behind terms like "reign" and "victory" as constitutive of historical experience literally signified by scriptural prophecy.
Where differences emerged in interpretation, they lay less in the kinds of
interpretive strategies adopted than in the historical range such strategies
were given to address. If, then, there is a misguided "system" at work behind figurism's conclusions according to Mangenot, it cannot be, as the
term baldly connotes, simply the "figurative" interpretation of Scripture.
More particularly, figurism's sin lay in the reach of its insistent application alone: that is, to the far boundary of scriptural figuration's use in the
parsing of contemporary events.

But how helpful is even this kind of definition in leading us to understand, for instance, the significance for Appellants and their Church of a
prodigious and prodigiously rejected episode like de Pâris and his miracles?
Even the application of biblical figures to the present does not stand
outside the accepted tradition of Catholic exegesis, at least insofar as

---

50. See Augustine's *City of God,* Book XX, esp. chapters 7–11.

it remains within the bounds of prudence. In what, then, lies the "imprudence" of figurism's practice? LeGros, from his side, points out the difficulty opponents of Appellancy must have in identifying figurism's defining error on this score. In explaining how arguments among Appellants over certain theological matters ought not to detract from their general integrity as a group — indeed, such disagreements point to the sincerity of their struggle, since they refute accusations of a "cabale" or "plot" — LeGros insists that Appellants commonly affirm essential truths of the faith which, in themselves, are central tenets of the Church's established teachings:

> They [Appellants] are in basic agreement, and it is hard to say exactly what is the thing among them that could distinguish minds so generally attached to the breadth of the Truth. What might it be? Could it be what is called "Figurism"? This might indeed be a serious dispute among them, if one were in fact dealing with that type of rash spirit who does not believe in the future conversion of the Jews, who sees nothing in the Church that would lead one to desire or hope for the coming of Elijah, and who imagines the common teaching of the holy Fathers and of theologians — that we are obliged to find Jesus Christ and the Church in all the Scriptures of the Old and New Testaments — to be in terrible error. But I dare say that this type of person is not a true Appellant. For those who are [Appellants] applaud the views of M. Duguet and his writings on Scripture. Then where lie their differences? Only in certain particular applications [of Scripture]: some find them beautiful and edifying, while others consider them to be inaccurate and inexact. But no one finds within [these applications] even a danger or hint of error, given that their implications and conclusions, in any case, hold nothing that is not in conformance with the Rule of Faith.[51]

Those "rash spirits" (*esprits téméraires*) of whom LeGros speaks, one observes, embody a particular imprudence of their own, refusing to see the present's shape, according to the witness of the Scriptures, as submitted to the authority of an experientially alien form, one in which the Church's lines are drawn in desperate and frustrated yearning. Perhaps it is merely the acceptance of submission such as this that lies at figurism's core. If so, what might this suggest?

Mangenot's description, in short, does at least point us to figurism's most striking aspects, that is, its figural applications of Scripture to concrete eschatological details of history, and it asks us properly to do some digging at this site. Current scholarship, at any rate, does little to cross this Mangenot line. The most serious, and really the only, contemporary attempt at a theological analysis of *figurisme* is Hervé Savon's brilliant chapter on Jansenist biblical interpretation in the multivolume history of the Bible, "Bible de tous les temps."[52] Along with Savon, Paul Catrice has provided some important historical analysis of aspects of *figurisme* in his

---

51. Nicolas LeGros, *Discours sur les Nouvelles Ecclésiastiques: Depuis leur origine jusqu'a présent* (np., 1759), 122f.

52. Savon, "Le figurisme et la 'Tradition des Pères,'" 757–85. More recently, C.-L.

study of Bossuet's attitude toward the future of the Jews, as has Bruno Neveu in his study of the abbé d'Étemare's collected *Pensées*. Finally, Marina Caffiero has provided an interpretation of *figuriste* millenarianism that is based on late eighteenth-century, especially Italian Jansenist authors.[53] But these scholars together, in the manner of other less theologically inclined students of Appellancy like Kreiser, tend to see such "figurism" as we have just encountered its practice in the François de Pâris devotional, as an interpretive posture toward Scripture dependent on a sectarian and millenarian set of convictions, convictions that in themselves determine the particular applications associated with Appellancy.[54] This has resulted in an assessment of the movement that, according to one's own sense of Scripture's normative meaning, will see "figurism" as a deformation and perversion of traditional figurative readings of the Bible (Savon), or as the logical consequence in irrationalism of such traditional figurative understandings as they are pressured by social circumstance (Kreiser et al.).

Savon's treatment is the most interesting for our purposes, in that it makes use of a number of debatable distinctions within Jansenist thinking on Scripture in order, in effect, to defend the "traditional" aspect of seventeenth-century Jansenist hermeneutics against what he emphasizes as being the innovative nature of Appellant interpretation. The latter's radical departure from Port-Royal's original commitments in this area, Savon argues, actually ended by contributing to the later eighteenth and nineteenth century's destruction of vitally religious exegesis. Savon is a deeply sympathetic student of Patristic theology — his work on Ambrose is deservedly well-regarded — and the "spiritual" interpretation[55] of Scripture

---

Maire's, *De la Cause de Dieu à la Cause de la Nation: L'Jansénisme au XVIIIe Siècle* (Paris: Gallimard, 1998).

53. Paul Catrice, "Bossuet et le 'Retour' des Juifs," *Mélanges de Science Religieuse*, 33 (1976): 162–91, and 34 (1976), 73–107; Bruno Neveu, "Port-Royal à l'age des Lumières: Les 'Pensées' et les 'Anecdotes' de l'Abbé d'Étemare, 1682–1770," *Lias* 4, no. 1 (1977): 115–53. Marina Caffiero, "Prophétie, millénium et révolution: Pour une étude du millénarisme en Italie à l'époque de la Révolution française," *Archives des Sciences Sociales des Religions* 66, no. 2 (1988): 187–99; and " 'Il Ritorno d'Israele': Millenarismo e mito della Conversione degli Ebrei nell'età della Rivoluzione Francese," in *Itinerari Ebraico-Cristiani: Società cultura mito* (Fasano: Schena Editore, 1987), 163–229. See also Catherine-Laurence Maire's selection of primary sources dealing with the Saint-Médard episode, *Les convulsionnaires de Saint-Médard: Miracles, convulsions et prophéties à Paris au XVIIIe siècle* (Paris: Éditions Gallimard/Julliard, 1985), 55–57. Maire properly counters the millenarian assessment of *figurisme*, but, to my mind, also mislocates the theological purposes of its practitioners (see below). Some extensive bibliographical references on *figurisme*, offered however without great critical order, can be found in Alfred-Félix Vaucher's study of Jesuit millenarianism, *Une célébrité oubliée: Le P. Manuel de Lacunza (1731–1801)* (Collonges-sous-Salève: Fides, 1968), esp. 76–85.

54. Neveu is more even-handed in his actual assessment of d'Étemare, whom he prefers to describe in terms of a balance of philosophical, literary, and theological perspectives; but he nonetheless feels it necessary, when it comes to the latter's specifically eschatological thinking, to assume for him and *figurisme* as a whole a niche within a stream of traditional "prophetic" social movements within the Church. See, 151, notes 111–15.

55. "Spiritual" readings of Scripture, for Savon, include the broad range of interpretive techniques used by the Fathers to relate literal referents within the divine text to a variety

that undergirded so much the readings of Scripture in the early centuries of the Church clearly has his support as a standard for continued use of the Bible.

The line of demarcation Savon draws between the traditionalist thinking of Port-Royal and Appellancy is marked by the writings of Duguet. Not only did the later self-styled "figurists" explicitly see Duguet as their mentor,[56] but, as Savon attempts to demonstrate, it was Duguet's writing on scriptural interpretation that, although it originally represented an attempt to maintain *la Tradition des Pères* (the Tradition of the Fathers) in the face of historical-critical attacks by scholars like Richard Simon, when assaulted by the program of *Unigenitus,* ended by reorienting itself in a direction that ultimately undercut that very tradition.[57] Using as his central text Duguet's *Règles pour l'intelligence des Saintes Ecritures* (1716) — a text we shall examine only at the end of our discussion of figurism — Savon shows how the work's main function, in its first part, of outlining the method by which Scripture is read as a unity referring to Christ through various prophetic figures, is clearly written in response to the dismissal of Patristic exegesis by "literalists" like Grotius and Simon. Although imbued with a Jansenistic spirit — Quesnellian in its succinct summaries of the theology of grace and the central place of Scripture within it — the work as a whole is devoid of the disputational flags signaling Appellant polemics, and instead takes as its guiding banner a meditative defense of the integrity and continuity of the Fathers' approach to exegesis.[58]

It is the second part of the *Règles* to which Savon draws our attention as indicating a crucial shift in perspective. Entitled "Application des Règles précédentes au Retour des Juifs" (Application of the preceding Rules to the Return of the Jews), this section has generally been attributed to Duguet as well, and, according to the book's preface, is to be read as a particular example of the way a figural method of interpretation might work

of significations governed by theological, moral, liturgical, and historical considerations and realities. Such techniques included, according to the usage of the time, typology, figuration, symbolization, parable, and allegory, methods identified as such interchangeably (see 758). For a discussion of these terms and their confusing inter-reference, Savon points us to a seminal article by de Lubac, " 'Typologie' et 'Allégorisme' " (in *Recherches de Science Religieuse* 34 [1947]: 180–226), in which de Lubac argues for a more supple understanding of Christian typology and allegory, which would see the two practices as analogous, if not even identical, methods of parsing biblical referents in terms of their participation in Christic reality. The distinction de Lubac draws here is with respect to a "pagan" understanding of allegory that is fundamentally fictional in its construal of signification. It is only this latter understanding of the term that deserves — and ever received in the Christian tradition until recently — the opprobrium of theological critics. As has been my own deliberate habit until this point, I shall continue to use the term "figurative," more or less in de Lubac's and Savon's encompassing "spiritual" sense, except where I wish to specify aspects of Jansenist thinking that are, if not peculiar, at least important to single out. We shall, in any case, be returning to a discussion of this terminology later in this chapter.

56. See Savon, "Le figurisme et la 'Tradition des Pères,' " 759, who refers to LeGros's comment quoted above.

57. Ibid., 768ff.

58. Ibid., 773ff.

itself out with regard to a question deemed of great importance to the Church. The rules are organized in terms of fourteen "vérités" concerning the Jews' return, and Savon points out how their Christocentric character, rendered figurally as Old Testament referents veiled in Jesus and the Church, now give way to a narrow concern with the predictive ordering of prophecy on the question of the Jewish nation. It is an ordering, according to Savon, that surpasses historically the subsuming fulfillment of the temporal events in the single spiritual truths of the New Testament, and instead presses to indicate how the notion of "historical fulfillment" must find its definition in the continued experience of the Church beyond its original establishment. In particular, the "vérités" attempt to demonstrate how Old Testament prophecies regarding the Israel "of the flesh" not only signify the Christian Church, but point more precisely even to the historical future of the Jewish nation itself at the end of time, as it is converted to Christ and fulfills a consummating mission on behalf of His Gospel. All this represents, in Savon's eyes, an exaggerated temporalizing of scriptural figures in a way that manages to separate the "horizontal" and "vertical" elements of patristic "spiritual" figuration — that is, of "typology" and "allegory" in the dichotomizing modern terminology de Lubac attacks — in favor of the strict historicizing of a politically motivated typology:

> As a matter of fact, among the Fathers as in the New Testament, it is impossible to separate these two forms of exegesis [the horizontal/typological and the vertical/allegorical]. It is only insofar as the temporal blessings promised to Israel are the image of spiritual and eternal blessings that they can be considered as the figure — or the "type" — of what Christ brought to His Church. Otherwise, the fulfillment of these prophecies is essentially referred to the future, a future that is both temporal and political. This referral to a future that is still earthly, this choice for a purely typological exegesis — linear, historical — seems to characterize fairly well the theology of today. We might well conclude, paradoxically, that the first among the moderns are these Figurists who awaited the return of Elijah to deal justly with the Bull *Unigenitus* and finally to save the crucified Truth.[59]

What explains this shift in perspective within the same book? Without our reviewing the details of his reasoning, Savon concludes that the *Règles*, that is, the first section of the book, was written by Duguet himself before the appearance of the bull. Whether or not Duguet himself saw the question of the Return of the Jews as crucial to his theology, the development of this eschatological theme among Appellants after the promulgation of *Unigenitus* drove him to accept an elaboration of his "rules" with respect to this question in a way that would limit the more extreme interpretations of the figure, e.g., in Romans 11, that were now cropping up. For this reason, he agreed to publish his *Règles* with the appended "Application," the latter of which, however, was written by his younger and long-time

---

59. Ibid., 784f.

collaborator, the abbé d'Asfeld. D'Asfeld, who is also the undisputed author of the book's general preface, is seen by Savon as a moderate figurist,
but nonetheless one whose millennial tendencies Duguet only reluctantly
and for the sake of party unity allowed to surface in a volume whose main
concern had been Christological and not historically prophetic. However
much he may have resisted theologically, it was Duguet's acquiescence on
this ideological application of his traditionally spiritual exegesis that laid
the groundwork for the later prophetism that engulfed the *laudatores* of
de Pâris's sanctity.[60]

Such is Savon's thesis of typological-millennial innovation on the part
of younger Appellants. And although he admits to the pneumatism of
Saint-Cyran's habit of creating "a secret and intimate link between biblical history and events of his personal life," set within the eschatological
framework of "the last days" in which the "the time for [the Church's]
upbuilding has past . . . and the time for her destruction has come,"[61] he
is at pains to circumscribe the significance of this tendency among early
Jansenists by insisting on the abbé's unwavering commitment to subjecting his personal interpretations "to the control [exerted by] the tradition."
In any case, it is to Port-Royal's classical defenders, Arnauld, Pascal, and
Nicole, and to *solitaires* like de Sacy that Savon turns to exemplify what he
calls "the spiritual sense's proper measure" as it was discerned in scriptural
exegesis.[62] Arnauld especially proves a helpful testimony in this regard, insofar as we have from his pen a work that carefully attacks a millennial
vision of the Church's near future, indeed a vision that included among
its central details events like the conversion of the Jews that were later
to attach themselves so prominently to Appellant figurism. *Remarques
sur les principales Erreurs d'un livre intitulé L'Ancienne Nouveauté de
l'Ecriture Sainte ou L'Eglise triomphante en terre* (Remarks on the main
errors of a book entitled "The Ancient Novelty of Holy Scripture or The
Church Triumphant on Earth") was published by Arnauld in 1665 as a
response to Nicolas Charpy de Sainte-Croix, whose popular apocalypticist
work cited in Arnauld's title first appeared in 1657. By underlining how
Arnauld carefully dissects Charpy's prophetic interpretations of Scripture
with a view to rejecting all broad millennial — that is, temporally established — figurative readings, Savon hopes to bring into relief the breadth
of the river spanned by Duguet's hermeneutic bridge.[63] The figurism of
Barbeau de la Bruyère's devotions thereby joins hands with Charpy's historicizing vagaries on the far side of a divide that separates a moderated
adherence to traditional spiritual guards in exegesis from the unleashed
projections of a striving (or perhaps fleeing) sectarianism.

---

60. Ibid., 771–84.
61. Ibid., 760–64.
62. Ibid., 764–68.
63. Savon here is really doing no more than following the lead of Léonard, who had
already seized on Arnauld's dissection of Charpy's millennialism. See Léonard, *Réfutation*,
460ff.

But there are two fronts on which I think we should question Savon's thesis of figurist innovation. The first would ask if it has indeed fairly judged what it sees as being a lack of theological coherence in Jansenist eschatological reasoning. For if, in fact, the spur toward prophetic reformulation among the figurists of *la Tradition des Pères* came largely from the afflictions poured out by *Unigenitus* and its aftermath, however much Savon savors "the proper measure" of patristic figural exegesis, he will be joining historians like Catrice and others in assigning to its fate the bare force of sociological oppression. *Le sens spirituel* itself will then seem but a toy in the hands of players more brutish than those lovers of God who normally claim its use. And having done that, one must secondly ask if one has not, in the process, deprived of Scripture's figurative reading the very commitment to historical coherence that maintained its supple usage, in de Lubac's view, over the centuries. The rejection of present circumstance in its describable detail as a legitimately figurated aspect of the biblical text's own meaning must necessarily cleave any coincidence of the "horizontal" and the "vertical" within the "spiritual sense." It is a dynamic such as this, not figurism's scrutiny of the Church's temporal experience in its exegesis, that would therefore contribute to the modern demise of an integrated exposition of Scripture.

The scholarly norm in this regard has been to discern a place for Appellant figurism among the branches of sectarian-millennialism's genealogical tree. It is notable, thus, that most modern commentators on figurism compare its conceptions and context with those of Pierre Jurieu, the celebrated Protestant pastor driven out of France in 1681 by the official persecutions of Protestants that preceded the Revocation of the Edict of Nantes. From his refuge in Holland, Jurieu engaged in polemics with Catholics back in France, like Arnauld and Bossuet. In addition, he battled with fellow Protestants over issues of ecclesiology.[64] Among his many writings to gain notoriety in this period was a two-volume work entitled *L'Accomplissement des Propheties ou la Delivrance Prochaine de l'Eglise* (The fulfillment of prophecy or the coming deliverance of the Church) (Rotterdam, 1686), which attempted to correlate texts from Revelation with historical events in the past and present, the chronological fixing of which enabled him to predict with some assurance (on his part) the Church's coming experience within history's course. Since the figurists are so often compared with Jurieu, whose ideas provoked the virulent opposition of an Arnauld, then their distance from classical Jansenism and its commitments must seem complete.[65] But a glance at Jurieu's prophetic

---

64. The only accessible contemporary English study of Jurieu is that of R. J. Howells, *Pierre Jurieu: Antinomian Radical* (Durham: University of Durham, 1983).

65. On the supposedly perspectival link between the figurists and someone like Jurieu, along with other Protestant millenarians, see Savon, "Le figurisme et la 'Tradition des Pères,'" 764; Catrice, "Bossuet et le 'Retour' des Juifs," pt. 2, 88–97; Caffiero, "'Il Ritorno d'Israele,'" 165ff.; Neveu, "Port-Royal à l'age des Lumières," 132 with notes; Elisabeth Labrousse, "Note sur Pierre Jurieu," *Revue de Théologie et de Philosophie* 3 (1978): 286ff.

practice in the *Accomplissement* shows, I think, that the distance between
his approach and Appellant figurism is as great, at least, as that between
the latter and Port-Royal.

Jurieu opens the work with a preface whose title summarizes his
general message: "Notice to all Christians on the coming end of the Anti-
Christian Empire of Popery and on the Arrival of the reign of Jesus Christ."
The message itself, as the preface's first lines indicate, is purposefully
given in the midst of grinding persecution:

> The afflicted Church seeks comfort: where might she find it except in the
> promises of God? When the present is filled with misery and sorrow, one
> must search the future. The promises of God are either general or particular.
> General promises are, for instance, those that assure us "in general" that
> God will not abandon His children, that His grace will never withdraw itself
> from the Church, that He will be with us to the end of world, that, when
> the mountains crumble, He will not leave us. But afflicted souls yearn for
> something more particularized; they want to see more closely the end of
> their miseries, given in particular promises. Now such promises and such
> knowledge as this are found only in the prophecies [of Scripture]. And it
> is incontestable that the prophecies contain promises for the deliverance of
> the Church: in fact, they note even the times and the circumstances of this
> deliverance.[66]

In so boldly (or "naively," in Howell's eyes) asserting the consolatory function of the book, Jurieu identifies the interpretive task as *responsive* to the
moment, the "affliction" of his fellow French Protestants. Rather prophetic
particularization" now serves to mark the historical "fulfillment" of such
textual forms. Historical events themselves thus provide the necessary
glossary and key to reading Scripture, whose words are mute, as unreferred
signifiers, apart from such experiential parsing. The relationship of figuration is thereby reversed from that asserted by Appellancy: the figures of
Scripture reflect particular events, of which they are signs; events do not
themselves reflect the shape of figures, whose form they share.

To speak, then, of *accomplissement* (fulfillment) as Jurieu does, indicates how the boundaries of scriptural meaning are set by the successive
unfolding of events, each in turn representing the instantiation of some
further portion or aspect of the word of God. The "particulars" of prophecy
correspond to the "particulars" of God's providential ordering of their
interpretation through history, "from age to age, year to year" by His
Spirit.[67] When Jurieu describes this pneumatic ordering of understanding
through time, however, he does so entirely in terms of the "violence" of
events themselves, whose pressure sets demands upon the turn to Scripture. The Spirit, as he says, imposes on him two historical realities: "the
cruel and horrible persecution that is currently ravaging the Church" and

---

66. The "Avis" is unpaginated. I shall refer to their number in parentheses. In this case,
(1–2).

67. Ibid., (3).

"agreement of so many prophecies [by modern interpreters, e.g., Ussher, Cotterus, Poniatouski, Drabitius], which, although obscure with respect to the truth and of an uncertain and doubtful origin, all predict a deliverance of the Church that will be quick, complete, and perfect."[68] In addition, the evolution of the modern age itself draws into its remarkable developments these pointed happenings so as to declare itself as the End of time whose measure must itself inform the meaning of the prophecies in the book of Revelation. Jurieu lists five "marks" of this final age which calls upon it the reference of Scripture: the miraculous advance of science and philosophy; the great voyages of discovery; the mass conversion of so many heathen into papist "semi-Christians" thus easing their ultimate passage into full sonship within Protestantism; the decadence of Islam and the appearance therein of messianic sects; and, finally, the inner rot of Popery itself.[69] This last is intimately tied to the Catholic persecution of Protestants in France. Jurieu, not surprisingly, devotes many pages to this episode, and the sin of the Roman Church quickly slides narratively into a description of the unparalleled quality of the Protestant suffering, "extraordinary" in so far as its "method" consists in every sort of harassment and torture, but always *short* of death; reformed pastors are even allowed to leave the country unharmed! "The best way to exterminate either a purported or a real heresy, is to chop off as many [of its followers'] heads as possible, to let the blood flow in buckets, to smother its most ardent exponents by massacring them. For if you let them live, and content yourself with having them offer some pretended oath of denial, all you have done is to create irreconcilable heretics."[70] That the normal horror of religious op- pression in this case holds such small mercies itself bears a providential stamp. The numbers of forced converts to Catholicism may be great, but the very possibility of survival for a few within this crushing onslaught moors the eschatological promise of Scripture to its substance. It is this "singularity" of persecution, then, within the history of Christendom that demonstrates the pertinence of scriptural prophecy in its terminal predic- tions. The order of analysis in all of this is clear: having established the present as the End Time from an examination of its shape, the *subse- quent* application to its circumstances of the biblical texts — notably the Book of Revelation — is demanded and assured accuracy.

The rest of the "Avis," and indeed, of the two long volumes that com- prise the work as a whole, do little beyond correlate particular texts and events within a general prophetic framework built around the Revocation and its immediate aftermath as the final affliction of the Church before its "deliverance" and the judgment of the papist Anti-Christ (Rev. 16). But within such a "particularized" framework Jurieu, following the lead of the English commentator Joseph Mede, constructs a necessarily chronological

---

68. Ibid. (4ff.).
69. Ibid., (7–14); on the final mark, (14–32).
70. Ibid., (27).

ordering of future events now tagged dependently on the scriptural verses, but ones in which *accomplissement* (fulfillment) signifies the datable: the return of Christ and beginning of His millennial reign on earth is fixed around 1715. The nature of the prophetic utterance's reference as temporal here simply reflects the decidedly "terrestrial" character of Jurieu's major concern, both in its pastoral and in its polemical aspect. Much of the long second volume of the *Accomplissement* constitutes a defense of millenarian thinking in general, seen in terms of the reign of Christ on earth. That this period and its preparation can be durationally measured provides the historical basis for expecting the Church's "deliverance" and its Roman Catholic oppressors' demise, both of which order the grammar of "consolation" that stands as the work's overall purpose. Much in the manner of St. Paul's defense of the bodily Resurrection's historicity in Romans 15, Jurieu sees the affirmation of millenarian temporality as the basis of Christian hope in the historical trustworthiness of God's promises. Exegetically, typological figuration serves to ground this consolatory premise.[71]

Jurieu's notable expository prediction of the Return of the Jews falls within this same dynamic.[72] This "dogma" of the Church, as Jurieu insists it is, receives a treatment of an extent unusual before the work of Appellant figurists.[73] But Jurieu's interest here is neither philosemitic[74] nor even figural, as with the Appellants. Typological instruments are brought to bear — e.g., St. Paul as the type for the future conversion (without evangelization) of the Jewish nation[75] — however Jurieu's real purpose, as he states himself in the title of the chapter, is to establish a "proof" for the millennial concept itself by maintaining the temporal character of the divine promises made to Israel. Although he is still willing to apply many of these same promises to the Christian Church, in the manner of traditional figurative reading, he insists that their literal meaning must yet await accomplishment if the reality of a carnal Messiah is not to be illusory.[76] If Scripture says that the Jews will "rule" the nations, whatever "spiritual" significance we might wish to attach to the promise must be bound up with its literal fulfillment in historical terms. If the prophesied punishments of the Jews were given temporal form, so too must be their promised blessings. By reappropriating this "judaizing" exegesis as foun-

---

71. Ibid., vol. 2, 286ff.

72. Ibid., 239–70. See Catrice, "Bossuet et le 'Retour' des Juifs," 89ff.

73. Although it had in fact played an important role in many millenarian expositions, such as Charpy de Ste.-Croix's. See our discussion on the Return of the Jews later in this chapter.

74. Although Jurieu notes that a major mark identifying Popery as the Anti-Christ is the Catholic Church's historical persecution of the Jews, especially during the Inquisition, he is equally careful, in the course of his chronological reckonings, to demonstrate how the various sufferings of the Jews themselves stand as a divine *accomplissement* within an order that demands a similarly tangible sequence of fulfilled promises of blessing. See ibid., 269ff.; 250ff.

75. Ibid., 256ff.

76. E.g., ibid., 248ff.

dational to any Christian understanding of these texts, Jurieu hopes to bolster the claim for a literal understanding of apocalyptic millennialism. Common sense, observing the experience of Israel, must demonstrate that God's "reign of grace" on earth, in the face of history's sorry chronicle for the world, has still not been established, yet must be in the future if God's goodness is to be affirmed:

> Those distinguished anti-millenarians are as repulsed by the idea of an earthly reign of God as I am by its denial. How can one reconcile with God's wisdom and goodness the fact that He has abandoned the world for such a long time, unless there yet remains a time for Him and for His reign? [...] Of course God has saved individuals throughout history, I admit; but that is not the same thing as "reigning. After all, truth and grace have never been dominant, they have never held sway, as it were, with the numbers and multitude on their side. For the number of worldly persons has always taken the field by far. Is it not reasonable, then, to imagine that God, after having abandoned six ages [of history] to the world and the devil, has at least reserved the seventh for truth and grace to have dominion, while in all the others, they were but slaves?[77]

Thus does "consolation" cut the bolt of prophecy into curtailed cloths fit to wipe away the tears vulgar complaint drips upon God.[78]

---

77. Ibid., 262–64.

78. Jurieu, obviously, is not unique in his espousal of a prophetic "hermeneutic of consolation." Appellants were often just as insistent that a proper understanding of the immediate eschatological import of scriptural prophecy would provide the hope necessary to afflicted defenders of the Truth battling the corrosive effects of the *Unigenitus* bull. This, after all, is one of the bases upon which *figurisme* is today read in parallel to Jurieu as the product of a "minority" mindset. But Appellant *figuristes*, as the nomenclature suggests, drew consolation in the present not from the shape of the present as such, into which redemption was injected, but from a discernment of a *figure* in Scripture to which the present was inevitably conformed. When, for instance, Jean-Baptiste de Beccarie de Pavie de Fourquevaux (to whom we will return later in the chapter) published his *Reflexions sur l'histoire de la Captivité de Babylone* (1727), he described his work in a subtitle as follows: "Wherein are given means for understanding many important passages in the Prophets; and wherein are offered reasons for comfort and confidence in the face of the great trials to which God sometimes permits His people to be exposed." The book as a whole, however, pursues this consolatory purpose aimed at fellow Appellants by presenting a long series of "Captivity" figures according to which the Church of today is to be understood, just as was the Church in Jesus' time. What brings hope, in viewing this set of comparisons, then, turns out not to be the immediate promises to "deliverance" of the oppressed, as explained by Jurieu, but the reality of conformity to Christ's own redemptive life:

"We have followed this method in comparing, within many passages, the condition of the cause of our Lord Jesus Christ among the Jewish people. In carefully making these comparisons, one can no longer be surprised that Jesus Christ allows his own truth and his own faithful followers to be treated, at times, in the same way He sought to be treated Himself. It is no longer possible to mistake the truth under the form of its occasional condemnation, even at the hands of legitimate pastors, once one has learned to recognize Jesus Christ as standing under a curse, which He Himself sought, at the hands of the leaders of a religion of which God was the author. We can find in the behavior of Jesus Christ and of His disciples a source of light for our own conduct in the face of the most difficult circumstances. And although they may seem to us somehow inappropriate, the glory God brings through these means is a powerful encouragement for us to hope that, even these scandals and this darkness within which we moan will prove a way that God will use to bring new brilliance to the Truth" (3d ed., Utrecht, 1735, xxiv–xxv). The prophetic referent here remains the *figure,*

Jurieu's work as a whole is, in fact, a disorganized affair, written in haste, and aiming at a number of contemporary targets in its attempt to promise triumphant relief in their own lifetime to the members of the Refuge and their compatriots still in France. Quite apart from the anti-papist barrage, the main element of Jurieu's *Accomplissement* criticized by Catholic commentators — and later alleged to contaminate Appellant figurism — was the demand of its obsessive theodicy that Christian comfort take the form of a temporal reversal of fortune, that, in short, the "saints" should "reign" in history. Arnauld, some years before Jurieu's work, had thus defined the "error" of Millenarianism in terms of the "rule of saints *on earth* with Christ before the End."[79] Even here, however, Arnauld was careful to point out that much hung on how one understood the nature of such a "rule." After all, saints like Irenaeus and Justin held to ostensibly millenarian views, without thereby falling into heresy.[80] Jurieu himself had taken pains to limit it, with respect to the Jews, to a "moral

---

which, although given hoped-for instantiation in the present, carries alone and in itself the substance of any divine, and hence consoling, *éclat.*

In addition to the works cited earlier, Jurieu's millenarianism is discussed in the context of Reformed eschatology in J. Van Den Berg, "The Eschatological Expectation of Seventeenth-century Dutch Protestantism with Regard to the Jewish People," appendix 3 in *Puritans, the Millennium, and the Future of Israel: Puritan Eschatology 1600 to 1660,* ed. Peter Toon (Cambridge and London: James Clarke & Co., 1970), 137–53, esp. 149ff. Van den Berg, after outlining the views of a number of representative Dutch theologians on the matter, concludes that "the idea of a general conversion of the main body of the Jewish people had become *communis opinio* in the circle of Reformed theologians in the Netherlands" (p. 148). Although Calvin himself, in addition to his insistent anti-chiliastic stance, had rejected an interpretation of Romans 11 that would see "all Israel" in anything but figurative terms, Dutch theologians followed Beza's ethnic reading of the Romans text, as referring in the future to the Jewish people *"in genere."* This perspective was widespread, despite the enormous variety of attitudes held specifically on the question of this conversion's place in chronological history: Was the millennium referred to in Revelation past? Was it yet to come? Would the Jews return to the geographical Israel? In what way would they function in the Gentile Church? In general, influential theologians like Voetius, Cocceius, and their followers eschewed a radical millenarianism that looked forward to an imminent historical reign of Christ on earth; at the same time, however, they tended to periodize history according to prophetic texts and their fulfillment, and so identify scriptural history, past and future, with the kind of sequential temporality that informed more "radical" millenarianism like Jurieu's and his French predecessor De Labadie's. The whole phenomenon of Christian milleniarian interest in the Jews, among Protestants in the seventeenth century and among Catholics (Jansenists especially) in the eighteenth century, remains to be studied. Given that this interest took such different shapes, however, from organized proselytization to more abstract typological theory, from the journalistic sensationalism concerning Sabbatai Zevi to Jurieu's consolatory props, it seems wise to avoid subsuming interpretations of its origins and significance. My own concern in this book is with the character of Jansenist Appellancy's more general attitude toward the interpretation of Scripture and history, an attitude which in itself held room for a range of motivations, whose specific meanings we are not yet in a position to discern.

79. See his *Seconde Apologie de Jansenius,* livre IV, chapters 8–10, 425–48.

80. Even the most cautious of scholars in Arnauld's circle agreed on this point: millenarianism in itself is not heretical, so long as the millennial rule is not understood in a purely "carnal" sense. See the astoundingly productive church historian and theologian Louis-Ellies Du Pin's "Dissertation sur les Millenaires," in his *Analyse de l'Apocalypse, Contenant Une nouvelle Explication simple et litterale de ce Livre* (Paris: Jean de Nully, 1714), 319ff., esp. 335–66.

influence" over the nations, rather than an outright political control. For Arnauld, however, it was more generally a problem of the underlying "carnality" one attributed to the millennium's character. Precisely the issue of a scriptural figure's relationship to historical experience was involved here, and Arnauld's response to Charpy de Ste.-Croix's book,[81] as Savon notes, provides an instructive look at how "classical" Jansenism might have understood the matter.

There is no question, on the face of it, that Arnauld rejects a broad millenarianism almost identical to Jurieu's in all but its historically contextual details. Charpy's vision lays out an imminent chain of events including the binding of Anti-Christ, the conversion of the Jews and their consolidation under a King of the race of Judah who stands as "Lieutenant-General" to Christ and who rules the nations from a rebuilt Jerusalem, the sanctification of all Christians, and, after a final revolt and the restoration of Original Justice, their immediate passage to Heaven.[82] And, as Savon correctly points out, Arnauld's rejection of this scheme is justified on the basis of *la Tradition des Pères* explicitly, against whose more modest uncertainty in interpreting apocalyptic prophecy predictively Charpy's aggressively precise claims move with unacceptable idiosyncrasy. The grand "principle of Religion," violated by these claims, is that Scripture be interpreted only by the "perpetual tradition" of the Church, which is founded initially on the expository exercises and conclusions of the Apostles themselves, that is, on Scripture's own internal framework of exegetical practice.[83]

Arnauld is concerned, however, with more than the naked authority that might control the reading of Scripture. What interests him is the apostolic pattern of figural applications that must, in his mind, regulate all subsequent attempts to decipher prophetic utterances, especially those of the Old Testament. And the pattern is simple: where temporal goods linked to the Messiah are promised to Israel, these are clear figures of spiritual goods given by the Son who is Jesus to those "true Israelites according to the Spirit," that is, to baptized Christians. Thus, any scriptural reference to the political character of a "rebuilt Jerusalem" in relation to the Nations can only be grasped in terms of the Christian Church's spiritual embrace of the world's peoples. This fundamental construction of prophetic meaning, wherein temporal promise refers to a spiritual good in Christ, stands as "the key to all the secrets of the Old Testament," and is the basis upon which *la Tradition des Pères* took its normative form.[84] Arnauld provides a lengthy set of scriptural examples of this flesh/spirit

---

81. Arnauld, *Remarques sur les principales erreurs d'un livre intitulé L'Ancienne Nouveauté de l'Ecriture Sainte, ou l'Eglise triomphante en terre etc.* (1st ed., 1665), in the *Oeuvres,* vol. 4–5, 321–63. See also Richard Popkin, *Isaac La Peyrère (1596–1676): His Life, Work, and Influence* (Leiden: E. J. Brill, 1987), 105f.

82. Ibid., 327f.

83. Ibid., 328f.; 331ff.; 346; 355ff.

84. Ibid., 339ff.

figurating dynamic as it appears to be explicitly understood in the New Testament, and insists that these applications be taken "as divine rules, which ought to lead to understand other similar passages, of which they [Jesus Christ and the Apostles] never spoke."[85]

Charpy's millenarian error, then — as with Jurieu later — derives from his adherence to the "Judaic" linkage of prophetic language to its temporal referents, with the result that he parses the particular Christian images of the book of Revelation in a way that is identical to the "sensual" hopes of the Old Testament.[86] But the figuring "rule" Arnauld upholds in place of this anachronistic method does not equate the "sensual" with the historical, as if the orthodox rejection of a millenarian earthly kingdom of Israel somehow demanded a rejection of the historical referent in prophetic discourse altogether. To attribute such an equation to someone like Arnauld is to contribute, I think, to the mistaken tendency to view all and any interest in eschatological figuration, as among the Appellants, with the chronologically obsessive concerns of a Jurieu. Instead, we must see with Arnauld that the flesh/spirit dichotomy reflects a divergence over two different *kinds* of historical referent, not the historical nature of such reference itself. Thus, Arnauld does not dispute the historical significance of prophecies dealing with the conversion of the Jews. What he insists upon, however, is that the context of prophetic fulfillments be located within the Christian Church as it has been formed in history by Christ Himself. And if this is the case, then two *historical* realities assert themselves as defining the character of the Jews' conversion. The first is that they shall become *one* with the Gentile Christians and not remain a separate people; the second is that this single Israel of Christ alone embodies the Church which greets the coming of the Lord at the end of time, a people whose "mixture" refers not to race but to the unsorted community of holiness and sin.[87] These two realities simply reflect the fact that the Incarnation's own history determines the figurated referents of prophetic particulars. Their "spiritual" nature derives from their Christic determination, but it is a determination that is nonetheless directed within the bounds of historical experience. It is in the peculiar *shape* of such experience that the figures fulfill themselves and manifest their divine accomplishment, a shape whose origin in Christ, Arnauld indicates, cannot be gleaned in terms of temporal triumph, but only confronted in the shadows of evil's confused oppressions.[88] The figurating transferal of Israel's promises to the "spiritual" realm of Jesus' life and followers thereby attempts to locate true "happiness" — "the clear vision and eternal possession of God by an unchangeable love" — not so much outside as inescapably within a world of diachronic movement, but one in which such passage swirls in the unevolving pull of hostile eddies

85. Ibid., 345; see 342ff.
86. See ibid., 330.
87. Ibid., 342 and 348ff.
88. See ibid., 338, 350.

that encircle and alone thrust into relief the forms of divine love. As with Saint-Cyran, we remember how Arnauld from early on in his career — as in the *Fréquente Communion,* the *Apologies* for Jansenius, and the discussion of the Holy Thorn miracle — submitted these figurated forms of Christian life to that larger figure of eschatological decadence, whose embrace was already measured in the Crucifixion's outline. The "spirit," in his dichotomy, perceives the "clarity" of God's visage here — but here, not somewhere else — while the "flesh" resists in favor of another, unrealized history of desire, whose fulfillment can only be explained in terms of an ordered sequence of temporally reparative events detached from God's own historical figure in Christ.

That Arnauld insists on labeling his version of spiritual figuration as "the literal sense" of Scripture should come as no surprise in light of this. Not only is such figuration "first order" in its meaning insofar as it represents the original "[sense] that the Holy Spirit intended to show us." But it is "literal" in that the referents of all scriptural language, including the Old Testament fundamentally, are revealed in the literal reading of New Testament texts and are understood in the application of the New Testament's literal figures — the life of Christ and His disciples — to such signifiers.[89] When later Arnauld defends the extensive reading by the laity of Scripture in translation against those for whom the "difficulty" of Scripture invites misinterpretation by the uneducated, he does so on the basis of these "literal" figures. The Gospels and the Epistles, he writes, present *faits historiques* (historical facts) whose forms are easily grasped by all, and whose direct application to all of life provides the only manner in which we can "dwell in Christ." The whole Scripture itself is grasped according to this pattern of application, by which alone a "firm hope" can be established among people.[90]

Granted that Arnauld's general theological interests do not focus on these themes, such figural "literalism" does, in large measure, act as a scriptural backdrop to much of the vast polemical literature he produced, informing the terrain of that historical landscape in which he consciously understood his battles on behalf of the Church to be waged. As against Charpy's, and to a larger extent Jurieu's, temporal schematizations of prophetic discourse, Jansenists continued to uphold eschatological reckonings that took human history as their substance, but they demanded that these historical reckonings themselves submit to the shapes figured in Christ's own historic existence as presented in Scripture. This fact points us once again to the penitential center of the Christian's life — and, indeed, the Church's life — as Jansenists understood it to be figurally em-

---

89. See ibid., 345f.

90. See Arnauld, *Difficultés Proposées à M. Steyaert Docteur et Professeur en Théologie de la Faculté de Louvain. Sur l'Avis par lui donné à M. l'Archeveque de Cambrai, Pour lui rendre compte de sa commission d'informer des bruits répandus contre la doctrine et la conduite des Prêtres de l'Oratoire de Mons en Hainaut* [Cologne, 1691], in *Oeuvres,* vol. 1/3, 615ff.

bodied, penitence not as a functional devotion, but as the historical form of the Church's participation in Christ's prophetically described existence. The figurism of the Appellants, then, as it decks the self-mortifying form of François de Pâris with the apocalyptic imagery of a final age, does no more than to perceive Pascal's grand figure of Justice and Mercy joined — the Crucifixion's fact — as fashioning time's own wanderings. Coming judgment, the Return of the Jews, the onslaught of the Anti-Christ, even the astounding outbreak of miracles — all of these assertions and the bib- lical analysis behind them acted to bolster their bold announcement in a posture very different from Jurieu's consolatory attack on history. As in Barbeau de la Bruyère's devotional, they lead to penitence, because the figures of these prophecies and images themselves, however realized in a temporal world, derive from the encoding figure of its Christ.

The distance, then, between Port-Royal and Saint-Médard is surely not obviously great, and when Duguet writes his *Règles* — the figurist hand- book — he does so almost descriptively (not constructively) of a practice well-rooted in the life of Jansenists before him. The figurating center of Scripture's texts, that is, the detailed form of Jesus Christ that itself cre- ates the sensible realm of history according to multiplied refractions of its image within the Bible, is consistently promoted by this tradition as the sole handle by which the interpretative task can be grasped. It is a task, moreover, in which the pages of the text and the borders of existence merge in such coherence that the conclusions of the exegete must inevitably snare as game the course of the Church's own experiential movements, the apprehended form of which penitence itself defines. What Arnauld and other Jansenist writers of the seventeenth century demonstrate is how, before Duguet, this practice necessarily presses the "spiritual" read- ings of Scripture into the sphere of eschatological constraint and temporal submission to its figures.[91] At work behind all of this is the Arnauldian

---

91. The exegesis of Jean Hamon, quintessential Port-Royal *solitaire,* is representative in involving a number of aspects congruent with later Appellant figurism: an identification of the form of Christ with the bare words and figures of Scripture, acceded to as the term of the Incarnation; an understanding of Christ's form in terms of humility and "annihilation" in the face of evil; a strong view of the Church as Christ's figural Body, thus subject to the same form of temporal vicissitudes as Christ, and to the same particularities of history, of which Scripture's own words are a part; finally, an appreciation of the circumstantial context of the Church's figurative life as formed in eschatological persecution. See his "De Trois Communions Spirituelles: Outre Celle Qui A pour objet JESUS-CHRIST dans le Saint Sacrement," in *Recueil de Divers Traitez de Pieté: Ou l'on verra les principales maximes de la Morale Chrétienne excellemment établies. Nouvelle Edition* (Paris: Jean-Baptiste Delespine & Jean Th. Herissant, 1740), vol. 1, 179–309; *De la Solitude,* 2d ed. (Amsterdam, 1735), 4–28, 42ff., 121ff., 300ff., 317–88; "De la vie de la Foi dans les grandes afflictions (sur ces paroles: *Justus ex fide vivit)*" and "De la Douleur des Maux de l'Eglise" [on Macc. 1], both in *Receuil de Divers Traitez de Pieté,* vol. 2, 1ff.; 362ff.; "Qu'il ne sert de rien de s'approcher des Sacrements, ou d'en être privé, même pour la cause de Jesus-Christ si l'on n'a d'ailleurs une solide et veritable pieté, qui seule est utile à tout," and "Que l'on ne doit jamais tout esperer de dieu que lorsque tout paroit desesperé du côté des hommes," in *Traitez de Pieté, composez Par M. Hamon. Pour l'Instruction et la consolation des Religieuses de P.R. A l'occasion des differentes épreuves auxquelles elles ont été exposées* (Amsterdam: Nicolas Potgieter, 1727), 467ff. and 440ff. See also Isaac Louis Le Mastre de Sacy, translator and commentator of the

scheme of historical decadence, in which sanctity as a pneumatic event is instantiated most fully in the Church's subjection to the eschatologically conforming pressures of the figure of Christ's assaulted form.

Jansenist applications of scriptural figures *in general* — including not only the resultant objects of application but the very act itself of obediently applying them in their affront to our expecting desires — depend on the governing impulse and form of a central Christic figure, revealing itself temporally within varying circumstances. But just this relation of application, however, renders confused the manner in which we are led to order the historical referents of text and experience chronologically, a factor that fuels Jansenist antipathy toward Juerieu's sequentialist scheme of fulfillment. The consistent and formative pull exerted by the governing figure — the historical life of Jesus the Christ — on all other referents of the biblical text and on the historical world they populate (e.g., Old and New Testament objects, persons, events, and prophetic images, the Christian Church, her experience, and the future promised to her) has the effect of de-"carnalizing" their reality in favor of a "spiritual" substance, apprehended in the fact of figural conformance. But even if these referents are not de-historicized in the process, that is, even if we insist that their descriptive contours remain experientially literal in reference, is not their decarnalized temporal succession nonetheless a dislocated one? If the history of "these last days" is also the history of the Church "throughout the ages," in Hamon's phrase,[92] which post-figures the Cross, and this one event in a punctuated chronology subsumes experientially all the details of its own pre-history, and if, finally, the relation of these events one to another is governed only by the limits of a non-sequential order of scriptural inter-reference founded in the New Testament collections — if, in other words, history in its course is both wholly figurated and continuously figurating by and in the scripturally described life of Christ, as Arnauld's Spirit/Flesh figuration of history insisted, then the notion of its single and underlying narrative continuity is perhaps illusory. If again, as I have earlier averred in discussing the descriptions of François de Pâris's holiness, the glory of God composes an embodied lectionary of variously tailored and alternately arranged texts, then history provides, according to earlier Jansenists, and in a way thoroughly consistent with the Saint-Médard hagiography, not their unifying temporal summary, but merely the consistent numbering of their verses, clipped, reordered, repeated, ever-referring.

And this is indeed the case for Jansenist expositors of Scripture, from Arnauld at least through the early Appellants. Further, the continuity of

---

Bible at Port-Royal, esp. his "Quel est l'usage qu'on doit faire de la vérité écrite," Lettre LXIV in his *Lettres Chrestiennes et Spirituelles de Messire Isaac Louis Le Maistre De Sacy* (Paris: Guillaume Desprez et Elie Josset), 1690, vol. 2, 648ff.; also the preface to his *Explication des Proverbes de Salomon,* nouvelle edition (Bruxelles: Eugene Henry Fricx, 1698), xi. On de Sacy and figural exegesis at Port-Royal in general, see David Wetsel, *L'Écriture et le Reste* (Columbus: Ohio State University Press, 1981), especially. chapters 1–3; on de Sacy's views in relationship to Pascal's hermeneutic, see chapters 4–6.

92. See Jean Hamon, "De la vie de la Foi," in *Recueil de Divers Traitez de Pieté,* 34–40.

this approach within the Jansenist tradition is striking, all the more so in the face of modern historians, like Savon, who have steadfastly wished to deny the linkage and have preferred to follow the same path as that pursued by certain of the Appellants' detractors, in pitting the texts of early Jansenists against their later disciples. Still, most Appellants along with their most obdurate opponents recognized the substantive genealogy in this case, for what was the glory of one was just as easily the sweeping indictment offered by the other.[93] And now, having suggested the plausibility of this single tradition, let us go on to explore the more consciously hermeneutical convictions with respect to Scripture that underlie this common vision of God's history.

---

93. Very early on in the debate over *figurisme*, defenders of the practice explicitly cited their fidelity to the exegetical tradition of the early Jansenists. See Jean-Baptiste de Beccarie de Pavie de Fourquevaux's published response to Léonard, *Lettre d'un prieur a un de ses amis, au sujet de la nouvelle Réfutation du Livre des Règles pour l'intelligence des saintes Ecritures* (Paris: Gabriel Valleyre, 1727), to which is appended a *Principes sur l'intelligence de l'Ecriture Ste*, both of which contain lengthy quotations from works by, e.g., Hamon, Arnauld, Nicole, and other Jansenists, as authorities in concert with Patristic sources supporting figural exegesis.

# Chapter Nine

# FIGURALISM AND THE BIBLE

## *Figurisme* as a Hermeneutical System

### *Figurisme*, Millennialism, and Historical Reference

By affirming, at least in general, the continuity of figuralist practice between Appellant hagiography and earlier Jansenism, we are now in a position to examine in more detail some of the substantive exegetical and theological commitments informing that practice as peculiar to Jansenism. To gauge the peculiarity of what I have just described in the preceding chapter as a representative Jansenist vision of figuralism, then, let us return to Savon's distinction of "vertical" and "horizontal" figurative readings. We remember that, following de Lubac, Savon had seen Patristic exegesis as holding the two perspectives, identified by the technical terms "allegory" and "typology," together as a single "spiritual" orientation toward the text, while figurism instead fixated upon the "purely typological, linear, and historical" understanding of scriptural reference and thereby fell into the "exaggerated" temporalizing of biblical imagery fundamental to political millenarianism. Yet the fashion in which Port-Royal writers like Arnauld and Hamon can correlate spiritual communion with an experienced, yet figurated eschaton belies the necessity for such a judgment, and suggests at least that millenarianism, in its fully historical commitments, is not antithetical to the "vertical" aspects of an integrated "spiritual" exegesis.

The vocabulary used in these discussions, however — as de Lubac himself was at pains to demonstrate — has become singularly disorienting. "Typology" is today generally defined, in Erich Auerbach's influential terms, as an interpretation of Scripture in which two historical events (or persons or objects) are given a connection within history of signification/ fulfillment, the first event (type) signifying the later (antitype), the latter of which somehow discloses and embodies the full meaning and purpose of the former.[1] Auerbach lays great stress on the "phenomenal historicity" of both type and antitype in their literal referents, in contrast to a more narrowly "allegorical" reading that might move in realms that are abstractly ethical or devotional. But while Auerbach's definition still pertains to the

---

1. Erich Auerbach, "Figura," in *Scenes from the Drama of European Literature* (Minneapolis: University of Minnesota Press, 1984), 11–76. See esp. 53f.

modern usage of "typology," it should be noted that Auerbach himself applied the above description to "figural" interpretation in general, and not to typology in particular. He thereby attempted not only to found the broad Patristic understanding of figural exegesis on a historical phenomenology — that is, on the historical referentiality today strictly associated only with typology — but, conversely, he also sought to imbue the understanding of such referentiality with a sense of supra-temporal reality. "Figura," Auerbach argues, is a word whose root connotation implies changeability and repeatability, in the sense of the malleable character of plastic form.[2] As historical phenomena, then, biblical "figures" in both the Old and the New Testament derived their existence from the creative orchestration by God of His works, and their historical inter-references were thus seen by theologians like Tertullian and Augustine as grounded in the divine atemporality of God's eternal providence. As *significant* phenomena, historical figures are not informed by *differentia temporis*.[3]

In explaining the relation of history to its providential significance, however, Auerbach makes use of the horizontal/vertical dichotomy, with the result that the figural "plasticity" he had earlier underlined as crucial to the term's meaning is confined to a fully non-temporal realm, leaving the linear nature of figural phenomenality intact. Thus, in its "horizontal" dimension of temporal succession, Auerbach asserts, figural history is incomplete, in that the figure, as figure, must always strain forward into the future for its fulfillment in the divine *veritas*; in its "vertical" dimension, however — the eternal present of God's knowledge — the relationship between sign and fulfillment is wholly instanced.[4] The historical *shape* of figural relationships given in scriptural referents must therefore remain one governed by temporal succession.

Modern explications of typology assume this sequentially chronological basis for the method's referential applications. Whether one characterizes figural arrangements of type and anti-type in the traditional relation of historical movement *ad perfectiorem*,[5] or whether one speaks of figural interpretation as working from the discernment of a "teleological pattern" of meaning within a "cumulative story,"[6] the histories that a figurative read-

---

2. Ibid., 13–23.

3. Ibid., 42f.

4. Ibid., 59; see also 45ff.

5. See Jean Gribomont, "Le lien des deux Testaments, selon la théologie de S. Thomas," *Ephemerides Theologicae Lovanienses* 22 (1946): 74ff.; Joseph A. Galdon, S.J., *Typology and Seventeenth-Century Literature* (The Hague: Mouton, 1975), 38ff.

6. Hans W. Frei, *The Eclipse of Biblical Narrative,* 27ff. Frei's masterful discussion in his first two chapters trades heavily on Auerbach's own analysis of figural interpretation. What becomes obscure, perhaps through nuance, are the fundamental changes Frei wishes to identify between the figural practices of Calvin, for instance, and a prophetic figuralist like the seventeenth-century theologian Cocceius (see 46ff.).

For Frei, the desire to discern the unitive meaning of the whole Bible, both Old and New Testaments together, in a way historically continuous with contemporary phenomena led Cocceius to impose upon the text's interpretive structure a "larger framework" of extra-biblical construction: "'salvation history' comes to be the meaning of the Bible" (50).

ing of Scripture will disclose will be limited by the possibilities imposed by temporal sequence. One of two results must follow. Either scriptural history will be seen as following a purely sequential course in the arrangement of its phenomenal references; and this, I take it, is the pattern followed by a strict millennialist like Jurieu. Or, scriptural figuration will be construed as referring to realities altogether other than the *given* shape of phenomenal (because necessarily sequential) history, because history and figural reference cohere too confusedly; and this, in my mind, lies behind the more modern separation from a figural hermeneutic of the *essential* assertion of a text's historical reference.[7]

---

Practically, this led to "Cocceius's extraordinary and baroque proliferation of figural reading," at the same time "extravagant," "decadent," "constant and cramped" (49). What is not clear in this description is how this "stress on the temporally differentiated sequence in the economy of salvation" really differed from what Frei sees as the more balanced figural hermeneutic of Calvin.

As with critics of the Figurists, the real problem for Frei seems to be the particular figural applications made by Cocceius, and not the manner of making them in itself. Frei sees Calvin's attitude as one for which "the pattern of meaning glimpsed in a historical event, or within two or more occasions figurally and thus meaningfully related, cannot be stated apart from the depiction or narration of the occasion(s)." The issue of proper figural application therefore turns on the organizing power of the "narrative": "The occurrence character and the theme or teleological pattern of a historical or history-like narrative belong together.[ ... ] Without this conviction to govern the figural reading of a sequence, it becomes a totally arbitrary forcing together of discontinuous events and patterns of meaning" (34). But to what "narrative" does Frei here refer? If, as he frequently uses the term, a narrative, at least in Scripture, is "history-like," it simply cannot be the case that Scripture itself, as a whole and single text, provides with any clarity the narrative moorings for such an "overarching" pattern as would control its figural construals. For Scripture, as a whole and single text, is not a history-like narrative but rather a collection (and even tangle) of such narratives along with many other texts and discourses that are hardly history-like in their narrative genre at all (including most of the Wisdom and much of the prophetic literature of the Bible). Calvin, no less than Cocceius, was obliged to apply to this collection a chronological pattern, informed no doubt by various scriptural narratives given in a hierarchy of influence, so as to allow for a coherent figural construction of the texts as a group; but the pattern applied was not, any more than it was for Cocceius, derived from the inherent temporal ordering of Scripture's referents. That the death of the Swedish king Gustavus Adolphus could have been, for Cocceius, the historical fulfillment of an Old Testament figure, strikes Frei as manifestly indicative of interpretive perversion (49). But the identification of the Catholic pope as Antichrist by Calvin, even though the latter's more Augustinian "amillennialism" demanded that he grant groups of individuals and events (versus punctiliar historical referents) over longer periods the role of figural fulfillments, is no less bold an imposition of contemporary experience upon the typological capacities of Scripture.

Calvin might well have been shocked by the exegeses of a theological descendent like Jurieu. But both would have shared, on Frei's terms, a confidence in the temporally sequential ordering of figural reference. And, in contrast to Appellant figurists, neither could have ever comprehended how the Church of Christ might suffer sin and live in joy at once — they were "protestants" not "appellants" after all — an understanding made possible only by seeing Scripture's "overarching" figurating pattern, not constituted by the sequential ordering of time, but as itself a figure by which alone the notion of "order" can be measured.

7. I am thinking here of those efforts today to locate figural interpretation in the "imaginative" sphere of human consciousness, which, while they grant the traditional typological procedure's intrinsic affirmation of its referents' historicity, are concerned less with these referents than with the creative character of the procedure itself. Stephen Crites's "Unfinished Figure: On Theology and Imagination" (in *Thematic Issue: Unfinished...: Essays in Honor of Ray Hart,* ed. Mark C. Taylor, JAAR Thematic Studies 48, no. 1 (1981): 155–84), for example, as the title suggests, claims that the theological significance of figural interpre-

In general, any assertion of prophetic historicity or of millenarianism broadly understood not in terms of the "carnal" reign of Christ on earth but more loosely simply as a belief in the fact of the millennium's durative referent in history however construed — and this would then include the historically cautious Augustinianism of Aquinas and Calvin as well as Jurieu's flamboyant ordering of dates — in general, then, such millenarianism has assumed an underlying chronological sequence in its figural ordering. Ernest Lee Tuveson's still valuable *Millennium and Utopia* demonstrates the conceptual ease with which a scholastic unwillingness to

---

tation lies in its ability to act as a vehicle of participation in the creative striving of the divine spirit. Figural practice is not a boundary-setting activity whose limits are given by the shape of historical figures and their figured referents, but an act of imagination using figural interpretation as a tool by which the unrealized and open possibilities of the future are constituted (see 172f.).

While, from a Christian point of view, Crites focuses on the normative character of certain scriptural figures in this life-giving process, e.g., the Resurrection, he does so because these figures, to his mind, embody the imaginative imperative (as against its enemies, figured in Paul's terms by the Law), and not vice versa (see 175ff.). Crites, to be sure, wants to argue that figural interpretation takes seriously historical phenomena, and is in fact wedded to them. But in his espousal of imaginative openness and creativity as the process by which these phenomena take life as figures, he argues that "the living, plastic form that is the immediate object of imagination and experience" can act as figure only "as [these figures] *appear,*" and not as they intrinsically instance or refer to some distinctly definable truth. If there is a limit set to the imaginative construal of reality, then, it is the limit of "appearance," which, in historical terms, is reduced to the relationships of temporal sequence ("prefigurement" and "fulfillment" in the future's unfinished sweep). Anything denying these limits trespasses into realms of "allegory" and "metaphysics," according to Crites, wherein "occult" truths become the oppressive arbiters of meaning (see 170f.).

But as Crites himself recognizes, the scriptural texts do not adhere to such clear-cut limits in their own narratives. The story of Jesus' birth, he notes, contains "few historical kernels" that are "salvageable," yet nonetheless constitutes "a masterful creation of the figural imagination, luminous and whole" (167). What "appears," then, as the properly rooted phenomena of history with which the imagination does its figural work, cannot be considered the historical referents of the text — actual events and persons like Herod and the massacred children — but the narratives *qua* narratives in which they are contained as figures. Unable to contain these actors and their deeds as history, time regurgitates them as figures for the use of the contemporary imaginative process, within whose unconstrained grasp divine truth can flourish. Directed by a view of historical reference situated within chronological succession, Crites must therefore understand the historical reference of Scripture's narrative as dealing with the figural constructions themselves, as imaginative acts whose authorial practice within time comprises the significance of their shape.

Therefore, literary analysis — still governed by historical-critical assumptions in all their sociological and political desiring — becomes theology's mentor. We must attend to the construction of texts within history, according to this attitude, and to their contextualized literary resonance; but we cannot presume or presume upon some world of signified historical referents that the text communicates (see 169). See also Richard Hays, *Echoes of Scripture in the Letters of Paul* (New Haven: Yale University Press, 1989), in which Hays argues for a "transcendental" (not a historical) "referent" to Scripture's figures, which lies in the *act* of interpretation itself (see esp. 160–69; 178ff.; 227, note 60; 229–30, note 80). See also, from increasingly explicit socio-political stances, Herbert Marks, "Pauline Typology and Revisionary Criticism," *Journal of the American Academy of Religion,* 52, no. 1 (1984): 71–92, and finally, although from a literary perspective now wholly divorced from theistic considerations, David Dawson's *Allegorical Readers and Cultural Revision in Ancient Alexandria* (Berkeley: University of California Press, 1992), esp. 1–17 (with notes), where figural interpretation is understood as a deliberate *strategy* of social subversion aimed at textual pretentions to revelatory discourse.

link apocalyptic prophecy with the present was able to transform itself into an eagerness for just such coordinations.[8] Tuveson, for instance, sees Luther as representative of a "revolution" in attitudes toward the book of Revelation that took place in the fourteenth through the sixteenth centuries, a remarkable change of exegetical perspective that now sought prophetic referents in the world of contemporary events.[9] But he shows how only a commonly presupposed conviction within the Christian tradition from its inception, that the world *did* have a temporal end whose ordered coming was adequately signified by Scripture's prophetic figures, could have allowed for the flowering of those contemporizing biblical explications so evident among Reformers and their popular audiences. The subsequent replacement of a more traditionally "pessimistic" reading of history's course — derived from the literal application of New Testament prophetic images to current events by someone like Cyprian — in favor of the historically developmental and "optimistic" interpretation of biblical figures adopted by a host of seventeenth- and eighteenth-century exegetes forms the substance of Tuveson's study. But the seeming distance of this passage only distracts, according to Tuveson, from a more basic agreement between the two orientations, one that identifies, in common, figural referents with particular moments in a temporal succession. Whether, as in the case of an Augustine or Luther, that succession was seen as descriptive of a *mundus senescens* or whether, as with the seventeenth-century Anglican historian Gilbert Burnet, it was attached to an ameliorative historical framework of progress, spiritual participation in Scripture's figural significations could easily become reduced to participation in the historical process itself. Thus it is that an antinomian chiliast like Jurieu, whose thought was strongly determined by the expectations of conflagrationary suffering, could have so comfortably taken as his exegetical mentor in apocalyptic reading the optimistically evolutionary theologian Joseph Mede, whose direction embraced with equal ease disciples like the "Cambridge Platonists" Henry More, and Ralph Cudworth.[10]

From one point of view, Jansenists simply followed the Cyprianic tradition of a "hermeneutic of decadence" in their application of eschatological

---

8. Ernest Lee Tuveson, *Millennium and Utopia: A Study in the Background of the Idea of Progress* (Berkeley: University of California Press, 1949), esp. chapters 1–3.

9. On the development of Luther's highly influential millennial thinking, glaringly apparent in his change of focus from his first preface to the book of Revelation (1522) to his second preface of 1542, see ibid. 24ff. Luther's periodized identification of Revelation's prophetic images with, e.g., various heretics from Marcion to Mohammed to the contemporary Turks and Roman pope, joined to specific historical signs, were popularized and disseminated throughout Europe and proved far more influential among subsequent writers in the long run than did Calvin's carefully calibrated use of such references. Luther's particularizing of scriptural prophecy's fulfillment within these kinds of events, however, already had a rooted tradition in medieval practice, most obviously among exegetes from, among others, the "Spiritual Franciscan" movement.

10. We have noted above Jurieu's personally acknowledged dependence on Mede's brand of millennialism. On Mede's influence on English apocalypticism, see Tuveson, *Millennium and Utopia,* 76ff.

figures. We have seen how Saint-Cyran's and Arnauld's work within this governing tradition functioned to orient much of their theological program. But, from another vantage point, we must also note how their willingness to blur the lines between the world's decay and the Church's apocalyptic deteriorations moved their thinking in a less traveled direction, at least on an acknowledged level. By pressing for what was practically a combination of Cyprianic historicism with Augustine's more explicit spiritualizing of eschatological figures, they ended by working with a multilayered collection of these figures that had for their referents at once the world, the Church, and the individual. The interpretive movement from scriptural figure and its original historical referent, to its governing form, Christ Jesus, to its contemporary refiguration as Christ's Body, the Church within the world, was a movement made with astonishing and certainly at times confusing fluidity.[11]

But the "fluidity" here is not some characteristic instrinsic to the nature of the figural imagination's reality-constituting function, as modern literary theologians might insist (see footnote 7 above). It is simply descriptive of the human act of apprehending scriptural referents, an act limited by the temporally distinguishing frame in which such apprehension necessarily works. On the other hand, there is no implication for the Jansenists thereby that the *res* of figural reference truly exist within a higher realm of divine "historical simultaneity" whose temporal fragmentations are but the created shadows of some deeper non-temporal and eternal order. This is to apply to their interpretive practice a metaphysical basis, however vague, that is quite simply irrelevant to its function. Rather, this practice asserts only the priority of figure over history, such that chronological sequence as a governing limit to the identification of figural reference drifts into an area of only occasional and purely secondary concern. The possibility of moving interpretively back and forth across a spectrum of figural referents certainly bespeaks an underlying simultaneity of *figure.* And as a result the referents themselves, however much they remain historical particularities, may or may not temporally coincide: the Church's woes in a given year figurally enact a predictively prophesied set of events historically located in the Last Days, but these themselves coincide with Old Testament events embodying the figure of Christ's own historical life and death. There is no demand, however, that any of these

---

11. Note how such a unitary movement was almost impossible among other figuralists like the New England Puritans, who insisted that the various orders of figural referents be kept conceptually separate because, in fact, they were mutually exclusive. Sacvan Bercovitch, for instance, shows how the devolution of a common typologizing commitment (as practiced by the early Church and then confusedly affirmed by some of the major Reformers) into a "vertical/spiritual" method (associated with, e.g., Roger Williams) and a "horizontal/ historical" method (associated with, e.g., John Cotton and most other New England Puritans) lay behind some of the bitterest religious conflicts of the period. The shared assumption that these perspectives were referentially incompatible, of course, is what made these conflicts inevitable. See Bercovitch's "Typology in Puritan New England: The Williams-Cotton Controversy Reassessed," reprinted in *The Marrow of American Divinity: Selected Articles on Colonial Religion,* ed. with intro. by Peter Charles Hoffer (New York: Garland, 1988), 189ff.

temporally distinguishable events represent distinctive, historically exclusive, and thereby sequentially limited "fulfillments" one of another. The events of the past, the present, and the future necessarily conform to a divinely given figure or set of figures, and the logic of their happenings as perceptible events susceptible to historical scrutiny is wholly determined by this conformance.

To borrow loosely from the vocabulary of structural linguistics, it could be said that temporal reality — historical experience — stands here, according to the Jansenists, as a "suprasegmental morpheme," the sequentially organized morphemic units of which do not carry the weight of fundamental signification, although their shapes are integral to that meaning. Instead, overall meanings which may enormously alter the referents of individual morphemes are provided by a controlling speaker's fashion of utterance, which stands "above" the "segmented" order of the units themselves. A famous example of such "suprasegmental" forms of meaning are the various significations provided a set of morphemes like "light-house-keeper," the tone, pitch, and rhythm of whose utterance governs their potentially disparate referents. This is only to indicate how the peculiarity of Jansenist figuralism turns on a specific conceptualization of history itself as a dependent phenomenon, dependent, that is, on the figurating control of its author, its divine "utterer," who is God.

It has always been recognized, of course, that typology, as an interpretive stance that took for granted the historicity of its referents, assumed the providential omnipotence of God in ordering events in a significant manner as described by Scripture. The further assertion, made in practice by Jansenists, that this ordering conforms to a governing (scriptural) figure whose shape necessarily and frequently defies the expectations of temporal succession, presupposes not only divine ordering of history, but history's phenomenal malleability in accordance with Scripture's enunciation of that figure. What Auerbach described as the "plasticity" of *figura* has been taken by literary theologians as referring to the creative control exercised by interpreters of biblical texts. For Jansenists, however, plasticity is located in the realm of figures' historical referents themselves: events, persons, and objects whose existence in time by definition follows the divine authorial control that makes their reality coincide with scriptural form. In terms of temporal sequence, then and for instance, the Curse of Adam in Genesis 3:17ff., the faithlessness of the Christian Church in Hebrews 6:4ff., and the Final Judgment in Matthew 7:17ff. are all shaped by the common figure of "thorns" and "thistles" and their destruction, and one can order their historical referents in terms of a chronology of Fall, Salvation (rejected?), and End. But, as the Hebrews text shows (v. 6), this figure is itself shaped around the form of the Crucifixion, whose own historical referent subsumes those of the others as their governing signification in time. In the words of Hebrews, Christian apostasy is a "crucifixion anew" of God's Son, but in a way that also instantiates in time the historically conclusive judgment of the Cross over sin's curse that punctuates the final "burning" of the eschaton. For Jansenists of Port-Royal, however, the significance of these figural relationships is not cognitive, as if their apprehension acted only as a theological pedagogy; rather, it is descriptive of the events themselves in their divinely appointed manifestation of the one controlling form — *en parresia en auto*, "the showing forth in the Cross" (Col. 2:15).

Pascal offers perhaps the most explicit example of a seventeenth-century Jansenist struggling conceptually with the phenomenon of a figurated history. To say, as he does, that "the figure was made on the basis of the Truth, and the Truth was recognized on the basis of the figure," might seem simply to state how a chronology of figures — the Old Testament in its historical referents, for instance — could gradually reveal a supra-historical reality like Christ. But, in founding the recognition of the Truth on figures — that is, on their historical orchestration — Pascal wants to say in addition that the Truth in relation to which history exists is manifested in time *only as* figure. Thus, while there is a stark contrast between the hiddenness of Truth in fully carnal terms and Truth's clear unveiling in fully spiritual terms, historical experience in its significant whole is formed according to the figural shape that alone can embody God within its temporal limitations: "among the Jesus, the Truth was only in figures; in heaven, it is unveiled. In the Church, [the Truth] is veiled, but recognized in its relation to the figure."[12] The "Church" here, of course, represents the body of the Elect throughout time, even among the Jews, and for this reason, acts as the explicator of God's ordering of *all* history, an order that is, as stated, figural before anything else. And apart from the unknown form of the beatific vision, the Truth willingly reduces itself to this exclusive shape.

From a phenomenological point of view, according to Pascal, the Truth's controlling, yet figural character — the Christ — leaves the world at descriptive loose-ends, in that this world's underlying reality can be properly enunciated only in terms that continually point away from themselves to a defining figural vocabulary that explicates, in its references to sin, redemption, and the Cross, the very impossibility of accurate self-knowledge. Rational thought can examine and attempt to delineate the processes and order of nature and history, but it will forever offer only arbitrary frameworks of understanding unless these are themselves subjected to the ordering figure of the Cross. The formal role of Pascal's "hidden God" comes to the fore just at this point:

> if the world existed in order to teach men about God, God's divinity would shine out in an incontestable way from [the world's] every aspect. But since [the world] exists only by Jesus Christ and for Jesus Christ and in order to teach men about both their corruption and their redemption, every [aspect of the world] blazes forth with the proofs of these two truths. And what appears in the world points neither to a full exclusion nor to a manifest

---

12. Pascal, *Pensées*, no. 826 (Lafuma numbering, *Oeuvres Complètes*, 605f.).

presence of divinity, but rather to the presence of a God who hides Himself. Everything is imbued with this character.[13]

In most contexts, then, how human reason construes the ordering of history will be irrelevant to its actual significance, except insofar as, apart from such construals' conformance to Christ's figure, their erroneous results themselves manifest the "character" of God's hiddenness, embodied in the Cross's submission, through charity, to human sin's oppressive weight. This embodiment, we will recall from our earlier discussion of Pascal's understanding of miracles, contains within it figures such as those of sight and blindness, faith and unbelief, mercy and judgment, and the like, all of which make possible, if not likely and essential, the continuance of such vain attempts at systematizing the temporal relations of phenomena.

Gabriel Widmer summarizes well the dependent relationship this attitude sets up between rational explication in its application to the interpretation of scriptural referents and the controlling figure of Christ. This latter figure orders historical experience according to its own form in such a way as to include the blinding limits of a chronological insistence incapable of figural discernment within its own contours:

> Pascal does not base his figurative hermeneutic on such an ontotheology [of a Platonist kind, wherein the sensible universe is founded upon the intelligible one]. It was a perspective that was, in any case, disappearing. Rather, he makes use of a critical reflection upon the differences between the new scientific spirit and theology [ ... ]. He accepts — because he himself had observed it — progress in scientific and technical research. But, from the start, he is opposed to any evolutionary conception of history itself. God, in effect, cannot exist in becoming, nor within the process of becoming. God is contemporaneous to the successive manifestation of each of the figures of His final revelation, and figurative relationships appear to Him as simultaneous, even as they become more clearly transparent to the approach of the Messiah. Furthermore, every historical moment is only repeating, in an indefinite way and within the most varied forms, the originating event of the Fall and of its inversion on the Cross. The only really new event [in history], and thus the only progress and genuine change there is, is the operation of grace that fulfills the figures — that of the crucified Messiah, that of the new humanity, that of the new creation. This vision of a repetitive history overwhelmed by the coming of Christ is based on the fact that, for Pascal the reader of Scripture and participant in the liturgy, "the Messiah has always been believed in" (282, see also 286), through the most diverse means.[14]

---

13. Ibid., no. 449, 558.

14. Gabriel Ph. Widmer, "L'herméneutique figurative de Pascal," in *In Necessariis Unitas: Mélanges offerts à Jean-Louis Leuba,* ed. Richard Stauffer (Paris: Les Editions du Cerf, 1984), 446f. Widmer's bibliographical notes, especially note 6 on 442, indicate some of the major and relatively recent work on Pascal and figuralism. In addition, see studies from earlier this century, e.g., M.-J. Lagrange's "Pascal et les prophéties messianiques," *Revue Biblique Internationale,* nouvelle série 3 (1906): 533–60; Jean Mesnard, "La théorie des figuratifs dans les 'Pensées' de Pascal," *Revue d'Histoire de la Philosophie et d'Histoire Générale de la Civilisation,* nouvelle série 35 (July–September 1943): 219–53; J. Coppens, "L'Argument des

In all of this, however, Pascal's pointed affirmations mark only the honing of practical instruments shared and utilized implicitly by most of his Port-Royal colleagues and their associates. The exegetical heritage of Appellancy, therefore — passed on through the dogmatic polemics of an Arnauld, the devotional writings of an Hamon or de Sacy, or the apologetic ruminations of a Pascal as we have described them — was shaped by convictions whose continued force provided the energy behind the explicit hermeneutical concerns of eighteenth-century Jansenists designated as *figurisme*. And we now can summarize these convictions, observed more in practice than in verbal definition, as including the following:

1. The relationship between temporal history (or Nature) and Scripture's referents is explicated only *functionally at best*. What determines such explication is therefore neither a metaphysical nor a hermeneutical "system," but simply the ongoing practice of subjecting the experiential apprehension and articulation of historical phenomena to the Christically governed figures of the Bible.

2. Temporal chronology, as it is identified or expressed in human discourse, represents nothing more than the experiential ratification of scriptural figures. And it has no ostensive reality as an ordered framework apart from its conformance to such figures.

3. What could be called the "eschatological pressures" evident in Jansenist descriptions of history — i.e., their broad millenarianism — derive from the intrinsically necessary historical expression(s) of this figural priority over temporal order. The historical "fact" that we are in the "last days" (and therefore that our experience must conform to the figures of eschatological prophecy) is verified by the relative nature of all consecutive chronologies as they are dependent upon the figural reality of Jesus Christ, whose redemptive Cross is inclusive and historically formative of the Final Judgment and history's own conclusion (even as it is so of all other historical events, however they are understood to be chronologically ordered).

4. The historical-critical problem of scriptural reference — already raised by the middle of the seventeenth century — is resolved positively on the side of affirming the historicity of all literal and figural referents. This is so because of the prior affirmation, underlying all figural reading of Scripture, of the divinely authorial realization of coincidence between all biblical images and their temporal referents, whose (occasional? frequent?) experiential irrationalism itself conforms to the enacted figure of Christ.

---

prophéties messianiques selon les Pensées de Pascal," *Ephemerides Theologicae Lovanienses* 22, no. 2 (1946): 338–61. Mesnard, in particular, usefully locates aspects of Pascal's figuralism in a revived Christian apologetic directed at Jews, under the influence of republished medieval texts like Raymond Martini's *Pugio Fidei;* he also illuminates the figurative nature, in Pascal's eyes, of Jewish history as a whole, a character that embodies the controlling elective will of God in molding historical phenomena so as both to obscure and to reveal His truth according to the governing figure of the Cross (225, 230f. 235ff.).

5. Finally, and most importantly, these convictions allow for and demand the adorative apprehension of God's glory within the temporally kaleidoscopic proliferation of figural enactments and of their diverse historical affronts to concupiscently perverted expectations. Because they stand as divinely authored coincidences of experience and scriptural signification, all events, if properly appreciated, are divine *éclats* of *sensibilité*, which is to say that the "historical process" cannot be summarized in terms of a project furthered through the instrumentalities of occasions, but is a bare conventional designation for a divinely collected anthology of figurated miracles. Figurated time and event can be, of course, and ought to be within the Church's proclamatory discourse, explicated narratively, according to the relationships of sequentially dependent forms: stories abound concerning the reality of divinely ordered experience. But this can be done only within the narrow limits of an individual occasion's passing exposition; grasped within the perspective of the "whole" Christ, and the whole of His Scripture's witness, such narratively susceptible events take form as figures whose relationships one to another defy sequential boundaries in their causal linkage.

Over and against these convictions, we can see how the suspicion aroused by and the disdain directed at the contemporizing of biblical figures entail, it would seem, an inescapable misunderstanding concerning the observed phenomena of miracle and sanctity. By explicitly (e.g., Léonard) or implicitly (e.g., Savon) denying scriptural figure a necessary and describable contemporary *accomplissement,* the phenomena of prodigious holiness in history are left to dangle perilously without firm support over the heads of onlookers, the Church as a whole included, seducing and finally crushing. Their religious referents as historical events are reduced to being but the behavioral signs of the *self-*referential pathology of spiritual pride: they are the results if not the actual embodiment of sectarianism's miasma of self-concern struggling against the current of social marginalization. All this, however, *does* represent misunderstanding, at least of those events as Jansenist convictions rendered their possibility. With the present divinely figurated in its whole and parts, as Jansenists believed, miracles and sanctity could hardly be considered, in the first place, to be bearers of some factional party's own self-reference. Like all else, but here with a uniquely characteristic *éclat,* these events in time referred to figures of a divine glory, whose Christic center demanded submission of all but their scriptural enunciation. Only a figurated present such as this, punctuated by marks of light, could claim the Word of God to be an evidence of anything at all.

We would, however, be guilty of a gross misrepresentation of Jansenist Appellancy especially, if we did not also recognize the central place held in their polemics and meditations by the very kind of spiritually self-referential locutions that have so distressed students of the movement: *pauci electi* or *reliqui fideles,* they would often call themselves — the few elect, the faithful remnant; they stood as Athanasius *contra mundum,* against the world; they were inheritors of the mantle of *defensores Causae Dei*, defenders of God's Cause; the End of the ages was indeed at hand, and it fell upon them, those who resisted *Unigenitus* and its doctrine, etc. To speak of prophetic *accomplissements* in eighteenth-century France and miracles in the midst of those who understood Scripture's fulfill-ment within their own era there cannot but press such discourse into self-reference. None of this can be denied. But the issue turns on where the self is located among such speech's referents. For if the talk, in all of this, is informed by Scripture's explicit *figural* significations, then self-reference also is informed by the self's place in the figure; the self's place in the figure, to repeat, and not the converse. "Reference" itself becomes a relative term, derivative in its fundamental connotation of the divine authorial signification.

We are here faced with the same ordering of reality and its apprehension as we have discerned to exist in the Jansenist description of chronology and figure: the latter is prior and defines the former. The referent in Jan-senist "self-reference" is, in the first place, not the self at all, but the figure that allows the self's experience to be in any way significant experience, that is, the historical figure of the Christ. The characteristically Appellant contemporizing of biblical figures through the discernment of their refer-ents in the life of the historical Church into and beyond the present — the "self" referred to in the Appellants' stream of prophetic interpreta-tion — ultimately serves the purpose, in their own mind, of overtly forging an interpretive path beyond the insidious *vanities* of any "disinterested" exegesis (which only obscures the visage Scripture aims to disclose), by insisting that historically contemporary experience itself be unremittingly and primarily referential of those figures in the Word upon which such ex-perience depends. To understand the subsuming nature of Christ's own figure given form in Scripture, is, quite simply, to allow for one's own historical subsumption within it.

## Duguet's *Figurisme*

This leads us back to Duguet, and to his acknowledged role at the helm of *figurisme*'s alarming ascendance, in Léonard's view, to the heights of ex-egetical fashion in the early eighteenth-century French Catholic Church. For if what I have just suggested is accurately reflective of some of the theo-logical dynamics underlying figurist prophetism, then Léonard's warning about its dangerous tendency toward idiosyncratic illuminism misses the mark. The Duguet of the *Règles* must instead, in this light, be seen as a man who simply sought to understand the Scriptures in a way that would include the present within God's own figurated self, a task that thereby answered the Christian (and hardly peculiarly Jansenist) voca-tion to glorify God in every moment. How this ties in with the more explicit millennialism of other Appellants will now follow and complete our chapter.

The *Règles* themselves cannot be read, as I hope it is by now clear, as somehow "programmatic" of a system of exegesis. They are, rather, expository of a given practice already rooted in Jansenist circles. Savon is probably correct in viewing the work's original composition as growing out of specific concerns Duguet may have held about the implications of the historical-critical methods adopted by Richard Simon — a member of the Oratory with which Duguet had early been associated — and by Grotius.[15] In this, he was following Bossuet's lead, and the work's first section, the "Rules" proper, sound themes that are less Appellant, in the political and prophetic sense, than they are simply Jansenist and Oratorian in their devotional springs. It is not unlikely therefore, as Savon suggests, that these "rules" predate their actual publication in 1716 by perhaps a decade and certainly seem to predate the official organization of Appellancy after the 1713 bull. Nonetheless, they would still reflect the practice of a confirmed Jansenist, who had left the Oratory in 1680s in part precisely because of the organization's official movement against the many Jansenist sympathizers in its midst.[16] And to this degree, they cannot simply be divorced from the trajectories of Appellant thinking taken by Duguet's friends and disciples, as if these latter were somehow artificially "attached" to his own work during the prepared publication of the *Règles*, in the form of the second prophetic section on the "Retour des Juifs," and then later defended and elaborated by students like d'Étemare. Having endured exile in Brussels in the 1680s (sharing lodgings with Arnauld and Quesnel), in Savoy in 1715, after joining the first Appeal against *Unigenitus*, in 1730 in Holland, and in between frequently hiding and traveling in secret because of his outlawed Appellant commitments, Duguet always framed his exegetical interests within his personal experience of the Jansenist struggle in the Church and the insecurities and threats this brought upon him and his colleagues.

We have already examined, in our chapter "The Form of Grace," something of Duguet's strikingly blunt reduction of God's glorious love to the bare outlines of Jesus' life, in its bounded historical particularities. We have noted also how the developing devotional theology of the Oratory, of Bérulle as passed through de Condren and Quesnel, probably lay be-

---

15. HervéSavon, "Le figurisme et la 'Tradition des Pères,'" in *Le Grand Siècle et la Bible*, ed. Jean-Robert Armogathe (Paris: Editions Beauchesne, 1989), 768–71, 779. Goujet, *Vie de M. Du Guet*, 26, tells us, without reference, that Duguet wrote the work in response to a request by a certain Abbé Charpentier, a relative of the great Jansenist historian Le Nain de Tillemont.

16. See Paul Chételat, *Étude sur Du Guet* (Paris: Ernest Thorin, 1879), 25ff. This remains the only real study of Duguet since the eighteenth century (although Sainte-Beuve, in vol. 5 of *Port-Royal* especially gives him some extensive treatment), and while it contains important references to and reproduction of many unpublished letters both of Duguet and of his acquaintances, the volume is wholly inadequate in its analysis of Duguet's thinking, even as Chételat's aversion toward the Saint-Médard episode causes him to paint a picture of Duguet's "moderation" in this affair that is obviously distorting of his personal motivations and commitments to Appellancy. Guny's article "Duguet" in the *Dictionnaire de la Spiritualité* is usefully accessible.

hind Duguet's writing on these themes. Here it is enough to show how these properly Quesnellian transpositions of Christic *anéantissement* implied for Duguet's mature works the explicit *figuriste* grasp of Scripture's eschatological molding of historical occasions.[17] The 1705 *Traité sur les dispositions pour offrir les SS. Mysteres, et y participer avec fruit* offers a good example of how decidedly Oratorian categories as applied to the issue of the Eucharistic "dispositions" could, in his hands, converge with the eschatological scripturalism of Port-Royal.[18]

Duguet preserves the popular enumerative treatment of the dispositions, laying out in his treatise a long list of attitudes appropriate to participation in (and celebration of) the Holy Communion, attitudes that, if read superficially, mostly fall into the class of spiritual and moral preparatives, e.g., "modesty and gravity," "untarnished chastity," "lively respect," etc. And while the work as a whole evidences little structural coherence apart from this traditional ethical catalogue, running consistently through it is Duguet's ready linkage of the dispositions described to the very form of Jesus' own life and "mysteries":

> Now, a priest with faith is convinced that all these mysteries live on and continue at the altar. We certainly do not have two sacrifices. That which JESUS-CHRIST has offered is the same one that we offer; they are the same humiliations, just as it is the same death. And the priest is not only a spectator to this; he is its pontiff and minister. What human injustice and cruelty accomplished, the priest continues through religious means and with a legitimate authority. The external violence is now over: but the priesthood of JESUS-CHRIST is eternal, and the priests that He has deigned to join to it do not possess [a priesthood] different from His. In their hands they hold what lies in the hands of JESUS-CHRIST; they offer to the Father all that the Son offers to Him.[19]

Taking up the traditional sacrificial imagery here, Duguet presses it into the use of that participatory vision of Jesus' mysteries: not only is the Eucharistic sacrifice per se invoked, but the whole of Jesus' historical existence is given form in the liturgical act, which becomes the conduit to the larger movement of the Christian's life into and within the details

---

17. Duguet, who was born in 1649 and lived until 1733, did not achieve the kind of recognized influence attested to by attacks on his work like Léonard's until after his fiftieth year. Only in the first decade of the eighteenth century did any of his works find published circulation, although already his "lectures" in Paris had gained a notable following. Thus, while it is tempting to assume an evolution in his own thinking on the basis of a chronological ordering of his books, virtually all of them date from the latter part of his life, and although events like the Appeal and Saint-Médard intervene during this last period, it seems unlikely to me that anything of substance in his basic theological orientations would have changed by this point. Add to this the fact that even from among his published works, many were but printings of lectures or privately circulated manuscript essays that had been composed many years earlier, and we are perhaps encouraged, for lack of detailed research into the origins of Duguet's writings, to interpret them as a whole, and not genetically.

18. In *Traitez sur la prière publisque et sur les dispositions,*, nouvelle edition (Liege: François Hoyous, 1715).

19. Ibid., 211.

of the Christ's incarnate circumstances. The "dispositions," we realize, refer to Jesus first, and only by some prior participation, to our own posture before Communion: "a sincere humility," "love of simplicity," "love of poverty" — each of these devolve into human dispositions only as they are participatory figures of the life of Christ. Indeed, this is well-worn devotional territory for the followers of Quesnel as they consider the Mass:

> We believe that we see Him born at Bethlehem, and we worship Him still, in His manger, even as we see Him on the altar as a newborn, wrapped in linens, barely recognized except by heavenly or humble spirits. His obedience before Mary and Joseph now go much further, for He respects, even among the most unworthy ministers, the promise He has made to His Church and the authority He truly wished to share with it.
>
> His hidden life, His silence, His obscurity are all continued in the Eucharist, even to a more perfect and marvelous degree. His long prayers in the wilderness, on the mountains, throughout the night — they were all interrupted from outside by the public demands of His ministry; but here they exist without interruption and constitute the merit and prize of all the prayers of the Church. His poverty blazes forth visibly in the simplicity of those symbols that act as His veil. His humility [ ... ] His mercy [ ... ] His compassion [ ... ]
>
> But the mysteries of His death, of His burial, and of His resurrection are all infinitely more tangible [*sensibles*]. He offers Himself, although still alive, with the same feelings of love and of faith for His Father, and of charity for men, that led Him to die upon the Cross [etc.].[20]

Duguet, familiarly, then applies these "continued" mysteries even more directly to the life of the Christian participant: receiving the Body and Blood is directly involved in the transformation of the *spectateur* [spectator] into the figurated *penitent,* the one in whom the form of Jesus is historically signified within the Body of the Church; that is, the Eucharist is the formative means by which, quoting Cyprian, *ad martyrii poculum idoneos facimus,* we make martyrs.[21] The final dispositions outlined, then, are those of "suffering" and "persecution," of "mortification" and "penitence," but explicated in terms of their experiential embodiment of Christ's own sacrifice. As a result of this shift in dispositional referent, Duguet moves from a commendation of a merely devotional preparation for the Eucharist, to the Christically participatory design of human history, that is, to the figurated realm of Scripture's description of that history. By reminding his readers that "the two most explicit figures of the Eucharist" are "the paschal lamb and the manna" — "the lamb is eaten with bitter herbs and the manna fell only in the wilderness; so that one had to be denied everything in order to be nourished"[22] — Duguet embarks on a summary reinterpretation of the Eucharist in terms of its figured and figurating role within the Bible's narratives. In its celebration, the Mass

20. Ibid., 246ff.
21. Ibid., 251ff.
22. Ibid., 267.

continually draws together the historical strands of Scripture's referents into the single informing figure of Christ Crucified.

Just this set of interconnections drives him to end the work on the same eschatological note that we have already argued as being necessitated logically by such a historically controlling center: the Body of Christ, which is His historically enacted figure, wherever it may be, now offers up its temporal limits to the constraining form of its Master, and the whole of prophecy's predictive and figurated discourse settles about the corners of this sacrificial plate. Speaking of the priest's duty to offer the sacrifice of the Mass in prayer for the whole of God's people scattered throughout the world, Duguet explains how such an intention concerning the Eucharist in itself embraces the experiential forms associated with prophetic *accomplissement:*

> At no time can one separate JESUS CHRIST from His Church, of which He is the bridegroom and the head. Even less so can one separate Him from the altar, where He offers Himself for the Church and offers the Church for Himself. Thus a priest [ . . . ] ought never to go up to the altar in the guise of a private person; he ought never to limit his intentions to a single diocese. Rather, he will remember the entire universe in which the family of Jesus Christ is scattered, where the good grain grows and bears fruit in the midst of a thousand perils.
>
> [ . . . ] He will share his compassion and heart far beyond the limits of the Church, and will plead with God that He might gather up those whom schism and heresy have separated from the Church, and that He might bring in to her the unbelieving nations promised to His Son. As for that nation which was once blessed, whose blindness caused her reproof, in whose place we now stand, and for whose conversion the prophets prayed so often and with such ardor — it seems as if the time has come to take pity upon her. Perhaps our own ingratitude toward Jesus Christ, and our own disdain of His teaching (which is better known and less followed now than at any other time) is a sign of this.[23]

The Christian is nourished for persecution and martyrdom, the unfaithfulness of the Church has etched marks of concern within the side of time, the Conversion of the Jews is probably at hand bringing to clarion pitch the promises made by prophets for the form of God's saving grace — and all of this, encompassing the years, flows outward in the Eucharistic act, itself fed by the well that is the life of Christ evangelically enfigured.

In the *Traité sur les dispositions* these eschatological notes are limited, even if they form the intrinsically motivated climax to an essay otherwise framed by the devotional categories of the Oratory. But throughout Duguet's published work, these notes are sounded, often with reverberating force, and they remain consistently articulated within the general prophetic pattern, associated with Appellancy, of historical synthesis ordered by Christ's figure. Duguet's masterwork, the *Traité de la croix de*

---

23. Ibid., 302f.

*N.-S. J.-C.*, which first appeared complete in its fourteen volumes in 1733, is imbued with such themes, and we should see them therefore as characteristic of, and not merely incidental to, his thinking.[24] The second volume of *Jésus crucifié* from this series continues a lengthy examination of the various references to the Passion made in St. Paul's letters, and for over fifty pages Duguet engages in the prophetic reading of Romans 11 for which later *figuristes* became notorious, and which stands as but a more detailed account of elements noted in the *Traité sur les dispositions:* the present condition of the Church and the "signs" of its destiny given therein, the Return of the Jews, and the consummation of God's plan in history.[25] Each of these topics, worked out in great detail and with enormous scriptural precision, conform in a more narrow compass to their treatment by Duguet in his posthumously published *Explication de l'Épitre de Saint Paul aux Romains.*[26] The degradation of the Gentile Church to a "small remnant" of the faithful, the imminent (if still undatable) conversion of the Jews through the intermediaries of Elijah and possibly Enoch, the restoration of the Nations to faith with the help of a believing Israel, and the gathering up of the elect to Christ — all of this is carefully explicated in both of these works, with a detail drawn from the current experience of the Church's life that, while hardly explicit, gains its force from the undercurrent of Jansenism's weary battle:

> It is true that many branches grafted in by grace to the natural olive tree will be cut off. Scripture says this too clearly for us to doubt it. And the reality of events has so confirmed what Scripture has predicted that we cannot claim that its predictions are somehow obscure: Africa as a whole wrenched from the Church; the Greek schism with all the subsequent Patriarchates in communion with it; the heresy of other Patriarchates, the desolation caused by Mohammedism among the sorry remnants of Christendom that remain, the ravages of recent heresies, which have removed all the northern kingdoms and entire provinces of Germany, the Low Countries, and Switzerland, not to mention the ancient wound within France's heart that has yet to close — all these ills, which resemble a terrible storm of hail and lightning, have struck countless branches and have ripped from the olive tree (though still standing despite these losses) a major portion of its beauty and dignity. And if there is anything surprising in all this, it is that God's mercy has yet to re-establish Israel within these many emptied spaces.

24. The *Traité* is made up of a number of previously published and collected books, appearing variously with different titles. As with other works of Duguet, the date of their actual composition remains confused. D'Étemare, later in life, mentions Duguet's *Jésus crucifié* as containing the fruit of Duguet's exegetical "method," and he is perhaps referring to the *Traité* as a whole, or to those particular volumes within it which we have earlier examined, the *Explication du mystere de la passion de N.-S. J.-C., Suivant la Concorde. Jesus Crucifié* (1728), and which may derive from lectures given in 1712, at which d'Étemare was present. See Bruno Neveu, "Port-Royal à l'âge des Lumières: Les 'Pensées' et les 'Anecdotes' de l'Abbé d'Étemare, 1682–1770," *Lias* 4, no. 1 (1977): 132–3.

25. In the *Explication du mystere de la passion*, part 2, 391–447.

26. Avignon, 1756. See the commentary on chapter 11 of the Epistle, 391–448. I have not been able to trace the origin of this work; it is perhaps a reworking of lecture notes, elaborated by another hand.

But the times, noted by the Prophet Hosea in a general way, for the Return of the Jews (and only God holds its secret) are more extended than we
might have thought [ . . . ] What we do know, and what our miseries will not
allow us to forget, is this: not only has charity become increasingly cold day
by day, but faith itself has become a rare thing, whose value is little understood, and for which we substitute human reasoning, foolish speculation,
and systems of thought unknown to our forebears. We know too that we
have, in many ways, undermined the gratitude we owe to JESUS CHRIST,
and that many now view His grace as something owed to them, and that
others are convinced that such grace is hardly even needed to make right the
human heart, able (as they believe) on its own to love and practice virtue,
and requiring grace only to render more noble their actions and to gain, by
their merits, a more supernatural (as opposed to some lower, though still
eternal) happiness. We know, as well, that in some people's minds Original
Sin is less a corruption of nature than it is a simple loss of external goods
which nature could well do without; that the goods of redemption are consequently a form of grace without absolute necessity, and since there is such
danger in receiving these goods without responding to them with an adequate righteousness and a persevering gratitude, it would almost be better
never to be baptized, so that, free from the obligation to maintain [baptismal]
innocence, one could hold on to a more certain, if lesser, dignity.

Each day gives birth to new errors, which tend to separate us from JESUS
CHRIST, to remove us from His grace, His liberty, and His rule, and to
establish instead a philosophical or Jewish form of righteousness. And this
downward spiral, which is taking on speed and coming up against few obstacles — for we worry about everything else except how to bring needed
healing for these ills — makes us worry if perhaps our time is near, or rather
makes us hope that the time of the Jews is not far.[27]

But the prophetic character of this kind of aggravated rumination, it
must be recognized, finds its settled purpose in the meditation upon
Christ's life and His Cross especially. The eschatological topic arises for
Duguet only within — or at least in strict theological dependence upon —
a more fundamental explication of the meaning of the Passion. Within
the context of *Jésus crucifié* in particular, his discussion of the Return
of the Jews hangs upon an effort to elucidate the "mystery of Christ" in
Ephesians 3:3f., which he refers back to the discussion by Paul in chapter
2 of the Gentiles' divine transposition, with the Jews, into a "new man."
This reality of the temporal and spiritual relation between Israel and the
Nations that touches upon the very shape of human history — and is also
explicated by Paul in chapters 9–11 of Romans — is shown by Duguet
to be given form in the figure of the Cross, that is, it is a "mystery" of
the Passion, by which alone the "dividing wall of hostility" between these
peoples was torn down, in the "flesh" of Christ (Eph. 2:14f.).[28] Delving
deeply into the historical reality of the Gentiles' separation from God and
consequent enmity with God's elect nation, demonstrating the historical

---

27. *Jésus crucifié*, 422–24.
28. Ibid., 347ff.

cost of their reconciliation through the suffering and death of the Incarnate Son, and emphasizing with passionate intensity the fragile temporal basis of this saving faith offered to the Nations — what was given belongs only to the giver and can be recalled — Duguet aims most of all to outline within the experience of the world's peoples, Israel at their center, the supporting boundaries of God's uniquely formative powers that trace the pattern of what theologians call divine "grace." It is *this* pattern of grace, embodied in the Cross of Christ, that structures the historical passage Paul delineates in Romans 9–11, and that explains Duguet's fascination with its vision of alternating election and reprobation among Jews and Gentiles. To be sure, Paul's "warnings" to his Gentile listeners that they too, as the unnatural grafts upon the olive tree of Israel's election, might be removed for unbelief, just as were the natural shoots, serve Duguet as undeniable "predictions" launched to reach their mark at least among the debris of the Catholic Church of his day.[29] But his confidence that scriptural "warnings" are indeed "predictions" for the Church is grounded less in his discernment, prejudiced or otherwise, of his own times, than it is in the recognition that history is essentially figured according to the form of Christ, and hence "the past is the model of the future" if, as Paul so clearly accepts in Duguet's view, that past's contours rightly limn the incarnate flesh of Christ.[30]

Thus, as with Pascal, the whole of the prophetic impulse in Duguet's work springs not so much from a conviction in the bare predictive quality of Scripture's discourse, as from one in the figural and figurating center of that discourse, which ensures that history's shape conforms and will conform to its own pattern. This figure, as with Pascal, is given in the historical Cross of Jesus Christ, is temporally ordered according to the epiphanic pattern of God's justice and mercy that the Cross embodies, and is theologically articulated in the notion of Grace, for which the Cross alone stands as the object of reflection. "Without the light cast upon the Scripture by the death and insults suffered by Jesus Christ, they [the Scriptures] would be unintelligible," Duguet notes in his long apologetic work, *Traité des Principes de la Foy Chrétienne.*[31] The single figure of the Cross, given in Scripture, not only exclusively illumines Scripture's meaning, but sheds its light in terms of the phenomenal shapes of history witnessed to in Scripture's words and cast in temporal forms inclusive of our futures, now shown to be joined and knotted to the lineaments of our Savior's flesh. Summarizing his comments on Romans 11:33, "O the depth of the riches and wisdom and knowledge of God! How unsearchable are his judgments and how inscrutable his ways!" Duguet writes:

> Note well that the profundity in question, which so astonishes St. Paul, is the profundity of the treasures and riches of God's wisdom and knowledge,

---

29. See ibid., 394f., 406ff.
30. Cf, ibid., 408.
31. Paris: Barthelemy Alix, 1736, 424ff.

which shine forth as fully as God's justice and mercy in the way Jews and Gentiles are successively called to faith.

No one can really give a reason as to why the nations were so long abandoned, even while God was showing Himself to a single people and appeared to be interested only in them. No one can explain why a people to whom all the Scriptures and promises had been entrusted and for whom existence itself lay in preserving a hope for the Messiah should be struck with blindness precisely in relation to this Messiah (although a small number of them did in fact receive Him). No one can understand why the Gentiles, who were completely ignorant of the Scriptures that promised the Messiah and who had not been able to listen to JESUS CHRIST or to see His miracles, believed in him so easily; while at the same time the Jews, instructed by His teaching and witnesses to His miracles, became day by day more unbelieving. No one can discover why the Gentiles, so full of zeal for the faith and so conscious of the sorry fate of the Jews, should come to find distasteful the very gifts given to them. Nor can one grasp how the Jews, who daily cast new clouds upon their ancient prejudices and for whom a willful stubbornness constitutes the greatest obstacle to their faith, should come to bow down before JESUS CHRIST.

But as in the past, all was readied by an infinite wisdom which has governed all these events, and which has established among them an admirable order and relation. So it is with all that remains to happen. Providence, which human reason cannot apprehend, guides and disposes all things according to its decrees. Its work advances day by day. Each event becomes the occasion and the season for another. Everything is tied together, and holds firm from the first link to the last. And one day, the Saints will wonder at this spectacle, wherein the entire work of their consummation—the riches of the wisdom and knowledge of God now laid out with order and economy, the unity of God's grand design now joining together His judgments and His ways—this great secret will no longer be hidden, even as its very brightness keeps it from their grasp.[32]

And this "great work"—whose plan was known to Him even before the ages: *Notum a saecula est Domino opus suum* [Acts 15:18], and was furthered by God "in the course of so many centuries"—Duguet tells us, is the final reconciliation of Jew and Gentile beyond their mutually distancing "invincible blindness," accomplished in "the single grace of JESUS CHRIST," "in His flesh" and "insofar as He is the cornerstone."[33] The rays of light inaccessible, even, will be found in nimbus form around this stark shape.

It is therefore impossible, it seems to me, to place an interpretive wedge between Duguet and his followers with regard to their respective prophetic interests: to read the Scripture according to the figure of Christ demanded a reading of history as located among those figurated referents of Scripture linked to Him. The prominence given to particular elements in such reading—to figures like Elijah, to events like the Appeal, to the Return

32. *Jésus crucifié*, 416–19.
33. Ibid., 443–47.

of the Jews or the demise of Gentile Christendom, etc. — varied among figurist writers. But the convictions underlying their use of Scripture were mostly held in common and centered together on this historically figurating role attributed to the form of Christ's life. And despite differences that developed among Jansenist theologians over the Saint-Médard episode, all remained committed to an affirmation of miracle and sanctity as both being of a piece with the eschatologically epiphanic character of the times in which they lived.[34] Any attempt, like Savon's, then, to take the *Règles* as a misused and misunderstood tool in the hands of extremist Appellants — the *figuristes* proper — must falter before the reality of this larger common mind.

## The *Règles* of Duguet

By leaving until this point our actual examination of the *Règles*, I have deliberately wanted them to speak for themselves, as much as possible, in the shadow of our previous discussion. After simply listing each "rule," my hope is that their functional (as opposed to "systematic") role in Jansenist figural devotion and theology will be relatively clear, and I will need only then to underline certain elements in the work's exposition that witness to its place within the continuum of this tradition. The concise form of these rules, as follows, is taken from the headings to each chapter; I append to each some of the scriptural examples Duguet uses in his explanatory sections:

FIRST RULE. We should see Jesus Christ everywhere the apostles saw Him. [The Virgin in Isaiah 7]

II. RULE. We should see Jesus Christ as visible, whenever certain features, suitable only to Him, point to Him. [Isaiah 9; 63]

III. RULE. Whenever the Scriptural expressions are too magnificent for their apparent subjects, this is proof that they have as their object something more august. [Isaiah 14:4; 41:18; 43:19, all on the Jews' return from Babylon]

IV. RULE. There are places where the prophetic sense is the only immediate and literal sense. [Ps. 22; 45:7]

V. RULE. Promises which have as their object a temporal happiness must be understood as images of spiritual goods. [Ps. 127; 128]

---

34. We shall be looking, in our next chapter, at some of the disagreements among Jansenists over the miracles and convulsions. Duguet himself, by this point near the end of his life, still pressed into periods of hiding and exile and no longer vitally engaged in the affairs taking place in Paris, was notably sceptical of the alleged prodigies. For at least a decade, from 1705 or so on, however, he was a careful recipient of the revelations offered by a self-styled prophetess, the Soeur Rose, whose inspired advice — always carefully given within scriptural bounds, even while it touched on contemporary and future events — Duguet considered seriously and respectfully. Having eventually felt disappointed in her prophesies by the outcome of events, he purportedly vowed in the face of Saint-Médard never to be "duped" again. See Chételat, *Étude sur Du Guet*, 57–63, and for references, Kreiser, *Miracles, Convulsions, and Ecclesiastical Politics in Early Eighteenth-Century Paris*, 289.

VI. RULE. Whenever the Scripture contains elements that, in the course of their narrative, do not make sense to us (according to our weak reason) or do not suit the notions we have of the persons involved, this is a sign that they hide a mystery. [Genesis 21, on Abraham driving out Hagar and Ishmael]

VII. RULE. There are things in Scripture that are so surprising and so mysterious that they make clear in themselves that the simple historical sense is not sufficient [to explain them]. [The entire story of Jacob through his return from Haran]

VIII. RULE. There are stories whose circumstances have such a visible relation to JESUS CHRIST that it is not possible to doubt that they represent Him. [The entire story of Joseph and his brothers, which also figures the Conversion of the Jews at the Endtime]

IX. RULE. The law, the tabernacle, the sacrifices, the priesthood, and the Jewish ceremonies were figures of Jesus Christ. [Hebrews]

X. RULE. When a story or prophecy is simple, natural, graceful [aisée], and when all of its parts are connected and joined in a single point of view, this is a sign that it should probably be applied to Jesus Christ. [Story of the Ark of Noah]

XI. RULE. Those parts of Scripture which speak of the inadequacy of circumcision, of the law, of the temple, of the sacrifices, of the ceremonies, of the privileges of being of the race of Abraham or of living in the promised land or of dwelling in Jerusalem — all these clearly disclose Jesus Christ and the righteousness of the Gospel. [Isaiah 1; 66]

XII. RULE. There are certain predictions of the prophets whose same language refers [at once] to very diverse events, far apart in time. [Psalm 2]

The first observation I would make concerns the language which informs these regulating maxims, language the understanding of which is itself an act of interpretive discernment: "visibility," "magnificence," "august," "spiritual images," "hidden mystery," "surprise," "representation," "simplicity," "disclosure." These are words all pointing to the character of meditative adoration that lies behind the act of figural exegesis Duguet is recommending: "discovering" Jesus Christ in the Scripture is an act of worship. In the opening of his introduction to the Rules, he summarizes the substance of Scripture and the nature of its proper reading:

> Nothing is truer than what we have learned from the Apostle Paul: that Jesus Christ is the end of the law; that He is predicted and figured in the whole Old Testament; the prophets had only Him in view; and that we do not understand the Scriptures that precede Jesus unless we discover Him within them everywhere, and unless we are satisfied only with an interpretation that leads to Him.[35]

The process of this "discovery" of Christ, however, is compared, in the first Rule, to the "parting" of the curtain (of, e.g., historically read referents in

---

35. Cited from the Migne edition, 15.

the texts) — "we must part the curtain, not rip it"[36] — a curtain which, in the context of the discussion as a whole, is nothing other than the Temple's own veil before the Holy presence of God. "The theologian's most sweet and sublime occupation is to search out Jesus Christ in the holy scriptures."[37] Figural exegesis itself is a form of worship.

As a form of worship, the discernment of figural reference within Scripture subordinates the whole process of historical conjunctions given or implied in the texts' ostensive signification to the controlling reality of the object of adoration, the form of Christ Jesus, as given explicit shape elsewhere in the Scripture. Although he notes the dangers of "purely allegorical explanations," which end by "substituting" "purely human" interpretations for Scripture's own intrinsic meanings, Duguet is far more concerned to combat attitudes that "exclude" or "neglect" the allegorical or figural meanings of texts.[38] Using Grotius's interpretation of Isaiah 9 as an example of historical reduction — seeing King Hezekiah and not Jesus the Christ as its referent — he offers a figural correction to this approach in his explication of Rule II, providing a lengthy meditation on the "names" given by Isaiah to the promised child.[39] With each term, Duguet turns his readers toward the apprehension of the redemptive life and death of Christ, seeking to confront them with sensible qualities of his existence as they evoke reverent astonishment:

> The Messiah will not have all of these names, but He will have all that they signify. He will Himself *be* a prodigy, and the object of every being's wonder. Not a single created intelligence will be able to comprehend His charity. His humility will be as surprising as His love. We shall never plumb the impenetrable and secret depths of divine nature's union with our own. The more we study His life — a mixture of greatness and weakness, worthy of God's holiness yet nonetheless accessible to sinners, able to make demons worship Him as Son of God, and able also to blind them to the point of crucifying Him — the more we shall be frightened at the profound wisdom that knew how to unite such apparently opposing extremes. But our wonder will only increase as we consider how all these means He chose for triumphing over the world and taking possession of His kingdom appeared so contrary to His plans, even as we note how much they conformed to His power, to His divine justice, His goodness, our own conversion, our consolation, our needs, and our example.[40]

---

36. Ibid., 26.
37. Ibid., 20.
38. Ibid., 21f.
39. Ibid., 28–30.
40. Ibid., 28. For the unremittingly inclusive character of Duguet's central figure, see his closing remarks to his introductory section: "I would ask that you note how, when I speak of Jesus Christ, I have in mind all that He is, and all that He has done, and all that He has suffered, and all that He has promised, and all that He has taught, and that I do not separate any of this from His Church. It is in this sense that He is the unique object of the Scriptures; and we must always assume this when we are trying to find Him in the sacred narrative and prophecies" (25).

The figure of the Cross itself, its affronting folly, the violence of its surprise, and the terrible efficacy of its power to save — all of these, if beheld in the relief of their scriptural utterance, reformulate the method by which the sacred text itself is to be read, demonstrating how divine "wisdom" reveals the "plans" of God in frequent contrarieties of self-giving and in humiliated passions. To begin first with this Christ, and to submit to Him in love, is in itself to recognize Scripture's composition along figural lines drawn tight about His form and ensnaring our attention to His shape. Such a recognition hearkens back to views of the Word wholly congruent with Port-Royal's.

The whole text of Scripture, in this light, acts as a kind of figural prophecy, because it is directed in its formulation as in the referents of its terms by the very One whose life is continuously disclosed in its words. The preface to the work as a whole, which is perhaps written by the abbé d'Asfeld and not by Duguet, properly turns to 1 Peter 1:10–12 as a central guiding text here:

> the prophets who prophesied of the grace that was to be yours searched and inquired about this salvation; they inquired what person or time was indicated by the Spirit of Christ within them when predicting the sufferings of Christ and the subsequent glory. It was revealed to them that they were serving not themselves but you, in the things which have now been announced to you by those who preached the good news to you through the Holy Spirit sent from heaven, things into which angels long to look.

Because given in and by the same Spirit who traces Christ's form, the *passiones, et posteriores glorias,* the sufferings and subsequent glory of the Christ, have formed the identical referents of all the words spoken and gathered in the various parts of Scripture, each moored within their own moments, yet each fitted to disclose the same Person in His time:

> The same Spirit of Jesus Christ filled the prophets and the apostles; and the former announced more obscurely and from a distance what He revealed more clearly through the latter. Each group gives witness to the other and offers a mutual authorization. They speak the same language and by the same Spirit sent from heaven. Their congruency is whole and perfect, and just as the apostles declare themselves to know nothing except Jesus Christ and to be sent to preach Him alone, so the prophets speak of nothing but Him and declare only His mysteries, into whose secrets even angels yearn to enter.[41]

The incompatibilities of prophetic reference with their historic circumstances are central "marks," for Duguet, of a truer, figural reference to Christ (e.g., Rules 3, 5, 6, etc.), and throughout the *Règles,* as in figurist writing in general, the *un*-fulfillment of prophecies within history, the confusing outcomes of obvious predictions, and the lack of clarity in the experience of providence's design all serve to unveil the unattended

---

41. Ibid., 11.

weakness by which God triumphs over sin within the world. Thus, the historical resolution of such prophecies — as, for instance, the prophetic depictions of a Jerusalem of such grandeur and virtue or of the blessings attached to human righteousness of such extent as would be materially impossible within the given experience of Israel and her saints — in the spiritual figure of Christ and His Church, indicates not an interpretation of "convenience," but a recognition of the Holy Spirit's authorial orchestration of history, as a referent of the text, around the figure of a God whose very wisdom given in the form of sacrificial love is "unveiled" in just such dazzling and dumbfounding incongruities.[42]

On this basis, one grounded in the historically given form of Christ whose own outline reached and held to the temporal dissonances between word and referents, whose own and single figure of divine humiliation was one of incarnate heterogeneity — a basis that was pneumatic in its ordering, as Léonard perhaps vaguely understood — on this lay the figurist confidence in construing historical experience prophetically, by freeing strands of temporal sequence given in a text from significations demanding constrictive chronological coherence, and allowing them to wrap themselves in discrete parallels about the shape of Christ. Where Duguet, in his introduction to the Rules, delineates the ways in which a text can operate prophetically, he does so with a deliberate goal of disengaging figures from any overriding structural logic apart from their ability to represent the life of Christ and His people, that is, His Body the Church.[43] Ostensibly proposing "limits" on figural applications, so as to protect the "literal" sense of a text, Duguet in fact sets out purposefully to qualify the distinction between historical and prophetic senses altogether, not so much to make the former impertinent as to affirm that history's shape is rendered by its own prophetic character.

The first move Duguet makes to this end is to call the whole of Scripture's meaning "literal," that is, to dispense with "literalness" as a useful term of contrast to the figural and to imbue the "letter" of the Word with a determinative integrity of meaning. "The letter can have two meanings [*sens*]," he writes, "the immediate and the prophetic." This "immediate" sense is discernible in both historical and prophetic genres and designates simply what seems the most obvious reading of a text: "the immediate meaning is the one that presents itself first; it acts as a veil for the second, and is its preparation." The immediate sense of a historical narrative is its literal referents, while the immediate sense of a prophetic discourse is its purely temporal referents as determined by the immediate context of the utterance. The "prophetic" sense of either genre, however, is the "ultimate" sense of all Scripture — Jesus Christ in the breadth of His life — and this object is different from and should not be confused with immediate referents. An "exact" interpretation will not mix the two senses.

---

42. See ibid., 15–17.
43. Ibid., 20–25.

"The objects of the one and of the other are different, but they stand in great relation to each other," he writes. But what then is their relation? The prophetic sense "ennobles" the immediate sense and is not "contrary" to it, to be sure, but in what way? Here is where Duguet seeks to collapse, not so much the distinction between the two, as the significance attached to each. Both senses, he says, are "founded on the letter," in such a way that the unifying character of their discernment is the text itself, a text authored by the Holy Spirit to point, as a whole and in its parts, to the person of the Christ. Certain texts and genres are not, in themselves, susceptible to prophetic interpretations, and many prophetic texts are understandable only according to their immediate senses. Finally, the prophetic interpretation of texts — historical or otherwise — is itself frequently accessible only through partial and "imperfect" figures, whose relation to the text as a whole or to other texts is often clouded or uneven. Only the *lettre* itself — the phenomenon of Scripture's text — and the referent of this text — Jesus Christ — can establish the unity and the logical linkage of individual passages and discourses within the Bible. And these are gleaned, less by an ordering of their parts than by the constant and shifting discernment of their figural applications in time. Referring to Scripture as a whole, and borrowing on a simile of Augustine wherein the parts of Scripture resemble the parts of a harp, Duguet writes:

> The whole body resounds with the name and the mysteries of Jesus Christ. But each part [of the body] is not resounding. History, though full of His figures, requires natural connections to sustain what promises and figures Him. Chronology, the succession of princes, battles, victories, purely temporal events — these are all necessary in order to unite into a single whole and to bring into evidence the different elements that announce and predict Jesus Christ. But what is mute by nature becomes filled with sound through its union with what resounds. We should never expect a sound from every part; but there is no part that does not contribute to the sound itself.[44]

It is hardly the case that the "chronologies" and "battles" and so on are irrelevant, let alone is their "necessity" that of a literary trope.[45] Rather, they are integral parts of a figural display whose exact sense may or may not be found to lie in immediate reference, but whose purpose derives always and in the first instance, whatever their proper sense, from their role in sustaining the unveiling of the primary form of God's Son. And this role, wherein immediate reference is assumed to "serve" a figure, calls out for holy scrutiny and the careful deployment of prophetic significations in all contexts of the Scripture. To revert to the musical metaphor, such immediate referents, without "natural" sound in themselves, are made to "ring in union" with the larger figure that encloses them.

---

44. Ibid., 23.
45. On Duguet's disdain for reading "incongruous" passages or images in Scripture as literary "metaphors" whose referents thereby remain centered in the immediate sense of the text, rather than as figures for the historical Christ, see his discussion under Rule III, in ibid., 30ff.

This dynamic accounts for the way Duguet articulates his final rule and embraces its significance: certain prophecies figure multiple historical events, often widely separated by time and space. As each event, as it were, "fulfils" the original prophecy, it becomes a figure in its own right, referring backward and forward in time, and among the various scriptural texts related to it. Such scriptural figures, therefore, are revealed as having "new" meanings by the succession of history, and their immediate and prophetic senses are often multiplied in retrospect by the conforming shape of events, each of which acts as "the image and guarantee of the others."[46] But even while historical experience in the present, then, must continue to stand as figurated signs of Scripture, it does so always controlled by and in reference to those original signs themselves.

In particular, the book of the Apocalypse stands, in Duguet's mind, as both the normative example of as well as the inclusive fund for such multiple figurating significations within history. Drawing together a range of figures from earlier texts of the Bible, applying both to the past and the present, St. John also discloses their figurating power on the future as well. The possibility of this variegated meaning is given and focused in the reality that lies behind all prophecy, that is, that the words of Scripture refer primarily to Jesus Christ in His mystery. The fullness of this mystery, obviously, includes the shape of the world's history. In a basic way, therefore, any given prophecy, while signifying immediately a given set of events in time, must also be significant of *any* time, insofar as such moments follow the lines of the single figure of Christ. The Apocalypse is the book of the Bible that most openly demonstrates and glories in this figurally inter-significating character of history as it receives its phenomenal form from Scripture. Duguet quotes pointedly from Bossuet's commentary on this final member of the canon:

> We can find the spirit of all the prophets and of all the men whom God has sent in the great apostle St. John. He received the spirit of Moses in order to sing the canticle of the holy people's new deliverance (*Apoc.*, XV, 3; *ib.* XI, 19; *ib.* VIII, 3), and to build up a new ark, and new tabernacle, a new temple and a new perfumed altar for God's honor. He received the spirit of Isaiah and of Jeremiah in order to describe the wounds of the new Babylon, and to astonish the whole universe with word of her fall (*ibid.*, XVI, 17 *et* 18). By Daniel's spirit he reveals to us the new beast, that is, the new empire that is the enemy and persecutor of the saints; and with this, he reveals her defeat and ruin. With the spirit of Ezekiel he shows us all the riches of the new temple wherein God wishes to be served, that is, [the temple] of heaven and of the Church (*ibid.*, XXI *et* XXII). . . . Every inspired man of God seems to have given to him [i.e., St. John] all that was rich and great, so that he might compose the most beautiful picture [*tableau*] imaginable of Jesus Christ's glory; and more than anywhere else, we can see clearly here how

---

46. Ibid., 69.

He is truly the end of the law; we can see here the truth of His figures, the body behind His shadows, the soul of His prophecies.[47]

Bossuet's description, using St. John as the object of an authorial "esprit" common to all the prophets, captures the adorative turning to Christ's image in the Scripture that compels the uncovering and exposition of its variegated figural ligatures, binding and loosening the events of time. And although such a vision need not engender a passion for contemporizing prophecy — as Bossuet's own case clearly shows — it unleashes its potential, even while erecting barriers (in theory) to any chronological tyranny in its reach. It is, after all, the determining figure of Christ that presses for contemporaneity in prophetic fulfillment, and not the prophecies themselves, or some engulfing character given in the act of prophecy. The second part of the *Règles*, then, which has been the source of so much subsequent and current discomfort is probably misunderstood if, as I have tried to warn against, it is read in parallel to typical millennial versions of prophecy, and not as an articulation of the peculiar *figuriste* subjection in conformity of historical experience to the single figure of Christ. While Savon may well be correct, on stylistic as well as strictly topical grounds, that the abbé d'Asfeld and not Duguet is responsible for the "Application des règles précédentes au Retour des Juifs (Application of the foregoing rules to the Return of the Jews)," Duguet's initial biographer, Claude-Pierre Goujet, seems also to be right in asserting that the "Application" "is also by M. du Guet, at least as far as its core goes."[48] And the "core," in this case, is the "mystery" of Christ, figurated in and through history, as given in the totality of Scripture. Here, then, follows a list of the fourteen "Truths" of the "Application":

FIRST TRUTH. God has promised to preserve the people of Israel until the end of the ages, through a miraculous protection.

II. TRUTH. This absolute and immutable promise is always tied to the promise of [Israel's] return.

---

47. Ibid., 72. The original text of Bossuet from which the quotation is taken can be found in the preface to his *L'Apocalypse Avec Une Explication* (1689), in his *Oeuvres Complètes de Bossuet*, ed. F. Lachat (Paris: Louis Vives, 1867), vol. 2, 302. On Bossuet's interpretation of Revelation, see Catrice, "Bossuet et le 'Retour' des Juifs," esp. "Suite," 98ff. Bossuet himself preferred to see most of the prophecies of St. John as pointing historically to events that were to take place in the life of the Church of the first few centuries, although he did not exclude — for the obvious principle cited by Duguet — interpretations that pointed to figurations extending far into the future. His main argument was against Protestant millenarians like Jurieu, whom he accused of a "judaizing" carnality less because of their contemporizing of prophetic fulfillment, than because of their association of that fulfillment with particular material blessings, e.g., the temporal reign of Christ on earth. He also wrote against their interpretation of the figure Babylon as referring to the Roman Catholic Church, using his own more temporally limited approach as a basis for his argument that the image more properly signified the pagan Roman Empire. See his *Avertissement aux Protestants sur leur prétendu Accomplissement des prophéties* (1689), and his *De Excidio Babylonis apud S. Joannen*, not published until 1772, both of which are found in his *Oeuvres complètes*, t. 3.

48. *Vie de M. Du Guet*, 26.

III. TRUTH. This return is a return to faith and true piety.

IV. TRUTH. This promise has not been fulfilled in the least by the return of the Jews from Babylon or by the conversion of those who came out of Babylon.

V. TRUTH. The promise, furthermore, has not been fulfilled at the time of Jesus Christ.

VI. TRUTH. The promises made to Israel after her abandonment [by God] have to do with her return.

VII. TRUTH. Those promises that predict an end to the blindness of the people of Israel can only be applied to her return.

VIII. TRUTH. Those promises made to the Jews after the calling of the Gentiles and the conversion of the whole earth have to do with their second vocation.

IX. TRUTH. The prophecies that predict all Israel's — and not only a small number's — conversion deal with the last times.

X. TRUTH. The promises of a constant conversion and of a faith that will last to the end of the ages are not consistent with the times of Jesus Christ.

XI. TRUTH. We must not defer the return of the Jews to the end of the ages, nor limit it to a few years before the last judgment.

XII. TRUTH. The prophecies which speak of the special holiness of those Jews brought back after the time of wrath, or of all the Jews, refer to the last days.

XIII. TRUTH. Only through the zeal and courage of the last Jews will all the nations receive the light of faith.

XIV. TRUTH. Once the Jews are converted, they will establish a unified form of worship throughout the earth; and they will wipe away, at least for a while, all vestiges of idolatry.

That the application chosen is constituted by the figures referring to the Return of the Jews, i.e., their conversion to Christ at the end of time, may seem at first perplexing and perhaps indicative of an alien millennial spirit thrust into the discussion. Missing is the grand elevation before the reader's heart of Christ's image through the various figures, a venerative offering strikingly evident in the "Rules" proper. In its place, in the "Application," we find an almost exclusive fixation on the Jewish nation as such, its origins, its history, and its fate, as gleaned from Old Testament prophecy. The *rappel des Juifs,* so prominent in *figuriste* writing, asserts itself here with its initial strangeness, arising seemingly from some subterranean store. It is, perhaps, all the more puzzling, from a historian's viewpoint, in that there is very little interest in Israel's destiny shown among the classical Jansenists before this point; must there not, therefore, be at work an influence from some other and extraneous current of millennial thinking that accounts for its appearance?[49]

But we have already seen that Duguet in his *Jésus crucifié* considered this theme at length, and in a way that flowed naturally from his Christologically oriented figuralism. Taken on its own, his discussion there mirrors someone like Pascal's earlier meditations on the figure of Justice and Mercy embodied historically in the Cross of Jesus as it is historically related to the experience of the Jewish nation. While Pascal himself was suspicious of millennialism,[50] the eschatological pressures of his own fig-

---

49. One frequently finds, e.g., in Kreiser, Neveu, Popkin et al., brief references to the occult "Joachimite" currents of millennialist tradition, stretching from the abbot of Fiora in the twelfth and into the eighteenth century, and into which Jansenist eschatology might presumably have plugged itself. Popkin, *Isaac La Peyrère,* provides the fullest overview of millennial thinking in France during the seventeenth and eighteenth centuries, as it interested itself in *le rappel des Juifs,* and he can find precious little that would lead us to suppose that Jansenists were drawing on any tradition other than their own application of scriptural figure to the life of their Church. Popkin uses as his point of reference to his survey Isaac La Peyrère's messianism. In 1643 La Peyrère published his *Du Rappel des Juifs,* part of an envisioned larger system that included his more notorious theories concerning the world's human population before Adam (the so-called "Pre-Adamites"). La Peyrère offered a prognostication of the world's future and end that included the conversion of the Jews to a kind of "Jewish Christianity," through the advent of a second Messiah, as well as the rebuilding of Jerusalem and the establishment of a universal rule from this center, with the French king playing a leading role. It also included elements of a specific civil and religious program for implementation within France and elsewhere aimed at facilitating this set of events. In the face of various competing hypotheses about La Peyrère's origins and purposes in the life-long elaboration of this set of theories, Popkin makes a good case for his being a Marrano at work on a "Marrano theology" that would somehow bridge the gap between Jewish and Christian particularisms, while creating a special providential role for Jewish converts alone. Whatever the case, Popkin demonstrates the influence that La Peyrère's ideas on these matters exerted on both English and Dutch Christian millennialists (e.g., Jurieu), on certain Iberian Catholics like the Jesuit missionary Vieira, as well as on Jewish messianists like Rabbi Menasseh ben Israel. But Popkin also finds *no* evidence of Peyrère's ideas regarding the future conversion of the Jews as having found any interested minds among French Catholics, even those who appear to have read the book at the time of its appearance. (La Peyrère was himself, until late in life, a supposed Calvinist.) And although Richard Simon, for instance, could see the connection between La Peyrère's ideas and the messianism of, e.g., Rabbi Mannasseh, La Peyrère showed little concern in disseminating his specifically prophetic scheme. *Du Rappel des Juifs* was not republished and proved extraordinarily rare in French libraries until the late eighteenth century, when it was rediscovered, among others, by the unusual revolutionary, the quasi-Jansenist Abbé Henri Grégoire. To the degree that French Catholics in the seventeenth and eighteenth centuries engaged in polemics over millennial themes with Protestants like Jurieu, they were dealing, it seems, indirectly with ideas influenced themselves, often only indirectly, by philosemitic chiliasm. While this may have included La Peyrère, it was more probably derived from the English millennialists who flourished around the era of the Commonwealth, but whom Jansenists do not seem to have read nor cared much about. And unless and until new evidence is found pointing otherwise, we must see Jansenist and Appellant interest in the Return of the Jews as *sui generis,* and derivative of their own figuralist theology. See Popkin, *Isaac La Peyrère,* esp. chapters 2 and 8, including their bibliographically laden notes.

50. See his pensée 575 (Lafuma): "Extravagances of the Apocalypticists and pre-Adamites and millenarians, etc. Whoever wishes to base their extravagant opinions on Scripture will do so on the basis of this example. It is said that this generation will not pass away until all this takes place. As for this, I would say that after this generation there will come another, and so on successively forever." Pascal was a member of the Prince of Condé's circle, along with *savants* like Marin Mersenne, Daniel Huet, and Grotius, at the time that La Peyrère was the

uralism along with that of other Port-Royalists, e.g., Arnauld, de Sacy, and Hamon, proved a coherent element in the explication of such larger and orchestrating figures as the Cross. And the preface to the *Règles,* it seems to me, hints at the logic of such coherence. For, after emphasizing, in a manner wholly consistent with the "rules" proper, the primary reference to Christ of all the Hebrew prophets and their writings, a final summary of the book's contents is offered: first, a statement on the purpose of the "rules," that is, that they help readers already presupposing the Christo-centric character of Scripture "find Jesus Christ in the ancient Scriptures, where they [i.e., the readers] were already quite convinced He was en-closed"; and next, the "application" is given on a theme and in a way that will demonstrate for the reader the historical continuity of this figure's formatively revealing presence among His people:

> To these rules — which form, as it were, a separate treatise and act as a kind of first section to the book — we have added some reflections taken from the explication of Psalm 101 on the conversion of the Jews to Jesus Christ. We thought it very appropriate to use them as a way of engaging the application of the foregoing rules, and as a way of helping one understand the Scriptures, which everywhere present the general return of the Jews as a great subject and marvelous event. For the Jews, according to St. Paul (*Rom.,* XI, v. 12 et 15), will one day act as the consolation of the Church and will make her rich. And we are therefore not permitted to be indifferent to this event. Especially since the righteous of the Old Testament took such a lively and tender interest in the conversion of the Gentiles, even though they knew that it [i.e., the Gentiles' conversion] would cost their nation very dearly.[51]

If, that is, Christ is the sole object of the Hebrew Scriptures, and His image is revealed in all of its parts for the sake of the future salvation of the Nations; and if, in addition, this revelation of the Messiah and all He was to suffer, just as Jesus explained on the road to Emmaus, was given in figure, so that the Jewish nation to whom it was spoken could only grasp it indirectly, through the figure of its own "blinding," then the fullness of this figural revelation will receive its historical stamp only as the Christic referent comprehensively grasps all of its historical figures, encompassing Israel as a whole in His salvation. Just as the Old Testament "righteous" figured the future redemption of the Gentiles in their words and lives — this is the historical basis for the prophetic announcement of the Messiah Jesus — so too must the Gentiles "interest" themselves in the future redemption of the Jews, in figural parallel with them, for the "consolation" of the Church and her consummation. The Return of the Jews, then, stands as the temporally religious guarantee of the figural

---

prince's secretary. While *Du Rappel des Juifs* was read or perused by many of them, what called for their comment appears to have been, not its millennialism, but the pre-Adamite theory first articulated in this work, and later presented by La Peyrère in published form shorn of the earlier prophetic framework.

51. *Règles,* 14.

reality of history as a whole, the singular trait by which the visage of Christ is unmistakably recognized, if only in hope.

The "Application," therefore, with its fourteen "Vérités," seeks more than anything else to bring into relief the figural unity of Scripture's historical referents, a unity that is "presupposed" by Christians, in the words of the preface, but whose articulation in devotional terms — the terms of prayer, of yearning, and of historical discernment — helps to undergird the Church's own central figural existence as it is wrapped around the person of Christ. And, in fact, the "Vérités" do little more than offer their own extended scriptural meditations from the perspective of the Jewish nation, using Old Testament texts quoted and referred to in Romans 9–11 and in the book of Revelation, on the themes of the figural relationship between Israel and the Gentiles, as already outlined by Duguet in *Jésus crucifié*. Among the exact topics taken over from Duguet's earlier work and amplified from the perspective of the Old Testament prophets exclusively, are: the clear need to look forward to a "second" fulfillment for the prophesied vocation of the Jews, since their return from the Babylonian exile does not account for a completion to even the "immediate" sense of relevant texts (see Vérité IV); the Christian Church's need of the Jews — both in the past and in the future, and thus the providential character of their preservation (Vérité V); the future joining of the Jews to the Gentiles in the future Church, according to Romans 11, but not the complete substitution of the former for the latter (Vérité VI); the danger of Gentile "pride," in presuming their "right" to salvation versus that of the Jews, when in fact even they risk exclusion from God's redemptive action (Vérité VIII); the prophetic distinction between the *petit reste* (small remnant) of the Jewish nation (i.e., the Apostles) who were converted by Grace for the sake of the Gentiles, and the whole of the Jewish nation whose conversion still awaits the Endtimes, see the story of Joseph bringing his brothers from Canaan into Egypt/Church (Vérité IX and XII); finally, the long temporal period that must be granted the Jews' conversion is not the prophesied "millennium," but corresponds to an extended notion of the "Endtimes" as being the "times of the Church," her own "last days" as she experiences persecution, demonic attack, and the need for divine aid (Vérité 11). This last topic, in particular, contains phraseology that is almost identical to passages in *Jésus crucifié*[52] and points to the way that the "Application" as a whole derives directly, in compositional terms, from Duguet's writing.

Assessing the peculiar character of the *Règles'* eschatological spirit, particularly in light of the perspective of the "Vérités," leads therefore to a conclusion at one with our general argument throughout this chapter: while the eschatological focus of *figurisme* is prominent, and while it is a focus bound by temporal terms, these terms themselves are significant only according to their figural shapes; eschatology thus becomes the theological expression of the figural nature of temporality itself. The treatment

---

52. See *Jésus crucifié*, 430ff.

of the Return of the Jews in the "Vérités," I claimed, is *sui generis* in comparison with other, more extensively propagated versions of the theme, and its peculiarity lies precisely in this fundamentally figural construal of the historical shape of the prophesied events involved. Unlike English Puritan and other Christian philosemitic concerns with the future conversion of the Jews, both in the seventeenth and eighteenth centuries, Jansenist Appellant exposition of related prophecies was never accompanied by practical programs aimed at either furthering such conversion or at preparing the ground for its possibility by easing Jewish-Christian relations.[53] Both Puritans and other Non-Conformists in the seventeenth century had placed great store in the millennial implications of the Jewish acceptance of Christ, and many enthusiastic millennialists from their midst organized themselves through mutual contacts and also pressed for various social reforms on behalf of Jews.[54] Jansenist Appellancy, however, never moved in this direction and, excepting certain extremist groups that grew up in the wake of the Saint-Médard convulsions, on the whole never attempted to identify individuals of the time with prophesied augurers of, or indeed fulfilled embodiments of, millennial figures.[55]

This conclusion is supported through several major and explicit affirmations provided by Fourquevaux in the first defenses given the *Règles* after Léonard's attacks.[56] The *Introduction abrégée*, in particular, sets out to explicate the *Règles'* vision of figural history by examining Romans 9–11 in the acknowledged light of Duguet's *Jésus crucifié*. The same parallels and dependencies between the two works that we have noted above

53. See Popkin, *Isaac La Peyrère*, esp. chapter 8. Pp. 107–14 give an account of the only practical use of the "Return" idea by a French Catholic, the abbé Grégoire, a remarkable exception that proves the rule here: Grégoire's "secular" application of many of La Peyrère's rediscovered ideas during the time of the French Revolution, ideas he had earlier explicated in more religious terms, ultimately gave rise to the reconvocation in 1806 of the Jewish "Sanhedrin" under Napoleon (who was now seen by some to be the "Jewish Messiah" of the Endtimes).

54. See Peter Toon,"The Question of Jewish Immigration," chapter 7 in *Puritans, the Millennium, and the Future of Israel*, ed. Peter Toon, 115–25.

55. There developed in the 1730s, as we shall see, highly historicized messianic views among a few (vocal) convulsionaries — e.g., the Vaillantistes and the Augustinistes, as well as others who began circulating specific predictions linked to secular events in France. These groups did indeed endow their leaders with just these roles or offer prophetic correlations of contemporary events with specific and limited messianic figures. See Kreiser, *Miracles, Convulsions, and Ecclesiastical Politics in Early Eighteenth-Century Paris*, 301–19. We will be examining the dispute among Appellants over these groups in the next chapter. At this point, however, it is important to see how the theological structure of *figurisme* was in fact distinguishable from such later phenomena.

56. Jean-Baptiste de Beccarie de Pavie de Fourquevaux, as noted earlier, replied to Léonard's *Réfutation* . . . with his *Lettre d'un prieur à un de ses amis au sujet de la nouvelle réfutation du livre des Règles pour l'intelligence des saintes Ecritures* (Paris: Gabriel Valleyre, 1727), and later responded to Léonard's *Traité* . . . with his *Nouvelles lettres d'un Prieur a un de ses amis, Pour la défense du Livre des Règles, pour l'intelligence des Saintes Ecritures* (Paris: Jacques Estienne, 1729). Finally, Fourquevaux offered a kind of organized theological rationale for the *Règles'* more diffuse presentation particularly in the "Application," in keeping with the intensifying eschatological interests of the Appellants, in his *Introduction abrégée a l'intelligence des propheties de l'Ecriture, Par l'usage qu'en fait S. Paul dans l'Epitre aux Romains* (n.p., 1731).

are underlined, and Fourquevaux adds nothing new to the discussion. On one issue, however, he brings to the fore what had until then been only a reticent attitude toward millennialism, and it is an attitude that is intimately tied to the whole prophecy of the Jews' Return. Following Duguet's lead, Fourquevaux emphasizes the long temporal duration that must be attached to the future conversion of the Jews.[57] But why the importance of this extended period? Duguet had generally insisted that it was linked to the needs, that is to say, to the decadence, of the Church, which the return of the Jews would largely alleviate, fulfilling Paul's words in Romans 11:15: "for if their rejection means the reconciliation of the world, what will their acceptance mean but life from the dead?" with the "resurrection" mentioned here seen as referring to the Church in the midst of her afflictions and disease. The *Règles,* as we saw, added the explicit distinction between the actual End with its Final Judgment, and the Endtimes, the latter of which includes the entire history of the Church, from its foundation, falling away, and restoration through the Return of the Jews, only after which can arrive the true End. The extended time accorded prophetically to the Return of Jews, therefore, is tied by Duguet directly to the condition of the Christian Church as it requires renewal, and to this degree is dependent on the reality, even present, of the Church's suffering.

This is the point Fourquevaux expands upon, by clearly differentiating the final "apostasy" predicted by, e.g., Paul in 2 Thessalonians 2 or 2 Timothy 3 that is linked immediately to the Last Day of Christ's Coming and Judgment, and the travails of the Church which are to be part of its eschatological figuration of its Lord, travails which are marked, figuratively, like the End, by apostasies as well. The Return of the Jews is prophetically related to this larger more general period of travail, within which the Church is restored through the final joining of the New Man of Jew and Gentile, in preparation for its ultimate testing. Were the Conversion of the Jews of short duration, to precede immediately the End of time, then the travails of the Church would offer no figurative value in giving rise to the joining of suffering or faithlessness to redemption in a single form, i.e., the history of the Church as it is presently experienced would offer no sign of hope on her own behalf for Christians in her embrace apart from any longing they might hold for the end of all things altogether. To hope for the Church, then, is to hope for the Return of the Jews and their mission on the Church's behalf; to hope for the *present* Church, in all of her present trials, is to recognize the extended temporal duration of both suffering and restoration. In writing of the specific "consolation" the doctrine of the extended conversion of the Jews offers Appellant Christians, Fourquevaux says:

> In the midst of such a trial [i.e., the present repudiation of the Truth of God's grace within the Church], we can feel illumined and strengthened as

---

57. *Introduction abregée,* 15, 40ff., 51ff., 58ff., 63ff. See Duguet, *Jésus crucifié,* 422 and 431ff.; and "Vérité XI" in the *Règles.*

we reflect on the fact that the Gentiles who have become Christian will fall into the same unbelief that led to the cutting off of the Jews. This infidelity consisted in misunderstanding the origin, and by consequence, the nature of righteousness.

Now the attack launched by so many Church people against these truths might seem an objection to them. But the objection itself turns into their proof, as one realizes that these truths must one day be combated and dishonored by the majority of the Gentiles; and that, far from casting doubt upon their importance, the sorry fate predicted for those thus ill-treating these truths clearly shows us how precious the truths are in the eyes of God and how important it is to remain inviolably attached to them.

We are no longer so distressed in seeing the truth and its defenders anathematized by the majority of the living God's ministers, if we have learned that Jesus Christ in His truth, and His defenders, must be treated by the Gentiles in the same way that He was by the Jews. We can follow our Savior outside the Camp carrying the insults of the Cross in His wake. Finally, by holding on to that vision of the great aid [i.e., the Return of the Jews] that God has in reserve for healing the ills caused by the faithlessness of the Gentiles, we can understand that the wounds of the Church are not incurable, that there is a balm that will be applied to them when they have become the most toxic, and that God will comfort the Church to a degree proportionate to the greatness of the sorrows that have tested her.[58]

From Fourquevaux's standpoint, only by untangling the various strands of prophetic reference — strands which, through the same figure, signify various events within history — can one properly perceive how figures of the End of time must also refer to the course of the Church's history as a whole. And only within such an extended course can the great figure of the Cross, which stands as God's grace in justice and mercy, take its historical form in the lives of people. The prophesied Return of the Jews, as itself a figure, therefore turns to the extended present for its referent, and not only to a punctuated future.[59] Phenomenal history is an embodiment of Grace itself, understood as the temporal effusions of its form. Taken as a whole, it manifests "the constant order and perpetual plan of God's designs, which is to blaze forth within His works His mercy and justice, by making them servants, at once, of the ruin of some and the resurrection of others, *in ruinam et resurrectionem.*"[60]

Even eschatological predictions, then, serve as figures of "the whole Christ" (*le Christ entier*), including not only His own flesh, but that of His Body, the Church, within time.[61] The Return of the Jews, by being a

---

58. Fourquevaux, *Introduction abregée,* 59f.

59. See ibid., 65.

60. Ibid., 3 and 43.

61. Ibid., 78. This is drawn from the *Règles,* 25. On 68–81 Fourquevaux attempts to delineate six "senses" to Scripture on this basis: the literal (immediate), Jesus Christ (the primary), and Jesus Christ as figurated in His Church (its formation, its renewal — including its decadence — and its consummation) and in the individual Christian soul. In fact, all this points, as with Duguet, to only a single sense, the figure of Christ, which is played out in a historically intermingling fashion through the Church's experience and temporal context.

part of this Whole Christ, is also figurally linked to the entire history of the Church, through a series of "proportional" relations, that must experientially verify, not contradict, the prolonged vicissitudes of the Church's life of faith and turmoil. What can be argued, in the face of this kind of account, is that the Return of the Jews, in Appellant hands, stands not so much as a "millennialist" vision at all, with a stress on the prospective experience of a unique temporal terminus, but as that vision's opposite, an insistent call to see the divine "ending" to history as being really a *set* of temporal arrangements in figural form that are both consistent with and experientially related to the whole history of the Church.

And such an alternative vision is attested to even by later Jansenist reflections on the millennium in particular, which, although they focus on this specific concept in a more exact fashion than the authors we have been examining, do so in a way that, because remaining tied to the latter's more general figural eschatology, acts to subvert their more patently chronological and predictive interests. In the 1770s, for instance, a typically learned and prolix exchange occurred between two Jansenists, the abbé Malot and the biblical scholar Laurent-Étienne Rondet (himself miraculously cured by the relics of the Appellant bishop of Senez). Rondet, in responding to an earlier work of Malot that predicted the Return of the Jews to begin in 1849, had advanced a relatively conservative Augustinian version of the millennium, which he identified as that period from the reign of Constantine through Luther, whose schism marked the unleashing of Satan. The present, therefore in Rondet's view, constituted the period of "final" persecution to precede immediately the Return of Christ.[62]

From Malot's side, Rondet seemed improperly and wholly opposed to the very notion of the millennium. For if the millennium itself composes the history of the Church, at least through the Reformation, there is nothing "special" about it: it is as full of schism, unfaithfullness, suffering, etc., as "normal" history. By contrast, Malot insisted that the millennium be understood as a "blessed" period for the Church, one in which her life reverted to the primitive purity of the Apostles.[63] The Return of the Jews with all of its missionary benefit for the Church, according to Malot, precedes this millennium, and in no wise can the latter be seen as anything but a "spiritual rule," indicated by the strengthening and renewal in the Church carried on by her repentant elder brethren into her midst. But, as only a time of "spiritual" rule, as figurally representative of the time of the Apostles, and, finally, as preceding the time of final persecution by Satan unbound wherein "only a few" are prophesied as remaining faithful, this millennium is, for Malot, something very different from a period of perfected faith for the Church: she is still filled with a "mixed" body of

---

62. See his *Dissertation sur le rappel des Juifs et sur le chapitre XI de l'Apocalypse*, 2 vols. (Paris, 1778).

63. Malot, *Dissertation sur l'époque du Rappel des Juifs, et sur l'heureuse révolution qu'il doit opérer dans l'Eglise, où l'on défend le sentiment des plus savans Théologiens et Interprètes de notre siecle sur ce point*, 2d ed. (Paris: Mequignon et Fils, 1779). See 239ff.

elect and non-elect, subject to suffering and injury, and in need of contin-ual penitence, prayer, and patience. Thus, while Malot claims, as against Rondet, that the millennium is a "special" time, his view of its relation to the Apostolic Church in its own un-millennially figured experience, means that, in most experiential respects, this final period of the Church's life is figurally identical to its history as a whole. And both Rondet and Malot, while they seek different temporal referents for the millennium, end by describing its historical character similarly, because each proceeds from the same figurist presuppositions: history, wherever located before Beatitude, figures and is figured by the form of Christ Jesus.[64]

## *Figurisme* as a Hermeneutic System

From the discussion we have just pursued, I hope that something of the consistent "grammar" of figurist thinking has become apparent, and in a way that lays out more fully the historical cloth on which the realities of miracle and sanctity were seen as designed, in the eyes of Jansenist Ap-pellants looking toward Saint-Médard. Taking LeGros's characterization of *figurisme* as that exegesis practiced according to the example of Duguet, we have observed the following at least. First, Duguet himself understood the referents of Scripture to be eschatologically oriented in a fundamental way that places prophecy, inclusive of predictive figuration, at the center of the Bible's general signifying discourse. The shape of temporal his-tory, past, present, and future is, according to Duguet, explicitly given in Scripture, and on this matter his exegetical practice gave a lead to all sub-sequent figurist writers, even at their most messianic and apocalyptically detailed. But second, the eschatological orientation of Duguet's figurism, precisely because of its figural foundation and limits, could never allow for a purely sequentialist and chronological explication of Scripture's histori-cal referents; the multiple strands of reference given by a single figure and

---

64. See Maire, *Les convulsionnaires de Saint-Médard*, 57: "The goal of the figurists is less to announce the millenarian reign of Jesus Christ on earth or the destruction of the Anti-Christ, than it is to do away, as far as possible, with epochal distinctions altogether, so as to bring into view and render triumphant the eternal truth of the primitive Church. The *figure* is the means of establishing a relationship of stated identity between the past and the present; it is a proof of history's repetition; it is evidence of the falsity of the bull *Unigenitus*."

Maire's rejection of crude millenarianism as the framework within which to understand *figurisme*'s interpretive goals is correct. But her alternative reading of its hermeneutic prac-tice as a "nostalgic" effort (see 189ff.) to recapture the purity of the Primitive Church within a "repetitive history" seems to miss two central figurist assertions: the central relationship between the figurating character of Jesus' life (not the early Church's) and historical phe-nomena in general, and the temporal integrity of these phenomena themselves, which are properly referred to in specific scriptural texts. Both of these assertions resist any notion of a "return to origins" or of a "repetition" in history. Rather, it is important to note how fig-urist understandings of history avoid both these extremes of diachronic sequencing as well as temporal cyclings. The point in between the two is staked out in a simple affirmation of divine authorial sovereignty over temporal orderings according to the shape of God's own historical form as embedded in Scripture.

intertwining with other figures sometimes with different, sometimes with identical referents, demanded an articulated eschatology that was temporally malleable and an eschaton that was extended retrospectively as well as prospectively. Third, Duguet's practice was clearly in continuity with the tradition of, in particular, Quesnellian Jansenism, itself deeply formed within the devotional theology of the "French School" of the Oratory. To this degree, it grew out of a set of attitudes common to many French theological writers of the period, Jansenist and otherwise, and formed a well-supported bridge between seventeenth- and eighteenth-century devotion. Finally, the figurist conceptions of the relation of Scripture and history with which Duguet operated stand as the same ground out of which grew the hagiographic representations of de Pâris's existence, and the figural interpretations of the miracles associated with his penitential witness.

If there are any "principles" associated with *figurisme,* they are two: the exclusively figurating character of Christ's scriptural life in history, and the consequent proliferation of figurated referents as they are phenomenally experienced according to Scripture's multiple articulations. These principles, however, are as much positive because of their tremendously restrictive role in theological systematics, as because of the actual theological affirmations they enable. Their functioning, whether formulated or not, works broadly to subordinate virtually all categories of phenomenal explication — historical, scientific, sociological, even metaphysical — to the given shapes of Scripture's words as they are discerned to figure Christ. Pascal, as we have seen, saw the issue most clearly in these terms. The experience of working rationally within the shadow of such subordination constitutes in itself the object of theological reflection and explication, the results of which, however, must also remain within the figural bounds given in the Scripture's depiction of Christ's life. Those strictly theological elements as outlined in the *Règles,* for instance, with which Léonard took early exception — e.g., the Holy Spirit's authorial control of Scripture's figuralist composition in its formative relation to history — are derived from such reflection, and only buttress it to the degree that they disclose themselves as internal to the character of the figure(s) scrutinized.

This theologically *un*systematic nature of *figurisme* — which is not to say untheological — is an important one to note. At root, it signals the submissive character attached to any and all figural reading of Scripture that is bound by the single Figure making possible the apprehension of relationship existing between historical experience and God, even the defiance of which proves an inescapable element of its expression. But far from indicating an obstinate retreat on the part of Appellant figurists into an eighteenth-century brand of fundamentalism, this submission of reason to scriptural figure instead seems more to be a hermeneutic expression of the religious conviction, uttered by Hamon for instance, that the "self-humiliation" of God in Christ's Incarnation is taken to its furthest extreme in the Word(s) of Scripture.[65] The relationship established between the reasoning mind and the Bible, then, both in its faithful and unfaithful forms, itself figures the reality of God's self-giving love into a world of sin. Port-Royal's use of figural readings of Scripture as themselves acts of figural conformity witnesses, ultimately, to the impossibility,

---

65. See Jean Hamon, "De Trois Communions Spirituelles. Outre Celle Qui A pour objet JESUS-CHRIST dans le Saint Sacrement," in *Receuil de Divers Traitez de Pieté*, 217. On Hamon's emphasis that "understanding" (*entendre*) Scripture is only secondary to submitting to its literal meaning in an act of adorative veneration of the Word incarnate within its vocables, see ibid., 222–26. Among Appellants, perhaps the most notorious practitioner of *figurisme* was the abbé d'Étemare, a writer whose breadth of intellectual interest, displayed in his vast output, belies any notion of figurism as a constraining rationalist system. Neveu's article "Port-Royal à l'âge des Lumières," goes far in demonstrating the inquisitive mix of philosophical, devotional, and dogmatic concerns and knowledge informing d'Étemare's production, the enormous exegetical portion of which remains almost deliberately diffuse in its meditative sweep. A comparison with another sophisticated typologist of the era, Jonathan Edwards, reveals in fact the Appellant's far less "naturalistic" metaphysical presuppositions underlying his scriptural interpretations.

At the same time, d'Étemare's overriding figuralist hermeneutic is wholly faithful to the example of his early mentor Duguet and ought to be seen as within the mainstream of Jansenist exegetical orientations. Savon has seen d'Étemare as the individual whose extreme prophetic views on the Return of the Jews was singled out for moderation by d'Asfeld, with Duguet's approval, in the "Vérités" section of the *Règles*. In particular, he cites d'Étemare's 1714 *Quatrième Gémissement d'une âme vivement touché de la Constitution de N.S.P. le Pape Clément XI du 8 septembre 1713* as a work whose passionate figural correlations of the immediate past and present—in the form of Port-Royal, its members, and the convent's destruction in 1711—with biblical events and individuals, including Christ Himself, were offensive to Duguet and required public correction. I am not in a position to judge Duguet's actual views on the book, and Savon relies on contemporary second-hand accounts concerning Duguet's comments, written by not disinterested parties, including, later, Duguet's niece Mme. Mol, who expended considerable (and seemingly deceitful) effort to rescue her uncle's reputation from the official opprobrium attached to Appellancy. (See Savon, "Le figurisme et la 'Tradition des Pères,'" 779ff., and 782 esp. On Mme. Mol's role in turning the elderly Duguet against his former friends and her role as an active spy for the police against Appellant convulsionaries in particular, see Kreiser, *Miracles, Convulsions, and Ecclesiastical Politics in Early Eighteenth-Century Paris*, 289f.) An examination of the *4e Gémissement* (or of the three *Gémissements* that precede it, also attributed by some to d'Étemare), however, reveals little that strays from Duguet's own discussions. The theme of the future "substitution" of the converted Jews for the now apostate Gentiles, for instance, which, drawing on Romans 9–11, is elaborated at length by d'Étemare, is seen by Savon as directly repudiated in the "Vérités." But we have already observed that Duguet himself pressed this idea to its scriptural limits in *Jésus crucifié* and affirmed himself the falling away of most of the Gentile Christians, although he explicitly stopped short of claiming that *all* the "unnatural" branches would be ripped off again. *Contra* Savon, d'Étemare goes no further (see the *4e Gémissement* . . . [2d ed., 1724], 130ff., 177ff., 197). In addition, the figures d'Étemare chooses to apply are standard with Duguet: e.g., Noah, Abraham, the Story of Joseph, Elijah, the Return of the Jews, et al. Quite explicitly, future temporal dates are not fixed for figural *accomplissements* (see 97), and the whole of the work, as it links together the past history of the Church, Port-Royal, the present persecution of Jansenists, and the future, does so according to the overriding scriptural figure of Christ, presented in the highly participatory fashion of the Oratory (e.g., xxvii ff., 177f., 221f.). In the face of scholarly caricatures of Appellant exegesis, one must conclude that abstracted logics derived from *figurisme's* practice, if sundered from the hermeneutic's profoundly devotional basis, are likely to deform its actual meaning and theological implications. See Neveu's article "Port-Royal à l'âge des Lumières" for a relatively detailed biography of d'Étemare, based on manuscript letters and reports of conversations. See esp. 132 for an account of his "vision," and what follows for his understanding of *figurisme*, as well as for some detailed references to some of his many "figurist" writings.

in Jansenist terms, of formulating an interpretive program apart from one's own immersion and participation in the Church's figural shaping as Christ's Body in time. They are identical acts, and their fate, inclusive of the suffering attendant upon sanctity and miracle, is common. To the degree, therefore, that any of these acts have a pneumatological basis, as is traditionally taught by the Church, it will be one that merges imperceptibly with the form and gives grateful way under the weight of the original figural frame borne by God. And all the wonder of this edifice, its temporal *éclats*, its kaleidoscopic opalescence, will array itself prostrate, *in ruinam et resurrectionem* at once. With this in mind, we turn to reflect upon the destiny of holy miracle at Saint-Médard, the final stage through which we can approach the episode as a form of the *ostensio Spiritus*, disclosing in its figural lines the content of our pneumatological speech and the limits of its expression.

## Chapter Ten

# MIRACLES, FIGURE,
# AND THE HOLY SPIRIT
## The Fate of Evidence

### Outline of the Chapter

Chapters 10 and 11 in this section comprise an integrated discussion of the actual conflict, in reflective terms, over the miracles (chapter 10) and Convulsions (chapter 11) of Saint-Médard. The overall purpose of this discussion is to bring into relief the pneumatological implications of the episode as it is examined within the category of its "historical fate," an essential element in determining the *ostensio Spiritus* phenomenologically, as we described it in our Introduction.

Chapter 10 begins with an attempt to outline systematically some of the pneumatological issues involved in the episode, as seen in Jansenist eyes. At particular issue is the character of Jansenist reformulations of pneumatic event as they derive from the experience of Saint-Médard. The provisional pneumatological structures described here will then be tested through their extraction from the actual discussion of events by participants and from the shape given to that discussion over time. The rest of the chapter involves an examination of the issue of miracles as "evidence," tracing the significance of this possibility both positively and negatively among defenders and opponents of the miracles. Through discussions of Gudvert and Colbert especially, on the Appellant side, and Languet and Lerouge on the other, we will see how the rejection of miracles as evidence by anti-Appellants carried with it an argument that questioned the value of deduction (or induction) from experience, apart from the infallibly guaranteed official authority of the Church, on the basis of a sceptical demonization of all historical phenomena. Appellant responses to this scepticism depended ultimately on a figuralist construal of belief and unbelief that attempted to maintain the value of experiential evidence, including miracles, even while accounting logically for their lack of persuasiveness in most cases.

This response lay directly behind the experience of the convulsions that grew out of the miracles. In demonstrating this connection in chapter 11, through a discussion of Carré de Montgeron's writing, the nature of pneumatic appearance in particular is defined in the context of the episode, a nature that is figurally characterized and apprehended within the shape of the conformance of historical experience to Christ's life. The pneumatology that derives from this notion of appearance is more concretely examined at this point, as we observe how traditional elements of its systematic exposition, like ecclesiology, are redefined in figurist terms and subsumed into a prophetic outlook and discernment on the fate of the Church's life in time, as it is shaped into the Body of Christ. We conclude the chapter by indicating how this kind of subsumption, demanded by the logic of the Saint-Médard episode in its evolution and fate, sharply reduces the proper scope of pneumatological assertion to bare scriptural affirmations, which depend on more primary Christological commitments. The systematic explication of this form of "kenotic" pneumatology is given in the dissertation's concluding chapter.

# Introduction:
## Systematic Issues in Appellant Pneumatology

At the end of our last chapter on *figurisme*, we stated that any pneumatological basis to holy miracle, in Appellant understanding, must be one that stands in broad identity with the historical experience of the Church's own shaping along the lines of Christ's scriptural form. This assertion, if true, involves a highly unusual grasp of the nature of the Holy Spirit itself, which although not unique to the tradition of the Church in its systematic basis, is uniquely developed here in its application. Our task in these last two chapters is to bring into relief more precisely the systematic character of Appellant pneumatology, in a way that was not possible in the first section of this book, precisely because here we will at last be able to moor the theological discussion in the historical experience of particular miracles, as they were seen by Appellants to be figurally constituted. We will, in effect, be confronting directly the central issue of the *ostensio Spiritus* as a phenomenon of history. Having examined, up to this point, the character of history as construed figurally by Jansenists, we can engage the miracles, their negation, and their historical fate within the bounds of their divinely constituted occurrence.

Even before we broach a description of the Appellant discussion of miracle, however, we can outline broadly in advance the systematic structure our own conclusions to this investigation will erect. It might be helpful, in the first place, to retrace some of the lines taken by our early chapter on Jansenist pneumatology in Section I in order to see the close conformance between the more general systematic tendencies evident there and the more particular ones initiated by a figural understanding of sanctity and miracle as we will explore it. We came to our study of pneumatology with a claim about Jansenist conceptions of grace in general: by and large, we said, these depended on a collapse of the traditional Thomistic distinction between uncreated grace and created "graces" as "effects in time." Drawing on the work of Gerberon, Arnauld, Quesnel, and Boursier, among others, we saw a consistent theological explication of grace, instead, as a single divine character, effective in time as "historically *subsuming*" of all divine-creaturely relational shapes. The paradigmatic manifestation of this character was, of course, the Incarnate Christ, whose own description as "love" itself, demanded the further conceptual merger, on the part of Jansenist theologians, of grace with divine charity.

The traditional link between charity and the Holy Spirit, we then saw, acted as a semantic bridge by which Jansenists, like Saint-Cyran originally, moved to attribute to the Spirit much of the theological weight borne by their formulations of *gratia figurans.* Just as the collapse of uncreated and created grace into a single divine character moved in a figuralist direction, so too did the inclusion of these elements, along with the practical focus of "charity" as the fulfillment of divine commands, into pneumatology, demand the latter's elaboration in terms of configurating narrative. The Holy Spirit, we saw, was defined (most often implicitly, but also explicitly) by writers like Fleury in his catechisms and Quesnel in his devotional work as the divine proximity within and by which were brought together a person's decisions and actions, in the context of historical experience, into the ordered shape of the forms of God's self-giving. Inasmuch as these forms are established through the historical figures of Christ's life, the Church — as His figurated mystical Body — stands as the preeminent historical focus for the ongoing reality of the Holy Spirit. Devotionally, we saw finally, this figurally bound "pneumatic ecclesiology" had as its consequence a turn toward historical discernment as the primary vehicle of adoration. But the object for this adoration, however, had as its only identifiable form of pneumatic presence the bald juxtaposition in coincidence of scriptural figure and the experiential circumstances of the Church. In short, the Holy Spirit lay secretly behind, or perhaps simply fused with, the experienced patterns of scripturally figurated history.

The Appellant experience of sanctity and miracle not only confirms the direction of these conclusions, but refines them in particular ways that both reflect the immediate context of the perceived *causa gratiae Dei* of the movement and integrate that perception into a more textured and sweeping vision of Christian existence in the Spirit. We can begin to get at the root of this experience's significance as we perceive how the figural construal of *both* holiness and miracle together aims at dissolving theologically significant distinctions between the two in much the same manner and to the same end as the Jansenist melding of uncreated and created grace.

In our exposition of the "features" belonging to Appellant miracle, we listed three in particular as being peculiar, in their common linkage, to the movement's experience. The miracles, we said, were consistently described in terms of their "circumstantial" location, their "figurative" character within and as a part of these circumstances, and the "epiphanic" quality they evinced in this positioning as a whole. Taken together, these features are simply synonymous representations from one perspective of the figural reality of the Church's life, and they stand in contrast to more traditional notions of miracle which have tended to dissect their meaning into a variety of functionalist and punctiliar moments of experience. Scholastic theology, following Thomas's treatment of the tradition, had made a sharp distinction between the various spiritual "gifts" and "virtues" of the Holy Spirit that constituted "sanctifying grace," and those gifts of the Spirit that denoted particular acts independent of the character of the performer. The former — *gratia faciens gratum* — associated the work of the Spirit with the sanctification of the Christian individual, and with venerated saints preeminently, through their growth in virtues as they are vitalized by pneumatic dispositions (e.g., Wisdom, Understanding, Fortitude, etc. as enumerated in Isaiah 11); the latter — *gratia gratis data* — stood as specific actions inspired by the Spirit in particular individuals for the furthering of special tasks in the Church's mission (e.g., prophecy, healing, etc., the "charismata" of St. Paul's discussion in 1 Corinthians 12).[1] Miracles in general were thus intrinsically disassociated from the pneumatic form of the Christian life, since they were not seen as linked essentially to holiness and could be performed by the wicked according to God's plan; and both the holy life and the performance of miracles were separately confined to individual and punctiliar movements of the Spirit. In contrast, the resolute subjection by Appellants of both holiness and miracle to broader circumstantial and figurative divine designs, the small parts of which stand individually only as adorative seams within the larger fabric, had as its systematic consequence the erasure of this traditional distinction between pneumatic life and pneumatic action. And the result of this dissolve is that the specifically *functional* pneumatological features of both disappear in favor not so much of some abstracted historical movement, as of particular figural coincidences or conformances within the Church's experience as a whole.

What we can see in the Appellant approach to sanctity and miracle is one way of overcoming what is, in fact, a rather odd tension in the Western Church's traditional understanding of the Holy Spirit. This tension is one that has pitted pneumatic experientialism with all of its palpable reorientings of personal history against the demands of an institutional order whose weight falls on relativizing the uncertainties of the miraculous beneath a nonetheless equally experientialist structure of moral concern. A glance at the typical origins of this tension discloses further the pneumatological importance of the Appellant attitude. For what is at stake in this contrast between the location of spiritual experience is ultimately the form of Trinitarian construal given to the Spirit's theological definition.

The early Messalian controversy (after A.D. 350) is one place to perceive the components that were to make up the scholastic tension between

---

1. Thomas deals with these matters, e.g., in the *Summa Theologiae* 1a2ae 62–70 (*gratia faciens gratum*) and 2a2ae 71–78 (*gratia gratis data* — the charismata).

holiness and miracle.[2] Arguably embodied at one remove in the writing of (Pseudo-)Macarius, Messalian attitudes to the Holy Spirit assumed the necessity of an individual's pneumatic possession as a condition of his or her freedom from sin. Such pneumatic possession was evident in the physical experience of sin's expulsion, in the cessation from temptation (understood as a conscious psychosomatic perturbation), and in a life of experienced *apatheia* in union with the Spirit. Messalians contrasted such pneumatic transformation, accompanied by "enthusiastic" phenomena of ecstasy — the Great Charism — with the inefficacy of water Baptism to free an individual from demonic enslavement. It was this last point of doctrine that brought them condemnation from much of the Church (e.g., at the Council of Ephesus). An orthodox opponent to the Messalians like Mark the Hermit instead countered their perfectionism with a defense of the "secretiveness" of the Holy Spirit's work in the Christian, beginning at Baptism. To the Messalian quest for experiential assurance, Mark upheld the intrinsic *uncertainty* of divine grace's operation, a fact that required continual self-scrutiny and penitence on the part of the Christian. He also replaced the experiential significance of pneumatic sensibility with the clear obligations of divine commands, as set forth in Scripture, the fulfillment of which was dependent upon grace, but in ways that were only retrospectively identifiable. The assurance of grace *in via* was, for Mark, attainable only through faith and hope. The reality of the Holy Spirit's life thereby remains hidden behind the devoted pursuance of the obedient life, even while the desire for its certain apprehension becomes characterized as misplaced and probably dangerous.

But it should be obvious here that both sides of the controversy lean toward a heavily experientialist approach to pneumatological definition: one ties the Holy Spirit to the direct realization of a sinless existence as its indwelling embodiment, the other to the struggling submission to a life of scriptural obedience. The difference lies, in part, on the possibilities for knowledge of God accorded to the respective experiences: the Messalians pursued the certainty of pneumatic assurance within sensible experience, while the orthodox located such assurance only within the trustworthiness of the scriptural commands themselves, to which the consistently ill-formed submission of human life could only give partial testimony.

It is significant that a Catholic commentator like Hausherr can fault the Messalians for their inability to distinguish *gratiae facientes gratum* — the "secret" and "mystical" workings of the Spirit to sanctify the Christian that Mark the Hermit properly upheld — from *gratiae gratis datae*, the purely sensible experiences of pneumatic charismata.[3] For this is just the distinction, as we have said, that was taken up by the Western scholastic

---

2. For an interpretive discussion, see Irenée Hausherr, "L'erreur fondamentale et la logique de Messalianisme" (1935), in *Études de Spiritualité Orientale* (Rome: Pontificium Institutum Studiorum Orientalium, 1969).

3. Ibid., 95. The scholastic terminology is Hausherr's.

tradition. But it is a distinction that, once elaborated in the highly pro-
fuse enumerations of spiritual "gifts" and "fruits" that was bequeathed to
Thomas, actually ends by favoring a broadly based experientialist pneumatology, although one so diffuse as to defy any integration outside of
individualist history. The graces of sanctification, understood in terms of
virtues, gifts, beatitudes, and spiritual fruits, all fall under the rubric of
a perfecting, if hardly perfectionist, movement of the soul toward union
with God, whose clear evidence, simply by their proliferous identification and analysis, can be seen as an institutionalized version (especially
in monastic existence) of an attenuated Messalianism; the carefully circumscribed understanding of the charismata, on the other hand, whose
descriptive presence precludes any evidence for their holiness and whose
significance lies in the uncertain discernment of their functions for the
Church in particular cases, judges the "gifts" as only possible and always
contestable evidence for institutional doctrine or sanctity, or — as in the
case of miracles performed by the wicked or demons — for diabolic enmity.
Pneumatology was here tied to two poles of evidentialism, one less assured
than the other, but both experientialist and functional at their base.

The Eastern Church, for the most part, never made the distinction
between sanctifying graces and the charismata, nor, despite Hausherr's
implication, was such a distinction somehow implicit in the Orthodox response to enthusiasm. Rather, as in the typical case of someone like John
of Damascus, miracle and sanctity were generally both seen as parts of a
single phenomenon of epiphanic witness to God's reality as the "Father
of lights," in whom all life resides. Relics, healings, exorcisms, and so on
were less functions derivative and/or confirmative of sanctity or truth, as
in the West, but stood instead as the historically connected manifestations of one gracious reality in which the "children of men" become the
"friends and children of God" within the visible contours of the world.[4]
And although the possibility of "false" wonders was acknowledged, especially in reference to the Antichrist, the whole problem of pneumatic
certainty and hiddenness never arose as a pressing difficulty.[5]

The Appellant confluence of sanctity and miracle was similarly founded
on the common epiphanic and adorative character of pneumatic experience. However, developing within the context of the scholastic distinction
we have been exploring, the issue of assurance and uncertainty that lay
embedded in the Western typology was addressed by Appellancy in a more
direct and theologically significant fashion than in the East. The governing rubric of figural history, buttressed by the more systematic scriptural

---

4. See John of Damascus, *The Orthodox Faith*, The Fathers of the Church 88 (Washington, D.C.: Catholic University of America Press), 37, 367ff.

5. This was, in part, perhaps due to the fact that Eastern theologians traditionally
held high, indeed optimistic, expectations about the infallible integrity of the institutional
Church, which was to remain free from the ravages of Satan, even in the form of Antichrist,
whose prophesied work would take place outside the Church's boundaries. See ibid., chapter
99 (pp. 398ff.).

science of the West, allowed Appellants to move beyond the almost arbitrary "command" biblicism of, say, Mark the Hermit, and provide a more coherent framework in which to locate what the latter had called the "mystical," that is, the "secret" workings of grace that had guarded against the quasi-pelagianism associated with enthusiasts like the Messalians. For the followers of François de Pâris, the distillate certainties of scriptural figure, in their englobing reach, became precisely definitive of Christian experiential *un*certainty, in such a way as to finesse the polarizing epistemological tendencies implicit in the scholastic typology (i.e., obvious virtues versus obscure charismata). Within the single frame of figural history, Appellant sanctity and miracle are conjointly given over to the experience of contestability, according to the inclusive character of God's justice and mercy in the Cross of Jesus, wherein human rejection and faith together mark features of a single divine figure. This figurally anticipated interpretive questioning of miraculous phenomena, however, is displaced from its scholastic location as arbiter of pneumatic experience's descriptive nature, a location in which evident sanctity and uncertain charismata each devolve into roles "confirmative" or "disconfirmative" of the other's functioning. Instead, the "problem" of both saints and miracles is subjected to the Appellant construal of the Church's history, which is itself nothing other than a species of exegesis of biblical forms. The clarity of the latter in every case ends by relativizing the significance of distinctions in pneumatic experience altogether, except insofar as they illuminate the historical sovereignty of the scriptural figures themselves.

Pneumatologically, this has important consequences. In the first place, the practical functionalism associated with Western reflections upon the Holy Spirit — the Spirit as the *agens* of the panoply of Christian actions or attitudes — fades within this Appellant framework. And as a specifically theological concern, it fades completely, and is not simply reattached to some other Person of the Trinity, as might be the case if Appellant figurism were but a tool of some Christological bias. Rather, *figurisme* as a substantive ecclesial scripturalism releases the functionalist aspect of pneumatology from theological play. To the degree that such an aspect continues to have any important theological role at all, *figurisme* relocates it within the broader context of the entire Trinity's three distinct Persons, shorn of appropriated qualities and actions.

The traditional ambiguities in distinguishing theologies of grace from pneumatology were, as we have indicated, extended positively by Jansenists into a kind of fusion. But the ultimate result of this fusion, within the figurist outlook on pneumatic gifts, was to defunctionalize the notion of grace as a whole and allow its practical categories to take their place in the general figural description of the Church's life within history. This description alone, structured around the scriptural realities of Israel and Jesus, includes within it all the embedded theologoumena that uphold Trinitarian speech and reference, but it is the descriptive enunciation in itself that remains the *summum* of adorative practice. In the second place, then, pneumatology, along with Trinitarian reflection in general, strays no further than scriptural reiteration. And insofar as one is willing to be pressed into pneumatological assertions on this basis, they can only form themselves around the notion of the Spirit's "kenotic" or self-emptying character.

This is so not because Appellant pneumatology ultimately proves itself to be a paralleling prop to kenotic Christologies of the Cross. Jansenist Christology, in fact, is based on the sacrificial scheme of historical sin and the divine justice of love, and not on concerns with the incarnational *modus* normally associated with theologies of divine *kenosis*. What is "kenotic" about Appellant pneumatology, instead, is the startling ease with which it accepts the burden of its systematic scriptural incoherence as the cost of its insistent enunciation in Scripture's figural terms. The Spirit bears its own reduction into a dangling Trinitarian qualifier to the Christic shape of salvation's history; but it is an appendage whose descriptive inextricability from the web of Israel's and the Church's experience necessarily testifies to the figure's own divine integrity. All traditional explorations of the relationship between the Spirit and the Word, which have often supported kenotic Christologies under the aegis of conceptions like "inspiration," "unction," "prophetic faith," and so on, must, in this view, end at a point of substantive retreat, in which the three original elements remain untouched logically: the Spirit, the Word, and the historical impression in practical terms of Scripture's words themselves. A "kenotic" — that is, figurally reductive — pneumatology, in Appellant terms, which sounds such distinct elements upon the lips the Christian Church, leaves all three of these just as they were, though with their divine integrity enhanced through unqualified assertion. If the *causa gratiae Dei* pleads, it is for the theological reticence of such plain description.

The systematic character of these points will be pursued in our concluding chapter, which will attempt some comparisons with certain modern pneumatologies. But with these conclusions thus anticipated at least *in abstracto*, we may now trace something of the historical fate of sanctity and miracle in Appellant thinking itself. And in so doing, we may observe, through an articulation of the *ostensio Spiritus* involved, the sublation of pneumatology into just such pleading for the simple Christian utterance of divine authorial presence in the scriptural shape of history.

## Miracles and Figurist Self-prophecy: Gudvert's *Jesus-Christ sous l'anatheme et l'excommunication*

We have already seen in our previous chapter how a retelling of the life of François de Pâris was incorporated into larger devotional and instructional material, whose character both in its parts and in its larger anthologizing was submitted to clear figurist shaping. This shaping, while clear enough, tended, nonetheless, to be somewhat indirect in its application, and the material itself is organized so as to lead the uninformed reader only gently into the realm of the Appellant *causa*'s theological under-pinnings. With an investigation of the more explicit concerns of *figurisme* behind us, however, we are now in a position to recognize in what way the reverse influence was not only at work in organizing the movement's self-expression, but in fact proved primarily exigent in this regard. By identifying the governing figures of scriptural history as the sole framework in which the actual manifestation as well as the significance of sanctity and miracle were to be gleaned, Appellant writers also set the heuristic limits in which the whole unfolding debate over the miracles and convulsions was, from their point of view *and even before its evolution,* to be understood.

Among the clearest and most popular *figuriste* descriptions of the Church was that given by Abbé Gudvert of Laon, and we may conveniently examine the way in which this simple application of scriptural form to the affairs of the French Church exemplifies the character of sanctity and miracle as figural inscription. It is an application, further, that discloses its own self-determining range as a kind of prophecy. Gudvert himself is known primarily in his role as a faithful toiler in the provinces for the Appellant cause rather than as a theologian. But his volume entitled *Jesus-Christ sous l'anatheme et l'excommunication* [Jesus Christ anathematized and excommunicated][6] enjoyed several editions in its first decade or so of publication, before slipping from view until the end of the century, when it was translated into Italian and used as a rallying cry for Jansenists involved in the reforming Synod of Pistoia (1786). We have already made mention, in our last chapter, of Marina Caffiero's description of *figurisme* as a method of millenarian exegesis informed by the myths of cyclical "rejuvenation." While this characterization is certainly mistaken, in our view, insofar as it touches upon the bulk of eighteenth-century French Appellancy, Caffiero's studies of "revolutionary" Jansenism in Italy have intriguingly drawn attention to the way in which aspects of *figurisme* were indeed applied to properly millenarian schemes by Catholic political radicals like Eustachio Degola and others. And the central place finally occupied by Gudvert's translated volume in these schemes points not so much to the nature of Gudvert's actual thinking, as to the fate to which such thinking and its objects prepares for itself within its own figural self-description.[7] For above all, Gudvert's book constitutes a meditation upon the patience required of the rejected Church at the hands of its rejecting brethren and the divine love by which God's truth submits to its own perversion.

The "Preface" states the figurist premise of the book as a whole, proceeding from the Mysteries devotions by now familiar to us:

---

6. Originally published in 1727.

7. On the Italian use of Gudvert, see Caffiero, "La Verità Crocifissa: Dal Sinodo di Pistoia al Millenarismo Giansenistico nell' Età Rivoluzionaria," *Rivista di Storia e Letteratura Religiosa* 25 (1989): 48–65.

We could never praise too much the devotion of those Believers who apply themselves to the honoring of both JESUS CHRIST's Passion and of the different circumstances of this Mystery. But few take note of one of these circumstances in particular that deeply merits their veneration: that is the fact that, given the death-sentence handed down by the Chief Priests, JESUS CHRIST was excommunicated and thus cut off from the People of God [ ... ] This condition had been figured by the scapegoat, who was driven out of the camp on the order of the High Priest, and who bore the sins of the whole people. And it was in keeping with the plan that God had established for satisfying His justice in the redemption of humanity that Jesus Christ should carry the punishment of excommunication that Adam had taken upon himself and his posterity through his sin.

It is this extraordinary condition of Jesus Christ — condemned in His person, anathematized and excommunicated, by the Chief Priests of the Old Law — which we present in this book for the devotion of the Faithful. After this, we present to them the same Jesus Christ, but this time condemned again in His Truth, and excommunicated through His defenders by a large number of the Priests of the New Law, in the Constitution *Unigenitus* [ ... ]

It is not our intention in this book to undermine the respect and obedience that the Faithful owe to the Pope and to Bishops, whose authority is derived from God Himself, and which we recognize and honor. Rather, we wish only to dispel the illusions cast upon [the Faithful] by the Constitutionaries, with the only apparent authority of their Constitution; and to arrest the progress of that seduction and mystery of iniquity that is at work within the bosom of the Church herself, in the midst of this time when we are warned of the renewal of Jesus Christ's Passion [ ... ]

Those who reflect seriously on these truths will recognize that the ills of the Church are greater than we had thought; they will be moved; they will pray ardently over her pressing needs; and to Jesus Christ in this condition of anathematization, where He manifests Himself today in His truth and His members as once He did in His own person — to Him, I say, they will offer homage as far as they are able, and they will pursue willingly the devotional acts we will suggest in this book.[8]

The "devotional acts" to which the preface refers are given at the end of the book and are elucidated according to the figural rubric that the Church, as Christ's Mystical Body, be molded according to the shape of Jesus' own historical existence:

But, for the same reason that He has taken upon Himself all of our troubles and weaknesses, He also desires that His Church, which is His mystical body, should bear, along with Him, all the [pain] that He endured in His natural body. He has shared everything between Himself and His Church, so that the resemblance between the Head and the members might be perfect. This is why He traces [His own form] upon this beloved Spouse, and why He imprints upon her all the aspects of His own being, so that she might bring

8. *Jesus-Christ sous l'anatheme et l'excommunication* (Amsterdam: Nicolas Potier, 1731), III–IX.

honor to and might re-present all the different conditions of life through which He passed for her sanctification.[9]

Enmeshed, therefore, in the figure of Israel's Synagogue in its relation to Jesus and his first disciples — including, for instance, the "man born blind" of John 9 — Christians are encouraged to submit to the shape of excommunication at the hands of the Church's authorities (i.e., the *Constitutionnaires* upholding *Unigenitus* and the pope himself). This involves both upholding the Truth of the Gospel, as condemned in various of the *Unigenitus* Propositions and unambivalent adherence to the unity of the Church, through the patient acceptance of official mistreatment aimed at Appellant sympathizers. *Les simples chrétiens* — simple Christians — require more than theological arguments for, but even the "efficacious" image itself of, the fact that accepting religious superiors in their promulgation of doctrinal error is sinful, even while such divinely appointed authorities demand respectful submission: look therefore to Jesus in the hands of His own people's religious leaders! The practical burden of Gudvert's argument in the book, then, is to explain the manner in which a faithful Catholic might thus maintain in his or her life the integrity of an "indefectible" and "visible" Church — the Israel of God's promise — even in midst of her patent apostate flailings. Only the Cross, fulfilled in Christ's own "anathematized" life and figured by the Church through her temporal molding in God's hands, provides the historical resolution to this tension.[10]

Beyond the simple sharpness of the exposition, however, there is nothing remarkable in Gudvert's book from a figurist standpoint. Indeed, this is just what makes instructive, for our purposes, the perusal of the essay's minor editorial transformations in the course of its republications. For the first edition, of 1727, aimed at nothing more than this presentation of the excommunicated figure of Christ itself, in all of its stark scriptural and contemporary relations: the Passion narrative, Deuteronomy 21, 1 Kings, Micah, Jeremiah, Galatians 3, Hebrews 13, along with *Unigenitus*, its Constitution in France, and the various measures taken against those refusing to subscribe. Taken as this whole, the call for a conscious submission to the divine conformities being established figurally between these various elements, especially that between Christ and His Church, becomes the book's overriding liturgical commission. To what degree, therefore, does this whole continue to exert its formative motions in succeeding editions?

---

9. Ibid., 3; see 2–12 as a whole. Gudvert, on 12, mentions a "prophecy" of Nicholas of Cusa, which "tells us at the beginning of this [eighteenth] century, the Passion of Jesus Christ will be renewed," a prediction that, quite apart from "the actual basis of his calculation," demonstrates the conformity of such convictions about the Church's potential shape with an officially sanctioned piety.

10. The "practices" involve prayer, study, Scripture's reading, and expressive figural submission. See ibid., 43–53.

The 1727 volume, written before the Saint-Médard episode began, makes no allusion to miracles, except in passing. Brushing aside the objection that Appellant opposition to a papal bull ought to require the confirmation of such a stance by miracle, just as Jesus' own doctrine so required it, Gudvert points out the redundancy of such prodigious manifestations on behalf of the Gospel once founded: with respect to those truths condemned by *Unigenitus*, "like the absolute power of God over our hearts as well as our bodies, there is no further necessity to ask for new miracles that might confirm the certainty [of such truths]." However, Gudvert does add that, nonetheless, several attested miracles of 1725, subjected to judicial inquiry, can be attached to the Appellant cause, as can some others, officially still unconfirmed, that occurred as a result of intercessory prayers made to the deceased P. Quesnel. While hardly "necessary" within the divine economy, these prodigies were clearly given by God as a "consolation" to His "afflicted Church," an ornamental *éclat* adorning the actual figure to which God's people were being subjected.[11] With the 1731 edition of the book, nothing is added to this brief consideration other than a small footnote, containing reference to miracles associated with the Appellant P. Rousse, as well as those taking place at the tomb of François de Pâris. The sum of this small addendum is the appearance of a new adjective linked to these events: "But what is happening today in our Kingdom's capital is as admirable as it is consoling."[12] What continues to define both the "admirable" as well as the "consoling" quality of these marvels, however, lies not in the miraculous outbreaks themselves, as if they served the function of discernment's rule within a contest of claims, but their linkage to a circumstantial train of historical experience whose figural conformance alone creates the bounds of divine manifestation:

> In the current affair, Appellants are providing a witness that is public, dazzling [*éclatant*], generous, perseverant, and worthy of the cause they are defending.[ ... ] God has prepared these remedies and these consolations, and it is up to us to gather them with care. This is what we have tried to do in this book. Those Servants of God who are the most faithful and the most sincere find themselves attacked in so many places, precisely by those whom God has given to them as their Pastors. [ ... ] Happy are those who, in resembling this aspect of Jesus Christ, find no obstacle in any of this, but rather use this unexpected situation as a way to be filled more and more with His spirit.[13]

The figure itself consoles and proffers resolution to the Church's ills; the historical *fact* of conforming testimony reveals the sovereign hand the redeeming God stretched across the body of His Son, whose own form enfolds the perfection of holiness. Insofar as the miracles provide conso-

---

11. Ibid., 38–40.
12. See 40.
13. Ibid., 59ff.

lation and exhibit that which astonishes, they do so in reference to and in dependence upon the larger "unexpected" consolation of faith's own figural conformance.

The 1739 edition of Gudvert's book, however, includes some major additions. It was from this version that the much later Italian translation was made, whose influence Caffiero traces in the millenarian tendencies in which participants at the Synod of Pistoia were caught. The volume is now almost twice as long as at its first printing. But a quick glance at these additions points out how the eschatological themes of *figurisme,* which Caffiero identifies as central to Gudvert's work (but absent from the initial editions), are here given over to the figural constraints of the original edition, and in a manner that moves entirely away from millenarian anticipation while remaining consistent with the primary purpose of the writing. To be sure, there are now several new pages devoted to the standard figurist teaching on the return of Elijah and the Conversion of the Jews, based on Romans 9–11. At the same time, however, these remarks remain faithful to the style of figural retrospective eschatology laid out by Duguet's *Règles,* according to which future promises of ecclesial transformation are made primarily dependent upon the pressures of historically Christic configuration, so that an odd (*surprenante*) conflation of "renewal" with "conformance" determines the sense of the scriptural prophecies. Indeed, the passage quoted by Caffiero — "through the gathering together of this ancient people [the Jews], and thus taking on new strength, the Church will discover her own perfect renewal, as in her first youth" — is really a paraphrase of Gregory the Great's text on the Conversion of the Jews, according to the figure of Job, frequently cited by figurists and given in whole at the end of the section from which "Gudvert's" citation is taken; the point of which, in fact, is the incapacity of "human remedies" for the Church's travails and the sole sufficient intervention of God's direct action, through the efficacious conversion of human hearts (Jansenistically understood): "who will allow me to become as I was in the days of my youth"? Job is quoted as saying through the pen of Gregory. The emphasis falls on the question of agency, "who?," and on the subsequent resolution given form in the "perfect resemblance between the times in which we now live and those wherein Jesus Christ appeared on earth in order to form His Church."[14] Nothing could be further from a millenarian fixation upon the cyclical return to a golden age than such a transposition of *ecclesia triumphans* into *ecclesia patiens.*[15]

---

14. *Jesus-Christ sous l'anatheme et sous l'excommunication, ou Reflexions sur le mystere de Jesus-Christ rejetté, condamné et excommunié par le Grand-Prêtre et par le Corps des Pasteurs de peuple de Dieu; Pour l'instruction et la consolation de ceux qui dans le sein de l'Eglise, éprouvent un pareil traitement* (Utrecht, 1739), 107–15. See Caffiero, "La verità crocifissa," 52.

15. See Caffiero's remarks, "La verità crocifissa,"53, which she ties to Eliade's conception of a Myth of the Eternal Return: "time as a cyclical renewal" and "return to original perfection," which is "frequently found at the center of millenarian eschatology."

In any case, these pages on eschatology are few and appear to be lifted almost verbatim in many places from Duguet's *Jesus crucifié*, whose figural import we have already examined. Far more lengthy are the preceding additions on the miracles. Where the first two editions of the work held these events to minimal scrutiny, they now make up almost half the volume as a whole. For the most part, however, these new sections confine themselves to recounting the course of the healings rather than analyzing their significance, and it is this method of exposition, within the context of the work, that now gives precision to the spare notions of "admiration" and "consolation" touched upon in the earlier version's discussion of the miraculous.

The book opens its expanded discussion with a setting of the scene: as the 1720s nears its end, there is increased persecution of the Appellants, but also increased conformity on their part to the figure of Christ's "excommunication." And as this double movement of oppressive grace went deeper, so too became more likely the visible showing of divine glory attached to such forms:

> In fact, given that God has decided to retrace the spectacle of His only Son our Savior Jesus Christ's sufferings and humiliations upon the person of His faithful servants, imprinting upon them these elements of such perfect resemblance, it seems most fitting that He should console them with such marvels as are connected with the miracles our divine Savior performed in instructing His Apostles.[16]

Although such miracles could never be either expected or desired on the part of Christ's servants, in one sense they were inevitable features of figural coincidence within the life of the Church. The year 1725, then, is given as the start of an accumulating series of marvels that seep out from the edges of the otherwise unembroidered garment of Appellant witness: on this date begin healings in Paris, then Amsterdam, then in the diocese of Reims, all associated with individuals and groups known for their faithfulness to the Appellant *causa* and culminating in the healings at Saint-Médard. An extended account is given of François de Pâris's sanctity, and then follow long pages on the various miracles, conversions, joys, and denials associated with his tomb. And in all of this, we are told, there worked a divine will to "declare in favor," publicly, for those whose faith had been condemned by *Unigenitus:*

> God has heard the groaning of His Church; He has taken in hand the cause of His oppressed servants; He has consoled them in a way that surpasses their thoughts, their desires, and all their hopes; and He has worked a multitude of miracles in their favor;
>
> [ ... ] God has finally broken His silence to speak in their favor;
>
> [ ... ] Since people have shut their ears to these first warnings given to them from on high, the Lord will not delay in working new marvels, yet more

---

16. *Jésus-Christ sous l'anatheme*, 1739, 57.

capable than the first of displaying before the whole earth the innocence of
the Appellants, and thereby the injustice of their persecutors.

[...] The moment people think they have smothered and discredited the
miracles of M. de Pâris, that is precisely when they will break out with a
new brilliance and will pierce the veils designed to cover them up;

[...] God has clearly demonstrated how He is the Sovereign Master of
people's wills, and the arbiter of all events; how He lifts up the poor, when
He pleases, from dust and refuse, in order to place him upon a throne of
glory, etc.[17]

The miracles, from the perspective of this account, console through their
provision of justificatory relief.

But the notion of clarity that pervades these descriptions of divine
purpose in the miracles, in which epiphany works in service of public vindication within the Church, is nuanced, and finally refashioned by the very
current of the cumulative recital. The "obvious" conclusion to be drawn
from the miracles is that the Appellant cause is divinely supported: "if
God renews in our day, through an unexpected mercy, the grace of miracle
in favor of the Appellants, what else can we conclude but that He holds
their cause as something precious in His sight"?[18] Yet, the "cause" itself
is cloaked in the mantle of anathematization, a "factual veil" that even
the miracles cannot pierce within the Church. For all the weight of the
marvelous placed upon their side, the balance of their setting within ecclesiastical life still tips against them, and increasingly so. A long quote from
St. Basil, on the reality of the faithful and persecuted "remnant" within a
hostile Church, used in the original edition, is now given a place within
the miracle accounts just at the moment where their visibility reaches its
brightest gleam.[19] Its new location, however, serves to punctuate a retrospective change in the movement of the miracles' performance, as the
author now reflects on the fact that, despite the clear evidence of the healings, at every stage of their display the opposition mounted. Were there
not arrests along with the miracles' accomplishment? Did not theologians
work in concert with the police to decry and limit their publication, investigation, and significance? Did not intelligent leaders within the Church
dare to attribute their form to the actions of the Demon, sowing doubt
along with blasphemy among the people? Was not the cemetery itself finally closed in an effort to forestall the miracles' proliferation? And, finally,
did not the convulsions which thereupon began to accompany the healings
in greater frequency, altering the course of their previously unquestionable
fulfillment in confusing and disturbing ways, tend to offer new weapons
of dispute to the miracles' opponents? For all God's prodigies on her behalf, the Gospel's Truth ends her "triumphal" entry into Jerusalem by
remaining an excommunicated outcast consigned to the Church's own
prisons.

---

17. Ibid., 58, 62, 64, 78, 80.
18. Ibid., 93.
19. Ibid., 97.

Thus, the recital of the miracles retreats, suddenly, before a larger question, hovering until now over the whole account, but here finally given a commanding posture as the "facts" themselves, however unimpeachable in their integrity, retire into the shadows of history's unrelenting rejection: does it make any sense to claim that the Church, promised guidance by the Holy Spirit, should grasp its heritage of blessing only through the hands of a few, in the midst of a general disease among her own members? "We must admit: the difficulty is real."[20] The very *shape* of besieged Appellancy, however proper its particular claims may be, seems incompatible with the nature of the Catholic Church's historical mission as normally understood.

But an answer to this question is, after all, the burden of Gudvert's volume from the beginning: the shape of the Church is precisely what provides the foundation of her hope, a shape at every turn given life by its conformity to her Lord's. And without attending to this shape, a figure that includes at the peak of its own transparency "Jesus Christ anathematized," all hope must surely vanish for the Christian. Thus, the account of the miracles reverts to the book's original figural reference: the times of "the Church's interior shadows and tempests,"[21] whose intrinsic linkage, historically, to the eschatological hope for the world's conversion through the Jews, becomes as well the figural reference of the miracles themselves. Joined to the witness of the "anathematized" of the Church, the brilliance of the marvelous partakes of the "clouds" of Jesus' own life, even as it participates in the still unrealized vision of God to which the saints of persecution now bear witness through their patience in the darkness. "God preserves the deposit of Truth within His Church during the days of trial and temptation, mainly through the struggles of these generous athletes. In this way He will cause the Truth to shine yet more brilliantly before the eyes of the whole world, once the storm is stilled and the torrent of violence, intrigue, and human passion has run its course."[22]

There is every reason to think that Gudvert himself was not personally responsible for the major additions of the 1739 edition of his book. An "Avertissement" by another hand provides a brief biography of the author, points out that his death took place in 1737, two years prior to the new edition, and makes no claims for his direct involvement in the book's changes. Further, as we noted, the fact that important new material, like the *figuriste* eschatology, appears to be drawn directly from other well-known sources, while much in the miracle accounts seems similarly assembled, leads me to believe that the volume's previous accessibility made it a convenient place in which to anthologize additional material central to popular Appellancy for widespread circulation: miracles, the penitential sanctity of François de Pâris, and the eschatologically figured

---

20. Ibid., 98.
21. Ibid., 98–109.
22. Ibid., 105.

nature of the Church. Yet, whoever the editor may have been, the placement of this material within Gudvert's work was not done haphazardly, and, indeed, the choice of the book itself as a repository for the new elements appears as a deliberate attempt to disclose their significance within Gudvert's original figural scheme.

In a way, then, that belies the superficial extent of the added miracle accounts, the "Avertissement" of this later edition draws attention to the fact that the new edition is published at a time when the forces of persecution have grown even stronger and acted even more oppressively than when the author first wrote his volume. No reference to the miracles is even made here. Rather, the new edition is required because the figure to which it calls faithful Christians remains the only source of "support" in a rapidly disintegrating era. Gudvert himself, next, is lifted up as an example of conforming sanctity in this regard, following the precepts of his own writing: he was driven out of his parish, deprived of his benefice, stripped of his functions, yet continued to uphold the Appeal. Finally, "even though he must have watched with pain as his parish was handed over to an interloper, he nonetheless let go of his cure of souls with joy, for he regarded it as a crushing burden; and he instead embraced a life in hidden retirement, in which he persevered until his death."[23] In this way, from the start of the volume, the kind of penitential patience celebrated later in François de Pâris is lifted up as a properly lived commentary on the "principles" of the book, which ends as in the original, with a daily devotional designed "to honor the Mystery of the excommunicated Jesus Christ": appropriate short texts from the Gospels and Acts, followed by the litany, "Jesus, anathematized and cursed, insulted and discarded by the people on our behalf, have mercy upon us." Through their recital, the miracles cannot go further than this plea. And as a result, joined with the holiness of particular individuals, they are subsumed together in a historical movement, the outline of which dampens the significance of peculiar lights in its midst in favor of a scriptural imposition of Christ's form, attentively discerned through faith, and whose shape alone can finally be honored in terms of "brilliance."

Gudvert's book, then, in the history of its own editorial transformation, offers a clear example of the way in which the phenomena of Appellant miracle, in their very recital, are given an intrinsic meaning drawn fundamentally from their figural construal. But the recital itself is nonetheless left standing, and is, indeed, still demanded, with all of the varying specifics and immediate ends for which its circumstantial detail is provided. Temporally and phenomenally, the miracles and the individuals involved remain discrete events and actors, and their narrative retains its own integrity and immediacy, even with the polemical and apologetic purposes of its fashioning left intact. None of these are somehow denied in their accurate connection with moments and episodes. The figural

---

23. Ibid., VI.

construal in which the miracles are subsumed is not, therefore, discovered through awaiting some final historical perspective that will provide a larger structure of meaning within which single elements will be fitted to some only now apparent task, a "consolatory" hope that will furnish a still-unforthcoming justification for innocent suffering and God's wisdom.

Rather, the figure is given from the start, in the scriptural forms of Jesus. The object and agent of *admirare* and *consolare* lies here, and cannot, therefore, be used to cast a mist about the forms of history whose unveiling will uncover God's "true" marks. Within the given figure, all the phenomenal realities associated with the miracles — saints, Appellant witness, debate, division, suffering — like all of those associated with the Church of Jesus Christ, take their places side by side without hermeneutic interruption, even in their obscurity, contestability, and malleable significance. They are *data,* the descriptive contours of God's sovereign promise, whose shape is grasped in advance through Christ. "Discernment," therefore, consistently called for by all parties in the Appellant dispute, is properly shifted in its object from the miracles themselves to the scriptural forms in which they are embedded, whether in their truth or falsity, their perspicuity or their murkiness. From these forms alone, in their divine embodiment and enactment, flow as one all "graces," "perfect gifts from above, coming down from the Father of lights" (James 1:17), coincident with the *charisma* that is Christ's own life for us and the showering glory of his death and resurrection (Eph. 4:8). But the integrity of historical narrative, including those that concern the manifestation of traditionally designated "graces," does not offer a significant divine referent apart from these scriptural forms, and to this degree, any associated pneumatological dependency cannot be affirmed apart from their simultaneous and exclusive enunciation. The *ostensio Spiritus,* even with its seemingly pneumatic events, is here given in forms that, fundamentally, are not pneumatologically defined at all.

In fact, *pneumatica* here are clearly subordinated to a figure bound to subvert their appearance. The very notion of a figure like "Jesus-Christ anathematized" coincident with the Church, entails, as we have indicated, a kind of prophecy about the fate of any miracles as might occur within the figure's outline, no less than of the kind of sanctity to which they might be joined. The editor of Gudvert's volume seems to recognize this in his "Avertissement" by remarking on the final "hidden life" of the author, without commentary on the vastly expanded account of the miracles newly incorporated into the text, and by allowing this account itself to flutter inefficaciously in the figural winds of the original project. And the book itself, it appears, along with the form of life advanced by its author, also eventually succumbs to the force of its own projections. For as Caffiero shows, its penitential figurism was rejected by the century's later "Patriotic" Jansenists, who, as splinters of a movement long since riven and disheveled, had reorganized themselves at the head of the approaching Revolution. Political activists now took the place of patient advocates for the Church's religious integrity. Italian Jansenist "Jacobins" resuscitated Gudvert's work, but took from it only its conveniently packaged eschatological additions, while using its figural villains — the High Priests of the Church and State — as a rallying cry for radical reform. Now in the hands of millenarian political optimists, the mutilated outlook of Gudvert's final litany allowed its ghost to migrate — ironically? obviously? graciously? — into another camp whose identity would have astonished only the most superficial and partisan readers of Duguet's earlier work: by the turn of the century, in the wake of Revolution's ravages upon the Church in France and Italy, Jesuits and ultramontanes like Joseph de Maistre were now those who saw the features of the Church's history given in the face of Christ's life-giving Passion, while "Jansenists" trailed eagerly the march of Bonaparte's armies through the ruins of a devastated Vatican.[24]

## Miracle and the Demonization of Experience: Colbert and Languet's Followers

The *fact* of the rejection of the Appellant miracles by Church authorities, then, was almost a theological given from the perspective of figurist devotion. That an earlier "debate" over miracles took place at all at Port-Royal with respect to the Holy Thorn, that this debate took place in the context of the monastery's own figural location in the Church's history, and that such a location was coincident with the continued Appellant *causa*, ought to have muted the sense of astonishment and indignation that followed in the wake of the Church's official incredulity with respect to the miracles of the 1720s, and then of Saint-Médard in particular. But such was not the case. Much as the recital in Gudvert's work reveals, healings in Paris, Amsterdam, and elsewhere, associated with liturgical activities at Appellant parishes or with pious individuals attached to the movement, like the P. Rousse and de Pâris himself, all provoked immediate celebration and rancorous opposition, sending printers to work with the voluminous arguments that ensued and driving the political forces of both Church and state to often acrid and mean maneuver.[25] But astonishment and indignation in the face of the miracles' rejection continued unabated throughout even the advent of the convulsions, even while the vision of

---

24. See Caffiero's articles, as cited in her contribution to *Jansénisme et Révolution* (Paris: Chroniques de Port-Royal, 1990). In that volume note also, in particular, those articles by Marcel Gauchet, Catherine Maire, Dale Van Kley, Yann Fauchois, Rita Hermon-Belot, Mario Rosa, and Dominique Julia. See also Frank Paul Bowman, *Le Christ Romantique* (Geneva: Librairie Droz, 1973), esp. 30ff.; and his *Le Christ des Barricades: 1789–1848* (Paris: Les Éditions du Cerf, 1987), 33–59. We will be returning to this point at the end of the next chapter.

25. The best and fullest account of this vigorous battle, we remind the reader, is B. Robert Kreiser's *Miracles, Convulsions, and Ecclesiastical Politics in Early Eighteenth-Century Paris* (Princeton: Princeton University Press, 1978), especially chapters 2 through 4. Good bibliographical remarks on the entire debate over the miracles and then over the convulsions can be found in Joseph Dedieu, "L'agonie du jansénisme," *Revue d'Histoire de l'Eglise de France* 14 (1928): 161–214.

the "humiliated saint" and the anathematized Christ asserted themselves on the sensibilities of the participants. Only gradually was an explicit understanding of the events, which allowed for the continuing contest of arguments while submitting it to the reticence of its figural meaning, developed by Appellant writers, an understanding capable of maintaining the traditional commitments to clarity normally associated with pneumatic events even as the concept of such clarity was transposed into the figural realm of Scripture's historical shapes.

Charles-Joachim Colbert provides what is perhaps the most succinct as well as the richest testimony to this developing sense concerning the miracles. Born in 1667 and bishop of Montpellier from 1696, Colbert was perhaps the most visible and influential Appellant leader within the hierarchy, until his death in 1738. As one the four original signers of the 1717 *Appel* itself, Colbert's stature remained commanding and irreproachable within the movement.[26] He was also, perhaps, the most consistent public defender of Appellant miracles, providing a whole series of pastoral instructions and official letters on their value and significance through the 1730s, which acted as regularly cited touchstones for the many other private pamphlets and volumes on the matter that circulated during this period. We have already mentioned Colbert's role in bringing into print for the first time, in 1727, some of Pascal's *Pensées* taken from his series on miracles. And in most respects, Colbert's own thought goes no further beyond, though now in a more organized fashion than his model, Pascal's attempt to hold together the evidentially epiphanic and figurally formative character of the miraculous that we have earlier examined and viewed in parallel with Arnauld's writing on the subject. Colbert's active participation in an episode of proliferated and opposed miracle far outstripped anything experienced by the seventeenth-century Port-Royalists, and just because of this grants to his reflections themselves something of the conformative shape — i.e., prophetic outcome — about which they eventually speak. This merging of theological inquiry with its own object in the form of their figural fate is what, finally, distinguishes Appellancy's vocation in relation to its classically Jansenist progenitors. Colbert, then, does not so much advance the argument as he does, in his inextricable tie to the historical current washing up the questions into view in the first place and lashed to colleagues in the Church's rush, fulfill it.

In 1725, a local woman by the name of Madame Lafosse was healed of long-standing paralysis and hemorrhage while attending a procession of the Holy Sacrament in the Paris church of Sainte-Marguerite.[27]

---

26. "Le Grand Colbert," as he was frequently called, has received little attention in his own right, since Valentin Durand's brief ecclesiastical biography, *Le Jansénisme au XVIIIe Siècle et Joachim Colbert, Évêque de Montpellier (1696–1738)* (Toulouse: Édouard Privat, 1907).

27. On the event and ensuing episode, see Kreiser, *Miracles, Convulsions, and Ecclesiastical Politics in Early Eighteenth-Century Paris*, 74ff., and Durand, *Le Jansénisme au XVIIIe Siècle*, 167ff.

Archbishop Noailles, following an official investigation, commended the miracle to the faithful in general terms as confirmative of God's presence in the Sacrament. But given that Sainte-Marguerite was a parish known for the Appellant sympathies of its leaders, Lafosse's healing was immediately appropriated by the movement as a sign of divine favor on its behalf. Colbert took the lead in this interpretation. In a pastoral letter written at the end of the year, he laid out a reading of the miracle that was firmly erected on the circumstantial evidentialism of the original 1656 Port-Royal *Reponse a un ecrit publié sur le sujet du miracle qu'il a plu a Dieu de faire a Port-Royal,* in which Pascal may have had a hand.[28]

Colbert begins with a somewhat unusual linkage of miracle to scandal in the Church, the premise of which both undercuts the bulk of the letter's evidentialism while also hinting at attitudes to follow in later writings. God's work in the world is infinite in variety and wisdom. Because of this, the faithful person is called to a constant attentiveness, scrutinizing nature and history in order to discern the enmeshed patterns of the divine "conduct" constructed by the "mass [*foule*]" of events guided by God's power. Here, the parameters for what we have called a "circumstantialist" context for the understanding of miracles is immediately laid out. Colbert then goes on to claim, more specifically, that such attentive discernment will necessarily take seriously the "intelligible language" of God's "silence," that is to say, the often lengthy periods of scandal and divine hiddenness in the life of the Church. By recognizing in advance the significant nature of these periods, the Christian will also be attuned to the particulars of their unwinding, particulars that will always include "occasional" miracles, the divine accompaniment to divine silence, for the sake of the weak, for the conservation of faith, and for the continued manifestation of God's glory. Indeed, a proportional relation exists between the evils of an age afflicting the Church and the unveiling of the marvelous. And are there days more evil than the present multiplication of "libertines," "heretics," and "false brethren" within the Church herself?[29]

Colbert thus sets up, in a crude fashion, a providential opposition between religious calamity and miracle. Not only does a reasoned assessment of the current age lead us to expect God's miraculous interventions, but any miracles in their very happening must attest to Gospel truths, rendered in polemical guise. While they occur within a providential pattern of historical event, miracles here do so in the purely functionalist role of argument and proof, whose meaning can, in large measure, be ascertained through propositional force detached from the shape of the healing and its actual reception. Thus, although Colbert devotes several pages to a description of Mme. Lafosse's experience, much of this discussion focuses

---

28. Colbert's letter, bound in his *Oeuvres*, vol. 2 (Cologne, 1740), is entitled "Lettre Pastorale de M. l'Evesque de Montpellier addressée aux fideles de son diocese à l'occasion du miracle operé à Paris dans la Paroisse de Sainte Marguerite le 31 Mai, jour du Saint Sacrement."

29. Ibid., 2–3.

on elements confirmative of the miracle's genuineness, which is designed
to buttress the main purpose of the letter: ways in which the healing "argues" against the era's opponents to true religion. The scepticism of the
libertines is confounded by clear evidence of the "finger of God" omnipo-
tently working in their midst and ordering nature; the heretics, that is,
Protestants left undefended by miracles of their own, are overturned by
the obvious blessing given by God to the prayers and doctrine (i.e., Eucharistic presence) of the Catholics; to false brethren bent on persecuting
the Appellants, the circumstances of the miracle, tied to Appellant priests
and indicative, through a figure, of (Jansenist) teaching on the sovereignty
of God over His creatures, declare from the heavens the rightness of the
cause of those opposing *Unigenitus*. Why did God choose *this* woman in
all of Paris to heal, if not to announce the truth implicated in the miracle's
context to the world?

> Join yourself to this triumph, my dear brothers! It is the triumph of inno-
> cence over slander and of truth over error. Go, and everywhere proclaim the
> great things that God has done in our midst [ ... ] Invite all creatures to
> glorify God along with you, to sing the praises of the Lord, to call upon His
> Name.[30]

But once having posited a divine "language of silence" for the Church,
was there not granted the possibility that miracles themselves might find
a phonetic role in the articulation of its obscurities? At this stage in the
discussion, however, it was a possibility Colbert could not or would not
consider, in large measure because the actual figural significance of such
providential speech was not yet tied, in his mind, to those scriptural forms
necessary to transpose the clarity of miracle into something beyond the
pure logic of theological *defensio*. Nor were Colbert's own figurist sensibilities sufficiently encompassing to provide such forms as necessary givens.
It seems probable, in this light, that his study of Pascal, among others,
had not advanced further than an appreciation of the latter's justificatory
posture toward the miracle of the Holy Thorn.

But if Colbert himself still, perhaps unconsciously, operated with a vision of the marvelous that managed to divorce its nature and occurrence,
as a functional tool drawn out of some divine arsenal of optional weapons,
from the larger fabric of God's providential purpose, his opponents unwit-
tingly pressed for just such an integration. They did so, to be sure, on
the basis of evidentialist presuppositions and with a view to demoting
miracles from any "useful" role in the course of doctrinal disputes. But in
so doing, they actually inflated the reach that a possible figural construal
of miracle might extend. Bishop Languet de Gergy of Soissons, later archbishop of Sens and an indefatigably bitter enemy of Appellancy and all of
its claims to supernatural witness, was the first to reply to Colbert's paean
to the Truth's miraculous "triumph." In 1726, he came out with a pas-

---

30. Ibid., 9.

toral letter[31] whose basic premise set, not only the wildly accusatory tone, but the whole framework of concern for almost all subsequent opposition to the miracles and, by extension, to the convulsions as well: the divine purposes of history are *insensible,* and all that transpires in time therefore ambiguous, except to the independent authority of the Church.

In view of Cardinal de Noailles's official acceptance of Lafosse's miraculous healing, Languet's tack lay not in questioning the divine origin of the event itself, but in casting doubt upon the evident purpose of the prodigy. God's performance of miracles, according to Languet, is in accordance with hidden ends that defy the easy linkage of confirmative miracle and its immediate circumstance. Indeed, miracles can "confirm" nothing, because their occurrence does not inherently manifest their end: miracles may happen, as God desires, in order to punish, confuse, and blind as readily as they may be worked as testimony on behalf of some contiguous cause. Languet adopts a form of historical dispensationalism in order to skirt the obvious scriptural objection to such a thesis on the basis of Jesus' own "confirming" miracles: while helpful in this role at the inception of the Gospel's preaching, miracles are no longer "needed" for such a function once both doctrine and the Church are established. The power of discernment, in times of contest, now resides wholly with the Church's *magisterium,* infallible in its judgments as rendered by bishops "united to the Pope." On this score, Appellancy has long been pronounced in error, and any miracle associated with it, however genuine, cannot be interpreted as a divine mark of vindication for its cause. Indeed, in light of its heretical location, Lafosse's healing must be seen as somehow marking the wrath of God by spreading a "seductive" veil upon the minds of those given over to the way of unrighteousness. As with the Eastern Church's response to Messalianism centuries before, Languet here insisted that experience itself cannot be clear; in a thoroughly Western fashion, however, he asserted that only the voice of the official Church can direct one's feet through the obscurity of the times.

It was precisely this epistemological wedge placed between experience and authority in religious matters that reflects what had already become, through the seventeenth century, a major "sceptical" feature in religious apologetic, working side by side and frequently in a complementary way with what we more normally associate with the "positivistic" elements of the Enlightenment.[32] Languet's argument, while it was hardly designed to question the capacity of the Church's human servants to investigate and pronounce upon the phenomena of the miraculous, nonetheless tended to consign them to the heap of general experience whose intrinsic opac-

---

31. *7e Lettre pastorale... donnée à l'occasion de divers écrits* (Paris, 1726); see Kreiser, *Miracles, Convulsions, and Ecclesiastical Politics in Early Eighteenth-Century Paris,* 77.

32. See our previous discussion on miracle, of Arnauld and Malebranche's epistemological debate. As always on this topic, the major work remains Richard Popkin's *The History of Scepticism, from Erasmus to Spinoza* (Berkeley: University of California Press, 1979). See also A. Monod's *De Pascal à Chateaubriand* (Paris: Alcan, 1915).

ity as religiously significant left only the Church's authority intact as its exegete. And while also considering divine control over events as a given, his logic moved to make inert even this assumption apart from ecclesial pronouncements.

It is pertinent to note, then, that the direction of the anti-miracle attack followed by Languet and others usually drifted away from this initial argument based on the inscrutability of God's earthly purposes even through genuine supernatural interventions, to an outright rejection of the "divinity" of the miracles altogether. As the prodigies associated with other Appellant saints and relics multiplied, culminating at Saint-Médard, but without ever meeting official acceptance as in the case of Mme. Lafosse, there was no longer any need to work with the assumption of their divine origin. The argument from the Church's authority remained decisive, as before, but now the miracles were simply attributed to other, non-divine sources: human imposture, natural causes, and, increasingly, the Devil himself. Languet later, in the wake of the convulsions, produced a large work in this vein, as did many others.[33] On the one hand, Languet and his circle defended the Church's refusal — on the part of the Diocese of Paris and of Rome — to investigate the miracles of François de Pâris, on the blunt basis that Appellants, as officially condemned, hold to nothing legitimate for which to be vindicated. On the other hand, they explained the seeming supernatural elements of the "miracles" in terms of forces — natural or evil — attention to which could only end by corrupting the observer. The simple syllogistic train of reasoning, requiring no attention or inquiry into claims for sanctity or miracle, went something like this: Appellants refuse to subscribe to official papal teaching; therefore they are out of communion with the Church; those out of communion with the Church cannot be saints; François de Pâris was an Appellant, and therefore he was not a saint. Any phenomena associated with him, then, have no relevance to the Church's life, and can at best derive from religiously nefarious sources. Archbishop Vintimille, Noailles's successor, repeatedly refused to initiate inquiries into the Saint-Médard miracles, despite official requests on the part of priests and others in the diocese that he do so; likewise, the Roman Inquisition, in an action upheld by the later Pope Benedict XIV, condemned de Pâris's cult, declared his miracles false, and forbade the printing of books dealing with him and his associated healings, without ever taking up an investigation. In both cases, the mere fact that Appellancy and its condemned doctrine were implicated justified their rejection out of hand.[34] The disappearance, here, of pneumatic

---

33. Jacques-Joseph Languet de Gergy, *Instruction pastorale au sujet des prétendus miracles du diacre de Saint-Médard et des convulsions arrivées à son tombeau*, 2 vols. (Paris, 1734–35). Also well known was the massive attack of Dom Louis-Bernard de La Taste, *Lettre Théologique aux écrivains défenseurs des convulsions et autres prétendus miracles du temps*, 2 vols. (Paris, 1740).

34. On Vintimille's refusal to accede to an inquiry and his condemnation of de Pâris and the miracles, see Kreiser, *Miracles, Convulsions, and Ecclesiastical Politics in Early*

claims beneath the weight of canonical prejudices of doctrine signaled the final reinterpretation of both sanctity and miracle into fully institutional terms. The pneumatic shape of the Church's life stood untouched and apart from the vicissitudes of her contextual disputes, with the result that it was divorced, not from historical existence as such, but from a history that could be seen as fully imbued with a positive divine significance.

Languet's rendering of miraculous phenomena as ambiguous, then, led to a de-divinizing of historical phenomena in general. In the course of the attack on Saint-Médard, in fact, it led to their outright demonization. Jean-Baptiste-Noël Lerouge, syndic of the Sorbonne from 1739, conveniently lays out in summary form many of the arguments of Languet and later La Taste as they had developed, in a volume of 1737 that, in the footsteps of Languet's first appeal to the "hidden God," once again seems to mimic the Appellant case for the miracles as God's speech in times of obscurity. But through extending that reasoning's inclusive grasp to the whole of "sensible" history, judging all phenomena suspiciously, he thereby drains the world of any comprehensible divine presence, in favor of the Church's detached magisterial determinations.[35] Lerouge's strategy is to fasten on the figurist eschatology of the Endtimes' disputes, and make the observation, logical in itself, that *all* phenomenal vindications of a given religious position in such days will be uselessly ambiguous, nay, even seductively so. For is it not prophesied that the Antichrist himself will perform miracles at that time?

---

*Eighteenth-Century Paris*, 122ff.; on the Inquisition's burning of the *Vie* of de Pâris and condemnation of his cult, see idem, 192ff. Cardinal Prosper Lambertini, later Pope Benedict XIV, reiterated the basis for such a summary rejection of Saint-Médard and her beloved deacon in a prominent addendum to his classic opus on beatification and canonization. After having described the undisputed Appellant associations of de Pâris and their common flagrant disdain for *Unigenitus* and the discipline of the Church, Benedict affirms the inherent incompatibility of such behavior with true sanctity and the consequent illegitimacy of private, let alone public, cults in his regard (otherwise allowed preliminary to official inquiries): "Notum est, annis praeteritis ex hac vita decessisse quemdam Diaconum nomine *Parisium*, et ejus corpus traditum fuisse sepulturae in coemeterio S. Medardi civitatis Parisiensis. Prodiit ejus vita, et in variis locis edita typis est. [ . . . ] Totus et universus rerum gestarum contextus eo unice collineabat, ut homo Apostolicae Sedi refragans, schismaticus, haereticus, acerrimus impugnator Constitutionis, quae incipit *Unigenitus*, pertinax Jansenistarum assecla, falsis ipsi attributis miraculis, imaginem solidae virtutis et sanctitatis praeseferret. Sancte ergo et prudentissime supra memorati Episcopi Gallicani abstinuerunt ab inquisitionibus juridicis, et sancte ac prudentissime insano et temerario cultui obstiterunt. Licet enim ex alibi dictis publicus tantum cultus prohibeatur erga non Beatificatos aut Canonizatos, nec publicus sit cultus, qui exhibetur in publico, sed qui exhibetur auctoritate Ecclesiae, et fama aut insignis virtutis, aut miraculi viam aperiat inquisitioni juridicae ab Ordinario assumendae; haec tamen, et similia sibi vindicant locum, cum agitur de Dei Servo, qui pie in Domino obiit, qui, dum viveret, non populari nec fictitio rumore, sed solida virtutum fama praefulsit. Quod si res sit de homine, de cujus fide et religione suspicio sit, tantum abest, ut cultus privatus erga eum permitti possit, vel ut de assertis ejus miraculis instituenda sit inquisitio, ut contra debeant Episcopi omnem cultum, licet privatum, amovere, et ab omnibus abstinere, quae indebito cultui proxime aut remote favere possint, juxta exempla a Nobis allata *lib. 2. cap. 8*."—*De Servorum Dei Beatificatione, et Beatorum Canonizatione* (1734–38), IV:1, c.7:20–21, in edition of 1841 (Prati).

35. *Traité dogmatique sur les faux miracles du temps, en reponse aux differens ecrits faits en leur faveur* (1737).

Lerouge's embrace of the apocalyptic figure is, at first glance, astonishing, but only until one recognizes that it serves merely to strengthen the *principle* of the Church's hierarchical authority in judging matters of doctrinal dispute. In fact, Lerouge has no interest whatsoever in examining the "parallel" of scriptural form and the Church's experience, in the sense of d'Étemare. It is simply the *axiom* at work in scriptural prophecy, that the Devil will perform seductive miracles, which Lerouge quarries for his purpose. And if the Devil "will," then at least the Devil "can." And if the Devil "can," then there is no basis upon which to turn to miracles now for any purpose other than corroborative of what the official Church has already taught. Making more precise, and inclusive, Languet's dispensational thinking on miracles, Lerouge sets the whole of the Church's history, after Apostolic times, in "the last days" of the Antichrist preceding Christ's Second Advent. If miracles were ever supportive of teaching before this time, they are so no more, but serve in this function only to seduce into error.[36]

Two affirmations about *pneumatica* are bound up with this claim: that miracles are susceptible to demonic agency, and that only the fulfillment of prophecy has any religiously evidential value. First of all, then, Lerouge must argue for the possibility that "true" miracles, in their phenomenological integrity, may be performed by demons. As we shall note later, this alleged demonic capacity for miracles proved an issue of enormous importance for Appellants, and one with which they take serious issue. And what is at stake in this particular element of the debate is the epistemological character of historical "facts" themselves — of human experience in its obdurate confrontations with phenomena — and, by extension, their receptivity for divine orchestration within figural coincidence.

Lerouge, like others attending to the question, turns to Aquinas's ambiguous definition of the miraculous for support of his position.[37] A "true" miracle, we are told, is "properly" attributed to God alone, since such an occurrence is understood as that which surpasses the forces of created nature and can therefore be enacted only by nature's divine Creator Himself. Since even Satan is a creature, he cannot perform "true miracles" in this sense. But, like angels, demons exist within an order of nature beyond human experience. Thus, says Thomas, it is "possible" to call something a "miracle" in a more general way without transgressing accepted semantic bounds, insofar as one refers to any event that "surprises" human cognitive faculties and stands beyond our natural capacity to understand and explain. Miracles thus broadly defined can and indeed *are* performed by demons.

Lerouge emphasizes here that, from the perspective of limited human apprehension — "in relation to us"[38] — there is nothing intrinsic to an

---

36. Ibid., 85ff.
37. Ibid., 75ff. Thomas discusses this in the *Summa Theologiae* 1a 114:4.
38. See Lerouge, *Traité dogmatique*, 17f.

event, "super"-natural only with respect to human experience, that can allow its divine or demonic origins to be distinguished. Further, Scripture itself teaches us that such fundamental confusion in the quest for attribution is demanded by the very purposes of God in history: Satan can seduce, especially in the Last Days, only if his works themselves bear a character capable of seducing. If God is indeed to punish people through such seductions — the general interpretation of biblical texts touching on the "blinding" of the Jews or the hardening of unbelievers' hearts — it can only be because such seductions are, from a human point of view, convincing. In fact, Lerouge goes so far as to assert, on the basis of Matthew 24:22ff., that what for all intents and purposes are "true miracles" will be more numerous and persuasive in their demonic form than in their divine form when the End finally comes upon us. Does not Jesus Himself tell us that some will be saved, *not* by discerning the "true" from the "false," nor by receiving from God convincing evidence of the truth (e.g., "stronger" miracles) over against the false, but for the sole reason that "God will cut short those days for the sake of the Elect"?[39]

Surrounded by such demonic prevarications, Christians must seek guidance from somewhere other than the miraculous, as they stumble through the shadowed hedges and ditches of history's disintegrating byways. Lerouge himself, in the course of his work, must finally let go of the logical pretension to miracle's probative value in general, even in the case of Jesus' own career, and the lines to his previous demarcation of apologetic dispensations fritter in a blur. To be sure, the actual *occurrence* of divine miracles, both past and present and of Jesus in particular, is never questioned, just as against Protestants Lerouge must insist on the genuinely divine origins of Roman Catholic prodigies.[40] But because he has already argued that God seduces individuals and whole peoples "mysteriously" and "secretly" through the instrumentality of demons,[41] the Christian Church's (and within it the Roman Church's) claims to divine miracles cannot be supported simply by an appeal to phenomenal self-evidence. The "facts" are intrinsically obscure, and history itself reveals, through the number of its incredulous children, that even the works of the Son of God cannot be properly identified on the basis of their own character. As Lerouge then reaches for some evidential measure of divine truth, including Christ's teaching, that lies beyond miracles, he is led along to his second main proposal: if we are to recognize God's side in the endless dispute among human beings over His will and wisdom, then we must look especially to the evidence of prophetic fulfillment.[42]

Lerouge here follows a tendentious reading of Augustine's famous apologetic letter to Volusianus (Ep. 137) and points out how, even in the case of Jesus, miracles could not plainly convince anyone of His divine

---

39. Ibid., 203ff.; 272ff.
40. See ibid., 244ff.
41. E.g., ibid., 203ff.
42. See ibid., 309ff.

mission because either their indistinguishability from pagan miracles —
e.g., in healing — or their completely unexpected and extraordinary character — e.g., his own Resurrection and Ascension — rendered them
unbelievable as uniquely divine works. The only universally persuasive
avenues of proof, according to Lerouge's interpretation of Augustine, are
the predictions of Scripture themselves, fulfilled in history and available
for all to examine.[43] We should recognize, however, that Augustine himself assigns persuasive distinctions in phenomena to the allocation among
people of "belief" and "unbelief," implicitly directed by God. Lerouge, on
the other hand, concludes from the different stands of faith adopted by
men and women in the face of Jesus that we must logically posit an
independent edifice capable of guarding these testimonies to the Christian claims for divinely ordered history through the prophecies, an edifice
that can only be the Church, guaranteed of infallible judgments amid
competing teachings.

Lerouge's elevation of prophecy's probative value over miracle has, in
fact, little practical power when applied to the divisions of the present.
He will say, for instance, that demonic miracles are predicted for the Last
Days, miracles designed to lead people away from the Church and en-
mesh them in false teachings.[44] Ought we not to view Appellant miracles
with such an expectation and under such a judgment? But the referents for
such predictions, as Lerouge himself realizes, are not immediately obvious
and can just as easily be located on opposite sides among the competing
parties. In fact, prophecies themselves cannot carry convicting weight, in
the same way that miracles cannot, without the adjudicating authority
of the Church to point the way. For just as demons can work miracles,
so can "false" prophets offer "true" predictions, in order to make effective their seduction.[45] The attempt to disengage miracle and prophecy as
pneumatic phenomena of different orders simply fails in the face of their
common human receptions. Lerouge's argument must ultimately end its
search amid many gropings for stability, at a demand that the Church's
teaching authority be preeminently critical in the realm of experience,
where no other means for certainty is available. Where shall we discover
the Truth? Who will pull us from the net of delusion that is cast at us
from every side of experience through the power of the Devil? "The authority of the Church alone, therefore, can guarantee the people's safety
from seduction."[46] The Holy Spirit fires the light of this necessary beacon.
Still, it is a desperate claim. For, if the Church can err in matters like the
bull *Unigenitus*, as Appellants insist she has, then "there is no more God
and no more Church; the promises are empty, and the Gates of Hell have
finally prevailed."[47] And so, while at one level of discussion, Lerouge can

---

43. Ibid., 409–15.
44. See ibid., 272ff., and 420ff.
45. See ibid., 17f.
46. Ibid., 247.
47. Ibid., 295.

lift up the Scriptures as the residence of knowledge, and even prophecy as the ordering form to history, he cannot dare even to trust these apart from the Church's official interpretation of their meaning. Although, in the Last Days, Elijah will return to teach people the true meaning of the Scriptures, we are told that he too will be put to death. This can only happen because of the intrinsic ambiguity of his own pedagogical referents.[48] All would be swept away, were there no visible Church to cling to among the gloomy conflicts over otherwise unglimpsed lights.[49]

Lerouge thus offers a reburnished version of an old anti-Protestant Counter-Reformation polemic, but now it is aimed at members of his own communion and recast into the eschatological framework of his opponents' writings. The recasting, however, is significant precisely in its rejection of any figurist basis to the predicted future of confusion: because the visible Church must remain immune from error — and visibly so for the sake of the Elect — neither can she conform to the painful and visible rending of her Master's own body. The figurist scheme of Christian apostasy, Jewish conversion, persecution, and End is reformulated in terms of a simple and continuous opposition between the official Church and the impostures of the Antichrist, whose seductive miracles and teachings will mimic Christ's own and draw away the Jews from the beginning. The Church remains steadfastly true, while the Jewish nation remains steadfastly unbelieving until their final confrontation with the Lord. Whereas the *figuristes* insisted on the figural continuity of Israel in Christian history, Lerouge maintains their traditional incompatibility in order to preserve the Church from the pain of Israel's scriptural disfigurement.[50]

The demonization of miracle, then, is bound to a fear of history's confusions. Lerouge must accept the "facts" of miracles and of their strange receptions. But more than and prior to this facing of the facts, he must first guard some clearing in the fog, untouched by the distresses of competing claims and failing tactics of persuasion. Having thus ranged the Church against the world and separated out the nature of experience for these two realms, Lerouge turns on Appellancy as a threat to inundate the former by the latter. He refuses to trust, as his opponents do, in a flood whose current might rush the other way. Only with this opposition set, and only within the context of an underlying trembling at history's self-promotion, can we begin to understand the vehemence of Lerouge's ilk arrayed against the supposed "atheism" of Appellant claims to miracle.

If, according to Lerouge's summary case in the introduction and conclusion to his work, we are to follow the Appellant line of argument, we will surely end in a position destructive of both Truth and Church.[51] His charges here are internally contradictory, as well as opposed to several

---

48. See ibid., 383ff. and 272ff.
49. Ibid., 248–51.
50. Ibid., 369ff.
51. See ibid., the "Avertissement" and 386ff., 417ff.

of his main points in the course of the volume, yet their common focus reveals the kind of anxiety that informs the treatise as a whole. For, in the first place, he says, Appellants dismiss the questioning of miracles on the basis of their "self-evidence," and thereby rule out the possibility of miracles' link to error from the start, thus preempting the exercise of judgment by the Church and encouraging "incredulity" in the possibility of any miracle at all. Second, by accepting as divine miracles what are in fact diabolical miracles, and doing so in the name of the Christian faith, Appellants encourage superstition and thereby open the gates to Satanic seduction. Finally, by endlessly debating the miracles, Appellants destroy any trust in the certain conclusions of discernment and any hope of true knowledge, and consequently encourage scepticism. There is a sense expressed in these tangled accusations that Appellancy is felt to represent too closely the troubled tides of the age, to cling too strongly in its religious apologetic to the rock of fideism, and somehow to place in question the capacity of a flailing Church to reach above the rising surf of unbelief. Both in its willingness to struggle with its claims and — seemingly at odds with this openness to contest — in its assertion of "invented faith," of grace given and found as part of the self-evident "facts" of experience, stumbled upon and tripped over, Appellancy painfully — mistakenly? — reminds Lerouge of the mysterious, inexplicable, and inescapably contradicting character of God's self-giving in the world.

Bruno Neveu has suggested that the seventeenth- and especially eighteenth-century quarrel over "infallibility" among Jansenist and anti-Jansenist parties with respect to the Five Propositions and *Unigenitus* as a whole missed the mark on what the papacy was actually pursuing in its magisterial pronouncements on the matter. Both groups focused "positivistically" on issues of *fait* and *droit*, according to which infallible judgments could be recognized only within certain strict limits, if at all, while Rome herself understood her teachings more as "intuitive pneumatic" judgments about the "occult" significance of dogmatic attitudes and propositions unrestricted by the details of "authorship," "intent," and so on.[52] But it seems from concerns like Lerouge's that the debate over miracles signals less a *crépuscule* [twilight] of pneumatological inquiry — Neveu's claim — than it does a profoundly differing understanding of pneumatic experience itself, where precisely the issue of its "occult" basis thrust inquiry into opposing areas of concern: the integrity of the Church in its independence from historical pressures (Lerouge et al.) or the figure of divinely ordered history in its coincidence with ecclesial form (figurist Appellancy). In one case, the character of the Holy Spirit informs the functions of the Church's resistance or leadership in a world whose integrity is identifiable apart from her; in the other, the fate of these functions, like

---

52. Bruno Neveu, "Juge Suprême et Docteur Infaillible: le Pontificat Romain de la Bulle *In Eminenti* (1643) à la Bulle *Auctorem Fidei* (1794)," in *Mélanges de l'École Française de Rome*, 93:1 (Rome, 1981), 221, 258ff.

the rest of the Christian life, reflects a set of forms already given universally to the world in the figure of her God and in connection to which the Holy Spirit can only be recognized in conformity with the expressions offered in His own self-giving.

## Miracles and the Figure of Their Inefficacy: The Figurist Counter-Argument of Colbert

We remember that Colbert had initially defended the miracle of Mme. Lafosse on the basis of its apologetic "triumph" over the enemies of the Christian faith, enemies in the service of the same "incredulity" and ultimate "atheism" which he himself was eventually accused of abetting by acknowledging the Church's own formative vulnerability to its ravages. As the number of miracles increased with Saint-Médard and their rejection by Church authorities and non-Appellants moved on apace through a progressive demonization of convicting experience, Colbert's arguments on behalf of the healings abandoned religious apologetic altogether and instead turned to an explication of the coincidental character of the Church's life and God's figural construal of human history as a whole. In doing so, he embraced positively the continuum of experience that people like Languet and Lerouge consigned to deceitful ambiguity. By insisting, on the one hand and as always, on the adequacy of traditional types of evidence within this continuum, but also charging, through their figural location, the epistemological query surrounding miracles with impotence, he thereby transposed ambiguity into a form of transparent conformity with God's own life of love, even "triumphing" over human sin.

In a pastoral letter dated February 1, 1733, Colbert offered the fully developed figurist version of the miracles, now properly responsive to the critiques of their opponents.[53] As the title suggests — "...au sujet des miracles que Dieu fait en faveur des Appellans" (...on the subject of miracles that God has performed in favor of the Appellants) — there has been no abandonment of the claim to vindication. But from the opening preamble, while Colbert locates the miracles within the contest over *Unigenitus*, he also places *Unigenitus* within the single contest of God's Truth as it struggles throughout history against its detractors:

> My dear brothers, we have been groaning for some time over the evils brought upon the Church by the Bull *Unigenitus*. There is nothing we can see within the space of seventeen centuries that compares to it. Each century has had its own scandal; but the scandal of the Bull appears to us, from whatever perspective one adopts, as the greatest God has ever permitted. It is great in its beginnings. Every century has had a hand in constructing it: *Mysterium jam operatur iniquitatis* [1 Thess. 2:7]. Every saint who has observed some part of it come into existence has been alarmed. It is great

---

53. "Instruction Pastorale au sujet des miracles que Dieu fait en faveur des Appellans de la Bulle Unigenitus," in Colbert's *Oeuvres*, vol. 2, 13ff.

in and of itself. It is no longer the case that one particular error has its partisans within the Church; now it is a whole mass of perverted dogmas that present themselves to us in the most seductive clothing. It is great in the results that it has achieved, so great as to make us tremble.

Within the figure of the Mystery of Iniquity, stretching back at least seventeen hundred years, the miracles will take their place amid a catalogued welter of phenomena announcing God's speech, alongside a bull whose own contours coincide with the comprehensive orchestration of a divinely wrought victory. Together they bear a common testimony:

> How many times and in how many ways has God not already spoken against the Bull *Unigenitus? Multifariam multisque modis olim locutus est* [Hebrews 1]. He has spoken already more than a century before [the Bull's] conception in famous Congregations [i.e., *De auxiliis*]. . . . God has spoken before its conception through bishops' Pastorals, which censured the corrupted advice of today's Casuists [ . . . ] God has spoken before its conception through the well-known Declaration of one of our Assemblies, where it established the opposite doctrine. Over and against the way that the Bull has justified distancing people from reading Holy Scripture, God has spoken through the vigorous attempts of France's most holy bishops precisely to place translations of Scripture within the hands of their people. God has spoken against the Bull from the day of its conception, through the fear and consternation it has caused in every place [ . . . ] God has spoken against the Bull since its conception through the Prophets, the Apostles, the Martyrs, the Confessors, the Doctors, and the Saints of every age and of every century, whose carefully gathered testimony stands as a witness against this horrible Decree. God has spoken against the Bull through His chief ministers [ . . . ] God had spoken against the Bull through the rising opposition of many thousands of Pastors, Doctors, Priests, Religious, and lesser Ministers [ . . . ] God has spoken against the Bull through the sufferings of those servants who have been exiled, banished, imprisoned, afflicted with punishments, thrown out, removed from their benefices, troubled, mistreated, prohibited, deprived of the sacraments, unjustly excommunicated [ . . . ] through the tears of penitents, through groaning, [ . . . ] through astonishment [ . . . ] through shame [ . . . ] through infinite sorrows [ . . . ] through vows [ . . . ] through testimonies [ . . . ] through the many fabricated attempts to accept it, reject it, take it up again, abandon it [ . . . ] through the joy that [the Bull] has caused among the supporters of error, the corrupters of morals, the enemies of the episcopacy and of our sacred liberties: *Dixerunt, Euge, euge* [They have said: Well done! Well done!]. In the same way, God has spoken against the Bull through that mass of writings, satires, booklets, theses, and official statements in which instruction is shamelessly given that, in times past, no one would even dare to have mentioned in the dark [ . . . ]
>
> Finally, God has spoken today against the Bull through miracles and prodigies, whose marvelously clarion voice calls forth the attention of the people, consoles the distressed soul, and sows fear in the camp of the enemy.[54]

---

54. Ibid., 13–14.

Of course, the drift of this magnificent declamation, which rhetorically rises to an explosion of discovery, where Saint-Médard figures in the historical revelation spoken of in Hebrews 1, is in fact to screw their "marvelous voices" into an edifice of repressive fury: next to the witness of blasphemy, they hold together the image of the Truth's disclosure in the world. God's decisive action on behalf of His cause, "on behalf of His servants," has, from the beginning of the exposition, been redescribed in terms of the figurist understanding of the Church's life and fate, subject to the "distresses" of an age — history in its sweep — bent upon her extinction. Miracles evince an *éclat* comparable to the witness of the worthies in Hebrews 11, triumphing in the splendor of "mocking, scourging, chains, imprisonment, stoning, being sawn in two, destitution, affliction, mistreatment": glory.

"Looking to Jesus, the pioneer and perfecter of our faith...." From this subversive flourish, Colbert's pastoral stakes out the familiar territory taken by the figurists: Israel, both in its blessings *and* its woes, is given in the Church's form, and all the promises showered upon her catch their gleam from the circumstances of her embattled and internally riven person. Having reached through Scripture for a range of texts that enclose this vast historical space — e.g., Isaiah 34:4, Joel 2:10, Ezekiel 32:7f, Daniel 8:10, Revelation 6:12, 12:14, etc. — Colbert draws down the prophetic images of nature's own involvement in this shape, her "darkening skies and stars" in the Last Days, and lays them on the Church as if the universe herself conformed to the Apostles' wanderings on the earth, "sounding out to all the lands" (Ps. 19:4/Rom. 10:18) even while being shouted down by unbelievers.[55] No longer does he seek to justify the miracles by their effective functions, defending their origins on the basis of some demonstrated apologetic efficacity. Now merely — although in great detail — does he seek to lay out their place within the *tableau* of the divinely inscribed surface of ordered experience, a whole whose configuration settles around the shapes of divine Mercy and Justice. When Colbert speaks of the "effects" of the miracles, all he means is that their historical location can and, for the Christian, ought to be tested in relation to these given figures.

As for the figure of Mercy, the miracles trace upon the mortal bodies of the diseased an image of the spiritual healing wrought by God in the heart. Associated with the tomb and relics of a well-known Appellant, they demonstrate the pneumatic attachment of God to opponents of the bull and point away from its claim to the Spirit's inspiration. "What a school!" Colbert exclaims: "without books, or writings, or polemical tracts, God instructs thousands of the faithful!" They illumine, touch, and convert those on whom God wishes to have mercy — and the fruit of their power lies before all eyes to see.[56] These "effects" retain all the phenomenal resiliency of traditional evidence, of course, capable of investigation and refutation.

---

55. Ibid., 17f.
56. Ibid., 23–25.

But Colbert sees no reason to press this aspect of his description. For the miracles' very position within such debate already points beyond the particular "graces" they might and do afford to some, and forms a partial element in a larger grace, fully moored in the phenomenal world of its experience, which is only completed by the "evidence" of their rejection. "There is a whole world on whom they [the miracles] produce an entirely opposite effect." Like Paul in Romans 9:2 bemoaning the Jews, Colbert remarks, we feel nothing but sorrow for our own people.

Is it not odd, he asks, that God should choose to multiply the miracles at a time when they would be *most* contradicted by the Church? Had Appellants themselves chosen moments for such blessing, would they not have sought them at the precise period of the bull's initial promulgation, to aid in strengthening opponents to its teaching? But God waited until both sides in the dispute were already taken, showing that the bull itself was part of a divine plan preliminary to some "great event": the display of His justice joined to His mercy, pulling the Church herself into the swirl of a far grander tide of redemption than the brief encouragements to a beleaguered faction (yes, but that too) — "for God has consigned all men," Israel, the Church, the human race, as prelude to a mercy shot even farther than the target of such incredulity. This is Bossuet's and Duguet's vision of a "universal history" and Christic "mystery" now imploded upon the tiny cemetery of a Paris neighborhood.[57]

By discerning the pressures of a governing figure whose shape enacts the range of responses to the miracles, Colbert overleaps the impasse faced by a Lerouge in confronting experience fraught with a seemingly intrinsic ambiguity. Historical phenomena are seen as serving a common end, with uncertain distinctions in their character deriving, not from the nature of their ultimate causal origins, but from the figural niches occupied by human beings in their apprehension. For this reason, Colbert can attack the accusation that François de Pâris's miracles are really works of the Demon. It is not demonic seduction per se that is ruled out by a figural construal of miracle; after all, Scripture is clear enough about the imminence of such delusions, and they too must form a part of the larger scheme that images the work of Christ. Rather, it is just this holding together of the Truth with its enemies into a single form that displaces confusion's agency from the character of events onto the human heart and reason, molded by belief or sin; Jesus, the Incarnate Lord, is unambiguous, except as rendered in the eyes of concupiscence, and even there, the form of God is unfettered in its explicit brilliance, if now received as a light that blinds.

Whatever demons do, then, cannot be called a "miracle," writes Colbert, leaning on the other side of Aquinas's famous definition; for only God can bring to pass something that outstrips the capacities of created nature, such as healing the incurable or raising the dead. But if, as Languet

---

57. Ibid., 25ff.

and Lerouge had argued, human reason has only a limited grasp of these capacities, how could one hope to distinguish the "true" miracles of God from the "tricks of the Demon"? The figurist point, however, is that there can be no muddied realm of apprehension in which the works of God and Satan coexist: a miracle of God, by definition, *is* self-evident just because there exists the broadest difference between divinity and creature, let alone perverted creature, because there exists the most intransigent lines of demarcation in the world that separate the discrete "facts" whose choreography compose the royal providence of the universe's King. If there are miracles, they will be known; conversely, if the devils play, this too is evident.

The imperative for investigation of phenomena, then, stands at the core of the Appellant attitude. Although the world can see that miracles are disputed, this reality lies at the level of a figural discernment that is founded first upon the facts themselves made object of dispute. An examination of these facts will yield their truths; and where this truth is then rejected, this too becomes a fact, one of unbelief, whose clear visage takes its place within the larger form. The a priori dismissal of the miracles, without inquiry, could only strike Colbert as a despairing evacuation from the world of divine facts, a loss of *jouissance* (delight) in the face of God, a deliberate eclipse of the glorious particularities of a Creator's touch. What demons do is discoverable by contrast with the image of the Lord; and the world to Him is subject. Examine, then, the alleged miracles! Bring in the doctors, gather up the testimony, compare the depositions, observe the effects on body and soul. But in all of this, at least trust in the clarity of God's power to invent the facts of history so as to display His self.

The disordered quality of Appellant arguments from such investigative "evidence," their lack of "program" for discernment, is witness to their faith in the inevitability of divine disclosure in the "facts" about the world. Colbert will later publish a set of seventeen "Règles" to aid in such discernment, mostly in response to the more troublesome question of the convulsions.[58] But these easily reduce themselves to four or five, and differ little from the more general and scattered standards he applied to the earlier miracles: Are they associated with sound teaching of the Gospel, with the name of Christ, with the increase of piety and devotion, with sanctity, with virtue? Is their occurrence well-attested by trustworthy witnesses, their form inexplicable by accepted natural causes, their circumstances compelling to the humble and sincere heart? Is Christ glorified and Christian faith strengthened? To questions like these, aimed at Saint-Médard, Colbert believes the answers are clear in the affirmative.[59]

The character of "evidence," in a figural — that is, figured and figurating — world, is, by definition, founded on "reciprocity" of form and

---

58. "Instruction pastorale sur les miracles en reponse à M. l'Archeveque de Sens [i.e., Languet]" (1736), in Colbert's *Oeuvres*, vol. 2, 202–5.
59. See the Lettre Pastorale of 1733, 40ff.

mutual disclosure among phenomena. This corresponds to "the great parallels" apprehended among events and things described by, among others,
d'Étemare's and Fourquevaux's explication of the *figuriste* scheme.[60] There
is an aspect of such evidence, then, that is uncovered through empirical
means. In themselves, events or phenomena are subject to the range of
examining criteria advanced by a given era's frame of "factual" reference:
physical, physiological, historico-critical, medical, etc. And so Colbert and
other Appellant defenders of the miracles make appeal to the various
"positivistic" methods of the day. But such criteria are always relative to
the shifting interplay of "mutual," "proportional," or "comparative" support provided by the range as a whole, by the "elongated perspective" in
d'Étemare's image, that is itself subject to the presupposed "relationship"
between historical event and scriptural form. Thus, the gathering of "evidence" is not strictly an inductive process (nor is it a method of strict
deduction). Governed by what we could call a figural "presumption," evi-

---

60. "Historical parallelism" is, of course, an axiom of figurist practice; see among many
of his works, d'Étemare's *Parallelle Abregé de l'Histoire du Peuple d'Israel et l'Histoire de
l'Eglise* (Liege, 1724), 1ff. which speaks of history in terms of a large *tableau* made up of specific images and discrete details, whose *trompe d'oeuil* particulars disappear into a larger and
different single image when viewed at a distance. (Arcimboldo's sixteenth-century *scherzi*
of "The Seasons" or "The Elements," portraits of human heads made up individually of
fruits, plants, metals, fire, etc. come to mind.) Within this larger image, each particular detail, whole in itself, achieves its purpose only as it "relates" to other details by means of
"proportion" and orchestrated placement: "This is how the person of Jesus Christ and the
events of His life are able to be represented through so many different moments, through
all the great characters and the majority of events in the Old Testament. Other aspects of
how God acts, and sometimes even the outcome to His plans for the Church, can similarly
be represented in summary within particular events" (3). Fourquevaux, in a similar manner, frequently speaks of *l'esprit de comparaison* (the spirit of comparison) as the basis for
all knowledge. See his *Reflexions sur l'Histoire de la Captivité de Babylone* (1727), 3d ed.
(Utrecht, 1735): "this [spirit of comparison] is a source of illumination in all the sciences;
and all the advances we have seen, both in the natural and in the theological sciences, are
due to it [ . . . ] Where does the success of this "spirit of comparison" come from in the sciences? In a word, here is an answer: The sciences have as their object all the different works
of God, whether earthly works or those of a more sublime order. Now the One who laid
out the Heavens with a sovereign intelligence, and who composed within the visible world
a realm of invisible beauty, did so with balance and measure, by imbuing all things with an
admirable proportion. He connected all things through aspects of resemblance, which mark
all His creatures as works of the same Wisdom and as gathered together through hidden
(though real) ties into a unity, despite the infinite variety manifest in them through the divine Wisdom. It is hardly surprising, then, that the more we compare God's works, the more
we discover a proportion among them. Even less surprising is the fact that these proportions
can teach us something: for they represent the traces of Wisdom's hand, which we cannot
come to know without growing in wisdom ourselves, to the degree that our knowledge of
these things itself grows" (pp. iv, viiif.). We should beware of reading too much into the
more metaphysical implications of this Classicist form of aesthetically fueled reflection. As
we have noted earlier in our discussion of *figurisme,* the governing category for *l'esprit de
comparaison* is an understanding of scriptural form, as depicting the reality of Christ, in its
relation to historical phenomena: "Holy Scripture contains its own account of these precious
works. And do we doubt that [Scripture] will not, therefore, have left us traces by which to
grasp this proportion? After all, it is Scripture that invites us so urgently to admire and
meditate upon them? [ . . . ] What we have just said already gives us many reasons why we
ought to study Scripture and the history of religion with that taste for carefully discerning
relationships [between things]" (p. x).

dence assumes the proportion between observed facts and a limited set of scriptural forms, the rigorous relating of which according to the governing figure of Christ, precludes major lapses into the arbitrary (an assumption clearly rejected by the *anti-figuristes*).

Colbert, therefore, attempts to avoid the hierarchy of evidences and probative criteria that opponents impose upon Christian disputes — and that was implicitly assumed by Appellants in the earlier stages of the polemic — by relating miracles, doctrine, conversions, sanctity, and other traditional standards in terms of "mutual" and "complementary" evidence. Miracles alone do not "prove" doctrine and sanctity such as François de Pâris's any more than articulated doctrine alone can determine the status of observed "facts." Since, in fact, the dispute over *Unigenitus* involves not simply the formulation of dogmatic principles, but the character of the Christian life, its moral imperatives, its form of witness, the nature of its Scripture's authority, and the properties of divine testimony in history, Colbert insists that each of these elements must be studied, not only on its own terms, but in their mutual "proportion," the synthetic clarity of which alone can provide a compelling argument for particular discernments. Since Appellants *can* "prove" their doctrine by the Bible's teachings, by the people's acceptance of its truth and their submission to it, by the occurrence of miracles associated with its defense, and by the witness of incontrovertible sanctity through penance in its adherence, and since each of these elements themselves, once elucidated singly in their discrete character, can "prove" themselves by their "mutual" conjunction and relation to the others, and since, finally this very proportionality of associative evidence can be discerned within a composing figure enunciated in Scripture's historical recitals and their inter-signification, *therefore* it is proper to speak of the entire shape of the episode, of each of its parts, including the miracles now, as a divine *demonstratio,* the embattled *Causa Dei* as its own ostensive evidence.[61]

Only such a figural demonstration can avoid the charge of circularity in claiming for itself as evidence the reality of its lack of persuasion. For just such a set of mutual empirical confirmations, bound to a figured and figurating form, must and does contain the observed facts of its own rejection, especially when that form is located within the inescapable figures of scriptural discourse and its referents. So offensive to Languet and his company in their forceful attempt to place a distancing ditch between the Church's purity and the muddying filth of the surrounding world, Colbert's demonstration required of the Church and world a common implication in the ordered division of humankind into belief and incredulity. For Lerouge, the presence of the ditch itself offered a sole and necessary apologetic approach to the confusions of experience outside the Church, careful and balancing in its passage. For Colbert, however, the joining of the Gospel and its rejection within a single figure, and one in which the

---

61. See Colbert's 1733 "Instruction pastorale," 43ff.

Church participated and which she embodied in her own integrity, offered the *éclat* of God's very present form. This figural conjunction was
itself a proof before and in the universe for which apologies were useful
only as passing, if observable, phenomena of practice. With the speaking
of the Truth, however articulated, in writing, in virtue, in preaching and
in healing, in word and miracle, will come obscurity and blindness. Together, they form the immovable figures lived by Jesus as He died in love
for sinners. The Cross shouts from the events of the Church's life within
the world. But just because of the divine depths from which it cries, its
unacknowledged echo forms the realm from which the towering image
of God emerges. God answers the bull with the "eloquence of fact, not
words," Colbert remarks, quoting Augustine. And the facts themselves?
He adds to these a verse from Job: "Here is but a small part of his doings,
here is but the whisper of his voice; who dares to contemplate the thunder
of his full magnificence?" (26:14, Knox trans.).

The effect of Colbert's overall approach, which remained the virtual
standard for all other Appellant defenses of the miracles, was, ironically,
to diminish logically their role in the *Causa*, relative to the cumulative
circumstantial evidence of the larger historical figure in which the debate
was taking place. With respect to pneumatology, the distinction of causal
origins, whether demonic or genuinely divine, while not rendered irrelevant, was elided with the practice of figural discernment. The result of this
was that traditional pneumatic categories — i.e., those of the *gratiae gratis
datae* — were ignored in discerning the miracles in favor of the synthetic
affirmations of the Spirit's figural authority, an authority visible, not so
much in phenomenal "marvels" or particular actions, however much these
are involved, as in the bare coincidence of scriptural and historical form.
D'Étemare describes this resultant pneumatological locus — and systematic reduction — for instance, when he speaks of the figurist practice of relating Israel and the Church historically through their scriptural paralleling:

> Let us assume that Scripture has been dictated by an all-knowing and all-
> seeing Spirit: who could doubt but that this divine Spirit has prepared for
> His Church consolations and teachings? And that He has done so by join-
> ing together, as the basis for teaching us, figurative events, which, over a
> distance, can have no proper proportion except with similar events given in
> the history of the Church? The only thing left to do, then, is to work hard at
> discovering the lengths to which God has wished to carry such similarities
> [*ressemblance*] and has desired to depict the history of one people in that
> of another. We must do this, however, by attempting, on the one hand, to
> follow these similarities organized by God's Spirit as far as possible, while,
> on the other, by trying hard to avoid falling into error by, for instance, dis-
> cerning similarities where the divine Spirit did not put them, or by rejecting
> them, however clearly we may have noted them already, because they did
> not go as far as we might like or were not sufficiently exact in chronological
> terms or given in the manner our imaginations would have preferred.[62]

---

62. *Parallelle Abregé,* 4–5.

The way, in a typically run-on and grammatically elaborate paragraph like this, that both historical experience and scriptural form merge as semantic referents, and that the Holy Spirit as omniscient author of an instructive text in particular becomes transposed into the very agent of historical conformity outside of the text, exemplifies the framework in which pneumatic events claim authority, precisely as pneumatic, only in their equalized juxtaposition with any number of other events along a plane defined — and authored — solely in terms of scriptural *ressemblance.*

Colbert's argument, then, had a strong effect on other Apellant apologists particularly in encouraging an accepted diminution of the miracles' vindicating role on behalf of the movement. In general, we find similar appeals to the figure of Justice and Mercy which, following Pascal via Colbert, are viewed to determine exclusively the experiential contours of the miraculous as particular pneumatic disclosure, and to limit its amplitude as divine phenomenon.

In conjunction with and dependent upon this typically *figuriste* application, we find Appellants attacking the notion of demonic miracles advanced by Languet, not only by appeal to the divinely self-evident distinctions between divine and creaturely works, but also through exegetical rejections of the Church/Antichrist opposition so strictly upheld by ecclesiastical apologists like the bishop of Soissons and by Lerouge. Dominique-Marie Varlet, for instance, follows this tack by relying on the figural ecclesiology of Appellancy that insists, in Augustinian fashion, on the "mixed" character of the Church through history.[63] This *corpus mixtum* of sinners and elect that composes the Church accounts for the possibility of error within her life. On the one hand, Varlet will argue against Protestants that such error does not compromise the divine promise of the Church's infallibility, but rather reflects an aspect of her historical conformity to the contested image of Christ over time.[64] On the other hand, his appeal to the *corpus mixtum* serves, not so much to deny the special historical evils of seduction reserved to the Endtimes, as to extend their character temporally — and thus figurally — into the continuous life of the Church from her inception, and to locate their power *within* her bounds, and not exclusively without. Priests and bishops — even the pope! — can, have been, and will be seduced throughout the Church's life (see the case of Pope Honorius and the Arians), and therefore the rejection

---

63. See his many writings on the subject. Varlet, a missionary in North America who was later appointed bishop of Babylon, was involved in supporting the struggling Catholic Church in Holland and finally, suspended from his duties, became embroiled in the "schismatic" Church of Utrecht. An ardent Appellant in contact with other leaders of the movement like Colbert and Soanen, Varlet penned a number of widely read defenses of the miracles in the form of letters, e.g., *Lettre de Monsieur l'Evesque de Babylone, aux Missionnaires de Tonquin* (n.p., 1734), *Lettre de Monseigneur l'Evesque de Babylone a Monseigneur l'Evesque de Montpellier Pour servir de réponse à l'ordonnance de M. l'Archevêque de Paris, rendue le 8 Novembre 1735 au sujet des miracles opérés par l'intercession de M. de Pâris* (Utrecht, 1736).

64. Varlet, "Lettre de Monseigneur l'Evesque de Babylone a Monseigneur l'Evesque de Senez" (on P. Courayer), 72ff.

of both true doctrine and divine miracles within the Church on the part of her leadership is hardly astonishing. Figurally, Antichrist is a continual threat, even as his wiles are obviously unmaskable to those within the single Body of Christ chosen for eternal life.[65]

The importance of this last, more specifically ecclesiological move that is taken together with its figural principle is to relegate particular pneumatic actions, however refulgent and convicting in their specificity, to the same signifying plane as their demonic contrasts. Now both, as a phenomenological ensemble, participate in the single figural formation of the Church's historical experience in a way that shifts the weight of her traditional pneumatic guarantees away from the pneumatic acts themselves — although these are by no means either denied or invalidated — and onto their coordination with other phenomena, including the antichristian, in embodying scriptural shapeliness. A space, conceptually at least, has been cleared within the Holy Catholic Church for the pneumatic explosion of confusion, dispute, division, violence, and rejection. This space, indeed, forms the arena for the convulsions that soon proliferated.

We might summarize the line of argument we have observed thus far as follows: if truth is demonstrated in *faits sensibles*, if the Cross epitomizes such demonstration, and if the Church's life derives from and continues it, then the very character of divine evidence is reformulated in terms of ostensive prods toward the contradiction that hangs on the opposition of belief and unbelief within the ecclesial communion itself. That the miracles of Saint-Médard took on the *appearance* of convulsionary phenomena in the 1730s, then, is, from the figurist perspective anyway, a reasonable outcome to the miracles' own sensible logic. To admit this, however, is already to link the convulsions to the *ostensio Spiritus* of Appellancy in an intrinsic way, something few subsequent theologians have done. In any case, the grammar of this outcome will now form the object of our section's final chapter, as we pursue the fate of pneumatic "evidence" construed prophetically, demonstrated phenomenally, and articulated pneumatologically.

65. Ibid., 58f. See also, "Lettre Contre les Dissertations choisies du P. HONORÉ, touchant la seduction genérale, pour servir d'apologie aux Lettres adressées à M. de Soissons" (1727), in *Lettres d'un Ecclesiastique de Flandres, a M. l'Evêque de Soissons* (n.p., n.d.), esp. 249–67. See also "Lettre de Monseigneur l'Evesque de Babylone a Monseigneur l'Evesque de Montpellier; Au sujet de l'Instruction Pastorale de M. l'Archevêque de Sens [i.e., Languet] contre les Miracles de M. de Pâris, &c" (1734), in *Ouvrages Posthumes de Monseigneur l'Evesque de Babylone; Où il est principalement traité des Miracles contre M. l'Archevêque de Sens* (Cologne, 1743), 41ff.

*Chapter Eleven*

# MIRACLES, FIGURE, AND THE HOLY SPIRIT

## The Pneumatic Appearance of Rejection

### The Miraculous Figure of Rejection: Carré de Montgeron and the Convulsions

If structures of theological commitment could ever give rise to practical demonstrations of faith that might be called "inevitable," then the convulsions of Saint-Médard ought to be so designated.[1] Just as it is inappropriate to view *Figurisme* as a millenarian form of compensatory Appellancy, so too would it be to label the convulsions that began in the early 1730s and continued after the cemetery's closing as a compensatory form of figurist miracle, desperately reactive to the failure of a cause. The necessary and positive link between the miracles and the convulsions was stressed by both proponents and adversaries of the latter, to the point even that many original supporters of the Saint-Médard healings who could not stomach the new developments of the convulsionaries ended by feeling forced to deny the first prodigies they had earlier so warmly accepted.[2] We need not belabor once again the point made in a prior chapter, that historians prone to attribute the unusual phenomena of both *figurisme*'s theological extravagance and Saint-Médard's experiential display of the marvelous to

---

1. I state this in as bald a way as possible, realizing my open violation of a principle of judgment on the convulsions held by almost all modern scholars from Dedieu (and even earlier, Sainte-Beuve) onward, who have tried to spare Jansenism the theological embarrassment of Saint-Médard. Obviously, opponents to Appellancy, from their own perch of hostility, have always thought otherwise.

2. The lines of debate, often bitter, among Appellants on these matters are still confusing to the historian, in large measure because polemical pamphlets and books were published or circulated anonymously and only sometimes granted openly accepted authorship. This allowed for participants in the controversy to adopt shifting positions as they deemed strategically appropriate. Further, pertinent correspondence remains voluminous, unedited, and scattered. Among well-known Appellants supportive of the convulsions were the bishops Colbert, Soanen, and Caylus; those clearly opposed were Bidal d'Asfeld, Besoigne, and Petitpied. Individuals like d'Étemare and Boursier held somewhat ambiguous positions, trying to conciliate factions, but tending to side with the convulsionaries, at least until the extent of some of their practices became notorious; as a result, the two of them attracted attacks from almost all parties. Many participants, in a manner more pronounced than these two, began on one side of the debate, but drifted to the other in the course of its development and the evolution of the convulsions.

the forces of psycho-social reflex fail to appreciate the apposite congruence, self-conscious in its percept, of religious reflection and event from the perspective of participants and observers. In this case, the clearing of the pneumatic ground, made possible by the figural construal of miracle, allowed for its transformation into a threshing floor for purely figural phenomena unhinged from the constraints of the traditionally functional charismata. In as tight an identification as possible, corporal experience in the convulsions became a cipher for scriptural form, the culminating testimony both to the historical range of its determinations and to the weight of its redemptive impression upon the back of human mortality.

We have already had occasion, near the beginning of this study, to touch upon the work of Louis-Basile Carré de Montgeron.[3] Without question, Montgeron's writings proved to be the most famous apology for the miracles of Saint-Médard and for their subsequent association with the convulsions. It was a vast work devoted entirely to the marvels, composed by a self-confessed "libertine" lawyer who had been sensationally converted at de Pâris's tomb. Montgeron wrote and published the last two volumes while he was in prison, arrested for his bold advocacy of the miracles and for violations, in the process, of parliamentary etiquette. As a whole, and especially the first volume, his *opus* reached educated audiences not only in France but throughout Europe, touching people who were otherwise ignorant of or impervious to the more purely theological debates about these matters being waged among Church leaders. The story of Montgeron's astonishing and indecorous approach at Versailles of Louis XV's person in 1737, presenting to him by hand the dedicated first volume of his work along with a small harangue on the miracles and the plight of Appellants, and of his subsequent incarceration until his death seventeen years later, gave to the work itself a scent of drama that intrigued observers and defenders of Saint-Médard alike.[4] British readers from afar, like Hume and Douglas, for whom the episode of Saint-Médard formed a touchstone for the philosophical discussion of miracles, relied on Montgeron's presentation of the facts; contemporary scholars themselves continue to see his arguments as somehow typical of an evolved "Enlightenment" approach by Christians to the supernatural;[5] art historians still consider the large folio volumes, ornamented with beautiful engravings by Jean Restout of healings and the *grands secours* [the "great

---

3. *La Vérité des Miracles opérés à l'intercession de M. de Pâris et autres Appellans, démontrée contre M. l'Archevêque de Sens* (Utrecht, 1737); *Continuation des démonstrations des Miracles Opérés à l'intercession de M. de PARIS et autres APPELLANS. Observations sur l'oeuvre des Convulsions Et sur l'état des Convulsionnaires*, 2 vols. (n.p., 1741–48).

4. See Kreiser, *Miracles, Convulsions, and Ecclesiastical Politics in Early Eighteenth-Century Paris*, 375–89; also Dedieu, "L'agonie du Jansénisme," 203ff.

5. See Jean-Robert Armogathe, "A propos des miracles de Saint-Médard: Les preuves de Carré de Montgeron et le positivisme des Lumiéres," *Revue de l'Histoire des Religions*, 87 (1971): 135–60. In a previous note we had occasion to question Armogathe's thesis in a preliminary way.

relief," symbolic acts of physical violence meant to contain and soothe the convulsions] to be masterpieces of book-production.[6] Montgeron's exposition of the movement from miracle to convulsion, then, is a historically patent example of the theological trajectories underlying the evolution of the Saint-Médard experience, and one which we will now use as our lens for its viewing.

Like that of all Appellants before him, Montgeron's purpose in defending the miracles is explicitly based on his conviction of their evidential value for the *causa.* This attitude is summed up in the dedicatory epistle to the king that opens the work. From the outset, it is important to note that the new "positivistic" posture a scholar like Armogathe attributes to Montgeron's apology is coherent with the sensibilities toward the "epiphanic" character of the miraculous that we identified in earlier Jansenists. His voluminous gathering of "evidence" on the miracles' behalf, in the manner of the official legal inquiry that never took place, is self-consciously derived from a faith in the nature of divine Truth as God's "Eternal Wisdom" (see Proverbs 8), whose being is grasped through her own self-expressing *éclat,* like the sun's rays, "living images of the Deity." While Montgeron seeks to offer the King "incontestable proofs" for the authenticity of the miracles, this is only because the miracles themselves participate in this sapiential brilliance. The empiricist quality of his initial project, then, is less a reflection of an era's intruding naturalism than it is of a traditional attitude toward the pneumatic expression of glory within history.[7] Still, within this realm of expression, the miracles can testify to the Truth as "positive" elements of reality. Since their divine purpose is *instruction* and *illumination,* they embody the kind of persuasive forces coincident with the character of human reasoning in a sensible world. If the "enemies" of the miracles pursue their nefarious mission only through attempts at suppressing the "witness" of the "facts," Montgeron's strategic response will simply be to marshal and publicize these unimpeachable evidences.[8] The power of "evidence," in such a project, depends simply on the inevitable efficacy of divine self-expression: "No, sire, God has not performed marvels of such brilliance only to let them fall into oblivion."[9]

This is the standard Appellant faith in the probative value of miracles as sensible epiphanies, forms of God's self-witness, to be found, with increasing qualifications, in Jansenist apologists from Pascal and Arnauld to Colbert. But even in his remarks to the King Montgeron inserts a warning whose import subverts a crude understanding of epiphanic "efficacy." Were not Jesus' own miracles rejected by authorities without adequate investigation? Did not this official rejection itself become the cause for the Jewish people's general rejection of the Christ, and therefore for their sin

---

6. See Augustin Gazier, "Restout et les miracles du diacre Pâris," *Revue de l'Art Chrétien* 62 (1912): 117–30.

7. Carré de Montgeron, *La Vériteé des Miracles,* "Epistre au Roy," i–ii.

8. Ibid., xv.

9. Ibid., xiii.

and rejection in turn by God (see John 15:22–24)?[10] Merely exposing the "facts" of the matter, then, while it may promise the conversion of some, confronts a more primary recalcitrance on the part of those in power. Montgeron's plea to the king is also a disguised prayer that the sovereign not be counted among the hard of heart.

The relationship of hardness of heart to "evidence," as it turns out, becomes a leitmotiv of the first volume's amassing of documentation for the Saint-Médard healings. Montgeron picks up previous Jansenist construals of sceptical "pyrrhonism" and links them, in an original way, with his own concerns over the convicting power of miracles. Especially in his "Essai de Dissertation sur la foi due au temoignage" (On faith owed to testimony)," he struggles to deal with the fact of the miracles' rejection in a way that will lead him toward the figural resolution of the problem we have already encountered among other Appellant apologists. Laying out a justification for the large *dossiers* of evidence to follow in his first volume, Montgeron outlines how we "know" things in general and at all. His epistemology identifies three main avenues of apprehension: immediate sense perception, direct revelation from God, and *la foi due au temoignage,* that is, the testimony of others. The use of these three instruments of reason are "divine" or "natural" laws, placed in the heart by God, on the basis of which the full purposes for human life can be pursued, that is, knowing God, loving God, and living in society before God. But since, in fact, these purposes far outstrip the normal appropriations of both sense experience and that of God's direct revelation, the bulk of our movement toward salvation is dependent upon this third "law" of belief in human testimony, the use of which distinguishes us from "beasts."[11] Montgeron cites Scripture for this conclusion, and the initial implication points toward his frequent claim, in the face of Languet and his circle, that proponents of the miracles have all the witnesses on their side and should *by reason* therefore be trusted and accepted.

Immediately, however, Montgeron admits that the persuasive power of testimony in matters religious is fraught with qualifying difficulties, precisely because the issue of "belief" and "unbelief" has come into play. As such, the power of sin to distort, through the passions, the "natural" usage of reason, undermines the human capacity to learn God's truth through the means of testimony. *Le Coeur* (the heart), in fact, is shown to be foundational even to "sense," to "discernment," and to "evidence" in general, with the primary arbiter of knowledge relocated from the simple exercise of natural abilities to the status of the individual's relationship of faith to God. "Pyrrhonism" itself is but the reflection of a more original *incrédulité* (unbelief) governed by sin's perversion of the heart, only the healing of which can provide the framework in which "reason," and especially the

10. Ibid., xiii–xiv.
11. "Essai," 1ff. The "Essai..." is part of the *Vérité des Miracles,* but is paginated separately.

reasoning based on testimony, can do its work.[12] Thus, Montgeron admits that he is taking up a self-contradictory and effectively pointless task, that is, to present the evidence for the miracles to those whose prior unbelief must make them incapable of seeing it for what it is:

> Here, then, is how those who refuse to believe in the present miracles have acted in the past and continue to act. These miracles have come too late for them. They have already made their decisions, they have already committed themselves to things of which they have neither strength nor desire to let go. Unfortunately for them, they see all kinds of advantages in remaining tied to their prejudices, and, looking to the Appellants, they see nothing but the crosses scattered on their way, crosses that fill them with fear. It is true that the miracles disturb them and frighten them. But even before the miracles took place, their heart was already set, and had seduced their mind, so that the brilliance of the evidence was unable to make any impression upon them, given that they had already willingly turned aside from all the proofs of the Truth. Thus, only vainly in their regard does God's voice everywhere resound with thunderous prodigies; for they refuse to hear it and to recognize it, they stop their ears and their eyes — something that is unforgivable in itself, since it is partially in their power to gain some understanding of all this at least through the witness of their senses.[13]

But his arguments are only seemingly self-contradictory and ineffectual, since their consequence, says Montgeron, here echoes the figure from Isaiah 6 and 65, previously alluded to in his use of Romans 10:16f., on *fides ex auditu*, the power of testimony: "Go and say to this people: hear and hear, but do not understand." In figural terms, the efficacy of evidential witness lies, not in its single gift of knowledge, but in its laying bare the set of human hearts toward God, whose position toward and among the "facts" arrange the shape of elected history. This itself is an effect that must be carried through.

The crucial detail for an understanding of Appellancy's unique regard for the evidential centrality of "sensible" phenomena, including miracles, lies in this position that the sensible holds in scaffolding the figural history of the human heart. We have already noted early in our discussion of miracle the way in which Montgeron's description of the healings at Saint-Médard reveal a figural significance in their very corporal details and in the responses taken in their face. In a striking account of his own conversion at François de Pâris's tomb, which stands as the first in his collection of evidences, he effectively uses this personal history as a way of modeling the miracles that follow: the "mysteries" of Christianity — immortality of the soul, divine atonement for sin, the resurrection of the body, eternal life in union with God — are all such as to "shock human reason," so that, on the one hand, *only* miracles could convince someone of the truth of "the Cross's ignominy," while on the other, the physical miracles themselves

---

12. Ibid., 2–5.
13. Ibid., 5.

only point to the fact that, "unless God changes the heart," the sublimity of such truths is unattainable.[14] And as we saw, Montgeron's accounts of the particular bodily marvels wrought at Saint-Médard go no further, but, after the minutiae of their witnesses have been displayed, they give rise to several like figural epiphanies: Mlle. Thibault's healing from paralysis discloses the ills of the Church and their promised remedy;[15] Marguerite-Françoise du Chêne's healing from tumors and bleeding reveals the figure of God's creative omnipotence as pointed to in the opening of Genesis;[16] Pierre Gautier's healing from blindness, and those who scoffed at it, indicates the Triumph of the Truth through martyrdom and the Cross;[17] the Demoiselle Hardouin's healing from apoplexies and paralysis, accompanied now by some convulsions, brings into relief the painful overthrow of atheism's opposition to the Lord,[18] and so on. In every case, the evidence, real though it is — "incontestable proof" — is joined to its own rejection in contestability as a singular witness to the power of God over the hearts of men and women: "But, O my God, what use will the Miracles be to us if You do not also touch our hearts at the same time?"[19]

This figural relativization of evidence, in the form of miracle, leads to an elevation of other forms of figural witness alongside the overtly glorious as inseparable players in this greater testimony to the electing power, the grace, of God. As is hinted at already in the first volume with respect to the healing of the Demoiselle Hardouin, accompanying convulsive agitations at the tomb pointed just to this consequence, wherein the figural aspect of physical phenomena linked to the Saint-Médard episode begins to predominate precisely in the space afforded by the epiphanic obscuring of the miracles' self-evidence:

> Heal our sins, for they have caused the affliction and desolation [of Sion]. Let us be participants in the mercies you have stored up for her. Perhaps those astonishing agitations from which your Servant [i.e., Hardouin] suffered at the tomb of the Blessed Deacon, and even at the foot of your Altar, are figures of the trials through which you wish your Elect to pass before you grant them your peace. May your will be done. Grant us, Lord, not to be ashamed at these trials, to bear them with courage, and to say, along with that holy King: "If this is how you would grant us life, punish us so that we might live" [Hezekiah, in Isaiah 38:16].[20]

When in the second volume, which now discusses the convulsions themselves as discrete phenomena, Montgeron appends a fourteen-page "Prayer," he barely mentions miracle and convulsion, and offers instead an

---

14. "Relation du miracle opéré sur l'auteur le 7 Septembre 1731," 21–23, in *La Vérité des Miracles*. . . .

15. *La Vérité des Miracles*, under "Thibault," 78–82.

16. Ibid., under "Du Chesne," 76ff.

17. Ibid., under "Pierre Gautier," 45.

18. Ibid., under "Hardouin," 24–29.

19. Ibid., "Thibault," 81.

20. Ibid., "Hardouin," 29.

extended depiction of the "contest" of "glory" with the "world," the long process by which the saints are made worthy to stand before the "light of God's light," through suffering. Here, the figurist eschatology of the Church's woes and internal apostasy, her seductions and divisions, her remnant, the promises of Elijah and the Jews' conversion, is given voice as an expression of the larger shape of Christic penitence:

> Ha! What happiness it is, what glory there is in suffering for such a cause! You have taught us, O my God, by the Mouth of Jesus Christ, that *happy are they who are persecuted for righteousness' sake, for theirs is the Kingdom of Heaven. Rejoice then,* He adds [ . . . ] They drew all their strength from the Cross and from the sufferings of Jesus Christ; and to these divine sufferings our own will be joined as well.[21]

All this forms the devotional prelude to the descriptive evidence of new phenomena, in themselves neither clear witnesses to glory nor to sin, except as they are joined in the experience of a rejecting Church. The "Prayer" as a whole, then, is an oddly muted turn away from the direct viewing of the marvels of Saint-Médard, otherwise so relentlessly promoted by Montgeron. And it must seem a strange commentary on their most spectacular manifestations, unless we recognize in this adorative pause a deferral to the subsuming figural character of the episode, wrenching particular moments of astonishment, *frayeur* (awe), incredulity, thanksgiving, bitterness, and boredom before events however judged, into the conformative images of the Savior's Body.

Montgeron himself explains how the convulsions began, and the providential course their experience would take, as a figure of Justice and Mercy.[22] This "mysterious work [ . . . ] that He purposed through His eternal decree" was, in its entirety, "an actual star by which He led a few to salvation, and a stumbling block for a host of others." As with Demoiselle Hardouin, in 1731, several remarkable healings took place at de Pâris's tomb accompanied by physical agitations. These healings began to multiply, but soon gave way to others whose progress was slower and whose effect was less perfect. Montgeron tells us that these "imperfect healings," used by critics as proof of their natural or demonic origins, designated "the slowness of most conversions, which usually do not take place except by degrees and by the soul's convulsions, which do not always heal all of its [the soul's] ills," a reality evidenced by the imperfect reception afforded the original miracles. Further, the convulsions began to occur among individuals who were not ill at all, something that pointed to the obvious divine goal of these new convulsive phenomena in general as lying beyond purely physical miracle. When the cemetery of Saint-Médard was officially closed in January 1732, the convulsions continued, now among worshipers in the church building, sometimes accompanied by physical healings, sometimes

---

21. *Continuation,* vol. 1, "Priere," 13.
22. *Continuation,* ibid., "Idée de l'Oeuvre des Convulsions," part 1, 57–60.

not, but taking place in an expanding circle of people. Montgeron is particularly careful to stress how the social background of those affected began
to shift as well: while in the earliest period, the miracles and convulsions
tended to occur among the educated and the nobility, now a larger and
predominant number touched "the humble folk [*les petits*], the simple,
the idiots," even children, a fact of not inconsiderable figural significance
itself in pointing to the "folly" of God's Wisdom and the favor granted to
the "little ones" of the world and Church.

What Montgeron calls the *deuxième époque* (the second stage) of the
convulsions next unfolds, as groups of Saint-Médardistes begin to meet in
private homes. The Pauline charismata appear for the first time: gifts of
knowledge, preaching, prophecy, and tongues become common, frequently
preceded in the speakers by convulsive experiences, many of which involve dramatic enactments of scriptural narratives or physical movements
prophetic of some future experience of the Church. In a later volume,
Montgeron relates how among these convulsive experiences and prophetic
utterances there gradually developed the practice of the *secours*.[23] Originally, some convulsionaries would seem to suffer enormous physical pain
in the course of their agitations and would ask for relief from bystanders
which, as time went on, included "prophetically" demanded actions of increasing violence to their persons, the result of which would be a return
to physical equilibrium, unaccompanied by marks of the "relief" (*secours*)
imposed upon their bodies. These *secours* included, first, physical pressure
to the stomach or back, then blows, then beatings, and finally punctures,
stabbings, even crucifixions (the so-called *grands secours* or *secours meurtriers*). Most of what was "miraculous" in these episodes, which involved
prophetic utterance and teachings as well, lay in the complete physical
invulnerability experienced by the suffering convulsionary.

The purpose of the convulsions, understood as comprehending the
range of experiences from simple agitation to the *grands secours*, is repeated by Montgeron in a consistent and clear fashion: as a divine *oeuvre*
in general, developing in the manner in which it has over time from the
first Saint-Médard healings to the final private meetings and their persecution by the authorities, the various actions and their fate represent
*simboles sensibles* and *touchantes* of the sufferings and agony of Jesus
Christ, of the woes of His Body, the Church, and of its future experiences of persecution and restoration. The eschatological "pressure" of the
*figuriste* attitude, following Duguet explicitly, makes of the prophetic dec-
larations concerning the coming of Elijah and the Conversion of the Jews
a necessary descriptive outcome to these immediate images.[24] Summarizing previous discussions of this material, Montgeron gives at the end of
his work the following "summary":

---

23. *Continuation* ... (vol. 2), "4e Partie des Observations sur les convulsions, où l'on
traite des Secours violens donnés aux Convulsionnaires et des Miracles qui en resultent,"
4–10.

24. See *Continuation* (vol. 1) part 1, 62ff., 109ff.

So! What is this System? What is this plan of God? This is how I explain it in my First Edition.

1. The work of the Convulsions has as its main purpose to announce the Coming of the Prophet Elijah, whom God has promised to send once the moral teaching of the Gospel has been almost wholly overthrown, and once the foundations of solid piety have been almost wholly destroyed within the midst of the Church herself — in a word, once all things will need to be restored.

2. The reprobation of almost all the Gentiles, once their unbelief and rebellion against the Miracles will have reached the same pitch as the Jews,' just as St. Paul has written in many places in his Epistles, when he describes how the Jews have been rejected because of their unbelief.

3. The sudden conversion of the entire Jewish People, and, through their preaching, the renewal of Religion throughout the world.

In my First Edition, I cite passages from Jesus Christ, St. Paul, M. de Pâris and M. Duguet, which offer proofs for this System.[25]

Montgeron is faithful to Duguet — who for his part rejected the divine origins of the convulsions — in insisting on the paradoxical relation existing between promised restoration of the Church through Elijah's return and preaching and the Church's increasing decrepitude ("in a word, once all things will need to be restored"). Like Duguet, he did not simply see a culmination of woes as the prophetic indicator of an imminent intervention. For although this temporal joining of extremes was similarly stressed as in much traditional millenarianism, the key element of the Jews' expected conversion acted as an extended historical drama, prying apart the easy linkage between travail and escape by inserting a new period of figural struggle for the Church, in which a final conformance between Bride and heavenly Groom might be established within the world before the Second Advent and in a manner always consistent with the scriptural forms of Jesus' redemptive body. If there is a "renewal" (*renouvellement*) of the Church just around the corner, it is one achieved in purity of figural coincidence within a fallen world, at one with the sufferings of the Apostles, a "restoration" of the early Church's martyred witness, not the refashioning of the heavenly Jerusalem come down to earth. To this expectation, the convulsions not only bear testimony in their symbolic gestures, but join themselves in participation:

> The scorn that we see today for the convulsions, for wonders, and even for miracles constitutes a most extraordinary disposition of mind. It is obvious that God permits it, justly, so that the Prophet can be rejected by almost the entire Catholic communion.
>
> The Word made flesh Himself predicted that when Elijah would come *to restore all things,* he would *suffer much, and would be rejected and scorned in the same way as it is written that the Son of Man must be.*

---

25. *Continuation . . .* (vol. 2), 306.

There is nothing, I think, more astonishing than this prophecy of Jesus
Christ.[26]

The very purpose of the miracles and the convulsions, in their particularities and histories, is to figure and be figurated by the Return of Elijah, to
conform to his own future history, to speak with *éclat* and be rejected, to
convert some and confuse most others, to usher in an era for the Church
when she and the world will move more deeply into the inscribed life
of the "Word Incarnate," itself "written" within the texts of Scripture's
prophecies.

The purely *figuriste* reading of prophecy here provides just the space
necessary for a pneumatic transposition away from physical epipiphany
and into providential mystery, as we have described it: miracles and convulsions merge as figural phenomena, whose significance as "spiritual"
testimonies is apprised only in their common mimetic determinations by
scriptural form, rather than in their internal individual character. Historical cause and figural meaning embrace, so that the internal character of
individual phenomena, distinctive though it may be, now becomes "instrumental" in only a secondary sense, forming the means by which God
engages the elective distribution of salvific grace among people:

> The essential difference between what the Prophet will do and what the
> convulsionaries now do lies in this: the Prophet will have much greater
> gifts, and on a very high plane; whereas the convulsionaries have almost no
> gifts at all, except of the lowest order. In fact, they seem to have received
> these gifts only for the purpose of rendering them despised. They have not
> even been used as instruments of God for the sake of performing miracles,
> except for the purpose of degrading those miracles in the eyes of most people,
> who, in our day, are hardly touched by marvels and regard [miracles] with
> an almost incomprehensible insensibility, perhaps because the latter have
> become too common.[27]

In effect, Montgeron suggests that distinctions between authentic miracles
and inauthentic ones, between divine prodigies and those of other origins,
between truly pneumatic and human gifts, distinctions otherwise so important for the Church to make, to regulate, and to act upon, are taken
up in the convulsions and figurally rendered incomprehensible.

Startling in its implications, this transposition allows for the explicit
and complete incorporation and transcendence of the argument from demonization taken from the miracles' (and convulsions') opponents. Call
"demonic" whatever you will in particular within the *oeuvre* — false
prophecies by convulsionaries, shocking displays of violence, occasional
impostures and deceits, schismatic and fanatical hangers-on (and if so,
they must be so called and rejected) — its figural construal demands that
even this indicating and naming be used to the historical glorification of
God. Indeed, the presence of the demonic — the difficult, confusing, and

---

26. Ibid., vol. 1, part 1, 124.
27. Ibid., 130f.

not always obvious presence of the demonic at work within the bizarre effects of convulsionary experience — was properly situated in a divine figure that must conform itself to Jesus' life, satanically abandoned by his own disciples, Peter among them, for the sake of the Cross's bearing up of sin:

> As I have already said, God issued great prophecies through the mouths of very criminal persons, like Balaam (among others),who hardly spoke by the immediate working of the Holy Spirit, since he was, in fact, forced to speak. Furthermore, God can allow the demon to influence the same person upon whom He has Himself just acted in a supernatural way. Jesus Christ rebuked St. Peter as being a "satan" — and therefore someone who spoke through Satan's prompting — almost at the same moment as Jesus declares that the confession Peter had just made of Him as the Christ was itself a revelation of the Father. All the mixture we see in the convulsions is nothing but the mixture of concomitance, which is hardly incompatible with God's work. God does not always completely remake the heart and soul of those upon whom He acts supernaturally, and whom He uses for His purposes.
>
> [ . . . ] I would add this as well: given that an infinity of circumstance clearly shows that God's plan for the convulsions has partly been aimed at using them as a means to bring scorn upon prodigies and miracles, and as a result to lead most of the Gentiles to reject the Prophet, there is every reason to assume that the obscurities here will yet thicken more and more.[28]

Montgeron himself was convinced of the generally divine character of most convulsionary practice. He even defended the *grand secours*, from the beatings to the stabbings, as wholly "religious" actions, in conformity with the Gospel. His was an extreme stance that led, with the publication of his last two volumes, to his gradual alienation from the center of the Appellant movement.[29] But the notion of a *mélange* (mixture) of divine and possibly demonic aspects to the convulsions, articulated in the quote above, became central to most defenders of the convulsions and encapsulates the theological transfer accomplished by Appellancy in general of the traditionally pneumatic into the figural realm. In theory, at least, Montgeron admitted that there existed a "mix" of divine and creaturely phenomena within the larger divine "oeuvre" embodied in the

---

28. Ibid., 133. See also 135.

29. Generally, Montgeron argues that the *grands secours* only transgress "conventional" boundaries of propriety, which are not in themselves reflective of divine law (e.g., when men apply pressure to a convulsive woman's body). To the charge that the *secours* in fact sin against the divine commandments that forbid both killing and tempting God (by applying actions that, in other situations would indeed end in death), Montgeron insists that the *secours* upheld the command of charity, since they are given only at the request of the convulsionary, in an effort to assuage their physical torment; further, they are applied only gradually, at every point testing the degree of the individual's invulnerability, and have, in any case, never resulted in injury or death. The last section of vol. 1 and the whole of vol. 2 of the *Continuation* deal with this issue: "4e Partie: Idée des Secours, mal a propos nommés Meurtriers." See especially vol. 1, 41, 57, 73, 80, and vol. 2, 4–10 for summary discussions. On the divine origin of other elements of the convulsions, see vol. 1, "Observations sur les Convulsions, Deuxième Partie. Idée de l'etat des Convulsionnaires. Du moins jusqu'à la fin du mois de Juillet 1737 [the time of Montgeron's incarceration]."

miracles and convulsions, itself a figure of the *corpus mixtum* of the Church's historical life as Christ's Body. And the very fact of a foundational *mélange* in her phenomenal existence, while it included the possibility of discernment among effects, nonetheless made the actual success of that discernment less important a sign of pneumatic presence than traditionally was the case.

Montgeron is not, as it turns out, consistent in his descriptive attributions of convulsionary experience. At some points in his work, he relies on a figural comparison with St. Paul's Corinthian brethren and their deployment of the charismata: the fact that abuses of these gifts occurred, leading to confusion within the Church, did not lead Paul to urge the rejection of the charismata themselves. "Test everything" and "do not quench the Spirit" (1 Thess. 5:19ff.).[30] To this degree, Montgeron continues to speak of the entire convulsionary phenomenon, as well as of its various particulars, in terms of a "gift" of the Spirit, and the particulars especially, as they correspond to traditional charismata, are singled out as distinguishable pneumatic blessings. But from the start, he labels these charismata — prophecy, glossolalia, teaching — "external gifts," and subordinates them to the general "plan" of the *oeuvre* as a whole.[31] Just as with the miracles, these gifts are open to investigation, and, cumulatively and associatively can serve to identify the nature of their circumstantial and figural location.[32] But more determinative of divine significance, and in a sense more substantive pneumatically because embodying in their ensemble the "mysterious" character of God's plan, are the convulsions themselves, the "agitations," the "ecstasies" and dramatic gestures. These, although generally divine in origin, Montgeron is clear to distinguish from the "particular gifts" of the Spirit:

> The involuntary agitations that are purely derived from the convulsions are neither sins nor do they render sinful. Consequently, it is hardly impossible that God should be their author.
>
> Nonetheless, these forced movements cannot be considered a "gift" either; rather, they appear to be a kind of penitence. Their character is humiliating at best; but they pertain to a supernatural condition that normally comes from God. First of all, God used them as the physical means by which He worked miraculous healings in the plain view of countless people. Afterward, He added to them different gifts; and frequently those most tormented by these violent agitations were themselves, and at the same time, illuminated by a supernatural light. Finally, through a host of prodigies, God declared that the condition of the good convulsionaries was entered under His protection. But let me repeat: these [physical] movements are, in

---

30. Ibid., part 1, 119.

31. See ibid., 24ff.

32. See the "Avant Propos" to ibid., part 2. See Catherine-Laurence Maire, *Les Convulsionnaires de Saint-Médard: Miracles, convulsions et prophéties à Paris au XVIIIe siècle* (Paris: Gallimard/Julliard, 1985), 186ff. on the ambiguity of the convulsionary *inspiration démonstrative*.

themselves and considered independently of the particular graces that often accompany them, rather a trial than they are an act of favor. They are perhaps even a kind of cloud with which God Himself has wished to obscure His works.[33]

Note how Montgeron is careful to qualify even the direct divine origins of the convulsions: it is not "impossible" that they come from God; they are "often" accompanied by divine gifts, etc. That they are, in fact, "perhaps" used by God to "obscure" his own works only renders their intrinsic character less obvious, but also relevant to the discernment of their figural purpose.

And when one realizes, in any case, that the distinction between a "convulsive condition" (*état convulsif*) (which embraces ecstatic speech and gesture, as well as prophecy[34]) and the "convulsive movements" (*mouvemens convulsifs*), (whose progress and group relation themselves constitute prophetic practice) is never hard and fast in Montgeron's mind, the whole theological structure ordering pneumatic graces can be seen as ineffective. This is the case especially, as we have observed, when both *état* and *mouvemens* are phenomenally susceptible to demonic or at least "natural" influence, which itself is open to the manipulations of sin. Montgeron at times defends the convulsions on the basis of their "forced" — i.e., externally caused — quality, just as he sometimes defends the convulsionaries on the basis of their retention of "free will," both conditions, however, being subject to potential perversions.[35] For all the various empirical tests applicable to the phenomena at the hands of, e.g., doctors, in an attempt to identify the nature of the experience as being supernatural, Montgeron will most often fall back upon the *mélange*'s need for figural discernment, a discernment governed by all the same constraints as Colbert's associative scrutiny of contested miracles: What are their results in terms of subsequent moral and religious virtues seen in the convulsionaries and in their companions? What is the relationship between their experiences and the teaching offered in their midst and promoted by their group? What are the experiential connections, historically understood, between the convulsions as a category of phenomena and various other Appellant circumstances? How, finally, can one integrate such events within the figural imperatives of the Church's own mission and prophetic fate?[36] On this score, pneumatic discernment, without losing its imperative in particular instances, gives way to figural perspicacity:

Must we not conclude that all these *Secours*, with the miracles and with what is absolutely supernatural in the Convulsions, are nothing but links

---

33. Ibid., part 3, 1. See also ibid., part 1, 24ff.
34. See ibid., part 2, 16–64.
35. See the opening remarks to ibid., 13ff.
36. See ibid., part 1, 76ff.; part 2, 44–76; vol. 2, part 4, 69ff.

in the same chain of marvels, and that God does not perform them without some plan that is worthy of His wisdom, His justice, and His goodness?

[ . . . ] It is easy to see that God's principal purpose [here] is to announce the coming of the Prophet Elijah to those to whom He wishes to give this grace; and at the same time, to render blind, with respect to this great event, those who deserve it. Their scorn, heaped upon the Convulsions, the true predictions, the prodigies, and the Miracles which constitute this *oeuvre*, will finally be directed at the Prophet, when he appears, and at all the marvels that will reveal his mission.[37]

As with all the Appellant apologies for the miracles, so too with those for the convulsions — Montgeron's defense, with all of its evidences and depositions and arguments from testimony, serves less as a convicting device than as an acknowledgement of the phenomenal basis to the divine Glory's own figurating power in a rebellious and alienated world. Its origin and end lie in the adorative posture of the creature gazing in wonder at the multifarious lights surrounding God's being, refracted as the scriptural forms embodied by the providentially ambiguous marvels of depicting experience. Swept aside by the movement of bodies in time according to these forms, pneumatic experience in itself disappears behind the straightforwardly "visible," behind the "sensible" and "palpable," the "touching" and "moving" (*ébranlante*), as graciously coincident with the scriptural catalogue. Montgeron, therefore, willingly lapses into simple descriptions of convulsionary actions, *tableaux* for the eyes linked to aural images drawn from the Bible, calling bystanders to *attention*, the only pneumatic imperative left with compelling recognizability. It is necessary to get a sense of these descriptions, because they form, ultimately, the verbal flesh of the pneumatic skeleton Montgeron is trying to extract from the *ostensio Spiritus*. Here, for instance, is one highly edited example of many such descriptions of convulsionary *représentations* he provides:

> It is worth noting that convulsionaries will often give spoken addresses prior to stimulating the senses with these edifying images. These talks are so admirable and deeply moving and uttered with a such real kind of force that they are able to affect and touch the most stubborn mind and heart and melt them like ice. I have seen, for example, one of them, holding up a crucifix, and speaking something like this:
>
> "Sinner, behold the enormity of your crimes: for their pardon required that a God should take flesh and suffer the cruelest torture. Listen to your Master, to your Savior, to your God as He speaks to you from the Cross: *I am the Wisdom eternally begotten from the bosom of the Father; I am the consubstantial splendor of His glory: He is made visible in me; through me and for me He has created all things.*
>
> [ . . . ] *It was for you, miserable and shameless creature, that I chose to suffer the cruelest pains; now profit from my blood by taking part in my sufferings. In suffering for you, I did not mean to free you from your own*

---

37. Ibid., vol. 2, 9.

*need to suffer; I did not promise my kingdom to cowards and to the unrepentant. Rather, I only wanted to render infinitely meritorious the work of penitence and every act of endurance performed to please me, to serve me, and to satisfy my righteousness. I take upon myself all the sufferings of my members; I join them to my own, and I present them to my Father as the offerings of His own Son.*

*[ . . . ] Ha! Hurry and profit from my blood; there is still time [ . . . ] Bury your face in the dust, even while you lift your eyes to the heavens. Behold the glory that is mine there: my bliss matches my omnipotence. I am inviting you to yearn after this supreme joy. I am offering you the chance to participate in my happiness, in my glory, and, in a sense, in my divinity. If you wish to reach this goal, therefore, scorn all those empty, frivolous, and vile pleasures that only dissipate, evaporate, and faint away the very moment you begin to experience them; and remember how the only true happiness is that which never ends."*

[ . . . ] Now, not only do the young convulsionaries speak these things with dignity, but they re-present upon their countenances the various feelings that are part of these discourses, in the liveliest and most compelling way, through gestures and through their whole bearing. First, there is the sense of majesty, which then gives way to a sense of compassion; when they speak of the tortures of the damned, they communicate a sense of horror which can be seen in the way they carry themselves; but immediately, as they proclaim the infinite happiness enjoyed by those whom the Son of God will join to Himself, their eyes shine with an almost heavenly joy.

After such addresses, the convulsionary will himself frequently become a living portrait of the passion of Jesus Christ. He will spread out his arms in the form of a cross, completely immobile for the duration of this re-presentation, and the whole attitude of his body will take the form of a crucifix.

His face, now become leaden, is painted in the characteristic details of a living and tender distress, borne with the most heroic patience and perfect resignation, seen now in his dying eyes and in the shuddering of his body.

When he has remained for a long time in this state, the pallor of death completely envelops his face: his dried lips take on a blackened color; his eyes, which are half-closed, seem altogether extinguished; no longer able to hold up his head, it falls on his chest. I have even seen one [convulsionary] who had drawn his tongue back so far into his throat that none of it was visible at all through his half-open mouth. I must also add that we have seen many convulsionaries whose hands, right before the eyes of bystanders, had marks form upon them, sometimes red, just in those places where Jesus Christ's own hands had been pierced by the nails.[38]

---

38. Ibid., vol. 1, part 2, 27–29. Other descriptions follow throughout this section. For an example of the figural significance to be gleaned from an episode of the *secours*, see a transcription of a prophetic account given by "Frère Hilaire," a well-known participant in the *oeuvre*, in vol. 3., 18ff. (The use of special "first names" among the "brethren" attending the convulsions, some of whose discourses were written down and then distributed in pamphlet form, became a distinctive trait of the developed convulsionary movement.) Both Maire's and Vidal's books contain lengthy citations from convulsionary discourses and descriptions of their physical figural enactments.

## The Convulsionary *Mélange*
## and the Figure of the Church

The effect of Montgeron's inclusion of these numerous *discours* and their placement within the described *peintures vivantes* (living paintings), of the convulsions and *secours*, is to attenuate any temptation the reader might have to dissect the phenomena a priori according to some applied criterion. "Attentiveness" is a devotional attitude to be adopted before the "facts," and the notion of the *mélange* is itself less a principle of discrimination to be brought to bear upon the "facts" than it is a simple "fact" of its own, descriptive of this observation. Indeed, a failure to appreciate how the *mélange* is not a regulative framework at all, but only a descriptive one, can easily lead to a perverted assessment not only of the *oeuvre* of the miraculous convulsions as a whole, but more particularly of the phenomenal status of the specific actions and practices that make up the *oeuvre* and in a sense are foundational to its meaning as *ostensio Spiritus.* All parties to the dispute over the miracles and convulsions pointed to some conception of a divine "plan" in order to justify the basis of their evaluative judgments. But the *figuriste* defense made a special appeal to the "facts" themselves as discrete and unadorned phenomena, whose "figural" construal was both possible and even necessitated (in their mind) only through protecting their experiential specificity prior to regulative analysis. The primacy of the *sensible,* the *littéral* [literal], and the *historique* in figurist commentary reflects the almost nominalist presuppositions held by its practitioners that undergirded their faith in divine sovereignty's capacity for figurating creation temporally. The incarnation of the Word, described in Scripture, proposes historical figures as revelatory priorities, but at the same time, such historical forms are given their shape as definable entities whose only common categorical character lies in their creaturely malleability before a configurating sovereign. In themselves, things are simply "what they are," and the attempt to distinguish them essentially in terms of, e.g., their particular pneumatic (as opposed to generally "supernatural" or "demonically natural" or humanly improvised) nature is bound to disengage them from their purely historical and thus primary figural moorings.

Montgeron frequently confuses matters in just such attempts, by trying to delineate in the wake of similar convulsionary defenses the nuances in pneumatic influence and epiphany of "divine instincts" leading to convulsionary speech, for instance, and to the outright "inspiration" of the prophets.[39] But on the whole, apologists for the convulsions like Montgeron inevitably fall back from such conceptual experiments, and like d'Étemare, content themselves with the presentation of that which is "plain":

---

39. This is the explicit burden of his arguments in the whole second (see 16ff., and 90ff.) and third parts of vol. 1.

the convulsions are convulsions, and nothing more... just as a fever is a fever, a cold is a cold [ ... ] the way that God has them [the convulsionaries] take a part in these gifts has something about it that is so base and broken that we could hardly qualify any of these elements, taken in themselves, as being sublime gifts.[40]

Although comments like these were used by opponents of the convulsions as admissions to their non-divine character, they are meant to be descriptive of no more than the *moiens phisiques* (physical means) mentioned by Montgeron, which, *in themselves* disclose only themselves, are to be noted as such, and finally must be judged according to the *ad hoc* associative "method" advocated by Colbert. Colbert, in fact, could provide "rules" for evaluating the convulsions that were no more exact ultimately than those for the miracles,[41] the sum of which deferred regulative precision to a kind of evangelically prudent attentiveness, issuing in patience — the very patience of the Church imaged in reverse by the figure Gudvert had pictured. In this regard, Montgeron and others frequently pointed approvingly to the example of Gamaliel, in Acts 5:33–39, whose advice to the Jerusalem Council bent on executing the apostles pressed instead for a watchful permission of the Christians' actions: if the plan — *oeuvre* — is of human origin it will fail; but if it is of God, no one will be able to stop it. "Waiting" and "seeing" properly set the limits to pneumatic definition, very much in line with Pauline categories for the apprehension of the Holy Spirit's self-demonstration.

But the notion of the *mélange* was in fact pressed into a non-descriptive role, one whose elevation to the status of regulative principle proved its incompatibility not only with the convulsions, but ultimately with the miracles as well and with the whole theological vision in which they shone. Simon Hervieux de la Boissière, for instance, was an Appellant who sought to counter Montgeron's defense of the *grand secours* on the very basis of the *mélange*, something theoretically that made perfectly good sense: the miracles of Saint-Médard may be authentic, and the healings of the convulsions too, but there is no reason to *assume* that the excess of the *secours* must necessarily be counted divine just because of

---

40. Cited from d'Étemare's *Exposé* ... (p. 3), in d'Asfeld's *Vains efforts des Mêlangistes ou discernans dans l'Oeuvre des Convulsions, pour défendre le système du mélange* (n.p., 1738), 84.

41. See his "Instruction pastorale sur les miracles en reponse à Monseigneur l'Archevesque de Sens," part 3, 202ff. Colbert's seventeen "rules" for evaluating the convulsions were frequently cited by both defenders and opponents, since he himself, as a believer in the divine origins of many convulsions, nonetheless upheld the existence of a *mélange* wherein both the good and bad could be discerned. Most of the rules are less regulative principles than the enumeration of an associative judgment already made, to wit, that the convulsions are properly seen as part of the single divine episode of which the non-convulsionary miracles form a part. The only *discrimen* he specifies is the general one of the "rule of faith," that must rule out any practices "that are contrary to the law of God" (which includes the vague category of *les moeurs* [customs]) (see Rules 11 and 12). Beyond this, Colbert promotes the example of the "Fathers of the Church" who "stayed attentive to the prodigies and extraordinary events of their times" (Rule 15).

their association with these genuine blessings.[42] An examination of the *secours* instead uncovers enough details to cast their divine character in doubt: "the wounding of modesty and shame," "tempting God," "pretensions to infallibility," etc. But Hervieux goes beyond a bare inquiry into the "facts" and the formulation of tentative conclusions; rather, he extends the experience of sensible ambiguity into an overriding historical determinant, not surprisingly ending up with supporting arguments and doctrinal frameworks similar to Lerouge's. Like Lerouge, he stresses the intrinsic lack of "clarity" of miracles in general,[43] and again like Lerouge, he gropes about for some kind of *discrimen* that can afford what epistemological certainty is lacking in phenomenal existence considered in itself.[44]

But, more importantly for the parallel, he inflates the otherwise merely prudential maxims of mitigated scepticism about the supernatural to a broad theological judgment about the nature of present experience in general eschatologically subject to demonically seductive manipulations.[45] The Appellant in Hervieux uses *Unigenitus* as an example of the Antichrist's deceiving power in the Church[46] — a fact which points up the inherent obscurity of most ecclesial existence in the Endtimes — but his conclusions reach after Lerouge's own solution of some kind of certain *magisterium.* To be sure, Hervieux does not opt, in this, for the latter's hierarchically promulgated pronouncements, but proposes something more akin to Anglicanism's supposed "three-legged stool" of Reason, Scripture, and Tradition, understood as the *analogia fidei.*[47] Still, it is a similar island of surety that he seeks, against the waves of a "manifest enthusiasm" rolling out from misplaced credulousness: "when dealing with authority [i.e., religion], all things have their motives and their rules — their motives, in terms of what might lead us toward this authority, and their rules, in terms of discerning what the authority says."[48] With respect to extraordinary religious phenomena like miracles, Hervieux must finally leave aside the descriptive aptness of the *mélange* altogether, and equate "pneumatic" authenticity with the utter "clarity" of self-evidence itself.[49] This is a conclusion that must in the end dispense with the very possibility of figural reality. We are hardly surprised, in light of this, to discover that his

---

42. See his *Preservatif Contre les faux principes et les Maximes dangereuses établies par M. de MONTGERON, pour justifier les secours violens qu'on donne aux Convulsionnaires* (n.p., 1750), "Avertissement," 3–16. There is a mention of Hervieux's treatise on miracles in Monod, *De Pascal à Chateaubriand,* 417f.

43. Ibid., 19f.

44. Ibid., main text, 15ff.

45. Ibid., 245ff.

46. See ibid., 271–3.

47. See ibid., 424ff.

48. Ibid., 432.

49. See his *De l'Esprit Prophétique: Traité dans lequel on examine la nature de cet Esprit, son objet spécial, les moyens par lesquels Dieu l'a communiqué & l'a fait reconnoître, tant par les Prophetes qui le recevoient, que par ceux à qui ils étoient envoyés* (Paris: Despilly, 1767), 12–17 and 80–85.

writings on these matters prove utterly devoid of the figurist perspective otherwise common to their Appellant defense.

That the *mélange* was a regulative principle was also assumed by those who attacked the convulsions without distinction. When it became evident that these included among them Appellants of considerable note like Jerôme Besoigne, who had initially supported the healing miracles, official *constitutionnaire* polemicists simply sat back and allowed their Jansenist enemies to fight it out among themselves. In early 1735 several prominent Appellant theologians led by Nicolas Petitpied and Bidal d'Asfeld, with government connivance, produced a short document condemning the convulsions outright. Known as the "Consultation des Trente sur les Convulsions," it became the basis for a sudden flurry of often vituperative debate within Appellant circles and did much to weaken the movement's cohesion in the wake of the Saint-Médard cemetery's closure.[50] For writers like Montgeron, the Consultation represented a foe of almost the same hateful stature as Languet, the archbishop of Sens, and many of the arguments he mounts in the *Continuation* have it in mind. It was, in any case, the Consultation that formulated the notion of *mélange* in terms of a mistaken principle of discrimination. By identifying as a fallacy the judgment that, with respect to "the condition of the Convulsionaries, [...] God is present in only a part of it, and the condition is therefore a mixed one,"[51] and arguing instead for the causal and non-divine "unity" of the phenomena, the Consultants set themselves over against both those few who defended the divine integrity of the convulsions as a whole and those in the majority who preferred to "discern" the mix of divine and non-divine elements within them. Only in an effort to distinguish itself from those who attacked and defended the *oeuvre* on the basis of its univocal character did this last group adopt the self-designation of *mélangiste*.[52]

The *mélange*, then, acted as an opposing "principle" for those, like the Consultants, who advocated the regulative premise of the *oeuvre*'s unity. Two related ideas governed their conviction on this matter: first, that evil "corrupts" that which is good (see 1 Cor. 5:6), and therefore any "mix" of unholy elements within the convulsions must render them unholy as a whole; and second, this idea is itself derived from the simple purity of God's own being, which is without "mixtures" in its nature and without contradictions in its works. The very conception of a divine *oeuvre mêlée* is an oxymoron.[53] The fact that some convulsionaries had drifted into clearly unorthodox practices, notably among two groups whose leaders had made messianic or at least firm "prophetic" claims of sorts, was not

---

50. See Kreiser, *Miracles, Convulsions, and Ecclesiastical Politics in Early Eighteenth-Century Paris*, 242–51.

51. *Consultation sur les convulsions* (n.p., n.d.), 2.

52. See *Vains efforts*, 4f. They were also, in the course of the debate over the convulsions, sometimes called *discernants*.

53. See the *Consultation*, 2; the *Réponse succinte a un ecrit intitulé: Examen de la Consultation sur les Convulsions*, attributed to Besoigne (n.p., n.d.), 5, 8, 9.

sufficiently countered by the fact of the *mélange* as Montgeron would insist, but merely demonstrated that the *oeuvre* in its entirety was driven by demonic forces.[54] Indeed, when one of the leaders of these splinter groups defended certain immoral convulsionary gestures by his followers — admitted "vile acts" — on the grounds that "they are a pen in God's hand, by which He writes down all the crimes of the Gentiles," such an attribution of excess to the divine "writer" could only be proof of the weak regulative reed that an appreciation of the *mélange* afforded.[55]

By this point, even an original proponent of *figurisme* like Bidal d'Asfeld was ready to give it up as subject to an "arbitrary fanaticism." D'Asfeld, to whom is attributed the *Vains efforts des Mêlangistes*, which, along with the Consultation, was the most highly visible Appellant attack on the convulsions, felt forced by the lack of interpretive self-regulation, seemingly inherent to figurist practice, to back off from its advocacy. But both he and the Consultation had by now translated its ad hoc applications into systematic rather than historically descriptive terms, something the practice could never — and was never meant to — logically sustain. In an astonishing assertion, the Consultation openly repudiated the very idea of figural embodiments, ignoring totally the prophetic examples of scriptural prophets like Isaiah, Jeremiah, and Hosea (an omission later anti-convulsionaries would be at pains to paper over):

> The Eighth Question asks whether the Convulsionaries can be regarded as "moving and speaking pictures" [*tableaux mouvans et parlans*] and whether God, through them, is re-presenting matters that concern the Church [ ... ]
>
> This pretension is, furthermore, nonsense: for what is its foundation? Where is the revelation that demands that we consider the Convulsionaries to be moving and speaking pictures? Who has ever heard, in the Church, talk of such pictures? What an opening to fanaticism it would be if we were allowed to embrace an attitude of such fantasy: we would see it pop up everywhere and multiply itself in a thousand ways according to the whims of each individual [ ... ]
>
> If this is the Spirit of God, where is the proof of it?[56]

"Where is the proof of it" (*Où en est la preuve*)? As with the miracles already, the convulsions were serving to batter *figurisme*'s descriptive visage with the demand for certainties and proofs, something it was not prepared to do purely on the historical grounds of the Church's own experience: self-evidence is a divine gift, whose own fate is open to investigation, but whose persuasiveness is subject to that history's determining figure. Opponents of the convulsions, like Besoigne, reveal their underlying Appellant commitments to such historical faithfulness by creating distinctions between the "ordinary" and therefore "mixed" life of the Church and

---

54. On the convulsionary "sects" of the Vaillantistes and Augustinistes, see Kreiser, *Miracles, Convulsions, and Ecclesiastical Politics in Early Eighteenth-Century Paris*, 304ff., 312ff., 326ff.

55. See *Consultation*, 7; *Vains efforts*, 156ff.

56. *Consultation sur les Convulsions*, 6.

her "extraordinary" life of supernatural revelations and phenomena, ever characterized by unsullied clarity.[57] But such maneuvers, whatever their intentions, ended only by decoupling pneumatic experience as a whole from the historical shape of ecclesial experience, and thus subverting one of the presuppositions of *figurisme*.

But the idea of the *mélange*, as we have previously noted, is rooted in the ecclesiological affirmation of the *corpus mixtum*, a description of the historical and human particulars dependent upon an electing God. It was for Appellants and especially those who defended the convulsions, as well as for the Augustinian tradition that bequeathed them the notion, a broadly pictorial representation of the Church's temporal existence, consistent with such scriptural parables of the Kingdom as the net with a great catch of fish (Matt. 13:47ff.). That the idea was transferred to more specifically pneumatic phenomena within the Body is indicative less of some confusion of categories than it is of the sublation of such phenomena within an ecclesial order subject to the historical reality the *mélange* describes. Pneumatic phenomena are not themselves evacuated of divine distinctions or robbed of their potential apprehension, but are simply positioned in a primary fashion within or behind the historical features of the Church's life, features which bear the form of the *corpus mixtum* as an at times overshadowing pall.

Modern theological systems generally link ecclesiology to pneumatology, or indeed make of it a subset of pneumatology, and for reasons that are not entirely without at least scriptural foundation. We would be remiss, then, if we did not stress this ecclesiological determination given to Appellant reflections on pneumatic experience. But in so doing, we must also realize how the ecclesiology of Appellancy in its turn, at least from one perspective, is determined by the broader figurist character of their theology (and, we might add, this is true even for Appellants who did not explicitly support the practice of *figurisme*, like a Besoigne). Ecclesiology, no less than pneumatology in this regard, is subject to a considerable reduction of articulated scope. Eighteenth-century Jansenist conceptions of the Church have in fact generated a good deal of scholarly interest of late, in general because of the political implications of their opposition to various "ultramontane" and occasionally even erastian models; their connections with Gallican, Enlightenment, Revolutionary, and, in the post-Vatican II era, even wished-for ecumenical versions of Christian polity and magisterium have demanded profitable historical and even theoretical scrutiny.[58] What most of these studies leave to the side, however,

---

57. See *Réponse succinte*, 16. Besoigne also composed four *Avis aux fideles sur le Mélange* and *Sur les Miracles du tems* (n.p., n.d.), which form clear presentations of the anti-convulsionary argument mounted by Appellant defenders of miracles.

58. Some overviews of this recent scholarship on Jansenist and Appellant ecclesiology, with extensive references, can be found in Jacques M. Gres-Gayer, "The *Unigenitus* of Clement XI: A Fresh Look at the Issues," *Theological Studies* 49 (1988): 259–82; Monique Cottret, "Aux origines du républicanisme janséniste: Le mythe de l'Eglise prim-

is just that figural construal of the Church that, to a large degree, explains many of the systematic inconsistencies of their various construals of ecclesial authority in the wake of *Unigenitus*, as well as the pneumatologically arid arguments made on their behalf.[59] For the same figural limits informing the issue of evidence and certainty in the episodes of the miracles and convulsions worked toward making sense, in a more general way, of the very shape of the Church's life, and of her character judged historically. We have already observed this dynamic at work in the thinking of Colbert and Varlet; and we have noted the horror with which a Lerouge could react against this threat to what he perceived as the only bastion for certain truth left amid the confusions of the world. It remains for us to uncover the avenue by which this vision of the Church directed Christians to a bare submission before her experiential forms, only the sum of whose figural coincidences could be properly, if distantly, called pneumatic.

The direction of ecclesiological argument among Appellants and their detractors moves from opposing premises. In contrast to Lerouge's assumption of the Church's infallibility which then must govern our evaluation of the Church's (necessarily pure) experience, the historical assertion of the Church as a *corpus mixtum* sets the empirical bounds within which Appellant ecclesiology must be, if not subsequently formulated, at least coincidentally related through the Scriptures. Nicolas LeGros, who ranks as one of the leading ecclesiologists of the movement, approaches the vexed issue of the "promises to the Church" from just such an angle. The *Constitutionnaires* who supported *Unigenitus* saw the bull's questioning as something that placed in doubt the promises made by Jesus to his Apostles that, e.g., He would be with them always (Matt. 28:20), or that the Spirit would lead them into all truth (John 16:13), or that the community led by Peter would be unassailable by Satanic error (Matt. 16:18). LeGros, in turn, replies that the very historical reality in the Church of error and travail requires either a revisioning of such promises in their "external" implications — LeGros's own strategy — or their complete rejection as inefficacious. The only way to maintain the glorious "extent" of the promises, that is, their "eternal" reach, is rather

itive et le primitivisme des Lumières," *Revue d'Histoire Moderne et Contemporaine* 31 (1984): 99–115; David Hudson, "The *Nouvelles Ecclésiastiques*, Jansenism and Conciliarism, 1717–1735," *Catholic Historical Review* 70, no. 3 (1984): 389–406; Bruno Neveu, "Augustinisme janséniste et Magistère romain," *XVIIe Siècle* 135 (1982): 191–209; idem, "Juge Suprême et Docteur Infaillible: Le pontificat romain de la Bulle *In Eminenti* (1643) à la Bulle (1794), *Mélanges de l'École Française de Rome* 93, no. 1 (1981): 215–75; C. B. O'Keefe, S.J., "The Jansenists and the Enlightenment in France," in *Religion in the Eighteenth Century*, ed. R. E. Morton and J. D. Browning (New York: Garland Publishing, 1979), 25–39; William H. Williams, "Jansenism Revisited," *Catholic Historical Review* 63, no. 4 (1977): 573–82; F. Ellen Weaver, "Jansenist Bishops and Liturgical-Social Reform," in *Church, State, and Society under the Bourbon Kings of France*, ed. Richard Golden (Lawrence, Kans.: Coronado Press, 1982). See also some of the essays in *Jansénisme et Révolution*, Actes du colloque de Versailles tenu au Palais des congrès les 13 et 14 octobre 1989 (Paris: Chroniques de Port-Royal, 1990). The latter part of Maire's recent volume, *De la Cause de Dieu*, covers much of this ground.

59. See the articles by Hudson and Neveu ("Juge Suprême . . .") cited above.

to subject their historical embodiments in the Church's life to limits of visibility that are, in the end, figural (and hence comprehensive of their own assault and weakness). The eschatological infallibility of the Church must necessarily involve her historical fallibilities, the temporal, material, and even moral constrictions imposed upon an as yet unfinished vocation toward righteousness and perfect love: "We cannot pretend that all the promises made to the Church are always fulfilled in such a way that the promised goods are all found, in every epoch, among the majority or even among the 'moral totality' of the Church's members, without mistaking the magnificence and extent of the promises themselves."[60]

To "promise" in this world, however divinely, is to submit the shape of what is offered to the same prophetic forms of scriptural description, in all of its range, as secular history. It is not simply the case that truth and error coexist within the bosom of the Church, though this is so. Nor is it simply the case that such coexistence obviously does nothing to rule out the reality of a distinct and finally triumphant truth. These are points that people like LeGros will argue for, against Languet and others in search of the Church's historical purity. But more fundamentally, the *corpus mixtum* reaching even to the Christian community's leadership is identified as theologically determinative by the historical congruence of the Church's experience of dispute and inner conflict with the form of Christ's own life within the Synagogue, the figure of which defines both the nature of "promise" and of its "fulfillment":

> If we pay attention to the discourses of our Savior, we will see that He is not interested in proving the unity of God, or the divine character of the Books of Moses, or the need to sacrifice in Jerusalem: He assumes these truths as a whole, and rather attacks the errors of the Pharisees. The entire Sermon on the Mount is a refutation of their moral teaching. The entire discourse after the Last Supper is meant to inspire in His disciples a spirit that is opposed to that of these false Doctors. He spoke with them; but at the same time, He reproached them for teaching and practicing poorly the true Religion which they possessed, and for abusing their holy ministry by being wolves in sheep's clothing. In doing this, He drew out their hatred toward Himself, a hatred that went so far as to excommunicate His disciples and to cause His own death as a blasphemer. He was, finally, a real martyr for these truths, which were contested within the midst of the Synagogue, even though they were never decided by a solemn judgment or by the consent of the Pastors who presided there.
>
> But in all this, He saved His disciples, and preserved them from taking part in this apostasy accomplished by the Mystery of Iniquity at work among the Jews revolting against these truths.
>
> I am well aware of the difference between the Synagogue, which was bound to be rejected, and the Church, which can never be. But this doesn't

---

60. [Nicolas LeGros,] *Lettres a Monseigneur l'Evesque de Soissons sur les Promesses faites a l'Eglise*, 2d ed. (Amsterdam, 1738), 4eme Lettre, 331ff.

mean that the vices of the Pharisees cannot, as St. Jerome says, be passed along to those who live and teach within the Church.[61]

Passages like this have implications, certainly drawn out by LeGros, for the Church's authoritative polity, pointing toward particular relocations of *magisterium* and decision, away from independent pontiffs or bishops or even councils and toward a looser arrangement of mutually confirming bodies of clergy over time. Yet beyond these interesting implications lies the more basic descriptive conformance LeGros wishes to erect and affirm between a martyred Jesus in the Synagogue of His own people, and the Christian Church that is His Body. And just as Gudvert's *Jesus anathematisé* was understood as a description of the Church rather than as a discriminating mark among two competing bodies, only one of which was the true Church, LeGros's figural ecclesiology was self-consciously distinguished from the form of Protestant dissent by its attempt to hold contestability within the bounds, not only of a parallel dispute in Israel, but of the shape given to the Truth by such dispute — submitted death. While the Church may eventually render judgment on some false teaching or opinion which then requires excommunication of the offenders, the bulk of her life expresses rather a "tolerance" for dispute and for the embattled defense of Truth within her midst, a tolerance colored by her calls to repentance, by her warnings, by her cries and tears and groanings, and finally, perhaps even by her own acceptance of the painful failure to convince, and so of her own self-exile in the midst of betraying children. "She tolerates those whom she loves," he writes, an attitude of unswerving faithfulness to the maintenance of communion with those in the wrong, to the point of bearing the sting of death at their hands:

> Error, therefore, can slip into the Church [...] The Church, in this case, urges us to flee, not by separating ourselves without authority from the communion of those whom she tolerates, but by placing an infinite distance between our attitudes and theirs. She wants us to leave everything in order to adhere to the doctrine of the Saints, who were like holy mountains, from whose slopes God waters the souls of the humble with His truth, righteousness, and peace. This is how she cries out against error.[62]

The promise of "infallibility" here, pneumatically guaranteed, has been given its historical fulfillment less in the functioning of an office than in the patient commitment by Christians — some at least — to extended attentiveness within the experiential limits of texts and events whose configurating ensemble makes of the evident "obscurities" within the Church something amenable to revelatory resolution: Scripture, tradition ("the voice of the dead"), living and prophetic testimonies, the witness of the faithful few, reasoning from the past, all join to form the *canal* of Truth,

---

61. Ibid., 3eme Lettre, 254–57.
62. Ibid., 243; see the entire section of 235ff. See also the anonymous *La Verité rendue Sensible a tout le Monde, Sur les contestations dont l'Eglise est agitée, et en particulier sur la Constitution UNIGENITUS,* 2d ed. (Utrecht, 1742), vol. 1, 67–79.

whose current shows itself associatively and passively in the attitude of its victims.[63]

More explicit figurist versions of this perspective can easily be cited. Fourquevaux, not surprisingly, offered detailed exegetical explications of the Church's character, all based on by now familiar figuralist assertions. The reflections on Romans 11 carried out by Duguet and others had early on in the century raised questions about a *figuriste* eschatology that had room for the real possibility of the "Gentiles'" reciprocal pruning from the root of Israel, preceding the Jews' regrafting into the tree: was this not a way of rendering conditional the promises made to the Church? Much of the continuing antipathy to *figurisme* as an exegetical method, long after the miracles and convulsions had faded as concerns, lay in this seeming repudiation of the Catholic Church's immovable indefectibility over time. Fourquevaux, who devoted individual books to the Romans texts,[64] also attempted more general scriptural analyses of the Church, which lead to the same conclusions as those of LeGros, without the more political particulars of the latter's discussion. Again, Fourquevaux works from the empirical basis of the Church's actual condition, and then attempts to establish *rapports* (connections) between this and scriptural forms, as he explains in this passage on the Church as Bablyonian captive:

> In a word, the condition of the Church is before our eyes. It is what it is, independent of what we compare it to. It is hardly the history of the Captivity, nor the prophecies made at that time, that prove the real existence today of a spiritual Babylon, or prove that the Church is awash in a deluge of evils, or that there is a Bull *Unigenitus*, or that this Bull condemns the truth, or that the Bull is nevertheless received to the letter by the majority of the Church's members, etc. But once we have seen these things and have then come to compare them, either with the event of the Babylonian Captivity or with the prophecies that concern it, and once we can see how the comparison is appropriate, and how it all fits perfectly, there is nothing to stop us from recognizing that a substantive Babylon exists in our midst, and that the figures and the prophecies [relating to it] are fulfilled.
>
> Are not these things more than they are, just because of what they are? If there really are terrible evils within the Church, are they there only because the Appellants notice them and weep over them? And will they all go away just because the Constitutionaries are uncomfortable with acknowledging them? The condition of the Church is what it is, and it won't change just because people think otherwise; rather, people should allow their thinking and their judgments to be formed on the basis of the true condition of things.[65]

---

63. See ibid., 269ff.

64. See his *Introduction abregée a l'Intelligence des Propheties de l'Ecriture, Par l'usage qu'en fait S. Paul dans l'Epitre aux Romains* (1731).

65. *Idée de la Babylone Spirituelle Prédite par les Saintes Écritures. Où l'on fait voir contre les Protestans et les Constitutionnaires que cette Babylone ne peut être l'Eglise Catholique, et que néanmoins elle doit se former dans le sein de cette même Eglise. Pour servir d'éclaircissement au Livre des Reflexions sur la Captivité de Babylone* (Utrecht, 1733), "Avertissement," 44f.; 55.

Having observed the character of the world and Church — d'Étemare's nominalist characterization of a cold as "just a cold" or a "fever" as "just a fever" in itself — the Christian at the same time holds this knowledge before the scriptural shapes of prophecy and history, the congruence of which is marked by an interior movement of Christ's Spirit within the mind, and which brings "understanding" of the truth:

> Whoever elaborates the connections of this work [i.e., the work of Jesus Christ throughout the ages] with Scripture, satisfies my mind; and in persuading my mind, he gains authority over it.
>
> He satisfies my mind, because he makes me see the connections — fitting, natural, and numerous — between the figure and the events that answer it. I have these events before my eyes: they exist, I see them, and I examine them carefully. And thus I have no doubts about them; for, as I hardly need point out, it is neither prophecy nor figure that assures me of these events, it is my own eyes. [ ... ]
>
> And if it is not just a few texts of Scripture that this person now elaborates for me, but rather if he speaks to me about all the rest with the same illumination, I am obliged to recognize that he has received an understanding that comes from being part of the gift Jesus made to His Apostles, when He opened their mind to understand the Scriptures. *Aperuit illis sensum ut intelligerent Scripturas.* Luke 24:45. Even I have a portion of this gift, and the Scriptures are opened to my eyes, if I can enter into such explications, and if I can understand them rightly and truly.
>
> But what would this gift end up really being, for teachers and disciples alike, if it were not at all joined to that force of persuasion based on the appropriateness of connections and resemblances?[66]

Fourquevaux is defending the application of the figure of Babylon to the Church's present history, a disputed application on ecclesiological grounds. But the pneumatological basis for this application, in his mind — the "gift" that enables such application — is the simple "light of persuasion" offered by the juxtaposition of scriptural form and ecclesial experience. Only on this basis can he speak of the historical "decline" of the Church in "conduct" (*moeurs*) and moral doctrine, as a religious claim compatible with her dominical "promises";[67] only on this basis do the particulars of the figure of Israel, in captivity, in suffering, and in purged restoration, bring clarity to specific ecclesiological assertions, whether against Protestants or advocates of the bull;[68] only on this basis can he finally bring particular evaluations to contested events within the Church — like the miracles — and finally resolve all of them into a single lapidary offering of thankfulness for God's protecting grace:

> I dare to say that whoever grasps well the extent to which Scripture was careful to predict and to figure the current woes of the Church will hardly be shaken in the midst of scandals; indeed, these scandals may even serve

---

66. Ibid., 15–18.
67. See *Reflexions sur l'Etat Present de l'Eglise* (Amsterdam: Nicolas Potier, 1731), 1–5
68. See ibid., 16–24.

to strengthen and solidify her [the Church]. [ . . . ] This same person will certainly not use the woes afflicting the Church as a pretext for abandoning her or insulting her; and he will never allow himself to be overwhelmed by the sheer extent of these woes and will remain faithfully attached to the Church's communion. All the disorder and confusion of the present day will strike this person neither as a matter of chance nor as an act of God's abandonment; but rather it will seem to him the result of God's wise plan, carefully followed and perfectly interconnected, not at all opposed to the promises God has made to His Church, but a proof even that God watches over her with enormous care, and that, as a result, He will never abandon her.[69]

By a grand reversal, uncertainty, doubt, and apostasy within the Church, each set alongside their submissive opposites in struggle and held together by the apprehended figure of their scriptural location, form together the most luminous evidence imaginable of God's faithfulness and truth, and the steadfastness of His promises.[70]

---

69. *Idée de la Babylone Spirituelle*, 24f.

70. This is not the context in which to attempt what would be a useful comparison between a figurist ecclesiology and Luther's. The respective understanding of the figure of "Babylon" in each, however, offers what might be an instructive contrast. It is not surprising, for instance, that Fourquevaux's use of the image was accused of a Protestant error, inasmuch as, from the beginning, Luther had prominently identified the woes of the Church with the "kingdom of Babylon." Further, Luther had also exhorted Christians to a "patient suffering" of these woes, without seeking to break the unity of the Church, so long as "liberty of conscience" might be maintained in speaking the truth. There is much similarity here with Appellant thinking. But Luther went so far as to "identify" the pope himself and the institutional Church led by the pope with Babylon and Antichrist (and not just as those seduced by him), and generally the structural relationship between this Babylon and the true Church was seen by him as one of finally only external contiguity. The Church was "in servitude" to Babylon, and Babylon lay "outside" her interior walls, as an oppressive force. See his *Pagan Servitude of the Church*, in *Martin Luther: Selections from His Writings*, ed. John Dillenberger (Garden City, N.Y.: Doubleday, 1961), 306ff. Fourquevaux attempted to distinguish his position from Luther's by stressing the *interior* location of the figural Babylon with respect to the Church, that it is *au sein de l'Eglise* (in the bosom of the Church). Thus, while Luther, like the Appellants, tied the Church's character to the Cross of Christ, this tendency often moved toward a vision of the true Church's *invisibility*, her "hiddenness" with respect to the phenomenality of holiness, recognizable only to faith, and visible in a broader sense only in her Sacraments and the Word. We have already noted something of his attitude toward saints and miracles that is consistent with this. (For some references in Luther's work to these matters, see Paul Althaus, *The Theology of Martin Luther* [Philadelphia: Fortress Press, 1966], 287–322.) Fourquevaux, however, in locating Babylon within the "bosom" of the Church, moves to the side of the more unilineal view of the Church's history implied by the "invisible/visible" distinction, and identifies error and contestability as interior aspects of the true Church's temporal existence in ways that are even conceptually inextricable from the "promises" given by God for her indefectibility. "Visibility," as we have observed, is a necessary feature of the true Church's life, but visibility now embraces the forms of rejection side by side with the forms of sanctity and marvel, both of which together outline a single and more immediately glorious figure. The Cross is resolutely a phenomenal and visible reality as figurated in the Body of Christ, the Church. The distinction of Appellant views here from Lutheran ones is, in any case, subtle and was admittedly not appreciated by the *constitutionnaires*. It is real, however, and its outplay in something like the episodes of Saint-Médard and the fate of Appellancy as an intra-Catholic and not an eventually separatist movement — although something like the "schismatic" Jansenist Church of Utrecht may or may not be an aberration — is not to be dismissed as casual.

If the hopeful attention preceding, and the authorial shape presiding at, and the penitential recognition proceeding from the Church's figural co-incidence in time traces the primary pneumatological boundaries to her character as an institutional instance of the *ostensio Spiritus*, then, as we have observed in Appellant narrative and argument, what we might call her more properly pneumatic aspects recede from view before a space left open to the spare enunciation of scriptural forms. They are forms which, together, disclose the figure of the Christ, along whose lines phenomenal existence, in all of its particularity, is stretched, identified with histories past and future, acting as prophecies, and named, quite properly now, according to their biblical referents. Pneumatic definition in this recessive space, defers in an *ad hoc* manner to such referents, but only to them, at least in what could be termed a straightforward way. "Testing the spirits" on the one hand, and "refusing to quench the Spirit," on the other, both end not so much in either verifying or in identifying pneumatic reference as in entering a realm of figural *ressemblance* where referents in time and scriptural discourse settle together, uninterrupted by deliberate decipherment, in their testimony to the Lord. What is meant by "Holy Spirit" is buried in — though not identified with — this adorative act that enumerates the divine reality of these interchanging referents, an interchange whose possibility undergirds the redemptive scope of the Incarnation's fate.

It is instructive, in this regard, to peruse an extended convulsionary work like that of the erudite lawyer Olivier Pinault. He was known in the *Oeuvre* by the name of "Frère Pierre," and a volume attributed to him entitled *Origine des maux de l'Eglise: Remedes qui doivent les guérir* (Origin of the Church's woes: Remedies for their healing)[71] appeared shortly before the Revolution, reportedly drawn from manuscripts composed over forty years before. The work is a loose arrangement of specific propositions, some of which are written in the tone of convulsionary discourses, stitched together as a broad argument about the Church, and its very genre stands as a typical culmination to figurist visions of *pneumatica*. Circling about the theme of the Church's incapacity to right herself, the book's spiraling pace of ecclesial self-recrimination ends abruptly with what the editor tells us is a (convulsionary?) peroration appended to the otherwise unfinished manuscript. The whole is perhaps among the most pointed and developed figurist descriptions of the Church that we have on record. As such, the end to which it points is arguably the significant detailing of only previously implied trajectories to the movement's reflections. Pinault simply exposes the consistently propagated hopes of their claims.

The historical framework adopted by the book is an extreme Augustinian version of the figurist eschatology, wherein the Mystery of Iniquity of 2 Thessalonians 2:7 "already at work" is seen as setting the circumstantial stage for the Church's life from her apostolic inception. The Last Days,

---

71. Paris, 1787.

while granted historical specificity for certain prophesied events still in the future, is nonetheless a time properly measured as the Church's own, in her temporal fullness. As with other figurists, and some Jansenists before them, the virtue of the "primitive Church," is not imagined in terms of its purity of faith in the Church as a whole, but rather in terms of the clarity of figural coincidence afforded by the apostles in their witness to a continually assaulted Gospel within the bounds of the Christian community. The *renouvellement* (renewal) of the Church in the latter days is thus not accurately described as a return to some lost "golden age" of "origins," in the manner of an Enlightenment utopianism or millenarian "cyclicism." But, as we already noted with respect to Duguet, the *jeunesse* (youth) of the Church lies not in the nature of her structures and communal life, but in her character of penitential martyrdom. This facet of the figurist vision is explicitly drawn out by Pinault.[72]

In stereotypically Appellant fashion, Pinault also elucidates the "Mystery of Iniquity" in its particularly "doctrinal" features, as the continual seduction of human beings by the delusions of creaturely independence and prideful self-construction, that is, by the doctrine of "works." In contrast, stands the "mystery" of divine wisdom (1 Cor. 2:7), given form in the Cross of Christ (v. 8), which is articulated in the doctrine of "grace" according to which "God alone will be exalted in all things on that day" (Isa. 2:11): "*Exaltabitur autem Dominus solus in die illâ.* This phrase says everything to whose who know how to grasp it. Everything, in the last analysis, comes down to this — all the beautiful perspectives that act as our key to understand the Scriptures."[73] Against this divine mystery of grace, have been arrayed from the beginning the forces of "Phariseeism" (the salvific value of human works), "philosophy" (the human search for happiness in a universe devoid of God), and "spirituality" (the reliance on a "disinterested" human love that seeks nothing sensible from God — e.g., Quietism), all three of which together form the "heads" of the satanic force of Iniquity rampant *within* the Church from the time of her birth, like an infection within a body.

Much of the book is devoted to tracing both the doctrinal guises taken by this evil Mystery within the history of the Church, as well as the pernicious and lamentable effects produced: heretics, schisms, corruptions, a full hundred pages of violent prose details these horrors, moving to "the consummation of the Mystery of Iniquity in the bull *Unigenitus*." Pinault can decry the hierarchy, the Curia, the papacy, individual popes even with the same truculence as a Wycliffe, Luther, or Calvin, except that he must include these Reformers themselves among the instruments of Satan, as among the divine punishments wielded against the Church for

---

72. See ibid., 24–45. Once again, I take issue with, e.g., Caffiero's view of figurist millenarianism, and even with Maire's more nuanced notion of an *eschatologie désespérée* (despairing eschatology) that is more "nostalgic" than imminent. See Maire, *Les Convulsionnaires de S.* Médard, 189ff. ("La nostalgie de l'Apocalypse").

73. Pinault, *Origine des maux de l'Eglise*, 191.

her unfaithfulness. The treatment of the Protestant Reformation, in fact, discloses the peculiar stance taken by dissenting Appellancy toward the official authorities of Catholicism.[74] The arguments against Protestant doctrine are themselves familiar and cant: the pelagianism of Zwingli, the "empty" justice promised by Lutheran notions of imputation, the prideful basis of Calvinist "inamissability," and the generally destructive stances taken by Reformers against the visible Church, etc. But Pinault admits the pressing need for reform first confronted by Wycliffe and Luther, in much the same terms as they. As with writers like LeGros, it is the possibility of "separation" that so disturbs him, and this is linked to the peculiar Jansenist commitments to "sensible" grace that distinguish their doctrinal and ecclesial attitudes from Protestantism. The Church is infallible, the pope cannot be Antichrist — Pinault bristles at such an identification, despite insisting that individual popes have been deluded by the Mystery of Iniquity — her unity, her sacraments, her structures, her emphasis on good works, her cult of saints and relics, her miracles, all these are affirmed against the Protestants because their sensible realities bespeak the Church's conformability in time to Christ's figural reality. This, after all, is the character of God's sovereign grace, that is, the fact that God can mold people and peoples in their phenomenal existences into the reflective shape of His love. God's efficacious sway over the very hearts of men and women, the basic proposition condemned by *Unigenitus*, demands the constant yearning and crying out for mercy and for conversion on the part of human beings and drives their lives into proper picturings of His love. But since this gracious sovereignty is enacted in the Cross of Christ, overturning all human efforts to enact its own transformation or be contented with its lot, any division or dissection of the Church so as to spare her such configurated similitude can only be a participation in revolt. The Church will be pressed, squeezed, refashioned in grace; but she cannot be sundered in faith.

From an Appellant perspective, Pinault's most remarkable assertions lie in his bleak assessment of the *causa* itself. Not only are the "woes of the Church" of such a weight as to be irredeemable by human efforts even on the part of saints, but they are so in part because the faithful remnant of Appellancy is not herself without deplorable blame for the Church's continuing and evolving disorder. Pinault accuses the "defenders of the Truth" with as much pride, factionalism, envy, and cowardice as any other group in the history of the Church, more degrading for its power among the otherwise informed and illuminated:

> Let us shed deserving tears for the fate of those who thus perish; but we should let them fall in such a way that they water us before anyone else. Do we not also, we Appellants, have reason to say: 'We walk like the blind against the walls; we grope along as if we had no eyes [ . . . ] We await the light, and behold, darkness [ . . . ]' (Isaiah 59, 10, 11, 9).

---

74. Ibid., 105ff.

When we refuse to apply these words to ourselves, words that God's servants, of far greater holiness than our own, applied to themselves, will not our cruel divisions, these internecine wars that rip us apart, these reciprocal accusations that we level one against the other — will not all this be enough to convince whoever knows us that there are no better [words] to describe the sorry state to which we now find ourselves reduced?

[...] The profession I make of being an Appellant obliges me to confess every truth, even those that are the most mortifying in our regard [...] Our cause will hardly lose its gleam; on the contrary, it will never seem more beautiful and more invincible than when others see it defended by people who confess their weakness, their lack of prudence, and their miseries, and thereby convince the universe that their cause is sustained, not by their merits and efforts, but by its own virtue.

[...] Given that we were little accustomed to suffer, and hardly enjoyed distress, we regarded these rather light first-fruits of the Cross as great sacrifices and heroic sufferings that deserved praises similar to those you ought to give to our martyrs. You know well, Lord, how skilled we were at offering ourselves a multitude of such tributes and at eliciting them from others whom we knew how to get to flatter us [...] Eloquence, finesse of language, biting expression, satires more suited to delighting the superficial mind than to bringing into the depth of the heart a sincere love for the holy truths it has been our joy to uphold.[75]

Such deformities within the movement only fed the blinding "clouds" placed about truly unambiguous signs like the penitential sanctity of François de Pâris, or the subsequent miracles granted in his name. So certain that these marvels would lead to the vindication of their commitments, Appellants allowed their already selfish passions to be carried away by an exultant gloating that gave rise, finally, only to further disintegration of the cause. Instead of seeing their appearance as "so many signs of a terrible judgment that you [God] will bring upon the world, beginning with your own house," instead of rushing toward lives of deeper penitence, they laughed in the faces of their opponents, thereupon to be struck down by the confusion brought to bear through the convulsions:

We thought that we deserved only triumph, and as a result we believed we could only triumph [...]

However a terrible cloud gathered over the tomb of Your Saint; day by day it was loaded with new thunderbolts that You prepared to hurl upon us without end. When the cloud first descended, it filled us with admiration and joy, because we assumed it could only be directed at the disappearance of our enemies. In our foolishness, we did not see that one of its principal effects would be to throw us down into the dust we hated and to divide us into a multitude of pieces each burdened with the weight of your indignation, whether real or apparent or passing.

Since that frightening time, O Lord, you have not ceased to thunder against us.[76]

---

75. Ibid., 165–67, 176–79, 192–93.
76. Ibid., 197f.

In all of this, Pinault is saying nothing fundamentally different from even Colbert. What he now openly stresses, however, is the way in which no possible remedy for the Church's woes is available to human strategies, even new ecumenical councils with the repeal of *Unigenitus*; even saints; even the miracles. The problem with the Church is now clearly shown to reside simply and most profoundly in the human hearts of her members: *Defecit Sanctus, diminutae sunt veritates a filiis hominum* (Ps. 11:1). 'There is no one who is holy; there is no more righteousness among the children of men.' Here is a picture that sums up all of our true woes."[77] And it is the unveiling of this reality that, in one action, by proving that "the condition of the church is incurable by any created power," also represents the exaltation of God's sole providence over the universe.[78] "Incurability" becomes a sign of grace, then, as it hands the Church over into the power of her redeeming Creator, much in the manner that St. Paul speaks of his own intractable ailments (see 2 Cor. 12:7–10). The practical signs of this redemption, however, are given in the figure of her ills themselves. Here is where Pinault goes even further than most *figuristes* in articulating the character of divine love historically enacted. Montgeron had always held out the return of Elijah, for which the Saint-Médard and convulsionary episodes were precursors, as being somehow continuous experientially with elements of the marvelous *éclat*. And while Elijah's fate was to be of a kind with Appellancy's in its rejection, there was always the implicit assertion — at times foolhardy and even petulant in tone — that, underlying this commonality was a yet deeper participation in a common "sensible delight" drawn from a core brilliance, however obscured. But Pinault sweeps even the convulsionary movement of which he is a leading member into the same "cloud" of rebellious failure, covering each portion of the canvas with a broad shadow so that the whole will hang as a single burden with an unwavering weight that sinks into the same void of irrecoverability wherein the Cross is struck. In a word, the Church as whole becomes a part, an impotent part at that, of the sacrifice "destined to assuage the wrath of the Lord" whose full and potent agent was the inexplicable and universally unexpected folly of the crucified Christ's love.[79] The "remedies" promised in the title of the book turn out to be none other than the tribulations of the just, which, in themselves, procure nothing but their own unmeasured end, to be "finally" taken up only in the body of the Lord. Without success one searches through the volume for some signal of another, "brighter" path, at this point tempted toward something like the aggrieved and exultant promise of Jurieu's grand reversal for his flock. But the Church, in Pinault's eyes, gives way only to God. The sole manner, within our histories, in which to point to such a move lies in the figure of Jesus' own passage.

---

77. Ibid., 233.
78. See ibid., 237, 261ff.
79. See ibid., 287ff.

Like other apologists for the miracles and convulsions, Pinault continues to assign particular events their phenomenal integrity and, in theory,
cogency. Miracles are miracles, and with proper scrutiny by the faithful, they can be discerned as such. But given the far point to which
the Church, holding in her bosom both conflicting (if unequal) mysteries of God's plan, is to be led, these distinctions gleaned become even less
critical to the meaning of the figure of which they are nominally part.
Whereas Montgeron still attempts to analyze the "condition" and character of convulsionary experience according to certain traditional pneumatic
categories, at several points by detailing the parallels between convulsionaries and canonized mystics like Madeleine de Pazzi, Philip Neri, and
the Blessed Marie d'Oignies,[80] Pinault abandons these commonly used
similitudes altogether, preferring instead to dwell upon contrasting particularities of figural positioning.[81] The pneumatic phenomena of the great
mystics, he argues, are to be regarded in general as the "fruit" of their
virtue, the mark of blessing showered upon their pursuit of perfected
love. As a result, their experiences were either free, on the whole, from
any aspect of *mélange,* or were evident embodiments of successful struggles waged against the Demon and granted as a sign of their virtue to
onlookers. Historically, one notes also, says Pinault, that the teachings
and experiences of mystics were rarely linked one to another, nor were
they consistently associated with any movement of reform or teaching.
They were, in this respect, traditional evidence of God's *gratia faciens
gratum,* distributed according to the particulars of God's individual election, possible and evident, figurally, because the full extent of the Church's
decadence was not yet to be revealed experientially. The entire nature of
the convulsionary phenomenon, however, contrasts with this: it is linked
to a specific set of circumstances in the Church's history, it makes use of
children, illiterates, and even the unjust as its instruments, and it takes
place at a period in the Church's life wherein the real sanctity of individuals, in any case, is necessarily overshadowed by the rage contained within
its coinciding figural events. Indeed, it is possible to see the virtuous clarity
of former mystical episodes as only the wasted gems of holiness scattered
along a road winding down to the Church's own sacrificial abyss, where
now sanctity, miracles, convulsions, and even the *grands secours* clasp
hands in a mutually enveloping mist: "God is quiet now, since the world
had no desire to hear Him; or, if God continues still to make us listen to
the voice of His signs, it happens more often than not in a darkness, the
secret of which it seems we penetrate only with shame."[82]

As with the miracles, prophecies, and *grands secours,* Pinault ever
maintains the divinely supernatural character of specific elements of the
*oeuvre,* while insisting that their gracious *éclat* lies primarily in their figu-

---

80. See Carré de Montgeron's *Continuation,* vol. 1, part 2, 22ff., and part 3, 14ff.
81. See the *Origines,* 344ff.
82. Ibid., 359.

ral referent of subjected justice that is God's love. Speaking of the common convulsionary phenomenon of "bleeding crucifixes," he writes:

> What thoughts are stirred up by such an astonishing miracle, one for which there are so few examples in Antiquity! Do we have here a case of Nature working with secret powers loaned to it from Unbelief, in order to free itself of what it doesn't wish to believe? Only madness would assert such a thing. Is it a case of the Demon receiving the power to use even the Cross of his victor to work his tricks? And what tricks, exactly, and in what circumstances? Religion can entertain only with horror such an idea, that is so contrary to the respect she inspires in us for the blood so worthy of our worship and so perfectly represented.
>
> [ ... ] As for us, whom the Lord has deigned to render more meek, let us offer Him ardent thanksgivings for such an instructive blessing. He makes the blood to flow from these miraculous images for two purposes: first, to alert us in the most palpable manner to the fact that His own blood continues to flow, in order to save us who live in the midst of these shadows of death that are today enveloping the whole earth; second, to show us that the times are now approaching when we shall see Him retrace upon His Mystical Body all His own wounds.[83]

Similar sentiments are expressed concerning the *grands secours*, which are enumerated in their astonishing bizarreness: eating of live coals, sleeping upon spikes, beatings, crushing weights, and so on. These are all both clearly wrought by God in their effects,[84] and the self-enacting signs of consolation to the Church as she enters into the form of His own gracious cure. Any concern for the detailing of pneumatic gift gives way before the conglomerated signs that the phenomena form for the Church's experienced vocation:

> To see beatings, stretchings, and other operations of extreme violence not only fail to kill, but in fact always to bring an end to actual pain, and often to heal long-standing and incurable illnesses, to reset bones and misshapen limbs, to heal cancers and violent headaches [ ... ] this is, for those who recognize God's hand in all these great marvels, the most sensible sign both of the divine aid that the witnesses to the truth will receive in the midst of persecution, and of the wonderful effect that trials will have on the Church. [ ... ] From this springs a disregard for the goods and honors of the world, the renunciation of pleasure, the scorn for glory, the hope for future blessings, the solid and courageous tarrying for the fulfillment of promises, and, as a result, a spirit of mourning and of prayer.[85]

Taken as a whole, the Church's gifted mission under the guidance of the Spirit is apprehended only in the reduction of individual sanctity and its gifts, as embodied for example in the mystics, to the submitted posture of adorative reception, in which God's grace is given sensibly through its figurated rejections. All that remains is the divine form proffered in its

---

83. Ibid., 402ff.
84. See ibid., 404ff.
85. Ibid., 424–25.

humanly abandoned luster: *exaltabitur autem Dominus solus in die illa.*
So apprehending, the Church will live:

> Since it pleased Him, O Holy Bride, to grant you such a large heart, may
> He grant you also what befits such a heart. And what is that? Himself,
> altogether. For only He is able to fill your heart. Whoever says everything
> himself, God entire, says all there is. What could we ever ask for you that
> is not already enclosed in this great totality [*ce grand tout*]? You would
> like countless children, O Holy Mother, you would like all the earth's in-
> habitants. But what is this compared to this great totality? You have been
> promised this great totality, it is yours, you will be given it. [ . . . ] You would
> like great Prophets [ . . . ] You would like victory over your enemies [ . . . ] You
> would like to see [God's] glory burst forth and reign through the earth. Yet
> you already possess the God of glory.[86]

*Le grand tout.* Ripped from attachments to anything less, the Church is
even now joined to the figure of her Lord's expiring offering, slipping from
the Cross "into Your hands."

## The Miraculous Self-Prophecy of Appellancy:
## The Holy Spirit Quiets Its Theologians

Gudvert's volume had presented an image of the Church suffering, and
indeed accepting, her own self-anathematization. Pinault, given a published voice fifty to sixty years later at the eve of the Church's visible
dissolution in the Revolution, restated this by drawing upon the concrete
events whose temporal locations together composed the history of this
submission, while also drawing down upon each the scriptural references
that fastened them in their gathering traces. In between, saints, miracles,
and convulsionary decrepitations ranged themselves as ancillary sparks
of saving decadence, alerting attentive members to the fact that bodies
and their shapes, Christ's own preeminently and originally, form their
own prophecies of self, through which God finally is exalted *solus*. The
Body, as a prophetic utterance of adoration, renders the *Ecclesia Spiritus*
an apprehended concept limited to the boundaries of its own phenomenal
expiration — its deeds, its words, its own conflicted formulations, just as
they appear — refusing, because impossible, to penetrate into some realm
of "secret grace," pointlessly posited because of the temptations to wrest
it from the sovereign hands of God, and the forms of which, in any case,
are already given. To these brief reflections we now turn, in an attempt
to summarize the character of the "historic fate" that joins together other
elements of the *ostensio Spiritus* into its figural appearance.

That the Saint-Médard episodes constituted a form of ecclesial self-
prophecy has been affirmed in various ways. Historians and social
scientists examining the events from outside a sympathetically theological

---

86. Ibid., 486.

and even overtly believing framework are still struck by the kind of determinative — "fulfilling" — dynamic that was embedded in Appellancy's
capture by the movement of the miraculous, through which aspects of its
own self-understanding shaped its fate conformatively. Joseph Dedieu's
famous and seminal "bio-bibliographical" article of 1928 caught this feature in its very title, "l'Agonie du Jansénisme (1715–1790)."[87] Beginning
his study with an observation on Sainte-Beuve's reluctance in his magisterial history of Port-Royal to take on the fortunes of Jansenism in the
eighteenth century, Dedieu comments on the unexpected devolution of a
movement begun so high-mindedly:

> Urged to continue his history of Port-Royal and of Jansenism in the eigh-
> teenth century, Sainte-Beuve replied that he did not feel brave enough to
> confront the immensely disgusting taste given off by the final heresy. In the
> quality of its defenders, in the value of its doctrine, in the pathetic character
> of its fate, the Second Jansenism hardly appears as the natural outcome of
> the wonderful Port-Royal.[88]

Dedieu himself takes up this challenge left behind, and in so doing
provides a picture of the almost inexorable self-destruction to which high-
mindedness is given. Bit by bit, with overwhelmingly accumulating detail
and reference, the essay describes a gradual and finally total degradation
of unity, principle, and reason.

> The torrent of miracles carried away with it the scrupulous care of the doc-
> tors. Prophets, only yesterday unknown, grabbed the attention of the crowds.
> A new team of theologians? Hardly; a band of visionaries. Jansenism slides
> into vulgarity.[89]
>     The premonitions of Duguet and of the abbé d'Asfeld were fulfilled to the
> letter. The convulsionaries, "a rabble that emerged from the dirt," smeared
> with filth the party that had protected and defended them against the voice
> of good sense.[90]
>     Miracles grab all the attention, take hold of every concern, monopo-
> lize every bit of energy. Jansenist theology, now emptied of its substance,
> becomes the refuge for the most absurd hypotheses.[91]
>     Jansenism tumbles down a fatal slope to the extreme consequences of
> the marvelous, which it had declared to be the touchstone of its truth.[92]

Dedieu's admiration for elements of classical seventeenth-century Jansenism notwithstanding, his more basic antipathy for its "heretical" impulses
leads him finally to draw a line of inevitable and inevitably ironic continuity between the golden age of rigorist *solitaires* and the convulsionary
disintegration of the movement at the time of the Revolution. Decrying

---

87. In *Revue d'Histoire de l'Église de France* 14 (1928): 161–214.
88. Ibid., 162.
89. Ibid., 186.
90. Ibid., 202f.
91. Ibid., 205.
92. Ibid., 212.

the "disarray" of Appellancy, Varlet and Pinault were nonetheless trapped within forces whose goal lay in the filling in of fears like theirs.

From a more contemporary sociological perspective, C.-L. Maire has traced an "order" to the temporal progress of the miracles and convulsions that is as fixed as Montgeron's providential reading of their evolution, only here the current of development follows the larger cultural and political tides sweeping eighteenth-century France and Paris in particular.[93] Like Dedieu, if more benevolently, she sees the sorry fate of Jansenism causally bound to that of the convulsionaries, yet now wrapped up in the general lot of religious belief in a time of ebbing faithfulness:

> In the final reckoning, the convulsionaries did terrible damage to the Jansenist cause: they are not strangers to the defeat or the complete division of the party. Similarly, they did no less of a disservice, in the end, to their own cause. In trying to save what they imagined to be the terrible and omnipresent God, they contributed powerfully to discrediting religion through their far too demonstrative corporeal extravagances: the tragedy of apologetics![94]

As they struggled "desperately" to experience the "presence" of a God whom the age had now hidden, their figural contortions grew ever more closely mimetic of such a forced impossibility's "agony."[95] It was an impossibility rendered by a shift in historical *mentalité*, however, to which their frustrated agitations gave a unique "prophetic" voice:

> The convulsionaries were not wrong in perceiving a terrible threat presenting itself through the *fracas* of the quarrel over *Unigenitus*, a push, as it were, to radically destroy true religion. There was a true insight in their aberrations. Their unreasonably despairing conviction that they were the last defenders of an untenable bastion — the truth of the Church of France — besieged from without, but also undermined from within, signals for us the reality of a situation that no one among their contemporaries was able, in fact, to apprehend: the beginnings of dechristianization. Prophets they were; and in their madness they acted as seismographic heralds of an inarticulate future that the evils of the age had put them in a position to sense.
> [ . . . ] Denigrators of the age and midwives of the age's spirit, no one could have felt more deeply the changing of a world. Christians at the end of time, over and against all.[96]

---

93. Catherine-Laurence Maire, *Les convulsionnaires de Saint-Médard: Miracles, convulsions et prophéties à Paris au XVIIIe siècle* (Paris: Gallimard/Julliard, 1985), 14ff.

94. Ibid., 18.

95. See ibid., 248f.

96. Ibid., 247, 250. With respect to the placement of Saint-Médard within the spread of "de-christianization" understood as a social transformation in ideas, a separate chapter at least could be written on the reaction of English thinkers to the miracles and convulsions taking place across the Channel. (See Colin Brown's *Miracles and the Critical Mind* [Grand Rapids: Wm. B. Eerdmans, 1984], 63ff., where he treats Saint-Médard in the context of the English Deists.)

I mention this here, however, more as a *warning* against pressing the use of such a sociological category too far, to the detriment of seeing the "fate" of Saint-Médard as part of a more deeply rooted and religiously circumscribed ecclesial phenomenon, that is, in the

That the Saint-Médardistes were somehow acting out a social-religious transformation seems to have been a judgment almost universally held even by the movement's immediate successors, commenting retrospectively on a set of occurrences inscribed into what had become an obviously

---

figural terms suggested by the participants themselves. Certainly writers like Hume and Conyers Middleton, both of whom dealt with the miracles associated with François de Pâris, attended to the issue on the basis of evidentialist logics independent of any basic Christian framework, and their reasons for doing so bear specific examination. But even Middleton, and those attacking from the more "orthodox" side, were exercised by a common concern, to wit, how to affirm Jesus' miracles while at the same time rejecting "papist" pretensions to the miraculous down to the present. Indeed, much of the peculiarly English — and by no means exclusively Deistical — eighteenth-century worry over miracles is tied to an earlier commitment to oppose one of the standard Roman Catholic apologetic props, and it dates from the Reformation–Counter-reformation polemic.

"Enthusiasm" as a menace to sound "religion" was, along with the notion's coinage in reference to certain seventeenth-century Anabaptist practices, a judgment applied just as pointedly to the Roman threat to English faith. Just as Roman Catholics feared that denying miracles could lead to Protestant dissidence, Anglicans believed that affirming their contemporary occurrence might lead to Catholic deceptions. George Lavington's famous *The Enthusiasm of Methodists and Papists Compar'd* (1749) uses all the *anti-miraculiste* and *anti-mélangiste* arguments of demonization against the Methodists, but does so by explicitly drawing on "enthusiastic" Roman Catholic admissions to the demoniacal and to the need for discernment as a proof *a fortiori* for Wesley's delusions. It is Methodism as a stepping stone to Papism. Serious Christians like Arthur Sykes labor to deny the Roman Church any claim to genuine miracles by erecting elaborate schemes of differentiation between apostolic and contemporary times with respect to the relation between teaching and confirming evidence, and between revelation and belief. Wesley himself accepted the authenticity of the miracles at Saint-Médard, but drew from their Appellant milieu an anti-papist message. And even vaguely sympathetic witnesses like Bishop Atterbury, present in Paris at the time, could not quite engage the question of Saint-Médard squarely, because of their fundamental reservations about anything convicting that might be tied to the Roman Church.

More than anything, the claims by French defenders of Saint-Médard, that the rejection of the miracles was bound most intimately to the providential patterns of the Church's life, of which the Reformation-Roman dismemberment of her body was itself paradigmatic, seems closer to the truth than the more modern claim that it was some cultural shift toward positivistic rationalism that undermined belief in the supernatural (though the latter may have a place in the former). As the fate of the Oxford Movement showed, from a wholly differing thematic perspective, the character of Anglican theological structures is as much defined by their originating crucible in the sixteenth-century division of the Church, and their historically polemical orientation toward another portion of this Church's divided self, as by anything else. As such, they are, at least in theory, susceptible to prophetic and figural evaluations. This theory is pursued at length in my book *The End of the Church: A Pneumatology of Christian Division in the West* (Grand Rapids: Wm. B. Eerdmans, 1998), where Jansenism appears, theologically, as a symbol (one among many) of integral judgment within a providentially straightened and pneumatically deprived Church.

English writers who dealt with Saint-Médard include: John Gordon, *Memoirs of John Gordon of Glencat, in the County of Aberdeen Scotland: Who was Thirteen Years in the Scots College at Paris, amongst the Secular Clergy* (London: John Oswald, 1733); Arthur Ashley Sykes, *A Brief Discourse Concerning the Credibility of Miracles and Revelation* (London: John and Paul Knapton, 1742); David Hume, *An Enquiry Concerning Human Understanding,* 1748 (Section X, with note); Conyers Middleton, *A Free Inquiry into the Miraculous Powers, Which are supposed to have subsisted in the Christian Church, From the Earliest Ages through several successive Centuries* (London: R. Manby and H. S. Cox, 1749); John Douglas, *The Criterion; or Rules by which the True Miracles Recorded in the New Testament Are Distinguished from the Spurious Miracles of Pagans and Papists* (London, 1752); William Paley, *A View of the Evidences of Christianity* (1794), in *The Works of William Paley, D.D.* (Edinburgh: Peter Brown and Thomas Nelson, 1833), Part I, Proposition II. Some of these works and the much larger literature regarding miracles in general from the period

grander slippage in the times, which if religiously deciphered, could only lead to a conclusion that the episode fell within some providentially embodied refractions of divine decree. Henri Grégoire, revolutionary, Constitutional bishop, long-lived observer of the rise and fall of Bonaparte, and Jansenist sympathizer, looked back at the convulsionaries in the early nineteenth century, and, in a manner not unlike Maire, saw their struggles — still sputtering exhaustedly during his day in corners of the nation — as a mysterious sign of scattered faith, coughing in the dust of organized dechristianization, and cast into a darkening future. Summing up the "convulsionaries, secouristes, discernans" etc., in his *Histoire des sectes religieuses*, he writes ambiguously of the providential significance and clarity given within movements of mass disaffection, however hysterical:

> Every event, great and small, has a part in the plan drawn by Eternal Wisdom and cooperates in its design.
>
> The same is true for the most common and ordinary events of life. All the more, then, ought we to reflect religiously upon those which, by their character and importance, have exerted a wide influence on society and which seem to stand outside the ordinary course of things. Whether they were motivated by attitudes of mercy, of punishment, or of justice, we should equally search among them for motives of worship, of love, and of thanksgiving.
>
> The same century in France saw the fanaticism of Cévennes and of the Convulsions: the first no longer exists; the second is winding down to its end. Humanity is furnished with a inexhaustible store of evil, corruption, curiosity, and love for the marvelous. This propensity will always find its nourishment, either in the cities, where passions are stirred up more than elsewhere and where so many unemployed languish; or in the countryside, where ignorance makes the mind more susceptible to all sorts of distractions.[97]

---

are treated in Colin Brown, *Miracles and the Critical Mind*. For contacts between England and French Jansenists, including later Appellants and some associated with Saint-Médard, see Ruth Clark's *Strangers and Sojourners at Port Royal: Being an account of the connections between the British Isles and the Jansenists of France and Holland* [1932] (New York: Farrar, Straus and Giroux, 1972). On the issue of "Enthusiasm" in general, see for example, Meric Casaubon's *A Treatise concerning Enthusiasme* [1655] (Gainesville: Scholars' Facsimiles and Reprints, 1970), and the study by Susie I. Tucker, *Enthusiasm: A Study in Semantic Change* (Cambridge: Cambridge University Press, 1972). On Methodism and its opposition with respect to "enthusiasm" and the miraculous, including convulsions, see Umphrey Lee, *The Historical Background of Early Methodist Enthusiasm* (New York: Columbia University Press, 1931); Albert M. Lyles, *Methodism Mocked: The Satiric Reaction to Methodism in the Eighteenth Century* (London: Epworth Press, 1960); D. Dunn Wilson, *Many Waters Cannot Quench: A Study of the Sufferings of Eighteenth-Century Methodism and their Significance for John Wesley and the First Methodists* (London: Epworth Press, 1969). See also Élie Gounelle, *Wesley et ses rapports avec les Français* (Lyons, 1898); Jean Orcibal, "Les spirituels français et espagnols chez John Wesley et ses contemporains," *Revue de l'Histoire des Religions* 139 (1951): 50–109.

97. Henri Grégoire, *Histoire des sectes religieuses qui sont nées, se sont modifiées, se sont éteintes dans les différentes contrées du globe, depuis le commencement du siècle dernier jusqu'a l'époque actuelle*, 6 vols., nouvelle édition (Paris: Baudouin Frères, 1828), vol. 2, 160f. For a brief discussion, with references, see Clark Garrett, *Respectable Folly:*

Joseph de Maistre, as is well known, advanced a theory of providential sacrifice from a side opposed to Grégoire, but it was not one superficially altogether different from Pinault's, except in its elevation of figure to historical principle. Looking at the Revolution in 1797, he called its genesis and progress clearly a "miracle," moving in directions wholly unanticipated, through forces otherwise inept, and along occult lines that only hindsight could, but surely must, ascribe to divine ordering.[98] Gathered up in the destructive onslaught of the Revolution, the Church, like the nation, was destroyed as an act of divine purgation, a joining of sinfulness with the atoning blood of the Son which alone effects redemption, but necessarily a redemption nailed to the split boards of human form that unswervingly press their scaffolding through history, adjusting temporally in a revolving manner, the frame of sacrifice:

> There is nothing but violence in the universe. Still, we are bloated with that modern philosophy that says that *everything is fine*, even though evil has ruined everything and, in a real sense, *everything is rotten*, because nothing is in its place. With the lowering of our created system's keynote, all the other keynotes have proportionately lowered as well, according to the laws of harmony. *All creatures groan*, and yearn, with effort and sorrow, after a different order of things.
>
> Those who observe the great calamities of the human race are led to such sad reflections. But we should be careful that we do not lose courage: there are no punishments that do not also purify; there is no disorder that ETERNAL LOVE does not turn against the principle of evil. It is a sweet thing, in the midst of a general chaos, to catch a sense of God's plans.
>
> [ ... ] There are no more priests: we drove them out, we cut their throats, we degraded them; we despoiled them, and those who escaped the guillotine, the stake, the daggers, the firing squads, the drownings, the deportations, now receive the alms they themselves once passed out. You worry about the force of custom, the rising power of authority, the illusions of the imagination: nothing is left of any of this; there is no more custom, no more master, each person's mind is their own. [ ... ] The churches are closed, or open only for noisy gatherings and the wild festivities of an unbridled populace. They have thrown over the altars; they have taken filthy beasts for walks through the streets, and clothed them with the vestments of priests; they have used holy chalices for abominable orgies; and where once the ancient faith surrounded altars with dazzled cherubim, now they place naked prostitutes on top of them. The philosophical spirit has nothing to complain about any longer: human fortune is on its side; everything is being done for it, and nothing for its rival. If it has won, it will not declare openly, like Caesar, *I came, I saw, and I conquered*; but it will have conquered nonetheless. It can clap its hands and proudly sit down upon an upturned cross. But if Christianity emerges from this terrible trial with greater purity and vigor, if the

---

*Millenarians and the French Revolution in France and England* (Baltimore: Johns Hopkins University Press, 1975), chapter 1, 23ff.

98. See his *Considérations sur la France*, in Joseph de Maistre, *Ecrits sur la Révolution*, ed. Jean-Louis Darcel (Paris: Presses Universitaires de France, 1989), 94.

Christian Hercules, strong through his own strength, takes up *the son of the earth*, and crushes him in his arms, *patuit Deus* [God is revealed].[99]

The Church's immolation, however, is sacrificially justified in all of this, not only for the sake of her future purity, but because of her own past crimes. Among these latter, both as cause and effect, de Maistre ruthlessly counts Jansenism, the Jansenists of Port-Royal especially, and by generation, the repulsive features of eighteenth-century Appellancy, including the miracles and convulsions. Beginning with Pascal and Arnauld, he subjects the heroes of the movement to unsparing insult, critically destroying even their literary reputations as a self-congratulatory overlay on mediocrity, because of their singular, if minor, attempt at resisting ecclesial authority:

> If the great lights of the seventeenth-century Port-Royal — the Pascals, the Arnaulds, the Nicoles (we must always return to this triumvirat) — could have seen, in the near future, the "ecclesiastical tabloids," the frolics of Saint-Médard, and the horrible scenes of the *secouristes*, they would die of shame and penitence. They were, after all, "respectable men" (even if distracted by the party-spirit), and certainly far removed — as are all the innovators of the world — from being able to predict the consequences of that first step taken against authority.
>
> In judging Port-Royal, it isn't enough, therefore, to cite the moral character of a few of its members, or to note the few more or less useful books that came out of this school. We must go on and weigh the evils to which it gave rise, and these evils are incalculable.
>
> [ . . . ] Among the terms of insult that [Bonaparte] liberally tossed about, the name of *Jansenist* held, in its way, first place. ("He is an *ideologue*, a *constituent*, a JANSENIST." This last epithet is the *maximum* insult. These three insults are actually quite remarkable as coming from the mouth of Bonaparte. On reflection, we cry out involuntarily: *The Demon's good sense sometimes frightens me!*) [ . . . ] Even though, during the French Revolution, the Jansenist sect acted as a kind of "second," the valet to the executioner, in principle it is perhaps more guilty than the vile workers who actually carried out the deed; for it was Jansenism that struck the first blows against the cornerstone of the building, through its criminal innovations. And in cases where error has such fatal consequences, the one who makes the argument is more guilty than the one who murders.[100]

---

99. Ibid., 121f., 139f. On de Maistre's view of the universal principle of "blood sacrifice," see his *Éclaircissement sur les sacrifices*, in his *Oeuvres Complètes* (Lyon, 1884), vol. 5. On some eighteenth-century precedents to this outlook, see Henry Vyverberg, *Historical Pessimism in the French Enlightenment* (Cambridge, Mass.: Harvard University Press, 1958).

100. Joseph de Maistre, *De l'Église Gallicane dans son rapport avec le Saint-Siége*, in his *Oeuvres Complètes*, vol. 3, 32f., 84f. De Maistre's criticism of even the "luminaires" is devastating: e.g., "*I will vomit you out*, says Scripture, in speaking about the lukewarm; I would say the same thing about mediocrity. I'm not sure how what is awful is less shocking than what goes on and on in mediocrity. Just open a book that comes from Port-Royal, and you will say right away, in reading the first page: *it's not good enough or bad enough to be from anywhere else*" (idem., 30). Much as he rails, throughout almost the entire first book of this work, against the unmerited stature of Port-Royal, there is a sense, quite accurate,

Examples like these could be multiplied among many commentators on the events befalling eighteenth-century French Christianity. In their partial ways, and from their own presuppositional vistas, they circle around the same self-prophecy of *figurisme*'s act of speech about the Church, of not only the content of her words, but of the very practice of their utterance. A figurist examination of *rapport* in all of this might finally take the judgments of her critics to this day as "confirmation" of the prophecy's fulfillment. In any case, the prophecy itself is distinguished from these other parallels of appraisal — and remains peculiar to its origins — in offering a purely religious construal of what it might mean in history to affirm *le grand tout de Dieu* (the great totality of God). Even de Maistre, for all his Christian thematizing of the principle of sacrifice, was more interested in the events themselves, and only because of this in the inductive movement from the events that bore his major scrutiny to some possible underlying cause. The prior affirmation of the creature, *exaltabit Dominus solus* — which someone like de Maistre never efficaciously affirmed — presents a prophecy of *le grand tout* that describes a disclosure of divine meaning unclothed of all humanly asserted historical determinants, and simply presentative of its divinely given phenomenal structures.

Theologically, the prophecy demands a kind of stasis of articulation, so notable to Jansenist dogmatics in its cramped range, judged even by the standards of its own day. There is no question, to be sure, that the "tone" of a Montgeron or Pinault is wildly unequal to that established by Arnauld or Saint-Cyran. But this admitted, as de Maistre also granted, there is a deeper and more fundamental commonality between these framers of the movement. For the reality of difference among historical phenomena is not at issue among Jansenists as a whole, and among the *figuristes* in particular. The times had changed, the style of dress and speech, the socially dug channels of emotion, even the patterns of obsecration and oblation. Those who visit Port-Royal today cannot but help to feel a disturbing twinge of dislocation on observing in one corner of the ancient barn that passes for a museum — almost all that is left from Louis XIV's razing — the familiarly spare portraits of Philippe de Champaigne's depictions of the nuns, whose austere lines still mold our modern imaginations of the early Jansenism, and then, on turning to the glass cases in the center of the bare floor, to behold in contrast the glittering rococo reliquaries of Appellant devotion, stuffed with bits of bone and hair and cloth gathered from François de Pâris's and de Sacy's and Hamon's and Soanen's corpses and musty wardrobes, circled with gilt and jewels, visually overwhelming the miracles to which they point. Every *thing* is different here. But things are givens. What is at issue is their figural import and the way this figural

---

that merited or not, Pascal's prose will prevail over his own. On some later assessments of Jansenism, in de Maistre's wake, see Charles Dédéyan, "L'Image de Jansénius et des Jansénistes dans le Romantisme Français," in *L'Image de C. Jansénius jusqu'à la fin du XVIIIe siècle*, ed. Edmond J. M. van Eijl (Louvain: Leuven University Press, 1987), 150–84.

import is articulated. And here the seeming stasis is just as real. Scholars like Dedieu to the contrary, the affirmations are the same, balanced on the blade of *Unigenitus*'s propositions; so too are practical dynamics of the penitential, for which the convulsions, for all their extravagance, were never seen as substitutes, but specific prods; and finally, behind all these, dredged up from the past's linguistic lockers in the translations of de Sacy and disbursed in Quesnel's *Reflexions Morales*, lay the same scriptural texts and referents, similarly appropriated — on these together they meditated, and by these they were sated. Joined to the undeniable distinctions of *faits*, such theological stasis marks one aspect of the more simple reality that is the recognized deployment of God's consistent sovereignty over creation, with "consistency" defined in terms of "figure," and one whose own notion makes no sense in other than scriptural terms. If the episode of Saint-Médard encloses a manifestation of the Spirit, it is clearly one apprehended less as a segregated moment or strictly limited set of events, than cumulatively, through the variety of phenomenological lenses aimed at scattered elements of human expectation, affirmation, passive experience, and negation caught up in these events. At the same time, all of these scattered elements are subject, in their unsorted coincidences and contradictions, to the singular outcome of a hidden order, to what St. Paul calls a "hidden wisdom" given by "eternal decree" in "him crucified" (2 Cor. 2:7, 2): to an *ostensio Spiritus*.

This prophetic *disclosure* of *le grand tout de Dieu* in history — with its twin aspects of phenomenal difference and theological univocity — can be framed pneumatologically in only a peculiar way. On the one hand, such a specifically pneumatological articulation can be done solely by acknowledging the functionalist impasse of traditional pneumatic markers in parsing such a divine appearance. Someone like Maire, from her socio-cultural perspective, has confirmed this characteristic of the developing experience of Saint-Médard which we mined from the more specifically theological dispute over the miracles and convulsions: there was at work a relativizing of pneumatic experience's evidential or revelatory essence, that allowed for the yet more gloriously disclosive divine purposes of phenomenal "obscurity."[101] Thus, to the degree that God's revelation is

---

101. See Maire, *Les convulsionnaires de Saint-Médard*, 248–49, for a description of pneumatic experience that coheres closely with aspects of our own conclusions, while gathered from a wholly divergent position and to a different end. Where Maire frames her judgments of the miracles and convulsions in terms of an increasingly frustrated human search for the sensual experience of God's direct presence — a search that is inscribed in socio-religious shifts of categorical possibilities defined by the phenomenon of dechristianization — our study prefers to rely on the figural construal of the episode offered by participants themselves, one which obviously bypasses the retrospective concerns over theistic experience formulated within modern secularizing intellectual cultures. Instead, we prefer to focus on providential conformances of historical phenomena to the reality of God's self-giving in Christ, conformances which are, by definition, to the side of or even over above identified psycho-cultural causal forces. The central place that the perceived influence of "deism" and "atheism" had in the apologies for the miracles and convulsions offered by, e.g., Colbert and Montgeron is clearly significant for a proper grasp of their understanding of the marvelous in its historical

defined historically in terms of the *éclat* of pneumatic experience, taken in itself as lapidary message, to that degree history itself will obscure God insofar as such clarity is inevitably contested. *Pneumatica* can fulfill no such clear functions. But, having acknowledged the impasse, then on the other hand, to the degree that such *éclat* is understood as being transcended figurally, in the forms of Christ's life culminating in the Cross — and is therefore allowed merely to dangle in historical and experiential ambiguity (though hardly insignificance, let alone nonexistence) — then pneumatology will orient itself around the enunciation of these consistent dominical patterns of divine sovereignty, "the remnant" when all pretenses to other functions are stripped away. *Le grand tout* is shown to be only, but also all, that is referred to scripturally, and on this basis affirmed ecclesially. This will lead to a pneumatology that must include a broad and varied range of affirmations, but ones that are unswervingly and unsystematically tethered to their biblical articulations.

That an *ostensio Spiritus* which is granted a central role in apprehending the Holy Spirit theologically gives rise to such a reductive pneumatology ought to surprise few who glance over the history of the discipline, even if the statement of its restrictions seems untraditionally patent. As a theological stepchild of Christology, occasionally adapted relative to the doctrines of creation or the Church or the "Christian life," pneumatology is most often no more than a set of enunciations about other matters, enunciations without figural weight or shape of their own, but always subject to the fated meanings of their associated and determining doctrines. *Pneumatica* themselves had generally proved arbitrarily identified experiences within such decentered schemes, which is something Appellant figurism now asserts openly, with the exception that their incapacities — "rejection" — are subsumed into a role of clarity the phenomena would otherwise be lacking. As part of the set of general pneumatological enunciations provided in the tradition, the *éclat* of the marvelous likewise carries no figural weight apart from its reticence, as

---

manifestations. But these influences, which might well be correlated with Maire's cultural "distancing" from the direct experience of the divinely supernatural must be viewed figurally themselves, according to people like Colbert.

The result of such a viewing will obviously reveal a categorically different grasp of God's historical form in presence, as opposed to one of either existential or cultural absence, than that suggested by Maire. Just as a figurist convulsionary like Pinault insisted, it must be seen as fortifying the Church of Christ, not undermining her. Further, I am not wholly convinced, in any case, that as clear a temporal ordering of the phenomena's development in terms of increasingly "desperate" searches for clarity as Maire presents, is accurate. Figurally, there is an obvious providential arrangement to these phenomena, as all participants for and against agreed. But convulsionary discourses, which for Maire represent the final level of reaching after pneumatic clarity — and were the last to flourish in the movement in terms of its temporal sequence — are often no more than spontaneous restatements of much earlier *figuriste* commentary from the decade and a half following *Unigenitus*. While this is not a historical point to be examined here, it suggests a much greater consistency of enunciation, even understood at its most pneumatically inspired, than Maire's determinative scheme of evolution acknowledges. It also follows our own argument for a pneumatological reduction to differentiated phenomena discretely held within a larger figural frame.

given in conjunction with the figure of Christ in His Church. What Appellancy demonstrates, in its ecclesially scriptural perspective on the Holy Spirit, is what had been a historical tendency in systematic reflection, now stated as a meaning embedded in the history of the Church's intellectual and political encounters with her faith: pneumatology is an *appropriately* theological dead-end, in a way that Christology, just as appropriately, cannot be. What is "appropriate," of course, is what conforms to the shape of God's own self-giving in love, a shape whose sovereign significance includes within itself the figural poverty of pneumatological reference as a historical phenomenon of revelation.

The self-prophecy, then, of Appellancy, that defines the historical fate of any *ostensio Spiritus* associated with Saint-Médard and that placed enormous value in the miracles of François de Pâris, is a focalized statement of this pneumatological impertinence, figurally speaking: it claims sanctity, cults, relics, miracles, and even convulsions; it adheres to them; it also affirms their transience, inefficacity, and arbitrarily nominal utilization in divine hands to configurate a conforming Church in time that cannot rely on or possess such marvels. Within this prophecy of self, indicating miracles through their celebration and apologetic defense is something that must give way to articulating figures discursively through the ostensively referring language of Scripture, a practice wherein the particularities of moments are ordered in the shadow cast by larger realities — those of Jesus and the history of His flesh and spirit. This ordering reality provides the *reason* why pneumatic experience is lost and pneumatological reflection abbreviated, and the reason is divinely uttered in the figure of the Church as Christ's Body, whose historical coincidence in time effects the subversion of all more expansive pneumatological schemes.

And we have seen how, within this self-prophecy, the Jansenist and later Appellant speech about the Holy Spirit reflects this predicted outcome. First, we have seen how the cramped functionalism of early Jansenist language identifying the Holy Spirit with Charity — e.g., Saint-Cyran's — was based on scriptural precedence (something unremarkable in itself) and more pointedly, on the perceived historical limitations imposed by ecclesial experience. Second, we have also seen how the subsequent systematic demotion of this language to the service of figural histories of the Church in Scripture moves in the predicted direction. Finally, we have seen how Appellant speech about the Spirit ultimately depended — unsystematically — on the penitential devotion of scriptural conformance as the typical extent of its overt theological application, forming the developmental limit to Jansenist pneumatological reflection as a whole.

One of the key theological "inflections" within this predictive movement of thought can be noted at that place where Quesnel took up the annihilationist pneumatism of the Oratory and applied it to the life of the Church in time. In so doing, the "sacrifice" and the "fire of the Holy Spirit" was shifted from the arena of the individual soul *coram Deo*, to the temporal forms of historical existence of the Body as it participated in the shapes of Christ's own life. We observed, in the chapter where this was discussed, how this inevitably involved a linkage of pneumatic agency and perhaps character, with the temporal coincidence of ecclesial existence and scriptural form, in short, with some kind of basic scriptural figuralism. What we left unclear at the time was how, if at all, such a pneumatology of historical figure escapes a continued functionalist construal of Spirit, now only granted a wider, historicizing canvas. What we can now add to the picture of this crucial shift is how the relegation of traditional pneumatic effects and functions, such as the miracles, to figurally super-seded positions did *not* result in a historicizing pneumatology. Instead, these phenomena were simply allowed to stand in their temporal loca-tions, maintaining a pneumatic identity that, because of their figurally determined contestability, in a sense kept any broader pneumatological implications they might hold limited to the same region of constrained scriptural form.

Quesnel's potentially inflating pneumatology of history's orchestrating agency never developed among Jansenists. This was in part, perhaps, be-cause its systematic basis was always confused with other categories, like Grace. The confusion, as we have suggested, is typical of the entire Chris-tian tradition in the West. And if held in place, as Jansenist fixation on the concept of Grace demanded that it would be, there remained always a check on appropriating the divinely figurating powers of providence to a single person of the Trinity. In Jansenist thinking and devotion, in any case, "grace" was neither a divine person, certainly, nor ever an entity — created or uncreated (vs., e.g., Rahner). Rather, "grace" was a description of a state of affairs, in the relation of Creator to His creatures. And this, we have argued, lies behind the emphasis by Jansenists from the beginning on the historical forms the description of whose divine order is connoted by the doctrine of grace. Ultimately, it accounts for their elevation of Scripture as the describer of divinely wrought historical form in both its overarching and specific features.

Quesnel's thinking, then, represents the historical threshold after which Jansenist pneumatology disperses itself into the varying and often inchoate channels of traditional reflection on the topic, which are none-theless held together by the specific reasoning of scriptural figurism's adorative descriptions of phenomena, ordered in Christ. There is an almost symbolic refraction of this theological eventuality given in the disappearance of pneumatic spirituality by Jansenists in the wake of Saint-Cyran in favor of scriptural meditation, which, however, continues to be designated in terms of the Holy Spirit's reality. "The Holy Spirit says in Scripture" becomes the constant and almost unthinking motif of Jansenist and Appellant discourse, expressive less of a new pneumatology of Scrip-ture than of the descriptive limits to which pneumatic designation could be uttered. Duguet, for instance, will still give counsel in the terms set by de Condren and the early Quesnel especially: in "preparing for" the Holy Spirit, "you call down from Heaven the fire that must consume [the sacrifice of your heart]."[102] But the image itself, in its pneumatic character, derives from "the Scripture, which is the most exact rule for the truth," and throughout most of his writing, he is content to offer pneumatological affirmations only in the context of his scriptural citations, guaranteeing their divine authorship and affording their figural congruities.[103] A Port-Royalist like Hamon's very notion of a "spiritual" communion on the basis of the Word is founded in this pneumatic bond between Scripture and its referent in Christ, but again, it goes no further than an assertion of divine authorship which, as we explicated earlier, derives from Scripture's historical participation, both in composition and in reception, in the figure of Christ Himself, "humiliated in the Word." The entire *figuriste* project justifies itself in the fact that the "Holy Spirit," in Scripture's texts, discloses God's truth in figural terms, drawing together not only literary images as an inter-significating instrument of revelation, but establishing even the divine *rapport* of historical phenomena and biblical reference.[104] Given the figurist understanding of temporal "malleability," by which divine sovereignty over history demands that all ostensive phenomena stand also, in their created aspect, as temporally and nonsequentially intersignificating figures, even a pneumatology of scriptural "inspiration" was never extensively developed by Jansenists, simply because the "mechanism" of divine influence in the writing of the Bible was as historically problematic as other pneumatic phenomena and subject to the same relativizing pressures.[105]

Appellant pneumatology as a reflective discipline, then, aims logically at leaving things just as they are, both phenomenally within history as a whole and doctrinally within the given speech of the Church. Both aspects,

---

102. In the 12e Lettre ("Préparation à recevoir le Saint-Esprit...") of his *Lettres sur divers sujets de Morale et de Pieté*, 5th ed. (Paris: Jacques Estienne, 1718), 264.

103. See even in the *Règles* (e.g., #1), figural *rapprochement* between prophets and apostles is justified in terms of their common "Spirit," something d'Asfeld examines closely in his preface, using 1 Peter 1:10ff. as his basis.

104. For a typical — and almost unconscious — example of this, see *Les Hexaples, ou les Six colonnes sur la constitution Unigenitus* (Amsterdam, 1721), IV (t. 1), 299ff., where the author (d'Étemare?) uses a *figuriste* approach to ground Appellancy's defense of Quesnel's doctrine of grace, by underlining the pneumatologically guaranteed scriptural figures of the Jansenist position on a matter that embraces the sovereignty of God over created form (e.g., the human heart). See also our earlier citation from d'Étemare's *Parallelle Abregé*, 4–5, on the "resemblance ordered by the Spirit of God" between historical form and scriptural reference.

105. Not, of course, that such divine inspiration was denied. But stated as such, in the restricted terms set by Scripture itself, further elaboration of the matter only led to the same conundra the figural resolution of which alone was evident in the debate over Saint-Médard. See Hervieux de la Boissière's *De l'Esprit Prophétique*, which appropriated the discussion of inspiration into the debate over the evidence of miracles, and thereby proved, at least in the context of Appellant discussion of the matter, the topic's empty future. The issue for Hervieux was less the Spirit, but what constituted valid marks for a "trustworthy" revelation, elements that contained the argument within familiar categories of phenomenal investigation, but also evacuated the subject of any intrinsically pneumatic characteristics. As an Appellant opposed to the convulsions, Hervieux ended by ridding his discourse even of figurist tools and demonstrated the futility of the phenomenalist argument apart from this last subsuming framework.

however, are "given" in the scriptural figures whose historical and semantically referring forms disclose the arena in which created life is bound to
God, by God. In this, the reductive pneumatic scope of affirming "that
which is" aims simply at the praise of God, whose grace is limited by the
contours of its single "donation" in Christ, to which givenness the Church
is joined in time. In no way, however, does any of this imply an affirmed
reduction of the Holy Spirit itself. Pneumatological kenosis continues to
affirm the Holy Spirit, and within as wide a spectrum of referring speech
as possible. But perhaps only and all of that, by lashing our bodies and our
tongues, even our thoughts, to a catalogue of glory seen juxtapositionally
in forms whose very limiting marks out the shape of infinite sovereignty.
It will be the purpose of our final chapter to take this question up in a
more constructive fashion.

We may conclude with a final observation, sketched out in the changing shape of Gudvert's volume over time, as it attempted to include, at
successive stages, the reality of pneumatic wonder in untraditional attitudes. Affronting expected pneumatological sensibilities, the book called
upon the Church both to suffer at the hands of its great high-priests and
to abandon miracles by refusing to "come down" from an elevated view of
the future of God's people, a view which commanded the stretch of historical promise in its punctured reach. The self-prophecy of Appellancy
implies that the fate of orthodoxy and the Church herself is linked in
part, either negatively or positively respectively, with the inflation and deflation of its pneumatological pretensions, with such inflation — *mirabile
dictu reapse* — supplying the burden under which simultaneously the
Gospel's deflationary truth achieves its clearest historical apogee of experiential fulfillment: the "demonstration of the Holy Spirit and of power"
(1 Cor.2:4).

# CONCLUSION

How shall we characterize the results of this inquiry into Saint-Médard and its governing theology? From one perspective, we must note the meagerness of the episode's historical outcome, the fact that both its positive phenomena and the arguments surrounding them have slipped into an obscurity that, if not uncommon for most events of the past, is striking for purported battles over pneumatic revelation. But there is also another way of viewing this poverty of result theologically, in a way suggested most forcefully by the Russian writer Pavel Florensky. We shall outline his version of kenotic pneumatology, and then examine its relation to Cappadocian sources. Finally, we will conclude with a description of four major features that must inform this kind of kenotic pneumatology as it elucidates and supports the kind of phenomena we have been investigating in this study.

## The Holy Spirit and Saint-Médard

The 1767 *Manuel des Pèlerins de Port-Royal Des Champs*, attributed to the abbé Gazagnes, laid out a pilgrimage route in and around Paris for those wishing to pray at sites associated with the great saints of Jansenism and early Appellancy.[1] Most of its thirteen stations are parish churches, like Saint-Médard, where the dead are buried. At the center of the journey are the ruins of Port-Royal des Champs and the "Grange" on the hill above, where Arnauld, Hamon, and the other *solitaires* prayed and wrote. But for the last two, now modestly maintained as museums, the rest of the churches are either destroyed, closed, or continuing their reduced ministries cut off from the memory of the search for sanctity carried out by their Jansenist forebears. Apart from arousing the restricted interest of a few social historians, as we have seen, Saint-Médard's unparalleled bevy of documented prodigies has slipped into the usual shadows of the quotidian past. To define the episode thus as "quotidian," of course, may seem in one sense already to have judged the events' distinction from the truly pneumatic disclosures associated with "genuine" sanctity and miracle. But the fate of Saint-Médard in this regard has become in our time the common end even of the "authentic" saint and healing. Few enemies of Appellancy could have imagined an era when St. Vincent de Paul or St. Francis Xavier

---

1. See an account of the pilgrimage route and its stations from over a century later, in André Hallays, *Le Pèlerinage de Port-Royal* (Paris: Perrin et Cie., 1914).

would share the same public neglect as the blessed deacon de Pâris. Like the occasional monument that still attests its occurrence to the inquiring tourist, pneumatic history as a whole — at least as it was given in the Church's long tradition — now presents itself as a set of scattered ruins among which to browse.

We must begin, however, with the positive character of this constricted activity. Gathering up surviving fragments from the events of Saint-Médard, we can see them as one of the few concluding resolutions to the phenomenological task this study has pursued. Taking as our object an episode generally deemed pneumatically challenging, we have tried to "see" through it the Holy Spirit in its self-demonstration and power, much as St. Paul describes his own ministry of proclaiming Christ as accomplished phenomenally through the *ostensio Spiritus*. To say that an episode is pneumatically "challenging" is not, however, to grant to it a full pneumatic character. The Church, we know, authoritatively rejected the integrity of de Pâris's sanctity, the genuineness of the miracles associated with him, and most certainly, the divine origins and direction of the subsequent convulsions. Were we to do the same, we might be decisively choosing to lay aside the question of *ostensio Spiritus* onto some other set of events and leaving Saint-Médard to the varied scrutinies of secular historians. But this is not the case. For even these rejections, as we have seen, involved the judgments of spiritual discernment that rarely escaped the ambiguities attached to disentangling divine and diabolic, supernatural and natural phenomena. Opponents were and perhaps are continuously called to find the strands of significance woven by God in the disputed events. In the devil's mirror there is always a divine visage staring back, not as its reflection but as the appearance of its judgment. In this light, then, even the disputes and facts of rejection, however valid as expressions of a rightly directed authority, prove phenomena properly gathered for the demonstration of some object of God's revelation. As St. Paul would have it, and as the Appellants themselves finally accepted positively, rejections, imprisonments, beatings, dangers, hardships, and anxieties (2 Cor. 11:23ff.) form the power of such manifestation more than anything. These later Jansenists, thus, were at last willing to hand over even their challenged claims to the dynamic of a providential figure, the appearance of which form alone was granted the ultimate authority of demonstration. Therefore, whether or not we accept the "genuineness" of Saint-Médard's wonders, their location within an identifiable phenomenological frame can and ought to provide the basis for a discernment of the Spirit, though one limited to the scattered, if patterned, debris of such contested data.

And we can go yet further in affirming the value of this data, as we realize through the course of this study the way in which the elements of the Jansenist vision and experience with respect to the episode coalesced into a larger prophetic statement confirmed by the unfolding of external events. While the pneumatica of Saint-Médard were taken seriously by many Appellants as positive divine actions, so too was their final shaping in rejection taken as a revelatory grace. Within the theological perspective of a historicizing grace, construed according to the governing form of Jesus' figure, these very pneumatica in their fullness as well as their elusiveness were translated into a pattern of appearance that, in the end, only the shape of the French Church's life could confirm. And this it did, through the outcome of her own figural conformance, though a conformance constituted by the very barrenness of phenomenal shapeliness left standing, by the fact that only fragments of what *might* have been a great pneumatic event, or its complete obverse, are left to tantalize the enquiring spirit. Upholding these, as we have seen, are the bare enunciations of scriptural terms, whose constancy carries the prophetic character of their figures. This is finally where the phenomenology of the Holy Spirit in this case has led us.

## Kenotic Pneumatology: The Model of Pavel Florensky

A pneumatology derived from these pieces will clearly be a limited one, but not merely because of a lack of data. In itself, the Spirit is known in this lack. Thus, the lack is an aspect of what is known. From the start, however, we must be clear in distinguishing such a limited pneumatology from what has often been described as a "kenotic" view of the Spirit, a way of conceptualizing the matter associated not least with British theologians of the last hundred years. Following a line first drawn in earlier expositions of "kenotic" Christologies like that of Gore, which had grappled with aspects of the incarnate Christ's limited human consciousness and dependence upon God, in terms of his self-emptying (see Phil. 2:7), writers like H. Wheeler Robinson applied the notion of *kenosis* to the life of the Holy Spirit too.[2] In this case, however, the category was used as an explicator of a more general divine character, not at all unique to the Spirit, by which God's transcendent self was communicated in love to human creatures, effecting a communion of "matter" and "spirit." Streeter was here taking up issues of divine immanence earlier worked over by, e.g., J. R. Illingworth.[3] While not unrelated to the more original Hegelian specula-

---

2. H. Wheeler Robinson, *The Christian Experience of the Holy Spirit* (London: Nisbet & Co., 1928). See esp. 83ff., and the whole of chapters 3, 5, 10, and 12. See also Alfred E. Garvie's *The Purpose of God in Christ and Its Fulfilment through the Holy Spirit* (London: Hodder and Stoughton, 1918), 95ff., 168ff., or his earlier *Studies in the Inner Life of Jesus* (1907). An important contribution of such British theologians was to push the category of *kenosis*, applied earlier to Christological reflection by nineteenth-century Lutherans (e.g., Gess and Thomasius) and later English writers, into the realm of pneumatology proper.

3. See Illingworth's *The Doctrine of the Trinity Apologetically Considered* (London: Macmillan and Co., 1909), chapter 10, on the logical aptness of considering God's "self-limitation" in transcendence as a function of His "self-affirmation" as "absolute personality."

tions concerning the negation of the Absolute Spirit in history,[4] on the whole these adumbrations of kenotic pneumatology proved to be species of a more generalized cultural vision of progress, theologized in terms of the spiritualizing transformation of the world and its institutions. Tags like Athanasius's famous dictum that "God became the bearer of flesh that men might become the bearers of the Spirit" were applied as patristic justifications for what was really an adapted evolutionary scheme.[5] In this context, the qualification "kenotic" is to be understood in reference to the "self-communicating divine transformation of creation," a kind of scientistic process of deification.

In contrast to this use of the term, our own phenomenological conclusions lead us to a characterization of pneumatology as "kenotic" in a primarily theo-logical, as opposed to (theologically) metaphysical, sense: it is, fundamentally, our Christian intellectual grasp of the Holy Spirit that is "emptied" in the face of the world's shape, a commentary on the capacities inherent in Christian existence, whose phenomenological basis points, to be sure, to a revelational reality — the Spirit's own self-giving — but is nonetheless descriptive only of the parameters of experienced speech within the Church. The clearest modern exponent of this understanding of kenotic pneumatology that I am adopting is the Russian theologian Pavel Florensky, whose own fate after the 1917 Revolution has been lost amid the welter of the unaccounted for within the Stalinist camps. Although it now appears that he died in 1937, the confusion over his final years, the hearsay and conflicting testimony to his disappearance, is itself a kind of historical commentary on the vision of experience he had earlier outlined. Florensky's chapter on the Holy Spirit in his idiosyncratic volume *The Pillar and Ground of Truth* (1914)[6] is by no means a systematic treat-

---

4. The Hegelian strand of self-styled kenotic pneumatologies doubtless deserves its own treatment. It is interesting to see its resurfacing, of sorts, among contemporary theologians working with aspects of "deconstruction," like Thomas Altizer; see his contribution "History as Apocalypse," to Altizer et al., *Deconstruction and Theology* (New York: Crossroad, 1982), and his *Genesis and Apocalypse* (Louisville: Westminster/John Knox Press, 1990), esp. chapters 4–7. (Altizer's fascination with Hegelian kenosis, to be sure, predates his appropriations of deconstructive categories: see the last chapter to his *The Gospel of Christian Atheism* [Philadelphia: Westminster Press, 1966].) As with the British immanentalists, however, the "kenotic" object of concern here is derived from a kind of apologetic for theism in general, and is not really tied to the Trinity, let alone the Holy Spirit, in particular. In any case, the semantic substance of this tradition is located far to the side of the theologically systematic discourse of the Christian Church in which the present study is being articulated, and although our own conclusions implicitly touch at the center of such an apologetic for theism and are explicitly critical of systematicians like Moltmann, whose thought has been formed within aspects of the Hegelian strand, we may rightly reserve that tradition's specifically pneumatological import for other students.

5. The phrase from Athanasius is found in his *De incarnatione Verbi*, chapter 8. The clearest example on this pneumatological trajectory is surely Charles Raven, many of whose works besides the seminal *The Creator Spirit* of 1927 trade heavily on this outlook.

6. A French translation of the whole is available as *La colonne et le fondement de la vérité: Essai d'une théodicée orthodoxe en douze lettres*, trans. Constantin Andronikof (Lausanne: Éditions L'Age d'Homme, 1975). An English translation of the material on the Spirit, by Ashleigh E. Moorhouse, to which our references will be made, appeared as "On the

ment of the subject, nor ought it to be taken, in itself, as representative of his larger theological project.[7] But, on its own limited terms, it proved an influential warning to subsequent Orthodox systematicians, and that through the use of an expositional method not unrelated to our own, although in this case, the "phenomenological" direction of his approach is mainly through the data of well-known theological discourse.

For Florensky, the actual *shape* of theological reflection on the Holy Spirit bespeaks a historical pneumatological constriction, whose cause he locates in the character of pneumatic revelation itself. Beginning with St. Paul, and passing through Justin, Origen, Athanasius, Basil, Gregory of Nyssa, and beyond, he shows how attempts to define the person — the very hypostasis — of the Holy Spirit have sputtered in vagueness and imprecision, in logical contradiction, in confusion with the Logos or the Father, in mixed assignations, or in reduction to the external spiritual gifts:

> One thing cannot fail to attract attention in the reading of the church's writings, something which seems strange at first but which later, in the light of pre-existing factors, manifests its inner necessity. It is this: that all the holy fathers and mystic philosophers speak of the importance of the idea of the Spirit in the Christian world view, but hardly one of them explains himself precisely and exactly. It is quite evident that the holy fathers know something from their own experience; but what is even clearer is that this knowledge is so deeply hidden away, so "unaccountable," so unspeakable, that they lack the power to clothe it in precise language. For the most part this applies to the dogmatists, since they must speak definitely and this is

Holy Spirit," in *Ultimate Questions: An Anthology of Modern Russian Religious Thought*, ed. with intro. by Alexander Schmemann (Chicago: Holt, Rinehart and Winston, 1965), 135–72.

7. In particular, it should be noted that Florensky elaborated a peculiar sophiology, which influenced someone like Bulgakov, and which similarly created confusions over the exact import of his pneumatology within his larger system. For our purposes, however, it is enough to see the broad reasoning behind his limitation of pneumatology and to note its location in the tradition. In what follows, particularly in the discussion of Cappadocian pneumatology in relation to Western versions (including Augustine), I am moving beyond Florensky's own remarks and applying some of his abstracted concepts, out of context to some degree, to proposals of my own devising. For more general discussions of Florensky's theology, see Zdzislaw Kijas, "La sophiologie de Paul A. Florensky," *Ephemerides Theologiae Lovanienses* 67, no. 1 (1991): 36–56; Robert Slesinski, "Fr. Paul Florensky: A Profile," *St. Vladimir's Theological Quarterly* 26, nos. 1 and 2 (1984): 3–27 and 67–88 (a summary of his volume *Metaphysics of Love* [Crestwood: St. Vladimir's Seminary Press, 1986]); Michael Silberer, O.S.C., *Die Trinitätsidee im Werk von Pavel A. Florenskij: Versuch einer systematischen Darstellung in Begegnung mit Thomas von Aquin* (Würzburg: Augustinus Verlag, 1984), esp. 169ff. and 181ff. The contemporary theological application of the term "kenosis" to the Holy Spirit seems to derive more directly from Bulgakov than from Florensky, with the suggestion that Florensky's more constricted use of the concept has been passed over; see the references to pneumatic *kenosis* in a recent article by James L. Buckley, "A Field of Living Fire: Karl Barth on the Spirit and the Church," *Modern Theology* 10, no. 1 (January 1994): 92ff. Buckley's desire to link the Holy Spirit's ecclesial operation to the consoling criticism of the Crucified Christ represents an undeveloped and functionalist parallel to certain aspects of Appellant ecclesiology and brings into relief, by contrast, the carefully controlled manner in which figurist conceptions of contestability within the Church prescind from expansive pneumatological assertion.

the nature of their work; they express themselves almost like dumb persons, or else become obviously confused.[8]

In opposition to this general *theological* obscurity, Florensky notes the extraordinary clarity with which ascetics and saints have *experienced* the Spirit, at "instants" alone where "separate people in separate moments [...] are lifted up out of time into Eternity." About such people, one can say: "for them history is ended."[9] If such knowledge of the Spirit is properly so-called, it is nonetheless a knowledge that "adorns only the supreme points of affliction"[10] and "proves once more that the Spirit is known only negatively outside of asceticism and discipline."[11] Known, but still not properly expressed, since even the saints, when articulating such experience, drift into blandness, imprecision, and downright error as they attempt to vocalize the illumination they have received.[12] Florensky's simple phenomenological conclusion is blunt:

> In general, on the average, usually, both in the personal life of the Christian (apart from his highest ascents) and in the everyday life of the Church (with the exception of Heaven's chosen ones), people hardly know the Holy Spirit as a Person, and then only dimly and in a confused way.[13]

All that remains for onlookers, for researchers, even for theologians, to grasp, are fragments, whose scattering embraces the muted lives of a disparate diaspora of saints.

This conclusion, however, is also a demonstration, an appearance somehow of the Truth: "I repeat, this is not a incidental feature of the history of theology, but the unfailing result of the fulfillment of the hours and days, an inevitable and certain indication of the comparatively unclear revelation of the Spirit as a hypostasis, an imperfection of life itself."[14] It is an appearance that, if recognized, would reflect speculation away from the "emptiness" of pneumatology as an intellectual discipline to the contemplation of the historical incoherence of pneumatic *éclat* itself. Florensky locates the emptiness of the Spirit's theological articulation in time to the character of its divine self-revelation as a historical phenomenon, an explanation whose historicizing of Trinitarian revelation we need not follow even if we wish to appreciate the necessary limits to pneumatic appearance it seeks properly to defend. To "see" the Holy Spirit "fully" in such a way as to provide the basis for an accurate communicative translation of its vision would, in Florensky's view, be "necessarily" coincident with the translation of human flesh into a complete pneumatic existence, a "full deification," an eschatological possibility only, whose realization would

---

8. Florensky, "On the Holy Spirit," 141.
9. Ibid., 140.
10. Ibid., 138.
11. Ibid., 149.
12. See ibid., 151ff.
13. Ibid., 139.
14. Ibid., 147.

indicate the "end of history."[15] In short, the "revelation of the Comforter" is a promise whose fulfillment is reserved for the end of time, leaving to the present unfolding of historical existence just those moments of incomplete illumination whose occurrence, precisely in their increasingly unsettling and dislocated imperfection, points to an inevitably nearing consummation of the ages. Phenomenal history itself, then, is replete with pneumatic "imperfections," whose own incoherence structures the progress of time in a "necessary" and "non-incidental" fashion, providing through its unassimilable and uncomfortable appearances the signals of divine sovereignty over temporal associations.[16]

From the positive perspective of pneumatological distinctions, made in contrast to clearer Christological definitions, Florensky takes as his point of departure the traditional theological characterization of the Spirit in terms of something like "procession" — "a term without meaning" whose purpose was only to give a "shadowy outline to the Word" by way of difference.[17] And in using such apophatic imprecisions as the definitional field in which to observe temporal pneumatic manifestations like miracles and holiness, Florensky argues for a deliberate dismantling of the logical articulation of such phenomena: moored to the conceptual pneumatological obscurities of the Trinitarian distinctions, which themselves feed off of scriptural Christology, the specificities of pneumatic acts can only testify to their own distinctive and "de-logocized" (i.e., unformed by the character of the Logos) origins and character, through their imperviousness to ordered knowledge.[18] "Here [in the Person of the Holy Spirit at its gifts] there is only interruptedness,"[19] loosely gathered phenomena that are "not a subject of knowledge for a science,"[20] and whose theoretical apprehension has more in common with — although can by no means be linked, except prophetically as a type, to — the mathematics of chaos than any other logical *topos*.

The emptiness of pneumatology, then, is both an essential feature of the order of divine revelation, but also a phenomenon that is itself a part of the distinctive appearance of the Spirit in time. Rather than only being a function of a dispensational apophaticism, Florensky's kenoticism in this area undergirds a set of discrete phenomena, including the traditional pneumatica, whose occurrence manifestly resists their own organization into anything other than a juxtapositional placement beside or within a clearer Christological order. The dispensational aspect of the *ostensio Spiritus* as Florensky sees it, therefore, involves the subordination of its own appearance in time to Christological forms, while both Christic and pneumatic appearances together are subject to the shape of eschatological

---

15. See ibid., 140.
16. See ibid., 147.
17. Ibid., 149.
18. See ibid., 151–56.
19. Ibid., 156.
20. Ibid., 155.

pressures toward an as yet unfulfilled completion of creaturely knowing. In terms of the Church's life, this means that the figures of holiness inscribed in the existence of saints display their pneumatic incoherence and Christic conformities at once, the whole sum of which indicates the completing act of divine sovereignty over human history.

To unbalance this juxtapositional subordination of form in any way, leads, in Florensky's mind, to the veiling of that act itself, a disequilibrium whose theological result is always error, and even heresy. In the words of our own observations concerning the Appellant "prophecy" of the Church's figure in time, the negative fate of orthodoxy is linked to the inflation of pneumatology. Appropriate theological coherence, instead, can be found only in a conscious restriction of speech to the *incompatibilities* of historical experience with clear pneumatic vision, only in the willing submission of pneumatological reflection to the realities of undeified flesh. Such a restriction gives rise to an intellectual agony that participates in the still applicable revelation of the Son's Incarnation: "If there were grounds for such speculation [on the Holy Spirit as has been illegitimately pursued in the past], if there were a real experience of life with the Holy Spirit, could what is now happening in Created Being" — the phenomenal shape of history — "take place?"[21] Clearly, it could not. And this limit to pneumatology by the revealed form of the Incarnate Lord's own historical fate governs Florensky's thought even when he attempts — seemingly against his own strictures — to relate the character of this bounded *ostensio Spiritus* to an intra-Trinitarian circle of eternal *kenosis* among the divine Persons. For while he engages in such experiments of otherwise forbidden speculation, he does so not in terms of the imagined moments of such immanent hypostatic self-emptyings themselves, but in terms of their congruent movement into moments of intra-Trinitarian "affirmation," in which each Personal sacrifice is linked to a revealed, that is, phenomenal glorification. In the case at hand, the historical sign of the crucified Son's "affirmation" is given in His unction by the Spirit, an act that *raises* His form into relief with respect to the world's opposing shape.[22] Positively, as in 1 Corinthians 2:2–4, the self-demonstration of the Spirit in power reveals the Son in His world-contradiction, while the actual glorification of the Spirit in its turn awaits a still unrealized conferral of meaning coincident with the "end of history."

## The Onomastic Character of Kenotic Pneumatology: The Cappadocian Claim

A kenotic pneumatology like Florensky's here is rooted in established traditions, including for instance the same Palamite strand that has made so

---

21. Ibid., 162.
22. Ibid., 168ff.

much of the distinction between the differentiated and unapproachable divine essence and the undifferentiated divine energies through which alone creatures come to know God. This is a tradition from which other recent Orthodox theologians like Vladimir Lossky have also been nourished, even as still more recent writers like Nissiotis and Zizioulas have deliberately left its orbit of influence.[23] And while it would be unfair to assess this pneumatology apart from an examination of such an, e.g., Palamite background, Florensky himself associates his thoughts on the matter with only one major predecessor in the tradition, Gregory of Nazianzus.[24] For our purposes, it is enough to see how this kind of appropriation of Cappadocian reflection can lead to pneumatological perspectives quite at odds with several current and highly visible appeals to the same sources, the shape of which we have been careful in trying to resist.

Gregory's Fifth *Theological Oration*, "On the Holy Spirit," in particular lies behind the dispensational structure of Florensky's thinking. In arguing within the treatise as a whole for the Holy Spirit's divinity, in chapters 21ff. Gregory tackles critics on the specific question of Scripture's own reticence concerning the Spirit's substantive equality with the Father. His main strategy in this section is to stress the pedagogically accommodating nature of God's revelation, in Scripture as in human history overall, a divine strategy that adjusts itself to the limited but growing capacities of human beings as only a *gradually* enlightening guide. Gregory thereby explains the anthropomorphisms of scriptural language about God (in contrast to the later Church's theological precision), and, more to his point, he provides a principle according to which the historically late attribution of divinity to the Holy Spirit, in a way that goes beyond the explicit warrant of Scripture, is explained in terms of the Trinity's own "gradual addition" in self-revelation within the Church.[25] The use of a Three-Age scheme, which culminates in a fourth era beyond history, is applied at this juncture[26] as an illustration of the progressive character of the Trinity's self-disclosure in time: each transition is marked by a scripturally symbolic "earthquake," from Pre-Law to Law (at Sinai), from Law to Gospel (at the Crucifixion?), and finally at the End of the Ages and the Consummation of all things (see Heb. 12:26ff.). Only within the Age of the Gospel, Gregory insists, does the Holy Spirit slowly work to reveal its own divine nature, the "greatest" of its promised teachings.[27]

It is Florensky, however, and not Gregory, who speaks of a "final" revelation of the Spirit given uniquely with the transition into the last Age. Nor should it be inferred from Gregory's dispensational imagery that he in any way connects the pedagogy of Trinitarian revelation to some intra-Trinitarian set of relations, relations which for him are both prior

---

23. See our comments on Zizioulas below.
24. See ibid., 163ff.
25. Gregory of Nazianzus, "On the Holy Spirit," *Theological Oration* V, chapter 26.
26. Ibid., chapter 25.
27. Ibid., chapter 26.

to and apophatically distinct from the entire reality of the economy of God's self-disclosure.[28] The *character* of the Holy Spirit is itself independent of the movement of human history, and Gregory stresses how the Spirit "functions" in a consistent range of works throughout all the various dispensations.[29] The only exception Gregory makes to this historically uniform set of operations is the Spirit's work in disclosing itself as a divine hypostasis. This exception, however, is important. For this historically limited and unique pneumatic operation is temporally and exclusively framed within the similarly unique Age of the Incarnation, the "earthquake" of the Gospel and the Church, wherein the Son's self-disclosure is finally made "clear." Here is where Florensky extrapolates from Gregory an analogy of progressive clarity, according to which one divine Person's hypostatic revelation takes place in tandem with intimations only of the next Person's reality; he therefore concludes that the Spirit's "full revelation" still awaits us.

What we need to observe in all of this is how for Gregory the coincidence of the Son's Age with the Spirit's unique work of self-disclosure commits him at the least to a pneumatology of limited expression. It is limited, first, by the fact that the Spirit's "unique" operation lies only in the appearance of its divinity, not in the meaning or implications of its nature. Insofar as this single revelation has semantic content, it remains tied, rather, to the temporally previous enunciations of the Spirit's life, which are bounded exclusively by the scriptural "names" attached to it through the course of the inspired writings. In Gregory's view, this means that the revelation of the Holy Spirit does not provide us with a new understanding of the Holy Spirit's work and character, but that it "merely" orchestrates the previously known scriptural names of the Spirit within a new act of divine worship or adoration: in the Church, we now respond to the Spirit as "God." And Gregory's pneumatology is of limited expression, secondly, in that, apart from this granting to the names of the Spirit a new context in adoration, the theological description of the Spirit must remain tied (to use expressions that are not his) to the narratively more coherent structures of Christology, where alone the "names" of Christ in themselves reveal a character of person from which pertinent Trinitarian relations can be explicated: the relation, that is, of Father and Son ("Spirit" having no concrete personal or relational meaning). To this degree, as with Florensky, to speak of the Christian "life in the Spirit" historically, is to refer back to the life of Christ, and to the conformances between such lives; the Spirit's *own* life remains an object of promise and praise, not of independent descriptive intelligibility.

On this view, it is a misreading of Gregory, then, to attach his imagistic dispensationalism to either an exposition of Trinitarian relations or to a historical vision of particular hypostatic operations. What his no-

---

28. See ibid., chapters 8f.
29. See his 41st Oration, "On Pentecost," chapter 11.

tion of the Spirit's limited self-disclosure as divine, within the life of the Church, establishes, to the contrary, is what we might call an "onomastic" pneumatology. Such a pneumatology goes no further than the "naming" of the Spirit's operations as given in their scriptural articulations, which act as disconnected points of phenomenal reference, the only decipherable historical context to which is formed by the narrative of the Christ. Within the terms of our own discussion, an onomastic pneumatology is "kenotic" insofar as it withholds itself from all explanatory frameworks apart from the bare naming — that is, adoring — of its revealed appearances in connection with the form of Christ.

Basil, more than anyone, demonstrates the limited character of this kind of pneumatology in his great work *On the Holy Spirit,* whose lengthy elaborations of the Spirit's "titles" is completely misunderstood once it is used as a basis for determining the hypostatic character, historical mission, and intra-Trinitarian relation of the Spirit's life. Florensky himself was aware of the fruitlessness of using titles to this end, although he did not note the way in which Basil's perspective was actually tethered to the same onomastic boundaries as Gregory's dispensational restrictions.

While freely employing Trinitarian analogies that seem to grant particular shapes to the hypostasis itself — analogies like the King, the King's Image, and the Spirit revealing them, or the Father, His Word, and the Breath of His mouth[30] — Basil's purpose in his treatise is, like Gregory's, only to defend the Spirit's divinity, not to elaborate a theology of Trinitarian relations. Indeed, given that the arguments against the Spirit's divinity that he is answering rely on linguistic *distinctions* in reference to Father, Son, and Spirit, Basil's brief is to demonstrate the way in which such distinctive appellations and prepositional orderings in prayer (e.g., "to" the Father, "through" the Son, "in" the Spirit) do *not* indicate substantive distinctions in the nature and even operative power of the Trinitarian Persons.[31] Thus, although much of the book is given over to an enumeration of the necessity to salvation of particular pneumatic functions, functions which in themselves could either be associated with the Father or the Son on theological or sometimes even scriptural grounds, or could be construed in terms of subordinate agency, Basil insists on their simultaneously appropriate reference to the Spirit and to the work of God in a single act[32] because, quite simply, the foundation of their enumeration lies in the articulated adorative practice of the Christian: they refer to God, and they are given by God in reference to the Spirit. Thus, the florid catalogues of the Spirit's "names," in chapters 9 and 23, are provided as the frameworks for a pneumatology that asserts nothing more than their placement as rungs for the "soul's ascent" in "prayer and wonder" to the contemplation of God's glory. The logic of Basil's argument ultimately rests on

---

30. Basil the Great, *On the Holy Spirit,* chapter 18.
31. See ibid., chapters 1–8.
32. See ibid., chapter 16.

the rhetoric of *anakolouthon*, the agrammatical concatenation of scriptural titles whose revelatory capacity coincides only with their adorative enunciation, and nothing more.[33] This corresponds exactly to the limited quality of Gregory's explication of pneumatic self-disclosure, within the Church, as an operation only of liturgical possibility and enactment: the Spirit gives itself as God through a set of properly referring names, but their reference does not extend beyond knowledge in worship.[34]

That phenomenal history supports such a naming does not, however, say that history's shape in whole or in expected part is visibly determined by such names. Florensky's insight was to perceive the manner in which Cappadocian theology, at least in the work of Gregory Nazianzus, had accurately disassociated pneumatological reflection from Trinitarian speculation, precisely because the phenomenological import — and basis — of the Spirit's onomastic self-revelation undercut any coherent application of "economic" schemata to the Trinity's instrinsic hypostatic existence. Any coherence of historical description lay exclusively in the figure of the Incarnation, a fact that did not, of course, exclude the Spirit from historical appearance, but only allowed that appearance to be expressed in scriptural terms whose orchestration was ungraspable except in the Christological terms given in the historically referred Incarnate Son. Modern attempts to use Cappadocian Trinitarian theology to establish a model for God's economic relations with the world appear, in this light, to be misguided, insofar as they understand the Trinity's articulated being as enlightening historical processes rather than, in Florensky's arguably correct reading of Gregory's pneumatology, seeing the Trinitarian theology inclusive of the Spirit's kenotic expression as obscuring history's phenomenal coherence.

This, at any rate, would be my criticism of works like that of Colin Gunton who, drawing on equally dubious if more muted versions of the same by, e.g., John Zizioulas, has tried to demonstrate how Cappadocian reflections on the Trinity as a social unity of particulars in communion have and ought to have profound implications, in terms of providing types, for our understanding of God's actual relation to the world in history, of human institutions, and of the character and nature of the Church in particular.[35]

---

33. See ibid., chapters 24–30.

34. We might note as well the similar treatment of the matter by Gregory of Nyssa, in his *On the Holy Spirit: Against the Macedonians*, in which the Holy Spirit is distinguished from the Father and Son only in terms of its not being "unoriginate" and "begotten"; the names and titles of the Spirit, given in Scripture for our worship, are not to be taken as providing semantic substance to its hypostatic distinction. It is from this treatise that Florensky borrows his ideas concerning the Spirit as Trinitarian "unction" in the process of the Persons' historical "affirmation," a topic whose implications, we noted, somewhat confuse his earlier argument. See Florensky, "On the Holy Spirit," 168ff.

35. Colin Gunton, *The Promise of Trinitarian Theology* (Edinburgh: T. & T. Clark, 1991), chapters 1, 4, 6, and 9 especially. Gunton's explicit goal is to show some of the ways a "Cappadocian" theology of the Trinity offers an "ontology" of far-reaching effects in our construal of the world as a whole. In many ways, his project follows the same method as earlier British immanentalists, though with a slightly differing content: while not using the category of "personality in otherness" associated with someone like Illingworth, and instead adopting

Reacting, in part, against the historical apophaticism inherent in the distinction drawn by Gregory Palamas between the unknowable essence of the Triune God and its "energies," through which human creatures can know God but only as the indistinct object that is common to all three Persons, writers like Zizioulas have made a strong break with the Orthodox tradition of pneumatological obscurity (because phenomenologically incoherent) in which Florensky himself is to be located. Instead, the movement from "immanent" to "economic" Trinities, and vice versa, following Rahner's "rule," passes through the presumed conformities of history with its Creator. But lines of passage like these, from intra-Trinitarian hypostatic particularities to the shape of phenomenal history, are just what the irrational configuration of temporal existence within the pneumatic reality of "interruptedness," identified by onomastic kenoticism, ought to preclude. And, as Florensky observes, simply to describe Created Being in terms of such a passage is to be confronted with the terms' phenomenological inadequacy; and despite the best efforts of thinkers like Rahner or Zizioulas or Gunton, it is to fail to escape the stuttering retreat that is content to gather fragments.

What is ironic in this kind of modern appeal to the Cappadocians is the way it ultimately appropriates their perspective of onomastic kenoticism to the same ends as did Augustine, a figure for whom writers like Gunton bear a peculiar disdain because of his alleged deformation of Trinitarian theology into a form of veiled Sabellian monism. It is true, especially in books IV and V of the *De Trinitate,* that Augustine struggles with little success to find ways of distinguishing the Persons of the Trinity in anything other than "accidental," as opposed to "substantive" ways. Augustine, however, was not trying to argue the divinity of any one Person as were the Cappadocians against, e.g., those who denied the Holy Spirit to be God, and he was thus in the patently more difficult position of attempting to present an exposition of the Persons' particularities that could escape the theological strictures imposed on such specifying by just the kind of arguments mounted by these earlier claims to the Trinity's divine unity. Far from erecting a burdensome theo-monistic tradition for the Western Church founded on the misplaced principle of *opera Trinitatis ad extra non sunt divisa,* Augustine himself labored to escape this already venerable warning bequeathed him by theologians like Basil and the two Gregories. He finally did so by ignoring the warning altogether and by adumbrating a pneumatology framed around such *ad extra* operations,

---

categories like Zizioulas's more patristically centered "being in communion," Gunton still wants us to believe that *some* such category derived from Trinitarian being will explain the shape of the world in its becoming. Thus, he too has a version of Trinitarian kenoticism (an "ontology of sacrifice") that expresses, not so much the shape of God's actual appearance as, primarily, the existence of a divine shapeliness around which all else is ordered. For Zizioulas, see his *Being as Communion: Studies in Personhood and the Church* (Crestwood, N.Y.: St. Vladimir's Seminary Press, 1985), e.g., 110–42, on the Holy Spirit.

more or less allowed to stand independently for substantive hypostatic characterizations.[36]

Beginning in V:11, Augustine applies a specific title to the Spirit's substantive hypostasis, that of "Gift," as a kind of deduction from the fact that the term "Spirit" itself can be used in common of the Father and Son, and thus must be described as that which they — the One who gives and the One to Whom it is given — have in common. By VI:5, this train of thought has taken him to the point of describing the Spirit, again hypostatically, as "Love" itself, the bond of "communion" or "friendship" between Father and Son: "it [the Holy Spirit] is more aptly called 'love'; and this is also a substance, since God is a substance, and 'God is love' [1 John 4:16]."[37] In doing this, however, Augustine takes what is very clearly an unappropriated scriptural appellation, and what is therefore on his own reasoning a Trinitarian "accident" common to all three Persons, and he limits and elevates it to a particular hypostatic characterization. And even while he recognizes the logical difficulties involved in this, as in XV:7 and 17, he deliberately insists on the warrant that scriptural synechdoche provides for such a push from name to limited substance (e.g., calling all the Bible "the Law," when only one part of it is properly so designated). Once having given himself such permission, it is an easy move to the kind of exegesis of John and 1 John that searches for a knowledge of the Spirit "in itself" through the identification of its functions, a move given even more scope when such functions can be located in the processes of human subjectivity (e.g., as "desire" of "will" in Book IX) which are both deduced from scrip-

---

36. However we explain this tension between Trinitarian essentialism and hypostatic functionalism, it is undeniably a presence in Augustine's thinking. Olivier du Roy, for instance, has argued that only Augustine's later appreciation of Pauline incarnationalism spurred him to move beyond his originally more congenial neo-Platonic interest in Trinitarian immanent relations, a development that encouraged him to make more central to his theology elements of economic function in his discussion of hypostatic substance (see du Roy, *L'intelligence de la foi en la Trinité selon S. Augustin: Genèse de sa théologie Trinitaire jusqu'en 391* [Paris, 1966]). Whatever the genetic background to the tension, however, its purely structural roots, in theological terms, are inescapable, something modern critics of Augustine seem unwilling to admit: in arguing against Arianism in the first four books of the *De Trinitate*, Augustine proposes the relational view of the immanent Trinity as a logical response to subordinationism, moving along lines of thought not dissimilar to the Cappadocians (see the many immanent relational analogies offered by, e.g., Gregory of Nyssa in his *On the Holy Spirit: Against the Macedonians*). This is the only controversial point that I am making here. If contemporary opponents of immanental essentialism are correct in their criticism, they must also realize that attempts to move *beyond* these kinds of arguments tend, as in Augustine's case (exemplified in later books of the *De Trinitate*), to lead to forms of pure hypostatic functionalism. They are two sides of the same coin. While there is an alternative, as I have argued, in the severe restraint of revelational onomastica, this option is not a popular one today. The problem, in any case, lies at the heart of the Trinitarian conception and not in the improper historical force of a single theologian. For Augustine's "Sabellian" tendencies must be recognized as *natural*, and not aberrational responses to basic conceptions of Trinitarian orthodoxy laid out by, e.g., the Cappadocians themselves, tendencies whose pull remains powerful (if veiled) even among those who are searching for an escape from Augustinian influence.

37. From the translation of A. W. Haddan, in *Nicene and Post-Nicene Fathers of the Christian Church*, ed. Philip Schaff, Series 1, vol. 3., 100.

turally described operations as well as reflective of the Trinitarian relations themselves. Much of the medieval slippage in pneumatology from Trinitarian naming to the graces of the sanctified life, a collapse of the Person of the Holy Spirit into the life of the Church or the individual Christian, can be derived from this Augustinian definition of the Spirit in terms of a function like divine Love or Grace and human Desire, which together fashion a theology grounded in the economy of creaturely ascent to the *visio Dei*. Curiously, given their Augustinian heritage, Jansenist Appellancy could conceive of the Church's figural travail and limitations just because, in resisting this primary substantializing of designated pneumatic functions, they also resisted the collapse of pneumatology into spirituality.

The transformation of an onomastic pneumatology into a functionalist one is surely a corruption, or at least an essential reworking, of Cappadocian commitments. It is one, however, that is not all that distant from those modern appeals made to Gregory of Nyssa and his circle's Trinitarian theology on the basis of its supposed support for structures of social relationship. We are led through such appeals, frequently, back to the identification of the *ostensio Spiritus* with the appearance of certain phenomenal operations in time, operations that, because of their dispensational location at least within the life of the Church, are given to historical systematizations. Moltmann's suggestion of a pneumatic "tendency" in history toward sociality, which at least correlates with the movement of evolution however much supported by Christic interventions, is premised on a vision of the Trinity's communion of Persons sustained by the peculiar role of the Spirit, a vision that is little different from the essentialized functions extracted from the Cappadocian theology by Zizioulas and Gunton. It is a premise, however, that is not only contradicted by Florensky's assertion of phenomenological obscurity, but also goes counter, as we have indicated in our introduction, to Moltmann's own fundamental theodicy.[38]

## Four Features of Kenotic Pneumatology

### 1. History as It Is

If we are now to characterize kenotic pneumatology, in the sense that we are elaborating the term, we can say first that it is arrayed against a certain

---

38. An inner tension in positions like that of Zizioulas, due perhaps to the way they adapt Cappadocian categories to modern theological ends basically at odds with their own traditional premises, can be seen in the manner non-Orthodox writers seize on the specifically pneumatological elements of these constructs as ways of forging bridges between them and liberal Protestant sensibilities. See for instance, Victoria Miller, "Ecclesiology, Scripture, and Tradition in the *Dublin Agreed Statement*," *Harvard Theological Review* 86, no. 1 (1993): 133f., where the author sees Orthodox pneumatology, represented in someone like Zizioulas, as one of the few places where the fundamentally non-organic and anti-progressive ecclesiology of the Eastern Church might be opened up to, e.g., Anglican developmental comprehensiveness. Cappadocian pneumatology, however, is, in my view, precisely the place such *aggiornamento* is excluded.

view of history, a view of history that schematizes phenomena in advance of their apprehension and their fate, so as to illustrate or embody principles of Trinitarian relation or operation. The fruit of such false schematization, while claiming history as an object of concern, is usually to be seen in the swallowing up of incongruous facts, the setting aside of repugnant events, and the willful ignoring of unsettling interventions of order whose trajectory of meaning is never allowed to congeal for view — in short, a fabricated history of the imagination is substituted for that experienced, if forgotten, by its unsystematized participants.

But kenotic pneumatology is not, in opposing such manipulations of experience, "anti-historical" or "ahistorical." We have already seen, in our section on Jansenist conceptions of grace, how the onomastic pneumatology of someone like Nicholas Cabrisseau, so clearly dependent on the method of Basil, was, for all its eschewal of systematic functionalism, firmly grounded in the recital of historical phenomena as the basis for our adorative response before the Spirit.[39] Adding to the traditional catalogue of scriptural titles, Cabrisseau had attached the laudatory list of miracles, saints, martyrs, holiness, courage, preaching, suffering, and healing culled from the Church's history as pneumatic objects of admiration. What, at the time, we called a Jansenist presupposition of "grace's pneumatological historicity" may well have informed the extension of this kind of catalogue, although in our subsequent study of Saint-Médard itself we stepped back from claiming for Appellant views of the Spirit some kind of subsuming pneumatic role in configurating history, as if, in Augustine's terms, Grace and the Spirit were one and the same. Nonetheless we must grant the fundamental way in which historical phenomena, in and of themselves, were seen in such onomastic adorative unveilings as structuring the very act of *ostensio Spiritus* in a restraining fashion. Cabrisseau, no less than Florensky although less reflectively, wishes to see pneumatology settle uneasily within the forms of historical experience, a coincidence to be marked by the juxtaposition of unexpected pneumatica within an otherwise inhospitable phenomenal environment, and held together theologically, not by a systemic coordination of history with the "effects" of the Spirit's operation so much as by the deferral of temporal form to the historical figure of the Incarnation.

## 2. The Deferral to Kenotic Christology

Such a deferral to the figure of the Incarnation is a second feature of kenotic pneumatology. It is not one, however, that marks a repudiation, through the backdoor as it were, of its overt opposition to historical schematizations, as if exchanging one set of (pneumatic) "principles" of temporal organization for another, equally functionalist, Christological one. The whole practice of *figuriste* exegesis that we have seen

---

39. See our earlier remarks on his 1740 *Instructions courtes et familieres sur le Symbole, pour servir de suite aux instructions courtes et familieres de Messire Joseph Lambert.*

undergirding Appellant pneumatology would be poorly grasped if it were understood as being reflective of an apprehended constructive force by which historical experience was oriented by an abstracted divine principle, e.g., a principle akin to the *theologia crucis* some interpreters attribute to Luther. St. Paul's articulation of the *ostensio Spiritus*, we recall, was that it might "demonstrate" itself in Christ crucified alone; but such a demonstration says no more than that the Spirit's appearance in power coincides with knowing such a Christ, and not that this Christ in the form of the one crucified is the *dynamis* of historical configuration. To see the Spirit is to know only this one. To know only the Crucified Christ, however, is not something that carries with it a knowledge of the principles of historical development; it is only, in the Gospel's terms, to share in His baptism and to drink His cup (Mark 10:38). This points merely to the *fact* of temporal conformance, and to nothing more; it points to the existence of figurated shapes in time, but not to the nature of time itself. It points, in short, only to the prospects of conforming attentiveness before the ostensibly variegated display of unrelated historical phenomena: passing through time, surrounded by the contradicting facts of lust and pride, of seeing and touching, we shall see Him as He is, for we shall be like Him, purified by the same purification He wrought within the world (1 John 3:2f). The figures of Christ, around which the experience of this world is indeed constructed and is discerned in *rapports* and associations, are simply given to the eyes of the faithful, and their truth is known as much in their obvious incongruities with the capacities of brute intelligence to apprehend their presence as in their evident disclosures to minds opened by grace.

It is not by accident, then, that the kind of kenotic pneumatology Florensky outlined was formulated within a theological context in which more familiar "kenotic" Christologies were being explored. Indeed, the experiments among Russian thinkers with such ideas, driven by traditional Orthodox commitments to ascetic conformities with Christ that had little in common with parallel "kenotic" projects among European Protestants of the time, provided the conceptual frame in which to confront the disordered data of historical experience as a divine significant.[40] According, then, to this Christological perspective, the "kenotic" Christ was seen as the "purely" human Christ, though yet God. He was the Christ opened most fully to and mired most deeply in the material of created being, because, as its Creator, the depth of His entry into the world reached definition only within the measure of an infinite participation. The kenotic Christ, in this perspective, is therefore not a form of the world's constructive configuration, overarching creation as the apprehended *telos* of its becoming. Rather, He is what the world of temporal experience *is* of its own, yet most fully. In no other way could one speak, as Scripture as-

---

40. See the fascinating book by Nadejda Gorodetzky, *The Humiliated Christ in Modern Russian Thought* (London: SPCK, 1938), esp. chapter 5, "Doctrinal writings on the Kenosis."

tonishingly testifies, of the fact that Christ was "made to be sin" (2 Cor. 5:21), or condemned sin "in his flesh" (Rom. 8:3), or "became a curse for us" (Gal. 3:13). These are statements, not about history itself, but about the absolute conformity of the figure of Christ to the events of time: emptied of the ordering of God's sovereignty, the Christ became lost among those phenomena whose forms litter the landscape of creation. Thus, to speak of the Cross as a "governing" or "regulating figure" in history, as figurist theology does, is to note only how the Cross of the incarnate Christ resembles, in its shape, the crosses of the two thieves surrounding it; they are phenomenally indistinguishable, except that one belongs to God. A supporting kenotic pneumatology moves only to the threshold where such resemblances and *rapports* spring into immediate view.

### 3. *Eschatological Designation of Christ's Figure*

But to see the form of God as figured in the scattered phenomena of the world, its sin, the temptations by the Devil and their judgment, to see the figure of Christ amid unaltered facts of experience, to apprehend at work a "demonstration" of the Spirit here, is clearly to make distinctions among facts and to note the difference of the Cross of Christ from those of other people. God and the world are not the same, though in every respect they may stand together. To see that they are not the same under such conditions of indistinguishability is itself the act of demonstration and the manifestation of the figural fact; it is to see that (in Appellant terms) the world is figurated, and its figure is given in the shape of its Redeemer. A kenotic pneumatology does not, therefore, merely reiterate the world, but, in Gregory of Nazianzus's scheme, it describes the world as it is, within the context of a Kingdom whose own shape is yet to be revealed: it describes the world as now contained by the particular figure of Him crucified. This is why the Resurrection is itself figurally absent from kenotic Christologies and pneumatologies: it is phenomenally imperceptible, except as that which makes possible the identification of the Christ amid the indistinguishable elements of history. While it is the Kingdom, the Power, and the Glory or, in Christological terms, the Resurrection, the Ascension, and the Parousia that ground the possibility of speaking of God within the world, their own realities are yet indescribable, and their facticity — even like the Spirit's — is apprehended in their demonstration of something other than themselves, of something temporally prior to their evidence, in short of Christ's incarnate figure. The opening of Romans describes this relation, by which we can proclaim the Resurrection, drawn in parallel with the Spirit, only insofar as we can understand their hidden reality as that which does indeed disclose the indistinguishable person of flesh as the one who, in this person, is God: "who was descended from David according to the flesh and designated Son of God, in power according to the Spirit of holiness by his resurrection from the dead, Jesus Christ our Lord" (1:3–4).

A third feature of kenotic pneumatology, then, is that it will speak of such "designations," such namings of Christ within the indistinguishable phenomena of the world — it will make the figural assertion that certain of these phenomena are indeed namings of Christ. The moment that God is seen in the world, but that such seeing of God is the only element of distinction given Him within the disparateness of events, this is the moment that the Cross is seen to be Christ's and that it thus achieves figural prominence. It is the moment of *pneumaticon*, the illumination and manifested power of the Holy Spirit, the triumph of the Resurrection, the opening of the Kingdom, yet, as Florensky notes, it is a moment only of "supreme affliction," because all that can be seen in such a moment is the fact of designation itself, that the Crucified One is Lord. All pneumatica fall within this act of retrospective designation, through which the glory of God reveals the figure of Jesus: the Church, most fully — hence the unusually limited character of Appellant ecclesiology — the fact of human holiness, the lives of saints, the acts of healing and of miracle, the gesturing of love. Themselves "hidden," in the sense of the Spirit's own disappearance among phenomena of a world without "cosmic" coherence, they mark themselves, not by the incontrovertible nature of their revelation, but by their simple standing within the conflicted data of existence, literally, their "suffering," a posture of juxtaposition which, only because of grace, does not cease to speak of Christ.[41]

## 4. Adoration and Scriptural Onomastica

It is, therefore, ultimately to a form of speech and act of speaking to which kenotic pneumatology is reduced. This, a final feature of its character, should not be assigned some basis in a theory of language or of the linguistic nature of knowledge or human apprehension. While it does not necessarily stand in opposition to elements of such theories, it does question their explanatory reach, for its own ground lies uniquely in the given relationship between pneumatic self-disclosure and the designated figures of its phenomenal context in which its self-disclosure is made. Because the *ostensio Spiritus* is given in the demonstration of Christ Crucified, because, that is, it is given in the shape of temporal phenomena as they are, only now designated by the figure of Jesus the Christ, the only divine permission to human knowledge provided in this self-disclosure is in the naming of described events by the appellations given in this figure. The onomastic character of pneumatology, as well as its limits within the scriptural fund, derive from a submission to the boundaries of this permission.

---

41. For a more detailed treatment of this particular feature of kenotic pneumatology, see Olivier Clément's neglected *Transfigurer le temps: Notes sur le temps à la lumière de la tradition orthodoxe* (Neuchâtel: Delachaux et Niestlé, 1959), Pt.3:2, "La tension entre le temps et l'éternité: Kénose de Saint-Esprit et Apocalypse," esp. 142ff. Clément's is one of few extended defenses of a kenotic pneumatology in the line of Florensky as I have described it. (Florensky's name does not appear in the work, however, which may indicate that aspects of his thinking in this regard do in fact derive from patristic sources common to the Church's larger tradition and still capable of exerting independent constructive influence.)

In the view of a seventeenth-century Jansenist like Jean Hamon,[42] the plain bending before these words, their devoted repetition and use apart even from understanding, contains the form of the Spirit's self-giving in the Church; it embraces the very act of Christic designation by which, through grace, the Incarnate flesh of Jesus is known within the world for no other reason beyond the fact of this knowing. "Truly this was the Son of God," says the centurion at the Cross (Mark 15:39), with no evidence to go on beyond the figure of an expiring man. And why? These words' designation refer, and nothing more can be said of them than this.

And while it might seem that this kind of reduction leads to an irrationally motivated enunciation, this is not the case. The act of speaking and the form of the speech are given, to be sure; they are not deduced nor are they constructed on an experimentally tested theory of the world's events. But they are *given*, they are handed over, and therefore they come bearing the traces of the One who gives, however obscure and however banal *except* in the fact that they are nothing else but given. In Basil's formulation, these words are given by God to refer to God, and their very vocalization embodies the relation of redemptive praise their brute reference indicates. In their incoherence, they truly demonstrate God, simply because they are God's, and this fact, thrown in among the otherwise mingled and perhaps meaningless sounds and referents, grants to them their lone distinction, one taken not on trust, but coincident with divine glory. This is why Gregory speaks of the Holy Spirit's self-revelation as one enacted wholly in worship, a knowledge whose terms are encountered only in adoration, the sole posture in which the canvas of phenomena and their descriptors can be gazed upon with the expression of aghast delight. Through the figures of Scripture, which themselves are but the scattered fragments of contested references, yet given and demonstrated in the emptying grasp of an otherwise unremarkable God, the world and what the world was once, is thus beheld. Only in the insistence on this otherwise incoherent speech does pneumatology render a faithful discussion of its object. Only by continually returning to this speech, and releasing at this place of rest the increments of its previous evolution, does the Holy Spirit show itself. Only here does it appear, not however as something we shall describe in some entitative fullness; but it will appear as the full range of references scriptural discourse offers, just some of which point out "here" or "there" as to the Spirit, and the sum of which together instead scatters such indicators around the more expansive figure of the flesh of God thrown into the world. We sift the world for light, we do not mold it, by speaking with such words as these; and in so doing

---

42. See Jean Hamon, *De Trois Communions Spirituelles. Outre Celle Qui A pour objet JESUS-CHRIST dans le Saint Sacrement*, in *Recueil de Divers Traitez de Pieté. Ou l'on verra les principales maximes de la Morale Chrétienne excellemment établies. Nouvelle Edition* (Paris: Jean-Baptiste Delespine & Jean Th. Herissant, 1740), vol. 1, 179–309. See the section, "De la Communion à la Parole de Dieu," esp. 217ff.

we are also shown the wonder of its passage, *in ruinam* (so we see) *et in resurrexionem* (so we are permitted to believe) the visage of its Lord.

Based on the realities of Saint-Médard, I think this proposal is a fair way to approach the "matter" of the Holy Spirit. And precisely because it is based on these realities, such a kenotic pneumatology can claim to maintain the facticity of events, even in the face of their severe and perhaps tragic discomfort. More importantly, our proposal strives to maintain the integrity of the divine objects of its speech: first, the Holy Spirit itself, by not making its power and its form dependent on our desires, and so reversing the relation that ought to obtain between the two; and second, the intention of the Spirit's care, the figure of the Christ, respecting that "which we have heard, which we have seen with our eyes and touched with our hands" (1 John 1:1). To delve into the world of Saint-Médard, as we have done, just as to delve into any bit of the world at all, without such fairness to the Spirit's own denuded showing of Another to Whom it is joined, is to fall into the same quagmire of inexplicable distinctions between light and darkness our words become when we *merely* look. Thus, by simultaneously upholding the contested givenness of phenomena while deferring their shape to the limited contours of Christ's scripturally rendered experience, the figurally restricted pneumatology here proposed allows for something presumably central to Christian faith as a whole: the articulated integration of historical experience with its divine significance. That pneumatology has, so frequently, been used as a realm in which to pry these two apart, either by limiting experience susceptible of pneumatic character, or by expanding the realm of explicating divine form to the point of the semantically unintelligible, ought at least to commend our alternative proposal for consideration. If the events of Saint-Médard could be seen as in some way contributing to such consideration, then perhaps, if only within this small scope, their consignment to the status of scattered *reliqua in ruinam* might indeed constitute a proper appearance of the Holy Spirit's vivifying self.

# BIBLIOGRAPHY

The following bibliography lists all works cited in the text, as well as a selection of other material used for this study, whose consultation proved especially useful. Only those specifics of place of publication, publisher, and date as were available for each book are provided. Generally accepted attributions of primary sources published anonymously are followed, placed in brackets; otherwise, works are listed by their title.

## Primary Sources of the Seventeenth and Eighteenth Centuries

Arnauld, Antoine. *De l'autorité des miracles*, in his *Oeuvres*, vol. 23.

———. *De la fréquente communion: où les sentiments des Peres, des Papes & des Conciles touchant l'usage des Sacremens de Pénitence & d'Eucharistie, sont fidellement exposés, pour servir d'adresse aux personnes qui pensent sérieusement à se convertir à Dieu; aux Pasteurs & Confesseurs zélés pour le bien des ames*, in his *Oeuvres*, vol. 27.

———. *Difficultés Proposés à M. Steyaert Docteur et Professeur en Théologie de la Faculté de Louvain. Sur l'Avis par lui donné à M. l'Archeveque de Cambrai, Pour lui rendre compte de sa commission d'informer des bruits répandus contre la doctrine et la conduite des Prêtres de l'Oratoire de Mons en Hainaut* [1691], in his *Oeuvres*, vols. 1–3.

———. *Dissertation sur la maniere dont Dieu a fait les fréquents Miracles de l'Ancienne Loi par le ministre des anges* [1685], in his *Oeuvres*, vol. 38.

———. *Le Fantôme de Jansenisme*, in his *Oeuvres*, vol. 25.

———. *Instruction sur la grace, Selon l'Ecriture et les Peres* [1700], in his *Oeuvres*, vol. 10.

———. (with Pierre Nicole) *La Logique ou l'Art de Penser, Contenant; outre les Règles Communes, plusiers observations nouvelles propres a former le jugement* [ed. of 1683], in his *Oeuvres*, vol. 41–2.

———. *Oeuvres de Messire Antoine Arnauld, Docteur de la Maison et Société de Sorbonne*. 43 vols., Paris: Sigismond d'Arney, 1775–83, repr. Brussels: Culture et Civilisation, 1964–67.

———. *On True and False Ideas*. Translated by Stephen Goukroger, Manchester: Manchester University Press, 1990.

———. *On True and False Ideas*. Translated by Elmar J. Kremer. Lewiston, N.Y.: Edwin Mellen Press, 1990.

———. *Reflexions philosophiques et théologiques sur le Nouveau Systeme de la Nature et de la Grace*, in his *Oeuvres*, vol. 39.

————. *Remarques sur les principales erreurs d'un livre intitulé L'Ancienne Nouveauté de l'Ecriture Sainte, ou l'Eglise triomphante en terre etc.*. [1655], in his *Oeuvres*, vols. 4–5.

[————.] *Reponse a un ecrit publié sur le sujet du miracle qu'il a plu a Dieu de faire a Port-Royal depuis quelque temps, Par une Sainte Epine de la Couronne de Notre Seigneur* [1655], in his *Oeuvres*, vol. 23.

————. *Seconde Apologie de Jansenius* [1645], in his *Oevures*, vol. 17.

————. *La Tradition de l'Eglise sur le sujet de la Pénitence et de la Communion* in his *Oeuvres*, vol. 28.

————. *Vera S. Thomae De Gratia Sufficiente et Efficaci Doctrina Dilucide Explanata*, in his *Oeuvres*, vol. 20.

————. *Vindiciae Sancti Thomae circa Gratiam Sufficientem*, in his *Oeuvres*, vol. 20.

Arnauld d'Andilly, Robert. *Les Vies des Saints Peres des deserts et de quelques saintes escrites par des peres de l'eglise et autres Anciens Auteurs Ecclesiastiques, traduites en françois par Mr. Arnauld d'Andilly*. Paris: la Veuve Jean Camisat et Pierre le Petit, 1647.

[Asfeld, Jacques Vincent Bidal d'.] *Vains efforts des Mêlangistes ou discernans dans l'Oeuvre des Convulsions, pour défendre le systême du mêlange*, 1738.

Atterbury, Francis. *Sermons and Discourses on Several Subjects and Occasions.* 5th ed., London: T. Woodward, 1740.

Baillet, Adrien. *Les Vies des Saints, Composées sur ce qui nous est resté de plus authentique et de plus assuré dans leur histoire.* 2e edition. Paris: Louis Roulland, 1704.

[Barbeau de la Bruyère, Jean-Louis.] *La Vie de M. François de Paris, Diacre*, 1731.

Barcos, Martin de. *Correspondance de Martin de Barcos, Abbé de Saint-Cyran Avec les Abbesses de Port-Royal et les Principaux Personnages du Groupe Janséniste.* Ed. Lucien Goldmann. Paris: Presses Universitaires de France, 1956.

[————.] *De la Foy de l'Esperance et de la Charité ou explication du Symbole, de l'Oraison Dominicale, et du Decalogue.* Anvers, 1688.

Beaumont, Christophe de. *Ordonnance de Monseigneur l'Archevesque de Paris, Rendu sur la Requeste du Promoteur général de l'Archevêché de Paris, au sujet des prétendus miracles attribuez à l'intercession du sieu Pâris Diacre, inhumé dans la Cimétiere de la Paroisse de Saint-Médard.* Paris: Pierre Simon, 1735.

Bérulle, Pierre de. *Oeuvres complètes du cardinal de Bérulle.* Montsoult: Maison d'Institution de l'Oratoire, 1960.

[Besoigne, Jerôme.] *Avis aux fideles sur le Mêlange*, n.d.

[————.] *Avis aux fideles sur les Miracles du temps*, n.d.

————. *Principes de la Pénitence et de la Conversion, ou Vie des Pénitens.* 3e édition, Paris: Desaint & Saillant et Simon, 1766.

[————.] *Réponse succinte a un ecrit intitulé: Examen de la Consultation sur les Convulsions*, n.d.

Bossuet, Jacques-Bénigne. *Discours sur l'histoire universelle.* Paris: Garnier-Flammarion, 1966.

————. *Oeuvres Complètes de Bossuet*. Paris: Louis Vives, 1867.

Boursier, Laurent-François. *De l'Action de Dieu sur les creatures: Traité dans lequel on Prouve La Premotion Physique par le Raisonnement. Et où l'on examine plusieurs questions, qui ont rapport à la nature des esprits & à la Grace*. Paris: François Babuty, 1713.

[————.] *Explication abregée des principales questions qui ont rapport aux affaires présentes*. 1731.

[Boyer, Pierre.] *La vie de M. de Pâris, diacre*. Bruxelles, 1731.

[Cabrisseau, Nicolas.] *Instructions courtes et familieres sur le Symbole, pour servir de suite aux instructions courtes et familieres de Messire Joseph Lambert*. Paris: Ph. N. Lottin, 1740.

Canisius, Peter. *Summa Doctrinae Christianae* [1569], Vienna, 1833.

————. *Catechisme ou Instruction Familière sur les principales veritez de la Religion Catholique, Par Demandes et Réponses. Trés-utile aux Nouveaux Convertis*. Paris, 1686.

Casaubon, Meric. *A Treatise concerning Enthusiasme* [1655], Gainesville: Scholars' Facsimiles and Reprints, 1970.

[Caussel, P.] *De la connaissance de Jésus-Christ, Considéré dans ses Mystères, et dans ce qu'il est par rapport à Dieu son Père, par rapport aux Créatures en général, aux Hommes en particulier, et aux Bienheureux dans le Ciel. Avec des Elévations sur chaque Mystere de Jesus-Christ, et sur chacune de ses Qualités*. Nouvelle édition. Paris: Delalain, 1780.

*Le Cathechisme de la Penitence, Qui conduit les Pecheurs à une veritable Conversion*. Paris: Helie Josset, 1676.

*Catechisme, ou Doctrine Chrétienne, imprimé par ordre des Monseigneurs les Evesques d'Angers, de la Rochelle, et de Luçon*, 1676.

*Catechisme sur l'Eglise pour les tems de trouble, Suivant les Principes expliqués dans l'instruction Pastorale de Monseigneur l'Evêque de Senez*. Nouvelle édition. Utrecht, 1739.

[Cerveau, R.] *Necrologe des plus Célébres Defenseurs et Confesseurs de la Vérité du Dix-Septieme Siecle*, 1760.

Colbert, Joachim. *7e Lettre Pastoral, donnée à l'occasion de divers écrits*. Paris, 1726.

————. *Instruction Pastorale au sujet des miracles que Dieu fait en faveur des Appellans de la Bulle Unigenitus* (1733), in his *Oevures*. Vol. 2, Cologne, 1740.

————. *Instruction pastorale sur les miracles en reponse à M.l'Archeveque de Sens*, in his *Oevures*, vol. 2, Cologne, 1740.

————. *Les Oeuvres de Messire Charles Joachim Colbert, evesque de Montpellier*. 3 vols., Cologne, 1740.

————. *Reponse a un ecrit publié sur le sujet du miracle qu'il a plu a Dieu de faire a Port-Royal*. In his *Oevures*. Vol. 2, Cologne, 1740.

Condren, Charles de. *L'Idée du Sacerdoce et du Sacrifice de Jesus-Christ donnée Par le R. P. De Condren Second Superieur General de l'Oratoire de JESUS. Avec quelques Eclaircissemens & une Explication des Prieres de la Messe Par un Prêtre de l'Oratoire*. Paris: Jean Baptiste Coignard, 1677.

————. *Lettres du P. Charles de Condren.* Ed. P. Auvray and A. Jouffrey. Paris: Éditions du Cerf, 1943.

*Conduite des Confesseurs dans le tribunal de la Pénitence, selon les instructions de S. Charles Borromée, et la doctrine de S. Fraínçois de Sales.* Paris: Gabriel Charles Berton, 1760.

*Consultation sur les convulsions,* n.d.

Douglas, John. *The Criterion; or Rules by which the True Miracles Recorded in the New Testament Are Distinguished from the Spurious Miracles of Pagans and Papists.* London, 1752.

[Doyen, Barthelémy.] *Vie de Monsieur de Paris Diacre du diocése de Paris. Nouvelle Edition Augmenté de plusieurs faits qui ne se trouvent dans aucune des précedentes.* 1733.

[Duguet, Jacques-Joseph.] *Explication de l'Épitre de Saint Paul aux Romains.* Avignon, 1756.

[————.] *Explication du mystere de la passion de N.-S. J.-C., Suivant la Concorde. Jésus Crucifié.* Paris: Jacques Estienne, 1728.

[————.] *Explication litterale de l'ouvrage des six jours.* Nouvelle édition. Bruxelles: François Foppens, 1731.

————. *Lettre de Mr. l'abbé Du Guet A un Professeur d'un College de l'Oratoire,* n.p., n.d.

————. *Lettre sur la grâce générale.* In *Recueil de Quatre opuscules fort importans de seu M. l'Abbé Duguet.* Utrecht, 1737.

————. *Règles pour l'intelligence des Saintes Ecritures* (1716). In J.-P. Migne, *Scripturae Sacrae Cursus Completus.* Vol. 27. Paris: Garnier Frères, 1877.

[————.] *Traité de la croix de N.-S. J.-C.,* 14 vols., 1733.

[————.] *Traité des Principes de la Foy Chrétienne.* Paris: Barthelemy Alix, 1736.

[————.] *Traitez sur la prière publisque et sur les dispositions.* Nouvelle Edition. Liege: François Hoyous, 1715.

Du Pin, Louis-Ellies. *Analyse de l'Apocalypse, Contenant Une nouvelle Explication simple et litterale de ce Livre.* Paris: Jean de Nully, 1714.

Edwards, Jonathan. *Images or Shadows of Divine Things.* New Haven: Yale University Press, 1948.

*Entretiens sur les miracles, des derniers temps, ou les lettres De Mr. Le Chevalier \*\*\*,* n.p., n.d.

[Étemare, Jean-Baptiste Le Sesne des Ménilles d'.] *Les Gémissements d'une âme vivement touchée de la destruction du saint monastère de Port-Royal-des-Champs.* [With Pierre Boyer] 3e édition, 1734.

[————.] *Histoire de la Religion, Representée dans l'Ecriture sainte sous divers symboles.* Bruxelles: Stryckwant, 1727.

[————.] *Parallelle Abregé de l'Histoire du Peuple d'Israel et l'Histoire de l'Eglise.* Liege, 1724.

[————.] *Quatrième Gémissement d'une âme vivement touché de la Constitution de N.S.P. le Pape Clément XI du 8 septembre 1713,* 1714.

[————.] *Remarques en forme de dissertations sur les Propositions condânées par la Bule Unigenitus. Ou IV Colone des Hexaples Dans laquelle on fait la comparaison de la nouvelle Doctrine des Jesuites autorisée par la Bule, avec la Doctrine de l'Eglise établie par l'Ecriture, les Sains Péres, et les Auteurs Eclesiastiques,* 1723.

[Feydeau, Matthieu.] *Cathechisme de la Grace.* In Antoine Arnauld, *Oeuvres,* vol. 17.

Fleury, Claude. *Catechisme historique, Contenant en Abregé l'Histoire Sainte et la doctrine Chrétienne.* Brussels: Fricx, 1727.

[Foinard, M.] *La Genèse en Latin et en François, avec une explication du Sens Litteral, et du Sens Spirituel, tirée de l'Ecriture et de la Tradition.* Paris: Pierre-Charles Emery, 1732.

[Fontaine, Nicolas.] *L'Histoire de Vieux et du Nouveau Testament, Avec des Explications édifiantes, tirées des Saints Peres pour regler les moeurs dans toutes sortes de conditions.* Paris: Pierre le Petit, 1680.

———. *Mémoires pour servir a l'Histoire de Port-Royal.* Utrecht, 1736.

[Fourmont, Étienne.] *Mouââcah, ceinture de douleur, ou réfutation d'un livre intitulé "Règles pour l'intelligence des saintes Écritures."* 1723.

[Fourquevaux, Jean-Baptiste-Raymond de Pavie de.] *Idée de la Babylone Spirituelle Prédite par les Saintes Écritures.* Utrecht, 1733.

[———.] *Introduction abregée a l'Intelligence des Propheties de l'Ecriture, Par l'usage qu'en fait S. Paul dans l'Epitre aux Romains,* 1731.

[———.] *Lettre d'un prieur a un de ses amis, au sujet de la nouvelle Réfutation du Livre des Règles pour l'intelligence des saintes Ecritures.* Paris: Gabriel Valleyre, 1727.

[———.] *Nouvelles lettres d'un Prieur a un de ses amis, Pour la défense du Livre des Règles, pour l'intelligence des saintes Ecritures.* Paris: Jacques Estienne, 1729.

[———.] *Principes sur l'intelligence de l'Ecriture Ste,* n.p., n.d.

[———.] *Reflexions sur l'Etat Present de l'Eglise.* Amsterdam: Nicolas Potier, 1731.

[———.] *Reflexions sur l'Histoire de la Captivité de Babylone.* 3e édition. Utrecht, 1735.

[Gaultier, J. B.] *La Vie de Messire Jean Soanen Evêque de Senez.* Cologne: 1750.

[Gazagnes, Abbé.] *Manuel des Pèlerins de Port-Royal Des Champs, "Au Desert."* 1767.

Gerberon, Gabriel. *Miroir de la Piété.* Liege, 1676.

Godeau, Antoine. *La Vie de S. Charles Borromée, Cardinal du Titre de Sainte Praxede, et Archevéque de Milan.* Paris: Andre Pralard, 1684.

Gordan, John. *Memoirs of John Gordon of Glencat, in the County of Aberdeen Scotland: Who was Thirteen Years in the Scots College at Paris, amongst the Secular Clergy.* London: John Oswald, 1733.

[Goujet, Claude-Pierre.] *Vie de M. Du Guet, Prêtre de la Congrégation de l'Orotoire, Avec le Catalogue de ses Ouvrages,* 1741.

[Gourlin, Pierre-Sébastien.] *Instruction Pastorale de Monseigneur l'Archevèque de Tours, sur la Justice Chrétienne, Par rapport aux Sacremens DE PENITENCE ET D'EUCHARISTIE.* Paris: Guillaume Desprez et Pierre Cavelier, 1749.

Grégoire, Henri. *Histoire des sectes religieuses qui sont nées, se sont modifiées, se sont éteintes dans les différentes contrées du globe, depuis le commencement du siècle dernier jusqu'a l'époque actuelle.* 6 vols. Paris: Baudouin Frères, 1828.

―――. *Les Ruines de Port-Royal Des Champs en 1809, Année Séculaire de la Destruction de ce Monastère.* Nouvelle édition. Paris: Levacher, 1809.

[Gudvert, Abbé.] *Jesus-Christ sous l'anatheme et l'excommunication.* Amsterdam: Nicolas Potier, 1731

[―――.] *Jesus-Christ sous l'anatheme et sous l'excommunication, ou Reflexions sur le mystere de Jesus-Christ rejetté, condamné et excommunié par le Grand-Prêtre et par le Corps des Pasteurs de peuple de Dieu; Pour l'instruction et la consolation de ceux qui dans le sein de l'Eglise, éprouvent un pareil traitement.* Utrecht, 1739.

Hamon, Jean. *De la Solitude.* 2e edition. Amsterdam: 1735.

―――. *Lettres sur divers sujets de Morale et de Pieté.* 5e edition. Paris: Jacques Estienne, 1718.

―――. *Receuil de Divers Traitez de Pieté. Ou l'on verra les principales maximes de la Morale Chrétienne excellemment établies.* Nouvelle edition. Paris: Jean-Baptiste Delespine & Jean Th. Herissant, 1740.

―――. *Traitez de Pieté, composez par M. Hamon. Pour l'Instruction et la consolation des Religieuses de P.R. A l'occasion des differentes épreuves auxquelles elles ont été exposées.* Amsterdam: Nicolas Potgieter, 1727.

Hermant, Godefroi. *Mémoires de Godefroi Hermant . . . sur l'Histoire ecclésiastique du XVIIe Siècle (1630–1663).* Ed. A. Gazier. 6 vols. Paris: Plon, 1905–10.

*Les Hexaples, ou les Six colonnes sur la constitution Unigenitus.* 6 vols. Amsterdam, 1721.

Houtteville, C. *La Religion chrétienne prouvée par les faits.* Nouvelle édition. Paris: Gregoire Dupuis, 1740.

[Hugot, N.] *Instructions sur les vérités qui concernent la grace de N.S. Jesus-Christ.* Paris, 1747.

Hume, David. *Enquiries Concerning Human Understanding and Concerning the Principles of Morals.* Ed. L. A. Selby-Bigge, Oxford: The Clarendon Press, 1902.

*[Instruction Theologique en forme de] Catechisme sur les Promesses faites a l'Eglise. Où l'on traite principalement de l'obscurcissement de la vérité, et où l'on répond aux principales objections soit des Protestans soit des Partisans de la Bulle Unigenitus.* Utrecht: Corneille Guillaume le Febvre, 1732.

*Instructions Générales en forme de Catechisme où l'on explique en abregé par l'Ecriture Sainte et par la Tradition, l'Histoire et les Dogmes de la Religion, la Morale Chrétienne, les Sacremens, les Prieres, les Cérémonies et les Usages de l'Eglise* ["Catéchisme de Montpellier"] nouvelle édition. Paris: Simart, 1739.

Jansenius, Cornelius. *Augustinus.* Louvain, 1640; repr. Frankfurt: Minerva GmbH, 1964.

[Joubert, François.] *De la Connoissance des Tems, par rapport a la Religion.* Utrecht: Corneille Guillaume le Febvre, 1727.

Jurieu, Pierre. *L'Accomplissement des Propheties ou la Delivrance Prochaine de l'Eglise.* Rotterdam, 1686.

[La Boissière, Simon Hervieux de.] *De l'Esprit Prophétique. Traité dans lequel on examine le nature de cet Esprit, son objet spécial, les moyens par lesquels Dieu l'a communiqué & l'a fait reconnoître, tant par les Prophetes qui le recevoient, que par ceux à qui ils étoient envoyés.* Paris: Despilly, 1767.

[———.] *Preservatif Contre les faux principes et les Maximes dangereuses établies par M. de MONTGERON, pour justifier les secours violens qu'on donne au Convulsionnaires,* 1750.

Lambertini, Prosper (Pope Benedict XIV). *De Servorum Dei Beatificatione, et Beatorum Canonizatione.* Prati, 1841.

Languet de Gergy, Jacques-Joseph. *Instruction pastorale au sujet des prétendus miracles du diacre de Saint-Médard et des convulsions arrivées à son tombeau.* 2 vols. Paris, 1734–35.

La Taste, Dom Louis-Bernard de. *Lettre Théologique aux écrivains défenseurs des convulsions et autres prétendus miracles du temps.* 2 vols. Paris, 1740.

[Le Clerc, Pierre.] *Vies intéressantes et Édifiantes des Religieuses de Port-Royal et De plusieurs PERSONNES qui leur étoient attachees Précédées De plusieurs lettres et petits Traités, qui ont été écrits pour consoler, soutenir et encourager ces Religieuses dans le tems de leur oppression, afin de servir à tous les fidèles qui se trouvent dans le tems de trouble,* 1750.

[LeGros, Nicolas.] *Abregé chronologique des principaux evenemens Qui ont précédé la Constitution* Unigenitus, *qui y ont donné lieu, ou qui en sont les suites. AVEC Les CI. Propositions du P. Quesnel mises en parallelle avec l'Ecriture et la Tradition.* Nouvelle Edition. 1732.

[———.] *Discours sur les Nouvelles Ecclésiastiques. Depuis leur origine jusqu'a présent.* 1759.

[———.] *Lettres a Monseigneur l'Evesque de Soissons sur les Promesses faites a l'Eglise.* 2e edition. Amsterdam, 1738.

[Léonard, Martin-Augustin.] *Réfutation du livre des regles pour l'intelligence des Stes Ecritures.* Paris: Jacques Vincent, 1727.

[———.] *Traité du sens litteral et du sens Mystique des Saintes Ecritures, Selon la Doctrine des Peres.* Paris: Jacques Vincent, 1727.

Lerouge, Jean-Baptiste-Noël. *Traité dogmatique sur les faux miracles du temps, en reponse aux differens ecrits faits en leur faveur,* 1737.

[Le Tourneux, Nicolas.] *L'Annee Chrétienne ou les messes des dimanches, feries et fetes de toute l'année En Latin & en François, Avec l'explication des Epitres & des Evangiles, & un Abregé de la vie des Saints dont on fait l'Office.* Nouvelle édition. Brussels: François Foppens, 1703.

Maistre, Joseph de. *Écrits sur la Révolution.* Ed. Jean-Louis Darcel, Paris: Presses Universitaires de France, 1989.

———. *Oeuvres Complètes.* Lyon, 1884.

Malebranche, Nicolas. *Oeuvres de Malebranche.* Ed. Geneviève Rodis-Lewis, Andrè Robinet, et al. 21 vols. Paris: J. Vrin, 1958–70.

———. *The Search after Truth.* Translated with commentary by Thomas Lennon and Paul J. Olscamp. Columbus: Ohio State University Press, 1980.

———. *Traité de la Nature et de la Grâce.* Ed. Ginette Dreyfus, in his *Oeuvres,* vol. 5, 1958.

[Malot, Abbé.] *Dissertation sur l'époque du Rappel des Juifs, et sur l'heureuse révolution qu'il doit opérer dans l'Eglise, où l'on défend le sentiment des plus savans Théologiens et Interprêtes de notre siecle sur ce point.* 2e édition. Paris: Mequignon et Fils, 1779.

Malvin de Montazet, Antoine de. *Catéchisme du Diocèse de Lyon.* Lyon, 1767.

[Martianay, Jean.] *Traité Methodique ou Maniere d'Expliquer l'Ecriture Par le secours de Trois Syntaxes La Propre, la Figurée, et l'Harmonique.* Paris: Jean-Baptiste Cusson, 1704.

[Mésanguy, François Phillipe.] *Exposition de la Doctrine Chrétienne, ou Instructions sur les principales Vérités de la Religion.* Cologne, 1754.

Middleton, Conyers. *A Free Inquiry into the Miraculous Powers, Which Are Supposed to Have Subsisted in the Christian Church, From the Earliest Ages through Several Successive Centuries.* London: R. Manby and H. S. Cox, 1749.

Montgeron, Louis-Basile Carré de. *Continuation des démonstrations des Miracles Opérés à l'intercession de M. de PARIS. Observations sur l'oeuvre des Convulsions et sur l'état des Convulsionnaires.* 2 vols. 1741–48.

———. *La Vérité des Miracles opérés à l'intercession de M. de Pâris et autres Appellans, démontrée contre M. l'Archevêque de Sens.* Utrecht, 1737.

Moreri, Louis. *Le grand dictionnaire historique* (with *Supplément* by Goujet and Drouel), Paris, 1759.

*Necrologe des Appellans et Opposans a la Bule Unigenitus, De l'un et de l'autre Sexe,* 1755.

[Neercassel, Jean van.] *Traité de la Lecture de l'Ecriture Sainte, Où l'on réfute la pratique des Protestans dans cette lecture, Et où l'on montre la solidité de celle des Catholiques. Avec un Dissertation De l'Interpréte de Ecriture Sainte.* Cologne: Balthazar Egmont, 1680.

Nicole, Pierre. *Essais de Morale.* Paris: Guillaume Desprez, n.d.

———. *Instructions theologiques et morales sur le premier Commandement du Decalogue: ou il est traité De la Foi, de l'esperance, et de la Charité.* Paris, 1710.

———. *Instructions Theologiques et Morales sur les Sacremens.* Nouvelle edition. Paris: Charles Osmont, 1719.

[Noë-Mesnard, Jean de la.] *Catechisme du Diocese de Nantes, par le Commandement de Monseigneur l'Ilustr. Rev. Messire Gilles de Beauvau, Evêque de Nantes. Composé par le Sieur Mesnard, Prêtre, Directeur du Seminaire de Nantes.* Nouvelle édition. Paris: Louis Roulland, 1705.

*Nouvelles Ecclésiastiques.* 1728–91.

Olier, Jean-Jacques. *Oeuvres Complètes de M. Olier.* Ed. J.-P. Migne, Paris: Ateliers catholiques, 1856.

Paley, William. *A View of the Evidences of Christianity* (1794). In *The Works of William Paley, D.D.* Edinburgh: Peter Brown and Thomas Nelson, 1833.

Pascal, Blaise. *Oeuvres Complètes.* Paris: Éditions Du Seuil, 1963.

[Pinault, Olivier.] *Origine des maux de l'Eglise: Remedes qui doivent les guérir.* Paris, 1787.

[Quesnel, Pasquier.] *Abregé de l'Histoire de la Congregation De Auxiliis, C'est-à-dire, Des secours de la Grace de Dieu, tenuë sous les Papes Clement VIII & Paul V.* Francfort: Frederic Arnaud, 1687.

[————.] *Jésus-Christ Penitent ou Exercice de Pieté pour le tems du Carême, pour une Retraite de dix jours. Avec des Reflexions sur les sept Psaumes de la Penitence et la Journée Chrétienne. Par un Prêtre de l'Oratoire de Jesus.* Paris: Lambert Roulland, 1688.

————. *Le Nouveau Testament en français, avec des réflexions morales sur chaque verset.* 1727.

————. *Plainte et Protestation du Pere Quesnel Contre La condamnation des Cent-une Propositions: Avec Un ample Exposé de ses vrais sentimens.* 2e édition. 1717.

*Rabat-joie des jansénistes ou Observations nécessaires sur ce qu'on dit être arrivé au Port-Royal au sujet de la sainte Epine, par un Docteur de l'Eglise catholique.* n.d.

*Recueil des miracles operés au tombeau de M. de Paris Diacre.* 1732.

*Reflexions sur la conduite de Dieu, Avec une explication de l'histoire de Gedeon. Chapter 6 du Livre des Juges.* 1732.

Rochechouart, Guy de Seve de. *Premiere Lettre Pastorale de Monseigneur L'illustrissime et Reverendissime Evéque d'Arras, Aux Curez, vicaires, et Confesseurs de son Diocése Touchant l'Administration du Sacrement de Penitence,* n.d.

[Rondet, Laurent-Étienne], *Dissertation sur le rappel des Juifs et sur le chapitre XI de l'Apocalypse.* Paris, 1778.

Sacy, Isaac Louis Le Maistre De. *Explication des Proverbes de Salomon.* Bruxelles: Eugene Henry Fricx, 1698.

————. *Lettres Chrestiennes et Spirituelles de Messire Isaac Louis Le Maistre De Sacy.* Paris: Guillaume Desprez et Elie Josset, 1690.

Saint-Cyran, Jean Duvergier de Hauranne, abbé de. *Lettres Chrétiennes et spirituelles.* Lyon, 1674.

————. *Theologie Familiere, Avec divers autres petits traitez de devotion.* Edition nouvelle. Paris: Jean le Mie, 1647.

Saurin, Jacques. *Sermons sur divers textes de l'Ecriture Sainte par Jacques Saurin, Pasteur a La Haye.* La Haye: Otton et Pierre van Thol, 1749.

*Second recueil des miracles operés par l'intercession de M. de Paris,* 1732.

Sykes, Arthur Ashley. *A Brief Discourse Concerning the Credibility of Miracles and Revelation.* London: John and Paul Knapton, 1742.

[Tronchay, Michel.] *Histoire Abregée de l'Abbaye de Port-Royal, Depuis la fondation en 1204 jusqu'à l'enlevement des Religieuses en 1709.* Paris, 1710.

Varlet, Dominique-Marie. *Lettre de Monsieur l'Evesque de Babylone, aux Missionnaires de Tonquin,* 1734.

————. *Lettre de Monseigneur l'Evesque de Babylone a Monseigneur l'Evesque de Montpellier Pour servir de réponse à l'ordonnance de M. l'Archevêque de Paris, rendue le 8 Novembre 1735, au sujet des miracles opérés par l'intercession de M. de Pâris.* Utrecht, 1736.

———. *Lettre de Monseigneur l'Evesque de Babylone a Monseigneur l'Evesque de Senez*, n.d.

———. *Lettre de Monseigneur l'Evesque de Babylone à Monseigneur l'Evesque de Senez*, 1736.

———. *Lettres d'un Ecclesiastique de Flandres, a M. l'Evêque de Soissons*, n.d.

———. *Ouvrages Posthumes de Monseigneur l'Evesque de Babylone; Où il est principalement traité des Miracles contre M. l'Archevêque de Sens*. Cologne, 1743.

*La Verité rendue Sensible a tout le Monde, Sur les contestations dont l'Eglise est agitée, et en particulier sur la Constitution UNIGENITUS*. 2e edition. 2 vols. Utrecht, 1742

[Ville-Thierry, Jean Girard.] *Le Veritable Penitent, ou les Sentimens et les devoirs d'une ame penitente contenus dans les sept Psaumes de la Penitence*. Paris: André Pralard, 1709.

## Secondary Sources Dealing with Jansenism, Its History, Theology, and Context

Abercrombie, Nigel. *The Origins of Jansenism*. Oxford: Clarendon Press, 1936.

Adam, Antoine. *Du mysticism à la révolte. Les Jansénistes du XVIIe siècle*. Paris: Fayard, 1968.

———. *Sur le problème religieux dans la première moitié du XVIIe siècle*. Oxford: Clarendon Press, 1959.

Ages, Arnold. *The Image of Jews and Judaism in the Prelude of the French Enlightenment*. Sherbrooke (Quebec): Éditions Naaman, 1986.

Angers, Julien-Eymard d.' *Pascal et ses Précurseurs. L'Apologétique en France de 1580 à 1650*. Paris: Nouvelles Éditions Latines, 1954.

Appolis, Émile. *Entre jansénistes et zelanti: Le "Tiers parti" Catholique au XVIIe siècle*. Paris: Éditions A. et J. Picard et Cie., 1960.

Armogathe, Jean-Robert. "A propos des miracles de Saint-Médard: Les preuves de Carré de Montgeron et le positivisme des Lumières." *Revue de l'Histoire des Religions* 87(1971).

Baasner, Frank. *Der Begriff "sensibilité" im 18. Jahrhundert: Aufstief und Niedergang eines Ideals*. Heidelberg: C. Winter, 1988.

———. "The Changing Meaning of 'sensibilité': 1654–1704." *Studies in Eighteenth-Century Culture* 15 (1986).

Ball, Bryan W. *A Great Expectation: Eschatological Thought in English Protestantism to 1660*. Leiden: E. J. Brill, 1975.

Barbier, Antoine-Alexandre. *Dictionnaire des Ouvrages Anonymes*. Paris: Paul Deffis, 1872.

Baroni, Victor. *La Bible dans la vie Catholique Depuis la Réforme*. Lausanne: A l'Enseigne du Clocher, 1955.

Batterel, Louis. *Mémoires domestiques pour servir à l'histoire de l'Oratoire*. Ed. A. M. P. Ingold and E. Bonnardet. 4 vols. Paris, 1902–5.

Becker, Carl L. *The Heavenly City of the Eighteenth-Century Philosophers*. New Haven: Yale University Press, 1932.

Bercovitch, Sacvan. "Typology in Puritan New England: The Williams-Cotton Controversy Reassessed." Reprinted in Peter Charles Hoffer, ed., *The Marrow of American Divinity: Selected Articles on Colonial Religion.* New York: Garland Publishing, 1988.

Bernos, Marcel. "Saint Charles Borromée et ses 'Instructions aux confesseurs.' Une lecture rigoriste par le clergé français (XVIe–XIXe siècle)." In *Pratiques de la confession: Des Pères du désert à Vatican II. Quinze études d'histoire.* Paris: Les Éditions du Cerf, 1983.

Betts, C. . *Early Deism in France. From the so-called "déistes" of Lyon (1564) to Voltaire's "Lettres Philosophiques" (1734).* The Hague: Martinus Nijhoff Publishers, 1984.

Blackstone, Daniel. "A la recherche du lien social: incrédulité et religion, d'après le discours janséniste à la fin du XVIIIe siècle." In J.-R. Derré et al.(eds.), *Civilisation chrétienne: approche historique d'une idéologie, XVIIIe–XXe siècle.* Paris: Beauchesne, 1975.

Blanc, Hippolyte. *Le Merveilleux dans le jansénisme, le magnétisme, le méthodisme et le baptisme américains.* Paris: Henri Plon, 1865.

Bocxe, Winfried. *Introduction to the Teaching of the Italian Augustinians of the Eighteenth Century on the Nature of Actual Grace.* Héverlé-Louvain: Augustinian Historical Institute, 1958.

Bonnot, Isabelle. *Hérétique ou saint? Henry Arnauld évêque janséniste d'Angers au XVIIe siècle.* Paris: Nouvelles Éditions Latines, 1984.

Bontoux, Françoise. "Paris janséniste au XVIIIe siècle: Les *Nouvelles Ecclésiastiques.*" In *Paris et Ile-de France* 7 (1955), Paris, 1956.

Bouillier, Francisque. *Histoire de la Philosophie Cartésienne.* (Paris, 1868). Reprinted New York: Garland, 1987.

Bowman, Frank Paul. *Le Christ des Barricades: 1789–1848.* Paris: Les Éditions du Cerf, 1987.

———. *Le Christ Romantique.* Geneva: Librairie Droz, 1973.

Bremond, Henri. *Histoire littéraire du sentiment religieux en France depuis la fin des guerres de religion jusqu'à nos jours. IV: La Conquête Mystique: L'Ecole de Port-Royal.* Paris: Bloud et Gay, 1920.

Brown, Colin. *Miracles and the Critical Mind.* Grand Rapids: William B. Eerdmans, 1984.

Buckley, Michael. *At the Origins of Modern Atheism,* New Haven: Yale University Press, 1987.

———. "Seventeenth-Century French Spirituality: Three Figures." In *Christian Spirituality: Post-Reformation and Modern.* Edited by L. Dupré and D. Saliers. New York: Crossroads, 1989.

Burns, D. M. *The Great Debate on Miracles From Joseph Glanville to David Hume.* Lewisburg, Pa.: Bucknell University Press, 1981.

Busson, Henri. *La pensée religieuse français de Charron à Pascal.* Paris: Librairie Philosophique J. Vrin, 1933.

Caffiero, Marina. "La Postérité du figurisme en Italie." In *Janénisme et Révolution.* Paris: Chroniques de Port-Royal, 1990.

————. "Prophétie, Millénium et Révolution." *Archives des Sciences Sociales des Religions* 66, no. 2 (1988).

————. "'Il Ritorno d'Israele.' Millenarismo e mito della Conversione degli Ebrei nell' età della Rivoluzione Francese." In *Itinerari Ebraico-Cristiani: Società cultura mito.* Fasano: Schena Editore, 1987.

————. "La Verità Crocifissa: Dal Sinodo de Pistoia al Millenarismo Giansenistico nell' Età Rivoluzionaria." *Rivista de Storia et Letteratura Religiosa* 25 (1989).

Campbell, Ted. "John Wesley and Conyers Middleton on Divine Intervention in History." *Church History* 55 (March 1986).

————. *The Religion of the Heart: A Study of European Religious Life in the Seventeenth and Eighteenth Centuries.* Columbia: University of South Carolina Press, 1991.

Cassirer, Ernst. *The Philosophy of the Enlightenment.* Princeton: Princeton University Press, 1951.

*Catholicisme. Hier, Augjourd'hui, Demain.* Paris: Letouzey et Ané, 1947–.

Catrice, Paul. "Bossuet et le 'Retour' des Juifs." *Mélanges de Science Religieuse* 33 and 43 (1976).

Ceyssens, L. "Le jansénisme: Considérations historiques préliminaires à sa notion." *Analecta gregoriana* 71 (1953).

Chadwick, Owen. *From Bossuet to Newman.* 2d ed. Cambridge: Cambridge University Press, 1987.

Chatellier, Louis. "Le miracle baroque." In *Histoire des miracles.* Angers: Presses de l'Université, 1983.

Chédozeau, Bernard. "La notion de 'juif' chez P. Nicole et 'l'enseignement du mépris.'" In *Les chrétiens devant le fait juif: Jalons historiques.* Edited by Jacques le Brun. Paris: Éditions Beauchesne, 1979.

Chételat, Paul. *Étude sur Du Guet.* Paris: Ernest Thorin, 1879.

Clark, Ruth. *Strangers and Sojourners at Port Royal: Being an account of the connections between the British Isles and the Jansenists of France and Holland* (1932). New York: Farrar, Strauss, and Giroux, 1972.

Cognet, Louis. *Le Jansénisme.* Paris: Presses Universitaires de France, 1968.

————. "Note sur le P. Quesnel et sur l'ecclésiologie de Port-Royal." *Irenikon* 21 (1948).

————. *La Spiritualité Moderne: 1. L'essor: 1500–1650.* Paris: Aubier, 1966.

Coleman, Francis X. J. *The Aesthetic Thought of the French Enlightenment.* Pittsburgh: University of Pittsburgh Press, 1971.

Cousin, Bernard. *Le miracle et le quotidien: les ex-voto provençaux images d'une société.* Aix-en-Provence: Sociétés, Mentalités, Cultures, 1983.

Coppens, Joseph. "L'Argument des prophéties messianiques selon les Pensées de Pascal." *Ephemerides Theologicae Lovanienses* 22, no. 2 (1946).

Cottret, Monique. "Aux origines du républicanisme janséniste: le mythe de l'Eglise primitive et le primitivisme des Lumières." *Revue d'Histoire Moderne et Contemporaine* 31 (1984).

Dagens, Jean. *Bérulle et les origines de la restauration catholique (1575–1611).* Paris: Desclée de Brouwer, 1952.

———. "Le XVIIe siècle, siècle de saint Augustin." *Cahiers de l'Association internationale des Études françaises* 3–5 (1953).

Dédéyan, Charles. "L'Image de Jansénius et des Jansénistes dans le Romantisme Français." In *L'Image de C. Jansénius jusqu'à la fin du XVIIIe Siècle.* Edited by Edmond J. M. van Eijl. Louvain: Leuven University Press, 1987.

Dedieu, Joseph. "L'agonie du jansénisme (1715–1790)." *Revue d'Histoire de l'Eglise de France* 14 (1928): 161–214.

———. "Le Désarroi Janséniste pendant la période du Quesnellisme." *Revue d'Histoire de l'Église de France* 20 (1934).

Delassault, Geneviève. *Le Maistre de Sacy et son temps.* Paris: Librairie Nizet, 1957.

Delumeau, Jean. *Le catholicisme entre Luther et Voltaire.* Paris: Presses Universitaires de France, 1971.

———. *Sin and Fear: The Emergence of a Western Guilt Culture. Thirteenth–Eighteenth Centuries.* New York: St. Martin's Press, 1990.

*Dictionnaire de Biographie Française.* Paris: Letouzey et Ané, 1933–.

*Dictionnaire d'Histoire et de Géographaie Ecclésiastique.* Paris: Letouzey et Ané, 1912–.

*Dictionnaire de Spiritualité, Ascétique et Mystique, Doctrine et Histoire.* Paris: Beauchesne, 1937–.

*Dictionnaire de Théologie Catholique.* Paris: Letouzey et Ané, 1930–50.

Dupré, Louis. "Jansenism and Quietism." In *Christian Spirituality: Post-Reformation and Modern.* Edited by Louis Dupré and Don E. Saliers. New York: Crossroad, 1989.

———. *Passage to Modernity: An Essay in the Hermeneutic of Nature and Culture.* New Haven: Yale University Press, 1993.

Durand, Valentin. *Le Jansénisme au XVIIIe Siècle et Joachim Colbert, Évêque de Montpellier (1696–1738).* Toulouse: Édouard Privat, 1907.

Eijl, Edmond J. M. van, ed. *L'Image de C. Jansénius jusqu'à la fin du XVIIIe Siècle.* Louvain: Leuven University Press, 1987.

Everdall, William R. *Christian Apologetics in France, 1730–1790: The Roots of Romantic Religion.* Lewiston, N.Y.: Edwin Mellen Press, 1987.

Fauchois, Yann. "Les jansénistes et la Constitution Civile du clergé." In *Jansénisme et Révolution.* Paris: Chroniques de Port-Royal, 1990.

Feller, François Xavier de. *Biographie Universelle.* Ed. Charles Weiss. Paris, 1847–50, 1860.

Ferreyrolles, Gérard. "L'influence de la conception augustinienne de l'histoire au XVIIe siècle." In *XVIIe Siècle,* (1992): 135:34:2.

Ferrier, Francis. "L'image de Jansénius dans l'Oratoire naissant: Jansénius et Gibieuf." In *L'Image de C. Jansénius jusqu'à la fin du XVIIIe Siècle.* Edited by Edmond J. M. van Eijl. Louvain: Leuven University Press, 1987.

Frijhoff, Willem. "La fonction du miracle dans une minorité catholique: Les Provinces-Unies au XVIIe siècle." *Revue d'Histoire de la spiritualité* 48 (1972).

Fumaroli, Marc. "Temps de croissance et temps de corruption: Les deux Antiquités dans l'érudition jésuite française du XVIIe siècle." *XVIIe Siècle* 131:33:2 (1981).

Garrett, Clark. *Respectable Folly: Millenarians and the French Revolution in France and England*. Baltimore: Johns Hopkins University Press, 1975.

Gay, Peter. *The Enlightenment: An Interpretation. The Rise of Modern Paganism.* New York: Random House, 1966.

Gazier, Augustin. *Histoire Générale du Mouvement Janséniste depuis ses origines jusqu'à nos jours*. 5e édition. Paris: Honoré Champion, 1924.

———. "Restout et les miracles du diacre Pâris." *Revue de l'Art Chrétien* 62 (1912).

Germain, Elisabeth. *Jésus Christ dans les catéchismes: étude historique*. Paris: Desclée de Brouwer, 1986.

Gilley, Sheriden. "Catholic Revival in the Eighteenth Century." In *Protestant Evangelicalism: Britain Ireland, Germany and America c. 1750–c. 1950. Essays in Honor of W. R. Ward*. Studies in Church History 7. Edited by Keith Robbins. Oxford: Basil Blackwell, 1990.

Golden, Richard, ed. *Church, State, and Society under the Bourbon Kings of France*. Lawrence, Kans.: Coronado Press, 1982.

Goubert, Pierre. *Louis XIV and Twenty Million Frenchmen*. New York: Random House, 1966.

Gouhier, Henri. *La Philosophie de Malebranche et Son Expérience Religieux*. Paris: J. Vrin, 1948.

Gounelle, André. *La Bible Selon Pascal*. Paris: Presses Universitaires de France, 1970.

Gounelle, Élie. *Wesley et ses rapports avec les Français*. Nyons, 1898.

Gres-Gayer, Jacques M. "The *Unigenitus* of Clement XI: A Fresh Look at the Issues." *Theological Studies* 49 (1988).

Guillén Preckler, Fernando. *Bérulle aujourd'hui, 1575–1975: Pour une spiritualité de l'humanité du Christ*. Paris: Beauchesne, 1978.

———. *"État" chez le cardinal de Bérulle: théologie et spiritualité des "états" bérulliens*. Rome: Gregorian University, 1974.

Guny, André. "Duguet." In *Dictionnaire de la Spiritualité, Ascétique et Mystique, Doctrine et Histoire*. Paris: Gabriel Beauchesne et Fils, 1937–. Vol. 3.

Hallays, André. *Le Pèlerinage de Port-Royal*. Paris: Perrin et Cie., 1914.

Hazard, Paul. *The European Mind: 1680–1715*. New York: New American Library, 1963.

Healy, P. J. G. *Jansenius' Critique of Pure Nature*. Rome: Gregorian University, 1964.

Hermon-Belot, Rita. "L'abbé Grégoire et le 'retour des Juifs.'" In *Jansénisme et Révolution*. Paris: Chroniques de Port-Royal, 1990.

Hilaire, Yves-Marie, ed. *Benoît Labre: Errance et sainteté. Histoire d'un culte 1783–1983*. Paris: Éditions du Cerf, 1984.

Howells, R. J. *Pierre Jurieu: Antinomian Radical*. Durham: University of Durham, 1983.

Hudson, David, "The *Nouvelles Ecclésiastiques*. Jansenism and Conciliarism, 1717–1735." *Catholic Historical Review* 70, no. 3 (1984).

Hurtubise, P. "Jansénisme ou janénismes." In *Modernité et non-conformisme en France à travers les âges*. Edited by Myriam Yardeni. Leiden: E. J. Brill, 1983.

Jacques, Émil. *Les Années d'Exil d'Antoine Arnauld (1679–1994)*. Louvain: Publications Universitaires de Louvain, 1976.

———. "Antoine Arnauld, défenseur de Jansénius." In *L'Image de C. Jansénius jusqu'à la fin du XVIIIe Siècle*. Edited by Edmond J. M. van Eijl. Louvain: Leuven University Press, 1987.

———. "Un anniversaire: l'édition des Oeuvres complètes d'Antoine Arnauld (1755–1783)." *Revue d'Histoire Ecclésiastique* 70, nos. 3–4 (1975).

James, E. D. *Pierre Nicole, Jansenist and Humanist: A Study Of His Thought*. The Hague: Martinus Nijhoff, 1972.

*Jansénisme et Révolution*. Paris: Chroniques de Port-Royal, 1990.

Knox, Ronald. *Enthusiasm: A Chapter in the History of Religion with Special Reference to the Seventeenth and Eighteenth Centuries*. New York: Oxford University Press, 1961.

Kolakowski, Leszek. *Chrétiens sans Église: La conscience religieuse et le lien confessionel au XVIIe siècle*. Paris: Gallimard, 1969.

Kreiser, B. Robert. *Miracles, Convulsions, and Ecclesiastical Politics in Early Eighteenth-Century Paris*. Princeton: Princeton University Press, 1978.

Kurland, Norman. "Antoine Arnauld's First Controversy; *De la Fréquante Communion*." In *The Dawn of Modern Civilization: Studies in Renaissance, Reformation, and Other Topics Presented to Honor Albert Hyma*. Edited by Kenneth Strand. 2d ed. Ann Arbor: Ann Arbor Publications, 1964.

Labrousse, Elisabeth. *Pierre Bayle*. Oxford: Oxford University Press, 1983.

———. "Note sur Pierre Jurieu." *Revue de Théologie et de Philosophie* 3 (1978).

Lagrange, M.-J. "Pascal et les prophéties messianiques." *Revue Biblique Internationale* 3 nouvelle série (1906).

Laporte, Jean. *La Doctrine de Port-Royal: La Morale (d'après Arnauld)*. 2 vols. Paris: J. Vrin, 1951–52.

———. *La Doctrine de Port-Royal (2:1): Les Vérités de la Grace (d'après Arnauld)*. Paris: Presses Universitaires de France, 1923.

Lee, Umphrey. *The Historical Background of Early Methodist Enthusiasm*. New York: Columbia University Press, 1931.

Lennon, Thomas. "Jansenism and the *Crise Pyrrhonienne*." *Journal of the History of Ideas* 38 (1977).

———. "Occasionalism, Jansenism, and Scepticism: Divine Providence and the Order of Grace." *Irish Theological Quarterly* 45, no. 3 (1978).

Lubac, Henri de. *Augustinianism and Modern Theology*. London: Geoffrey Chapman, 1969.

———. "'Typologie' et 'Allégorisme.'" *Recherches de Science Religieuse* 34 (1947).

Luneau, Auguste, *L'Histoire de Salut chez les Pères de l'Église: La Doctrine des Ages du Monde*. Paris: Beauchesne, 1964.

Lyles, Albert M. *Methodism Mocked: The Satiric Reaction to Methodism in the Eighteenth Century*. London: Epworth Press, 1960.

Maire, Catherine-Laurence. "Agonie religieuse et transfiguration politique du jansénisme." In *Jansénisme et Révolution*. Paris: Chroniques de Port-Royal, 1990.

————. *Les Convulsionnaires de Saint-Médard: Miracles, convulsions et prophé-ties à Paris au XVIIIe siècle.* Paris: Gallimard/Julliard, 1985.

————. *De la Cause de Dieu à la Cause de la Nation: Le Jansénisme au XVIIIe Siècle.* Paris: Gallimard, 1998

Mangenot, Émile. "Figurisme." In *Dictionnaire de la Théologie Catholique.* Vol. 5:2.

McManners, John. *The French Revolution and the Church.* London: SPCK, 1969.

Mesnard, Jean. "Le classicisme Français et l'Expression de la Sensibilité." In *Expression, Communication and Experience in Literature and Language.* Edited by Ronald G. Popperwell. London: Modern Humanities Research Association, 1973.

————."La théorie des figuratifs dans les 'Pensées' de Pascal." *Revue d'Histoire de la Philosophie et d'Histoire Générale de la Civilisation* 35 nouvelle série (1943).

Monod, Albert. *De Pascal à Chateaubriand.* Paris: Alcan, 1915.

Morra, Gianfranco. *Catechismi giansenisti.* Forli: Edizioni di Ethica, 1968.

Nadler, Steven M. *Arnauld and the Cartesian Philosophy of Idea.* Manchester: Manchester University Press, 1989.

Neveu, Bruno. "Augustinisme janséniste et Magistère romain." *XVIIe Siècle* 135 (1982).

————. "L'érudition écclésiastique du XVIIe siècle et la nostalgie de l'antiquité chrétienne." In *Religion and Humanism.* Studies in Church History 17. Edited by Keith Robbins. Oxford: Basil Blackwell, 1981.

————. "Juge Suprème et Docteur Infaillible: le Pontificat Romain de la Bulle *In Eminenti* (1643) à la Bulle *Auctorem Fidei* (1794)." *Mélanges de l'École Française de Rome* 93, no. 1 (1981).

————. "Port-Royal à l'age des Lumières. Les 'Pensées' et les 'Anecdotes' de l'Abbé d'Étemare, 1682–1770." *Lias* 4, no. 1 (1977).

*Nouvelle Biographie Générale.* Paris: Firmin Didet, 1853–66.

O'Keefe, C. B. "The Jansenists and the Englightenment in France." In *Religion in the Eighteenth Century.* Edited by R. E. Morton and J. D. Browning. New York: Garland Publishing, 1979.

Orcibal, Jean. *Le cardinal de Bérulle: évolution d'une spiritualité.* Paris: Éditions du Cerf, 1965.

————. "Gerberon." In *Dictionnaire de la Spiritualité,* vol. 6.

————. *Jean Duvergier de Hauranne, Abbé de Saint-Cyran et son temps (1581–1638).* 2 vols. Paris: J. Vrin, 1947–48.

————. "Les Jansénistes face a Spinoza." In *Revue de Littérature Comparée* 23 (1949).

————. *Jansénius d'Ypres (1585–1638).* Paris: Études Augustiniennes, 1989.

————. "Néo-platonisme et jansénisme: du De libertate du P. Gibieuf à l'Augustinus." *Nuove recerche storiche sul giansenismo, Analecta Gregoriana* 71 (1954).

————. "L'Originalité théologique de John Wesley et les spiritualités du continent." *Revue Historique* 222 (1959).

————. *Port-Royal entre le miracle et l'obéissance: Flavie Passart et Angélique de St-Jean Arnauld d'Andilly.* Paris: Desclée de Brouwer, 1957.

————. "Qu'est-ce que le Jansénisme?" *Cahiers de l'Association Internationale des Études Françaises* 3–5 (July 1953).

————. "La signification du miracle et sa place dans l'ecclésiologie pascalienne." *Chroniques de Port Royal* 21/22 (1972).

————. *La Spiritualité de Saint-Cyran avec ses écrits de piété inédits.* Paris: Librairie Philosophique J. Vrin, 1962.

————. "Les spirituels français et espangnols chez John Wesley." *Revue de l'Histoire des Religions* 139 (1951).

————. "Thèmes platoniciens dans l''Augustinus' de Jansenius." In *Augustinus Magister.* Vol. 2. Paris: Congrès International Augustinien, 1954.

Palmer, R. R. *Catholics and Unbelievers in Eighteenth Century France.* Princeton: Princeton University Press, 1939.

Perry, Elisabeth Israels. *From Theology to History: French Religious Controversy and the Revocation of the Edict of Nantes.* The Hague: Martinus Nijhoff, 1973.

Picot, Michel Joseph Pierre. *Mémoires pour servir a l'Histoire Ecclésiastique, pendant le Dix-Huitième Siècle.* Seconde Édition. Paris: Adrien le Clerc, 1816.

Platelle, Henri. *Les chrétiens face au miracle: Lille au XVIIe siècle.* Paris: Les Éditions du Cerf, 1968.

Plongeron, Bernard. "Benoît-Joseph Labre au miroir de l'hagiographie Janséniste en France (1783–1789)." In *Benoît Labre: Errance et sainteté. Histoire d'un culte 1783–1983.* Edited by Yves-Marie Hilaire. Paris: Éditions du Cerf, 1984.

————, ed. *Le Diocèse de Paris. T. 1: Des Origines à la Révolution.* Paris: Beauchesne, 1987.

————, ed. with Claude Savart. *Histoire des saints et de la sainteté chrétienne.* Paris: Hachette, 1987.

————. *Théologie et Politique au Siècle des Lumières.* Geneva: Librairie Droz, 1973.

Popkin, Richard. *Isaac La Peyrère (1596–1676): His Life, Work, and Influence.* Leiden: E. J. Brill, 1987.

————. *The History of Scepticism, from Erasmus to Spinoza.* Berkeley: University of California Press, 1979.

Preclin, E. (with E. Jarry). *Les Luttes politiques et doctrinales aux XVIIe et XVIIIe siècles.* 2 vols. In *Histoire de l'Église depuis les origines jusqu'à nos jours.* Edited by Augustin Fliche and Victor Martin. Paris: Bloud et Gay, 1955–56.

Rockwood, Raymond, ed. *Carl Becker's Heavenly City Revisited.* Ithaca: Cornell University Press, 1958.

Rosa, Mario. "Jansénisme et Révolution en Italie" In *Jansénisme et Révolution.* Paris: Chroniques de Port-Royal, 1990.

Sainte-Beuve, C.-A. *Port-Royal.* 3 vols. Paris: Gallimard, 1953–55.

Savon, Hervé. "Le figurisme et la 'Tradition des Pères.'" In *Le Grand Siècle et la Bible.* Edited by Jean-Robert Armogathe. Paris: Éditions Beauchesne, 1989.

Saward, John. "Bérulle and the 'French School.'" In *The Study of Spirituality.* Edited by C. Jones, G. Wainwright, and E. Yarnold. London: SPCK, 1986.

———. *Perfect Fools: Folly for Christ's Sake in Catholic and Orthodox Spirituality.* Oxford: Oxford University Press, 1980.

Schwartz, Hillel. *The French Prophets: The History of a Millenarian Group in Eighteenth-Century England.* Berkeley: University of California Press, 1980.

Séché, Léon. *Les derniers Jansénistes depuis la ruine de Port-Royal jusqu'à nos jours (1710–1870).* 3 vols. Paris: Perrin et Cie, 1891.

Sellier, Philippe. "La Bible de Pascal." In *Le Grand Siècle et la Bible.* Edited by Jean-Robert Armogathe. Collection Bible de tous les temps 6. Paris: Éditions Beauchesne, 1989.

———. *Pascal et Saint Augustin.* Paris: Librairie Armand Colin, 1970.

Shiokawa, Tetsuya. *Pascal et les miracles.* Paris: Librairie A.-G. Nizet, 1977.

Stella, Pietro. "Augustinisme et orthodoxie des congrégations *De auxiliis* à la bulle *Vineam Domini.*" In *XVIIe Siècle* 135:34:2 (1982).

Stephen, Leslie. *History of English Thought in the Eighteenth Century.* New York: G. P. Putnam's Sons, 1876.

Tans, J. A. G. "Quesnel et Jansénius." In *L'Image de C. Jansénius jusqu'à la fin du XVIIIe Siècle.* Edited by Edmond J. M. van Eijl. Louvain: Leuven University Press, 1987.

Tavenaux, René. "Port-Royal, Les Pauvres et la Pauvreté." In *Actes du Colloque sur le Jansénisme, Organisé par l'Academia Belgica Rome, 2 et 3 novembre 1973.* Louvain: Publications Universitaires de Louvain, 1977.

———. *La Vie Quotidienne des Jansénistes aux XVIIe et XVIIIe siècles.* Paris: Librairie Hachette, 1973.

———. "Les Voies de la sanctification chez les premiers jansénistes." In *Histoire et Sainteté.* Angers: Presses de l'Université d'Angers, 1982.

Thomas, Jacques-François. *La Querelle de l'Unigenitus.* Paris: Presses Universitaires de France, 1950.

Tocanne, Bernard. *L'Idée de Nature en France dans la Seconde Moitié du XVIIe Siècle: Contribution à l'histoire de la pensée classique.* Paris: Klincksbieck, 1978.

Tocqueville, Alexis de. *The Old Régime and the French Revolution.* Garden City, N.Y.: Doubleday, 1955.

Toon, Peter, ed. *Puritans, the Millennium, and the Future of Israel: Puritan Eschatology 1600 to 1660.* Cambridge and London: James Clarke & Co., 1970

———. "The Question of Jewish Immigration." In *Puritans, The Millennium and the Future of Israel: Puritan Eschatology 1600–1660.* Edited by Peter Toon. Cambridge and London: James Clarke & Co., 1970.

Tucker, Susie I. *Enthusiasm: A Study in Semantic Change.* Cambridge: Cambridge University Press, 1972.

Van Den Berg, J. "The Eschatological Expectation of Seventeenth-Century Dutch Protestantism with Regard to the Jewish People." In *Puritans, the Millennium, and the Future of Israel: Puritan Eschatology 1600 to 1660.* Edited by Peter Toon. Cambridge and London: James Clarke & Co., 1970.

Van Kley, Dale. *The Jansenists and the Expulsion of the Jesuits from France, 1757–1765.* New Haven: Yale University Press, 1975.

Vaucher, Alfred-Félix. *Une célébrité oubliée: Le P. Manuel de Lacunza y Diaz (1731–1801), de la Société de Jésus, auteur de "La Venue du Messie en gloire et majesté.* Nouvelle édition. Collonges-sous-Salève: Fides, 1968.

Vaussard, Maurice. *Jansénisme et gallicanisme aux origines religieuses du resorgimento.* Paris: Letouzey et Ané, 1959.

Vidal, Daniel. *Miracles et Convulsions Jansénistes au XVIIIe Siècle. Le Mal et sa Connaissance.* Paris: Presses Universitaires de France, 1987.

Vyverberg, Henry. *Historical Pessimism in the French Enlightenment.* Cambridge, Mass.: Harvard University Press, 1958.

Wainwright, William J. "Jonathan Edwards and the Language of God." *Journal of the American Academy of Religion* 48, no. 4 (1980).

Walsh, John. "John Wesley and the Community of Goods." In *Protestant Evangelicalism: Britain, Ireland, Germany and America c. 1750–c. 1952.* Edited by Keith Robbins. Studies in Church History Subsidia 7. Oxford: Basil Blackwell, 1990.

Ward, W. R. "Orthodoxy, Enlightenment, and Religious Revival." In *Religion and Humanism.* Edited by Keith Robbins. Studies in Church History 17. Oxford: Basil Blackwell, 1981.

———. "The Relations of Enlightenment and Religious Revival in Central Europe and in the English-Speaking World." In *Reformers and Reformation: England and the Continent c. 1500–c. 1750.* Edited by Derek Baker. Studies in Church History 2. Oxford: Basil Blackwell, 1979.

Weaver, Ellen. *The Evolution of the Reform of Port-Royal. From the Rule of Cîteaux to Jansenism.* Paris: Éditions Beauchesne, 1978.

———. "History and Historians at Port-Royal." In *The Divine drama in History and Liturgy.* Edited by Horton Davies and John Booty. Allison Park, Pa.: Pickwick Publications, 1984.

———. "Jansenist Bishops and Liturgical-Social Reform." In *Church, State, and Society under the Bourbon Kings of France.* Edited by Richard Golden. Lawrence, Kans.: Coronado Press, 1982.

———. "Liturgy for the Laity: The Jansenist Case for Popular Participation in Worship in the Seventeenth and Eighteenth Centuries." *Studia Liturgica* 19, no. 1 (1989).

———. "Saint-Cyran's 'Prière du Pauvre' vs Nicole's 'Oraison Mentale': A Conflict over Styles of Prayer at Port-Royal." *Citeaux: Commentarii Cistercienses* 24 (1978).

———. "Scripture and Liturgy for the Laity: The Jansenist Case for Translation." *Worship* 59, no. 6 (November 1985).

Wetsel, David. *L'Ecriture et le Reste.* Columbus: Ohio State University Press, 1981.

Widmer, Gabriel P. "L'herméneutique figurative de Pascal." In *In Necessariis Unitas: Mélanges offerts à Jean-Louis Leuba.* Edited by Richard Stauffer. Paris: Les Éditions du Cerf, 1984.

Williams, William. "Jansenism Revisited." *Catholic Historical Review* 63, no. 4 (1977).

Wilson, D. Dunn. *Many Waters Cannot Quench: A Study of the Sufferings of Eighteenth-Century Methodism and Their Significance for John Wesley and the First Methodists.* London: Epworth Press, 1969.

## Other Works, Cited in the Text or Consulted

Althaus, Paul. *The Theology of Martin Luther.* Philadelphia: Fortress Press, 1966.

Altizer, Thomas. *Genesis and Apocalypse.* Louisville: Westminster/John Knox Press, 1990.

———. *The Gospel of Christian Atheism.* Philadelphia: Westminster Press, 1966.

———. "History as Apocalypse." In *Deconstruction and Theology.* Edited by T. Altizer et al. New York: Crossroad, 1982.

Aquinas, Thomas. *Summa Theologiae.* Blackfriars Edition, New York: McGraw-Hill Book Co., 1964.

Auerbach, Erich. *Scenes from the drama of European Literature.* Minneapolis: University of Minnesota Press, 1984.

Augustine, Saint. *La Città di Dio.* With intro. by A. Trapè, R. Russell, and S. Cotta. Rome: Città Nuova Editrice, 1978.

———. *The City of God.* Translated by Marcus Dods. New York: Random House, 1950.

———. *On the Holy Trinity.* Translated by A. W. Haddan. In *A Select Library of the Nicene and Post-Nicene Fathers of the Christian Church.* Edited by P. Schaff. First Series, Grand Rapids: Wm B. Eerdmans, 1988.

*Augustinus Magister.* 3 vols. Paris: Congrès international augustinien, 1954.

Balthasar, Hans Urs von. *The Glory of the Lord.* Vol. 1. San Francisco: Ignatius Press, 1982.

———. *A Theology of History.* New York: Sheed and Ward, 1963.

Basil the Great. *The Treatise de Spiritu Sancto.* Translated by Blomfield Jackson. In *A Select Library of Nicene and Post-Nicene Fathers of the Christian Church.* Edited by P. Schaff and H. Wace. Second Series. Vol. 8. Grand Rapids: Wm. B. Eerdmans, 1978.

Bellarmine, Robert. *Opera Omnia* [1873], repr. Frankfurt: Minerva GmbH, 1965.

Bochet, Isabelle, *Saint Augustin et le désir de Dieu.* Paris: Études Augustiniennes, 1982.

Bonner, Gerald. "The Desire for God and the Need for Grace in Augustine's Theology." In *Atti I. Congresso Internazionale su S. Agostino nel XVI centenario della conversione.* Rome: Institutum Patristicum "Augustinianum." 1987.

Breton, Stanislas. "Mythe et imaginaire en théologie chrétien." In *Le Mythe et le Symbole de la Connaissance Figurative de Dieu.* Paris: Éditions Beauchesne, 1977.

———. "Révélation, Médiation, Manifestation." In *Manifestation et Révélation.* Paris: Éditions Beauchesne, 1976.

Brown, Peter. *The Cult of the Saints: Its Rise and Function in Latin Christianity.* Chicago: University of Chicago Press, 1981.

———. "The Saint as Exemplar in Late Antiquity." In *Saints and Virtues.* Edited by John Stratton Hawley. Berkeley: University of California Press, 1987.

Buckley, James. "A Field of Living Fire: Karl Barth on the Spirit and the Church." *Modern Theology* 10, no. 1 (January 1994).

Burns, J. Patout. *The Development of Augustine's Doctrine of Operative Grace.* Paris: Études Augustiniennes, 1980.

Cahill, P. Joseph. "Hermenutical Implications of Typology." *Catholic Biblical Quarterly* 44, no. 2 (April 1982).

Calvin, John. *Commentary on the Gospel of John.* Translated by William Pringle. Grand Rapids: Baker Book House, 1979.

Cerfaux, Lucien. *Problèmes et Méthode d'Exégèse Théologiques.* With J. Coppens and J. Gribomont. Louvain: Publications Universitaires de Louvain, 1950.

Charity, A. C. *Events and their Afterlife: The Dialectics of Christian Typology in the Bible and Dante.* Cambridge: Cambridge University Press, 1966.

Chéné, J. *La Théologie de Saint Augustin. Grace et Prédestination.* Le Puy et Lyon: Éditions Xavier Mappus, 1961.

Clark, Francis. "Grace-Experience in the Roman Catholic Tradition." *Journal of Theological Studies* 25 new series (1974).

Clément, Olivier. *Transfigurer le temps. Notes sur le temps à la lumière de la tradition orthodoxe.* Neuchâtel: Delachaux et Niestlé S.A., 1959.

Coffey, David M. *Grace: The Gift of the Holy Spirit.* Manly, Australia: Catholic Institute of Sydney, 1979.

Coppens, Joseph. *Les Harmonies des deux Testaments: Essai sur les Divers Sens des Ecritures et sur l'Unité de la Révélation.* Tournai: Casterman, 1949.

Crites, Stephen. "Unfinished Figure: On Theology and Imagination." In *Thematic Issue: Unfinished...: Essays in Honor of Ray Hart.* Edited by Mark C. Taylor. JAAR Thematic Studies 48/1, 1981.

Dawson, David. *Allegorical Readers and Cultural Revision in Ancient Alexandria.* Berkeley: University of California Press, 1992.

Doré, Joseph, ed. *L'Ancien et le Nouveau.* Paris: Les Éditions du Cerf, 1982.

Dubarle, Dominique. "Pratique du Symbole et Connaissance de Dieu." In *Le Mythe et le Symbole de la Connaissance Figurative de Dieu.* Paris: Éditions Beauchesne, 1977.

Florensky, Pavel. *La colonne et le fondement de la vérité: essai d'une théodicée orthodoxe en douze lettres.* Translated by Constantin Andronikof. Lausanne: Éditions L'Age d'Homme, 1975.

———. "On the Holy Spirit." In *Ultimate Questions: An Anthology of Modern Russian Religious Thought.* Edited by Alexander Schmemann. Chicago: Holt, Rinehart and Winston, 1965.

Frei, Hans. *The Eclipse of Biblical Narrative: A Study in Eighteenth and Nineteenth Century Hermeneutics.* New Haven: Yale University Press, 1974.

———. "The 'Literal Reading' of Biblical Narrative in the Christian Tradition: Does It Stretch or Will It Break?" In *The Bible and the Narrative Tradition.* Edited by Frank McConnell. New York: Oxford University Press, 1986.

Galdon, Joseph A. *Typology and Seventeenth-Century Literature.* The Hague: Mouton, 1975.

Garvie, Alfred E. *The Purpose of God in Christ and Its Fulfilment Through the Holy Spirit.* London: Hodder and Stoughton, 1918.

Gorodetzky, Nadejda. *The Humiliated Christ in Modern Russian Thought.* London: SPCK, 1938.

Gousmett, Chris. "Creation Order and Miracle according to Augustine." *Evangelical Quarterly* 60 (1988).

Grant, Robert. *Miracle and Natural Law in Graeco-Roman and Early Christian Thought.* Amsterdam: North-Holland Publishing Co., 1952.

Greer, Rowan. *The Fear of Freedom: A Study of Miracles in the Roman Imperial Church.* University Park: Pennsylvania State University Press, 1989.

Gregory Nazianzen. *Select Orations.* Translated by C. G. Browne and J. E. Swallow. In *A Select Library of Nicene and Post-Nicene Fathers of the Christian Church.* Edited by P. Schaff and H. Wace. Second Series. Vol. 7. Grand Rapids: Wm. B. Eerdmans, 1983.

Gregory of Nyssa. *Select Writings and Letters.* Translated by W. Moore and H. A. Wilson. In *A Select Library of Nicene and Post-Nicene Fathers of the Christian Church.* Edited by P. Schaff and H. Wace. Second Series. vol. 5, Grand Rapids: Wm B. Eerdmans, 1988.

Gregory the Great. *Dialogues.* Translated by Odo John Zimmerman O.S.B. New York: Fathers of the Church, Inc., 1959.

Grelot, Pierre. *Sens Chrétien de l'Ancien Testament: Esquisse d'un Traité Dogmatique.* Tournai: Desclée & Co., 1962.

Gribomont, Jean. "Le Lien des deux testaments, selon la théologie de S. Thomas." *Ephemerides Theologicae Lovanienses* 22 (1946).

Gunton, Colin. *The Promise of Trinitarian Theology.* Edinburgh: T. & T. Clark, 1991.

Hanson, Anthony Tyrell. *Jesus Christ in the Old Testament.* London: SPCK, 1965.

Hardon, John. "The Concept of Miracle from St. Augustine to Modern Apologetics." *Theological Studies* 15 (1954).

Hays, Richard, *Echoes of Scripture in the Letters of Paul.* New Haven: Yale University Press, 1989.

Hausherr, Irenée. "L'erreur fondamentale et la logique de Messalianisme" (1935). In *Études de Spiritualité Orientale.* Rome: Pontificium Institutum Studiorum Orientalium, 1969.

Hegel, Georg Wilhelm Friedrich. *The Philosophy of History.* Translated by J. Sibree. New York: Dover Publications, 1956.

Hodgson, Peter C. *God in History: Shapes of Freedom.* Nashville: Abingdon Press, 1989.

Hove, Aloïs van. *La doctrine du miracle chez saint Thomas et son accord avec les principes de la recherceh scientifique.* Paris: J. Gabalda, 1927.

Illingworth, J. R. *The Doctrine of the Trinity Apologetically Considered.* London: Macmillan and Co., 1909.

John of Damascus. *The Orthodox Faith.* Fathers of the Church 37. Washington, D.C.: Catholic University of America Press, 1958.

John Paul II, Pope. *L'Esprit Saint* [Encyclical *Dominum et vivificantem.*] Paris: Éditions du Cerf, 1986.

Kieckhefer, Richard. "Imitators of Christ: Sainthood in the Christian Tradition." In *Sainthood: Its Manifestation in World Religions.* Edited by Richard Kieckhefer and George D. Bard. Berkeley: University of California Press, 1988.

Kijas, Zdzislaw. "La sophiologie de Paul A. Florensky." In *Ephemerides Theologicae Lovanienses* 67, no. 1 (1991).

King-Farlow, John. "Historical insights on miracles: Babbage, Hume, Aquinas." *International Journal for Philosophy of Religion* 13, no. 4 (1982).

Lécuyer, Joseph. "La causalité efficiente des mystères du Christ selon Saint Thomas." *Doctor Communis* 6 (1953).

Luneau, A. *L'Histoire de Salut chez les Pères de l'Église: La Doctrine des Ages du Monde.* Paris, 1964

Luther, Martin. *Martin Luther: Selections From His Writings.* Ed. John Dillenberger. Garden City, N.Y.: Doubleday, 1961.

———. *Luther's Church Postil.* Translated by John Nicholas Lenker. Minneapolis: Luther In All Lands Co., 1905.

———. *On the Bondage of the Will.* Translated by Philip S. Watson. In *Luther and Erasmus: Free-Will and Salvation.* Edited by E. Gordon Rupp and Philip S. Watson. Philadelphia: Westminster Press, 1969.

Mailhiot, M. D. "La pensée de saint Thomas sur le sens spirituel." In *Revue Thomiste* 59, no. 4 (1959).

Marello, Jacques. "Création-Révélation et Manifestation." In *Manifestation et Révélation.* Paris: Éditions Beauchesne, 1976.

Marks, Herbert. "Pauline Typology and Revisionary Criticism." *Journal of the American Academy of Religion* 52, no. 1 (1984).

McGrath, Alistair E. " 'Augustinianism'? A Critical Assessment of the So-called 'Medieval Augustinian Tradition' on Justification." *Augustiniana* 31 (1981).

Mersch, Émil. *The Whole Christ: The Historical Development of the Doctrine of the Mystical Body in Scripture and Tradition.* Milwaukee: Bruce Publishing Co., 1938.

Miller, Victoria. "Ecclesiology, Scripture, and Tradition in the *Dublin Agreed Statement.*" In *Harvard Theological Review* 86, no. 1 (1993).

Molinari, Paul. *Saints: Their Place in the Church.* New York: Sheed and Ward, 1965.

Moltmann, Jürgen. *The Future of Creation.* London: SCM Press, 1979.

———. *The Spirit of Life.* Minneapolis: Fortress Press, 1992.

———. *The Trinity and the Kingdom.* San Francisco: Harper and Roy, 1981.

———. *The Way of Jesus Christ.* Minneapolis: Fortress Press, 1993.

Monden, Louis. *Signs and Wonders. A Study of the Miraculous Element in Religion.* New York: Desclee Co., 1966.

Mourant, John. "Augustine on Miracles." *Augustinian Studies* 4 (1973).

O'Donnell, John J. *Trinity and Temporality. The Christian Doctrine of God in the Light of Process Theology and the Theology of Hope.* Oxford: Oxford University Press, 1983.

Pailin, David. "Abraham and Isaac: A Hermeneutical Problem Before Kierkegaard." In *Kierkegaard's "Fear and Trembling": Critical Appraisals.* Edited by Robert L. Perkins. University, Ala.: University of Alabama Press, 1981.

Prenter, Regin. *Spiritus Creator.* Philadelphia: Muhlenburg Press, 1953.

Radner, Ephraim, *The End of the Church: A Pneumatology of Christian Division in the West.* Grand Rapids: Wm. B. Eerdmans, 1998.

Raven, Charles E. *The Creator Spirit. A Survey of Christian doctrine in the light of Biology, Psychology and Mysticism.* Cambridge: Harvard University Press, 1927.

Reeves, Marjorie. *The Originality and Influence of Joachim of Fiore.* In *Traditio,* 1980.

Robinson, H. Wheeler, *The Christian Experience of the Holy Spirit.* London: Nisbet & Co., 1928.

Rondet, Henri. *The Grace of Christ.* Westminster, Md.: Newman Press, 1967.

Roy, Olivier du. *L'Intelligence de la foi en la Trinité selon S. Augustin: Genèse de sa théologie Trinitaire jusqu'en 391.* Paris, 1966.

Shepherd, William C. *Man's Condition. God and the World Process.* New York: Herder and Herder, 1969.

Sherry, Patrick. *Spirit and Beauty: An Introduction to Theological Aesthetics.* Oxford: The Clarendon Press, 1992.

Silberer, Michael. *Die Trinitätsidee im Werk von Pavel A. Florenskij. Versuch einer systematischen Darstellung in Begegnung mit Thomas von Aquin.* Würzburg: Augustinus Verlag, 1984.

Slesinski, Robert. "Fr. Paul Florensky: A Profile." *St. Vladimir's Theological Quarterly* 26, nos. 1 and 2 (1984).

———. *Metaphysics of Love.* Crestwood: St. Vladimir's Seminary Press, 1986.

Suenens, Léon Joseph. *A New Pentecost?* New York: Seabury Press, 1974.

Thils, Gustave. *Christian Holiness. A precis of ascetical theology.* Tielt (Belgium): Lannoo Publishers, 1961.

Tuveson, Ernest. *Millennium and Utopia: A Study in the Background of the Idea of Progress.* Berkeley: University of California Press, 1949.

Vogel, Winifried. "The Eschatological Theology of Martin Luther" Parts I and II. In *Andrews University Seminary Studies* (Autumn 1986 and Summer 1987).

Vooght, Paul de."Les miracles dans la vie de saint Augustin." *Recherches de Théologie Ancienne et Mediévale* 11 (1939).

———. "La notion philosophique de miracle chez saint Augustin." *Recherches de Théologie Ancienne et Mediévale* 10 (1938).

———. "La théologie du miracle selon saint Augustin." *Recherches de Théologie Ancienne et Mediévale* 11 (1939).

Ward, Benedicta. *Miracles and the Medieval Mind: Theory, Record, and Event 1000–1215.* Philadelphia: University of Pennsylvania Press, 1987.

Wilson, Stephen, ed. *Saints and Their Cults: Studies in Religious Sociology, Folklore, and History.* Cambridge: Cambridge University Press, 1982.

Wolterstorff, Nicholas. "Evidence, Entitled Belief, and the Gospels." *Faith and Philosophy* 6, no. 4 (1989).

Yon, Ephrem Dominique. "Le Symbole et la Croix." In *Le Mythe et le Symbole de la Connaissance Figurative de Dieu.* Paris: Éditions Beauchesne, 1977.

Zizioulas, John. *Being as Communion: Studies in Personhood and the Church.* Crestwood, N.Y.: St. Vladimir's Seminary Press, 1985.

# Index

# OTHER TITLES OF INTEREST
## *from The Crossroad Publishing Company*

**Lorenzo Albacete**
**GOD AT THE RITZ**
*Attraction to Infinity*

**A Priest-Physicist Talks about**
**Science, Sex, Politics and Religion**

A prominent priest and columnist for the *New York Times Sunday Magazine* offers his commentary on a variety of topics where current events and pop culture touch the spiritual: the bombings at the World Trade Center, the Chicken Soup series, Germaine Greer, and Charles Darwin, among others. In the book, he also provides a reasonable explanation for suffering and weighs in on the science-religion debate that is raging today.

0-8245-1951-5, $19.95 hardcover

**Carlo Maria Martini**
**ON THE BODY**
*A Contemporary Theology of the Human Person*

As parents, teachers, and catechists, we all struggle to relate the Church's teachings on sexuality to our children, to our students, and to ourselves. Martini provides straightforward answers in a conversational style meant to be accessible even to those without much theological training. The result is this compact, articulate, and very spiritual book that will be of use to anyone looking for theologically accurate answers to difficult questions about sex and the body. The content for this work comes out of the cardinal's years as a bishop, and from his experience, he regards the topic as being central theologically, anthropologically, and pedagogically. Above all, the book addresses the excessive concern that consumes our fitness-oriented body culture and that has become such a huge phenomenon in our time.

0-8245-1892-6, $14.95 paperback

crossroad

# OTHER TITLES OF INTEREST
### from The Crossroad Publishing Company

**Bernard McGinn**
**THE MYSTICAL THOUGHT OF MEISTER ECKHART**
*The Man from Whom God Hid Nothing*

Centuries after his work as a preacher, philosopher, and spiritual
guide, Meister Eckhart remains one of the most widely read mystics of the Western tradition. Yet as he has come to be studied
more closely in recent decades, a number of different Eckharts have
emerged. Is he the prophet of the God known only in radical negation and darkness, or of the intimate God in Christ born in the
human soul? Are his evocative German sermons the truest form of
his mystical vision, or do we find the key to his vision in the more
scholastic, seemingly drier Latin works? For the first time, Bernard
McGinn, the greatest living scholar of Western Christian mysticism,
brings together in one volume the fruition of decades of reflection on
these questions, offering a view of Eckhart that unites his strands as
preacher, philosopher, and theologian.

0-8245-1914-0, $45.00 hardcover

Please support your local bookstore,
or call 1-800-707-0670 for Customer Service.

For a free catalog, write us at

THE CROSSROAD PUBLISHING COMPANY
481 Eighth Avenue, Suite 1550
New York, NY 10001

Visit our website at
*www.crossroadpublishing.com*

All Prices Subject to Change

crossroad